Lecture Notes in Computer Science 16213

Founding Editors

Gerhard Goos
Juris Hartmanis

AF181228

Editorial Board Members

Elisa Bertino, *Purdue University, West Lafayette, IN, USA*
Wen Gao, *Peking University, Beijing, China*
Bernhard Steffen, *TU Dortmund University, Dortmund, Germany*
Moti Yung, *Columbia University, New York, NY, USA*

The series Lecture Notes in Computer Science (LNCS), including its subseries Lecture Notes in Artificial Intelligence (LNAI) and Lecture Notes in Bioinformatics (LNBI), has established itself as a medium for the publication of new developments in computer science and information technology research, teaching, and education.

LNCS enjoys close cooperation with the computer science R & D community, the series counts many renowned academics among its volume editors and paper authors, and collaborates with prestigious societies. Its mission is to serve this international community by providing an invaluable service, mainly focused on the publication of conference and workshop proceedings and postproceedings. LNCS commenced publication in 1973.

Alessandro Gianola · Renata Guizzardi ·
José Borbinha · Miguel Mira da Silva ·
José Barateiro
Editors

Enterprise Design, Operations, and Computing

29th International Conference, EDOC 2025
Lisbon, Portugal, September 9–12, 2025
Revised Selected Papers

Springer

Editors
Alessandro Gianola
INESC-ID, IST, Universidade de Lisboa
Lisbon, Portugal

José Borbinha
INESC-ID, IST, Universidade de Lisboa
Lisbon, Portugal

José Barateiro
Nova LINCS and University of Algarve
Faro, Portugal

Renata Guizzardi
University of Twente
Enschede, The Netherlands

Miguel Mira da Silva
NOV, IST, Universidade de Lisboa
Lisbon, Portugal

ISSN 0302-9743 ISSN 1611-3349 (electronic)
Lecture Notes in Computer Science
ISBN 978-3-032-15139-1 ISBN 978-3-032-15140-7 (eBook)
https://doi.org/10.1007/978-3-032-15140-7

© The Editor(s) (if applicable) and The Author(s), under exclusive license
to Springer Nature Switzerland AG 2026

This work is subject to copyright. All rights are solely and exclusively licensed by the Publisher, whether the whole or part of the material is concerned, specifically the rights of translation, reprinting, reuse of illustrations, recitation, broadcasting, reproduction on microfilms or in any other physical way, and transmission or information storage and retrieval, electronic adaptation, computer software, or by similar or dissimilar methodology now known or hereafter developed.
The use of general descriptive names, registered names, trademarks, service marks, etc. in this publication does not imply, even in the absence of a specific statement, that such names are exempt from the relevant protective laws and regulations and therefore free for general use.
The publisher, the authors and the editors are safe to assume that the advice and information in this book are believed to be true and accurate at the date of publication. Neither the publisher nor the authors or the editors give a warranty, expressed or implied, with respect to the material contained herein or for any errors or omissions that may have been made. The publisher remains neutral with regard to jurisdictional claims in published maps and institutional affiliations.

This Springer imprint is published by the registered company Springer Nature Switzerland AG
The registered company address is: Gewerbestrasse 11, 6330 Cham, Switzerland

If disposing of this product, please recycle the paper.

Preface

EDOC 2025 was held from September 9–12 in the lovely city of Lisbon, Portugal. This was the 29th edition of the International Conference on Enterprise Design, Operations, and Computing, continuing its tradition as a prominent forum for researchers and practitioners in the field of Enterprise Computing.

As in 2024, EDOC 2025 was co-located with the IEEE Conference on Business Informatics (CBI), bringing together two leading conferences in a shared program. Once more, the decision to organize these two conferences in tandem was successful, allowing the exploration of synergies between the two communities and creating new collaboration opportunities. Moreover, the joint program featured shared keynotes, technical sessions, and social events, providing participants with a unique opportunity to engage with cross-disciplinary insights in an intellectually stimulating environment.

The EDOC 2025 proceedings include 19 research papers selected from 73 submissions, reflecting a rigorous selection process with an acceptance rate of 26%. EDOC had two rounds of submissions: 4 research papers were accepted from 19 submissions after an early call, and 15 from 54 submissions after the second call. Each submission was thoroughly evaluated through a single-blind review process by at least three members of the program committee.

EDOC 2025 highlighted emerging research and practical advances in Enterprise Computing. Some contributions explored trending topics such as applied Agentic AI for enterprises. The field of Business Process Management saw advancements in business process governance, modeling, and optimization, with particular focus on process mining. Research on Cyber-Physical Resilience highlighted the crucial role of conceptual modeling in enhancing healthcare systems. Further topics included risk-aware enterprise architecture, sustainable transformation to reduce environmental impact, and innovative approaches to identity, accountability, and ontology-based security governance.

An important moment was the announcement of the Best Paper Award, given to Antoine Leblanc, Jacques Robin, Nourhène Ben Rabah, Zequan Huang, and Bénédicte Le Grand for their excellent paper titled "Rethinking Cybersecurity Ontology Classification and Evaluation: Towards a Credibility-Centered Framework." The paper stood out for the use of a very systematic methodology from which the authors drew coherent conclusions and relevant results to determine which existing Cybersecurity Ontology is most relevant for certain applications. Two other papers were announced as distinguished papers: the one by Maximilian Niedermeier, Holger Wittges, and Stefanie Rinderle-Ma, titled "Automating Access: LLM-based Permission Request Processing for the Enterprise"; and the one by Isadora Valle, Tiago Prince Sales, Eduardo Guerra, Luiz Olavo Bonino da Silva Santos, Maya Daneva, Henderik Proper, and Giancarlo Guizzardi, titled "Mapping the pain: How modelers experience and respond to common domain modeling frustrations."

Another noteworthy element in this year's conference was a panel discussion on "Interoperability in Health", chaired by José Borbinha (INESC-ID, IST, University of Lisbon, Portugal), where Zoran Milosevic (Deontik, Australia), Henrique Martins (ISCTE, Portugal), Mário J. Silva (INESC-ID, IST, University of Lisbon, Portugal), and Jean Paul Sebastian Piest (University of Twente, The Netherlands) shared their insights and sparked a lively and engaging discussion with the audience.

As in previous years, a separate post-conference volume is published, featuring papers from the Forum, Tools, and Doctoral Symposia along with Workshop contributions. This provides a platform for continued dialogue and exploration of new ideas and perspectives.

We are honored to feature the abstracts of invited talks from three esteemed, joint CBI-EDOC, keynote speakers: Manuel Dias, from Microsoft (Portugal), explored the landscape of methods and applications of GenAI in Businesses, in his talk titled "Generative AI – What's next?". Stefanie Rinderle-Ma, from Technical University of Munich (Germany), gave a keynote titled "AI-augmented Process Mining and Automation", which described different projects and results on the use of AI to automate Business Process and BP Mining in particular. Stefanie even delivered to the audience some glass coasters manufactured by a robot developed in one of these projects. Luiz Olavo Bonino, from University of Twente (The Netherlands), explored how FAIR principles can be applied to the diverse enterprise dimensions as focused on Enterprise Architecture in his speech titled "The impact of the FAIR principles on Enterprise Architecture: A critical reflection".

We would like to extend our deepest gratitude to the organizing committees of both EDOC and CBI for their tireless efforts in ensuring the success of this joint event. Special thanks go to the local organizing team at the University of Lisbon, whose dedication made the smooth execution of the conference and the warm atmosphere possible. We are also grateful to our sponsors, Turismo de Lisboa, for their generous support, which contributed significantly to the success of the event.

Finally, heartfelt thanks to the authors, reviewers, and participants. Your invaluable contributions and engagement made EDOC 2025 a memorable and impactful event. We look forward to the ongoing discussions, collaborations, and innovations that will arise from this year's conference.

November 2025

Alessandro Gianola
Renata Guizzardi
José Borbinha
Miguel Mira da Silva
José Barateiro

Organization

General Chairs

José Borbinha	INESC-ID, IST, Universidade de Lisboa, Portugal
Miguel Mira da Silva	INOV, IST, Universidade de Lisboa, Portugal

Program Committee Chairs

Alessandro Gianola	INESC-ID, IST, Universidade de Lisboa, Portugal
Renata Guizzardi	University of Twente, The Netherlands

Proceedings Chair

José Barateiro	NOVA-LINCS, Universidade do Algarve, Portugal

Publicity Chairs

Rob Bemthuis	University of Twente, The Netherlands
André Vasconcelos	INESC-ID, IST, Universidade de Lisboa, Portugal

Forum Chairs

Andrey Rivkin	Technical University of Denmark, Denmark
Jelena Zdravkovic	Stockholm University, Sweden

Workshop Chairs

Cláudia Antunes	IST, Universidade de Lisboa, Portugal
Andrea Marrella	Sapienza University of Rome, Italy

Doctoral Consortium Chairs

Selmin Nurcan	Université Paris 1 Panthéon–Sorbonne, France
Raimundas Matulevicius	University of Tartu, Estonia

Industry and Case Reports Chairs

Zoran Milosevic	Deontik, Australia
Rui Dinis Sousa	University of Minho, Portugal

Tools and Demos Chairs

Luis Sousa	INESC-ID, IST, Universidade de Lisboa, Portugal
Simone Agostinelli	Sapienza Università di Roma, Italy

Journal-First Chairs

Faiza Bukhsh	University of Twente, The Netherlands
Marco Montali	Free University of Bozen-Bolzano, Italy

Steering Committee

Alan Wee-Chung Liew	Griffith University, Australia
Colin Atkinson	University of Mannheim, Germany
Dimka Karastoyanova	University of Groningen, The Netherlands
Georg Grossmann	University of South Australia, Australia
Giancarlo Guizzardi	University of Twente, The Netherlands
Henderik A. Proper	TU Wien, Austria
João Paulo A. Almeida	Federal University of Espírito Santo, Brazil
Manfred Reichert	University of Ulm, Germany
Marten van Sinderen	University of Twente, The Netherlands
Remco Dijkman	Eindhoven University of Technology, The Netherlands
Selmin Nurcan (Chair)	Paris 1 Panthéon-Sorbonne University, France
Sylvain Hallé	Université du Québec à Chicoutimi, Canada
Zoran Milosevic	Deontik, Australia

Program Committee

Alexander Knapp	Universität Augsburg, Germany
Alfred Zimmermann	Reutlingen University, Germany
Andrea Marrella	Sapienza University of Rome, Italy
Aniruddha Gokhale	Vanderbilt University, USA
Ben Roelens	Open Universiteit, Ghent University, Belgium
Chiara Di Francescomarino	University of Trento, Italy
Christian Zirpins	Karlsruhe University of Applied Sciences, Germany
Claudenir M. Fonseca	University of Twente, The Netherlands
Claudio Di Ciccio	Utrecht University, The Netherlands
Colin Atkinson	University of Mannheim, Germany
Emilio Sulis	University of Turin, Italy
Evangelos Ntentos	University of Vienna, Austria
Fabrizio Fornari	University of Camerino, Italy
Fatih Turkmen	University of Groningen, The Netherlands
Georg Grossmann	University of South Australia, Australia
Giancarlo Guizzardi	University of Twente, The Netherlands
Giuseppe Di Lucca	University of Sannio, Italy
Glenda Amaral	University of Twente, The Netherlands
Guido Governatori	Central Queensland University, Australia
Ítalo Oliveira	University of Twente, The Netherlands
Jean Paul Sebastian Piest	University of Twente, The Netherlands
Jan Mendling	Humboldt-Universität zu Berlin, Germany
João Luiz Rebelo Moreira	University of Twente, The Netherlands
João Paulo Almeida	Federal University of Espírito Santo
Julio Cesar Nardi	Federal Institute of Espírito Santo, Brazil
Lam Son Lê	Vietnamese-German University, Vietnam
Ljiljana Brankovic	University of New England, Australia
Lorenzo Rossi	University of Camerino, Italy
Luís Ferreira Pires	University of Twente, The Netherlands
Luise Pufahl	TU Munich, Germany
Madhushi Bandara	University of Technology Sydney, Australia
Manfred Reichert	University of Ulm, Germany
Marek Suchánek	Czech Technical University in Prague, Czechia
Mark Mulder	The Enterprise Engineering Company 2, The Netherlands
Mathias Weske	Hasso Plattner Institute, University of Potsdam, Germany
Mattia Fumagalli	University of Bozen-Bolzano, Italy
Nicolas Herbaut	Université Paris 1 Panthéon-Sorbonne, France

Oscar Pastor	Universidad Politécnica de Valencia, Spain
Paolo Ceravolo	University of Milan, Italy
Pedro Paulo F. Barcelos	University of Twente, The Netherlands
Rajeev Raje	Indiana University Indianapolis, USA
Remco Dijkman	Eindhoven University of Technolog, The Netherlands
Roberto Nai	University of Turin, Italy
Ronny Seiger	University of St.Gallen, Switzerland
Rüdiger Pryss	University of Würzburg, Germany
Ruth Breu	University of Innsbruck, Austria
Sagar Sunkle	Tata Consultancy Services, India
Schahram Dustdar	Vienna University of Technology, Austria
Simon Hacks	Stockholm University, Sweden
Stefan Tai	TU Berlin, Germany
Sylvain Hallé	Université du Québec à Chicoutimi, Canada
Tiago Prince Sales	University of Twente, The Netherlands
Vinay Kulkarni	Tata Consultancy Services Research, India

Keynotes

Generative AI – What's next?

Manuel Dias

Microsoft, Portugal
manuel.dias@live.com

Abstract. Generative AI is accelerating innovation across industries, moving beyond content creation to enable intelligent agents that can perceive, reason, and act autonomously. These AI agents are transforming how work gets done (automating complex tasks, orchestrating workflows, and collaborating with humans to solve problems in entirely new ways). With the rise of multimodal models and Retrieval-Augmented Generation, AI systems are becoming more capable, context-aware, and proactive, unlocking new possibilities for product design, customer engagement, and decision-making. As these technologies mature, the next wave of innovation will be driven by the seamless integration of AI agents into daily operations, creating smarter businesses, faster innovation cycles, and entirely new business models.

AI-augmented Process Mining and Automation

Stefanie Rinderle-Ma

Technical University of Munich, Germany
stefanie.rinderle-ma@tum.de

Abstract. Process mining and automation have become major technological trends, propelled by recent breakthroughs in artificial intelligence. In particular, generative AI, especially large language models, offers significant potential to revolutionize process discovery from textual data and empower domain experts to build process models through natural language interactions with chatbots. Additionally, process technologies now enable the collection of richly contextualized data, such as sensor inputs, which can be harnessed to enhance process behavior prediction and improve functions like compliance monitoring. This presentation introduces the core principles of conversational process mining, demonstrates how contextualized process data can be captured in a manufacturing environment, and explores key research directions, including predictive compliance monitoring.

The impact of the FAIR principles on Enterprise Architecture: A critical reflection

Luiz Olavo Bonino

University of Twente, The Netherlands
l.o.boninodasilvasantos@utwente.nl

Abstract. The FAIR Principles, which aim to improve the Findability, Accessibility, Interoperability and Reusability of digital objects, have become a cornerstone of responsible data stewardship. However, their relevance and potential can extend beyond (meta)data management alone. This presentation will explore how FAIR can serve as a foundational lens through which to rethink and reconfigure Enterprise Architecture. By interpreting FAIR as a set of systemic requirements rather than isolated data practices, we can derive actionable architectural principles that support improved organizational agility, transparency, and cross-boundary collaboration. The talk will examine how FAIR can influence the design of enterprise systems, promote semantic and structural interoperability, and inform governance models that ensure consistent data stewardship across business units. Ultimately, we argue that embracing the FAIR principles is not just a matter of better data management—it can be a transformative strategy for architecting organizations that are ready for the challenges and opportunities of the knowledge-driven economy.

Contents

Enterprise Architecture

Towards a Taxonomy for Enterprise Architecture Debts

Jürgen Jung[1] and Simon Hacks[2(✉)]

[1] Faculty of Computer Science and Engineering, Frankfurt University of Applied Sciences, 60318 Frankfurt, Germany
jung.juergen@fb2.fra-uas.de
[2] Department of Computer and Systems Sciences, Stockholm University, 164 25 Kista, Sweden
simon.hacks@dsv.su.se

Abstract. Enterprise Architecture (EA) plays a vital role in aligning business and IT, yet its implementation often encounters challenges due to evolving needs and past architectural decisions. These challenges, termed Enterprise Architecture debt (EA debt), arise from short-term decisions or misalignments that hinder progress toward an optimal architecture. This study proposes two taxonomies: one to characterize EA debt descriptively and another to assess its impact. The taxonomies were developed using systematic literature reviews and refined with practitioner feedback. They offer a structured approach to identify, describe, and evaluate EA debts, enabling organizations to address them systematically. The study demonstrates the application of the taxonomies through a real-world case example, illustrating their potential to support strategic and operational decision-making. These contributions aim to enhance the theoretical foundation and practical management of EA debts, fostering better alignment of architectures with organizational goals.

Keywords: Enterprise Architecture · EA Debt · Taxonomy

1 Introduction

Digital transformation introduces opportunities and challenges, particularly in achieving business-IT alignment (BITA) [1]. A holistic perspective is crucial for BITA, as it enables organizations to understand the relationships between products, employees, and business models [2]. Enterprise Architecture (EA) provides such a perspective by offering methods to align business with IT and operationalize business strategies [3,4]. EA enhances transparency by incorporating business views, application landscapes, and technological representations [3,5].

EA is widely implemented in large organizations, supported by extensive research [6,7]. However, EA often evolves organically, resulting in complex architectures. Moreover, EA is perceived as bureaucratic, potentially limiting agility and innovation [8,9]. Conflicts between EA's long-term objectives and the

© The Author(s), under exclusive license to Springer Nature Switzerland AG 2026
A. Gianola et al. (Eds.): EDOC 2025, LNCS 16213, pp. 3–22, 2026.
https://doi.org/10.1007/978-3-032-15140-7_1

immediate needs of individual projects often arise. These conflicts can include (1) Complex application landscapes, (2) Outdated or incomplete documentation, and (3) Procedures and organizational structures that inhibit innovation.

These challenges can stem from appropriate past decisions but have become impediments due to change. To address this, Hacks et al. proposed Enterprise Architecture debt (EA debt) to describe the impacts of such decisions [10]. Like technical debt (TD), EA debt captures the gap between the current EA (as-is) and the desired EA (to-be). However, EA debt adopts a broader scope, including technical systems, processes, organizational structures, and compliance frameworks.

Research on EA debt has developed along two streams: technical and socio-technical aspects [11]. Technical research has introduced concepts like EA Smells (e.g., patterns indicating potential problems), tools for identifying such smells [12,13], and methods for handling debts [14,15]. Socio-technical research focuses on processes for managing EA debt, including identification, prioritization, and resolution [11]. Jung et al. [16] developed a workshop format to uncover debts that cannot be detected through models alone, later refined by Daoudi et al. [17] to improve efficiency and evaluate organizational impact. Specifically, current socio-technical contributions focus on process (e.g., who should meet, how often, and with which artifacts) but pay little attention to content, what exactly constitutes an EA debt, how it should be cataloged, and how its business impact can be compared across cases.

This study builds on this concept with the specific objectives of characterizing EA debts descriptively and assessing their impact. Therefore, we develop two taxonomies that provide a structured way to describe EA debts, understand their context, and evaluate their consequences. Our study offers two tightly coupled taxonomies: the characterization taxonomy standardizes debt descriptions across architectural layers, while the impact taxonomy translates those descriptions into comparable, decision-oriented impact profiles. These help organizations systematically address EA debts and align their architectures with strategic goals.

The remainder of this paper is organized as follows: First, we explore the concept of EA debt in more detail and review related research. Next, we present the research method used to develop the taxonomies. We then demonstrate their application using a real-world example. Finally, we discuss related work and conclude with the implications of this research.

2 Research Method

The taxonomy was developed using the method provided by Nickerson et al. [18] in combination with two SLRs and practitioner interviews (cf. Fig. 1)[1]. The initial steps are defined as follows: (1) Meta-characteristic: The taxonomies are intended to support enterprise architects and decision-makers concerning describing and assessing EA debts. Based on this characterization, follow-up

[1] A documentation of the two SLRs and the resulting concept matrices can be found here: https://github.com/simonhacks/ead_taxonomy.

actions on how to mitigate EA debts can be defined. (2) Ending conditions: The result after each iteration will be checked against the objective ending conditions listed in [18]. Furthermore, the authors focused on the three subjective conditions[2]. The other two (comprehensive and extendible) have not been ignored, but their evaluation could not be performed extensively due to the size of the corresponding domain.

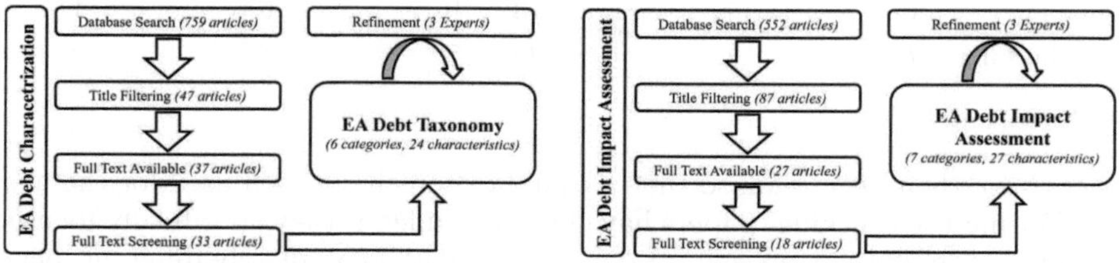

Fig. 1. Macro Research Process

The first iteration for each taxonomy has been initiated with an SLR to get an overview of current research [19–21]. The first SLR focused on existing taxonomies for TDs to establish a foundational understanding of classification approaches relevant to EA debt. The second explored the impact of EA to identify dimensions and characteristics critical for assessing the consequences of EA debt. These reviews were necessary to ensure the resulting taxonomy for EA debts is comprehensive and grounded in prior research. Later iterations of Nickerson's method (after conducting the SLR) have been conducted by the paper's authors based on additional literature from the authors' libraries and feedback from practitioners.

Two distinct searches have been done as part of the SLR. They were performed between September 2nd and 17th, 2024, by accessing the same three databases: Springer Link[3], Science Direct[4], and IEEE[5]. The queries differed slightly as the user interface of each database offered different possibilities. Springer allows searching in the complete dataset while Science Direct can specifically search in selected fields (e.g., *title* and *abstract*) and IEEE in meta-data.

The first search aimed to identify existing TD taxonomies from the literature. The number of papers from each database is shown in Table 1. After the initial query with the search term ("technical debt" AND (taxonomy OR classification)), there was a total number of *759*. The results were then filtered based on publication type[6] and whether the search terms appeared in the title. Available

[2] Concise (adequate size of the taxonomy for practitioners), Robust (meaningful differentiation between EA debts), and Explanatory (helpful characterization for practitioners).

[3] link.springer.com.

[4] www.sciencedirect.com.

[5] ieeexplore.ieee.org.

[6] Only scientifically peer-reviewed articles were considered.

Table 1. Combined Results from Searching for *Technical Debt and Taxonomy* and *Enterprise Architecture and Impact*

Metric	Technical Debt and Taxonomy			Enterprise Architecture and Impact		
	Springer Link	Science Direct	IEEE	Springer Link	Science Direct	IEEE
# search results	553	187	19	372	167	13
after filter	26	7	14	66	10	11
available	17	7	13	16	10	11
after checking	*14*	*6*	*13*	*7*	*6*	*5*

papers have then been read, so that *33* publications have been used for the next step. During the checking, papers have been excluded if they specifically focused on source code, did not present a taxonomy, or had a completely different focus.

The final set of papers has been analyzed to extract elements of taxonomies or classifiers for TDs that are also relevant to EA debt. These were collected in a concept map together with the corresponding publication. Such a map is an established tool for extracting relevant concepts from a set of publications [19, 22]. Concepts related to details in software development or programming have been excluded. Typical kinds of TDs usually include *code*, *test*, or *build* [23,24], but are on a too detailed level and usually not subject to an EA.

The resulting concept matrix contains 23 entries, grouped into five categories as shown in Table 1 in the online appendix. The categories are supposed to be reflected as dimensions for the taxonomy. Two concepts (*usability* and *environment*) could not be added to a reasonable category. *Usability* relates to the property of a software system and might be an effect of an EA debt. *Environment* is quite generic and might be subject to different categories (e.g., business, organization, or technology).

The second search focused on finding papers that presented research concerning the impact of EA in the organization. From the resulting *552* publications, those from the past 10 years with the search term (impact AND "enterprise architecture") in the title have been filtered, resulting in *37* available titles. These have been read, and *18* publications have been chosen for getting an overview on *impact* expected from EA. Some titles have been excluded as they were technical or related to special topics (e.g., dynamic capabilities).

The concept matrix has been created based on identified recurring concepts in the literature (cf. Table 2 online appendix). Building categories is ambiguous, as the same terms might have different meanings. *Quality* might, for example, refer to a company's products [25] or processes [26–28] but also to its IT [29] or EA [30,31]. *Usage* is a general term that relates explicitly to using the EA function in an organization. Therefore, it has been categorized as *collaboration* rather than *business*. However, some other papers mention the usage of a *resource (usage)*, which can relate to business [32] or, specifically, IT resources [31].

The results from the literature review[7] were the input for the first iteration of the two EA debt taxonomies. Then, practitioners with long experience in EA refined them (cf. Table 2). The final result from this iterative approach is presented in the subsequent Sect. 3.

Table 2. Details on Practitioners involved in the Taxonomy Refinement

ID	Domain	EA Experience	Formal Education
1	Logistics	25 years	PhD in Engineering
2	Consulting	17 years	PhD in Information Systems
3	Finance	13 years	Masters in Computer Science and Software Engineering

3 EA Debt Taxonomy

The two taxonomies are shown in Table 3 and 4. The first one is supposed to describe an EA debt to understand its context. It can be used to determine which kinds of changes might be required in case the EA debt needs to be resolved. The second one aims to assess the impact of an EA debt, i.e., understanding the necessity for resolving it. The single dimensions of the taxonomies might influence each other. However, this is not the focus of this work and needs to be further analyzed in future studies, such as case studies.

We chose to use two separate taxonomies because they serve different goals. The first one helps describe the EA debt and where it comes from. The second focuses on why the debt is important and how urgently it should be fixed. If we combine both into one, it could mix up these different viewpoints and make it harder to understand the debt clearly. Keeping them separate makes it easier for researchers and practitioners to describe, assess, and prioritize EA debts clearly and organized.

3.1 Taxonomy for Characterizing an EA Debt

Dimensions for characterizing an EA debt cover several aspects, like the awareness of its creation, its position in the EA, or its current phase in the lifecycle. EA frameworks usually separate the entire architecture into several layers [33]. Hence, such a distinction between *business*, *application*, and *technical* layers are incorporated as individual dimensions into the taxonomy.

Business. The business layer reflects concepts for describing the business ecosystem of an organization [34]. It encompasses concepts like business processes or actors to reflect what is required to run the business and create value.

[7] See tables in the online appendix: https://github.com/simonhacks/ead_taxonomy/blob/main/Appendix.pdf.

Table 3. Taxonomy for EA debt characterization

dimension	characteristics
business	organization | process | product | business capability | business motivation
application	IT system | data | interface | service
technology	hardware | network | location | standard | interoperability
collaboration	skill | capacity | policy | documentation
consciousness	intentionally | unintentionally
life cycle	identified | in analysis | in mitigation | resolved

Many concepts are available, but only a few have been chosen to keep the taxonomy concise. *organization* and *process* are included to cover a static and a dynamic view. Both can also be found in the context of TD taxonomies [36–40,42–45]. *Product* (and services sold to customers) refers to the outcome of a company's processes and its value-add towards a customer. *Business capability* is an abstract representation of the certain ability of a company to do something. It may include and represent various business execution concepts (e.g., routines or resources) [46]. Using *business capability* was suggested by practitioner 2 to keep the taxonomy compact. He also suggested using *business motivation* as defined in the business motivation model by Simon [34] rather than listing individual elements, like strategy, (business) objective, or mission. Characteristics in the *business* dimension are not exclusive, as a given EA debt might be located in different concepts simultaneously.

Application. The application dimension relates to software-technical artifacts of the IT landscape [3]. An *IT system* reflects a software system consisting of a set of related applications (e.g., server applications and clients) [37]. IT systems manage and process *data* [47]. Different IT systems can be integrated by *interfaces* [48]. A (software) *service* is a special interface for exposing functionality externally.

Technology. Most papers mention *infrastructure* [23,24,39,40,42,45,49–51] and one *interoperability* [41] as relevant aspects of TD. Even though the term *infrastructure* has a slightly different meaning in the software development area, infrastructure is also a relevant concept in EA. It has been perceived as too generic so that the taxonomy includes specific infrastructure or technology components from the TOGAF standard [52]. Infrastructure is divided into *hardware* and computer *networks* as well as *locations* representing data centers. *Standard* only refers to technology standards or protocols agreed upon in an organization. The term *interoperability* might incorporate networks and standards but be left as a separate characteristic as the reason for interoperability issues might not be that easy to determine.

Collaboration. Collaboration among actors in an organization may be the reason for an EA debt [17]. This aspect is separated from the business dimension as it does not necessarily refer to an architectural layer but to how people work together. In case of lacking capabilities (i.e., missing training [53]), the reason for an EA debt might be in required *skills*. If required skills are available but lacking manpower, then there is an EA debt with lacking *capacity* [53]. A *policy* debt occurs if existing rules hamper efficient collaboration. First, these were called *regulation*, but based on feedback from practitioner 3, it was renamed so as not to confuse it with external regulations like laws. Missing or flawed *documentation*[8] is one of the most frequently mentioned kinds of EA debt [16].

Consciousness. There are different terms for describing the origins of a specific TD. Most seem to be traced back to a blog post by Martin Fowler in 2009 [54]. Fowler introduces the terms *reckless* and *prudent* for indicating the severity of a TD (i.e., is it worth considering for paying back) [43,55–58]. Even though these terms are widely used, they are not considered for the EA debt taxonomy at this stage as they are mixed in an assessment. The second pair of terms, *deliberate* and *inadvertent*, considers the awareness of the team creating the TD [43,50,55–57,59]. Others use the term *self-admited* for characterizing a TD as being created on purpose [37,47,51,60–65]. Some practitioners do not feel comfortable using these terms[9], especially as they mix an objective description with an impact assessment. Hence, the taxonomy is reduced to indicating whether the EA debt has been created intentionally.

Life Cycle. The taxonomies presented in the paper are supposed to support a framework for managing EA debts [11]. Each EA debt might already be subject to a given phase within the management cycle: An EA debt is *identified* if it is known to an organization. Still, no action has been initiated to deal with it. After starting an assessment concerning its impact and potential measures for repayment, an EA debt is in status *in analysis*. Any EA debt subject to a mitigation action is in status *in mitigation*. If an EA debt has been mitigated or decided not to be relevant (anymore) to the actual strategy, it is in status *resolved*.

3.2 Taxonomy for Assessing the Impact of an EA Debt

The first version of the taxonomy for assessing the impact of an EA debt was created based on the literature review categories (Table 2 online appendix). The dimensions seemed redundant, and the taxonomy was not concise. It was reviewed with the authors of the article and three academics and practitioners within five iterations, resulting in Table 4. The performance dimension was excluded because it is also covered by the *IT* and *finance* dimensions. Some characteristics of the *management* dimension got removed as some of them address similar topics (*strategy* and *business objectives* as they are part of a strategy). The first three rows represent the ArchiMate-like three-layer architecture model as in Table 3. *Technology* got renamed to *IT infrastructure* as the second one seemed to be more precise for management (based on the feedback of practitioner 2).

[8] After discussing the term with practitioner 3, we would like to highlight that documentation refers to architecture models, as well as enterprise and technical documents.

[9] Practitioner 1: "What do these words mean at all?".

Table 4. EA debt taxonomy for impact assessment

dimension	characteristics
business	outcome | efficiency | maturity | resilience
application	data | application function | IT system | portfolio
IT infrastructure	effectiveness | efficiency | reliability | scalability
management	strategy | resource usage | decision making | project
financial	revenue | cost | stability
partner	customer | supplier | collaboration | regulatory body
risk & compliance	security | legal | industry regulation | ESG

Business. The *business* dimension shows the impact on the business domain in the company. *Outcome* summarised *product* and *service* [25,26,28,30] as well as their quality [26–28,31,48]. *Efficiency* measures the resource usage compared to the outcome, summarising *efficiency* from the literature review [32,66], *business performance* [67] and *productivity* [25]. As outcome and efficiency rather reflect the present situation, *maturity* was added to reflect the company's capability to sustain its future business model (as proposed by practitioner 2). The ability to react to changes in the environment is covered by *resilience*, summarising *innovation* [26–28,68,69], *adaptability* [31], *agility* [25–28,32,69–71], and *change* [68,72].

Application. The resulting characteristics of the *application* dimension are structured according to the application layer in ArchiMate [5]. *Data* [25–28] is the core concept of the passive structure in the application architecture and can be affected by EA debts hampering proper data management. The functionality implemented by IT systems is represented by *application function*, indicating whether an EA debt impacts the implementation of systems. *IT system* (*application component* in ArchiMate) represents a deployable software system implementing application functions (i.e., *solution* [30,73], *application* [25,30,32,48,66,74,75] or *information system* [76,77]). In addition to ArchiMate concepts, there is a characteristic for the *application portfolio* [30,48,69,73] as some EA debts affect several systems or even the conceptualization of the application landscape.

IT Infrastructure. The term *technology* (analog to the lower layer in ArchiMate) was changed to *IT infrastructure* as technology may refer to any technology used in a company. Characteristics are partially derived from the literature review: *effectiveness*, *efficiency*, and *reliability* [31]. Two participants suggested eliminating *quality* as the first three are already quality attributes. However, scalability [78] was added during one of the iterations to address the technology's ability to scale with increasing demand.

Management. The *management* dimension collects different levels of management within a company. Developing [30] and monitoring the achievement [31,48,72,73,75,77,79,80] of *strategy* addresses long-term objectives. EA debt effects on *resource usage* [25,30–32,67,81] and *decision making* [67,72,80] relate to the operational management of the company. A *project* is relevant to perform changes and is often not related to daily business. Nevertheless, EA debts in any areas depicted in Table 3 may hamper project execution [29,30,48,69,71,73,75,82,83].

Financial. The *financial* dimension can be used to indicate the impact on *revenue* [25–28,47] or *cost* [25–28,31,32,48,66,69,70]. As both cover short-term or present indicators, (financial) *stability*[10] [31] has been added to cover the impact on long-term financial stability. *ROI* (return on investment) [32,66], and market share [32] are excluded as the impact of an EA debt is hard to determine.

Partner. External (business) partners might also recognize the impact of EA debts. Especially a negative impact on *customers* [26–28,31,32,69] should be avoided, as it could damage the company's reputation. Usually, less severe but still relevant is the impact on suppliers and collaborators. A *supplier* delivers goods or provides a service to the company so that there are dependencies (IT interfaces or interaction as part of value creation). A *collaborator* also interacts with the company but is not part of the value chain (e.g., common work in standardization bodies). Furthermore, there is a need to integrate *regulatory bodies* as the company needs to interact with them. Typical examples are the tax authority or customs organizations (international trade) [84].

Risk and Compliance. The two categories *risk* and *compliance* from Table 2 online appendix have been consolidated. Risk can have many flavors and might lead to a too-detailed taxonomy. A *risk* [26–28,48] exposed by an EA debt is not an isolated, abstract phenomenon but is associated with at least one of the further dimensions. *Security* [31,69] addresses IT and incorporates any security aspect in the company. Compliance can have various dimensions, three of which have been included in the taxonomy after discussions with four practitioners. *Legal* [31] compliance is defined by laws issued by the government of a nation. *Industry regulations* [31] are agreed upon by business partners within a given industry and must be adhered to. Potential consequences of not adhering to them are fines or a loss of reputation. *ESG* (environmental, social, governance) [85] captures further responsibilities of a company besides those enforced by laws. Examples for such responsibilities are *social responsibility* [26–28] or *environmental sustainability* [76].

4 Demonstrating the Taxonomies

The two taxonomies are demonstrated using a real-world example based on experiences in an e-commerce company. Some years ago, the company's IT department introduced a service-oriented middleware, an Enterprise Service Bus (ESB) [86]. The initial motivation is based on the idea that the IT department shifts from developing software applications towards software services. Such a design accelerated IT system development by reusing existing services. The ESB was

[10] We named this characteristic sustainability first, but after feedback from practitioner 3, we renamed it to stability as sustainability is a term with a much broader meaning.

introduced with a support team and the regulation to make its usage mandatory for any system integration. Management feared people would not shift towards a service-oriented mindset without such a regulation.

Table 5. Example Application of EA debt Taxonomy

dimension	characteristics
business	organization | process | product | business capability | business motivation
application	**IT system** | data | interface | service
technology	hardware | network | location | standard | **interoperability**
collaboration	skill | **capacity** | **policy** | documentation
consciousness	intentionally | **unintentionally**
life cycle	**identified** | in analysis | in mitigation | resolved

After two years with the ESB, it became apparent that IT projects were slowing down while costs were increasing, both leading to dissatisfied (IT) project managers. After an initial investigation, the situation with the ESB as an EA debt can be characterized as shown in Table 5. The ESB has not been introduced as a workaround; therefore, the ESB being an EA debt happened *unintentionally*. For the time being, it is located solely in the IT environment; therefore, none of the characteristics of the dimension *business* applies. ESB as *IT system* is a significant part of the EA debt, and the data were unaffected. Even though ESB as integration middleware focuses on providing interfaces, it was decided that the interfaces were no EA debt but rather the IT system itself. Only two web services were implemented and used. Any other integration only focused on data exchange and was implemented using the message queue component in the ESB product. The ESB was not used as an ESB but as message-oriented middleware, which was possible because the software product[11] also includes a corresponding module.

Further aspects of the EA debt have been identified on the *collaboration* side. The *capacity* of the ESB team was too low, resulting in project delays. The *policy* forcing IT teams to use the ESB appears to be one of the key reasons for using the service-oriented middleware as a message queue. The real integration need is to exchange data rather than to provide functionality to other systems. There is no specific aspect on the technology level, but people perceive *interoperability* as part of the EA debt. Furthermore, there are no guidance or assessment criteria for using an ESB as an integration platform. The EA debt has been identified at the current stage, but no further action has been planned.

The impact of service-oriented middleware on the company is shown in Table 6. Arrows indicate a supporting (↑) or a non-supporting (↓) impact on the corresponding characteristic. In this case, the ESB supports the corporate strategy as the management aims to provide a service-oriented IT infrastructure,

[11] webMethods by Software AG.

Table 6. Example Application of EA debt Taxonomy for Assessing the Impact

dimension	characteristics
business	outcome | efficiency | maturity | **resilience** ↑
application	data | application function | IT system | **portfolio** ↓
IT infrastructure	effectiveness | **efficiency** ↓ | reliability | scalability
management	**strategy** ↑ | resource usage | decision making | **project** ↓
financial	**revenue** ↓ | **cost** ↓ | stability
partner	**customer** ↓ | **supplier** ↓ | collaboration | regulatory body
risk & compliance	security | legal | industry regulation | ESG

including offering web services to customers via an external API (application programming interface). However, there were various complaints from project managers as the ESB hampers project execution, as it causes time delays and additional budget requirements. Consequently, the organization also perceived an increased cost, which is against the savings objective.

At the same time, the sales department complained about lost revenue as the partner integrations were not implemented on time. An impact on the financial stability of the organization could not be recognized. The same holds for *business outcome*, *efficiency*, or *maturity* as the ESB is a middleware IT solution, and the impact on the business processes is rather indirect. There only was a positive impact on *resilience* as the architecture allowed for faster adaptation to new business needs by reusing existing software services. Project delays affected not just a single *IT system* but the application *portfolio* as most systems depend on others, including the ESB. The delay of one project resulted in the delay of others, making application portfolio management difficult.

Consequently, IT as an organizational unit was perceived as *ineffective*. Interfaces to systems already connected with the ESB could be implemented more easily than a solution without ESB. However, integrations with business partners were hampered as each partner interface needed to be developed by or at least with the understaffed ESB team.

An overall assessment of the impact shows that a service-oriented architecture strategy was followed and that the implementation of services and data interfaces allowed for easier adaptation of the IT landscape. This was the initial intention of introducing the service-oriented middleware. Nevertheless, the organization's setup of the ESB causes financial issues and project delays. The priority of solving the EA debt becomes even higher as external partners are affected by the delays. After assessing the urgency, measures for dealing with the EA debt can be derived from the taxonomy characterizing the EA debt as soon as corresponding EA smells [12] are classified according to the taxonomy. Even though the IT system is central, debt also affects the organization. The team needs to be extended, and the regulations for using the ESB require rework.

5 Discussion

The study follows a structured methodology, combining SLRs with practitioner feedback to refine the taxonomies. This approach ensures that the taxonomies are informed by existing research and practice. Furthermore, applying the taxonomies to a real-world example involving a service-oriented middleware project in an e-commerce company illustrates their potential practical use. This example demonstrates how organizations can identify the sources of EA debts and plan appropriate mitigation strategies.

The taxonomies are designed with practitioners in mind, offering clarity and usability. Their alignment with established frameworks, such as ArchiMate, enhances their relevance and makes them suitable for integration into current enterprise architecture practices.

The taxonomies presented in this study are designed to be concise, robust, and explanatory, making them practical for researchers and practitioners. Their conciseness is reflected in the clearly defined dimensions and characteristics, which focus on key aspects of EA debts without adding unnecessary complexity. This ensures they are straightforward and can be applied across various organizational contexts. The robustness of the taxonomies comes from their foundation in SLRs and practitioner input, which helps ensure they are relevant and adaptable to real-world scenarios. The taxonomies provide a structured way to differentiate between various types of EA debts by including dimensions such as business, application, technology, and collaboration. Lastly, their explanatory nature is evident in their ability to guide users in identifying EA debts, understanding their potential impacts, and planning mitigation strategies.

While the study makes meaningful contributions, some limitations may affect its generalizability and applicability. One concern is the scope of the literature reviews. The reviews were conducted using specific search terms and a limited selection of databases (Springer Link, ScienceDirect, and IEEE). This approach might have excluded relevant studies using alternative terminology or published in other venues.

The reliance on a small group of practitioners for feedback may also limit the diversity of perspectives incorporated into the taxonomies. The insights provided by the three practitioners may not fully reflect the challenges organizations face across different industries and contexts.

Although the twin taxonomies were developed with Nickerson et al.'s structured procedure [18], several threats to validity arise from the authors' unavoidable subjective judgments. First, the decision to stop iterating once the artifacts seemed"concise, robust, and explanatory" was evaluated by the authors themselves, so their personal experience determined which dimensions or characteristics survived each round. Second, in the systematic literature reviews, the authors had to cluster heterogeneous terms into six concept categories, yet many terms legitimately fit more than one category, meaning the final mapping reflects interpretive choices that other researchers might contest.

Additionally, the taxonomies are primarily conceptual and have not yet undergone extensive empirical validation. While grounded in literature and practitioner feedback, broader testing in diverse organizational environments would strengthen their practical utility.

Using a single case example to illustrate the taxonomies poses another limitation. While the example highlights the frameworks' application in an e-commerce context, it may not capture the complexity or variety of EA debts encountered in other sectors, such as healthcare or manufacturing.

Finally, as enterprise architecture practices evolve, the taxonomies must be periodically updated to address emerging issues such as sustainability, artificial intelligence, and regulatory changes. These areas may introduce new dimensions not currently included in the frameworks.

6 Related Work

Related work in EA can be categorized into efforts that structure EA through taxonomies or ontologies. Zimmermann and Zimmermann [87] developed an ontology tailored for service-oriented architectures, focusing on aligning architecture metamodels with standards to ensure adaptability and scalability. Similarly, Hinkelmann and Maise [88] introduced the ArchiMEO ontology to bridge EA and information management, offering a framework to integrate data and processes with architecture components for better decision-making and operational consistency. Syynimaa [89] proposed a taxonomy categorizing EA purposes based on practical applications and strategic value, emphasizing the need for EA to drive organizational efficiency, support decision-making, and enable innovation. These works highlight structured approaches to improving EA alignment, modularity, and measurable value.

The second category of related research focuses on structuring the domain of TD. Lenarduzzi et al. [23] review TD prioritization and propose a taxonomy categorizing debt types, strategies, and influencing factors, highlighting the need to balance new development with debt repayment. Tom et al. [50] expand on this by presenting a taxonomy of TD types, including code, design, and architecture, along with a framework for proactive management. Alves et al. [90] introduce an ontology to standardize TD identification and classification, aiming to improve stakeholder communication and decision-making. Ampatzoglou et al. [91] explore the financial implications of TD, linking costs and repayment metrics to specific debt types, offering insights into the economic trade-offs of debt management. Together, these works provide a comprehensive understanding of TD, from categorization to prioritization and financial evaluation.

Our work differentiates itself from the research above by integrating the fields of EA and TD by developing two taxonomies specifically addressing EA debts. While prior works in the EA domain focus on structuring EA through ontologies or taxonomies that align architectural components with business goals or practical applications, this study addresses the concept of "debt" within EA. Unlike these works, which emphasize the alignment, modularity, and strategic use of EA, this study introduces a novel perspective by framing the challenges in EA as "debts" that need identification, characterization, and impact assessment.

Similarly, while TD research provides taxonomies and frameworks for managing debts in software development, this work extends the debt concept to the enterprise level, encompassing broader organizational dimensions such as business, collaboration, and compliance. Additionally, the focus on integrating characterization and impact assessment into a cohesive framework differentiated our work from previous work, offering practitioners a practical, dual-purpose tool that bridges theoretical insights from EA structuring and TD management into a unified approach.

7 Conclusions

This paper introduces two taxonomies to categorize EA debts: one for characterizing EA debts and another for assessing their impacts. The taxonomies were developed rigorously, including SLRs and iterative refinement with practitioner feedback. A practical case example demonstrates their applicability in identifying, describing, and mitigating EA debts in real-world scenarios. The frameworks aim to help organizations improve their understanding of EA debts and take informed actions to minimize their long-term risks and costs.

There is no specific order in which the two taxonomies should be used. If EA debts are not known yet, it might be beneficial to start to identify symptoms and note them in the taxonomy for the impact of EA debts. There might be several reasons causing the symptoms and, consequently, several EA debts, each of which can be characterized by the first taxonomy. Starting the EA debt investigation with the first taxonomy (characterizing EA debts) seems reasonable if debts are already known but not documented (or understood) in detail. The interplay of the two taxonomies will be further elaborated during the development of the EA debt management method as introduced in [11].

The proposed taxonomies have the potential to impact both scientific research and practical enterprise management. For researchers, they provide a structured foundation to explore the under-researched domain of EA debts. By formalizing key dimensions and attributes, the taxonomies open avenues for empirical validation, development of new models, and integration with other frameworks in the EA and TD field. For practitioners, the taxonomies offer actionable tools to address EA debts systematically, fostering better decision-making, resource allocation, and alignment of architecture with organizational goals. Including characterization and impact assessment allows organizations to take a comprehensive approach to managing EA debts and balancing strategic and operational needs.

Future work can focus on several areas to enhance the applicability and relevance of this research. First, broader empirical validation is necessary to test the taxonomies across diverse industries, organizational sizes, and cultural contexts. Second, integrating these taxonomies into existing EA management tools could improve their accessibility and adoption in practice. Third, the frameworks should be updated regularly to reflect evolving challenges, such as the rise of artificial intelligence, sustainability concerns, and data privacy requirements.

Finally, extending the taxonomies to include quantitative metrics for evaluating the severity and priority of EA debts could further support organizations in making data-driven decisions. These efforts will strengthen the theoretical foundation of EA debt management and ensure its continued relevance and usefulness in an ever-changing organizational landscape.

Disclosure of Interests. The authors have no competing interests to declare that are relevant to the content of this article.

References

1. Tabrizi, B., Lam, E., Girard, K., Irvin, V.: Digital transformation is not about technology. Harvard Bus. Rev., 2–7 (2019)
2. Morakanyane, R., Grace, A., O'Reilly, P.: Conceptualizing digital transformation in business organizations: a systematic review of literature. In: 30th Bled eConference: Digital Transformation - From Connecting Things to Transforming our Lives, BLED 2017, pp. 427–444 (2017). ISBN 9789612860431
3. Lankhorst, M.: Enterprise Architecture at Work: Modelling, Communication and Analysis, 4th edn. Springer, Heidelberg (2017)
4. Lapalme, J.: Three schools of thought on enterprise architecture. IT Prof. **14**(6), 37–43 (2012). ISSN 1520-9202
5. Wierda, G.: Mastering ArchiMate: A Serious Introduction to the ArchiMate Enterprise Architecture Modeling Language, version 3.0.1. R&A, The Netherlands, edition iii. tc1 edition (2017)
6. Kaisler, S., Armour, F.: 15 years of enterprise architecting at HICSS: revisiting the critical problems. In: Proceedings of the 50th Hawaii International Conference on System Sciences 2017, pp. 4807–4816 (2017)
7. Kotusev, S.: Enterprise architecture: what did we study? Int. J. Coop. Inf. Syst. **26**(4) (2017)
8. Wierda, G.: Chess and the Art of Enterprise Architecure. R&A (2015). ISBN 978-90-819840-5-8
9. Bente, S., Bombosch, U., Langade, S.: Collaborative Enterprise Architecture: Enriching EA with Lean, Agile, and Enterprise 2.0 Practices. Morgan Kaufmann (2012). ISBN 978-0-12-415934-1
10. Hacks, S., Hofert, H., Salentin, J., Yeong, Y.C., Lichter, H.: Towards the definition of enterprise architecture debts. In: 2019 IEEE 23rd EDOCW, pp. 9–16. IEEE (2019). ISBN 978-1-7281-4598-3
11. Alexander, P., Hacks, S., Jung, J., Lichter, H., Steffens, U., Uludag, Ö.: A framework for managing enterprise architecture debts - outline and research directions. In: Koschmider, A., Michael, J., Thalheim, B. (eds.) Proceedings of the 10th International Workshop on Enterprise Modeling and Information Systems Architectures. CEUR workshop proceedings, Kiel, Germany, 14–15 May 2020, vol. 2628, pp. 5–10 (2020)
12. Salentin, J., Hacks, S.: Towards a catalog of enterprise architecture smells. In: WI2020 Community Tracks, pp. 276–290. GITO Verlag (2020)
13. Smajevic, M., Hacks, S., Bork, D.: Using knowledge graphs to detect enterprise architecture smells. In: Serral, E., Stirna, J., Ralyté, J., Grabis, J. (eds.) PoEM 2021. LNBIP, vol. 432, pp. 48–63. Springer, Cham (2021). https://doi.org/10.1007/978-3-030-91279-6_4

14. Yeong, Y., Hacks, S., Lichter, H.: Prioritization of EA debts facilitating portfolio theory. In: CEUR Workshop Proceedings, vol. 2511 (2019). ISSN 16130073
15. Liss, L., Kämmerling, H., Alexander, P., Lichter, H.: Towards a catalog of refactoring solutions for enterprise architecture smells. In: Joint Proceedings of SEED 2021 & QuASoQ 2021 Co-Located with 28th Asia Pacific Software Engineering Conference 2021, Taipei [Virtual], 6 December 2021, vol. 3062, pp. 60–69 (2021)
16. Jung, J., Hacks, S., Gooijer, T., Kinnunen, M., Rehring, K.: Revealing common enterprise architecture debts: conceptualization and critical reflection on a workshop format industry experience report. In: 2021 IEEE 25th International Enterprise Distributed Object Computing Workshop (EDOCW), pp. 271–278 (2021)
17. Daoudi, S., Larsson, M., Hacks, S., Jung, J.: Discovering and assessing enterprise architecture debts. Complex Syst. Inf. Model. Q. **35**, 1–29 (2023)
18. Nickerson, R.C., Varshney, U., Muntermann, J.: A method for taxonomy development and its application in information systems. Eur. J. Inf. Syst. **22**(3), 336–359 (2013). https://doi.org/10.1057/ejis.2012.26
19. Okoli, C.: A guide to conducting a standalone systematic literature review. Commun. Assoc. Inf. Syst. **37** (2015). Article 43. http://aisel.aisnet.org/cais/vol37/iss1/43
20. Brocke, J.V., Simons, A., Niehaves, B., Riemer, K., Plattfaut, R., Cleven, A.: Reconstructing the giant: on the importance of Rigour in documenting the literature search process. In: ECIS 2009 Proceedings, p. 161 (2009). https://aisel.aisnet.org/ecis2009/161
21. Oosterwyk, G., Brown, I., Geeling, S.: A synthesis of literature review guidelines from information systems journals. In: Proceedings of 4th International Conference on the Internet, Cyber Security and Information Systems (2019). https://api.semanticscholar.org/CorpusID:210909597
22. Wu, F., Weld, D.S.: Automatically refining the Wikipedia infobox ontology. In: Proceedings of the 17th International Conference on World Wide Web, WWW 2008, pp. 635–644. Association for Computing Machinery, New York, NY, USA (2008)
23. Lenarduzzi, V., Besker, T., Taibi, D., Martini, A., Fontana, F.A.: A systematic literature review on technical debt prioritization: strategies, processes, factors, and tools. J. Syst. Softw. **171** (2021)
24. Li, Z., Avgerioua, P., Liang, P.: A systematic mapping study on technical debt and its management. J. Syst. Softw. **101**, 193–220 (2015)
25. Espinosa, J.A., Boh, W.F., DeLone, W.: The organizational impact of enterprise architecture: a research framework. In: 2011 44th Hawaii International Conference on System Sciences, pp. 1–10 (2011). https://doi.org/10.1109/HICSS.2011.425
26. Plessius, H., van Steenbergen, M., Ravesteijn, P., Versendaal, J.: Areas where enterprise architecture contributes to organizational goals – a quantitative study in The Netherlands. In: Sales, T.P., Proper, H.A., Guizzardi, G., Montali, M., Maggi, F.M., Fonseca, C.M. (eds.) Enterprise Design, Operations, and Computing. EDOC 2022 Workshops. Springer, Cham (2023)
27. Plessius, H., van Steenbergen, M., Ravesteijn, P., Versendaal, J.: A longitudinal view on the perceived contribution of enterprise architecture in The Netherlands. In: Proceedings of the 28th International Conference on Enterprise Design, Operations, and Computing (EDOC 2024), Vienna (Austria), 10–13 September 2024 (2024)
28. Plessius, H., van Steenbergen, M., Ravesteijn, P., Versendaal, J.: The development of an instrument to assess the areas where enterprise architecture contributes

to organizational goals. Inf. Syst. Manag. **42**(3), 1–18 (2024). https://doi.org/10.1080/10580530.2024.2387578
29. Lange, M., Mendling, J., Recker, J.: An empirical analysis of the factors and measures of enterprise architecture management success. Eur. J. Inf. Syst. **25**(5), 411–421 (2016)
30. Arnold, I.: Enterprise Architecture Function: A Pattern Language for Planning, Design and Execution. Springer, Cham (2022)
31. Ziemann, J.: Fundamentals of Enterprise Architecture Management: Foundations for Steering the Enterprise-Wide Digital System. Springer, Cham (2022)
32. Niemi, E., Pekkola, S.: The benefits of enterprise architecture in organizational transformation. Bus. Inf. Syst. Eng. **62**(6), 585–597 (2020)
33. Winter, R., Fischer, R.: Essential layers, artifacts, and dependencies of enterprise architecture. In: 2006 10th IEEE International Enterprise Distributed Object Computing Conference Workshops (EDOCW'06), p. 30 (2006). https://doi.org/10.1109/EDOCW.2006.33
34. Simon, D.: Introduction: demystifying business architecture. In: Simon, D., Schmidt, C. (eds.) Business Architecture Management. MP, pp. 1–17. Springer, Cham (2015). https://doi.org/10.1007/978-3-319-14571-6_1
35. Ahmad, M.O., Gustavsson, T.: Nexus between psychological safety and non-technical debt in large-scale agile enterprise resource planning systems development. In: Jarzębowicz, A., Luković, I., Przybyłek, A., Staroń, M., Ahmad, M.O., Ochodek, M. (eds.) Software, System, and Service Engineering, pp. 63–81. Springer Nature Switzerland, Cham (2024)
36. Dong, Q.H., Vogel-Heuser, B., Neumann, E.-M.: Including validation of process control systems' engineering into the technical debt classification. Forschung im Ingenieurwesen **88**(1) (2024)
37. Nielsen, M.E., Østergaard Madsen, C., Lungu, M.F.: Technical debt management: a systematic literature review and research agenda for digital government. In: Viale Pereira, G., et al. (eds.) EGOV 2020. LNCS, vol. 12219, pp. 121–137. Springer, Cham (2020). https://doi.org/10.1007/978-3-030-57599-1_10
38. Mendes, T.S., Gomes, F.G.S., Goncalves, D.P., Mendonca, M.G., Novais, R.L., Spínola, R.O.: VisminerTD: a tool for automatic identification and interactive monitoring of the evolution of technical debt items. J. Br. Comput. Soc. **25**(1) (2019)
39. Alves, N.S., Mendes, T.S., de Mendonça, M.G., Spínola, R.O., Shull, F., Seaman, C.: Identification and management of technical debt: a systematic mapping study. Inf. Softw. Technol. **70**, 100–121 (2016)
40. Rios, N., de Mendonca Neto, M.G., Spinola, R.O.: A tertiary study on technical debt: types, management strategies, research trends, and base information for practitioners. Inf. Softw. Technol. **102**, 117–145 (2018)
41. Yang, Y., Michel, R., Wade, J., Verma, D., Törngren, M., Alelyani, T.: Towards a taxonomy of technical debt for cots-intensive cyber physical systems. Procedia Comput. Sci. **153**, 108–117 (2019). 17th Annual Conference on Systems Engineering Research (CSER)
42. Codabux, Z., Vidoni, M., Fard, F.H.: Technical debt in the peer-review documentation of R packages: a rOpenSci case study. In: 2021 IEEE/ACM 18th International Conference on Mining Software Repositories (MSR), pp. 195–206 (2021). https://doi.org/10.1109/MSR52588.2021.00032
43. Slupczynski, A., Hacks, S.: Towards a knowledge base of terms on enterprise architecture debt. In: Sales, T.P., de Kinderen, S., Proper, H.A., Pufahl, L., Karastoy-

anova, D., van Sinderen, M. (eds.) Enterprise Design, Operations, and Computing. EDOC 2023 Workshops, pp. 194–210. Springer Nature, Cham, Switzerland (2024)
44. Rios, N., Spínola, R., Mendonca, M., Seaman, C.: The practitioners' point of view on the concept of technical debt and its causes and consequences: a design for a global family of industrial surveys and its first results from Brazil. Empir. Softw. Eng. **25**(5), 3216–3287 (2020)
45. da Fonseca Lage, L.C., Kalinowski, M., Trevisan, D., Spinola, R.: Usability technical debt in software projects: a multi-case study. In: 2019 ACM/IEEE International Symposium on Empirical Software Engineering and Measurement (ESEM), pp. 1–6 (2019). https://doi.org/10.1109/ESEM.2019.8870180
46. Offerman, T., Stettina, C.J., Plaat, A.: Business capabilities: a systematic literature review and a research agenda. In: 2017 International Conference on Engineering, Technology and Innovation (ICE/ITMC), pp. 383–393 (2017). https://doi.org/10.1109/ICE.2017.8279911
47. Muse, B., Nagy, C., Cleve, A., Khomh, F., Antoniol, G.: FIXME: synchronize with database! An empirical study of data access self-admitted technical debt. Empirical Softw. Eng. **27**(6) (2022)
48. Jung, J., Fraunholz, B.: Masterclass Enterprise Architecture Management. Springer, Cham (2021)
49. Martini, A., Besker, T., Bosch, J.: Chapter 4 technical debt tracking: current state of practice: a survey and multiple case study in 15 large organizations. In: Bosch, J., Carlson, J., Holmström Olsson, H., Sandahl, K., Staron, M. (eds.) Accelerating Digital Transformation: 10 Years of Software Center, pp. 87–118. Springer International Publishing, Cham (2022)
50. Tom, E., Aurum, A., Vidgen, R.: An exploration of technical debt. J. Syst. Softw. **86**(6), 1498–1516 (2013)
51. Kleinwaks, H., Batchelor, A., Bradley, T.H.: Ontology for technical debt in systems engineering. IEEE Open J. Syst. Eng. **1**, 111–122 (2023). https://doi.org/10.1109/OJSE.2023.3316395
52. The Open Group: The TOGAF Standard: Content, Capability, and Governance, 10th edn. Van Haren Publishing, Hertogenbosch (2022)
53. Ciancarini, P., Russo, D.: The strategic technical debt management model: an empirical proposal. In: Kruglov, A., Masyagin, S., Sillitti, A., Succi, G. (eds.) Open Source Systems, vol. Ivanov, pp. 131–140. Springer International Publishing, Cham (2020)
54. Fowler, M.: Technical debt quadrant (2009). https://martinfowler.com/bliki/TechnicalDebtQuadrant.html
55. Vidoni, M., Cunico, M.L.: On technical debt in mathematical programming: an exploratory study. Math. Program. Comput. **14**(4), 781–818 (2022)
56. Brown, D.A.R.: What Is Technical Debt?, pp. 3–14. Apress, Berkeley, CA (2024)
57. Codabux, Z., Williams, B.: Managing technical debt: an industrial case study. In: 2013 4th International Workshop on Managing Technical Debt (MTD), pp. 8–15 (2013). https://doi.org/10.1109/MTD.2013.6608672
58. Slupczynski, A., Alexander, P., Lichter, H.: Defining and evaluating prudence and recklessness of enterprise architecture debt. In: Filipe, J., Śmiałek, M., Brodsky, A., Hammoudi, S. (eds.) Enterprise Information Systems, pp. 237–261. Springer Nature, Switzerland, Cham (2024)
59. Franco, E.F., Hirama, K., Armenia, S., dos Santos, J.R.: A systems interpretation of the software evolution laws and their impact on technical debt management and software maintainability. Software Qual. J. **31**(1), 179–209 (2023)

60. Cassee, N., Zampetti, F., Novielli, N., Serebrenik, A., Di Penta, M.: Self-admitted technical debt and comments' polarity: an empirical study. Empirical Softw. Eng. **27**(6) (2022)
61. Xiao, T., Zeng, Z., Wang, D., Hata, H., McIntosh, S., Matsumoto, K.: Quantifying and characterizing clones of self-admitted technical debt in build systems. Empirical Softw. Eng. **29**(2) (2024)
62. Sharma, R., Shahbazi, R., Fard, F.H., Codabux, Z., Vidoni, M.: Self-admitted technical debt in R: detection and causes. Autom. Softw. Eng. **29**(2) (2022)
63. Zampetti, F., Serebrenik, A., Di Penta, M.: Automatically learning patterns for self-admitted technical debt removal. In: 2020 IEEE 27th International Conference on Software Analysis, Evolution and Reengineering (SANER), pp. 355–366 (2020). https://doi.org/10.1109/SANER48275.2020.9054868
64. Ebrahimi, A.M., Oliva, G.A., Hassan, A.E.: Self-admitted technical debt in Ethereum smart contracts: a large-scale exploratory study. IEEE Trans. Software Eng. **49**(9), 4304–4323 (2023). https://doi.org/10.1109/TSE.2023.3289808
65. Fucci, G., Cassee, N., Zampetti, F., Novielli, N., Serebrenik, A., Di Penta, M.: Waiting around or job half-done? Sentiment in self-admitted technical debt. In: 2021 IEEE/ACM 18th International Conference on Mining Software Repositories (MSR), pp. 403–414 (2021). https://doi.org/10.1109/MSR52588.2021.00052
66. van der Merwe, A., Gerber, A., van der Linde, J.: The impact of managerial enterprise architecture decisions on software development employees. In: Proceedings of the First International Conference on Enterprise Systems: ES 2013, pp. 1–7 (2013). https://doi.org/10.1109/ES.2013.6690093
67. Lagerström, R., Sommestad, T., Buschle, M., Ekstedt, M.: Enterprise architecture management's impact on information technology success. In: 2011 44th Hawaii International Conference on System Sciences, pp. 1–10 (2011). https://doi.org/10.1109/HICSS.2011.187
68. Castro, S., Jung, J.: Towards measuring success of enterprise architecture decisions: survey among practitioners and outline of a framework. Enterp. Archit. Prof. J. (2021)
69. Gong, Y., Janssen, M.: The value of and myths about enterprise architecture. Int. J. Inf. Manage. **46**, 1–9 (2019)
70. Gong, Y., Janssen, M.: Why organizations fail in implementing enterprise architecture initiatives? Inf. Syst. Front. **25**(4), 1401–1419 (2023)
71. Möhring, M., Keller, B., Schmidt, R., Sandkuhl, K., Zimmermann, A.: Digitalization and enterprise architecture management: a perspective on benefits and challenges. SN Bus. Econ. **3**(2), 46 (2023)
72. Alwadain, A., Fielt, E., Korthaus, A., Rosemann, M.: Empirical insights into the development of a service-oriented enterprise architecture. Data Knowl. Eng. **105**, 39–52 (2016). Knowledge Engineering for Enterprise, Integration, Interoperability and Networking: Theory and Applications
73. Jager, E.: Getting Started with Enterprise Architecture: A Practical and Pragmatic Approach to Learning the Basics of Enterprise Architecture. Apress, Berkeley, CA (2023)
74. Graves, T.: Everyday Enterprise Architecture: Sense-making, Strategy, Structures, and Solutions. Apress, Berkeley, CA (2023)
75. Anthopoulos, L.G., Gerogiannis, V., Fitsilis, P.: The impact of enterprise architecture's absence in e-government development: the Greek case. In: 2010 International Conference on Information Society, pp. 122–127 (2010). https://doi.org/10.1109/i-Society16502.2010.6018808

76. Gampfer, F., Jürgens, A., Müller, M., Buchkremer, R.: Past, current and future trends in enterprise architecture-a view beyond the horizon. Comput. Ind. **100**, 70–84 (2018)
77. Gong, Y., Yang, J., Shi, X.: Towards a comprehensive understanding of digital transformation in government: analysis of flexibility and enterprise architecture. Gov. Inf. Q. **37**(3), 101487 (2020)
78. Luke, E.: Defining and measuring scalability. In: Proceedings of Scalable Parallel Libraries Conference, pp. 183–186 (1993). https://doi.org/10.1109/SPLC.1993.365568
79. Pattij, M., van de Wetering, R., Kusters, R.: Enhanced digital transformation supporting capabilities through enterprise architecture management: a fsQCA perspective. Digit. Bus. **2**(2), 100036 (2022)
80. Rijo, R., Martinho, R., Ermida, D.: Developing an enterprise architecture proof of concept in a Portuguese hospital. Procedia Comput. Sci. **64**, 1217–1225 (2015). Conference on ENTERprise Information Systems/International Conference on Project MANagement/Conference on Health and Social Care Information Systems and Technologies, CENTERIS/ProjMAN / HCist 2015 October 7–9 (2015)
81. Hook, D., Gustafsson, P., Nordstrom, L., Johnson, P.: An enterprise architecture based method enabling quantified analysis of it support system's impact on maintenance management. In: PICMET 2009 - 2009 Portland International Conference on Management of Engineering & Technology, pp. 3176–3189 (2009). https://doi.org/10.1109/PICMET.2009.5262273
82. Foorthuis, R., van Steenbergen, M., Brinkkemper, S., Bruls, W.A.G.: A theory building study of enterprise architecture practices and benefits. Inf. Syst. Front. **18**(3), 541–564 (2016)
83. Al-Kharusi, H., Miskon, S., Bahari, M.: Enterprise architects and stakeholders alignment framework in enterprise architecture development. IseB **19**(1), 137–181 (2021)
84. Hinkelman, E.G.: Dictionary of International Trade: The Handbook of the Global Trade Community, 14th edn. World Trade Press (2024)
85. Li, T.-T., Wang, K., Sueyoshi, T., Wang, D.D.: ESG: research progress and future prospects. Sustainability **13**(21) (2021). ISSN 2071-1050. https://doi.org/10.3390/su132111663. https://www.mdpi.com/2071-1050/13/21/11663
86. Ji-Chen, J., Ming, G.: Enterprise service bus and an open source implementation. In: 2006 International Conference on Management Science and Engineering, pp. 926–930 (2006). https://doi.org/10.1109/ICMSE.2006.313995
87. Zimmermann, A., Zimmermann, G.: Enterprise architecture ontology for services computing. Serv. Comput. (2012)
88. Hinkelmann, K., Maise, M.: Connecting enterprise architecture and information objects using an enterprise ontology. In: Proceedings of the International Conference on Enterprise Information Systems (2013)
89. Syynimaa, N.: Taxonomy of purpose of enterprise architecture. Centaur - University of Reading (2010). https://centaur.reading.ac.uk/36289/
90. Alves, N., Ribeiro, L., Caires, V.: Towards an ontology of terms on technical debt. In: Proceedings of the International Conference on Managing Technical Debt. IEEE (2014). https://ieeexplore.ieee.org/abstract/document/6974882/
91. Ampatzoglou, A., Ampatzoglou, A., Chatzigeorgiou, A., Avgeriou, P.: The financial aspect of managing technical debt: a systematic literature review. Inf. Softw. Technol. **64**, 52–73 (2015). ISSN 0950-5849. https://doi.org/10.1016/j.infsof.2015.04.001. https://www.sciencedirect.com/science/article/pii/S0950584915000762

Leveraging Enterprise Architecture for Business-IT Alignment: A Case Study of a Re-Engineering Project

Cristian Manuel Avram, Erik Perjons, and Simon Hacks(✉)

Stockholm University, Stockholm, Sweden
{perjons,simon.hacks}@dsv.su.se

Abstract. This study investigates the role of Enterprise Architecture (EA) in enhancing business-IT alignment during a large-scale re-engineering project at a European agency. Using a qualitative case study approach, the research analyzes insights from business and IT stakeholders involved in the Surveillance Systems Re-engineering (SSR) project. Focus group sessions were conducted to identify the strengths, weaknesses, and practical recommendations for EA implementation. The findings are organized across four dimensions of alignment: Communication, Governance, Partnership, and IT Scope & Architecture—adapted from Luftman's maturity model. Results show that EA contributes significantly to mutual understanding, learning acceleration, and strategic alignment but is challenged by complex methodologies, rigid modeling languages, and organizational readiness issues.

Keywords: Enterprise Architecture · Business-IT Alignment · Public Sector IT · Case Study Analysis

1 Introduction

Organizations have long been concerned with aligning business goals and IT strategies, especially as IT has become a key factor in their success [8]. Many researchers argue that business-IT alignment is one of the most important success factors for modern organizations [9]. However, the challenge remains: how can organizations achieve this alignment in practice? As Chen [7] points out, most practical efforts still focus on fixing misalignments rather than building strong, integrated systems from the beginning.

This paper presents a case study of the European Centre for Disease Prevention and Control (ECDC), a public health agency that undertook a large-scale IT transformation project. The Surveillance Systems Re-engineering (SSR) project aimed to modernize and integrate several existing disease surveillance and control applications into a unified platform called the Surveillance Portal (SuPo). The goal was to combine two major types of systems, indicator-based and event-based surveillance, into one shared interface, improving communication and efficiency.

© The Author(s), under exclusive license to Springer Nature Switzerland AG 2026
A. Gianola et al. (Eds.): EDOC 2025, LNCS 16213, pp. 23–39, 2026.
https://doi.org/10.1007/978-3-032-15140-7_2

The systems involved in this project contained large amounts of data submitted by EU member states and information gathered from external sources such as newspapers, social media, and the web. The SSR project also involved integrating data analysis tools such as a data warehouse, business intelligence (BI) software, and extract-transform-load (ETL) processes. Due to its complexity, the project was divided into several sub-projects, including system development, data migration, and integration with analytical tools.

The need for such a large-scale re-engineering effort arose from several problems: high IT costs caused by fragmented development across business units, limited business value due to poor system integration, and outdated technologies that were expensive to maintain. ECDC implemented an Enterprise Architecture (EA) framework to address these issues. This framework was intended to help define a clear vision for the future IT landscape, support decision-making, and bridge the gap between business needs and IT solutions.

Although business-IT alignment is widely discussed in the academic literature, most research either focuses on its theoretical benefits or offers general strategies for achieving it. As Chan and Reich [6] observed, business-IT alignment "remains an elusive goal." Practical examples of achieving this alignment, particularly through tools like EA, are still limited. EA has been recognized as a promising method for improving alignment in complex projects [4,22,28]. Still, there is little evidence of how it works in practice, especially in projects involving integrating multiple applications and large-scale data analysis.

This study aims to address this gap by exploring the role of EA in improving business-IT alignment during the SSR project at ECDC. It investigates the strengths and weaknesses of applying EA in this context and provides recommendations for other organizations planning similar initiatives.

The main research question is:

What impact does Enterprise Architecture have on business-IT alignment in large-scale re-engineering projects?

To support this inquiry, two sub-questions are addressed:

1. *What are the strengths and weaknesses of Enterprise Architecture from a business-IT alignment perspective?*
2. *What can be recommended to other organizations planning to implement Enterprise Architecture for better business-IT alignment?*

This paper aims to contribute to the practical understanding of business-IT alignment by presenting lessons from the SSR project. While the findings are especially relevant to organizations that collect, analyze, and report large amounts of data, they may also apply to any organization interested in using EA to align IT with business goals.

The remainder of this work is structured as follows. Section 2 reviews the relevant literature on EA and business-IT alignment. Section 3 outlines the research methodology. Section 4 introduces the case organization and describes the context and objectives of the SRR project. Section 5 presents the empirical results. Section 7 discusses the main findings and limitations and suggests future research.

2 Related Work

Recent literature shows a growing interest in the relationship between EA and business-IT alignment. This trend reflects the increasing maturity of both domains, which were not sufficiently developed until about a decade ago to support combined research efforts. As EA and business-IT alignment have evolved, researchers have increasingly explored how they interact and support one another.

Ross [21] suggests that business-IT alignment is a key return on investment from EA, highlighting alignment as a direct outcome of architectural efforts. In their systematic review, Zhang et al. [28] emphasize the business need and IT to align rapidly and continuously. They argue that EA contributes to this by offering a coherent view of the past, present, and future states of business and IT and that, along with business process management and ontology, EA is one of the key techniques to address alignment challenges.

Several studies have examined the practical benefits of EA on alignment. For instance, Alaeddini and Salekfard [1] analyze EA initiatives in Iran, concluding that EA improves alignment in real-world projects. Bradley et al. [4] also find that EA maturity positively affects alignment, suggesting that this combination enhances enterprise agility. In a comparative study, Zarvic and Wieringa [27] evaluate various EA frameworks for their ability to support alignment. At the same time, Iacob et al. [17] and Wegmann et al. [26] go further by proposing methods and tools designed to facilitate alignment through EA.

In addition to enabling alignment, some scholars argue that EA can help sustain an already established alignment between business and IT [13,16,24]. Other studies demonstrate broader benefits of combining EA with alignment practices, such as reducing organizational complexity [23], enhancing enterprise agility [10], increasing return on IT investment [5], reducing uncertainty [23], and improving system availability and resilience [15].

Clarke et al. [11] provide further evidence by surveying practitioners on the perceived benefits of EA. Their findings indicate a strong belief that EA improves the relationship between business and IT and contributes positively to IT value and organizational re-engineering. The study also finds that the outcomes are beneficial regardless of whether organizations adopt standard or custom EA frameworks. Notably, EA is reported to have a stronger influence on business-IT alignment than technology choices.

Recent research has added new insights to this area. Beese et al. [3] present a longitudinal case study at Commerzbank, demonstrating how portfolios of control mechanisms can anchor EA more effectively in an organization and adapt to strategic shifts. Andrén et al. [2] explore strategic alignment through a case study, highlighting the practical challenges of aligning IT and business strategies. Fragoso and Vasconcelos [14] introduce a governance-oriented lens on EA, emphasizing the dynamic interplay between temporary and permanent roles in enterprise transformation. Őri and Szabó [20] offer a comprehensive systematic literature review of business-IT misalignment, identifying patterns, symptoms, and potential remedies through EA-driven approaches.

Despite these positive assessments, some studies present a more critical view. For instance, Vicente et al. [25] argue that combining EA with other methodologies, such as ITIL, may lead to redundant efforts and wasted resources. Moreover, several authors highlight ongoing challenges. Choi et al. [10] note that the effects of EA on alignment are not always apparent, particularly in dynamic business environments. Others point to weaknesses in the theoretical foundations of EA [26], the limitations of current modeling languages, and the practical difficulties in implementing and managing EA initiatives. The lack of empirical, practice-based research also makes it difficult to evaluate the effectiveness of EA in supporting business-IT alignment in real-world settings.

Overall, the literature reflects a broad consensus that EA has the potential to improve business-IT alignment significantly. However, it also highlights the need for more empirical research to understand the practical implications and limitations of applying EA in complex organizational contexts.

3 Research Method

This study adopts a qualitative research strategy, with a case study approach selected to investigate the impact of EA on business-IT alignment in a real-world, complex organizational setting. The aim is not to test specific alignment theories but to gather practical insights into how EA influences alignment by examining a large-scale transformation project.

Following Denscombe [12], the selected strategy was evaluated against suitability, feasibility, ethics, usefulness, and appropriateness criteria. A case study approach is particularly suited for exploring complex social units in depth, allowing for collecting detailed accounts of events and interactions that may not emerge through broader strategies. ECDC, specifically its SSR project, represents a bounded and self-contained case aligned with these principles.

Focus group sessions were chosen as the primary data collection method to capture insights from professionals with deep knowledge of the SSR project. This interactive approach encourages the exchange of experiences and viewpoints, enabling participants to build on each other's reflections, especially valuable for revealing consensus and disagreement on key issues.

Expert sampling, a form of purposive sampling, was used to select participants. Individuals were identified through the institutional memory of the SSR project, using the modeling records in Sparx Enterprise Architect software. Two focus groups were conducted, one with IT staff (four participants, one providing input in writing) and one with business users (two participants). Questions were sent in advance to encourage thoughtful responses, and participants were fully informed of the research purpose and consented.

Each focus group session lasted approximately one hour. Discussions were recorded using multiple devices to avoid data loss, and transcripts were produced on the same day. Transcriptions included verbal and non-verbal elements to retain contextual depth. Separating groups by area (business vs. IT) helped foster open dialogue and honest feedback.

Thematic analysis was used to analyze the qualitative data, following a structured three-step process: (1) Transcription: Verbatim transcripts of each session were created in Microsoft Word, preserving content and emotional nuance. (2) Coding: After reviewing the transcripts, codes were assigned to relevant text segments as in-document comments. (3) Theme Identification: Codes were grouped into themes using Microsoft Visio, clustered around four dimensions of business-IT alignment inspired by Luftman's maturity model [19]: Communication, Governance, Partnership, and Scope & Architecture. Themes were organized under three headings: strengths, weaknesses, and recommendations, to facilitate clear presentation and interpretation of findings.

The focus group discussions were structured around four of Luftman's six dimensions of business-IT alignment [19], selected for their direct relevance to the use of EA at ECDC: (1) Communication: Exploring how EA facilitated or hindered mutual understanding and knowledge sharing between business and IT. (2) Governance: Investigating the role of EA in supporting business involvement in IT decision-making and resource allocation. (3) Partnership: Examining how EA contributed to a shared understanding of IT's role in the organization. (4) Scope and Architecture: Assessing whether EA helped IT staff understand architectural decisions from a business perspective. These dimensions guided the data collection and analysis processes, ensuring consistency and depth in addressing the research question.

As one of the researchers works at ECDC and participated in the SSR project, there is potential for observer bias. However, this position also provided privileged access to data and participants. The single-case nature of the study limits generalizability; however, many public organizations face similar challenges and operate under comparable conditions, which supports broader relevance. Finally, the analysis was conducted manually to maintain focus on the content rather than on learning new software tools, balancing time and depth of analysis.

4 Case Description

The ECDC is a European Union agency established in 2005 to identify, assess, and communicate threats to human health from infectious diseases. Known for its independent assessments and rapid risk evaluations, ECDC operates under the European Commission and collaborates with international organizations such as the U.S. CDC, Chinese CDC, EFSA, EMA, and Africa CDC.

ECDC collects structured indicator-based data from EU/EEA countries and complements it with unstructured event-based data from global sources. These combined datasets support a comprehensive understanding of disease trends, aiding EU Member States in shaping national public health policies. ECDC also works closely with laboratories across Europe to evaluate their diagnostic capacities.

Several specialized IT systems support the organization's work. The main platform, The European Surveillance System (TESSy), receives daily reports on 52 diseases – additional systems, such as EPIS, TTT, and EWRS, support epidemic intelligence and emergency response. Until 2012, these systems were developed independently by different business units, leading to overlapping functionality and limited integration. This fragmentation caused recurring technical issues and inefficiencies.

ECDC established a centralized Information and Communication Technology (ICT) unit to address these challenges in 2012. The new unit unified IT governance and introduced standardized business analysis, project management, and software development methods. By 2013, it became clear that a complete revision of ECDC's IT landscape was needed. This marked the beginning of the SSR project.

The SSR project aimed to modernize and integrate key IT applications to provide a sustainable foundation for future development. ECDC adopted The Open Group Architecture Framework (TOGAF) [18], a widely used and flexible EA framework to manage its complexity. The Architecture Development Method (ADM) within TOGAF was tailored to match the stages of the SSR project.

All data collection, analysis, and reporting applications were re-evaluated under the EA initiative, resulting in 40 defined projects. The SSR project was planned over seven years, three years for analysis, and four years for implementation, marking a major transformation of ECDC's IT environment and a strategic effort to align technology with business needs.

5 Results

The results of the focus group sessions are presented as a unified interpretation without attributing specific responses to either business or IT participants. This approach was intentional, as the objective of the work is to provide an integrated account of the identified benefits, challenges, and recommendations. Differentiating the responses by role could suggest a comparative analysis of the two perspectives, which is not the aim of this study.

5.1 Communication

Strengths. EA played a critical role in enhancing **communication** between business and IT at ECDC. It established a **shared language** that enabled constructive dialogue, mutual understanding, and knowledge exchange across organizational levels. As one participant noted, *"the introduction of an Enterprise Architecture framework at that point in time in ECDC created conditions for the establishment of a constructive dialogue between business and IT."* This improved communication was not limited to project settings but extended throughout the organization, supported strongly by top management who demonstrated strategic commitment to overcoming early implementation challenges.

EA also enabled the **sharing of a common view**, helping individuals from diverse professional backgrounds align on shared goals. This shared understanding positively influenced organizational culture and fostered more efficient problem-solving and collaboration, particularly at managerial levels.

Furthermore, EA contributed to **accelerating the learning process**. IT staff became more familiar with business concepts and strategic goals, while business users gained a broader understanding of how IT could support operational improvements. One participant reflected that *"IT staff had a view on only those small fractions of the organization [..] Now [..] they are much better equipped supporting the business."*

Finally, EA introduced **consistency and standardization** by applying layered architectural models and a unified methodology. The modeling practices helped translate complex discussions into visual representations, bridging the communication gap and ensuring continuity across development efforts. As described by a participant, *"a lot of problems we experienced in the past [..] were channeled by following a common methodology [..] into visual models."*

Weaknesses. Internal limitations significantly shaped the impact of EA on business-IT alignment at ECDC. One key issue was the **limited organizational maturity, skills, and knowledge**, which constrained EA's effectiveness. Although EA introduced valuable practices, its rollout was hindered by a lack of internal expertise and immature project methodologies. As one participant noted, *"at that time it was very much an IT exercise, so the architecture was sort of within the IT unit, and not that much related to the business activities."* This lack of clarity regarding EA's role led to a reliance on external consultants and politicizing EA-related decisions.

A second limitation arose from the **complexity of the EA methodology and modeling language**, which inhibited collaboration. The learning curve associated with frameworks like TOGAF, combined with the limited time available for training, created confusion and miscommunication. Business participants struggled to grasp the modeling language at the same level as IT staff, weakening shared ownership of architectural representations. Furthermore, EA was seen as a barrier to innovation in new technology adoption. One participant reflected that this part of the work *"didn't really bring in a lot of innovation."*

Another recurring issue was the **improper tailoring of the EA framework** to ECDC's context. The rigid application of methodology without adjusting to organizational needs led to reduced engagement, especially from the business side. Since IT staff understood EA faster, they naturally took the lead, resulting in a potential disconnect from business activities. As expressed by a participant, *"you could restrict a bit [..] the working relationship and the individual freedom, so it could be some push back."*

Finally, participants raised concerns about the **incorrect application of EA increasing the business-IT gap**. If the adoption process began with poor tailoring and insufficient foundational understanding, trust between business and IT eroded. In such cases, architectural decisions pushed top-down risked being accepted without comprehension or buy-in. Introducing unnecessary architectural layers made the framework feel overly complex and misaligned with organizational size. As one participant emphasized, *"if you apply it like rigidly, then you risk to overdo certain things or overlook other things."*

Recommendations. The focus group participants highlighted several key recommendations for improving the implementation and impact of EA at ECDC. A primary theme was the need to **assess organizational readiness** before adopting an EA framework. Participants emphasized that EA should not be introduced solely to comply with external recommendations or to imitate other organizations. Instead, a thorough readiness assessment is required, including evaluating leadership awareness, organizational structure, and maturity of internal processes and projects. As one participant explained, *"the need for us [..] to approve the architecture framework was the recommendation of the auditors [..] but that doesn't have any impact or affect anything else."* Another noted that EA had real value when responding to organizational needs, such as the SSR project.

A second recommendation was to **focus on business aspects** during EA implementation. Since EA involves a specialized vocabulary and technical modeling, IT staff must intentionally support business stakeholders in understanding these concepts. Using accessible language and linking architectural practices to business goals increases engagement and relevance for non-technical participants.

Finally, participants stressed the importance of **consistency and time**. Maintaining alignment around common goals is essential; even small divergences, if left unaddressed, can lead to significant misalignment over time. All architectural roles within the organization must share a unified understanding of the framework and its application. Agreements and decisions should be formally documented, and any deviations from them should be justified through impact analysis and clear rationale.

5.2 Governance

Strengths. Several key strengths were identified within the governance dimension that demonstrates the positive impact of EA at ECDC. First, EA significantly **increased transparency** in IT investment decisions. By clarifying where and why IT resources were being allocated, EA enabled business units better to understand the benefits and potential consequences of investment choices. This led to a more collaborative approach, where businesses accepted the timelines required for strategic changes, and IT efforts shifted from justifying investments to refining prioritization processes. As one participant observed, *"it helps a lot to understand what are the key elements of the system and therefore focus on what is really relevant and essential for building all the solutions."*

A second strength was the **increased safety and confidence** that EA brought to planning and delivery. Once a shared vision of the target architecture was established, business and IT could define intermediate architectural plateaus, providing clear direction and milestones. This long-term perspective helped build trust in the process and offered reassurance that projects were progressing within a defined, structured framework. As one participant explained, *"we accept the time needed for completing the various steps and we are happy to invest in the project because we are confident the project will deliver."*

Finally, EA played a significant role in **empowering the business units**. It clarified roles and responsibilities within projects and supported decision-making by offering a comprehensive overview of architectural priorities. Business units were better positioned to make informed decisions based on a clearer understanding of their needs and constraints. As summarized by one respondent, *"now business has a better view to base their decisions on."*

Weaknesses. Despite the benefits observed, participants also identified several governance-related weaknesses that hindered the effective implementation of EA at ECDC. A key concern was the **lack of a practical approach**. While EA aimed to provide clarity in project planning and justification, it often resulted in complex and bureaucratic procedures in practice. Securing funding became burdensome, and detailed project planning sometimes devolved into abstract or philosophical debates. The process also led to the production of excessive documentation, which was not always perceived as adding value. As one participant noted, *"we needed to provide further justifications [..] as if the rationale and the vision and description of the benefits [..] was not sufficient for meeting the agency requirement."*

Another issue was the **lack of adherence to architectural principles**, particularly regarding project staffing and continuity. When new participants joined ongoing projects, previously agreed decisions were frequently reopened for discussion. Without enforcing prior architectural choices, significant time was lost revisiting foundational topics instead of advancing delivery. Moreover, while EA opinions were formally included in project documentation, they were often overlooked or disregarded. One respondent remarked, *"we have the enterprise architecture opinion [..] but it is very rare that someone reads it."*

Finally, there was a reported **lack of clarity regarding the role of EA** within the broader governance framework. EA was introduced during evolving internal governance, which caused misalignment and friction. Aligning EA governance with the existing structures proved difficult and delayed the start of critical programs. As one participant observed, *"alignment of this EA governance with the existing governance was a problem [..] it has delayed the start of the program."* These challenges resulted in EA's only marginal role in resource allocation and strategic decision-making, ultimately weakening its intended impact on business-IT alignment.

Recommendations. Participants identified several recommendations to improve the governance-related aspects of EA implementation. One of the most emphasized suggestions was the need to **rely on dedicated, internal resources**. EA initiatives require individuals who understand the organization's technical and business dimensions. Participants stressed the importance of assigning two clearly defined roles: an enterprise architect and an active business-side driver. When these roles were not internally available, as in the case of ECDC, reliance on external consultants proved insufficient, as one participant explained, *"had we done SSR today having [ECDC staff] here and in the driver seat [..] it would have been a completely different situation."* The recommendation also stressed that project visibility should not lead to assignments based on personal preference; instead, human resources should be aligned with the organization's strategic needs.

Another key recommendation was to **link EA to organizational size and maturity**. EA frameworks are often extensive and should not be implemented entirely unless the organization has reached an appropriate level of readiness. Participants emphasized the importance of unfolding the EA framework gradually and only expanding its scope when scaling is warranted. As one respondent noted, *"EA doesn't really have to add much [..] it may sort of give some facilitating parts."*

A third recommendation was to **learn from experience**. Participants suggested starting with smaller, focused EA initiatives, allowing organizations to build experience, refine the framework, and stage learning.

5.3 Partnership

Strengths. In the partnership dimension, participants highlighted how **EA promotes in-depth reflections** by reducing the perceived divide between business and IT. At ECDC, the already narrow boundary between the two functions was further diminished by introducing EA, which fostered constructive dialogue and mutual understanding. EA enabled business stakeholders to better communicate with IT, enhancing collaboration and rapport across domains. One participant noted, *"there was a very tiny limit between business and IT [..] because IT was fully integrated with the business."* Moreover, EA provided a neutral ground to surface and resolve historical role ambiguities, enabling both sides to re-evaluate their responsibilities in a more structured and objective manner.

Additionally, EA was found to be instrumental in **clarifying roles and responsibilities**. It helped define decision-making authority and established a shared framework for follow-up and accountability through documented agreements and architectural outputs. Participants pointed to the importance of these written references in ensuring continuity across project phases. As one focus group member explained, *"having some decisions written, having some EA outputs from the previous phases helped to follow up [..] without that, I don't think we could have reached the situation we have reached."* The objectivity brought by EA was considered particularly valuable, as it allowed business and IT stakeholders to engage in meaningful, role-specific discussions based on shared understanding.

Weaknesses. Participants identified several EA limitations in supporting the business perspective during the project lifecycle at ECDC. A key issue was the **lack of support in traditional analysis**. While EA was extensively tailored for the organization, limited architectural expertise led to reliance on conventional analysis approaches. As a result, detailed *AS IS* models were prioritized over meaningful *TO BE* planning. Time pressure and low business maturity further contributed to superficial future-state modeling and fragmentation across business and data layers. As one participant reflected, *"that TO BE situation described initially was not that good. That was not different from the AS IS."*

In addition, EA showed **limited applicability in contradictory situations**, particularly in areas with low flexibility, such as technological choices. EA did not prevent prolonged or repetitive discussions in these contexts, which often lacked practical value. Some participants perceived these conversations as formalities driven by compliance rather than meaningful planning. One participant described, *"we have faced many times some [..] useless discussions because ultimately if there is no freedom [..] we should just not even have the discussion."*

Lastly, the focus group highlighted a general **uncertainty for the future** stemming from EA's inability to address emerging issues such as shadow IT and cloud technology integration. EA's emphasis on describing the current state created a barrier to envisioning disruptive or transformative architectures. The lack of strategic foresight among project participants meant that innovation was often reduced to incremental change. As one respondent summarized, *"we achieved some small changes here and there between the AS IS and TO BE"*, rather than considering fundamentally new approaches.

Recommendations. A key recommendation from participants was the need to **tailor the EA framework to support meaningful changes**. EA frameworks are typically comprehensive and generic, and their successful implementation depends on the ability to adapt them to the organization's specific needs, size, and maturity level. Skilled staff capable of shaping the methodology appropriately are essential for this process. As one participant emphasized, *"it is a bit an art of the enterprise architect to make the best of the methodologies that are provided."*

Moreover, participants suggested that EA adoption should be closely aligned with the project or program in which it is introduced. The success of EA in fostering partnership maturity and communication was noted to be context-dependent and influenced by how well the framework was adapted to the organizational setting. The importance of flexibility was repeatedly highlighted. One participant remarked, *"if you apply it like rigidly, then you risk to overdo certain things or overlook other things."* Another added that EA's effectiveness depends on its *"fit for purpose"* application and the ability to adapt based on the project's objectives.

5.4 IT Scope and Architecture

Strengths. Participants reported that EA strongly impacted aligning IT scope with business needs, particularly through two mechanisms. First, **EA encouraged exploration** by reducing resistance to change. Through its structured and integrative approach, EA helped both business and IT better understand each other's constraints and possibilities. The business side became more open to revisiting established working methods, while IT gained better insight into business priorities. As one participant noted, *"even if it is working well, it could work better"*, illustrating a shift in mindset towards continuous improvement.

Second, **EA influenced working relationships**, particularly in the context of requirements elicitation. EA introduced a more collaborative and structured approach to defining business needs, leading to improved mutual understanding. Business stakeholders could better articulate their needs within the broader organizational context, and IT staff were more responsive in shaping appropriate solutions. According to one participant, *"the way requirements from the business were collected was different than before [..] to really understand what the needs were."* EA helped establish a shared language and facilitated cross-functional dialogue that was previously lacking. Importantly, it also created space for business users to take a more active and leading role in shaping IT-related decisions. This opportunity had not always been accessible before EA's implementation.

Weaknesses. Although EA contributed significantly to bridging business and IT at ECDC, participants also identified notable limitations in its implementation, particularly within the IT scope and architecture dimension. One concern was that **EA generated undesired situations**, especially when business stakeholders were expected to take on a leading role without sufficient preparation or support. Time constraints often led to superficial engagement from the business side in reviewing technical architecture and software specifications. As one participant noted, *"we ended within the IT deliveries that was very little reviewed by the business and very little explained to the business [..] probably a missed opportunity."*

Another barrier was that the **architectural modeling language brought complexities** that hampered communication between IT and business units. EA's modeling tools and notation were perceived as overly technical, leading to misunderstandings and reducing the business side's ability to contribute meaningfully. As one participant remarked, *"sometimes those [models] can be [..] too complicated and people get too much involved."* The discussions often devolved into debates over technical syntax rather than strategic architectural alignment, limiting their effectiveness and inclusion.

A further issue was the **limited coverage of applications** under the EA framework. While the core, custom-built applications received in-depth modeling attention, many smaller systems, including commercial off-the-shelf applications, were excluded from the EA process. This created an incomplete picture of the IT landscape and undermined efforts to improve integration and consistency across systems. As one respondent stated, *"many systems, particularly systems that have been bought or rented, have not (yet) been covered."*

Recommendations. Participants provided several recommendations to strengthen the impact of EA on aligning IT with business needs. A key suggestion was to **focus on the future state**. Emphasis should be placed on developing a comprehensive vision of the *TO BE* architecture rather than investing excessive time in documenting the *AS IS* situation. One participant summarized this by stating, *"I would spend really less time on [..] the AS IS and much more emphasis on defining the TO BE from the business."*

In addition, participants stressed the importance of **focusing on the business architecture**. EA initiatives should begin by mapping business processes, goals, and needs before transitioning into technical modeling. This approach ensures that EA is perceived not as an IT-centric tool but as an organization-wide discipline. As one participant put it, *"you need to somehow decide: is this a tool that you use for the IT or is this a tool that you use for everything that happens in the organization?"*

Finally, participants recommended efforts to **blend EA into the organizational culture**. EA should not be treated as a separate or isolated initiative but embedded into the business and IT's daily routines and decision-making processes. This integration would make EA a natural part of planning and executing work. A participant noted that over time, *"EA could disappear because it would be embedded in the routine way of working."*

6 Lessons Learned

Following, we present a collection of the main lessons learned based on the previously presented results:

Begin only when the organization is ready, and for the right reasons. ECDC introduced EA largely because external auditors recommended it. Where tailoring and foundational understanding were thin, trust between business and IT actually worsened; architectural decisions were accepted "top-down" with little buy-in, and the framework quickly felt heavier than the value it delivered. Focus-group participants, therefore, insist on a formal readiness check: judge leadership appetite, process maturity, and cultural openness, and postpone rollout until genuine business drivers, such as spiraling maintenance costs or a pressing need for integration, make the case obvious.

Put permanent people, not consultants, in the cockpit. Reliance on external architects meant that critical know-how walked out the door when contracts ended. Participants stressed the need for "two clearly defined roles: an enterprise architect and an active business-side driver," both embedded inside the organization and backed by the authority and time to act. Without these champions, design decisions were repeatedly reopened and momentum leaked away.

Shrink the framework to fit, then let it grow organically. EA brought a common language and accelerated learning, but only when it was trimmed to what people could absorb. Where the organization tried to apply TOGAF or ArchiMate in full, models became "too complicated," debates slid into syntax, and business users disengaged. Practitioners recommend starting with the minimum set of viewpoints that solve today's problem and expanding only as capability matures.

Embed governance in what already exists and make decisions visible. EA raised confidence once business and IT shared a vision of the target landscape and could release funding in "architectural plateaus", intermediate milestones everyone understood. Transparency in investment choices shifted discussions from budget justifications to prioritization of value, further cementing trust. Conversely, adding parallel EA steering boards delayed programs and created friction; alignment works better when architectural checkpoints are woven into established portfolio or project boards.

Translate architecture into plain language and pictures that matter. At its best, EA dissolved the traditional business-IT divide by giving both sides a shared vocabulary and set of visuals. At its worst, it drowned dialogue in technical notation. The antidote is an "architecture playbook" that pairs simplified diagrams with one-page narratives, uses workshops to build models collaboratively, and hides metamodel complexity from casual readers. Consistency over time is essential: even small deviations from agreed designs, if not documented and justified, snowball into costly detours.

Watch the blind spots—shadow IT, cloud, and COTS. Because the modeling effort focused on custom systems, commercial-off-the-shelf and cloud services were left outside the architectural map, leaving integration risks unaddressed. Successful programs maintain an "innovation runway": they sandbox emerging technology and bring winning patterns into the governed architecture before they become systemic.

Make EA disappear by making it routine. The ultimate measure of success is that EA is no longer perceived as a special project. Participants envisaged a future where architectural principles surface automatically in annual planning, procurement check-lists, and change control: "EA could disappear because it would be embedded in the routine way of working". Regular alignment pulses keep frameworks, road-maps, and designs relevant as strategies evolve.

7 Discussion and Conclusions

This study explored EA's strengths and weaknesses in shaping the business-IT relationship at ECDC. The study also formulated recommendations for future EA initiatives at ECDC and similar public organizations based on focus group insights from both business and IT perspectives.

The findings reveal a varied perception of EA across the four analyzed dimensions: Communication, Governance, Partnership, and IT Scope and Architecture. While the Communication and IT Scope dimensions received the most attention, they did so for opposite reasons; Communication emerged as the most problematic, whereas IT Scope and Architecture were primarily associated with successful outcomes. These differences suggest uneven implementation maturity and varying stakeholder expectations.

A notable observation was that certain elements, such as the EA framework and modeling methodology, appeared in the strengths and weaknesses categories. EA was appreciated for creating a *common language*, enhancing *constructive dialogue*, and supporting *accelerated learning*. At the same time, it was criticized for imposing a *rigid modeling language* (e.g., ArchiMate), being difficult to tailor, and placing too much pressure on underprepared business units.

The way EA was introduced at ECDC contributed to these mixed outcomes. Initially driven by audit recommendations rather than an internal need, EA was deployed during the high-stakes SSR project. This accelerated implementation also led to *knowledge gaps*, reliance on external consultants, and difficulties in bringing business staff up to speed. Despite this, EA helped reduce long-standing misalignments by offering *transparency*, clarifying *decision-making roles*, and guiding *project prioritization*.

However, challenges persisted. At deeper modeling levels, the complexity of the language limited business engagement, and documentation efforts often replaced real collaboration. Furthermore, EA struggled to address *shadow IT* or propose *transformative architectural designs*, especially in emerging technologies like cloud computing.

From a cross-dimensional perspective, the most frequently praised aspects were EA's ability to *facilitate communication*, *standardize practices*, and *support learning*. In contrast, the main obstacles included the *modeling language*, the *methodological complexity*, and the *lack of internal expertise*.

Recommendations for other organizations include conducting a thorough *readiness assessment* before implementation, *focusing on the future state* rather than the current one, and *investing in internal capacity building*. The success of EA depends heavily on tailoring the framework to organizational size and maturity, clearly articulating the business case, and embedding EA practices into the routine work culture. Passionate, well-informed staff can act as change agents, ensuring EA evolves as a flexible tool rather than a bureaucratic constraint.

This study acknowledges several limitations related to reliability, validity, and generalizability. Regarding reliability, the timing and setting of the focus group sessions, held at different times and under varying participant conditions, may have influenced the responses. Additionally, one of the researcher's dual roles as both investigator and member of the IT unit may introduce potential bias, although mitigated by their neutral role as a business analyst. Regarding validity, while focus groups provided rich qualitative data, the limited number of participants (six) and the absence of IT infrastructure staff may constrain the breadth of perspectives. External validity is further limited by the small sample size relative to the organization's workforce, though participants were purposefully selected based on their deep involvement in the re-engineering project. On generalizability, the findings are context-specific but likely relevant to other public organizations managing large-scale IT transformations, particularly those involving data warehousing, ETL, and business intelligence platforms.

Future research could build upon the current study in several meaningful directions. First, a natural extension would incorporate all six of Luftman's alignment dimensions, as this study focused on only four. Second, since the ArchiMate modeling language was perceived as a barrier to collaboration, a comparative study assessing the impact of different modeling languages on EA adoption could yield valuable insights. Third, including the perspectives of IT infrastructure staff, who were not represented in this study, could enrich the findings, especially given their technical involvement in architecture implementation. Fourth, with ECDC currently outsourcing parts of its IT capabilities, investigating how IT outsourcing affects business-IT alignment in public organizations presents another relevant avenue. Lastly, as emerging technologies reshape IT environments, exploring how cloud adoption influences Enterprise Architecture and business-IT alignment would address a timely and evolving challenge.

Disclosure of Interests. The authors have no competing interests to declare that are relevant to the content of this article.

References

1. Alaeddini, M., Salekfard, S.: Investigating the role of an enterprise architecture project in the business-it alignment in Iran. Inf. Syst. Front. **15**, 67–88 (2013)
2. Andrén, S., Lindström, E., Hugosson, A., Rönnqvist, S., Lagerström, R., Hacks, S.: Assessing alignment between business and it strategy: a case study. In: PoEM (Forum), pp. 1–12 (2020)
3. Beese, J., Haki, K., Schilling, R., Kraus, M., Aier, S., Winter, R.: Strategic alignment of enterprise architecture management-how portfolios of control mechanisms track a decade of enterprise transformation at commerzbank. Eur. J. Inf. Syst. **32**(1), 92–105 (2023)
4. Bradley, R.V., Pratt, R.M., Byrd, T.A., Simmons, L.L.: The role of enterprise architecture in the questforit value. MIS Quart. Execut. **10**(2) (2011)
5. Buchanan, R.D., Soley, R.M.: Aligning Enterprise Architecture and it Investments with Corporate Goals. OMG Whitepaper, Object Management Group, Needham (2002)
6. Chan, Y.E., Reich, B.H.: It alignment: what have we learned? J. Inf. Technol. **22**(4), 297–315 (2007)
7. Chen, H.M.: Towards service engineering: service orientation and business-it alignment. In: Proceedings of the 41st Annual Hawaii International Conference on System Sciences (HICSS 2008), pp. 114–114. IEEE (2008)
8. Chen, H.M., Kazman, R., Garg, A.: Bitam: an engineering-principled method for managing misalignments between business and it architectures. Sci. Comput. Program. **57**(1), 5–26 (2005)
9. Chen, Q., Chen, H.M.: Exploring the success factors of ECRM strategies in practice. J. Database Market. Customer Strat. Manage. **11**, 333–343 (2004)
10. Choi, J., Nazareth, D.L., Jain, H.K.: The impact of soa implementation on it-business alignment: a system dynamics approach. ACM Trans. Manage. Inform. Syst. (TMIS) **4**(1), 1–22 (2013)
11. Clarke, M., Hall, J.G., Rapanotti, L.: Enterprise architecture: a snapshot from practice. Int. J. IT/Business Align. Govern. (IJITBAG) **4**(1), 1–10 (2013)
12. Denscombe, M.: EBOOK: The good research guide: For small-scale social research projects. McGraw-Hill Education (UK) (2017)
13. Fischer, R., Aier, S., Winter, R.: A federated approach to enterprise architecture model maintenance. Enterprise Modell. Inform. Syst. Architect. (EMISAJ) **2**(2), 14–22 (2007)
14. Fragoso, B., Vasconcelos, A.: An enterprise architecture approach to temporary and permanent governance continuum. In: International Conference on Enterprise Design, Operations, and Computing, pp. 101–116. Springer (2024)
15. Gerow, J.E., Grover, V., Thatcher, J., Roth, P.L.: Looking toward the future of it-business strategic alignment through the past. MIS Q. **38**(4), 1159–1186 (2014)
16. Gerow, J.E., Thatcher, J.B., Grover, V.: Six types of it-business strategic alignment: an investigation of the constructs and their measurement. Eur. J. Inf. Syst. **24**(5), 465–491 (2015)
17. Iacob, M.E., Meertens, L.O., Jonkers, H., Quartel, D.A., Nieuwenhuis, L.J., Van Sinderen, M.J.: From enterprise architecture to business models and back. Softw. Syst. Model. **13**, 1059–1083 (2014)

18. Josey, A.: TOGAF® version 9.1-A pocket guide. Van Haren (2016)
19. Luftman, J.: Assessing business-it allignment maturity. In: Strategies for information technology governance, pp. 99–128. IGI Global Scientific Publishing (2004)
20. Őri, D., Szabó, Z.: A systematic literature review on business-it misalignment research. IseB **22**(1), 139–169 (2024)
21. Ross, J.W.: Creating a strategic it architecture competency: learning in stages. MIS Q. Exec. **2**(1), 5 (2008)
22. Ross, J.W., Weill, P., Robertson, D.: Enterprise architecture as strategy: Creating a foundation for business execution. Harvard business press (2006)
23. Strnadl, C.F.: Aligning business and it: The process-driven architecture model. Information systems management **23**(4) (2006)
24. Trienekens, J.J., Kusters, R.J., Cuenca, L.: Measuring business-it alignment, framework development and case study results. In: Information System Development: Improving enterprise communication, pp. 1–16. Springer (2014)
25. Vicente, M., Gama, N., da Silva, M.M.: The value of itil in enterprise architecture. In: 2013 17th IEEE International Enterprise Distributed Object Computing Conference, pp. 147–152. IEEE (2013)
26. Wegmann, A., Balabko, P., Lê, L.S., Regev, G., Rychkova, I.: A method and tool for business-it alignment in enterprise architecture. In: CAiSE Short Paper Proceedings. vol. 2005 (2005)
27. Zarvić, N., Wieringa, R.: An integrated enterprise architecture framework for business-it alignment. Designing Enterprise Architect. Frameworks: Integrating Business Processes IT Infrastructure **63**(9), 1–9 (2014)
28. Zhang, M., Chen, H., Luo, A.: A systematic review of business-it alignment research with enterprise architecture. IEEE Access **6**, 18933–18944 (2018)

Integration of Data Science Projects in Enterprise Architecture Modeling

Matthias Pohl[1(✉)], Christian Haertel[2], Daniel Staegemann[2], and Klaus Turowski[2]

[1] German Aerospace Center, Institute of Data Science, Jena, Germany
matthias.pohl@dlr.de
[2] Otto von Guericke University, Magdeburg, Germany
{christian.haertel,daniel.staegemann,klaus.turowski}@ovgu.de

Abstract. Data Science (DS) technologies provide crucial competitive advantages in contemporary business environments through optimized processes. However, DS-based service systems require collaborative efforts between IT and business divisions, necessitating structured frameworks to bridge organizational gaps and ensure alignment between technical requirements and business objectives. This research examines the integration of DS systems within Enterprise Architecture (EA) models to address complex implementation challenges. EA modeling provides an indispensable, structured framework for ensuring the optimal performance of DS systems, particularly in the context of digital transformation initiatives, and enables the seamless integration of data science capabilities into organizational frameworks. This work presents a thorough literature review that critically examines existing research on integrating DS projects into EA models, offering a comprehensive view of DS integration to enhance architectural frameworks. Future work will demonstrate these holistic models in practical enterprise applications and conduct case studies to refine the model and evaluate the effectiveness of conceptual modeling approaches.

Keywords: Enterprise Architecture · Data Science · Literature Review · Digital Transformation · Organizational Framework

1 Introduction

Data Science (DS), commonly referred to as Data Analytics, in conjunction with Machine Learning (ML) [41] and the increasingly influential domain of Artificial Intelligence (AI), provides a crucial competitive advantage in the contemporary business environment. The implementation of these advanced technologies is associated with the optimization of business processes, which can lead to enhanced operational efficiency [31,63], cost reductions, and elevated levels of customer satisfaction [38,39]. This strategic deployment of DS technologies underscores their significance in driving sustainable competitive advantage [28] in an increasingly data-driven world.

© The Author(s), under exclusive license to Springer Nature Switzerland AG 2026
A. Gianola et al. (Eds.): EDOC 2025, LNCS 16213, pp. 40–58, 2026.
https://doi.org/10.1007/978-3-032-15140-7_3

DS-based service systems require a collaborative effort between IT and business divisions, fostering a common understanding of projects that is crucial for success [11,15]. Enterprise Architecture (EA) modeling provides a structured framework that bridges the gap between these divisions, ensuring that DS initiatives align with both technical requirements and broader business objectives [45,53]. Due to the unique challenges that DS systems face in achieving reliability, EA modeling is indispensable for ensuring optimal performance [11,45,53]. In a climate where digital transformation requires organizations to transform their business and operating model, the importance of EA modeling becomes even more pronounced. It enables the seamless integration of data science capabilities into the overall organizational framework, ensuring that technological advancements are embedded within the structure and operations of a company [45]. Furthermore, successful digital transformation relies on effectively incorporating technology into the EA. DS systems must engage with not only other ML models but also traditional software components. This multifaceted interaction requires developers to utilize multiple models to analyze different views of the ML system [11,21]. EA modeling provides the architectural framework necessary to coordinate these complex interactions, thereby enhancing the ability of organizations to deploy scalable and efficient DS solutions [11,46,53,66].

This research examines the integration of DS systems within EA models to address the complex challenges. To facilitate this inquiry, a thorough literature review will be conducted to systematically analyze and synthesize existing methodologies articulated in the scientific literature, thereby providing a cohesive overview of the current state of knowledge in this domain. The investigation will be guided by a central research question:

How can Data Science projects, their goals, and tasks be integrated into Enterprise Architecture models according to scientific literature? **(RQ)**

Following the introduction, a concise background on EA and DS is provided for context. In Sect. 3, we examine the key concepts underlying the methodology of a structured literature review (SLR), focusing on essential frameworks and processes. Sections 4 and 5 outline the sequential steps of the SLR, from formulating a keyword search to data extraction. Finally, Sect. 6 presents a comprehensive perspective on integrating DS within EA, exploring the interactions between these fields and their implications.

2 Prerequisites

Initially, key concepts around the research topic must be discussed. For this paper, this includes the theoretical background on EA and DS projects.

2.1 Enterprise Architecture

EA is a strategic planning discipline that helps organizations align their information systems and technological assets with operational goals [1]. Various models and methodologies exist within EA, with The Open Group Architecture Framework (TOGAF) being particularly prominent [8]. TOGAF offers a comprehensive set of methods and tools for developing and governing EA, facilitating a structured approach to defining the architecture of an organization, IT systems, and services. ArchiMate[1] is a powerful modeling language closely aligned with TOGAF, enabling the creation of integrated models that illustrate business processes, organizational structures, information flows, and technical infrastructure. Additionally, the Zachman Framework [65] is one of the earliest and most influential EA frameworks, featuring a matrix that cross-references stakeholder perspectives with architectural focus areas, such as data, functions, and networks. This approach ensures that diverse stakeholder concerns are addressed, aligning architectural vision with business needs.

2.2 Data Science Projects

Briefly, DS aims to synthesize "useful knowledge directly from data" [4]. Therefore, data analytical modeling is a fundamental aspect of DS [48], providing a structured framework for extracting insights from complex datasets. At its core lies the exploration of relationships among variables using techniques that range from neural networks to advanced statistical methods. The principle of mapping inputs to outputs, which underpins diverse applications across various fields, including healthcare and finance [14,16].

In DS, analyses are typically categorized by purpose. Descriptive Analytics focuses on understanding historical events and identifying patterns, often using visual formats like graphs and dashboards. Predictive Analytics, on the other hand, applies statistical models and ML to forecast future events, enabling organizations to anticipate potential outcomes. Prescriptive Analytics takes this a step further, offering actionable recommendations and strategies to optimize future scenarios [6,32].

Additionally, the objectives of data analytics practices can be classified based on their applications. The goals of data analysis are essential as they define the purpose of a DS project, guiding its direction and ensuring that insights align with stakeholder needs and business outcomes. A DS project follows a structured methodology with key process steps, for instance data understanding, data preparation, data modeling, evaluation, model deployment, following the CRISP-DM methodology [48]. In the field of data science, the processes essential to a project are deeply interconnected and function as a cohesive framework throughout its various project phases. As a result, the terminology used to describe these processes and the project itself is often interchangeable.

It is essential to note that while the terms "Data Analytics", "Data Mining", and "Data Science" are often used interchangeably, they have distinct meanings in this context. Data Analytics specifically refers to the application of analysis to solve defined problems using statistical tools to generate insights for decision-making. In contrast, DS and DS projects encompass a broader perspective, inte-

[1] https://www.opengroup.org/archimate-forum.

grating data processing, management, and analysis. Essentially, DS involves all activities of the Data Analytics lifecycle [4].

3 Methodology

To investigate the integration of DS projects into EA models, a structured literature review following commonly used methodology [3,62] is conducted. According to these guidelines, the procedure starts with the *review scope*, which was outlined in the introduction. Afterward, the step called *conceptualization of the topic* involves discussing key concepts relevant to the field of interest [62]. The lessons learned from this task provide further useful inspiration for the *search process*. This activity consists of two branches: the keyword/database search, which involves multiple established databases in the field of information systems, and the citation search, covering both backward and forward searches to work toward "a more complete census of relevant literature" [64]. Following the systematic collection of relevant items, a rigorous *literature analysis* will be conducted in accordance with the established research framework. The resulting *research agenda* will summarize key findings, highlight significant research challenges encountered, and outline potential avenues for future exploration.

4 Literature Review Process

In line with the methodology presented in Sect. 3, this research topic is conceptualized through an examination of the foundational principles of DS and EA models (see Sect. 2). For the keyword search, the following query term was used to search in title, abstract and keywords of research items:

"enterprise architecture" AND "model" AND ("data analytics" OR "data science" OR "artificial intelligence" OR "machine learning")

A set of exclusion criteria was established to systematically filter and evaluate the items retrieved in the course of the research. The investigation is concentrated on studies pertaining to the intersection of EA and DS, thereby omitting any works that explore both domains in isolation. Additionally, brief papers that lack substantial foundational contributions to either field are excluded. Furthermore, the selection will be restricted to peer-reviewed scholarly articles, specifically journal and conference papers, ensuring a robust and credible basis for the analysis.

Figure 1 summarizes the entire search and filtering process. These were aligned with the PRISMA guidelines [34]. The search process was conducted systematically across a range of common scientific databases, namely Scopus, Web of Science, IEEE Digital Library, and ACM Digital Library. In total, 574 items were retrieved, reflecting a diverse array of research contributions within the field. To ensure the selection of relevant articles for the research endeavor, a set of clear inclusion and exclusion criteria was meticulously defined. These criteria targeted research works published in the English language, subjected to rigorous peer review, and situated within the domain of computer science, aligning closely with the predetermined set of keywords pertinent to our study. The retrieved publications were then filtered through a multi-stage process to evaluate their relevance to the research topic. After eliminating 56 duplicate entries, the initial screening phase involved reviewing abstracts in relation to the research focus, resulting in the exclusion of 467 articles that were deemed not relevant.

A detailed full-text analysis was subsequently performed, further refining the selection to 46 items that met the criteria established for analysis. To enhance this pool of literature, both forward and backward citation searches were executed, identifying an additional set of potential candidate papers (BW: 29, FW: 15). Each of these candidates underwent careful assessment for eligibility based on the established criteria. Ultimately, the citation searches added 8 studies that enriched the comprehensiveness of the literature review. As a result, these efforts culminated in a final collection of 54 articles that form the basis of the systematic literature review (SLR), providing a solid foundation for the subsequent analysis and discussion.

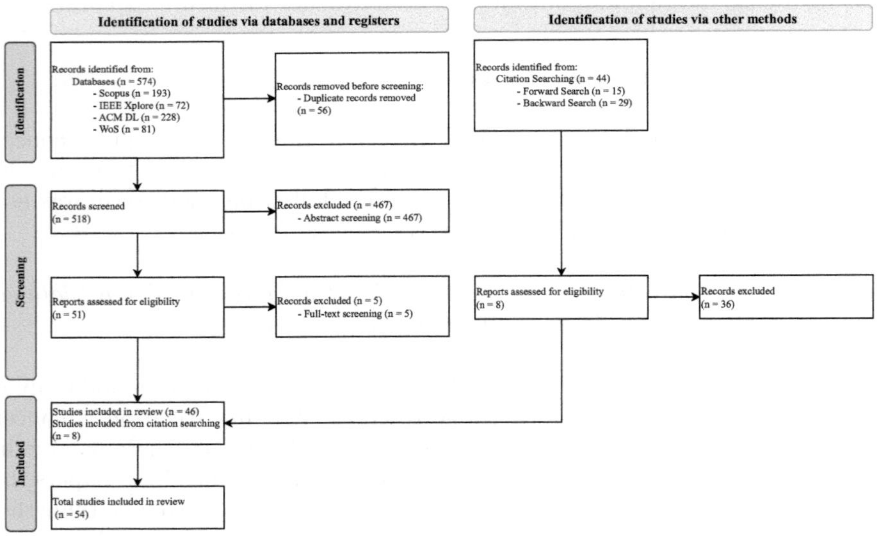

Fig. 1. Filter process of retrieved literature according to PRISMA.

5 Results

An initial overview of the results will precede a rigorous analysis and synthesis of the relevant literature [62]. The analysis of the retrieved scientific literature revealed three distinct thematic categories.

The first category examines EA as a crucial enabler for the integration and adoption of DS in enterprises. This research primarily employs literature analysis to establish foundational concepts, highlighting how a structured architectural framework can support data-driven decision-making and foster innovation.

The second thematic cluster focuses on applying DS methodologies to enhance the understanding of EA models. By utilizing advanced analytical techniques, researchers aim to improve stakeholder comprehension of complex models and leverage ML to inform strategic EA development. Additionally, this research addresses the challenge of automating EA modeling through data science techniques, creating a more efficient design process that adapts to organizational needs.

The third thematic category aligns closely with the research objectives of the paper at hand, exploring innovative approaches to integrate DS processes within EA frameworks. This integration fosters collaboration among business units, DS teams, and IT departments, ensuring alignment between enterprise goals and data-driven initiatives.

A detailed compilation of the results, accompanied by their respective categorizations, is systematically presented in Table 1. Furthermore, a timely overview of the analyzed work is provided.

5.1 Data Science Adoption Supported by EA Modeling

DS is a vital component of modern business strategy, prompting a reevaluation of EA to better integrate with complex data environments [23]. Research shows that traditional EA approaches need enhancement to support the dynamic, data-intensive nature of DS-driven enterprises [44,45,56,66]. To stay competitive in a DS-focused digital landscape, organizations must refine their capabilities to identify market trends, seize new opportunities, and adjust resources and strategies as needed. In this context, EA plays a crucial role by providing the foundational support necessary for navigating transformations and achieving strategic goals, ultimately improving **organizational agility and resilience** in a fast-changing tech environment [35,42].

Organizations are increasingly adopting **data-driven business models** that utilize advanced DS technologies like ML, Big Data Analytics, and the Internet of Things (IoT) [42,47]. These innovations enhance traditional products and generate value by deriving insights from data [49]. EA is essential in this shift, enabling secure data access through open interfaces and ensuring system interoperability while promoting resilience in a changing technological landscape [23,47]. Additionally, EA provides strategic architectural blueprints that guide the development of DS initiatives in alignment with organizational goals [23].

EA modeling should align with broader digital transformation efforts, recognizing that DS is just one part of a larger ecosystem contributing to innovation and efficiency [66]. EA models must effectively **integrate big data technologies** that collect, store, and analyze vast datasets from various sources, as these are essential for DS applications that rely on large volumes of data for training and operation. Utilizing Big Data enhances the performance and accuracy of

Table 1. Results of SLR categorized into (I) Data Science Adoption supported by EA Modeling, (II) Application of Data Science on EA Modeling, (III) Integration of Data Science into EA Models

Year	Ref	I	II	III
2014	[46]	●	○	○
2015	[11]	○	○	●
2016	[24]	○	●	○
2018	[25]	○	●	○
–	[33]	○	●	○
2019	[2]	○	●	○
–	[27]	○	○	●
–	[59]	○	○	●
–	[60]	○	○	●
2020	[61]	○	○	●
2021	[42]	●	○	○
–	[66]	●	○	○
–	[56]	●	○	○
–	[22]	○	○	●
–	[26]	○	○	●
–	[54]	○	○	●
–	[51]	○	○	●
–	[56]	○	○	●
2022	[9]	○	●	○
–	[45]	●	○	○
–	[50]	●	○	○
–	[30]	○	○	●
–	[57]	○	○	●
–	[55]	○	○	●
–	[21]	○	○	●
2023	[47]	●	○	○
–	[49]	●	○	○
–	[29]	○	○	●
–	[58]	○	○	●
–	[52]	○	○	●
–	[18]	○	○	●
2024	[10]	○	○	●
–	[12]	○	●	○
–	[37]	○	●	○

(*continued*)

Table 1. (*continued*)

–	[43]	○	●	●
–	[44]	●	●	○
–	[7]	○	●	○
–	[23]	●	○	○
–	[36]	○	○	●
–	[23]	○	○	●
2025	[13]	○	●	○
–	[5]	○	●	○
–	[35]	●	○	○
–	[40]	●	○	○

DS systems [50]. Intelligent digital systems are built on interconnected service ecosystems. EA modeling should adopt **service-dominant logic**, focusing on collaborative value creation among stakeholders. This underscores how DS can drive innovation and facilitate value co-creation through improved services and customer engagement [56,66].

DS applications have specific prerequisites that vary by archetype within an IT landscape of an organization, making it crucial to understand these requirements for successful implementation [49]. While some prerequisites can be discerned through EA models, others may highlight **organizational readiness** gaps [45]. To enhance the success of DS adoption, EA models should provide detailed information to support a robust **requirements engineering** process and assess organizational readiness prior to implementation. Different DS applications demand distinct requirements from an organizational IT infrastructure. Thus, EA models must be sophisticated enough to accurately identify and document these prerequisites, ensuring preparedness for targeted DS deployments [45].

Finally, the interest in EA Analytics is growing, as it utilizes advanced DS technologies to discover, analyze, and optimize architectural frameworks. This approach complements traditional top-down EA methodologies, allowing organizations to better understand and adapt to evolving business needs [46]. Moreover, traditional manual modeling techniques are increasingly insufficient in AI-enabled environments. EA Mining techniques, which leverage Data Mining to automatically generate architectural models from sources, are becoming essential for maintaining relevant EA representations. Researchers emphasize that these methods are critical for organizations aiming to stay agile and responsive in their EAs [44]. Relevant studies are further discussed in Sect. 5.2.

5.2 Application of Data Science on EA Modeling

Traditional EA modeling primarily relies on manual processes, leading to challenges in keeping models current as the business environment evolves. This dependence often results in discrepancies between documented architecture and the operational landscape [44]. Organizations struggle with the substantial manual effort required to create and maintain EA models, especially given the increasing complexity of their IT ecosystems [25]. This complexity emphasizes the need for more efficient modeling approaches that provide accurate and accessible architectural information amid swift changes in business and technology. There has been an ongoing search within the EA documentation field for solutions to reduce manual effort and promote automation in EA model creation and maintenance [25]. A key role of effective EA management is to lead the automation of modeling tasks, ensuring models are continuously updated with changes in organizational reality [44]. By utilizing technology for automation, organizations can maintain a flexible EA framework that reflects their current state and future goals.

A variety of innovative methodologies employ ML techniques to autonomously create EA models from existing operational data. Key approaches include extracting insights from the extensive data generated by applications, using ML algorithms to identify patterns that inform EA frameworks [37]. Further work highlights the analysis of log files from API gateways, which reveals usage patterns and performance metrics to help optimize architecture based on actual data, and outlines the conversion of operational database data into structured architectural models, offering visual insights for improved decision-making and strategic planning [37,44]. Another approach utilizes ML methods for detecting and classifying applications within complex IT environments, providing a clearer view of application portfolios [25].

DS is transforming dynamic EA models by allowing them to autonomously adapt to external and internal constraints while maintaining alignment with enterprise goals and stability. This adaptability is enhanced by ML, which enables models to evolve through experience [9]. Predictive Analytics support decision-making by analyzing historical data to forecast trends [5]. Additionally, multi-agent systems help to manage complex organizational dynamics, effectively navigating interdependencies within operational environments [5]. ML is essential for identifying similar EA model components, thereby preventing unnecessary repository expansion. By employing similarity measures based on component properties and usage context, organizations can enhance architectural consistency [2]. Association Rule Mining and other Data Mining techniques allow practitioners to uncover patterns within EA data [37].

Specialized ontologies for EA mining have been developed to define concepts and relationships that enable the automatic generation of architectural models from operational data sources, improving the relevance of the models to actual business practices [44]. Generative AI (GenAI) is nowadays seen as crucial for effective EA, offering improvements in efficiency and decision-making while requiring new skills from EA professionals [7].

Although the use of AI and ML in Enterprise Architecture shows great promise, the field is still in its early stages, presenting opportunities for exploration in automation, adaptable frameworks, and intelligent model management.

5.3 Integration of Data Science Into EA Models

This category primarily investigates the integration of DS methodologies within EA. It explores how DS processes can be systematically embedded in architectural frameworks to enhance decision-making and improve operational efficiency.

The research by Takeuchi et al. addresses the challenge of developing reusable knowledge and patterns for machine learning-based service system projects to improve implementation effectiveness across various enterprise functions [53–55,57–59,61]. The proposed EA modeling approach highlights the TOGAF framework [1,8] as a fundamental methodology, and effectively integrates business layer elements, application layer components, as well as extensions to create comprehensive representations of ML project models using ArchiMate. In ML service system projects, collaboration among multiple stakeholders is essential. Such projects require the establishment of a common understanding that bridges business and technical perspectives. Thereby, it is crucial to enable effective communication and foster cooperation among diverse teams, including data scientists, business analysts, and IT professionals. To equip project practitioners with a thorough perspective on complex ML initiatives, metamodels are constructed by synthesizing various ML service system models. The approach makes a contribution to aligning business and IT objectives by extending metamodels to include business models alongside the technical architectures of ML systems. To validate the effectiveness and practicality of these modeling approaches, real-world project cases and examples are employed. These case studies demonstrate the applicability of the proposed methodologies, highlighting their effectiveness in navigating the complexities and challenges commonly associated with ML project environments.

Furthermore, Husen et al. developed a multi-view modeling framework specifically for ML system development, which uses a metamodel as its backbone to ensure consistency across different views of EA [18–20]. In the development of ML systems, developers often utilize multiple models to address various perspectives and functionalities. This approach can lead to inconsistencies and conflicting information among the models, creating challenges for the cohesive integration and evaluation of the system. A supplementary case study was conducted with a specific focus on enhancing the metamodel framework by incorporating support for activity-driven analysis within the context of an optical character recognition (OCR) system. The extensibility study employed an in-depth process mapping technique and provided a clearer visualization of the adaptability of the framework, demonstrating how it can be effectively modified to meet varying analytical needs and incorporate new features.

Geerdink et al. introduce a solution reference architecture designed to guide organizations in leveraging big data technology and predictive analytics to enhance performance [11]. The architecture was developed using a design science approach for designing information systems artifacts [17] and is claimed as the first reference architecture specifically for Big Data and predictive Analytics. Other reference architectures typically consist only of software component diagrams, while the model of Geerdink et al. provides comprehensive coverage, including components, interfaces, architectural patterns, principles, and best practices. The research methodology combined extensive literature research with qualitative data analysis, utilizing grounded theory in expert interviews to provide robust empirical support.

Idowu et al. provide a unified meta-model built on Eclipse Modeling Framework that serves as a blueprint for ML asset management [21]. Traditional version control systems are insufficient for managing the diverse asset types required in ML model development and experimentation. The research presents the Experiment Management Meta-Model (EMMM), which unifies conceptual structures and relationships extracted from a systematic analysis of 17 existing ML experiment management tools. The metamodel represents a superset of conceptualized structures that captures asset types, their relationships, and evolution history across ML experiments, addressing key ML concerns, including versioning, traceability, auditability, collaboration, and reproducibility of experiments.

6 Holistic View on Integrated Modeling of Data Science Processes in Enterprise Architecture

The analyzed research on integrating DS processes into EA reveals a significant gap in providing a comprehensive view that addresses DS implications. Existing methodologies either focus on the business architecture level [51–55,58], incorporating conceptual DS processes [21], or maintain a high-level perspective that overlooks the details of DS processes and infrastructure [11,18].

In response to the findings presented in Sect. 5.3, a combined approach is proposed. This framework aims to integrate the various layers of architecture outlined in EA frameworks (e.g., TOGAF [8]) with relevant DS methodologies [48]. The goal is to create a cohesive understanding of how DS can be effectively woven into the overall architecture, ensuring both strategic and operational elements are aligned (see Fig. 2).

The combined architectural approach can be precisely articulated as follows: In the context of TOGAF, enterprise design is structured into three principal layers. The Business Architecture layer outlines the essential business processes, while the Technology Architecture combines the hardware and software technologies that support enterprise operations, providing the necessary infrastructure for effective business and systems integration. Notably, the Information Systems layer is further divided into two critical subcomponents, Data Architecture and Application Architecture. Data Architecture focuses on the systematic organization and management of data assets to support business processes and decision-making. In contrast, Application Architecture addresses the design and interrelation of software applications within the enterprise, emphasizing their alignment with organizational objectives and seamless integration.

The **Business Architecture** is depicted through a detailed diagram that is segmented into two primary components. On the left side, it illustrates a typical structure of business processes, featuring both an event-driven diagram and a business unit diagram [8]. This section highlights a central business process that

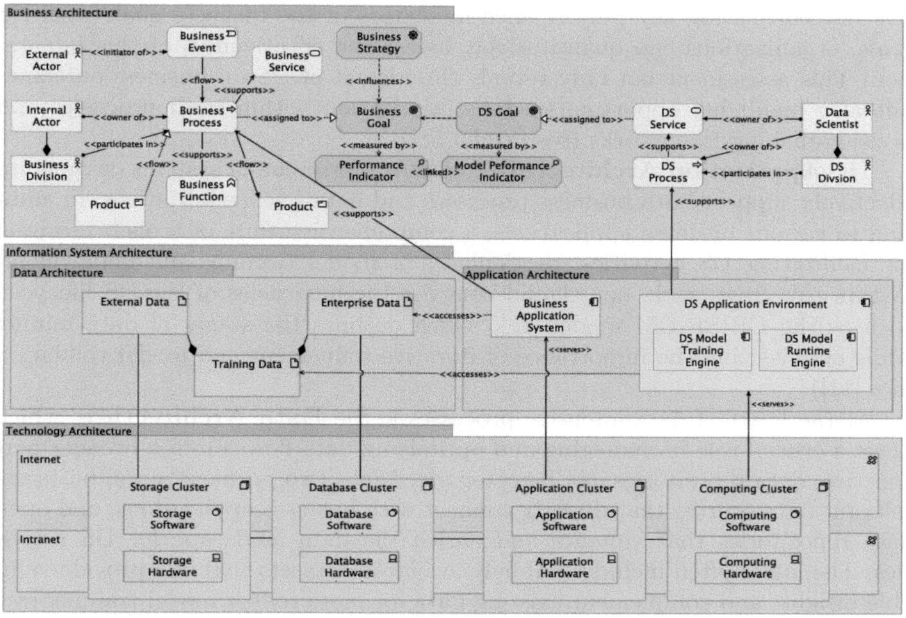

Fig. 2. Holistic View on Integrated DS Processes in EA.

is integral to the operations of an enterprise, supported by essential **business functions** and services that ensure its effective execution and alignment with organizational strategic objectives. Fundamentally, the **business process** acts as a transformation mechanism, converting an **input**, typically represented as a product or service, into a valuable **output**. This transformation is initiated by an actor responding to a specific **business event**, which subsequently triggers the process workflow. It is important to note that each business process is owned by an **internal actor**, usually associated with a particular **business division**, thereby providing clear accountability and defining roles and responsibilities.

On the right side of the architecture, a foundational representation of a **Data Science service** is showcased, managed by a **Data Scientist** within either the IT or **Data Science division** of the organization. This service exemplifies how DS can enhance decision-making and operational efficiency across the business. The realization of a DS service often depends on a framework of multiple **Data Science business processes**. These processes are defined through established DS methodologies, enabling a systematic approach to data analysis and interpretation. By following these methodologies, organizations can ensure that their DS initiatives are not only effective but also aligned with their broader business goals, ultimately driving valuable insights and fostering innovative solutions (see [51–55,58]).

To effectively align the objectives of business processes with DS services, it is crucial to connect these goals in an integrated framework from an EA perspective. By correlating key performance indicators of the business goals with DS goals, organizations can quantitatively assess the effectiveness of this integration. This assessment not only reveals the impact of DS on business outcomes but also highlights opportunities for optimization within both processes and decision-making frameworks (see [51–55,58]).

The **Application Architecture** consists of interrelated systems designed to effectively support both business processes and data science initiatives. In addition to various business applications, a comprehensive suite of tools is essential for facilitating DS activities, particularly in model training and deployment. Within this framework, one should consider the intricacies of the DS lifecycle, such as the CRISP-DM model [48], which outlines the stages of data mining while emphasizing the importance of iterative refinement and model validation (see [11]).

At the heart of data-intensive processes is the **Data Architecture**, which plays a crucial role in managing and optimizing data flow. From a broader perspective, data repositories can be categorized into two primary types: business-relevant data sources that directly connect with business applications, and open data repositories that enhance and enrich the data landscape for DS activities. The latter often includes publicly available datasets that can provide valuable insights and complement existing data for more robust model training (see [11,21]).

On a foundational level, it is essential to consider the **Technology Architecture** to ensure optimal performance. A diverse range of hardware and software technologies is crucial for developing robust business applications and compute-intensive DS solutions. This encompasses not only the processing capabilities required for advanced Analytics but also the infrastructure necessary for scalable data storage and effective database management. Specifically, data storage solutions and database technologies play a vital role in supporting the intricate, data-driven processes. Proper integration and maintenance of these technologies are crucial for maximizing efficiency and achieving organizational goals. A storage cluster will efficiently manage unstructured data, ensuring optimal accessibility, while a dedicated database cluster will enhance query performance and maintain data integrity for structured data. Additionally, a computational cluster will support resource-intensive application tasks. These clusters will be interconnected through a secure organizational intranet, utilizing advanced internet technologies to facilitate seamless communication and data exchange (see [11]).

7 Discussion

The perspective presented in Sect. 6 integrates existing research that primarily focuses on both business architecture [21,53,58] and high-level architectural concepts [11,18,19]. The proposed framework seeks to establish a cohesive architecture that integrates technological advancements into business processes within an EA in the context of DS projects. This alignment ensures that technology supports organizational objectives and promotes operational agility.

To enhance this holistic view, it is crucial to provide a more **detailed examination** of the Application Architecture and Technology Architecture. This level of specificity is essential for effectively incorporating particular DS applications and realizing their technical implementations. Additionally, this approach should **extend to the methodologies** utilized in DS and their respective processes, especially at the Business Architecture level.

As we integrate relevant business processes, the complexity of the Business Architecture will inevitably increase. Consequently, it is essential to **refine the established EA model** concepts, with a focus on capturing and integrating these processes to ensure the architecture can adapt to the evolving business environment.

The **establishment of key performance indicators** also presents a significant challenge, particularly in defining the connections between business performance indicators and model performance indicators. This task requires identifying definitive and cohesive performance indicators that fuse both business and technical viewpoints. Alternatively, a mechanism for directly integrating technical performance indicators into business performance metrics may need to be developed, or vice versa. Identifying an appropriate conceptual framework or tool to address this intricate challenge remains an open question, demanding further investigation and innovative approaches.

8 Conclusion

This work provides a thorough literature review that critically examines existing research on integrating DS projects into EA models. In addition to previous research, it presents a comprehensive view of integrating DS to enhance architectural frameworks.

Looking ahead, it is planned to demonstrate these holistic models in practical applications within various enterprises. Additionally, a case study will be conducted to refine the model and rigorously evaluate the effectiveness of conceptual modeling, providing valuable insights into the practical implications of integrating DS projects into EA.

Disclosure of Interests. No funds, grants, or other support were received, and the authors have no relevant financial or non-financial competing interests to disclose.

References

1. Ahlemann, F., Stettiner, E., Messerschmidt, M., Legner, C.: Strategic enterprise architecture management. Springer, Heidelberg (2012). https://doi.org/10.1007/978-3-642-24223-6. http://link.springer.com/10.1007/978-3-642-24223-6
2. Borozanov, V., Hacks, S., Silva, N.: Using machine learning techniques for evaluating the similarity of enterprise architecture models. In: Giorgini, P., Weber, B. (eds.) CAiSE 2019. LNCS, vol. 11483, pp. 563–578. Springer, Cham (2019). https://doi.org/10.1007/978-3-030-21290-2_35

3. Brendel, A.B., Trang, S., Marrone, M., Lichtenberg, S., Kolbe, L.M.: What to do for a literature review? - A synthesis of literature review practices. In: AMCIS 2020 Proceedings (2020)
4. Chang, W.L., Grady, N.: NIST big data interoperability framework: Volume 1, definitions (2019). https://doi.org/10.6028/NIST.SP.1500-1r2
5. Chen, J., Zhao, L.: AI- driven innovation in enterprise architecture: a multi-agent system approach to adaptive design. In: Proceedings of the 2024 8th International Conference on Electronic Information Technology and Computer Engineering, pp. 768–774. Association for Computing Machinery, New York, NY, USA (2025). https://doi.org/10.1145/3711129.3711261
6. Delen, D., Ram, S.: Research challenges and opportunities in business analytics. J. Bus. Anal. **1**(1), 2–12 (2018). https://doi.org/10.1080/2573234X.2018.1507324
7. Denni-Fiberesima, D.: Navigating the generative AI-enabled enterprise architecture landscape: critical success factors for AI adoption and strategic integration. In: Alareeni, B., Hamdan, A. (eds.) Navigating the Technological Tide: The Evoluation and Challenges of Business Model Innovation, vol. 3, ICBT 2024. LNNS, vol. 1082, pp. 210–222 (2024). https://doi.org/10.1007/978-3-031-67434-1_20. iSSN: 2367-3370
8. Desfray, P., Raymond, G.: Modeling Enterprise Architecture with TOGAF: A Practical Guide Using UML and BPMN. Morgan Kaufmann, Amsterdam; Boston (2014)
9. Ettahiri, I., Ajallouda, L., Doumi, K., Zellou, A.: Toward dynamic enterprise architecture model using MAPE-K, control theory and machine learning to achieve autonomic adaptiveness. In: 2022 International Conference on Computational Modelling, Simulation and Optimization (ICCMSO), pp. 42–47 (2022). https://doi.org/10.1109/ICCMSO58359.2022.00022
10. Fitriani, L., Khodra, M.L., Surendro, K.: TOGAF-based enterprise architecture framework for utilizing artificial intelligence. In: 2023 International Conference on Computer, Control, Informatics and its Applications (IC3INA), pp. 90–95 (2023). https://doi.org/10.1109/IC3INA60834.2023.10285801
11. Geerdink, B.: A reference architecture for big data solutions - introducing a model to perform predictive analytics using big data technology. Int. J. Big Data Intell. **2**(4), 236 (2015). https://doi.org/10.1504/IJBDI.2015.072160. http://www.inderscience.com/link.php?id=72160
12. Glaser, P.L., Sallinger, E., Bork, D.: EA ModelSet – a FAIR dataset for machine learning in enterprise modeling. In: Almeida, J.P.A., Kaczmarek-Heß, M., Koschmider, A., Proper, H.A. (eds.) The Practice of Enterprise Modeling. LNBIP, vol. 497, pp. 19–36. Springer Nature, Switzerland, Cham (2024). https://doi.org/10.1007/978-3-031-48583-1_2
13. Glaser, P.L., Sallinger, E., Bork, D.: The extended EA ModelSet–a FAIR dataset for researching and reasoning enterprise architecture modeling practices. Softw. Syst. Model. (2025). https://doi.org/10.1007/s10270-025-01278-1
14. Goodfellow, I., Bengio, Y., Courville, A.: Deep Learning. Adaptive Computation and Machine Learning. The MIT Press, Cambridge, Massachusetts (2016)
15. Haertel, C., Pohl, M., Nahhas, A., Staegemann, D., Turowski, K.: Toward a lifecycle for data science: a literature review of data science process models. In: Proceedings of the Pacific Asia Conference on Information Systems (PACIS). AIS (2022)
16. Hastie, T., Tibshirani, R., Friedman, J.: The Elements of Statistical Learning. Springer Series in Statistics, Springer, New York (2008)
17. Hevner, A.R., March, S.T., Park, J., Ram, S.: Design science in information systems research. MIS Q. **28**(1), 75–105 (2004)

18. Husen, J., Washizaki, H., Yoshioka, N., Tun, H., Fukazawa, Y., Takeuchi, H.: Metamodel-based multi-view modeling framework for machine learning systems. In: Proceedings of the 11th International Conference on Model-Based Software and Systems Engineering, pp. 194–201. SCITEPRESS - Science and Technology Publications, Lisbon, Portugal (2023). https://doi.org/10.5220/0011699600003402
19. Husen, J.H.: Integrated multi-view modeling for reliable machine learning-intensive software engineering. Software Qual. J. **32**(3), 1239–1285 (2024). https://doi.org/10.1007/s11219-024-09687-z
20. Husen, J.H., et al.: Extensible modeling framework for reliable machine learning system analysis. In: 2023 IEEE/ACM 2nd International Conference on AI Engineering – Software Engineering for AI (CAIN), pp. 94–95. IEEE, Melbourne, Australia (2023). https://doi.org/10.1109/CAIN58948.2023.00022
21. Idowu, S., Struber, D., Berger, T.: EMMM: a unified meta-model for tracking machine learning experiments. In: 2022 48th Euromicro Conference on Software Engineering and Advanced Applications (SEAA), pp. 48–55. IEEE, Gran Canaria, Spain (2022). https://doi.org/10.1109/SEAA56994.2022.00016
22. Ilin, I., Levina, A., Borremans, A., Kalyazina, S.: Enterprise architecture modeling in digital transformation era. In: Murgul, V., Pukhkal, V. (eds.) EMMFT 2019. AISC, vol. 1259, pp. 124–142. Springer, Cham (2021). https://doi.org/10.1007/978-3-030-57453-6_11
23. Kamalabai, N.E., Donoghue, I., Hannola, L.: Sustainable enterprise architecture: a critical imperative for substantiating artificial intelligence. In: 2024 Portland International Conference on Management of Engineering and Technology (PICMET), pp. 1–12 (2024). https://doi.org/10.23919/PICMET64035.2024.10653061. iSSN: 2159-5100
24. Kearny, C., Gerber, A., van der Merwe, A.: Data-driven enterprise architecture and the TOGAF ADM phases. In: 2016 IEEE International Conference on Systems, Man, and Cybernetics (SMC), pp. 4603–4608. IEEE (2016). iSSN: 1062-922X
25. Landthaler, J., Uludağ, Ö., Bondel, G., Elnaggar, A., Nair, S., Matthes, F.: A machine learning based approach to application landscape documentation. In: Buchmann, R.A., Karagiannis, D., Kirikova, M. (eds.) PoEM 2018. LNBIP, vol. 335, pp. 71–85. Springer, Cham (2018). https://doi.org/10.1007/978-3-030-02302-7_5
26. Martel, Y., et al.: Software architecture best practices for enterprise artificial intelligence (2021). https://doi.org/10.18420/INF2020_16. http://dl.gi.de/handle/20.500.12116/34722. iSBN: 9783885797012 Publisher: Gesellschaft für Informatik, Bonn
27. Mattila, J., Parkinson, S.: An approach for enterprise architects to analyse opportunities and constraints for applying artificial intelligence in military transformations (2022)
28. de Medeiros, M.M., Hoppen, N., Maçada, A.C.G.: Data science for business: benefits, challenges and opportunities. Bottom Line **33**(2), 149–163 (2020). https://doi.org/10.1108/BL-12-2019-0132
29. Molnár, B.: An analysis of the concept of cognitive enterprise architecture foundation of cognitive enterprise archtecture. In: 2023 14th IEEE International Conference on Cognitive Infocommunications (CogInfoCom), pp. 000107–000112 (2023). https://doi.org/10.1109/CogInfoCom59411.2023.10397536. iSSN: 2473-5671
30. Mukherjee, P.K.: Artificial intelligence based smart government enterprise architecture (AI-SGEA) framework. In: Sk, A.A., Turki, T., Ghosh, T.K., Joardar, S., Barman, S. (eds.) Artificial Intelligence. CCIS, vol. 1695, pp. 325–333. Springer Nature, Switzerland, Cham (2022). https://doi.org/10.1007/978-3-031-22485-0_30

31. Müller, O., Fay, M., vom Brocke, J.: The effect of big data and analytics on firm performance: an econometric analysis considering industry characteristics. J. Manag. Inf. Syst. **35**(2), 488–509 (2018). https://doi.org/10.1080/07421222.2018.1451955
32. Nalchigar, S., Yu, E.: Business-driven data analytics: a conceptual modeling framework. Data Knowl. Eng. **117**, 359–372 (2018). https://doi.org/10.1016/j.datak.2018.04.006. https://linkinghub.elsevier.com/retrieve/pii/S0169023X18301691
33. Nardello, M., Møller, C., Gøtze, J.: Understanding enterprise architecture with topic modeling - preliminary research based on journal articles:. In: Proceedings of the 20th International Conference on Enterprise Information Systems, pp. 640–648. SCITEPRESS - Science and Technology Publications, Funchal, Madeira, Portugal (2018). https://doi.org/10.5220/0006693106400648
34. Page, M.J., et al.: The Prisma 2020 statement: an updated guideline for reporting systematic reviews. BMJ (Clin. Res. Ed.) **372**, n71 (2021). https://doi.org/10.1136/bmj.n71
35. Pathak, S., Krishnaswamy, V., Sharma, M.: A dynamic capability perspective on the impact of big data analytics and enterprise architecture on innovation: an empirical study. J. Enterprise Inf. Manag. **38**(2), 532–563 (2025). https://doi.org/10.1108/JEIM-01-2024-0059. https://www.emerald.com/insight/content/doi/10.1108/JEIM-01-2024-0059/full/html
36. Piest, J.P.S., Jinzaki, M., Masuda, Y., Toriya, M., Nakamura, O., Toma, T.: Multiple use case analysis of an AI hospital using the AIDAF and intelligence amplification design canvas. In: Sales, T., DeKinderen, S., Proper, H., Pufahl, L., Karastoyanova, D., VanSinderen, M. (eds.) Enterprise Design, Operations, and Computing, EDOC 2023 Workshops, IDAMS, IRESEARCH, MIDAS4CS, SOEA4EE, EDOC Forum, Demonstrations Track and Doctoral Consortium. LNBIP, vol. 498, pp. 5–22 (2024). https://doi.org/10.1007/978-3-031-54712-6_1. iSSN: 1865-1348
37. Pinheiro, C., Guerreiro, S., Mamede, H.S.: A survey on association rule mining for enterprise architecture model discovery. Bus. Inf. Syst. Eng. **66**(6), 777–798 (2024). https://doi.org/10.1007/s12599-023-00844-5
38. Pohl, M., Haertel, C., Turowski, K.: Value creation from data science applications - a literature review. In: Hinkelmann, K., López-Pellicer, F.J., Polini, A. (eds.) Perspectives in Business Informatics Research, pp. 327–338. Springer Nature Switzerland, Cham (2023). https://doi.org/10.1007/978-3-031-43126-5_23
39. Pohl, M., Staegemann, D.G., Turowski, K.: The performance benefit of data analytics applications. Procedia Comput. Sci. **201**, 679–683 (2022). https://doi.org/10.1016/j.procs.2022.03.090
40. Qiu, Y., Liu, Y.: Exploring the path to building intelligent enterprises in the digital era. In: Proceedings of the 2024 15th International Conference on E-Business, Management and Economics, ICEME 2024, pp. 202–206. Association for Computing Machinery, New York, NY, USA (2025). https://doi.org/10.1145/3691422.3691467
41. Rahlmeier, N., Hopf, K.: Bridging fields of practice: how boundary objects enable collaboration in data science initiatives. In: Wirtschaftsinformatik 2024 Proceedings, vol. 55 (2024)
42. Rashed, F., Drews, P.: How does enterprise architecture support the design and realization of data-driven business models? An empirical study. In: Ahlemann, F., Schutte, R., Stieglitz, S. (eds.) Innovation through Information Systems, Vol III: A Colleciton of Latest Research on Management Issues. LNISO, vol. 48, pp. 662–677 (2021). https://doi.org/10.1007/978-3-030-86800-0_45. iSSN: 2195-4968
43. Rehman, Z., Tariq, N., Moqurrab, S.A., Yoo, J., Srivastava, G.: Machine learning and internet of things applications in enterprise architectures: solutions, challenges,

and open issues. Exp. Syst. **41**(1), e13467 (2024). https://doi.org/10.1111/exsy.13467. https://onlinelibrary.wiley.com/doi/10.1111/exsy.13467
44. Pinheiro, C.R., Guerreiro, S.L.P.D., Mamede, H.S.: A lightweight ontology for enterprise architecture mining of API gateway logs. IEEE Access **12**, 128585–128601 (2024). https://doi.org/10.1109/ACCESS.2024.3456119
45. Sandkuhl, K., Rittelmeyer, J.D.: Use of EA models in organizational AI solution development. In: Aveiro, D., Proper, H.A., Guerreiro, S., De Vries, M. (eds.) Advances in Enterprise Engineering XV. LNBIP, vol. 441, pp. 149–166. Springer International Publishing, Cham (2022). https://doi.org/10.1007/978-3-031-11520-2_10
46. Schmidt, R., Wißotzki, M., Jugel, D., Möhring, M., Sandkuhl, K., Zimmermann, A.: Towards a framework for enterprise architecture analytics. In: 2014 IEEE 18th International Enterprise Distributed Object Computing Conference Workshops and Demonstrations, pp. 266–275 (2014). https://doi.org/10.1109/EDOCW.2014.47. iSSN: 2325-6605
47. Schubert, V., Kuehner, S., Krauss, T., Trat, M., Bender, J.: Towards a B2B integration framework for smart services in Industry 4.0. Procedia Comput. Sci. **217**, 1649–1659 (2023). https://doi.org/10.1016/j.procs.2022.12.365
48. Shearer, C.: The CRISP-DM model: the new blueprint for data mining. J. Data Warehouse **5**(4), 13–22 (2000)
49. Stahl, B., Häckel, B., Leuthe, D., Ritter, C.: Data or business first?–Manufacturers' transformation toward data-driven business models. Schmalenbach J. Bus. Res. **75**(3), 303–343 (2023). https://doi.org/10.1007/s41471-023-00154-2
50. Suroso, J.S., Jericho, I., Suroso, M.F.A., Reynaldy, R., Wang, G., Kristanto, J.: Big data based information system design in hospitality. In: 2022 IEEE International Conference of Computer Science and Information Technology (ICOSNIKOM), pp. 01–05 (2022). https://doi.org/10.1109/ICOSNIKOM56551.2022.10034870
51. Takeuchi, H., Doi, T., Washizaki, H., Okuda, S., Yoshioka, N.: Enterprise architecture based representation of architecture and design patterns for machine learning systems. In: 2021 IEEE 25th International Enterprise Distributed Object Computing Workshop (EDOCW), pp. 245–250. IEEE, Gold Coast, Australia (2021). https://doi.org/10.1109/EDOCW52865.2021.00055
52. Takeuchi, H., Husen, J.H., Tun, H.T., Washizaki, H., Yoshioka, N.: Enterprise architecture-based metamodel for a holistic business—IT alignment view on machine learning projects. In: 2023 IEEE International Conference on e-Business Engineering (ICEBE), pp. 8–15. IEEE, Sydney, Australia (2023). https://doi.org/10.1109/ICEBE59045.2023.00013
53. Takeuchi, H., Husen, J.H., Tun, H.T., Washizaki, H., Yoshioka, N.: Enterprise architecture-based metamodel for machine learning projects and its management. Future Gener. Comput. Syst. **161**, 135–145 (2024). https://doi.org/10.1016/j.future.2024.06.062
54. Takeuchi, H., Ichitsuka, A., Iino, T., Ishikawa, S., Saito, K.: Assessment method for identifying business activities to be replaced by AI technologies. Procedia Comput. Sci. **192**, 1601–1610 (2021). https://doi.org/10.1016/j.procs.2021.08.164
55. Takeuchi, H., Imazaki, K., Kuno, N., Doi, T., Motohashi, Y.: Constructing reusable knowledge for machine learning projects based on project practices. Intell. Decis. Technol. **16**(4), 725–735 (2022). https://doi.org/10.3233/IDT-220252. https://journals.sagepub.com/doi/full/10.3233/IDT-220252
56. Takeuchi, H., Ito, Y., Nishiyama, R., Isomura, T.: Modeling of machine learning projects using archimate. In: Zimmermann, A., Howlett, R.J., Jain, L.C.,

Schmidt, R. (eds.) Human Centred Intelligent Systems. SIST, vol. 244, pp. 222–231. Springer, Singapore, Singapore (2021). https://doi.org/10.1007/978-981-16-3264-8_21
57. Takeuchi, H., Ito, Y., Yamamoto, S.: Method for constructing machine learning project canvas based on enterprise architecture modeling. Procedia Comput. Sci. **207**, 425–434 (2022). https://doi.org/10.1016/j.procs.2022.09.077
58. Takeuchi, H., Kaiya, H., Nakagawa, H., Ogata, S.: Practice-based collection of bad smells in machine learning projects. Procedia Comput. Sci. **225**, 517–526 (2023). https://doi.org/10.1016/j.procs.2023.10.036
59. Takeuchi, H., Yamamoto, S.: AI service system development using enterprise architecture modeling. Procedia Comput. Sci. **159**, 923–932 (2019). https://doi.org/10.1016/j.procs.2019.09.259
60. Takeuchi, H., Yamamoto, S.: Business AI alignment modeling based on enterprise architecture. In: Czarnowski, I., Howlett, R.J., Jain, L.C. (eds.) Intelligent Decision Technologies 2019. SIST, vol. 143, pp. 155–165. Springer, Singapore (2019). https://doi.org/10.1007/978-981-13-8303-8_14
61. Takeuchi, H., Yamamoto, S.: Business analysis method for constructing business–AI alignment model. Procedia Comput. Sci. **176**, 1312–1321 (2020). https://doi.org/10.1016/j.procs.2020.09.140
62. vom Brocke, J., Simons, A., Niehaves, B., Reimer, K., Plattfaut, R., Cleven, A.: Reconstructing the giant: on the importance of Rigour in documenting the literature. In: ECIS 2009 (2009)
63. Wamba, S.F., Gunasekaran, A., Akter, S., Ren, S.J.F., Dubey, R., Childe, S.J.: Big data analytics and firm performance: effects of dynamic capabilities. J. Bus. Res. **70** (2017)
64. Webster, J., Watson, R.T.: Analyzing the past to prepare for the future: writing a literature review. MIS Q. **26**, 13–23 (2002)
65. Zachman, J.A.: A framework for information systems architecture. IBM Syst. J. **26**(3), 276–292 (1987). https://doi.org/10.1147/sj.263.0276
66. Zimmermann, A., Schmidt, R., Sandkuhl, K., Masuda, Y.: Architecting intelligent digital systems and services. In: Zimmermann, A., Howlett, R.J., Jain, L.C. (eds.) Human Centred Intelligent Systems. SIST, vol. 189, pp. 127–137. Springer, Singapore (2021). https://doi.org/10.1007/978-981-15-5784-2_11

Business Process Management

Business Process Optimization: A Systematic Review of Combining Concepts from Business Process Management and Operations Research

Michel Kunkler(✉), Felix Schumann, and Stefanie Rinderle-Ma

TUM School of Computation, Information, and Technology, Technical University of Munich, Garching, Germany

{michel.kunkler,felix.schumann,stefanie.rinderle-ma}@tum.de

Abstract. Business Process Management and Operations Research are two research fields that both aim to enhance value creation in organizations. While Business Process Management has historically emphasized on providing precise models, Operations Research has focused on constructing tractable models and their solutions. This systematic literature review identifies and analyzes work that uses combined concepts from both disciplines. In particular, it analyzes how business process models have been conceptualized as mathematical models and which optimization techniques have been applied to these models. Results indicate a strong focus on resource allocation and scheduling problems. Current approaches often lack support of the stochastic nature of many problems, and do only sparsely use information from process models or from event logs, such as resource-related information or information from the data perspective.

Keywords: Business Process Optimization · Process Improvement · Business Process Management · Operations Research · Systematic Literature Review

1 Introduction

One major goal in Business Process Management (BPM) is process optimization and improvement [32]. Another research discipline targeting the operational performances of organizations is Operations Research (OR). OR *"is concerned with quantitative (mathematical) models and their solution"* [33]. [32] points out that OR *"is generally concerned with controlling an existing process without necessarily changing it, while BPM is often concerned with making changes to an existing process in order to improve it"* [32]. Nevertheless, *"many process improvement problems can in fact be traced back to typical problems investigated by OR"* [2]. Hence, BPM approaches such as [2,29] promote the idea of applying OR techniques on business processes.

© The Author(s), under exclusive license to Springer Nature Switzerland AG 2026
A. Gianola et al. (Eds.): EDOC 2025, LNCS 16213, pp. 61–83, 2026.
https://doi.org/10.1007/978-3-032-15140-7_4

Despite the shared goal of improving the operational performance of organizations, so far, both disciplines have followed distinct optimization approaches. An OR project as described by [39] is a finite sequence of steps designed to serve a specific optimization goal. When a problem appears intractable for some solution method, an OR practitioner can either change the solution method (e.g., to a heuristic) or simplify the model [99]. In contrast, a key concept in BPM is the BPM lifecycle [32], which categorizes means to operationalize business processes into four recurring phases, i.e., the process (re-)design, system configuration, process enactment, and process diagnosis phase. The output of one phase is taken as input for the next phase and the cycle is continuously executed to reach ongoing improvement.

Existing surveys on Business Process Optimization focus on the improvement of the enactment phase of the BPM life cycle. [92] analyze methods of resource allocation and scheduling of business process in particular for the cloud computing domain. [84] analyze the BPM data sources that are used as input for resource allocation approaches of business processes. Here a specific focus is on the used process models and data for different allocation algorithms during enactment.

This work focuses on the model depicted in Fig. 1, which combines the OR-driven optimization project methodology presented in [39] with the BPM life cycle. By following this model, our survey enhances existing surveys by considering business process optimization as a holistic, continuous effort, which can affect the (re-)design and the enactment phase. The integrated model is based on the idea in [32], that *quantitative analysis* methods can be applied to the (re-)design and the enactment phase (①) and are based on data obtained during process diagnosis. We further enhance this definition by also looking at data gathered during enactment and (re-)design ②.

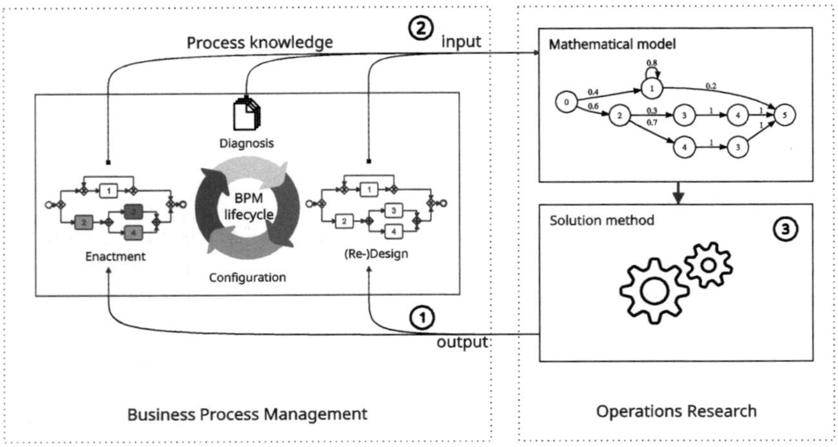

Fig. 1. Quantitative optimization of business processes using OR methods

We design the research questions for this systematic literature review in coherence with Fig. 1 and analyze the application of OR techniques in the context of business process improvement. The first objective is to provide an overview of the targeted optimization phase, i.e., is the (re-)design or the enactment of a process optimized through the application of an OR method (see ①). We do not perceive the configuration and diagnosis phases as directly applicable to OR techniques, as the diagnosis phase is concerned with aggregating data post-ex, and the configuration phase with implementing a process model (see Fig. 1). The second objective is to survey how mathematical models are obtained from process data and in which form this data is structured. To this end, we distinguish data collected during process enactment, such as event streams/logs and runtime data, as well as during process (re-)design, i.e., process models. In particular, we are interested in which process mining techniques, which process modeling techniques, and which process perspectives are suitable or even required for the creation of an OR model (see ②). The third objective is to survey the solution methods used to solve the optimization problem, i.e., mathematical models obtained from process-related data (see ③).

The survey at hand contributes to the BPM community, as the results indicate which data baseline in the form of models is necessary for business process optimization from an OR perspective and discusses missing modeling standards. It contributes to the OR community, as the results indicate how mathematical models and solution techniques can be applied to business processes and, therefore, optimize meaningful real-world use cases.

The remainder of this work is structured as follows: In Sect. 2 we outline the search strategy of the literature review. The findings are presented in Sect. 3. In Sect. 4 we present identified challenges that should be considered by future research. Related work is presented in Sect. 5. Section 6 discusses and concludes the systematic literature review.

2 Research Method

The Systematic Literature Review (SLR) follows the guidelines by [51] and starts with defining research questions based on the integrated model depicted in Fig. 1. The first research question **RQ1** asks **which BPM life-cycle phase is addressed when applying optimization techniques from OR on business processes.** It seeks to provide insights into the types of optimization problems that have been predominantly proposed and addressed so far or present promising opportunities for future research. The second research question **RQ2** asks **how business processes are modeled or mined to deliver data for the application of OR techniques.** In detail, it aims to identify the most suitable business process modeling and mining techniques for creating mathematical optimization models, especially considering different process perspectives, i.e., control-flow, resources, time, and data. The third research question **RQ3** focuses on **which solution techniques are used to optimize business processes** and aims to identify mathematical solution approaches that align with business processes, including approximations or optimal solutions.

We search *Scopus* and *Web of Science* acknowledged as world-leading comprehensive databases [113]. The following search queries are designed to find relevant works for answering **RQ1–RQ3**.

For Scopus, we use:

```
TITLE–ABS–KEY (
    ("BUSINESS PROCESS MANAGEMENT" OR "WORKFLOW MANAGEMENT" OR "PROCESS MINING"
        OR "PROCESS ANALYTICS") AND
    ("OPERATIONS RESEARCH" OR "OPERATIONAL RESEARCH" OR "SCHEDULING"
        OR "ALLOCATION" OR "ROUTING" OR "OPTIMIZATION" OR "OPTIMISATION")
)
```

For Web of Science, we use:

```
TS=(
    ("BUSINESS PROCESS MANAGEMENT" OR "WORKFLOW MANAGEMENT" OR "PROCESS MINING"
        OR "PROCESS ANALYTICS") AND
    ("OPERATIONS RESEARCH" OR "OPERATIONAL RESEARCH" OR "SCHEDULING"
        OR "ALLOCATION" OR "ROUTING" OR "OPTIMIZATION" OR "OPTIMISATION")
)
```

In order to address the combination of BPM and OR fields, the search queries consist of keywords targeting the BPM field and the OR field, connected by a logical 'AND'. For both fields, terms that are used interchangeably are included, such as *Business Process Management* and *Workflow Management*. Moreover, language bias is avoided by using, e.g., *Operations Research* and *Operational Research*. In a test run, the term *Business Process* yielded an infeasible amount of results, often unrelated to the BPM discipline, and is therefore disregarded from the search strings. The term *Process Mining* is included in order to address the process enactment phase.

The keywords are used to search within the title, abstract, and keywords of publications. The search was conducted in September 2025, resulting in 3 650 initial studies. After removing duplicates, 2 639 publications remain for the title, keywords, and abstract screening. The screening is based on inclusion and exclusion criteria. From a technical point of view, we consider peer-reviewed publications in English and exclude position papers. From a content perspective, we consider publications that regard formalized process models or event logs and are concerned with quantitative optimization techniques. Analogously, we exclude papers on manual optimization or manual re-engineering. Finally, we exclude papers on grid and cloud computing and scientific workflows as the corresponding optimization techniques are concerned with "the transportation and analysis of large quantities of data" [14]. The inclusion and exclusion criteria are applied to titles, keywords, and abstracts of search results and rated by the authors on a Likert-5 scale [62]. All publications that are ranked higher than 3 are chosen for reading the full text. Full-text copies are obtained for 179 publications, while the full text could not be obtained for six publications. After reading the full texts, 87 studies are excluded due to not meeting the inclusion criteria, resulting in 92 publications[1] put into further assessment.

Based on a full-text review of the 92 selected publications, we extract data in order to ensure a systematic approach in answering research questions **RQ1–RQ3**. The data set can be found in[1].

[1] https://github.com/Schlixmann/SLR_OR_BPM.

- **RQ1 – Targeted BPM life-cycle phase:** We assess whether the proposed process optimization approach affects the design phase, e.g., planning an optimal amount of resources prior to enactment, or the enactment phase, e.g., allocating resources to process activities during its enactment (`life cycle phase` ∈ {`enactment, design`}). Moreover, we assess the problem by categorizing it into `category` ∈ {`Action recommendation, Resource planning, Resource allocation, Scheduling, Process navigation, Process model selection, Batching, Control-flow re-engineering, SLA Planning`} Initial categories were discussed during the review protocol design and refined after all relevant publications were read. OR categories are derived from [39], i.e., scheduling, batching, resource planning, and resource allocation. As BPM problems are typically concerned with changing the process model [32], we decide on the following categories from a process-driven perspective, i.e., selection of the best process model, control-flow re-engineering, process navigation, action recommendation, resource allocation (present in BPM and OR), and SLA planning.
- **RQ2 – Optimization input:** We assess the existence of (i) a `process model` ∈ {`yes, no`}, ii) an `event log` ∈ {`yes, no`}, iii) the `workflow patterns` ∈ {`sequence, AND, XOR, deferred choice`}, iv) `multiple process instances` ∈ {`yes, no`}, v) `resource modeling` ∈ {`yes, no`}, vi) `resource performance indicators` (RPI) ∈ {none, single, complex}, vii) `resource grouping` ∈ {`pooled, individual, both`}, viii) `time profiles` ∈ {`yes, no`}, and ix) `data perspective` ∈ {`yes, no`}. If, for example, a process model is available, we review which workflow patterns are supported in the optimization model. For the resource perspective, we extract how resources are represented, e.g., as individual resources and/or as pooled resource groups.
- **RQ3 – Solution method:** We assess x) which solution approach is applied and xi) `optimality` ∈ {`yes, no`}. Since publications often combine several algorithms to obtain a solution, we do not use a structured field to extract the proposed solution approaches. We extract whether the applied method finds an optimal solution to the mathematical model or an approximation and how this solution is found, e.g., by heuristics.

3 Results

This section presents the analysis of the included studies on the research questions **RQ1–RQ3** based on the categorizations presented in Sect. 2.

3.1 RQ1: Targeted BPM Life-Cycle Phase

73% of the publications target optimization problems in the enactment phase and 27% the design phase. Figure 2 shows the distribution of the publications on a timeline, grouped by *life cycle phase*. The majority of publications addressing quantitative optimization methods in BPM have been published since 2011. The number of publications that address optimization in the enactment phase peaked in 2016, while the number of publications that address optimizations in the design phase has been rather constant every year since 2017.

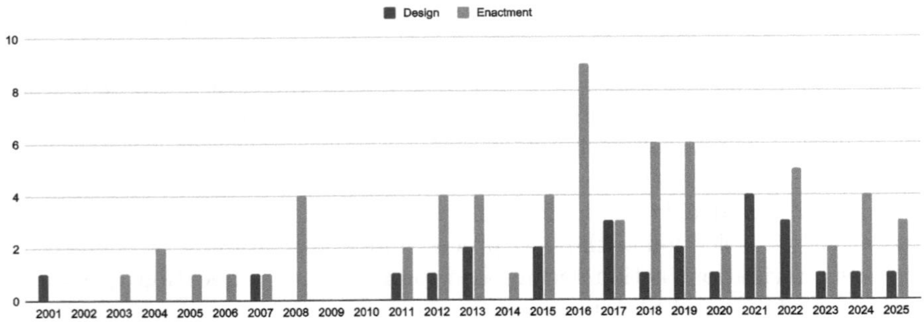

Fig. 2. Publishing year and life cycle phase

Figure 3 shows the number of publications for each of the nine *problem categories*. The majority of publications are concerned with *scheduling* and *resource allocation* in the enactment phase, and with *control flow re-engineering* and *resource planning* for design time. In the following, a description of the individual problem categories and their publications is presented.

Design phase: *Process model selection* comprises [90,91], which are concerned with finding the best-performing process model from a set of feasible process models. *Control flow re-engineering* publications present quantitative optimization approaches for re-engineering the control flow of a process. In this category, [76,100] propose techniques to parallelize activities in an automated way to speed up the process execution. Conversely, [104] propose an automatic approach to sequentialize activities, such that an allocation algorithm is prevented from assigning an unsuitable or expensive resource to an activity when a well-suited resource is unavailable because it is executing a parallel activity. Two publications are concerned with (re-)engineering decision points: [16] aims to find optimal conditional values for exclusive choices, while [98] aims to move the decision points to the earliest possible points to enhance planning certainties. [1] investigates strategies to find an optimal task order in knock-out processes where the outcome is, e.g., to approve or disapprove a loan. [58] suggest splitting a process model into a subset of process models so that the process models have a minimal inter-process coupling. These smaller processes can be used individually for further scheduling or allocation techniques. Lastly, [97] presents an approach that finds the minimal number of change operations needed to transform a control flow model into another one. *SLA planning* in [18] is concerned with an automatic approach for proposing SLAs based on business processes. *Resource* *planning* publications aim to plan either the number of resources needed for process execution or the properties of resources, e.g., their locations. Finding the optimal number of resources is the goal of [5,15,60,66,73,78,82], while finding optimal properties is the objective for [35,50,87]. [20,68] propose approaches that can be used to evaluate the effect of replacing a resource with another one. [53] is concerned with identifying bottleneck resources. *Batching* addresses the problem of finding optimal batch sizes for activities. It is the only category considered in the enactment and design phases. [83] focuses on a static batch size determined during design time. In contrast, [79] introduces a dynamic method that adjusts the batch size during the enactment phase.

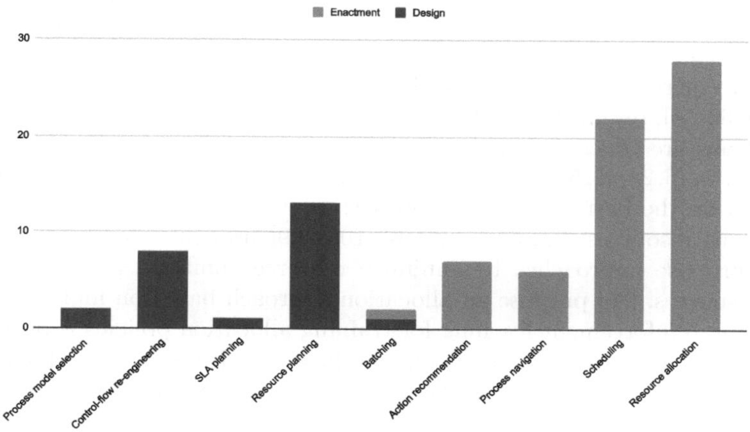

Fig. 3. Problem categories and life cycle phases

Enactment phase: *Action recommendation* refers to the execution of a next task in a process instance or for a resource or to initiate a new process instance. [12] recommend the most suitable next activity to a resource, i.e., a user. The pool of possible activities can stem from different process instances with different priorities or service-level agreements that must be obeyed. Similarly, [44] recommend the most suitable intervention for aggressive patients in a clinical process. [101] recommend skipping process activities, e.g., when a deadline can only be met if checking the credibility of a customer is skipped. [10] recommend whether a new process instance should be spawned or not, i.e., an offer be accepted or not. [56,88,89] focus on recommending time points for maintenance tasks. *Process navigation* proposes a viable process path, e.g., a set of activities required to complete a process instance. [48,49,72] are primarily concerned with (resource) deadlocks that might occur during the process executions and suggest identifying feasible execution strategies that are not exposed to deadlocks by using Monte Carlo simulation. [22,112] present approaches to select the optimal branch at deferred choices. Similarly, [11] conceptualizes robot movements as a process model and addresses the optimal navigation through the process model. *Scheduling* comprises approaches that schedule the execution of business processes in advance and, in doing so, typically also plan the allocation of resources to tasks. [23,55,96,103,106] focus on instance-level scheduling, i.e., planning the starting times of process instances. While [106] aims to balance the resource workload, [103] aims to maximize the number of instances that can be finished in a given timeframe. The other publications focus on scheduling at task level, i.e., they consider a process model for scheduling the execution of activities and propose either to solve constraint programming (CP) formulations [7,13,46,94], answer set programming (ASP) formulations [36–38], or (mixed) integer linear programming ((M)ILP) formulations [8,27,34,40,69]. [86] formulate the scheduling problem as a Markov reward process and propose to find an approximate solution via stochastic approximation methods. [69,75] propose to use metaheuristics, [41,42] multi-agent systems, and [19,93] propose to incrementally build schedules via heuristics. *Resource allocation:* In [9,30,31,54,73], resources are allocated to one specific type of activity. The other publications are concerned with allocating resources to tasks, i.e., instantiated activities: In [6,28,45,59,64,65,67,85,102,107,108,110,111], allocation decisions are based on the best matching of properties of tasks to resources or resources to previous resources. Similarly, [21,63,105,109] propose allocation heuristics. [24,26] propose approaches to minimize resource conflicts and maximize the active resources. [80] propose an allocation approach based on multi-agent auction. Using reinforcement learning for training allocation policies is proposed in [43,73,74]. Finding the best match among the available resources and unassigned and future tasks by formulating the problem as a minimum-cost maximum-flow problem is presented in [54,77]. [6] propose two resource criteria driven allocation approaches, i.e., immediately allocating a task to the resource with the best resource criteria matching, and allocating a set of tasks (batch) to resources such that the best matching for all tasks is achieved.

3.2 RQ2: Optimization Input

Finding a mathematical model that precisely depicts reality and maintains computational tractability is key to solving an OR problem. In the following, we investigate for which process representations and process perspectives mathematical optimization models are currently obtained that are later solved through various techniques.

Information sources, Workflow Patterns, and Multiple Instances: 53 of the publications formalize the *process model (i)* in an imperative and 3 in a declarative way. 38 publications do not specifically mention the usage of a process model. 13 publications mention an *event log (ii)* as information source and 43 publications describe the discovery of a process model from an event log. 30 publications use/mention both process model and event log as an information source. Assessing the expressive power of the proposed models and associated mathematical formulations is based on selected *workflow patterns (iii)* used in the process models, i.e., sequence, parallel split and synchronization, exclusive split, and merge, as well as deferred choice. Workflow patterns are conceptualized in OR problems in two distinct ways. One option is to formalize them as constraints into mathematical models directly. Solutions are then obtained from the mathematical model by using *analytical optimization* techniques. The sequential pattern, for example, can be formalized as a constraint in a constraint programming formulation such that no activity may be scheduled before its predecessor has been finished. The second approach is to conceptualize workflow patterns in simulation models, where only the simulation model is aware of the workflow constraints. The optimization model itself then learns a policy based on the outputs of the simulation model, e.g., by using reinforcement learning techniques. This approach is known as *simulation optimization* [4]. Of the 56 publications that formalize the control-flow perspective for optimization, 23 use *simulation optimization* techniques, and 33 use *analytical optimization* techniques.

Table 1 summarizes the workflow patterns for the 53 publications using an imperative modeling approach, differentiated by life cycle phases design and enactment. All 53 publications incorporate the sequential pattern in their analytical or simulation models. 44 publications additionally conceptualize and consider information from parallel splits and their synchronizations. 21 publications consider exclusive choices and their merges, and 11 publications consider the deferred choice pattern, with a focus on the enactment phase.

Table 1. Workflow patterns

	Design	Enactment	$\sum$
Sequential	15	38	53
AND	12	32	44
XOR	10	11	21
Deferred Choice	1	10	11

Exclusive choices are interesting because, unlike AND-splits, where all subsequent branches are executed, the branch chosen at an exclusive choice can typically not be foreseen during design time or at model instantiation, consequently creating *uncertainty* for OR models. In [98], data-flow analysis is conducted to move decision points to the earliest possible points to reduce the number of possible paths of a process as early as possible. [16] optimize the conditions of exclusive choices themselves to maximize the value contribution of a process. In the context of scheduling and planning, 10 publications conceptualize exclusive choices for the application of *analytical optimization* techniques and 10 for *simulation optimization* techniques. For exclusive choice gateways, analytical approaches most commonly use probabilistic techniques such as transition probabilities to handle individual branches [9,16,25,37,38,78]. [13] schedule the execution of a business process until an exclusive choice is reached. [38] combine the idea of rescheduling and using transition probabilities. They propose considering the most likely branch of an exclusive choice when it exceeds a predefined threshold. In resource planning for emergency processes, the work of [60] considers the worst-case branch for estimating the maximal number of simultaneously required resources. Another non-probabilistic approach is presented in [20]. Under the assumption that resources affect the data perspective of processes, their approach finds associations between resources and the control flow path. Exclusive choices in *simulation models* are considered in the works of [15,20,30,34,63,66,68,70,73,106], but only [30,70,73] describe in detail how they set up their simulation model or provide an artifact.

Another dimension in which the performance of business processes can be improved is through optimization across multiple process instances. A multi-instance view is known in simulation approaches as multi-entity simulation. In process mining, a comparable multi-case approach is rare [71]. 52 publications claim to consider *multiple instances (iv)* for the optimization, but most works do not further describe how information from multiple instances is formalized.

Process Perspectives: A key approach to quantitative business process improvement is to optimize a process not only over the control-flow, but also over other perspectives. Intuitively, the focus is often set on the planning, allocation, and modeling of *resources (v)* that execute process tasks. 78 papers model resources and use them as input to solve their mathematical model. For the 78 publications, we investigate in detail how resources are modeled, including *resource performance indicators (RPI) (vi)*, e.g., execution time. Moreover, we analyze if resources are considered as individual instances or groups, e.g., as (*resource grouping (vii)*), if their availability schedules (*time profiles (viii)*) are modeled, e.g., following a shift plan.

18 of the 78 publications target the optimization of the design phase. A resource is modeled as an individual instance in 6 of these publications. In [68], the difference between modeling resources as individuals and modeling resources as groups is assessed for simulation models and finds that the individual modeling of each resource leads to simulation models closer to actual event logs. In terms of modeling RPIs, 5 publications model multiple RPIs, and 4 publications model a single performance measure. 9 publications fully disregard the performance of resources. 11 publications, where optimization affects the design phase model resources in a grouped manner, [68] uses a hybrid model. In terms of time profiles, only [5] models a notion of a schedule for the design phase. Here, the waiting times in an emergency department are optimized by improving the overall schedule design.

60 publications consider resources as input for an optimization model to improve the enactment phase of business processes. 24 approaches model a single RPI. The resource performance is fully disregarded in 15 publications. Different modeling approaches for the RPIs are chosen. An advanced modeling is described in [6]. The authors employ the structure of resource process cubes, where each dimension represents one RPI of a resource. These cubes enable the usage of online analytical processing (OLAP) operations to obtain insights into resource performance. When targeting the enactment phase, 45 approaches use individually modeled resources. In 11 publications, resources are pooled, and 4 publications combine individual and pooled modeling. E.g., [36,63] enable an aggregation of RPIs for a group, if not enough information for an individual resource is present. 13 publications model time profiles as part of their resource modeling. Many of those publications are concerned with scheduling, especially in the healthcare domain, e.g. [19,27,34].

The *data perspective (ix)* is (partly) modeled by 28 approaches. [98] models data dependency graphs. In [16], information from the data perspective is used to improve the decision at XOR-Gateways. [38] uses the data perspective to decide if a fragmentation for better allocation should be done at a decision point or not.

3.3 RQ3: Solution Method

Some publications set up a simple formal model on which the application of optimal solution techniques is tractable. Other publications present complex mathematical models to which only approximate solution methods can be applied. Optimal solutions are preferred when the search space is small, mostly due to a small number of input variables from the model or due to a small number of objective variables with a small value range. The first is the case when information is strongly aggregated. [9], for example, use risk and cost information of each task as input for allocating control resources that reduce overall costs, to tasks. The latter is the case when, e.g., only starting times of instances are to be scheduled, instead of scheduling all tasks from all instances [106]. Some publications propose optimal solutions, even when the algorithmic complexity is NP-hard. [36,37] propose to use logic programming and [94] constraint programming to find optimal schedules for imperative process models. Similarly, [13,46] suggest using constraint programming for scheduling on descriptive process models.

Approximate solutions are the preferred solution method when the search space is intractably large or when the problem is subject to uncertainties under which searching for an optimal solution seems to be infeasible. Approximate solutions are especially present in publications that relate to resource allocation and scheduling, resource planning, or process navigation. Linear programming relaxation is used for resource allocation in [24,25]. [102] argue against scheduling allocations in business processes due to the problem complexity and that "various unpredicted factors" can occur during the execution. Therefore they propose to conduct on-the-fly resource allocation by matching resource properties to task properties. Other approaches propose the use of metaheuristics; [22,75] propose ant-colony optimization for process navigation and scheduling. [31] proposes a genetic algorithm for planning the number of resources for each activity. [16] proposes an evolutionary algorithm to find good conditional values for decision points. Overall, metaheuristic approaches find their solution by using simulation-optimization techniques that require a simulation of the process. However, most approaches do not describe in detail how complex the simulation models become.

Overall, data provided from process models and from event logs is only sparsely used: In particular, fundamental workflow patterns like XOR gateways are often not considered in optimization models or are only abstracted in a very simple fashion. As of today, no publication explicitly aims at scheduling tasks by considering different scenarios that can occur when taking either of the XOR branches. Similarly, no publication addresses that transition probabilities of XOR gateways might change depending on data attributes and leverages this information for further planning. Moreover, resource-related information such as their performances or availabilities is rarely modeled or learned from event logs.

4 Open Challenges and Research Directions

This section discusses research gaps when combining BPM and OR identified by the literature review.

4.1 Targeted BPM Life-Cycle Phase

Challenge: Existing optimization approaches affect either the design or the enactment phase of the BPM life cycle. Some resource planning approaches test if adding a resource enhances the process performance by employing a simulation model that uses an allocation algorithm [5]. However, during enactment, neither the quality of the found plan is determined, nor the simulation model is updated. Future holistic approaches should combine optimizations in the process (re-)design phase, e.g., by providing optimized process models, and the enactment phase, e.g., by providing an optimized process execution.

Research Direction: A holistic approach creates an optimization cycle that covers both the enactment and design phase and serves multiple optimization purposes successfully along the BPM life cycle. This also requires the development of a feedback strategy between the design and enactment phases.

4.2 Process Models

Challenge: Information provided by the process model currently finds only limited use for decision making. Especially in the context of resource allocation and scheduling, 38 of 66 publications consider information from process models, but only 17 consider the basic workflow patterns, exclusive choices, and merges. From the 17 publications that consider exclusive choices, 7 conceptualize them in analytical models. Of these, only [37,38] propose to build schedules beyond the points of exclusive choices. However, these schedules are only built when a branch is expected to be selected with a likelihood that surpasses a predefined threshold. Existing optimization approaches disregard exclusive choices in process models and, hence, the stochasticity of the problem.

Research Direction: Full support of conceptualizing exclusive choices in optimization approaches supports the application of stochastic optimization techniques for an analytical solution approach, e.g., stochastic linear programming. Moreover, simplifying the transfer from process models to optimization models offers the opportunity to embed optimization during process execution.

Challenge: Conceptualizing the control-flow perspective as a simulation model is another approach pursued in some publications that can be used, e.g., for what-if analysis or to find solutions to combinatorial optimization problems via simulation optimization techniques. Most surveyed publications that use simulation models do not describe in detail how a simulation model is built from a process model or an event log. Creating simulation models is generally considered complex and time-consuming [47]. If a simulation model does not depict reality, a solution based on the simulation model will never be applicable in reality. Some approaches circumvent the issue by, e.g., suggesting to replay event logs instead of building complex simulation models [3].

Research Direction: Precise simulation models should be discovered automatically. Recent approaches combine log-replay methods (e.g., [17]) with simulation methods to build hybrid simulation models. This appears to be a promising research direction to ease the simulation model-building process and should be further studied for simulation improvement. Other recent approaches have suggested using event log data to improve the modeling of resources in simulation models, such as capturing the availability of human resources [68]. Further research should additionally focus on process performance aspects, such as learning the processing and waiting times of activities, to simulate more than only control-flow aspects.

4.3 Resource Modeling

Challenge: When modeling a resource perspective, existing work mostly relies on data tailored to the specific optimization use case, resulting in a variety of performance data representations. A structure named in multiple works is the resource profile, e.g., [6], but the structure of resource profiles is not clearly defined. A generally agreed-upon resource representation is missing. A common approach to mining and modeling resource data cannot be identified among the publications. Following this, the optimization and simulation approaches become highly specialized to the given problem, and general solutions, which can be easily adapted and reused, are non-existent. Further, current process optimization approaches lack a sophisticated analysis of the interaction between resources, resource and task performance, and, even further, resource and process performance.

Research Direction: A standardized modeling approach for resources, which connects resource data and process execution data, fosters the creation of general optimization and simulation models. Resource performance can be analyzed during process runtime. This could enable on-the-fly optimizations based on resource usage adaptations. Moreover, resource and process performance should be analyzed, mined, and optimized in a combined manner. If BPM wants to become more proactive [81], a more general resource model is needed that is linked to the control-flow to improve forecasting, optimization, and simulation models. This can enable advanced allocation algorithms from the OR field to outperform reactive approaches.

Challenge: [68] shows that an individual representation of resources can lead to improved resource allocation. Often, data on individual resources is missing, and such an individual consideration of resources becomes impossible. When using a pooled approach, no direct connection of resource performance and process performance is possible and the outcome of optimization approaches suffers.

Research Direction: Hybrid approaches combine individual and pooled resource data to address the challenge of missing data. The pooling of resources can be used to extrapolate missing data. Two existing approaches propose and evaluate a hybrid format between pooled resource representation and individual resource representation [25,63]. A fluid approach between treating resources individually or in a pooled way can adress the trade-off between performance and missing data. AI approaches can also support the generation of missing data.

4.4 Solution Techniques

Challenge: Current approaches often do not model stochastic properties sufficiently due to two reasons. Firstly, the set of tasks required for finishing a process instance is often assumed to be known upfront. Model-induced uncertainty, e.g., due to exclusive choices, is often not considered. Secondly, task durations are often assumed to be deterministic, and solution methods work only with their expected values. As real-life problems often have stochastic properties and uncertainties, it appears worth exploring the potential for applying stochastic optimization methods. Currently, only approaches that use simulation-optimization (metaheuristic) techniques have considered stochastic task durations. Whether finding optimal solutions, e.g., via stochastic linear programming, can practically be applied is questionable, as incorporating stochastic properties into the problem formulation will likely increase the problem complexity. As, e.g., the benchmarking results from [37] revealed that solving a deterministic scheduling problem for a process instance with 64 activities and 32 resources could already not finish within 2 h of time, one can expect that for a stochastic formulation only small problem types will be solvable in a feasible amount of time. Recent advancements in deep reinforcement learning have shown remarkable results for different kinds of optimization problems [61]. Future work could explore how deep reinforcement learning approaches can be applied to solve optimization problems in the context of business process management.

Research Direction: Stochastic approaches better represent real-world scenarios, but can often not be solved sufficiently. Deep reinforcement learning can be employed to address this trade-off [61]. Stochastic approaches could also address incorporating uncertainties introduced by XOR-Gateways in process models. Additionally, incorporating information from the process model into *simulation optimization approaches* might help improve their performance.

5 Related Work

Multiple surveys have focused on the topic of business process optimization [52,84] taking a specific method from BPM and analyzing how it has been used to improve business processes. This SLR offers a broader scope in terms of optimization techniques since it is not limited to approaches prevalent in the BPM world. By incorporating OR into the research questions, the optimization-driven research area of OR as a whole is analyzed for possible optimization approaches that could advance automated business process optimization in the future. In the following, we discuss further research directions that are related but beyond the scope of this SLR.

Prescriptive Process Monitoring is defined as *"a family of techniques to optimize the performance of a business process by triggering interventions at runtime"* [95]. [52] find that prescriptions can i.a. refer to the resource perspective, e.g., which resource to choose from the pool of possible resources to execute a task. In contrast to our work, [52] focus on optimization during process enactment, but not during design. Further, the focus is on the BPM field and does not consider the combination with OR optimization approaches.

Resource allocation strategies for business processes during the enactment phase have been surveyed in [84]. The strict focus on resource allocation emphasizes the importance of resources for business process optimization. Yet, important factors for resource allocation, such as the modeling of resources, have been excluded. In contrast, this SLR investigates how multiple different optimization approaches can contribute to quantitative business process improvement and provides insights on typical solution methods.

6 Conclusion, Discussion, and Outlook

This SLR aims at providing a holistic picture of the current state of research in process optimization at the intersection of BPM and OR. We examined the targeted life-cycle phase of optimization approaches in existing literature (**RQ1**), how the control-flow, resource and data perspective of business process models and event logs have been conceptualized as mathematical models (**RQ2**), and which solution techniques have been applied for finding optimal or near-optimal solutions (**RQ3**). **RQ1**: Existing works address optimization problems in either the design or enactment phase, with the majority addressing the enactment phase and, in particular, resource allocation and scheduling problems. No approach has yet investigated a holistic approach concerned with both phases, mutual goals of both phases or carrying information from one phase over into the optimization of the other. Furthermore, most works focus on a single optimization objective. Future work should consider multi-objective optimization with interaction among all life-cycle phases. **RQ2**: Important information from process models or event logs is often disregarded when constructing an optimization model. Results show that in the control flow perspective, most works do not consider complex workflow patterns, such as the exclusive choice pattern. From the resource perspective, information on the effect of resources on the execution performance of tasks or processes is often missing. While the event log is mainly used to structure control-flow data, no such consensus is found for the resource and data perspective. To combine several perspectives into one model a standardized data structure would be helpful. **RQ3**: Optimization techniques strongly depend on their mathematical model. As many approaches set up simplified mathematical models, optimal solution techniques have been widely used. However, as simple models often neglect implications from the control flow, resource, and data perspective, solving larger, more holistic models with optimal algorithms is infeasible.

Discussion and Limitations: First, BPM and OR are both broad fields with rather specific terms that were not explicitly part of the search strings. [57], for example, list the top 40 keywords used in the European Journal of Operations Research. However, as using all keywords was not feasible for this research, this study is limited to a subset that the authors deemed most relevant. Further, the nomenclature between the two fields differs. We addressed this by identifying and including interchangeable terms in the search strings (see Sect. 2). Secondly, optimization approaches from cloud computing might be applicable to business process management. However, due to the size of the research field and the potential bias that could be introduced by that, the authors decided to exclude the field.

This SLR shows that a better specification of the interface between OR and BPM is required. Since many optimization approaches focus on allocating processes and process tasks over resources, a more general representation of resources, their availabilities, and performance implications is required from BPM. The same accounts for the data perspective. Future optimization approaches should focus on developing solution techniques that can better handle the complexity represented in process models and stochasticity created during process execution. Even if an optimal solution can not be found for these more complex models, a better representation of real-world use cases can be achieved.

Acknowledgement. This work was partly funded by the Deutsche Forschungsgemeinschaft (DFG, German Research Foundation) - GRK2201 - Projektnummer - 277991500.

Disclosure of Interests. The authors have no competing interests to declare that are relevant to the content of this article.

References

1. van der Aalst, W.M.P.: Re-engineering knock-out processes. Decis. Support Syst. **30**(4), 451–468 (2001)
2. van der Aalst, W.M.P., La Rosa, M., Santoro, F.M.: Business process management. Business Inform. Syst. Eng. **58**(1), 1–6 (2016)
3. van der Aalst, W.M.P., Low, W.Z., Wynn, M.T., ter Hofstede, A.H.: Change your history: Learning from event logs to improve processes. In: Computer Supported Cooperative Work in Design, pp. 7–12 (2015)

4. Amaran, S., Sahinidis, N.V., Sharda, B., Bury, S.J.: Simulation optimization: a review of algorithms and applications. Ann. Oper. Res. **240**(1), 351–380 (2016)
5. Antunes, B.B.P., Manresa, A., Bastos, L.S.L., Marchesi, J.F., Hamacher, S.: A solution framework based on process mining, optimization, and discrete-event simulation to improve queue performance in an emergency department. In: Business Process Management Workshops, pp. 583–594 (2019)
6. Arias, M., Munoz-Gama, J., Sepúlveda, M., Miranda, J.: Human resource allocation or recommendation based on multi-factor criteria in on-demand and batch scenarios. Europ. J. Indust. Eng. **12**(3), 364–404 (2018)
7. Avanes, A., Freytag, J.C.: Adaptive workflow scheduling under resource allocation constraints and network dynamics. VLDB **1**(2), 1631–1367 (2008)
8. Bae, H., Lee, S., Moon, I.: Planning of business process execution in business process management environments. Inf. Sci. **268**, 357–369 (2014-06-01)
9. Bai, X., Krishnan, R., Padman, R., Wang, H.J.: On risk management with information flows in business processes. Inf. Syst. Res. **24**(3), 731–749 (2013-09)
10. Banaszak, Z.A.: Workflows management for project-driven manufacturing. IFAC Proc. Volumes **36**(3), 149–154 (2003)
11. Bando, T., Nishi, T., Alam, M.M., Liu, Z., Fujiwara, T.: Automatic generation of optimization model using process mining and petri nets for optimal motion planning of 6-DOF manipulators. In: Intelligent Robots and Syst, pp. 11767–11772 (2022)
12. Barba, I., Weber, B., Del Valle, C., Jiménez-Ramírez, A.: User recommendations for the optimized execution of business processes. Data Knowl. Eng. **86**, 61–84 (2013)
13. Barba, I., Valle, C.D., Weber, B., Ramirez, A.J.: Automatic generation of optimized business process models from constraint-based specifications. Int. J. Cooperative Inf. Syst. **22**(2) (2013)
14. Barker, A., van Hemert, J.: Scientific workflow: a survey and research directions. In: Parallel Processing and Applied Mathematics, pp. 746–753 (2008)
15. Boareto, P.A., et al.: Simulation Optimization-Based model for Decision-Making in the stroke clinical pathway. Comput. Indust. Eng. **204**, 111164 (Jun 2025)
16. Bolsinger, M., Elsäßer, A., Helm, C., Röglinger, M.: Process improvement through economically driven routing of instances. Business Process Manage. **21**(2), 353–378 (2015)
17. Camargo, M., Dumas, M., González-Rojas, O.: Learning accurate LSTM models of business processes. In: Business Process Management, pp. 286–302 (2019)
18. Cho, M., Song, M., Müller, C., Fernandez, P., del Río-Ortega, A., Resinas, M., Ruiz-Cortés, A.: A new framework for defining realistic SLAs: An evidence-based approach. In: Business Process Management Forum,. pp. 19–35 (2017)
19. Cho, M., Song, M., Yoo, S., Reijers, H.A.: An evidence-based decision support framework for clinician medical scheduling. IEEE Access **7**, 15239–15249 (2019)
20. Choueiri, A.C., Santos, E.A.P.: Discovery of path-attribute dependency in manufacturing environments: a process mining approach. J. Manuf. Syst. **61**, 54–65 (2021)
21. Combi, C., Pozzi, G.: Task scheduling for a temporal workflow management system. In: Temporal Representation and Reasoning, pp. 61–68 (2006)
22. Comuzzi, M.: Ant-colony optimisation for path recommendation in business process execution. J. Data Semant. **8**(2), 113–128 (2019)
23. Cunzolo, M.D., et al.: Robust solutions via optimisation and predictive process monitoring for the scheduling of the interventional radiology procedures. Int. Trans. Oper. Res. **32**(4), 2189–2214 (2025)

24. Delias, P., Doulamis, A., Matsatsinis, N.: A joint optimization algorithm for dispatching tasks in agent-based workflow management systems. In: Enterprise Information Systems, pp. 199–206 (2008)
25. Delias, P., Doulamis, A.D., Doulamis, N.D., Matsatsinis, N.F.: Optimizing resource conflicts in workflow management systems. IEEE Trans. Knowl. Data Eng. **23**(3), 417–432 (2011)
26. Delias, P., Grigori, D.: Formulating the potentials of clustering of event data over multiple entities for decision support: a network embeddings approach. J. Decision Syst., pp. 1–23 (2023)
27. Di Cunzolo, M., et al.: Combining process mining and optimization: a scheduling application in healthcare. In: BPM Workshops, pp. 197–209 (2023)
28. Diamantini, C., Pisacane, O., Potena, D., Storti, E.: Combining an LNS-based approach and organizational mining for the resource replacement problem. Comput. Oper. Res. **161**, 106446 (2024)
29. Dijkman, R., Senderovich, A., van Jaarsveld, W.: 1st International workshop on data-driven business process optimization (BPO 2022). In: BPM Workshops. Lecture Notes in Business Information Processing, vol. 460, p. 336 (2023)
30. Djedovic, A., Karabegovic, A., Avdagic, Z., Omanovic, S.: Innovative approach in modeling business processes with a focus on improving the allocation of human resources. Mathematical Problems in Engineering (2018)
31. Djedović, A., Žunić, E., Avdagić, Z., Karabegović, A.: Optimization of business processes by automatic reallocation of resources using the genetic algorithm. In: Telecommunications, pp. 1–7 (2016)
32. Dumas, M., Rosa, M.L., Mendling, J., Reijers, H.A.: Fundamentals of Business Process Management, Second Edition. Springer (2018)
33. Eiselt, H.A., Sandblom, C.L.: Operations Research: A Model-Based Approach. Springer (2010)
34. Guastalla, A., Sulis, E., Aringhieri, R., Branchi, S., Di Francescomarino, C., Ghidini, C.: Workshift scheduling using optimization and process mining techniques: An application in healthcare. In: Winter Simulation Conference, pp. 1116–1127 (2023)
35. Halawa, F., Chalil Madathil, S., Khasawneh, M.T.: Integrated framework of process mining and simulation–optimization for pod structured clinical layout design. Expert Syst. Appl. **185**, 115696 (2021)
36. Havur, G., Cabanillas, C., Mendling, J., Polleres, A.: Resource allocation with dependencies in business process management systems. In: Business Process Management Forum, vol. 260 (2016)
37. Havur, G., Cabanillas, C., Polleres, A.: Benchmarking answer set programming systems for resource allocation in business processes. Expert. Sys. Appl. **205** (2022)
38. Havur, G., Cabanillas, C.: History-aware dynamic process fragmentation for risk-aware resource allocation. In: On the Move to Meaningful Internet Systems, pp. 533–551 (2019)
39. Hillier, F.S., Lieberman, G.J.: Introduction to Operations Research. McGraw-Hill Education (2020)
40. Hirsch, M., Ortiz-Peña, H., Nagi, R., Sudit, M., Stotz, A.: On the optimization of information workflow. In: Springer Proceedings in Mathematics and Statistics, pp. 43–65 (2012)
41. Hsieh, F.S.: Location-aware workflow scheduling in supply chains based on multi-agent systems. Technol. Appl. Artif. Intell. 441–448 (2016)

42. Hsieh, F.S.: A hybrid and scalable multi-agent approach for patient scheduling based on petri net models. Appl. Intell. **47**(4), 1068–1086 (2017)
43. Huang, Z., van der Aalst, W.M.P., Lu, X., Duan, H.: Reinforcement learning based resource allocation in business process management. Data Knowl. Eng. **70**(1), 127–145 (2011)
44. Hundogan, O.A., Verhoef, B.J., Theeven, P., Reijers, H.A., Lu, X.: Reinforcement learning for optimizing responses in care processes. Data Knowl. Eng. **157**, 102412 (2025)
45. Ismaili-Alaoui, A., Benali, K., Baïna, K., Baïna, J.: Business process instances scheduling with human resources based on event priority determination, In: Big Data, Cloud and Applications (2018)
46. Jiménez-Ramírez, A., Barba, I., Del Valle, C., Weber, B.: Generating multi-objective optimized business process enactment plans. In: Advanced Information Systems Engineering, pp. 99–115 (2013)
47. Juan, A.A., Faulin, J., Grasman, S.E., Rabe, M., Figueira, G.: A review of simheuristics: extending metaheuristics to deal with stochastic combinatorial optimization problems. Oper. Res. Perspect. **2**, 62–72 (2015)
48. Julia, S., De Oliveira, F.: A p-time hybrid petri net model for the scheduling problem of workflow management systems. In: Systems, Man and Cybernetics, pp. 4947–4952 (2004)
49. Julia, S., de Oliveira, F.F., Valette, R.: Real time scheduling of workflow management systems based on a p-time petri net model with hybrid resources. Simul. Model. Pract. Theory **16**(4), 462–482 (2008)
50. Kinast, A., Doerner, K.F., Rinderle-Ma, S.: Combing metaheuristics and process mining: improving cobot placement in a combined cobot assignment and job shop scheduling problem. Procedia Computer Science, pp. 1836–1845 (2022)
51. Kitchenham, B.A.: Systematic Review in Software Engineering: Where We are and Where we Should Be Going. University of Durham, New York, NY, USA, Tech. rep. (2012)
52. Kubrak, K., Milani, F., Nolte, A., Dumas, M.: Prescriptive process monitoring: Quo vadis? PeerJ Comput. Sci. **8**, e1097 (2022)
53. Kumbhar, M., Ng, A.H.C., Bandaru, S.: A digital twin based framework for detection, diagnosis, and improvement of throughput bottlenecks. J. Manufact. Syst. **66**, 92–106 (2023)
54. Kunkler, M., Rinderle-Ma, S.: Online resource allocation to process tasks under uncertain resource availabilities. In: 6th International Conference on Process Mining, ICPM 2024, Kgs. Lyngby, Denmark, October 14-18, 2024, pp. 137–144. IEEE (2024)
55. Kurakado, H., Nishi, T., Liu, Z.: Data-Driven Scheduling of Cellular Manufacturing Systems Using Process Mining with Petri Nets. In: Advances in Production Management Systems. Production Management Systems for Volatile, Uncertain, Complex, and Ambiguous Environments, pp. 17–28. Springer Nature Switzerland, Cham (2024)
56. Kurscheidt Netto, R.J., de F. R. Loures, E., dos Santos, E.A.P.: Enabling the use of shop floor information for multi-criteria decision making in maintenance prediction. In: Industrial Engineering and Operations Management, pp. 435–447 (2023)
57. Laengle, S., et al.: Forty years of the European journal of operational research: a bibliometric overview. Eur. J. Oper. Res. **262**(3), 803–816 (2017)

58. Lee, D., Park, J., Pulshashi, I.R., Bae, H.: Clustering and operation analysis for assembly blocks using process mining in shipbuilding industry. In: Asia Pacific Business Process Management - First Asia Pacific Conference, AP-BPM 2013, Beijing, China, August 29-30, 2013. Selected Papers. Lecture Notes in Business Information Processing, vol. 159, pp. 67–80. Springer (2013)
59. Lee, J., Lee, S., Kim, J., Choi, I.: Dynamic human resource selection for business process exceptions. Knowl. Process Manage. **26**(1), 23–31 (2019)
60. Li, H., et al.: Mining emergency event logs to support resource allocation. IEICE Trans. Inf. Syst. **104-D**(10), 1651–1660 (2021)
61. Li, Y.: Deep reinforcement learning: An overview. arXiv preprint arXiv:1701.07274 (2017)
62. Likert, R.: A technique for the measurement of attitudes. Archives of psychology (1932)
63. Lin, H., Fan, Y., Loiacono, E.T.: A practical scheduling method based on workflow management technology. Int. J. Adv. Manuf. Technol. **24**(11), 919–924 (2004-12-01)
64. Liu, R., Kumar, A., Lee, J.: Multi-level team assignment in social business processes: An algorithm and simulation study. Inf. Syst. Front. **24**(6), 1949–1969 (2022)
65. Liu, X., Chen, J., Ji, Y., Yu, Y.: Q-learning algorithm for task allocation based on social relation. In: Process-Aware Systems, pp. 49–58 (2015)
66. Liu, Y., Zhang, H., Li, C., Jiao, R.J.: Workflow simulation for operational decision support using event graph through process mining. Decision Support Syst. **52**(3), 685–697 (2012)
67. Liu, Y., Wang, J., Yang, Y., Sun, J.: A semi-automatic approach for workflow staff assignment. Comput. Ind. **59**(5), 463–476 (2008)
68. López-Pintado, O., Dumas, M.: Business process simulation with differentiated resources: does it make a difference? In: Business Process Management, pp. 361–378 (2022)
69. Low, W.Z., et al.: Revising history for cost-informed process improvement. Computing **98**(9), 895–921 (2016-09-01)
70. López-Pintado, O., Dumas, M., Berx, J.: Discovery, simulation, and optimization of business processes with differentiated resources. Inf. Syst. **120**, 102289 (2024)
71. Martin, N., Depaire, B., Caris, A.: The use of process mining in a business process simulation context: Overview and challenges. In: 2014 IEEE Symposium on Computational Intelligence and Data Mining, pp. 381–388 (2014)
72. Medeiros, F.F., Julia, S.: Constraint analysis based on energetic reasoning applied to the problem of real time scheduling of workflow management systems. In: ICEIS 2017 - Proceedings of the 19th International Conference on Enterprise Information Systems, Vol. 3. pp. 373–380. SciTePress (2017)
73. Middelhuis, J., Bianco, R.L., Sherzer, E., Bukhsh, Z., Adan, I., Dijkman, R.: Learning policies for resource allocation in business processes. Inf. Syst. **128**, 102492 (2025)
74. Neubauer, T.R., da Silva, V.F., Fantinato, M., Peres, S.M.: Resource allocation optimization in business processes supported by reinforcement learning and process mining. In: Intelligent Systems, pp. 580–595 (2022)
75. Ng, C.: Business process optimization using the ant colony system. Manag. Decis. Econ. **39**(6), 629–637 (2018)
76. Niedermann, F., Radeschutz, S., Mitschang, B.: Design-time process optimization through optimization patterns and process model matching. In: Commerce and Enterprise Computing, pp. 48–55 (2010)

77. Park, G., Song, M.: Prediction-based resource allocation using LSTM and minimum cost and maximum flow algorithm. In: Process Mining, pp. 121–128 (2019)
78. Peters, S.P.F., Dijkman, R.M., Grefen, P.W.P.J.: Resource optimization in business processes. In: Enterprise Distributed Object Computing Conference, pp. 104–113 (2021)
79. Pflug, J., Rinderle-Ma, S.: Application of dynamic instance queuing to activity sequences in cooperative business process scenarios. Int. J. Coop. Info. Syst. **25**(1), 1650002 (2016)
80. Pla, A., López, B., Murillo, J.: Multi-attribute auction mechanism for supporting resource allocation in business process enactment. In: STAIRS 2012 - Proceedings of the Sixth Starting AI Researchers' Symposium. Front. Artif. Intell. Appl. **241**, 228–239 (2012)
81. Poll, R., Polyvyanyy, A., Rosemann, M., Röglinger, M., Rupprecht, L.: Process forecasting: towards proactive business process management. In: BPM, pp. 496–512 (2018)
82. Prokofyeva, E., Zaytsev, R.: Clinical pathways analysis of patients in medical institutions based on hard and fuzzy clustering methods. Business Inform. **14**(1), 19–31 (2020)
83. Pufahl, L., Bazhenova, E., Weske, M.: Evaluating the performance of a batch activity in process models. In: Business Process Management Workshops, pp. 277–290 (2015)
84. Pufahl, L., Stiehle, F., Ihde, S., Weske, M., Weber, I.: Automatic resource allocation in business processes: a systematic literature survey. Inf. Syst. **132**, 102541 (2025)
85. Reijers, H.A., Jansen-Vullers, M.H., Zur Muehlen, M., Appl, W.: Workflow management systems + swarm intelligence = dynamic task assignment for emergency management applications. In: Business Process Management, pp. 125–140 (2007)
86. Reveliotis, S.A.: Real-time management of complex resource allocation systems: necessity, achievements and further challenges. Annu. Rev. Control. **41**, 147–158 (2016)
87. Rismanchian, F., Lee, Y.H.: Process mining–based method of designing and optimizing the layouts of emergency departments in hospitals. HERD **10**(4), 105–120 (2017-07-01)
88. Ruschel, E., Santos, E., Loures, E.: Mining shop-floor data for preventive maintenance management: integrating probabilistic and predictive models. Proc. Manufact. **11**, 1127–1134 (2017)
89. Ruschel, E., Santos, E.A.P., Loures, E.d.F.R.: Establishment of maintenance inspection intervals: an application of process mining techniques in manufacturing. J. Intell. Manuf. **31**(1), 53–72 (2020)
90. Satyal, S., Weber, I., Paik, H.y., Di Ciccio, C., Mendling, J.: AB-BPM: Performance-driven instance routing for business process improvement. In: Business Process Management. pp. 113–129 (2017)
91. Satyal, S., Weber, I., Paik, H.y., Di Ciccio, C., Mendling, J.: AB testing for process versions with contextual multi-armed bandit algorithms. In: Advanced Information Systems Engineering, pp. 19–34 (2018)
92. Schulte, S., Janiesch, C., Venugopal, S., Weber, I., Hoenisch, P.: Elastic business process management: State of the art and open challenges for BPM in the cloud. Futur. Gener. Comput. Syst. **46**, 36–50 (2015)

93. Senderovich, A., et al.: Conformance checking and performance improvement in scheduled processes: a queueing-network perspective. Inf. Syst. **62**, 185–206 (2016)
94. Senderovich, A., Booth, K.E.C., Beck, J.C.: Learning scheduling models from event data. In: Automated Planning and Scheduling, pp. 401–409 (2019)
95. Shoush, M., Dumas, M.: Prescriptive process monitoring under resource constraints: A causal inference approach. In: Process Mining Workshops, pp. 180–193 (2022)
96. Silva, F., Grilo, C., Martinho, R., Rijo, R.: Scheduling molds manufacturing processes through process mining. Proc. Comput. Sci. **239**, 2348–2358 (2024)
97. Song, W., Chen, F., Jacobsen, H.A., Zhang, C.: Identifying a minimum sequence of high-level changes between workflows. IEEE Trans. Serv. Comput. **15**(4), 2425–2438 (2022)
98. Subramaniam, S., et al.: Improving process models by discovering decision points. Inf. Syst. **32**(7), 1037–1055 (2007)
99. Taha, H.: Operations Research: an Introduction. Global Edition, Pearson Education (2017)
100. Wang, M., Zhang, X., Zhu, L., Liao, L.: Trust-based workflow refactoring for concurrent scheduling in service-oriented environment. Concurr. Comput.: Pract. Exper. **25**(13), 1879–1893 (2013)
101. Weinzierl, S., Dunzer, S., Zilker, S., Matzner, M.: Prescriptive business process monitoring for recommending next best actions. In: Business Process Management Forum, pp. 193–209 (2020)
102. Wibisono, A., Nisafani, A.S., Bae, H., Park, Y.J.: On-the-fly performance-aware human resource allocation in the business process management systems environment using naïve bayes. In: APBPM, pp. 70–80 (2015)
103. Xu, J., Liu, C., Zhao, X., Yongchareon, S., Ding, Z.: Resource management for business process scheduling in the presence of availability constraints. ACM Trans. Manage. Inf. Syst. **7**(3) (2016)
104. Xu, J., Liu, C., Zhao, X., Ding, Z.: Incorporating structural improvement into resource allocation for business process execution planning. Concurr. Comput.: Pract. Exper. **25**(3), 427–442 (2013)
105. Xu, J., Huang, Z., Yu, Y., Pan, M.: A performance analysis on task allocation using social context. In: Liu, J., Chen, J., Xu, G. (eds.) 2012 Second International Conference on Cloud and Green Computing, CGC 2012, Xiangtan, Hunan, China, November 1-3, 2012, pp. 637–644. IEEE Computer Society (2012)
106. Yaghoubi, M., Zahedi, M.: Tuning concurrency of the business process by dynamic programming. In: Software and Computer Applications, pp. 1–5 (2018-02-08)
107. Yang, H., Wen, L., Liu, Y., Wang, J.: An approach to recommend resources for business processes. In: On the Move to Meaningful Internet Systems, pp. 662–665 (2012)
108. Yeon, M.S., Lee, Y.K., Pham, D.L., Kim, K.: Experimental verification on human-centric network-based resource allocation approaches for process-aware information systems. IEEE Access **10**, 23342–23354 (2022)
109. Zeng, D.D., Zhao, J.L.: Effective role resolution in workflow management. INFORMS J. Comput. **17**(3), 374–387 (2005-08)

110. Zhao, W., Liu, H., Dai, W., Ma, J.: An entropy-based clustering ensemble method to support resource allocation in business process management. Knowl. Inf. Syst. **48**(2), 305–330 (2016)
111. Zhao, W., Yang, L., Liu, H., Wu, R.: The optimization of resource allocation based on process mining. In: Advanced Intelligent Computing Theories and Applications, pp. 341–353 (2015)
112. Zheng, H., Li, L., Wang, B., Ruan, T.: Enterprise workflow modeling based on priced timed petri nets. In: Edge Comput. Scalable Cloud, pp. 106–110 (2018)
113. Zhu, J., Liu, W.: A tale of two databases: the use of web of science and scopus in academic papers. Scientometrics **123**(1), 321–335 (2020-04-01)

Modelling and Estimating Inter-Case Effects in Business Processes Stochastically

Sander J. J. Leemans[1(✉)], Michael Grohs[2], and Jana-Rebecca Rehse[2]

[1] RWTH Aachen University, Aachen, Germany
s.leemans@bpm.rwth-aachen.de
[2] University of Mannheim, Mannheim, Germany
{michael.grohs,rehse}@uni-mannheim.de

Abstract. When analysing business processes through process mining, cases are typically considered in isolation. A case is seen as one process execution, whose control-flow is only influenced by case-specific features. However, this isolated view on cases does not consider inter-case effects, which likely occur when cases compete for the availability of a fixed number of shared resources. In this paper, we study the stochastic implications of (1) transition life cycles and (2) resources. That is, we extend stochastic Petri nets with the notion of a transition life cycle to capture the non-atomicity of resources executing transitions. This then allows us to describe the competition between cases for resources stochastically and analyse how scarcity of resources influences the behaviour of real-life processes. We provide an according automated discovery method, and evaluate our technique on multiple real-life event logs by showing its applicability and feasibility, and demonstrating that new types of insights can be obtained for real-life processes.

Keywords: stochastic Petri nets · stochastic process mining · inter-case effects · resource mining

1 Introduction

Process mining describes a family of analysis techniques aimed at gaining insights into business processes in organisations [9]. It relies on the idea that each execution of a process in an information system can be digitally recorded and extracted in the form of an event log. This event log then contains data on numerous process executions, each captured as a separate case [15]. Analysing the patterns in these cases can reveal new insights about the true process execution [9]. For example, we can discover a process model that describes the control flow of the process. When extended by a stochastic perspective, such a model also contains the frequencies of choices at given decision points [17].

This traditional view on a process considers cases *in isolation* [30]. Each case is seen as a separate process execution, whose progression is only influenced by

© The Author(s), under exclusive license to Springer Nature Switzerland AG 2026
A. Gianola et al. (Eds.): EDOC 2025, LNCS 16213, pp. 84–102, 2026.
https://doi.org/10.1007/978-3-032-15140-7_5

case-specific features, such as attributes or control flow decisions. A discovered process model hence describes the control flow for each case individually. Similarly, choice frequencies in a stochastic process model only depend on features of the case itself, not others [19]. However, this isolated view on cases does not account for potential inter-case effects, i.e., changes in the control flow of one case that are influenced by what happens in other cases. These effects are likely to occur because different cases of the same process are inherently connected by resources, which are typically responsible for the execution of an entire process instead of a single case [15]. For example, if a process is handled by a fixed number of resources shared between cases, we can assume that a high overall load on the process will influence the decisions made in individual cases, such as choosing a faster casual check of a document over a time-consuming thorough one. Hence, these inter-case effects are important for describing and analysing a process, but they are not considered in existing process mining techniques.

In this paper, we introduce a new stochastic modelling formalism that is able to capture inter-case effects that occur because cases compete for the availability of limited resources. In order to model resources and the competition for their availability, we must consider transitions as non-atomic, i.e., going through a life cycle, which gives them a duration. Therefore, the new modelling formalism combines the notion of a transition life cycle with explicit resources and intra-case stochastics. Based on this modelling formalism, we provide a discovery technique that can capture inter-case effects by estimating how the control flow of an individual case is influenced by the availability of resources in the process. By evaluating our technique on multiple real-life event logs, we show its applicability and demonstrate that new types of insights can be obtained for real-life processes.

The remainder of this paper is structured as follows. After introducing the preliminaries in Sect. 2, we describe our new modelling formalism stochastic labelled resource Petri nets (SLRPN) in Sect. 3. Section 4 introduces a discovery algorithm for SLRPN, which is evaluated in Sect. 5. We report on related work in Sect 6, before concluding the paper in Sect. 7.

2 Preliminaries

Let S be a set. We denote 2^S for the set of all sub-sets of S, including $\emptyset$ and S. A multiset X over S is a function that maps the elements of S to the natural numbers. Given two multisets X, X', we denote $\bar{X} = \{x \mid X(x) > 0\}$ (*set of multiset*), $\forall_x (X \uplus X')(x) = X(x) + X'(x)$ (*multiset union*), $X \Subset X' \equiv \forall_x X(x) \leq X'(x)$ (*multi-sub-set*), $S^+ = \{X'' \mid S = \bar{X''}\}$ (*set of all multisets*), and $\forall_x [\,](x) = 0$ (*empty multiset*). If $X' \Subset X$, then $\forall_x (X \setminus X')(x) = X(x) - X'(x)$ (*multiset difference*).

An *activity instance* is the execution of a process step (an *activity*). An activity instance has a life cycle consisting of several stages that the instance passes through during execution. In this paper, we use the activity instance life cycle shown in Fig. 1. First, an activity instance is *enabled*, which indicates that from the process's control-flow perspective, it is ready to be executed. The next stage is *enqueue* (e), which indicates that the instance will be executed eventually, and it has joined a queue waiting for execution. The difference between enabled and enqueued instances occurs, for example, at decision points, where all alternative paths are enabled, but only one is enqueued. Once an instance *starts* (s), a resource has begun with its actual execution. The *complete* (c) stage indicates that the resource has finished the execution. Please note that while more elaborate life cycle models exist [1], they would make this paper needlessly complex; nevertheless, the ideas and concepts presented in this paper can also be applied to such more elaborate life cycles.

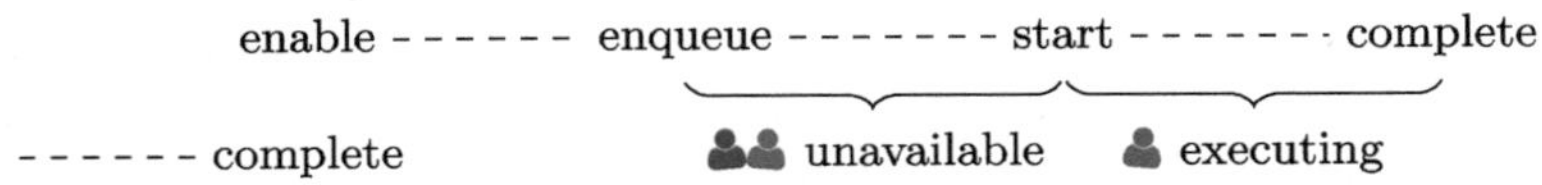

Fig. 1. Life cycle of an activity instance.

An *event* is the combination of an activity, a life cycle stage, a resource involved and a time stamp, denoted as $\text{activity}^{\text{life cycle stage}}_{\substack{\text{resource}\\ \text{time stamp}}}$. If a particular detail is not relevant in a context, we may replace it with a $\bullet$ for brevity of notation. As enablement is induced by a model, event logs will not contain events with a life cycle stage of enable. Similarly, resources are relevant only for start and completion events.

A *trace* is a sequence of events denoting the stages executed for a case in the process. An *event log* is a sequence of traces.[1] Figure 2 shows an example of an event log with two traces and two resources (and).

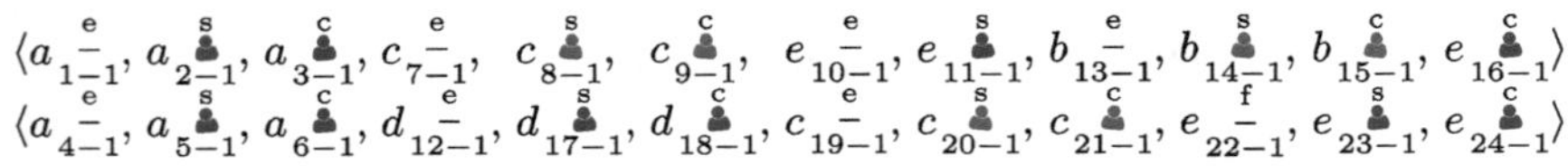

Fig. 2. Example event log.

Definition 1 (Labelled Petri net). *Let P be a set of places, T such that $P \cap T = \emptyset$ be a set of transitions, let $F\colon (P \times T) \cup (T \times P) \to \mathbb{N}$ be a flow relation, let $M_0 \in P^+$ be an initial marking, let Σ be an alphabet of activities such that $\tau \notin \Sigma$, and $\lambda\colon T \to \Sigma \cup \{\tau\}$ be a transition labelling function. Then (P, T, F, M_0, λ) is a* labelled Petri net *(LPN).*

We denote ${}^\bullet t = [p \mid (p,t) \in F]$ and $t^\bullet = [p \mid (t,p) \in F]$. A transition t such that $\lambda(t) = \tau$ is a *silent* transition, otherwise it is a *labelled* transition. We assume the standard semantics of labelled Petri nets [3]. That is, the state of a

[1] Note that we assume the traces to be ordered, though this order is arbitrary.

labelled Petri net is denoted by a multiset of places (a *marking*). A transition t is *enabled* in marking M if $^\bullet t \Subset M$. An enabled transition can *fire*, which changes the marking to $M' = M \uplus t^\bullet \setminus {}^\bullet t$. A *run* of a labelled Petri net is a transition sequence that bring the net from initial marking M_0 into a marking with no enabled transition (a *deadlock*). The LPN example in Fig. 3b has two runs.

A *life-cycle labelled Petri net* (LLPN) provides an abstract view of a labelled Petri net, while incorporating life cycle stages. An LLPN can be transformed into an LPN by replacing every visible transition with a sequence of three transitions, connected by places, each representing a life cycle stage, as illustrated in Fig. 4.

Definition 2 (Life-cycle labelled Petri net). *A life-cycle labelled Petri net (LLPN) is a tuple* (P, T, F, M_0, λ)*, such that* (P', T', F', M_0) *is an LPN with:*

$$T_\tau = \{t \mid t \in T \wedge \lambda(t) \neq \tau\}$$

$$T_\lambda = T \setminus T_\tau$$

$$P' = P \cup \{p'_{t^e}, p'_{t^s} \mid t \in T_\lambda\} \qquad T' = T_\tau \cup \{t^e, t^s, t^c \mid t \in T_\lambda\}$$

$$F' = \{(p,t) \mid (p,t) \in F \wedge t \in T_\tau\} \cup \{(t,p) \mid (t,p) \in F \wedge t \in T_\tau\} \cup$$

$$\{(p,t^e) \mid (p,t) \in F \wedge t \in T_\lambda\} \cup \{(t^c,p) \mid (t,p) \in F \wedge t \in T_\lambda\} \cup$$

$$\{(t^e, p'_{t^e}), (p'_{t^e}, t^s), (t^s, p'_{t^s}), (p'_{t^c}, t^c) \mid t \in T\}$$

Visually, we distinguish LLPNs from LPNs with transitions having double borders; an example is shown in Fig. 3a with its translation to an LPN in Fig. 3b.

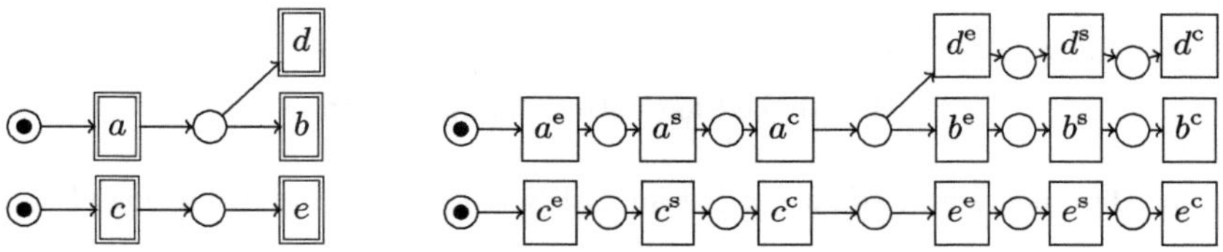

(a) An LLPN. (b) Translated to an LPN.

Fig. 3. Life cycle labelled Petri net and its translation to a labelled Petri net.

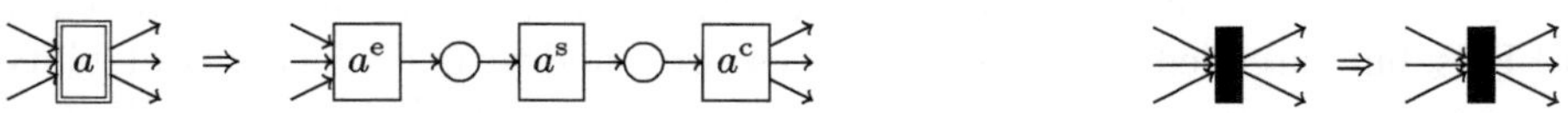

Fig. 4. Transformation of an LLPN to an LPN.

To establish if a trace conforms to a given LPN (or, by extension, an LLPN), we can compute an *alignment* between them. An alignment is a step-wise comparison of the trace and a possible execution path of the model. It consists of a sequence of steps, each made up from a pair of a (trace) event and a (model) activity, or an empty symbol $\gg$, if an event or activity is without counterpart [3].

A cost function assigns costs to each step, typically one unit cost for every $\gg$. An alignment is optimal if no other possible alignment has a lower cost.

Figure 5a shows an example aligned log for our LLPN (Fig. 3a) and event log (Fig. 2): the first trace does not contain any empty symbols (the trace fits the LLPN fully), while the second trace has two $\gg$ as the $f\,{}_{22-1}^{\overset{\text{e}}{-}}$ event does fit the model, and the e^{e} transition firing is missing from the run.

In an alignment, the sequence of steps taken for the model is, by construction, a run. If we combine this run, where available, with the corresponding resources and timestamps of the event log, we get an *aligned run* consisting of *aligned events*. The sequence of all aligned runs (one optimal alignment for a trace) is an *aligned log*. Notice that an aligned log differs from an event log in two key aspects: it fully "agrees" with the model, and it contains runs with transitions rather than activity labels. Figure 5b shows an aligned log for our running example.

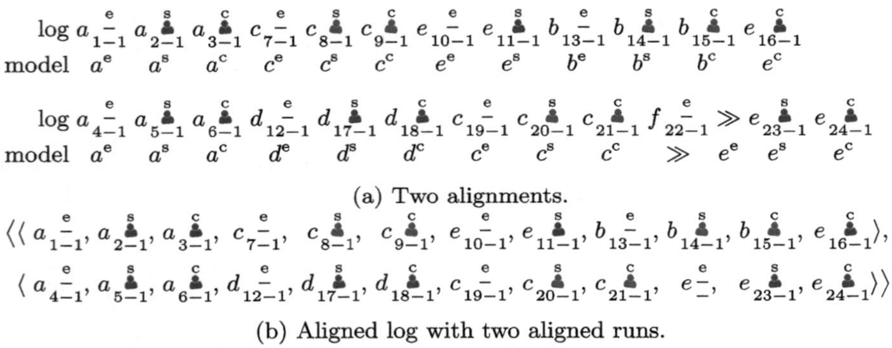

Fig. 5. Alignments and aligned log of an LLPN (Fig. 3a) and an event log (Fig. 2).

3 Modelling Transition Life Cycles, Resources and Stochastic Intra-Case Effects

In this section, we introduce our modelling formalism. This formalism is based on LLPNs, but extended by two novelties: resources and their stochastic availability. We first define its syntax: a stochastic labelled resource Petri net (SLRPN) is an LLPN extended with a resource function R that assigns a set of resources that can execute a particular transition, and a weight function, which assigns a weight to a transition, based on the available resources.

Definition 3 (SLRPN). *$(P, T, F, M_0, \lambda, R, w)$ is a stochastic labelled resource Petri net (SLRPN), where (P, T, F, M_0, λ) is an LLPN, $R\colon T \to 2^{\mathcal{R}}$ is a resource function such that $\forall_{t \in T} R(t) \neq \emptyset$, and $w\colon T \times 2^{T \times R} \to \mathbb{R}^+$ a weight function.*

We require that every labelled transition t has at least one resource that can execute it: $|R(t)| \geq 0$. Figure 6a shows an example of an SLRPN: the double borders indicate that each transition is to be interpreted as a life cycle (as in LLPNs). Furthermore, the labelled transitions are annotated with the set of resources that can execute it (👤 and 👤). Finally, each transition is annotated with the parameters of their weight function (which will be defined in Sect. 3.3).

Given that traces in an SLRPN are not independent, we need to define both their control-flow and stochastic semantics from scratch. After that, we introduce the weight functions that we consider in the remainder of this paper.

3.1 Semantics Control Flow

The state of a single case is a multiset M of places (*marking*, $M\colon P^+$) combined with a map A of the resources that are busy for each transition in the context of the case ($A\colon (T \times (R \cup \{\bot\})^+$). As a transition may be started multiple times concurrently, A is a multiset. The state of an SLRPN is a collection of such (M, A) combinations. The initial state S of an SLRPN is an empty collection: $S = [\,]$.

A new case being initiated in the SLRPN in state S involves adding an initial marking and no in-use resources (assuming an enabled transition in M_0):

$$S' = S \uplus [(M_0, [\,])] \tag{1}$$

Figure 1 shows the life cycle of an execution of a transition: once it is enabled, it may enqueue, then it waits for a resource to start the execution, which at some point completes. In a case state $(M, A) \in S$, a transition $t \in T$ is *enabled* if ${}^\bullet t \subseteq^{+} M$ (2). In a case state $(M, A) \in S$, a transition t can *enqueue* if it is enabled. Then, a new state S' is obtained by removing the old (M, A) and inserting the updated (M', A') into S (5); the new marking M' is the result of consuming the tokens necessary to fire t (3); and the new resource mapping A' sees t mapped to $\bot$, indicating that t is not assigned to a resource yet (4).

$$\text{if } {}^\bullet t \subseteq^{+} M \text{ then} \tag{2}$$

$$M'_{t^e} = M \setminus {}^\bullet t \tag{3}$$

$$A'_{t^e} = A \uplus [(t, \bot)] \tag{4}$$

$$S' = S \uplus [(M'_{t^e}, A'_{t^e})]) \setminus [(M, A)] \tag{5}$$

A resource r is *available* in S if it is not allocated to a transition (7). In a state S with an instance (M, A), an enqueued transition (6) can *start* if an available resource r (7) can execute t (8). Then, a new state S' is obtained in which the new (M', A') indicates no change in marking M (9), and that t is now being executed by r (10).

$$\text{if } (t, \bot) \in A \wedge \tag{6}$$

$$r \notin \{r' \mid (M, A) \in S \wedge (t' \to r') \in A\} \wedge \tag{7}$$

$$r \in R(t) \tag{8}$$

$$\text{then } M'_{t^s} = M \tag{9}$$

$$A'_{t^s} = A \uplus [(t, r)] \setminus [(t, \bot)] \tag{10}$$

$$S' = S \uplus [(M'_{t^s}, A'_{t^s})] \setminus [(M, A)] \tag{11}$$

In a state S with instance (M, A) a transition t started with resource r (12) can *complete*. If the completion causes the instance to enter a deadlock (15), the instance is completed and is removed from the state atomically with the completion of the last transition. Then, a new state S' is obtained in which the new (M', A') includes a new marking M' that adds the tokens produced by t (13), and the new resource mapping without (t, r) (14).

$$\text{If } (t, r) \in A \text{ then} \quad (12) \qquad M'_{t^c} = M \uplus t^\bullet \quad (13) \qquad A'_{t^c} = A \setminus [(t, r)] \quad (14)$$

$$S' = S \setminus [(M, A)] \uplus \begin{cases} [(M'_{t^c}, A'_{t^c})] & \text{if } \exists {}^\bullet t' \Subset M'_{t^c} \vee (t', y) \in A'_{t^c} \\ [] & \text{otherwise} \end{cases} \quad (15)$$

As a silent transition merely updates a net's state instead of representing the execution of an activity, the life cycle does not apply to it. Rather, it behaves like a standard Petri net transition: if the transition is enabled (16), it can *fire*, which yields a change in marking according to the consumed and produced tokens (17) and no change in resource availability (18).

$$\text{if } {}^\bullet t \Subset M \text{ then} \quad (16)$$

$$M'_{t^c} = M \uplus t^\bullet \setminus {}^\bullet t \quad (17) \qquad A'_{t^c} = A \quad (18) \qquad S' = S \uplus [(M'_{t^c}, A'_{t^c})]) \setminus [(M, A)] \quad (19)$$

Multi-run Language. Having defined the control flow, we next characterise the potential behaviour of an SLRPN. As a SLRPN expresses the behaviour of several cases at the same time, we need a new notion of language that captures this. A *run* in an SLRPN is a sequence of such stages that brings a process instance from marking M_0 to a deadlock marking (15). As each transition stage is atomic, an SLRPN expresses a total order of transition stages (*events*) for a set of runs, referred to as a *multi-run*. Given a number of cases, we refer to the set of all possible multi-runs of an SLRPN as the *multi-run language* of it.

Figure 6b shows a multi-run that was constructed from the two aligned runs of our example SLRPN. Figure 6c shows a visual representation of this multi-run. Please note that this visual representation of the behaviour of an SLRPN deviates from the formal concepts in three ways: (i) whereas we visualise the enablement of the initially enabled transitions at the start of the run, even though a multi-run does not specify when these enablements occur, (ii) whereas we annotate events with their run, though an SLRPN provides no way to distinguish between its running instances, which is similar to standard Petri nets, and (iii) whereas we visualise a connection between events of a transition through horizontal lines, though this connection is not present in an SLRPN.

3.2 Semantics Stochastics

The stochastic behaviour of an SLRPN can be considered in two ways: at the level of the entire system (i.e., as a distribution of multi-runs) and at the level of the individual traces (i.e., as a distribution of runs). An SLRPN does not contain

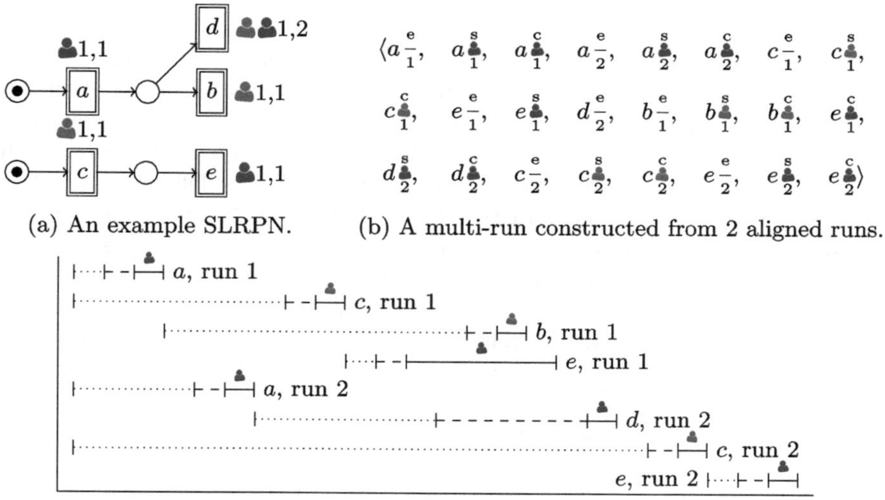

(a) An example SLRPN.

(b) A multi-run constructed from 2 aligned runs.

(c) A visualisation of the multi-run.

Fig. 6. Example of an SLRPN and its semantics.

enough information to fully describe its inter-case behaviour: for instance, the arrival rate and how to prioritise cases when they are competing for resources is not modelled. Therefore, we define the stochastic behaviour over individual runs, and leave the system-level distribution for future work.

We consider a particular instance (M, A) in the state of an SLRPN. Several labelled transitions may be enabled, queued or started, for which the next stage would be to enqueue, start or complete, respectively, and several silent transitions may be enabled. Each of these stages has a weight of $w(t, A)$ of occurring, for a particular transition t. Then, the probability for each of them to happen first is:

$$P(t \text{ progresses a stage} \mid M, A) = \frac{w(t, A)}{\sum_{{}^\bullet t' \Subset M \vee (t', y) \in A} w(t', A)} \tag{20}$$

Note that the weights are only relevant for what happens next *for a particular trace*, not which trace is handled next. Also note that we do not consider the availability of resources directly in this definition – (7) and (8) are not included –; rather, we leave this to be modelled stochastically in the weight function w. The probability of a run is the product of likelihoods of the stage in the run:

$$\begin{aligned} P(\langle t_1^x, \dots t_n^x \rangle \mid M, \langle A_1, \dots A_n \rangle) = \\ P(t \text{ progresses a stage} \mid M, A_1) P(\langle t_2^x, \dots t_n^x \mid M', \langle A_2, \dots A_n \rangle) \\ \text{with } M' = \begin{cases} M \setminus {}^\bullet t & \text{if } t_1^e \\ M & \text{if } t_1^s \\ M \uplus t^\bullet & \text{if } t_1^c \end{cases} \end{aligned} \tag{21}$$

3.3 Weight Function

In this paper, we consider weight functions of a particular, limited form. If, in a process, the choice for a transition t is made, t is enqueued. That is, by moving into the enqueueing stage, it is decided that t must be executed eventually. This decision may depend on the load in the process, such as when major fraud checks are scaled back if the process is busy. Thus, the modelled weight of the enqueueing stage can depend on the load of the process. Similarly, if there is a large queue for a transition, then starting the execution of a transition may be delayed, which can be modelled with a lower weight, depending on the load of the process. In contrast, once a resource is executing a transition, in our assumed modelled world, completion will not depend on the load of the entire process.

Accordingly, we choose our weight function as follows: for the enqueueing and starting stages of labelled transitions, we limit the weight functions we consider in this paper to the following form:

$$w(t, A) = b(t)u(t)^{\rho(t,A)} \quad (22) \qquad \text{with } \rho(t, A) = \frac{|\{r \mid (t', r) \in A \wedge r \in R(t)\}|}{|R(t)|} \quad (23)$$

where b_t is the *base weight* and u_t is the *utilisation weight*. Intuitively, b is the weight that b gets to be executed, while u is the adjustment to that weight based on the current resource utilisation. Both of these weights are constant for each transition. $\rho(t, A)$ represents the fraction of resources that could execute t but are currently executing other tasks (resource utilisation). For silent transitions and completion stages of labelled transitions, we use the weight function $w(t, A) = b(t)$, that is, without influence of the load of the process.

Figure 6a shows these weights annotated to the transitions in the model in the form of $b(t), u(t)$. For instance, given $\rho(d, A)$, the start stage of the transition d has a weight of $1 \cdot 2^{\rho(d,A)}$. In the context of the multi-run in Fig. 6b, run 2 has a probability of $\frac{\sqrt{2}}{32(\sqrt{2}+2)} \approx 0.013$, as illustrated in Fig. 7.

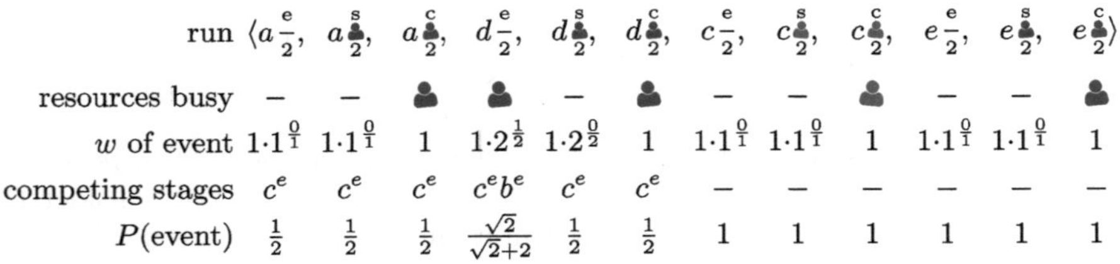

Fig. 7. Computation of the probability of a run in our example SLRPN.

4 Discovering SLRPNs

In this section, we introduce a stochastic discovery technique that takes an event log and a control-flow model (LPN or LLPN), and returns an SLRPN. Formally:

given (P, T, F, M_0, λ) as in Def. 3 and an event log L, mine a resource model R and estimate the $b(t)$ and $u(t)$ parameters for w.

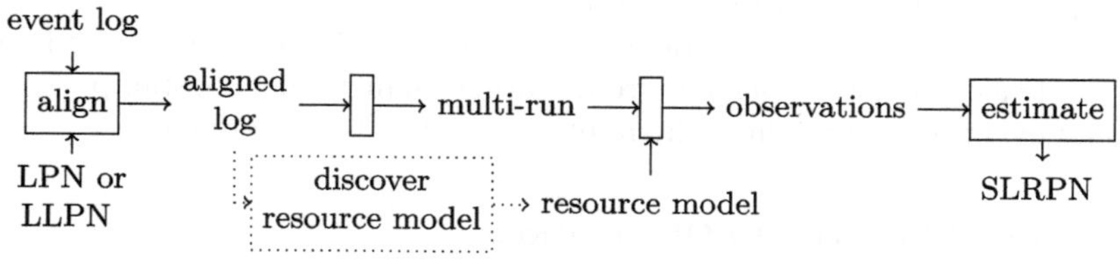

Fig. 8. Discovery approach for SLRPNs.

Figure 8 illustrates our approach: from an event log and an LPN or LLPN, first an aligned log is constructed using an alignment computation. Second, a multi-run is derived from the aligned log. Third, a resource model R is discovered from the multi-run. This step is optional; a resource model can also be provided if it is for instance developed using domain knowledge. Fourth, from the multi-run and the resource model, a collection of observations is gathered. Finally, weight parameters are estimated to construct an SLRPN.

In the remainder of this section, we introduce these steps in more detail.

4.1 Alignments

In this first step of the SLRPN discovery, we start with an event log and create an aligned log. To this end, we need to transform traces into runs. Traces are not guaranteed to map to runs 1-on-1, as (i) there may be multiple runs that support a trace (e.g., in case of duplicated labels or loops of silent transitions [17]) or (ii) the trace may contain deviations, such that there may be several ways to align trace and a run from the model with the same minimal cost. We apply an alignment computation (detailed in Sect. 2) to rectify this: for each trace, a least-deviation run of the model is computed [3], using the transformation of LLPNs to Petri nets of Definition 2, which yields an aligned log.

In case the given event log does not contain enqueueing, starting and/or completing events, they should not be considered as deviations and be given a 0 cost in the alignment computations. In case the input model is an LPN, it can simply be interpreted as an LLPN.

4.2 From Aligned Log to Multi-run

An aligned log is a sequence of sequences of aligned events, whereas a multi-run is a sequence of aligned events. Thus, we need to flatten the aligned log to obtain a multi-run. That is, from an aligned log $\langle\langle e_1, \dots e_n\rangle, \langle f_1, \dots f_m\rangle \dots\rangle$, we obtain a multi-run by merging the aligned runs into a single multi-run, while sorting them by timestamp. Ambiguities in the sorting, e.g., due to equivalent or missing timestamps (which in turn can be due to deviations, and the absence of enqueue or start events) are resolved arbitrarily. We choose a stable sorting algorithm, which considers first the timestamps of aligned events (inter-case), but does not violate the intra-case order of aligned events.

For readability, in the remainder of this paper, we will annotate aligned events with the trace they were derived from, rather than their timestamp. Figure 2 shows an event log from which the multi-run in Fig. 6b is derived.

4.3 From a Multi-run to Observations

Next, from a multi-run, we extract the observations we need for fitting the weight parameters of the SLRPN. To this end, we replay each aligned event $t\,\vdots$ on the structure of the SLRPN (which is equal to the LLPN), while keeping track of: (i) The marking, which is specific to the aligned run. From the marking, we record the transitions that were enabled at firing of the transition of the event. (ii) The resources that are busy.

Intuitively, we capture the number of times a stage t^x was executed, versus how often it could have been executed as it was enabled. The observation data is a function $O\colon 2^{T\times\{\mathrm{e,s,c}\}} \times (T \to [0,1]) \to (T \times \{\mathrm{e,s,c}\})^+$. That is, for each combination of a set of enabled stages and a set of resource utilisations, it records a multiset of stages that were executed. Table 1 shows the observations for our running example. For instance, line one shows that when the LLPN allowed b^{e}, d^{e} and c^{c} to occur and the resource utilisation of b was 1.0 and of d was 0.5, then we observed that c^{c} was executed once, and nothing else.

Table 1. Observations for our example.

enabled	utilisation	executed
$\{b^{\mathrm{e}}, d^{\mathrm{e}}, e^{\mathrm{s}}\}$	$\{b \to 0.0, d \to 0.0, e \to 0.0\}$	$[e^{\mathrm{s}}]$
$\{e^{\mathrm{e}}\}$	$\{e \to 0.0\}$	$[e^{\mathrm{e}}]$
$\{a^{\mathrm{c}}, c^{\mathrm{e}}\}$	$\{c \to 0.0\}$	$[a^{\mathrm{c}2}]$
$\{b^{\mathrm{e}}, d^{\mathrm{e}}, c^{\mathrm{e}}\}$	$\{b \to 0.0, d \to 0.0, c \to 0.0\}$	$[c^{\mathrm{e}}]$
$\{b^{\mathrm{e}}, d^{\mathrm{e}}, e^{\mathrm{e}}\}$	$\{b \to 0.0, d \to 0.0, e \to 0.0\}$	$[e^{\mathrm{e}}]$
$\{e^{\mathrm{c}}\}$	$\{\}$	$[e^{\mathrm{c}2}]$
$\{c^{\mathrm{c}}\}$	$\{\}$	$[c^{\mathrm{c}}]$
$\{b^{\mathrm{e}}, d^{\mathrm{e}}, c^{\mathrm{c}}\}$	$\{b \to 1.0, d \to 0.5\}$	$[c^{\mathrm{c}}]$
$\{a^{\mathrm{e}}, c^{\mathrm{e}}\}$	$\{a \to 0.0, c \to 0.0\}$	$[a^{\mathrm{e}2}]$
$\{c^{\mathrm{e}}\}$	$\{c \to 0.0\}$	$[c^{\mathrm{e}}]$
$\{a^{\mathrm{s}}, c^{\mathrm{e}}\}$	$\{a \to 0.0, c \to 0.0\}$	$[a^{\mathrm{s}2}]$
$\{b^{\mathrm{s}}, e^{\mathrm{c}}\}$	$\{b \to 0.0\}$	$[b^{\mathrm{s}}]$
$\{d^{\mathrm{c}}, c^{\mathrm{e}}\}$	$\{c \to 0.0\}$	$[d^{\mathrm{c}}]$
$\{b^{\mathrm{c}}, e^{\mathrm{c}}\}$	$\{\}$	$[b^{\mathrm{c}}]$
$\{d^{\mathrm{s}}, c^{\mathrm{e}}\}$	$\{d \to 0.0, c \to 0.0\}$	$[d^{\mathrm{s}}]$
$\{c^{\mathrm{s}}\}$	$\{c \to 0.0\}$	$[c^{\mathrm{s}}]$
$\{b^{\mathrm{e}}, d^{\mathrm{e}}, c^{\mathrm{s}}\}$	$\{b \to 0.0, d \to 0.0, c \to 0.0\}$	$[c^{\mathrm{s}}]$
$\{e^{\mathrm{s}}\}$	$\{e \to 0.0\}$	$[e^{\mathrm{s}}]$
$\{b^{\mathrm{e}}, d^{\mathrm{e}}, e^{\mathrm{c}}\}$	$\{b \to 0.0, d \to 0.5\}$	$[b^{\mathrm{e}}]$
$\{b^{\mathrm{e}}, d^{\mathrm{e}}, c^{\mathrm{e}}\}$	$\{b \to 0.0, d \to 0.5, c \to 0.0\}$	$[d^{\mathrm{e}}]$

4.4 Mining a Resource Model

If no domain knowledge on resources is available, a resource model must be discovered from a log. Although many techniques can discover a control-flow model from an event log, techniques that yield a resource model (R) are less common. Therefore, we then provide three baseline methods to discover a resource model from an event log. Finally, we show how the weight parameters can be fitted to obtain an SLRPN. A complete overview of methods for discovering resource models from an event log is beyond the scope of this paper, though we provide three simple baseline methods, each requiring a different level of information in the event log. We list them in decreasing order of required information.

M1 In the first case, each event in the multi-run is annotated with the resource that executed it; that is, if each event is $a \overset{x}{\underset{\bullet}{r}}$ for a resource r, for $x \in$

{start, complete}. From a multi-run MR, the resources that can execute a transition t are all resources that executed t at least once: $R(t) = \{r \mid t\,\overset{x}{\underset{\bullet}{r}}\!\in MR\}$.

This method is obviously prone to noise and over-fitting, and a threshold $f \in [0, 1]$ could be used to filter spurious resources, by filtering all resources that appear f times or less than the resources that executed t the most times: $R'(t) = [r \mid \underset{\bullet}{t}\,\overset{x}{r}\!\in L]$ and $R_f(t) = \{r \mid R'(t)(r) \geq f \max_{r'} R(t)(r')\}$.

M2 In the second case, the events in the log do not contain resource information, but a life cycle distinguishes start and end events, that is, each event is $\bullet\overset{\text{s}}{\underset{\bullet}{\bullet}}$ or $\bullet\overset{\text{c}}{\underset{\bullet}{\bullet}}$. In this case, we make the assumption that each transition has a dedicated set of resources that are not shared with other transitions, that is, for $t \neq t'$, $R(t) \cap R(t') = \emptyset$. Then, an estimation of the number of resources for a transition t is the maximum number of concurrently executed t's in the multi-run MR. That is, we count the maximum number of "open" start events for t for which no end event t was seen yet: $c(t, \langle\,\rangle) = 0$

$R(t) = \{r_{t,y} \mid y \leq \max_{\sigma\cdot\sigma'=MR} c(t, \sigma)\}$

$c(t, \sigma \cdot \langle t' \overset{\text{c}}{\underset{\bullet}{\bullet}} \rangle) = c(t, \sigma) - \left\{\begin{smallmatrix} 1 & \text{if } t=t' \\ 0 & \text{if } t\neq t' \end{smallmatrix}\right.$ $\quad c(t, \sigma \cdot \langle t' \overset{\text{s}}{\underset{\bullet}{\bullet}} \rangle) = c(t, \sigma) + \left\{\begin{smallmatrix} 1 & \text{if } t=t' \\ 0 & \text{otherwise} \end{smallmatrix}\right.$

M3 If the events in the log contain neither resource information nor life cycle information, one can take enablements instead. To this end, for every event $e_j = t_j \overset{\text{c}}{\underset{\bullet}{\bullet}}$ in each aligned trace, we search for the first event $e_i = \bullet\overset{\text{c}}{\underset{\bullet}{\bullet}}$ that happened before e_j (24), such that after e_i, t_j was enabled until e_1 (25): Let $\langle e_1, \ldots, e_n\rangle \in L \wedge \forall_{k\geq 1} e_k = t_k \overset{\bullet}{\underset{\bullet}{\bullet}} \wedge M_k = M_{k-1} \uplus t_k^{\bullet} \setminus {}^{\bullet}t_k$, then for each

$$1 \leq i < j \leq n \text{ such that} \qquad e_i = t_i \overset{\bullet}{\underset{z}{\bullet}} \wedge e_j = t_j \overset{\text{c}}{\underset{y}{x}} \text{ and} \quad (24) \qquad \forall_{i\leq x<j} {}^{\bullet}t_j \Subset M_j x \quad (25)$$

insert $t_i \overset{\text{s}}{\underset{y}{x}}$ between i and $i + 1$. With this log transformation, strategy 4.4 can be applied to discover a resource model.

In the remainder of this paper, without loss of generality, we assume that for each event in the log, where relevant, a resource that executed it is available.

4.5 From Observations to an SLRPN

From the observations, we estimate the weight parameters for an SLRPN by constructing an optimisation problem. In this problem, we pose one equality for each enabled transition in each observation. The optimisation then assigns values to the weight parameters $b(t)$ and $v(t)$ for each transition t, such that the equalities are met as closely as possible. The equalities are:

$$\forall_{(E,Y)\to Z\in O} \forall_{t^x \in \bar{E}} \frac{Z(t^x)}{||Z||} = \frac{b(t)u(t)^{\psi(y)}}{\sum_{(t'^{x'},y')\in E} b(t')u(t')^{\psi(y')}} \tag{26}$$

with weight $Z(t^x)$, where $\psi(y) = \left\{\begin{smallmatrix} 0 & \text{if } x=\text{c}\vee t \text{ is silent} \\ y & \text{otherwise} \end{smallmatrix}\right.$. For $x = \text{c}$, the fixed utilisation is $\psi(y) = 0$. This will numerically disregard the utilisation parameter

$u(t)$, which we do not consider for completions. Similarly, silent transitions do not have a utilisation factor. In our example, for the observed stages $\{b^e, d^e, c^c\}$ with resource utilisation $\{b \rightarrow 1.0, d \rightarrow 0.5\}$ and fired stages $[c^c]$, we, e.g., derive the equation $\frac{1}{1} = \frac{b(c)}{b(b)u(b)+b(d)u(d)^{0.5}+b(c)}$ with weight 1.

The optimisation problem minimises a total distance, e.g., least squares, of both sides of each equation, where each equation (and hence distance) is weighted proportionally to how often the transition with stage t^x was observed. This results in a non-convex optimisation problem, for which solvers are available. These solvers typically approximate, but do not guarantee, an optimal solution.

5 Evaluation

We evaluate our discovery technique threefold: we describe its implementation, its feasibility, and show that it can discover novel types of insights.

Implementation. Our approach has been implemented in the ProM framework [8], and its source is available https://github.com/promworkbench/StochasticLabelledPetriNets. The implementation assumes the presence of completion stages only. The other (enqueue, start) stages are optional, and their presence can differ arbitrarily. As a solver, the Levenberg Marquardt implementation of Apache Commons is used, as partial derivatives for (26) are easy to compute. To ensure consistency, a resource annotated on the start event is ignored and instead the resource of the first same-activity completion event is used. This may not work reliably on models which allow for a concurrent execution of a transition with itself. If a completion event contains no resource, it is processed without; if an activity never has a completion event with a resource, it will not get a utilisation weight.

Feasibility. To test the feasibility of our approach, we applied it to several publicly available real-life logs, most of which can be obtained from https://www.tf-pm.org/resources/logs. The logs were selected to contain a resource perspective. Our implementation was applied to these logs on an AMD-5965wx CPU and Ubuntu 22.04 with 80GB of RAM available for the experiments. The discovery of the control-flow models was performed using the Inductive Miner - infrequent on default settings. Loading the log and discovering the control-flow are not included in the time measure. The alignment time was measured separately.

Table 2 shows the results of this experiment. Unsuccessful were the Road Fines log (no resource information on non-first events), Sepsis (anonymised to groups), the BPIC13-op and BPIC13-cp logs (our solver did not converge), and the BPIC18-gd log (alignment did not finish). Run time seems to correlate with the number of observations, which in turn depends on the number of resources (as a different set of resource utilisations means a new observation) We conclude that our implementation is feasible in practice, and that the limiting factors are similar to those of the alignment computations.

Practical Insights. To demonstrate the practical value of our approach, we apply it to multiple well-known real-life event logs. Figure 9 shows the discovered

Table 2. Results of our feasibility experiment.

Log	weight parameters	resources	multi-run size	observations	equations	alignment time (s)	run time (s)
Fig. 2	10	2	24	20	14	0	0
BPIC12-a	30	62	198 562	522	822	0	16
BPIC13-in	40	1435	254 320	15 000	17 972	19	4 569
BPIC17-o	22	145	625 837	2 124	3 997	2	100
BPIC18-ea	32	67	1 031 874	5 708	7 981	96	486
BPIC18-pd	32	111	479 426	10 676	14 636	6	2 541
BPIC20-dod	52	3	194 521	121	130	1	5
BPIC20-int	118	3	279 558	186	177	19	5
BPIC20-ppt	98	3	77 721	148	136	4	0
Mobis [4]	92	353	152 186	2 420	3 335	297	227

SLRPN for the BPIC12-a sublog, which describes a loan application process. It contains 60849 events across 10 activities in 13087 cases, executed by 62 resources. From that model, we learn multiple things about this process. First, we see that the acceptance transition has a utilisation weight below 1 (0.9263). This means that the higher the load in the process, the fewer application will be accepted. However, since the weight is still close to 1, this effect is not particularly strong. Conversely, we see that the decline transition has a utilisation weight of 25.0943. This means that the higher the load in the process, the more application will be declined. Given the size of this utilisation weight, this effect is rather strong. Finally, we also see that the cancellation transition has a utilisation weight of 0.5672, which means that the higher the load in the process, the more applications will be cancelled. This is particularly interesting because the cancellation of an application is initiated by the customer, not by the resources in the process. Nevertheless, it appears that the load in the process indirectly also affects the customer. One could hypothesise that higher load causes longer waiting times, such that customers either find a better offer for a loan or are generally dissatisfied with the service quality, leading to a cancellation.

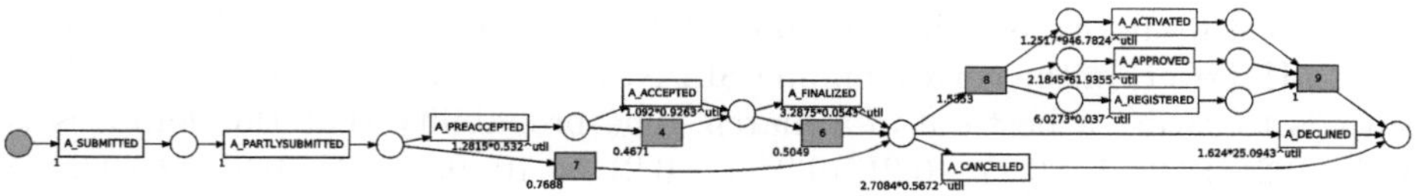

Fig. 9. Discovered SLRPN for the BPIC12-a log.

Figure 10 shows the discovered SLRPN for the BPI17-a log, which describes a loan offering process. This log contains 193 849 events from 8 activities in 31 509 cases, executed by 120 resources. The insights in this model mainly stem from comparing the weights of the three transitions for acceptance, cancellation, or refusal of offers with their respective parallel silent transitions. These silent transitions by definition are not dependent on resource utilisation, which is why they do not have a utilisation weight. However, the weights of the parallel non-silent transitions tell us that, for example, acceptance of an offer is more frequently

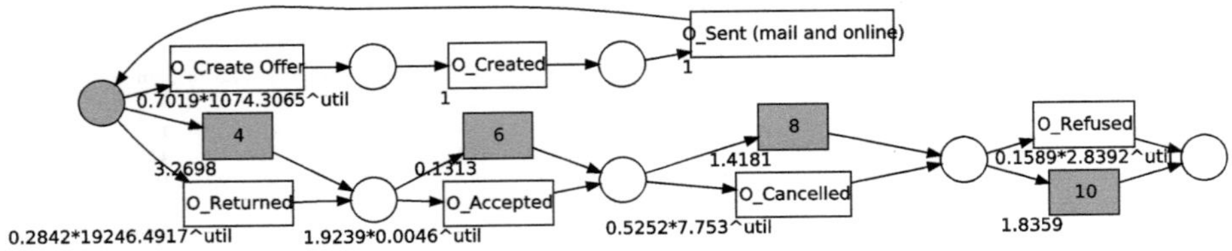

Fig. 10. Discovered SLRPN for the BPIC17-o log.

skipped when the load in the process is higher. Conversely, offers are more frequently cancelled by the employee or refused by the customer under a higher load, hinting to similar effects as above.

Discussion. The results of our evaluation may be influenced by a couple of factors. First, the absence of explicit enqueue or start events in the event logs requires us to make assumptions about when transitions are actually enqueued and started. These assumed events may not represent the actual execution of a process. Similarly, when ordering multiple runs into a multi-run, ties might have to be solved arbitrarily, which also introduces a risk of misrepresentation. Finally, the presence of duplicate labels or silent transitions in the process model may introduce arbitrariness into the alignment, which can have the same effect.

Indirect conflicts occur when prioritisation is present in a formalism [5]. For instance, if transition a has priority over transition b, the structure of the net may prevent b from firing at all, or the decision may be made by firing a structurally seemingly unrelated transition c [5, Fig. 9]. Our SLRPN formalism has a, perhaps counter-intuitive, closely related phenomenon in the representation of life cycle stages. Consider for instance the SLRPN shown in Fig. 11a, where a and b compete for execution (their utilisation weights are not relevant here; therefore, we can project the SLRPN down to a stochastic labelled Petri net [17]). Intuitively, one would expect that the probability that b completes before a would be 0.2. However, in the corresponding SLPN, we see that for b to complete first, b needs to "win" a best-out-of-5 match. The probability that this happens is $0.2^3 + 0.2\binom{3}{2}0.2^2(1-0.2) + 0.2\binom{4}{2}0.2^2(1-0.2)^2 = 10 \cdot 0.2^3 - 15 \cdot 0.2^4 + 6 \cdot 0.2^5 = 0.05792$. Figure 11c illustrates the relation of the base weight of transition b in the SLRPN and the probability of b completing first: it is not a straight line, and it is biased towards the highest-weighted transition: if b has a higher base weight in the SLRPN, then it will have an even higher probability of completing first. This phenomenon is present whenever transitions are concurrent in an SLRPN, and different model structures inhibit more elaborate stochastic dependencies.

6 Related Work

Stochastic Process Mining. Stochasticity in processes may come from uncertainty in logs and probabilities of choices in process models. In uncertain event logs,

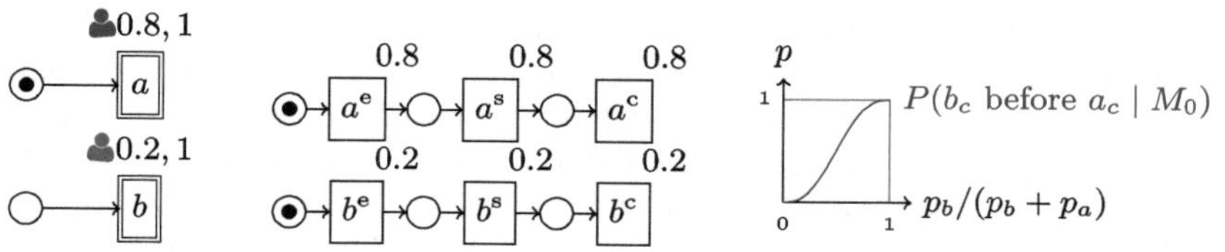

(a) An SLRPN. (b) Corresponding SLPN [17]. (c) Probability of b completing first.

Fig. 11. Stochastic "indirect conflict" in SLRPNs.

recorded events are considered indeterminate events whose existence and features follow a stochastic distribution and are not assigned a deterministic value [10]. Applications of uncertain event data include conformance checking against deterministic models [21]. In stochastic Petri nets (SPN), choices are annotated with probabilities. Given a Petri net, these probabilities can be estimated from event logs [6,23], or SPNs can be discovered from scratch [7]. Extensions of SPNs include long-distance [18] or data dependencies [19] within cases. Finally [17] addresses the problem of confusion, i.e., unclear probabilities due to concurrency effect. None of these approaches considers inter-case effects based on transition life cycles and resource availability.

Transition Life Cycles. Most process mining approaches assume that events and activities are atomic, though some consider their life cycles, such as to distinguish concurrent and interleaving behaviour [16], which may help to explain waiting times [15] or queues [28].

Inter-Case Effects of Resources. Resource-aware process models capture resource scarcity by restricting control flow based on resource availability [13]. Corresponding conformance checking techniques reveal deviations to such models [30], and simulation approaches obtain key performance indicators in resource-constrained environments [2] (our approach could provide a more refined stochastic perspective in simulation). Other approaches find an optimal resource allocation in resource-constraint processes with inter-case dependencies [12] or detect inter-case reasons for bottlenecks [31]. Furthermore, life cycles were used to explain waiting times caused by scarcity of resources [15]. In contrast to our work, stochastic effects of resource scarcity on decisions in models were not examined. [26] models and estimates delays due to inter-case dependencies, though does not explain *decisions* in the model based on inter-case dependencies; our approach could be combined with [26] in the future. Common literature defines the availability of a resource explicitly using a schedule, which may include regular working hours, holiday, weekends, and breaks, and can either be provided by the user or discovered from a log [20,27]. We model resource availability implicitly (23) by the number of available resources at any point in time. This is similar to resource utilisation used in queuing theory [9,29], with the difference that SLRPNs have no notion of time, and hence, do not need to consider arrival rates.

Inter-Case Features for Predictive Process Monitoring have been used to improve prediction quality. For example, inter-case features have been used in combination with conventional intra-case features to predict the remaining time of cases [24]. This approach has been extended to unknown case characteristics [25]. Furthermore, [11] uses time-window based encoding for inter-case features in time prediction that considers process variant dependencies. Similarly, inter-case dynamics in process segments that cause high prediction errors have been used to increase performance of remaining time prediction models [22]. Lastly, [14] encodes resource experience from event logs as an inter-case feature for predictive purposes. All of these approaches consider inter-case dependencies but do not regard stochastic effects and transition life cycles.

7 Conclusion

In this paper, we introduced stochastic labelled resource Petri nets (SLRPN) that model inter-case effects that may occur when individual cases of a process compete for shared resources. To this end, we combine transition life cycles with explicit resources and intra-case stochastics. We provided a SLRPN discovery algorithm that estimates how the control flow of a case is influenced by the availability of resources. Our evaluation shows that the discovery technique is technically feasible and able to obtain new insights in real-life logs.

Future work should, firstly, consider inter-case stochastic behaviour. This involves extending the (semantics of) SLRPNs with likelihoods of which run executes which stage next. A conceptual hurdle is that, currently, SLRPNs do not distinguish between traces, and that an arrival rate must be modelled. Secondly, most (stochastic) conformance checking techniques assume independence between runs/traces. Therefore, techniques that consider inter-case dependencies may differ substantially from existing ones. Thirdly, our approach requires alignments to establish which run belongs to a given trace. However, as shown in Sect. 5, many arbitrary choices may influence the results. It would be interesting to develop stochastic discovery techniques that do not depend on alignments. Lastly, whereas we model resource availability implicitly and detect its impact on the control-flow of cases, we did not aim to optimise inter-case control-flow decisions in presence of scarce resources. However, our notion of SLRPNs could be helpful when determining an appropriate schedule of cases, often referred to as resource capacity planning or scheduling in operations research [32]. Therefore, we want to investigate the application of SLRPNs to optimise inter-case decisions in presence of resource scarcity or resource availability costs [33].

Disclosure of Interests. Not applicable.

References

1. IEEE standard for extensible event stream (xes) for achieving interoperability in event logs and event streams. IEEE Std 1849-2016, pp. 1–50 (2016). https://doi.org/10.1109/IEEESTD.2016.7740858
2. van der Aalst, W.M.P.: Process mining and simulation: a match made in heaven! In: SummerSim, pp. 4:1–4:12. ACM (2018)
3. van der Aalst, W.M.P., Adriansyah, A., van Dongen, B.F.: Replaying history on process models for conformance checking and performance analysis. WIREs Data Mining Knowl. Discov. **2**(2), 182–192 (2012)
4. Baier, S., et al.: The mobis-challenge 2019 (2020)
5. Balbo, G.: Introduction to stochastic petri nets. LNCS, vol. 2090, pp. 84–155. Springer (2000)
6. Burke, A., Leemans, S.J.J., Wynn, M.T.: Stochastic process discovery by weight estimation. In: ICPM Workshops, pp. 260–272. Springer (2020)
7. Burke, A., Leemans, S.J.J., Wynn, M.T.: Discovering stochastic process models by reduction and abstraction. In: Petri Nets, pp. 312–336. Springer (2021)
8. van Dongen, B.F., de Medeiros, A.K.A., Verbeek, H.M.W., Weijters, A.J.M.M., van der Aalst, W.M.P.: The prom framework: A new era in process mining tool support. In: Petri Nets, pp. 444–454. Springer (2005)
9. Dumas, M., Rosa, M.L., Mendling, J., Reijers, H.A.: Fundamentals of Business Process Management, Second Edition. Springer (2018)
10. Gal, A.: Everything there is to know about stochastically known logs. In: ICPM (2023)
11. Grinvald, A., Soffer, P., Mokryn, O.: Inter-case properties and process variant considerations in time prediction: a conceptual framework. In: Enterprise, Business-Process and Information Systems Modeling, pp. 96–111. Springer, Cham (2021)
12. Havur, G., Cabanillas, C., Mendling, J., Polleres, A.: Resource allocation with dependencies in business process management systems. In: BPM Forum, pp. 3–19. Springer (2016)
13. Hee, K., Sidorova, N., Voorhoeve, M.: Resource-constrained workflow nets. Fund. Inform. **71**, 243–257 (2006)
14. Kim, J., Comuzzi, M., Dumas, M., Maggi, F.M., Teinemaa, I.: Encoding resource experience for predictive process monitoring. Decis. Support Syst. **153**, 113669 (2022)
15. Lashkevich, K., Milani, F., Chapela-Campa, D., Suvorau, I., Dumas, M.: Why am i waiting? data-driven analysis of waiting times in business processes. In: CAiSE, pp. 174–190. Springer (2023)
16. Leemans, S.J.J., Fahland, D., van der Aalst, W.M.P.: Using life cycle information in process discovery. In: BPM Workshops, pp. 204–217. Springer (2015)
17. Leemans, S.J.J., Maggi, F.M., Montali, M.: Reasoning on labelled petri nets and their dynamics in a stochastic setting. In: BPM, pp. 324–342. Springer (2022)
18. Leemans, S.J.J., Mannel, L.L., Sidorova, N.: Significant stochastic dependencies in process models. Inf. Syst. **118**, 102223 (2023)
19. Mannhardt, F., et al.: Modelling data-aware stochastic processes - discovery and conformance checking. In: Petri Nets. pp. 77–98. Springer (2023)
20. Martin, N., Depaire, B., Caris, A., Schepers, D.: Retrieving the resource availability calendars of a process from an event log. Inf. Syst. **88**, 101463 (2020)
21. Pegoraro, M., Uysal, M.S., van der Aalst, W.M.: Conformance checking over uncertain event data. Inf. Syst. **102**, 101810 (2021)

22. Pourbafrani, M., Kar, S., Kaiser, S., van der Aalst, W.M.P.: Remaining time prediction for processes with inter-case dynamics. In: Process Mining Workshops, pp. 140–153. Springer (2022)
23. Rogge-Solti, A., van der Aalst, W.M.P., Weske, M.: Discovering stochastic petri nets with arbitrary delay distributions from event logs. In: BPM Workshops, pp. 15–27. Springer (2014)
24. Senderovich, A., Di Francescomarino, C., Ghidini, C., Jorbina, K., Maggi, F.M.: Intra and inter-case features in predictive process monitoring: a tale of two dimensions. In: Business Process Management, pp. 306–323. Springer (2017)
25. Senderovich, A., Francescomarino, C.D., Maggi, F.M.: From knowledge-driven to data-driven inter-case feature encoding in predictive process monitoring. Inf. Syst. **84**, 255–264 (2019)
26. Senderovich, A., Weidlich, M., Gal, A.: Context-aware temporal network representation of event logs: Model and methods for process performance analysis. Inf. Syst. **84**, 240–254 (2019)
27. Senderovich, A., Weidlich, M., Gal, A., Mandelbaum, A.: Mining resource scheduling protocols. In: Sadiq, S., Soffer, P., Völzer, H. (eds.) BPM 2014. LNCS, vol. 8659, pp. 200–216. Springer, Cham (2014). https://doi.org/10.1007/978-3-319-10172-9_13
28. Senderovich, A., Weidlich, M., Gal, A., Mandelbaum, A.: Queue mining for delay prediction in multi-class service processes. Inf. Syst. **53**, 278–295 (2015)
29. Senderovich, A., Weidlich, M., Gal, A., Mandelbaum, A., Kadish, S., Bunnell, C.A.: Discovery and validation of queueing networks in scheduled processes. In: Zdravkovic, J., Kirikova, M., Johannesson, P. (eds.) CAiSE 2015. LNCS, vol. 9097, pp. 417–433. Springer, Cham (2015). https://doi.org/10.1007/978-3-319-19069-3_26
30. Sommers, D., Sidorova, N., van Dongen, B.: Exact and approximated log alignments for processes with inter-case dependencies. In: Petri Nets, pp. 99–119. Springer (2023)
31. Toosinezhad, Z., Fahland, D., Köroğlu, Ö., Van Der Aalst, W.M.: Detecting system-level behavior leading to dynamic bottlenecks. In: ICPM, pp. 17–24. IEEE (2020)
32. Vieira, B., Hans, E.W., van Vliet-Vroegindeweij, C., Van De Kamer, J., Van Harten, W.: Operations research for resource planning and-use in radiotherapy: a literature review. BMC Med. Inform. Decis. Mak. **16**, 1–11 (2016)
33. Yamashita, D.S., Armentano, V.A., Laguna, M.: Scatter search for project scheduling with resource availability cost. Eur. J. Oper. Res. **169**(2), 623–637 (2006)

State-Aware Object-Centric Process Mining: Enhancing OCEL 2.0 with Explicit State Transitions

Dina Kretzschmann[1], Alessandro Berti[1](✉), and Wil M. P. van der Aalst[1,2]

[1] Process and Data Science (PADS), RWTH Aachen University, Aachen, Germany
{dina.kretzschmann,a.berti,wvdaalst}@pads.rwth-aachen.de
[2] Celonis, Munich, Germany

Abstract. Modern organizations manage complex processes involving multiple object types, event types, and dynamic attributes, such as stock levels, patient vital signs, or machine status, which define critical object states (e.g., *Understock*, *Patient at Risk*, *Machine Down*). While object-centric process mining (OCPM) with OCEL 2.0 captures these attributes, it does not systematically model state transitions, limiting insights into process dynamics. We propose *State-Aware Object-Centric Process Mining (SA-OCPM)*, an extension of OCEL 2.0 that introduces (1) *object state transition events* to log changes (e.g., *Normal* to *Understock*, *Patient at Risk* to *Stable*, *Machine Down* to *Running*) and (2) *object state-aware events* to refine events with state context (e.g., *Goods Receipt (Understock), Patient Admission (Patient at Risk), Maintenance Start (Machine Down)*). Implemented in a commercial platform, SA-OCPM enables precise analysis of *when*, *why*, and *how* processes deviate from the optimum, as demonstrated in a logistics case study revealing inefficiencies like prolonged understock. SA-OCPM's state-based approach enhances diagnostic granularity and is applicable to domains like healthcare, manufacturing, and customer relationship management.

Keywords: State-Aware Object-Centric Process Mining · OCEL 2.0 · Process Mining · Inventory Management

1 Introduction

Modern organizations manage complex processes involving object types (e.g., materials, patients, machines), event types (e.g., goods receipt, patient admission, maintenance start), and dynamic attributes (e.g., stock levels, vital signs, machine status) that define critical *object states* like *Understock*, *At Risk*, or *Down*. These states impact outcomes, e.g., a material shifting to *Understock* causes order delays, a patient to *Critical* needs urgent care, a machine to *Idle* signals inefficiencies, and a client to *Churned* risks revenue loss. Understanding *when*, *why*, and *how* these transitions occur is key to process optimization. Object-centric process mining (OCPM), based on OCEL 2.0 [2], models object types, event types, and their interactions and attributes, surpassing case-centric

© The Author(s), under exclusive license to Springer Nature Switzerland AG 2026
A. Gianola et al. (Eds.): EDOC 2025, LNCS 16213, pp. 103–118, 2026.
https://doi.org/10.1007/978-3-032-15140-7_6

methods. Yet, OCEL 2.0 captures attributes (e.g., stock levels, risk scores) without systematically modeling *object states* or transitions, limiting detection of changes like low stock and links to inefficiencies, thus impeding root cause analysis and insights.

To address this gap, we propose *State-Aware Object-Centric Process Mining (SA-OCPM)*, a structured extension of OCEL 2.0 that explicitly incorporates object states and their transitions. SA-OCPM enhances OCPM by introducing: (1) *object state transition events*, which mark changes like a material shifting from *Normal* to *Understock*, and (2) *object state-aware events*, which refine existing events with state context, such as relabeling *Goods Receipt* as *Goods Receipt (Understock)*. These extensions enable precise tracking of state dynamics, revealing the catalysts and consequences of critical transitions. SA-OCPM is particularly suited for objects with measurable, dynamic attributes that form discrete state sets, such as materials (with stock-based states), patients (with health-based states), or machines (with operational states).

Problem Statement. Existing OCPM approaches, despite modeling objects, events, and attributes, do not explicitly capture *object states* or their transitions, limiting the ability to analyze how state changes drive process behavior. This gap obscures critical insights, such as why a material enters an *Understock* state or how a patient becomes *At Risk*, impeding targeted interventions.

Research Questions. This study addresses the following questions to advance state-aware process analysis:

RQ1: *State Modeling:* How can object states be defined and integrated into OCEL 2.0 to enable precise tracking of state transitions in object-centric process mining?

RQ2: *Transition Analysis:* How can state transitions be detected, represented, and analyzed to uncover *when*, *why*, and *how* processes deviate from desirable states?

RQ3: *Practical Impact:* How does SA-OCPM, applied to domains like inventory management, demonstrate effectiveness and generalizability in identifying and addressing inefficiencies?

Contributions. We introduce SA-OCPM, extending OCEL 2.0 by defining object states (e.g., *Normal*, *Understock*) from dynamic attributes using domain-specific models like Min-Max inventory rules, generating *object state transition events* to log state changes (e.g., *ST CHANGE Normal to Understock*), and refining events into *object state-aware events* (e.g., *Goods Issue (Understock)*) to embed state context. Formalized in Definitions 2 and 3 and implemented in Celonis, SA-OCPM reveals inefficiencies like prolonged *Understock* in a logistics case study, generalizing to domains like healthcare and manufacturing for enhanced process intelligence.

The paper is organized as follows: Sect. 2 reviews related work. Section 3 details SA-OCPM's framework and formalization. Section 4 presents the implementation. Section 5 presents the case study and results. Section 6 concludes with future research directions.

2 Related Work

In this section, we review literature relevant to our proposed *State-Aware Object-Centric Process Mining (SA-OCPM)*, focusing on its advancements in modeling and analyzing object state transitions within object-centric process mining.

Object-Centric Process Mining: OCPM extends traditional case-centric approaches [1] by modeling multiple object types and their interactions [2]. Techniques include artifact-centric models [17], object-centric behavioral constraint models [16], and object-centric DFGs/Petri nets [3,6]. Commercial tools like Celonis Process Sphere leverage OCPM for complex process analysis [2]. While OCEL 2.0 captures dynamic attributes (e.g., stock levels), it lacks explicit mechanisms to model state transitions, limiting insights into process dynamics driven by state changes. SA-OCPM addresses this by introducing state transition events and state-aware events, enabling precise tracking of *when*, *why*, and *how* state changes impact processes.

Data-Driven Process Analysis and State-Based Modeling: Data-aware process mining integrates contextual attributes to analyze process behavior. Methods include decision rule discovery [11], multi-perspective process models [20], and simulation-based approaches [18]. State-based models, such as finite state machines [13] and interactive discovery [12], capture dynamic conditions in domains like healthcare [32] and manufacturing [10]. However, these approaches often focus on case-centric states or lack systematic integration of state transitions within object-centric frameworks. SA-OCPM extends OCEL 2.0 by defining states via domain-specific models (e.g., Min-Max inventory rules) and embedding state transition events, enhancing causality analysis across multiple object types.

Inventory Management and Logistics in Process Mining: Process mining has been applied to optimize inventory and logistics [1,25]. Early case-centric approaches [19,29] evolved into OCPM to handle multiple object types [2,23], as seen in case studies [7,15]. However, OCPM models can become complex due to numerous elements, and prior work [14] introduced activity transformations that complicated analysis. The segmentation framework by [8] addresses this by decomposing object-centric event logs into focused segments based on object relationships, event types, and temporal intervals, simplifying analysis and revealing localized patterns like understock and overstock issues in inventory management. SA-OCPM builds on this by incorporating state-aware events and transition events, enabling focused analysis of state-driven inefficiencies, such as prolonged *Understock* states, in domains like inventory management. Unlike segmentation, which isolates process fragments, SA-OCPM embeds state dynamics directly into the event log, enhancing granularity in tracking *when*, *why*, and *how* state changes impact logistics processes.

Root Cause Analysis and Performance Insights: Root cause analysis in process mining links outcomes to underlying causes using causal modeling [24], machine learning [22], graphical models [30], and domain knowledge [5,25]. These methods are based on models which do not explicitly consider state transitions, limiting their ability to capture dynamic data interactions across objects. SA-OCPM integrates state transitions directly into the event log, enabling precise identification of catalysts (e.g., supplier delays causing *Understock*) and their process impacts, offering a more granular and actionable approach to root cause analysis.

3 State-Aware Object-Centric Process Mining (SA-OCPM)

We propose *State-Aware Object-Centric Process Mining (SA-OCPM)*, a structured extension of the OCEL 2.0 standard to explicitly incorporate object states and their transitions. Unlike traditional OCPM [2], which models objects, events, and their interactions but does not systematically exploit state dynamics, SA-OCPM enhances OCEL 2.0 by introducing (1) *object state transition events* to mark changes in object states (e.g., from *Normal* to *Understock*) and (2) *object state-aware events* to refine existing events with state-specific labels (e.g., *Goods Receipt (Understock)*). This approach, formalized in Definitions 2 and 3, enables

(a) Non-Enriched Object-Centric Event Log

Ev.ID	Mat.	POi	Activity	Supplier	Speed	Stock	Timestamp
E01	M001	PO001	Create Purchase Order Item	Supplier A	Low	75	2025-01-01 09:00
E02	M001	–	Goods Issue	–	–	65	2025-01-02 10:00
E03	M001	–	Goods Issue	–	–	55	2025-01-03 11:00
E04	M001	–	Goods Issue	–	–	45	2025-01-04 12:00
E05	M001	PO001	Goods Receipt	Supplier A	Low	165	2025-01-10 14:00

(b) State-Aware Object-Centric Event Log

Ev.ID	Mat.	POi	Activity	Supplier	Speed	State	Stock	Timestamp
E01	M001	PO001	Create Purchase Order Item (Normal)	Supplier A	Low	Normal	75	2025-01-01 09:00
E02	M001	–	Goods Issue (Normal)	–	–	Normal	65	2025-01-02 10:00
E03	M001	–	Goods Issue (Normal)	–	–	Normal	55	2025-01-03 11:00
E06	M001	–	ST CHANGE Normal to Understock	–	–	Understock	45	2025-01-04 12:00
E04	M001	–	Goods Issue (Understock)	–	–	Understock	45	2025-01-04 12:00
E07	M001	PO001	ST CHANGE Understock to Overstock	Supplier A	Low	Overstock	165	2025-01-10 14:00
E05	M001	PO001	Goods Receipt (Overstock)	Supplier A	Low	Overstock	165	2025-01-10 14:00

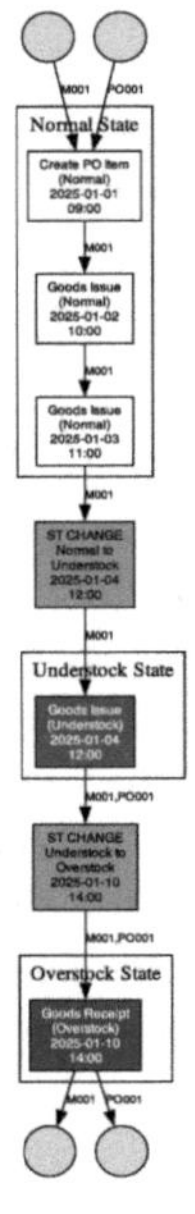

Fig. 1. Comparison of non-enriched (Table 1a) and state-aware (Table 1b) object-centric event logs for inventory management (material with normal stock: 50150), alongside a visualization of the enriched log (right). The state-aware event log incorporates state data and transition events, detailing *how Understock* resulted from delayed replenishment and *Overstock* from excessive order size, *why* (e.g., Supplier A's delays or low delivery speed), and *when* transitions occurred with precise timestamps.

precise analysis of *when*, *why*, and *how* processes evolve due to state changes, addressing the limitations of OCPM in capturing dynamic data-driven conditions.

Conceptual Framework: SA-OCPM extends OCEL 2.0, which already models objects, events, and attributes (including data attributes like stock levels or risk scores) as per Definition 1 [2]. While OCEL 2.0 supports dynamic data attributes via the π_{ovmap} function, these are typically used for static or descriptive purposes rather than dynamic state modeling. SA-OCPM introduces a systematic approach to define and track object states, derived from domain-specific data attributes, and integrates them into the event log. This is achieved through two key mechanisms:

1) *Object State Transition Events*: New events are generated to explicitly record when an object's state changes, as defined in Definition 2. For example, a material transitioning from *Normal* to *Understock* due to a stock level dropping below a safety threshold triggers a state change event (e.g., *ST CHANGE Normal to Understock*). These events, timestamped at $t-\epsilon$, link to the affected object and capture the old and new states, enabling traceability of state dynamics.
2) *Object State-Aware Events*: Existing events are refined by appending the object's state at the time of occurrence, as specified in Definition 2. For instance, a *Goods Receipt* event executed when a material is in an *Understock* state is relabeled as *Goods Receipt (Understock)*. This preserves the original event identity while embedding state context, facilitating state-specific process analysis.

Definition 1 (Object-Centric Event Log (OCEL)). *Let $\mathcal{U}\sigma$ denote the universe of all strings. An object-centric event log (OCEL) is a tuple $(E, O, A, OT, \pi_{act}, \pi_{time}, \pi_{ot}, \pi_{omap}, \pi_{vmap}, \pi_{ovmap}, \leq)$, where E is a finite set of unique events, O is a finite set of unique objects, A is a finite set of activities, OT is a finite set of object types, $\pi_{act} : E \rightarrow A$ assigns to each event an activity, $\pi_{time} : E \rightarrow \mathbb{R}$ assigns each event a timestamp, $\pi_{ot} : O \rightarrow OT$ assigns each object to an object type, $\pi_{omap} : E \rightarrow \mathcal{P}(O)$ assigns each event to a set of related objects, $\pi_{vmap} : E \times \mathcal{U}\sigma \nrightarrow \mathcal{U}\sigma \cup \mathbb{R}$ assigns values to event-attribute pairs, $\pi_{ovmap} : O \times \mathcal{U}\sigma \times \mathbb{R} \nrightarrow \mathcal{U}\sigma \cup \mathbb{R}$ assigns values to object-attribute-timestamp triples, and $\leq \;\; \subseteq E \times E$ is a total order on events defined by $e_1 \leq e_2 \iff \pi_{time}(e_1) \leq \pi_{time}(e_2)$, with tie-breaking for equal timestamps.*

An OCEL, as in Definition 1, structures process execution data involving multiple interacting entities, with events (E) as process occurrences (e.g., "Order Created"), objects (O) as involved entities (e.g., orders, products), activities (A) as event types linked by π_{act} (e.g., "Create Order"), and object types (OT) categorizing objects via π_{ot} (e.g., "Order"). The function π_{time} assigns timestamps to events, π_{omap} links events to related object sets (e.g., "Ship Package" to order "o1" and package "p1"), π_{vmap} assigns attribute values to event-attribute pairs (e.g., "Channel" as "Online"), π_{ovmap} assigns time-varying attribute values to object-attribute-timestamp triples (e.g., "StockLevel" for "Product X" at time t_1), and $\leq$ orders events temporally by timestamps.

Definition 2 (State-Aware OCEL). *Given an OCEL $OCEL_{base} = (E, O, A, OT, \pi_{act}, \pi_{time}, \pi_{ot}, \pi_{omap}, \pi_{vmap}, \pi_{ovmap}, \leq_{base})$ and a specific object attribute name $\bar{a} \in \mathcal{U}\sigma$ such that for all $o \in O$ and for all $t \in \mathbb{R}$, $(o, \bar{a}, t) \in \text{dom}(\pi_{ovmap})$ and $\pi_{ovmap}(o, \bar{a}, t) \in \mathcal{U}\sigma$ (this means the attribute $\bar{a}$ is always defined for every object o at every time t, and its value is always a string representing the state of o at t). A state-aware object-centric event log is a tuple $OCEL_{state} = (E', O, A, OT, \pi'_{act}, \pi'_{time}, \pi_{ot}, \pi'_{omap}, \pi'_{vmap}, \pi_{ovmap}, \leq')$ where:*

- *$E' = E \cup E''$ is the extended set of events.*
- *$E'' = \{e_{(o,t)} \mid o \in O, t \in \mathbb{R}$ such that $\pi_{ovmap}(o, \bar{a}, t) \neq \pi_{ovmap}(o, \bar{a}, t - \epsilon)\}$ is a set of newly generated* ***state change events****. Here, ϵ is a small positive real number representing the time duration just before t. (The condition ensures that $\pi_{ovmap}(o, \bar{a}, t)$ and $\pi_{ovmap}(o, \bar{a}, t - \epsilon)$ are both defined due to the global assumption on $\bar{a}$).*
- *The sets O, A, OT, and the function π_{ot} are inherited from $OCEL_{base}$. The function π_{ovmap} is also inherited and primarily used for determining states and attribute values.*
- *$\pi'_{act} : E' \to A \cup \mathcal{U}\sigma$ is the activity assignment function, defined as:*
  - *$\pi'_{act}(e) = \pi_{act}(e) \oplus$ "(" $\oplus\, \pi_{ovmap}(o, \bar{a}, t) \oplus$ ")" for $e \in E$.*
  - *$\pi'_{act}(e_{(o,t)}) =$ "STCHANGE " $\oplus\, \pi_{ovmap}(o, \bar{a}, t - \epsilon) \oplus$ " to " $\oplus\, \pi_{ovmap}(o, \bar{a}, t)$ for $e_{(o,t)} \in E''$, where $\oplus$ denotes string concatenation.*
- *$\pi'_{time} : E' \to \mathbb{R}$ is the timestamp assignment function, defined as:*
  - *$\pi'_{time}(e) = \pi_{time}(e)$ for $e \in E$.*
  - *$\pi'_{time}(e_{(o,t)}) = t - \epsilon$ for $e_{(o,t)} \in E''$.*
- *$\pi'_{omap} : E' \to \mathcal{P}(O)$ is the object mapping function, defined as:*
  - *$\pi'_{omap}(eBullet) = \pi_{omap}(e)$ for $e \in E$.*
  - *$\pi'_{omap}(e_{(o,t)}) = \{o\}$ for $e_{(o,t)} \in E''$.*
- *$\pi'_{vmap} : E' \times \mathcal{U}\sigma \nrightarrow \mathcal{U}\sigma \cup \mathbb{R}$ is the event attribute value assignment function, defined as:*
  - *$\pi'_{vmap}(e, attr) = \pi_{vmap}(e, attr)$ for $e \in E$ and $(e, attr) \in \text{dom}(\pi_{vmap})$.*
  - *$\pi'_{vmap}(e_{(o,t)}, attr) = \pi_{ovmap}(o, attr, t - \epsilon)$ for $e_{(o,t)} \in E''$ and $(o, attr, t) \in \text{dom}(\pi_{ovmap})$. (If $attr = \bar{a}$, this gives the new state, which is guaranteed to be defined).*
- *$\leq' \subseteq E' \times E'$ is a total order on the extended set of events, defined as $e_1 \leq' e_2 \iff \pi'_{time}(e_1) \leq \pi'_{time}(e_2)$, with a suitable tie-breaking mechanism if needed.*

A State-Aware OCEL, as in Definition 2, extends a standard OCEL by incorporating a state attribute $\bar{a}$ (e.g., "Stock Status"), always defined for every object at all times $t \in \mathbb{R}$, with string values representing object states. It includes original events E and new state change events $E'' = \{e_{(o,t)} \mid o \in O, t \in \mathbb{R}, \pi_{ovmap}(o, \bar{a}, t) \neq \pi_{ovmap}(o, \bar{a}, t - \epsilon)\}$, where ϵ is an small positive duration.

For original events, $\pi'_{act}(e) = \pi_{act}(e) \oplus$ "(" $\oplus\, \pi_{ovmap}(o, \bar{a}, t) \oplus$ ")", while for state change events $e_{(o,t)} \in E''$, $\pi'_{act}(e_{(o,t)})$ = "STCHANGE " $\oplus\, \pi_{ovmap}(o, \bar{a}, t - \epsilon) \oplus$ " to " $\oplus\, \pi_{ovmap}(o, \bar{a}, t)$. Original events retain their timestamps via π'_{time}, while state change events are timestamped at $t - \epsilon$. The function π'_{omap} preserves original event-object mappings and assigns $\{o\}$ to state change events $e_{(o,t)}$. Event attributes via π'_{vmap} and temporal order $\leq'$ are updated accordingly, making state changes explicit events to facilitate analysis of state transitions and their impact.

Definition 3 (Coalesced State-Aware OCEL). *A Coalesced State-Aware OCEL, denoted $OCEL_{coal}$, is derived from a State-Aware OCEL $OCEL_{state} = (E', O, A, OT, \pi'_{act}, \pi'_{time}, \pi_{ot}, \pi'_{omap}, \pi'_{vmap}, \pi_{ovmap}, \leq')$ (where $E' = E \cup E''$, and E'' is the set of individual state change events) by applying a coalescing transformation. The $OCEL_{coal}$ shares the core components O, A, OT, π_{ot}, and π_{ovmap} with $OCEL_{state}$. The transformation primarily affects the event set and its related mappings as follows:*

- Event Coalescing*:*
  - *Original process events $E \subseteq E'$ from $OCEL_{state}$ are preserved.*
  - *All individual state change events $e'' \in E''$ that share an identical timestamp $t^* = \pi'_{time}(e'')$* and *an identical activity label $\pi'_{act}(e'')$ are grouped. Each such group is replaced by a single new coalesced state change event, $e_c^{(t^*,a)}$, where $a = \pi'_{act}(e'')$ is the common activity label of the grouped events.*
  - *The resulting event set is $E_{coal} = E \cup E''_{coal}$, where E''_{coal} is the set of all such unique coalesced state change events.*
- Properties of New Coalesced Events ($e_c^{(t^*,a)} \in E''_{coal}$) *in $OCEL_{coal}$:*
  - Timestamp*: The event $e_c^{(t^*,a)}$ is assigned the timestamp t^*.*
  - Related Objects*: It is related to the union of all objects that were related to the individual e'' events merged at t^* with activity a, i.e., $\pi''_{omap}(e_c^{(t^*,a)}) = \bigcup\{\pi'_{omap}(e'') \mid e'' \in E'', \pi'_{time}(e'') = t^*, \pi'_{act}(e'') = a\}$.*
  - Activity*: It is assigned the common activity label a, i.e., $\pi''_{act}(e_c^{(t^*,a)}) = a$.*
  - Attributes*: Its attributes can be defined to summarize the merged changes (e.g., a count of affected objects, a list of the specific state transitions involved) or may be sparsely defined/omitted if detailed attribute information for these coalesced events is not critical.*
- Mappings for Original Events*: For events $e \in E$, all their mappings (activity, time, related objects, attributes) remain unchanged from $OCEL_{state}$.*
- Overall Structure*: The new functions $\pi''_{act}, \pi''_{time}, \pi''_{omap}, \pi''_{vmap}$ and the temporal order $\leq''$ for $OCEL_{coal}$ reflect these changes.*

To manage complexity in logs with frequent state changes, SA-OCPM includes a coalescing transformation (Definition 3), which groups simultaneous state change events into single coalesced events. This simplifies analysis by highlighting collective state transitions across multiple objects, as illustrated in Fig. 1, where state transitions (e.g., *Normal* to *Understock*) are visualized alongside state-aware events.

Defining Object States: Object states are encoded as an OCEL attribute $\bar{a} \in \mathcal{U}\sigma$, always defined for every object at all times (Definition 2). States (e.g., *Normal*, *Understock*, *Overstock*) are derived during ETL or computed using mathematical models (e.g., optimization or decision rules) based on attribute values. Suitable object types have dynamic, measurable attributes impacting process behavior. Examples include:

- *Materials (Inventory)*: States like *Understock*, *Normal*, *Overstock* from stock levels via Min-Max model [28].
- *Patients (Healthcare)*: States like *Stable*, *At Risk*, *Critical* from clinical metrics (e.g., vital signs).
- *Machines (Manufacturing)*: States like *Running*, *Idle*, *Down* from operational metrics (e.g., uptime).
- *Customers (CRM)*: States like *Active*, *At Risk*, *Churned* from engagement metrics (e.g., purchase frequency).

Objects like orders may aggregate states from related objects (e.g., materials). SA-OCPM focuses on objects with discrete state sets derived from attributes like stock levels or risk scores, ensuring broad applicability.

4 Implementation

This section outlines the implementation of *State-Aware Object-Centric Process Mining (SA-OCPM)* within the Celonis Execution Management System (EMS)

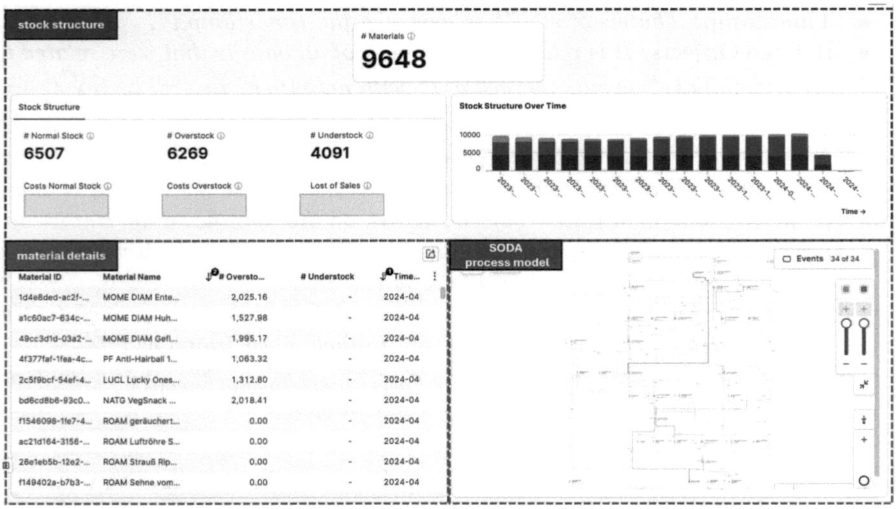

Fig. 2. Celonis Dashboard highlighting context-specific metrics (stock structures, material details) and a state-aware object-centric process model.

to enrich object-centric event logs with state information for granular process analysis.

SA-OCPM begins with loading source data, such as inventory tables from enterprise systems or simulated datasets (e.g., Zenodo artifacts). Object types (e.g., materials (*MAT*), purchase orders (*PO_ITEM*)) and event types are defined in the Celonis Object-Centric Data Model, including their relationships.

State-related information is materialized through custom transformations:

- *Attribute Computation:* Scripts compute dynamic attributes like Economic Order Quantity (EOQ) and Safety Stock (SS) for state definitions, e.g., for material-plant combinations in inventory management.
- *State Transition Events:* SQL scripts detect state changes (e.g., *Normal* to *Understock*) based on attributes, generating *object state transition events* (e.g., *ST CHANGE Normal to Understock*).
- *State-Aware Events:* Transformations postfix activity names with the object's state (e.g., *Goods Receipt* to *Goods Receipt (Understock)*) using query languages like PQL.

These transformations, orchestrated via Celonis Data Jobs, update the process intelligence graph. The enriched event log supports advanced analysis, including state-aware process visualization (e.g., via Multi-Perspective Process Explorer), conformance monitoring (e.g., Min-Max policies), and automated actions (e.g., Action Flows for understock replenishment).

Scripts for state transitions and state-aware events, including SQL and PQL snippets, are available in an OSF dataset (https://osf.io/7wm2y/?view_only=dd7ca32c15cf4b80884afce82d37357e). A simulated OCEL and source data are provided on Zenodo (https://doi.org/10.5281/zenodo.15535073).

5 Case Study

To evaluate the practical impact of *State-Aware Object-Centric Process Mining (SA-OCPM)*, we applied it to an inventory management scenario at a leading European pet retailer, with 2024 revenues of approximately 4.8 billion €. Conducted in collaboration with the retailer, this study targets inefficiencies tied to object states like *Understock* and *Overstock* across omnichannel operations, which lead to significant financial losses. Leveraging SA-OCPM, we extend prior work [14] by integrating *object state transition events* and *object state-aware events* to analyze state-driven process dynamics, capturing *when*, *why*, and *how* inefficiencies emerge.

5.1 Mathematical Models for Inventory States

To systematically analyze inventory dynamics within SA-OCPM, we define object states, i.e., *Understock*, *Normal*, and *Overstock*, derived from dynamic attributes using the Min-Max method [4,27]. These states, computed from object-centric event data as outlined in Sect. 3, enable precise tracking of state transitions, revealing the catalysts and consequences of inefficiencies. Maintaining *Normal* state balances availability and cost, while *Overstock* increases holding costs and *Understock* risks lost sales [9,21,31].

The Min-Max method uses four key metrics for each material m:

- *Economic Order Quantity (EOQ)*: Minimizes ordering and holding costs, calculated as $\mathrm{EOQ}_m = \sqrt{\frac{2D_m S}{H}}$, where D_m is annual demand, S is fixed cost per order, and H is holding cost per unit [26].
- *Safety Stock (SS)*: Buffers demand and lead time variability, given by $\mathrm{SS}_m = z \times \sigma_m \times \sqrt{l_m}$, where z is the service level factor, σ_m is demand standard deviation, and l_m is lead time [33].
- *Reorder Point (ROP)*: Triggers replenishment, defined as $\mathrm{ROP}_m = d_m \times l_m + \mathrm{SS}_m$, with d_m as average demand [27].
- *Maximum Stock Level (Max)*: Limits excess inventory, computed as $\mathrm{Max}_m = \mathrm{EOQ}_m + \mathrm{SS}_m$ [27].

Using these, we define the state for material m at time t:

- *Understock*: $\text{Inventory Level}_{m,t} < \mathrm{SS}_m$, signaling insufficient stock.
- *Normal*: $\mathrm{SS}_m \leq \text{Inventory Level}_{m,t} \leq \mathrm{Max}_m$, reflecting optimal levels.
- *Overstock*: $\text{Inventory Level}_{m,t} > \mathrm{Max}_m$, indicating excess.

These states, encoded as attribute $\bar{a}$ in the State-Aware OCEL (Definition 2), enable *object state transition events* (e.g., *ST CHANGE Normal to Understock*) and *object state-aware events* (e.g., *Goods Receipt (Understock)*), linking state changes to process behavior for root cause analysis.

5.2 Object-Centric Event Log

The State-Aware OCEL, constructed via SA-OCPM in Celonis (Sect. 4), spans December 2022 to April 2024, covering the central warehouse in Germany. It includes 34 event types, enriched with object states (*Understock*, *Normal*, *Overstock*), derived from dynamic attributes per Sect. 3. The log captures 36,439,490 events across two object types: *materials* (9,648 instances) and *purchase order items* (33,242,938 instances). Relationships are defined as materials linking to zero or more purchase order items (**0..***), and each purchase order item linking to one material (**1..1**), enabling tracking of state dynamics.

Object state-aware events (e.g., *Goods Issue (Understock)*) refine activities with state context, while *object state transition events* (e.g., *ST CHANGE Normal to Overstock*) explicitly log state shifts, capturing the moment, prior state, and new state per Definition 2. These link to process activities, ensuring traceability of state-driven dynamics. Table 1 lists event types, associated states, and occurrence counts.

Table 1. Overview of event types in the State-Aware OCEL, enriched with object states (*Understock*, *Normal*, *Overstock*) and *object state transition events* per Definition 2, alongside occurrence counts during December 2022 to April 2024.

Goods Issue (Overstock)	24,289,441
Goods Issue (Normal)	8,428,451
Create Sales Order Item (Overstock)	1,684,667
Create Sales Order Item (Normal)	680,844
Goods Issue (Understock)	210,264
Create Purchase Suggestion Item (Overstock)	198,908
Goods Receipt (Overstock)	188,841
Create Purchase Order Item (Overstock)	173,095
Create Purchase Suggestion Item (Normal)	144,586
Create Purchase Order Item (Normal)	121,903
Goods Receipt (Normal)	119,561
Create Sales Order Item (Understock)	93,324
Create Purchase Suggestion Item (Understock)	18,967
Goods Transfer Out (Overstock)	13,822
Create Purchase Order Item (Understock)	9,614
ST CHANGE Normal Overstock	9,396
ST CHANGE Overstock Normal	8,881
ST CHANGE Understock Normal	7,262
ST CHANGE Normal Understock	6,463
Goods Transfer Out (Normal)	5,477
END OVERSTOCK	4,604
END NORMAL	4,093
START OVERSTOCK	3,872
START NORMAL	3,849
Cancel Goods Receipt (Overstock)	3,619
START UNDERSTOCK	1,892
Goods Receipt (Understock)	1,199
Cancel Goods Receipt (Normal)	963
END UNDERSTOCK	916
ST CHANGE Understock Overstock	286
Goods Transfer Out (Understock)	263
Cancel Goods Receipt (Understock)	111
ST CHANGE Overstock Understock	55
Create Purchase Requisition (Normal)	1

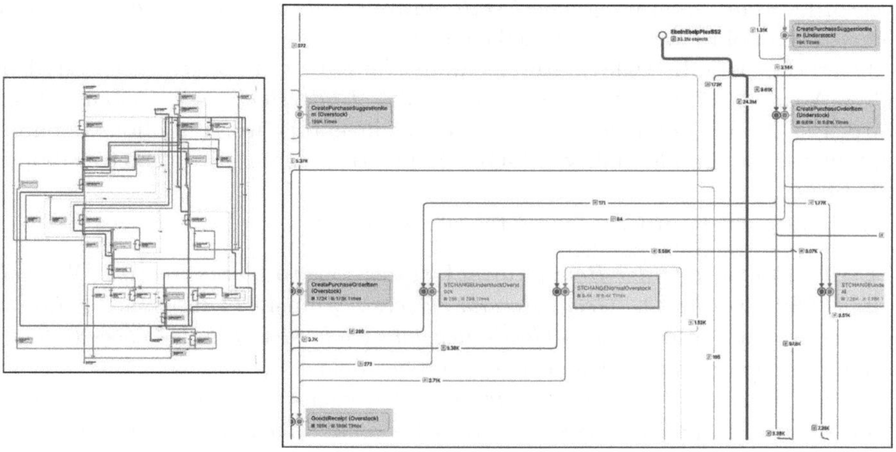

Fig. 3. State-aware object-centric process model derived via SA-OCPM. The left figure (a) displays the full model with Celonis object coloring (e.g., material in orange, purchase order item in dark green), extended to show object states: blue (*Overstock*), purple (*Understock*), white (*Normal*), and light green for *object state transition events* per Definition 2. The right figure (b) zooms in to increase readability.

5.3 Process Discovery

Using SA-OCPM, we derived a state-aware, object-centric process model in Celonis with the Multi-Perspective Process Explorer, leveraging the State-Aware OCEL from Sect. 5.2. This model integrates *object state-aware events* and *object state transition events*, capturing how processes evolve under specific state conditions, per Definition 2.

For clarity, we applied a semantic color-coding scheme in Celonis, as shown in Fig. 3. Object types are colored per Celonis defaults (orange for materials, dark green for purchase order items), with manual extensions for states: white for *Normal*, purple for *Understock*, blue for *Overstock*, and light green for *object state transition events*. This visualization highlights state-specific patterns and critical transitions, enhancing diagnostic precision.

The model reveals state-driven behaviors obscured by traditional OCPM. For example, *object state-aware events* like *Goods Receipt (Overstock)* show contributions to prolonged inefficiencies, while *object state transition events* track shifts (e.g., *ST CHANGE Normal to Understock*), supporting targeted analysis of bottlenecks and conformance under specific states, explored further below.

5.4 Main Results

The objective is to identify catalysts of inefficient object states in inventory processes. Using SA-OCPM, we analyze interactions between materials and purchase order items, leveraging *object state-aware events* and *object state transition events* to pinpoint state-driven inefficiencies.

Over the period, 9,648 materials were tracked, with states distributed as 38.5% *Normal*, 37.2% *Overstock*, and 24.3% *Understock* (see Celonis Dashboard, Fig. 2). These inefficient states impact inventory worth millions of euros, anonymized for confidentiality. SA-OCPM identifies materials prone to suboptimal states.

The state-aware process model reveals patterns:

- *Create Purchase Order Item (Normal)* transitions to *Goods Receipt (Normal)* in 97,589 cases, but to *Goods Receipt (Overstock)* in 4,473 cases (4.4%) due to excessive quantities, and to *Goods Receipt (Understock)* in 247 cases (0.24%) due to demand underestimation or supplier delays.
- *Create Purchase Order Item (Overstock)* worsens to *Goods Receipt (Overstock)* in 151,478 cases (98%), driven by poor forecasting, with rare shifts to *Goods Receipt (Normal)* (1,124 cases) or *Goods Receipt (Understock)* (7 cases) from unexpected demand or supplier issues.
- *Create Purchase Order Item (Understock)* shifts to *Goods Receipt (Normal)* in 3,276 cases (75%), fails to resolve in 692 cases (16%) to *Goods Receipt (Understock)*, and overcompensates to *Goods Receipt (Overstock)* in 413 cases (9%), signaling reactive ordering.

Analysis of *object state transition events* highlights inefficiencies. In 210,186 cases, materials lingered in *Understock* with active demand but no purchase order, causing 1,460 unfulfilled sales orders. Additionally, 122 materials remained in *Understock* despite multiple *object state-aware events* like *Goods Receipt (Understock)*, due to insufficient quantities. In 1,520 cases, multiple purchase orders during *Overstock* led to excess, reflecting poor synchronization. Recovery

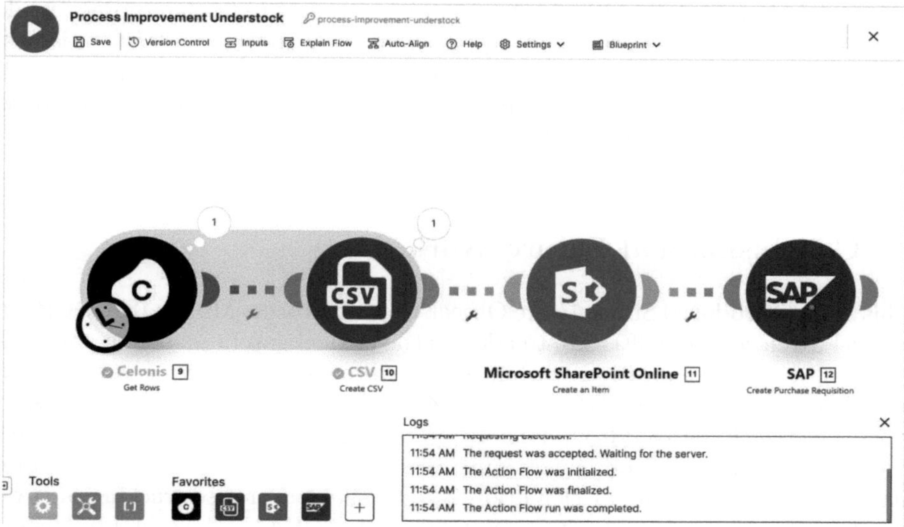

Fig. 4. Celonis Action Flow for Stock Replenishment. Detects understocked materials with demand, generates a CSV list, stores it on SharePoint, and aims to trigger a purchase requisition in SAP. Detection works fully; storage and requisition steps await system integration.

times averaged 246 d for *ST CHANGE Overstock to Normal* and 87 d for *ST CHANGE Understock to Normal*, indicating slow corrections.

SA-OCPM's explicit modeling of states and transitions uncovers inefficiencies missed by standard OCPM, such as persistent *Understock* or excessive *Overstock*. By integrating *object state-aware events* and *object state transition events* per Definitions 2 and 3, SA-OCPM pinpoints catalysts like inaccurate forecasting and supply delays, offering actionable insights for optimization across domains with dynamic attributes.

5.5 Process Improvements

To boost inventory efficiency, targeted measures are implemented as automated *Action Flows* in Celonis, triggering interventions based on state-aware, object-centric insights from real-time data. However, full operationalization is pending due to limited integration with systems like SAP.

For example, an Action Flow in Celonis detects understocked materials with active demand but no purchase order. It compiles these into a CSV file, stored on SharePoint, and aims to create a purchase requisition in SAP. Currently, the final steps remain non-operational due to integration gaps.

Forecasting models now incorporate state awareness to avoid excess purchase orders for overstocked materials and align quantities with demand, reducing stock imbalances. Synchronized purchasing prevents redundant orders, while improved demand forecasting and supplier reliability address understock issues.

Purchasing processes proactively replenish understocked materials with active demand to prevent shortages. Data-driven, state-oriented interventions via Celonis swiftly correct inefficient stock states, boosting inventory responsiveness and supply chain agility.

6 Conclusion and Future Work

This study introduced State-Aware Object-Centric Process Mining (SA-OCPM), a novel extension of OCEL 2.0, to address the critical gap in modeling and analyzing object state transitions within complex processes. Revisiting our research questions, we first tackled **RQ1**. We defined object states (e.g., *Normal*, *Understock*, *Overstock*) derived from dynamic attributes using domain-specific models like the Min-Max method, integrating them into OCEL 2.0 through a state attribute $\bar{a}$ as formalized in Definition 2. This enabled precise tracking of state changes via *object state transition events* (e.g., *ST CHANGE Normal to Understock*). For **RQ2**, SA-OCPM detects and represents state transitions through new events and refines existing ones as *object state-aware events* (e.g., *Goods Receipt (Understock)*), per Definitions 2 and 3. Analysis in Celonis revealed when transitions occur (e.g., timestamps of shifts to *Understock*), why they happen (e.g., supplier delays, poor forecasting), and how they impact processes (e.g., unfulfilled sales orders). Finally, for **RQ3**, our logistics case study at a European pet retailer demonstrated SA-OCPM's effectiveness, uncovering inefficiencies like prolonged *Understock* (e.g., 210,186 cases with active demand but no purchase order) and excessive *Overstock* due to unsynchronized orders.

SA-OCPM advances process mining by embedding state dynamics directly into event logs, enhancing diagnostic granularity and enabling state-driven interventions. Future work will focus on automating state detection with machine learning to adapt to complex, non-linear state boundaries, integrating SA-OCPM with real-time systems like SAP for seamless process adjustments, and extending the framework to multi-object state interactions for deeper insights across interconnected entities.

Disclosure of Interests. The authors have no competing interests to declare that are relevant to the content of this article.

References

1. van der Aalst, W.M.P.: Process mining: data science in action. Springer (2016)
2. van der Aalst, W.M.P.: Object-centric process mining: unraveling the fabric of real processes. Mathematics **11**(12), 1–11 (2023)
3. van der Aalst, W.M.P., Berti, A.: Discovering object-centric Petri nets. Fundam. Informaticae **175**(1–4), 1–40 (2020)

4. Asana, I.M.D.P., Radhitya, M.L., Widiartha, K.K., Santika, P.P.: Inventory control using ABC and min-max analysis on retail management information system. Proc. J. Phys.: Conf. Ser. **1469** p. 012097 (2020)
5. Badakhshan, P., Wurm, B., Grisold, T., Geyer-Klingeberg, J.: Creating business value with process mining. J. Strateg. Inf. Syst. **31**(4), 101745 (2022)
6. Berti, A., van der Aalst, W.M.P.: OC-PM: analyzing object-centric event logs and process models. Int. J. Softw. Tools Technol. Transf. **25**(1), 1–17 (2023)
7. Berti, A., Jessen, U., Park, G., Rafiei, M.: Analyzing interconnected processes: using object-centric process mining to analyze procurement processes. Int. J. Data Sci, Anal (2023)
8. Berti, A., Kretzschmann, D., van der Aalst, W.M.P.: Segmentation for Optimizing Long-Lifecycle Processes in Object-Centric Process Mining (2025)
9. Brabänder, C.: Modell 4: Kontinuierliches Bestandsmanagement. Stochastisches Bestandsmanagement, pp. 75–92 (2020)
10. Celik, U., Yurtay, Y.: Improvement of assemble-to-order model processes with process mining: dynamic analysis and hybrid approaches. IEEE Access (2025)
11. De Leoni, M., van der Aalst, W.M.P.: Data-aware process mining: discovering decisions in processes using alignments. In: Proc. ACM Symp. Appl. Comput, pp. 1454–1461 (2013)
12. van Eck, M.L., Sidorova, N., van der Aalst, W.M.P.: Discovering and exploring state-based models for multi-perspective processes. In: La Rosa, M., Loos, P., Pastor, O. (eds.) BPM 2016. LNCS, vol. 9850, pp. 142–157. Springer, Cham (2016). https://doi.org/10.1007/978-3-319-45348-4_9
13. Hompes, B.F.A., van der Aalst, W.M.P.: Lifecycle-based process performance analysis. In: Panetto, H., Debruyne, C., Proper, H.A., Ardagna, C.A., Roman, D., Meersman, R. (eds.) OTM 2018. LNCS, vol. 11229, pp. 336–353. Springer, Cham (2018). https://doi.org/10.1007/978-3-030-02610-3_19
14. Kretzschmann, D., Berti, A., van der Aalst, W.M.P.: A data-driven framework for retail inventory optimization: integrating object-centric process mining and mathematical models (2025)
15. Kretzschmann, D., Park, G., Berti, A., van der Aalst, W.M.P.: Overstock problems in a purchase-to-pay process: an object-centric process mining case study. In: CAiSE Workshops, pp. 347–359. Springer (2024). https://doi.org/10.1007/978-3-031-61003-5_29
16. Li, G., de Carvalho, R.M., van der Aalst, W.M.P.: Automatic discovery of object-centric behavioral constraint models. In: BIS, pp. 43–58. Springer (2017)
17. Lu, X., Nagelkerke, M., Van De Wiel, D., Fahland, D.: Discovering interacting artifacts from ERP systems. IEEE Trans. Serv. Comput. **8**(6), 861–873 (2015)
18. López-Pintado, O., Murashko, S., Dumas, M.: Discovery and simulation of data-aware business processes. In: Proceedings of International Conference on Process Mining (ICPM), pp. 105–112. IEEE (2024)
19. ER, M., Astuti, H.M., Wardhani, I.R.K.: Material movement analysis for warehouse business process improvement with process mining: a case study. In: Bae, J., Suriadi, S., Wen, L. (eds.) AP-BPM 2015. LNBIP, vol. 219, pp. 115–127. Springer, Cham (2015). https://doi.org/10.1007/978-3-319-19509-4_9
20. Mannhardt, F.: Multi-perspective process mining. Ph.D. thesis, Eindhoven Univ. Technol. (2018)
21. Meyer, J.C., Sander, U., Wetzchewald, P.: Bestände senken, Lieferservice steigern: Ansatzpunkt Bestandsmanagement. FIR e. V. an der RWTH Aachen (2019)

22. Nadim, K., Ragab, A., Ouali, M.S.: Data-driven dynamic causality analysis of industrial systems using interpretable machine learning and process mining. J. Intell. Manuf. **34**(1), 57–83 (2023)
23. Oldenburg, F., Hoberg, K., Leopold, H.: Process mining in supply chain management: state-of-the-art, use cases and research outlook. Int. J. Prod. Res., 1–16 (2024)
24. Qafari, M.S., van der Aalst, W.: Root cause analysis in process mining using structural equation models. In: Del Río Ortega, A., Leopold, H., Santoro, F.M. (eds.) BPM 2020. LNBIP, vol. 397, pp. 155–167. Springer, Cham (2020). https://doi.org/10.1007/978-3-030-66498-5_12
25. Reinkemeyer, L.: Process mining in action. Process Min. Action Princ. Use Cases Outlook (2020)
26. Riza, M., Purba, H.H.: Mukhlisin: the implementation of economic order quantity for reducing inventory cost. Res. Logist. Prod. **8**(3), 207–216 (2018)
27. Rizqi, Z.U., Khairunisa, A.: Integration of deterministic and probabilistic inventory methods to optimize the balance between overstock and stockout. Proc. IOP Conf. Ser.: Mater. Sci. Eng. **722**, 012060 (2020)
28. Scarf, H.E., Arrow, K.J., Karlin, S.: A min-max solution of an inventory problem. Rand (1957)
29. Schuh, G., Gutzlaff, A., Cremer, S., Schoppen, M.: Understanding process mining for data-driven optimization of order processing. Procedia Manuf. **45**, 417–422 (2020)
30. Tang, J., Liu, Y., Lin, K.Y., Li, L.: Process bottlenecks identification and its root cause analysis using fusion-based clustering and knowledge graph. Adv. Eng. Inform. **55**, 101862 (2023)
31. Tempelmeier, H.: Bestandsmanagement in supply chains. BoD–Books on Demand (2005)
32. Valero-Ramon, Z., Fernandez-Llatas, C., Valdivieso, B., Traver, V.: Dynamic models supporting personalised chronic disease management through healthcare sensors with interactive process mining. Sensors **20**(18), 5330 (2020)
33. Waters, D.: Inventory control and management. Wiley (2003)

Confidentiality-Preserving Verifiable Business Processes Through Zero-Knowledge Proofs

Jannis Kiesel(✉) and Jonathan Heiss

Information Systems Engineering, Technische Universität Berlin, Berlin, Germany
{jaki,jh}@ise.tu-berlin.de

Abstract. Ensuring the integrity of business processes without disclosing confidential business information is a major challenge in inter-organizational processes. This paper introduces a zero-knowledge proof (ZKP)-based approach for the verifiable execution of business processes while preserving confidentiality. We integrate ZK virtual machines (zkVMs) into business process management engines through a comprehensive system architecture and a prototypical implementation. Our approach supports chained verifiable computations through proof compositions. On the example of product carbon footprinting, we model sequential footprinting activities and demonstrate how organizations can prove and verify the integrity of verifiable processes without exposing sensitive information. We assess different ZKP proving variants within process models for their efficiency in proving and verifying, and discuss the practical integration of ZKPs throughout the Business Process Management (BPM) lifecycle. Our experiment-driven evaluation demonstrates the automation of process verification under given confidentiality constraints.

Keywords: Zero Knowledge Proof · Business Process Management · Carbon Footprinting

1 Introduction

Inter-organizational business processes are fundamental to modern supply chains and collaborative ecosystems [10,21]. Yet they face a critical paradox: organizations require transparency to verify process integrity and build trust, while simultaneously needing to protect confidential business information from competitors and partners. This tension is particularly important in regulated domains such as carbon footprinting [2], healthcare data sharing [9], and financial compliance [24], where regulatory frameworks increasingly mandate verifiable reporting while organizations cannot afford to expose sensitive operational data, proprietary methodologies, or competitive advantages. Traditional approaches to this challenge rely on either full disclosure to intermediaries, which creates confidentiality risks and limits scalability, or manual data validity checks. The result is a fundamental trust deficit that hinders effective inter-organizational collaboration [20,22] and forces organizations to either compromise on confidentiality or accept unverifiable claims from partners.

© The Author(s), under exclusive license to Springer Nature Switzerland AG 2026
A. Gianola et al. (Eds.): EDOC 2025, LNCS 16213, pp. 119–136, 2026.
https://doi.org/10.1007/978-3-032-15140-7_7

While the challenges of integrating confidential, yet verifiable, inter-organizational processes are relevant across various domains, this paper adopts the carbon footprinting issue as a representative use case.

1.1 Running Example: Product Carbon Footprinting

Product Carbon Footprints (PCF) quantify the Greenhouse Gas (GHG) emissions associated with a specific product throughout its lifecycle, from raw material extraction to disposal (cradle-to-grave) [2]. By measuring and reporting these emissions, PCFs help manufacturers identify opportunities to reduce their environmental impact and enable consumers to make more carbon-conscious purchasing decisions. Regulatory frameworks such as the EU Supply Chain Directive,[1] the Greenwashing Directive,[2] and the Corporate Sustainability Reporting Directive (CSRD)[3] increasingly mandate reliable PCF reporting.

The GHG Protocol [2] provides standards and tools to footprint GHG emissions. It differentiates three organizational scope boundaries to attribute GHG-emitting activities:

- Scope 1 emissions are direct *internal* GHG emissions from sources controlled by an organization, such as fuel combustion of manufacturing facilities.
- Scope 2 emissions are indirect *internal* emissions from purchased electricity, steam, etc., that an organization consumes.
- Scope 3 emissions include all other indirect *external* emissions in a company's value chain, such as those from suppliers, product use, and waste disposal.

PCF standards mandate a business process activity-centric approach for calculating and tracking carbon emissions [2], which we refer to as *footprinting*. To calculate an accurate PCF, organizations must collect emissions data across a product's entire value chain, particularly for Scope 3 emissions, which account for the majority of emissions. However, suppliers cannot provide full transparency in their calculation of PCFs, as disclosing sensitive business activity information may compromise confidential business process specifications [15]. Due to the lack of transparency, suppliers must be assumed to greenwash their reported Scope 3 emissions. This hinders trusted cooperation and requires organizations to verify the reported Scope 3 emissions.

In the example shown in Fig. 1, a material pre-processing supplier provides raw material inputs to a production company. To calculate a product's PCF, the production company relies on Scope 3 data from the supplier, Scope 2 data from their electricity provider, and Scope 1 emissions from the production process.

Derived Requirements. Key footprinting principles such as *consistency* and *transparency* must be met [2]. The underlying Business Process Management system is therefore required to facilitate these encompassing principles. Therefore, the reporting enterprise's footprinting process must:

[1] https://eur-lex.europa.eu/eli/dir/2024/1760/oj/eng.
[2] https://eur-lex.europa.eu/eli/dir/2024/825/oj/eng.
[3] https://eur-lex.europa.eu/eli/dir/2022/2464/oj/eng.

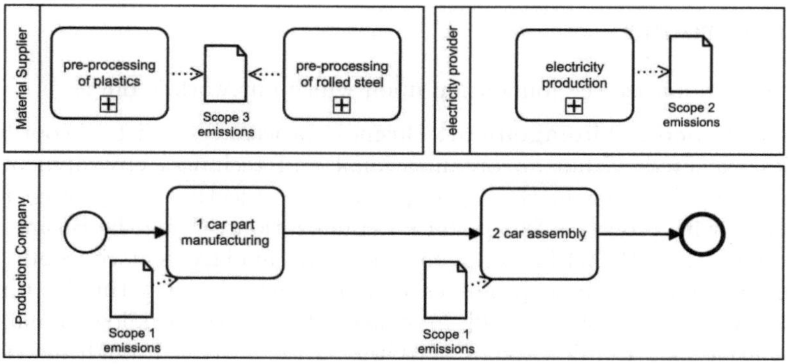

Fig. 1. Car production process example for a cradle-to-gate process derived and reduced for clarity from the example process map of [2].

1. *Validate* that the Scope 3 emission data of all process inputs were computed based on compatible footprinting standards to ensure consistency,
2. *Prove* the PCF computation *integrity* such that it can be verified to facilitate trust, and
3. Ensure that sensitive process data, such as used electricity, materials, and process specifications, remain *confidential* while making the footprinting *transparent*.

1.2 Solution Approach

Zero-knowledge proofs (ZKPs) verify the correctness of a computation without requiring access to the underlying inputs, utilizing cryptographic protocols. Recent advancements in ZKPs and related developer tools have been significant, mainly driven by blockchain applications, where ZKPs help address scalability and privacy issues. Beyond blockchains, ZKPs hold great promise for trustworthy and confidentiality-preserving inter-organizational data sharing [15]. Despite their potential, ZKPs' cryptographic complexity and enterprises' unfamiliarity with the technology pose challenges for their adoption within processes.

This paper addresses the problem of trust and confidentiality in data outputs of business processes with the example of carbon footprinting and contributes in the following ways:

- First, we outline confidentiality-preserving verifiable processes.
- Second, we present a service architecture to integrate ZKP technologies within business process engines.
- Finally, we evaluate the performance and feasibility of our implementation.

Our contributions unfold as follows: We provide background information in Sect. 2 and related work in Sect. 3. Next, we present ZKPs for confidentiality-preserving verifiable processes in Sect. 4. Afterward, we present our service architecture implementation in Sect. 5. Finally, Sect. 6 evaluates our proposed solution, and Sect. 7 concludes.

2 Background

Below, we summarize the foundation upon which our work is built.

Business Process Management: Business processes consist of coordinated activities executed within an organizational and technical environment by a single organization to achieve a specific business objective. They often involve interactions with processes from external organizations. Using the Business Process Management (BPM) lifecycle, encompassing management concepts, methods, and techniques, these processes can be efficiently structured, standardized, repeated, and automated [30]. In orchestrator-based Workflow Management Engines (WMEs), atomic process activities are executed through distributed, horizontally scalable service tasks. The WME manages the propagation of activity data, while event data, generated by application systems or business process execution platforms, is recorded in event logs. Camunda[4] is a widely used and extensible open-source WME that features a built-in orchestrator-worker architecture.

Zero-Knowledge Proofs: ZKPs describe a class of protocols that enable one party (*prover*) to convince another party (*verifier*) of the correctness of a statement without disclosing private arguments. This adds the notion of "zero knowledge." Non-interactive ZKPs furthermore allow this with a single message. While ZKPs were invented in the 80s [13], they have received immense attention in recent years for their suitability to mitigate the confidentiality and scalability limitations of blockchain technology [19,20,28]. For that, zkSNARKs, as described in [12], are particularly suitable, which allow the verification of arbitrary large computations at constant costs (succinctness). STARKs, as introduced in [1], address some limitations of zkSNARKs, removing trust assumptions from the initial setup of zkSNARKs and adding post-quantum security [7].

Zero-Knowledge Virtual Machines: STARKs serve as the foundation for *zero-knowledge virtual machines* (zkVMs), which provide developers with tools to build ZK-enabled applications without needing to understand the underlying cryptographic complexities. In contrast to application-specific circuits like e.g. ZoKrates [8], zkVMs encode a virtual machine's instruction set as a circuit [5]. ZkVMs translate programs written in common programming languages like Rust into a suitable binary format and execute it within virtual machines (VM) with zk-instructions natively supported in the VM's instruction set. Apart from the outcome of the original program, zkVMs deliver a ZKP as proof of correct execution. They provide a convenient tool for specifying code using higher-level programming languages and abstract many security and performance issues.

Risc0: In this work, we leverage Risc Zero (Risc0)[5] as an established zkVM available at the time of writing, which utilizes zkSTARKs. Risc0 is built upon the RiscV instruction set,[6], which is an open-source standard for VMs and, hence,

[4] camunda.com.
[5] risczero.com.
[6] riscv.org.

promises interoperability with many programming languages. The procedure for Risc0 can be described in the following steps [3]:

1. *Compilation*: The prover specifies a program in Rust, called the *guest program*, which is compiled into an executable format for the RISC-V instruction set. Each method in a *guest program* is compiled into an Executable and Linking Format (ELF) binary before execution begins.
2. *Execution*: The executor runs the ELF binary and records the session, which is the execution trace, i.e., a complete record of the computation containing complete snapshots of the state of the zkVM at given moments in time.
3. *Proving*: The prover checks and proves the validity of the session, outputting a *receipt*. The *receipt* serves as a succinct proof of validity for executing the application. Receipts can be passed to third parties and verified to attest to the cryptographic validity of the application's output.
4. *Verification*: The verification algorithm receives an *ImageId* as a parameter; the *ImageId* serves as a cryptographic identifier for the expected ELF binary.

3 Related Work

We consider the related work on trust-enhancing approaches for choreographies and ZKP approaches within BPM.

Blockchain platforms have primarily addressed the issue of trust and verifiable computing between organizations. Enacting collaborative business processes on permissioned blockchains was first proposed by Weber et al. [28] by translating BPMN process models to smart contracts and was extended in [11,16]. Sturm et al. [26] proposed a system that enables on-chain execution of business processes using generic smart contracts populated with specific process models. By storing the process specification directly on-chain, their approach improves transparency and trustworthiness compared to earlier solutions, such as Weber et al. [28]. However, this increased transparency comes at the cost of confidentiality, as all participants must agree on and expose a globally shared process specification, making the approach unsuitable for scenarios involving sensitive data or proprietary logic.

To preserve the confidentiality of private process data in a public blockchain environment Marangone et al. [18] adopt an Attribute-Based Encryption (ABE) approach and extend it to a Multi-Authority ABE approach [17]. While their method effectively protects sensitive data contents, it still requires disclosure of process specifications and metadata.

For concealing process states, Toldi and Kocsis [27] employ ZKPs and the ZoKrates toolkit [8] to implement "zero-knowledge workflows," in which encrypted process states derived from BPMN models are stored on-chain to enable confidential collaboration across organizations. While their approach successfully conceals private process data, it suffers from high on-chain computational costs and limited scalability, rendering it impractical for real-world deployment. Moreover, it exposes process specifications and metadata to other parties.

Building on Toldi and Kocsis, Petto et al. [23] significantly enhance efficiency and eliminate the need for process-specific smart contracts by embedding the process model as a private input within the ZKP, thereby ensuring the confidentiality of the process specification. ZKPs also find adoption in service-oriented approaches for trustworthy and privacy-preserving data exchanges across organizations in the context of collaborative business intelligence [25], IoT data preprocessing [14], cloud-native scalability [6], or chained trusted compute units [4].

Concealing sensitive data and process internals, even utilizing encryption, remains a challenge on-chain as other organizations can observe which accounts interact and how often with whom [28]. Solution approaches to this carry their own issues, such as new account addresses for each process instance hindering the possibility of creating reputable accounts [28]. To the best of our knowledge, we are the first to introduce a blockchain-less architecture that supports scalable, verifiable, and confidential process execution without exposing any process data or metadata to other parties.

4 Confidentiality Preserving Verifiable Processes

In line with the running example and derived requirements of Sect. 1.1, we introduce a confidentiality-preserving verifiable process model starting with a baseline model, and then extend it through validity and integrity.

4.1 Baseline Process

Consider a simplified footprinting process for the PCF of a car as shown in Fig. 2. The footprinting process consists of four activities. First, in 0, the Scope 3 emissions from the material supplier are validated. Then, in 1 and 2, the manufacturing emissions and assembly emissions are calculated using the internally assessed Scope 1 direct emissions and Scope 2 emissions provided by the electricity provider. Finally, in 3, the Scope 1, 2, and 3 emissions of the process are aggregated to the total PCF.

The validation in 0 faces the following problem: To validate the Scope 3 emissions of the supplier, the production company must have access to the supplier's

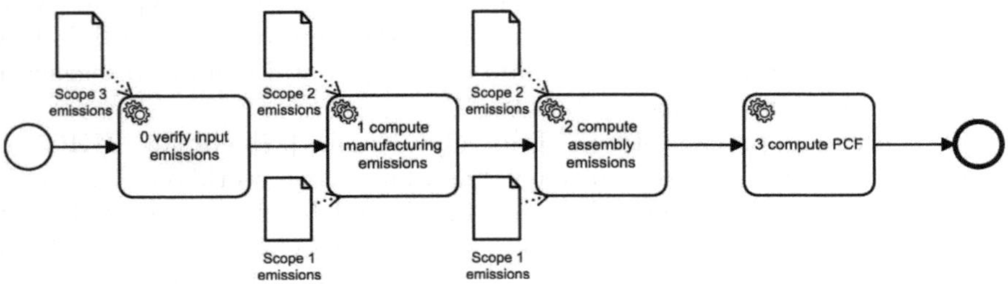

Fig. 2. Footprinting process for the car production process of Fig. 1. It resembles the composite verifiable process strategy outlined in **b**).

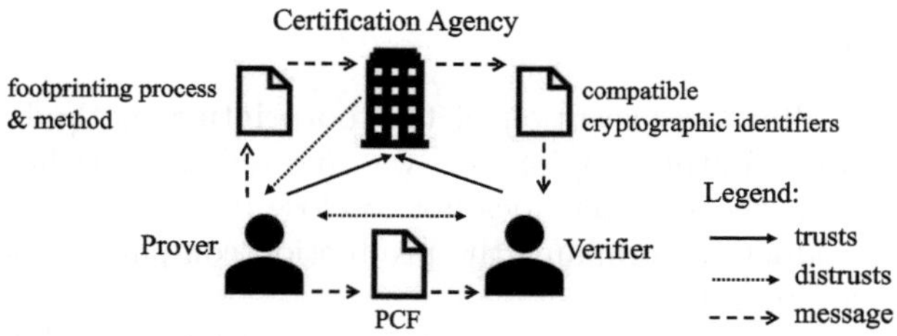

Fig. 3. Trust relationships and artifact exchange.

sensitive business activity data to validate that the footprinting was carried out according to a compatible standard and verify that the Scope 3 emissions were computed correctly. In this baseline process, verification and validation must be conducted manually by an emission footprinting expert, which increases the process's cost and decreases its performance as it cannot be fully automated. However, the supplier cannot provide confidential business information necessary for the PCF validation to the production company. In the absence of process transparency, the production company must trust in the reported Scope 3 emissions validity and computational integrity.

4.2 Adding Validity

To resolve the conflict between transparency and confidentiality, we introduce a footprinting certification agency which acts as a trusted third party among all process participants.[7] In Fig. 3, the supplying company is the *Prover* and the production company is the *Verifier*.

Before the process is enacted, the proving party discloses its footprinting process and calculation method to the certification agency, which audits the process and method. It attests conformance of the process and method with a PCF standard through a signed footprinting certificate, which is returned to the proving party. Whenever the footprinting process changes, the certification agency performs a new audit and certifies the validity of the PCF standard for the changed process. On process enactment, the proving party sends their reported Scope 3 emission data, along with the footprinting certificate, to the verifying party. The verifying party trusts the certification agency and therefore only needs to validate the compatibility of the Scope 3 emission certificate with its footprinting process.

Sharing the footprinting process with the certification agency facilitates the transparency principles of PCF standards. At the same time, the private process activities of the prover and their data remain confidential from other parties as they are not shared.

[7] Utilizing a certification agency aligns with industry standards for PCF processes as outlined in the Catena-X Product Carbon Footprint Rulebook, carbon-transparency.org/resources/catena-x-product-carbon-footprint-rulebook.

4.3 Adding Integrity

The supplier can alter the execution of the footprinting method to greenwash their PCF even if the footprinting process was audited and certified by a trusted third party. Because the supplier does not disclose its footprinting process and method to the production company, the production company must trust in the supplier's footprinting integrity.

To remove this trust assumption, we propose to utilize ZKPs for all footprinting methods that require verification by other parties. The footprinting process activities of the supplier are executed from within zkVM guest programs. Shown in Fig. 3, the footprinting process and footprinting method, in the format of a zkVM guest program, are shared with the certification agency. The certification agency generates the proving and verification keys for the guest program of the footprinting process. It provides the proving key to the prover and the verification key to the verifier.

Upon process enactment, the prover executes the footprinting guest program, proves its computational integrity using the proving key, and sends the proof, which includes the Scope 3 emissions, to the verifier. The ZKP guarantees the integrity of the computation of the Scope 3 emission data. The verifier, in activity 0 of Fig. 2, verifies the ZKP using the verification key. Because the verifier trusts in the footprinting validation of the certification agency, verifying the ZKP using the certified verification key also validates that the footprinting process is consistent with the PCF standard.

In turn, the production company must also prove the PCF of the assembled car to the customer, and cannot disclose confidential business information. Therefore, for the remaining footprinting process, the production company assumes the role of the prover and executes all its footprinting activities within zkVM guest programs, which are also certified by the certification agency. In 1 and 2, the prover verifies the Scope 2 emissions from the electricity provider and computes and proves the Scope 1 emissions of the production activities. Finally, in 3, the prover aggregates all footprinted emissions from previous footprinting activities and creates a ZKP that contains the total PCF of the car.

5 Integrating ZkVMs Into Workflow Management Engines

We propose extending WMEs with zkVM-enhanced tasks to perform verifiable computations of activities.

5.1 System Architecture

Our architecture comprises the prover and verifier with their respective WMEs and dedicated modular proving and verification task workers as shown in Fig. 4.[8]

[8] Our architecture implementation artifact within the Camunda Platform is open-source available here: github.com/curiousjaki/verifiable-processes-demo.

A proving task worker contains the proving zkVM host and the zkVM guest program. In contrast, the verification task worker consists only of a verification zkVM host with the verification keys of the trusted certification agency. The WME orchestrates the verifiable process, handles errors and logs, and propagates the resulting ZKPs between the proving and verification activities as process variables. Using the service task approach, our proposal leverages horizontal scaling orchestrated by the WME or an external load balancer. Generally, utilizing zkVMs within business processes can be distinguished into two phases: setup and operation.

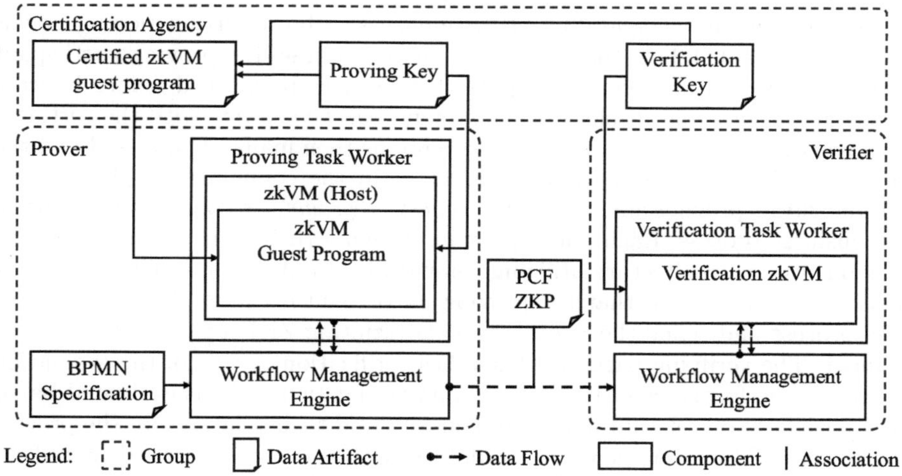

Fig. 4. Architecture for extending WMEs with zkVM task workers.

Setup: In the setup phase, the certification agency audits and certifies the *provers'* guest program and generates the proving and verification keys. The verification key is shared with the verifier.

Operation: Upon executing a verifiable process, the *provers'* WME calls the zkVM host to run the certified guest program in a guest zkVM. The zkVM host provides the private and public data inputs to the guest program. In the context of our running example, the footprinting guest program receives the private business data, such as resource amounts and public emission factor data. The guest program then returns the PCF as part of the public data output of the guest program. The zkVM host then creates a computational integrity proof of the guest program using the proving key, resulting in a ZKP that includes the public data output of the guest program. The ZKP size and proving runtime are determined by the complexity of the guest program and the size of the data input, and are constrained by the WME and its variable data store size. Upon successful proof generation, the ZKP is returned to the WME and then propagated to the verifying party. The *verifiers'* WME then sends the ZKP to a verification task worker. The verification zkVM determines the correct verification key, verifies the presented ZKP, and extracts the public data output.

5.2 BPM Lifecycle

Integrating ZKPs within existing BPM practices allows the utilization of the managerial aspects of the BPM lifecycle for ZKP management. In the following, we map ZKP procedures to BPM lifecycle phases outlined around the lifecycle of Weske [29] with its Design & Analysis, Configuration, Enactment, and Evaluation phases. The proving and verifying participants align their verifiable process *design* and *configuration* lifecycle phases with the certification agency as described in Sect. 4.2. In the design and analysis phase, the proving participant identifies external process data inputs that need to be verified before internal processing occurs and discloses their proving *guest programs* with the certification agency. The validity of the *guest program* is then manually assessed and the proving and verification keys are generated. In the configuration phase, task-specific zkVM proving and verification *guest programs* are configured as part of the business process. Each participant implements their own proving and verification system architecture utilizing compatible zkVM systems. The enactment phase is extended such that the proving participant executes the defined business process and sends the *guest programs* resulting ZKP to the verifying participant. The verifying participant handles verification errors. In the evaluation phase, the performance of the proving and verification tasks is evaluated based on their effects on relevant quality dimensions and their relevance to the process control flow. Moreover, new private data inputs and outputs are identified for the following iteration of the BPM lifecycle.

6 Evaluation

We quantify the computational overhead of integrating zkVMs in processes through an experiment, evaluate the confidentiality and transparency requirements of Sect. 1.1 qualitatively, and discuss threats and validity limitations.

6.1 Modeling Alternatives for Verifiable Processes

We investigate three alternatives to the carbon footprinting process approaches visualized in Fig. 2 and Fig. 5:

a) **Single-step proving:** All verifiable processing steps are carried out within one verifiable activity. In our running example, the single activity verifies Scope 3 and Scope 2 emissions, computes the Scope 1 emissions of all business activities, and proves the computational integrity of its footprinting in a single ZKP with its public PCF output.

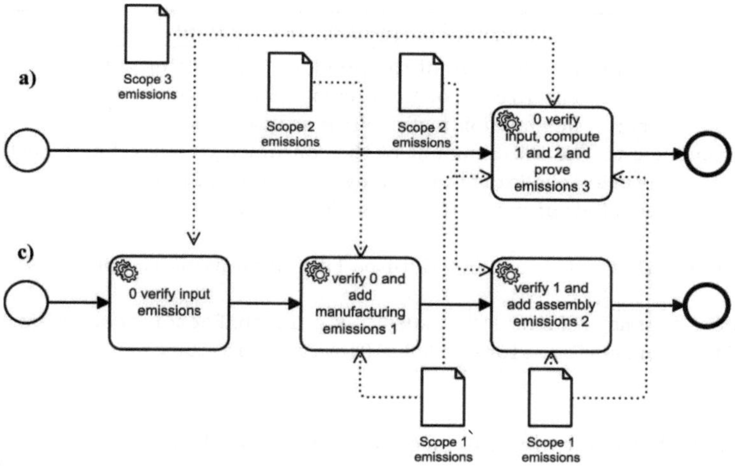

Fig. 5. Verifiable process modeling alternatives **a)** single-step and **c)** chained for the PCF example process of Fig. 1.

b) **Composed proving:** A verifiable activity proves a single business activity, with a final activity composing all prior proofs. This approach is the example footprinting process outlined in Fig. 2. This composing approach introduces the notion of process-centricity as the different footprinting activities prove individual business activities. The process notion enables the assessment of carbon footprints on a per-activity basis, allowing for the analysis of ZKP performance through a process mining lens.

c) **Chained proving:** Altering the composed approach, individual verifiable activities can be chained, where each verifiable activity verifies the prior proof and aggregates the prior's public data output with its computation result. In our example, the verification activity 0 generates a proof containing the Scope 3 emissions. The footprinting activity 1 verifies the proof of activity 0, and computes its business activity footprint and aggregates it with the output of the proof of 0. Then, 2 verifies the proof of 1, computes its business activity, and aggregates it with the public data output of 1 and so on, omitting the need for a final aggregation step. This approach is suitable for processes that may not entirely complete or exit early due to errors, as a cumulative PCF of the enacted activities is continuously present.

6.2 Verifiable Carbon Footprinting Guest Program

In our chained footprinting example of Fig. 5, each footprinting activity computes an activity's Scope 1 emissions in a dedicated zkVM *guest program* as illustrated in Algorithm 1. The proving method processes private data such as the emission factors and resource amounts. As the *guest program* is executed

Algorithm 1. Simplified Carbon Footprinting zkVM Guest Program

```
▷ previousImageId: The ImageId of the previous footprinting activity
▷ previousReceipt: The Receipt of the previous footprinting activity
▷ emissionFactor: The emission factor of the utilized resource
▷ resourceAmount: The total amount of the consumed resource for the activity
if VERIFY_ZKP(previousVerificationKey, previousZKP) then
   totalPreviousEmissions ← previousZKP.totalEmissions
else
     return False                 ▷ Returns False if verifying the previous ZKP fails.
end if
currentEmissions ← COMPUTE_EMISSIONS(emissionFactor, resourceAmount)
     return currentEmissions + totalPreviousEmissions
```

within a zkVM, its outputs are encoded within a ZKP generated by the zkVM host. The ZKP includes the public PCF computation outputs required by the footprinting standard and ensures the integrity of the program's computation.

With our *chained* approach, we designate the outputs of prior computations as inputs of successive proving and verification activities. The *chaining* is facilitated within a respective *guest program* through proof composition, where the ZKP of a previous activity is provided to the zkVM guest as private data input. The *guest program* thereupon verifies the ZKP within the zkVM host and encodes the verification success within its own ZKP. The resulting outputs include the cumulative emissions of the entire process instance and the specific emissions of the current activity. Thus, the last footprinting activity output becomes the PCF data output of the footprinting process, which is then used as input for successive footprinting processes of verifying parties, as Scope 3 emission data. The *composed* approach utilizes the same composition approach but in a dedicated final composition *guest program*. The proof composition of the *chained* and *composed* approach enables the efficient verification of the entire footprinting process. A verifying party merely needs to verify the ZKP of the last footprinting activity to ensure the validity and computational integrity of the prover's footprinting process.

6.3 Quantitative Evaluation

We have implemented all the approaches presented in Sect. 6.1 to evaluate their practical feasibility on the example of Risc0 in the popular Camunda WME.[9] We chose Risc0 for its mature state, open-source availability, and rich development support, and opted for Camunda for its wide adoption, extensibility, and inherent orchestrator-worker architecture. For Risc0 zkVMs, the proving and verification keys are the same, referred to as *ImageId.*

We have generated processes of start and end events and activities connected with message flows, omitting gateways and other BPMN elements. In our experiment, we created processes with one to thirty activities to measure how process

[9] camunda.com.

length impacts footprinting proving performance. Our footprinting *guest program* multiplies a resource input with an emission factor, generating a carbon footprint, which is then aggregated with a previously calculated PCF as outlined in Algorithm 1. All experiments were conducted on an 8-core Apple M3 processor with 16GB of LPDDR5 memory, utilizing a Risc0 zkVM version 1.2.5.

For the *single step* approach, only one proving activity is carried out with varying resource input variables proportional to the number of activities within the process. Our results of Table 1 show that we could not observe the effect of the number of variables passed into the *guest program* on the proof size and proving runtime overhead, suggesting near-constant costs for each process instance.

In the *composite* approach, the proving activities are followed by one final composing activity, which is not required in the *chained* approach as it composes the previous receipt in each proving activity. Table 1 shows that the generated receipts and proving runtime overheads of the *composite* and *chained* approach increase linearly with the number of activities verified within the process. The *composite* approach yields a larger proof size due to our recursive implementation of the *composite* proof aggregation method. Other composition methods yield proof sizes comparable with the *chained* approach but require specific composition *guest programs* per number of activities of a given process.

As shown in Fig. 6, the proving overhead of the *chained* approach per activity is higher than the composite and single-step approaches, caused by the proof chaining in each activity. However, it is more efficient on a process level than the *composite* approach as shown in Table 1. The overhead of the final composition step in the *composed* approach depends on the number of previous receipts to verify and compose, which decreases the overall process instance performance. It is less efficient than the *chained* approach at three activities and doubles the overhead of the *chained* approach at 30 activities.

For a carbon footprinting process involving 30 business activities without proof generation, the execution time is 0.06 s for the single-step approach, 1.90 s for the composed approach, and 2.19 s for the chained approach. With proof generation, the process instance runtimes are much larger. In the composed

Table 1. Process proving overhead in sec and proof size in MB.

No. of Activities	Single Step		Composite		Chained	
	sec	MB	sec	MB	sec	MB
1	6.25	0.24	6.71	0.24	6.63	0.24
5	6.18	0.24	51.42	2.19	33.57	1.22
8	6.66	0.24	93.37	**3.65**	54.22	1.95
9	7.02	0.24	106.86	**4.13**	60.93	2.19
10	6.4	0.24	120.51	4.62	67.61	2.43
15	6.51	0.24	203.24	7.05	102.13	3.65
16	6.49	0.24	220.12	7.54	109.02	**3.89**
17	6.7	0.24	239.71	8.03	115.99	**4.13**
20	6.48	0.24	304.87	9.48	138.27	4.86
25	6.37	0.24	384.15	11.92	174.45	6.08
30	6.87	0.24	464.04	14.35	211.52	7.3

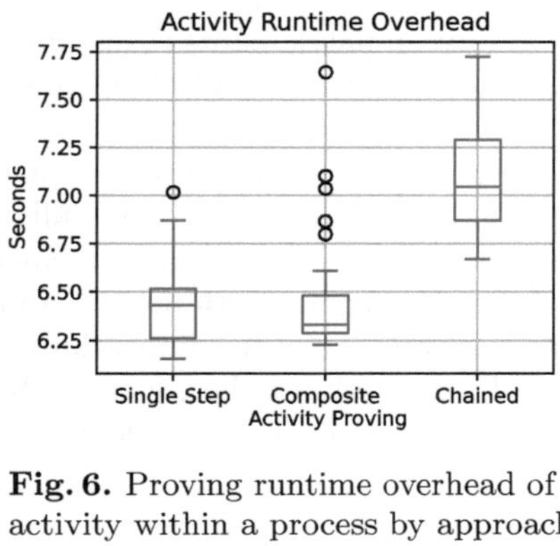

Fig. 6. Proving runtime overhead of an activity within a process by approach.

approach for example, the total process runtime was 465.94 s and the proof generation accounted for 99.6% of the total runtime, highlighting the proving overhead of the zkVM. In contrast, the verification duration of receipts increases linearly with the proof size, rather than with the approach, ranging from 0.04 s for a small proof of a process involving one activity to 0.73 s for verifying a composite proof of 30 activities.

Our results show that the different approaches entail significant performance and feasibility constraints. Messaging standards such as gRPC and WMEs such as Camunda have message and variable size limitations of 4 MB.[10] This constraint prevents the propagation of proofs by WMEs for processes with a larger number of activities. In our implementation with Risc0, we reached this limit in our *composite* and *chained* approaches at 8 and 16 activities, respectively.

6.4 Qualitative Evaluation

As with blockchain approaches, where enterprises must agree on a blockchain platform, our ZKP approach requires enterprises to agree on the zkVM vendor and version. In contrast to blockchain, computation remains within each participant's organizational boundaries, allowing participants with different confidentiality concerns to collaborate without an all-in commitment.

Our different PCF approaches show tradeoffs in their performance and applicability to real-world scenarios. The *single step* approach benefits from near-constant proving runtime overheads and proof sizes and, therefore, the highest integrability in standard WMEs. However, it only creates a verifiable computation at the end of a process, thereby prohibiting process management tools from managing the footprinting. The *composite* approach performs worse than the *chained* approach for proof size and instance duration. Both enable process-centric footprinting. The chained approach additionally ensures that the footprinting is *consistent* throughout at runtime, leveraging the integrity guarantees of zkVMs. Despite the proving and composition overheads, we argue that the *single-step* and *chained* approaches are viable for process-centric verifiable PCF between organizations due to their guarantees of confidentiality and efficient verifiability. Alternative PCF approaches require full processing transparency between participants to ensure validity, or involve time-consuming manual spot-checking, and do not allow for complete verification of PCF computation integrity.

While our evaluation focuses on carbon footprinting as a representative use case, the proposed approach is equally applicable to other regulated domains such as health data sharing and financial compliance, thanks to our system's adaptability to varying data models and validity requirements.

This work entails several limitations. First, our evaluation process is relatively simple, which may limit the generalizability of the results to more complex process models. Furthermore, we do not evaluate the usability or organizational

[10] docs.camunda.io/docs/components/concepts/variables/#variable-size-limitation.

adaptability of our proposed implementation, both of which are crucial for practical adoption. Specifically, our static zkVM setup does not account for dynamic process changes that may occur in practice.

6.5 Degree of Confidentiality

Similar to Petto et al. [23], our proposed contributions eliminate the need to disclose process specifications to all involved participants, as seen in trust enhancing approaches for processes in related work [27,28]. With our proposed setup, only the ZKP verification key for the last verifiable activity needs to be revealed to verifying participants. All other business process properties, the *guest program*, and verifiable process must only be disclosed to the certification agency which ensures the process confidentiality. The process specification, metadata, and private data inputs are preserved from other participants. This ensures the required *integrity* and *transparency* attributes for the confidential process.

7 Conclusion and Future Work

This paper uses the example of verifiable carbon footprinting to present zkVMs as a service technology within business processes to enable trustworthy, verifiable computations while preserving private data and process confidentiality in a novel, blockchain-less approach. We evaluate three approaches to verifiable processes on the example of carbon footprinting processes. Our results demonstrate that our proposed architecture ensures the integrity and confidentiality of process executions at the expense of increased processing overheads. Dedicated footprinting activities ensure the required transparency for PCFs, while chained ZKPs provide the necessary degree of data confidentiality and verifiability. Our prototypical implementation demonstrates the fundamental capability of proving and verification within WMEs. It reveals practical integration challenges, particularly for chained composite proofs due to large proof sizes.

For future work, we envision advancements that strengthen the approach's validity through verifiable data authenticity and a platform to facilitate a more holistic setup of ZKP technology among participants. We envision extending our work to explore the implications of our proposal on inter-organizational process management practices.

Additionally, we anticipate integrating hierarchical process models and enabling conditional routing and dynamic process adaptations through verifiable path validations. Complementary to this, the role of process control flow and process structure on the suitability of the presented modeling alternatives may be further explored. Moreover, this work could be extended by utilizing zkVMs as a vessel to enable verifiable executions of choreographies. Broader, we expect that ZKPs within BPM enable more verifiable process conformance for auditing and analysis purposes.

Disclosure of Interests. The authors have no competing interests to declare that are relevant to the content of this article.

References

1. Ben-Sasson, E., Bentov, I., Horesh, Y., Riabzev, M.: Scalable, transparent, and post-quantum secure computational integrity. Cryptology ePrint Archive, Paper 2018/046 (2018). https://eprint.iacr.org/2018/046
2. Bhatia, P., Cummis, C., Brown, A., et al.: Product Standard. GHG Protocol (2011). https://ghgprotocol.org/product-standard
3. Bruestle, J., Gafni, P.: RISC Zero zkVM: Scalable, Transparent Arguments of RISC-V Integrity (2023). https://dev.risczero.com/proof-system-in-detail.pdf
4. Castillo, F., Heiss, J., Werner, S., Tai, S.: Trusted compute units: a framework for chained verifiable computations. In: 2025 IEEE International Conference on Blockchain and Cryptocurrency (ICBC), pp. 1–9 (2025). https://doi.org/10.1109/ICBC64466.2025.11114627
5. Dokchitser, T., Bulkin, A.: Zero knowledge virtual machine step by step. Cryptology ePrint Archive, Paper 2023/1032 (2023). https://eprint.iacr.org/2023/1032
6. Domenech, A.A., Heiss, J., Tai, S.: Servicifying zk-snarks execution for verifiable off-chain computations. In: 2024 IEEE International Conference on Blockchain and Cryptocurrency (ICBC), pp. 670–671 (2024)
7. Eberhardt, J., Heiss, J.: Off-chaining models and approaches to off-chain computations. In: Proceedings of the 2nd Workshop on Scalable and Resilient Infrastructures for Distributed Ledgers, pp. 7–12 (2018). https://doi.org/10.1145/3284764.3284766
8. Eberhardt, J., Tai, S.: ZoKrates - Scalable Privacy-Preserving Off-Chain Computations. In: 2018 IEEE International Conference on Blockchain (2018). https://doi.org/10.1109/Cybermatics_2018.2018.00199
9. Fdhila, W., Stifter, N., Judmayer, A.: Challenges and Opportunities of Blockchain for Auditable Processes in the Healthcare Sector. In: Business Process Management: Blockchain, Robotic Process Automation, and Central and Eastern Europe Forum, pp. 68–83. Springer International Publishing, Cham (2022). https://doi.org/10.1007/978-3-031-16168-1_5
10. Flynn, B.B., Huo, B., Zhao, X.: The impact of supply chain integration on performance: a contingency and configuration approach. J. Operat. Manag. **28**(1) (2010). https://doi.org/10.1016/j.jom.2009.06.001
11. García-Bañuelos, L., Ponomarev, A., Dumas, M., Weber, I.: Optimized execution of business processes on blockchain. In: Carmona, J., Engels, G., Kumar, A. (eds.) BPM 2017. LNCS, vol. 10445, pp. 130–146. Springer, Cham (2017). https://doi.org/10.1007/978-3-319-65000-5_8
12. Gennaro, R., Gentry, C., Parno, B., Raykova, M.: Quadratic span programs and succinct NIZKs without PCPs. In: Johansson, T., Nguyen, P.Q. (eds.) EUROCRYPT 2013. LNCS, vol. 7881, pp. 626–645. Springer, Heidelberg (2013). https://doi.org/10.1007/978-3-642-38348-9_37
13. Goldwasser, S., Micali, S., Rackoff, C.: The knowledge complexity of interactive proof-systems. In: Proceedings of the seventeenth annual ACM Symposium on Theory of Computing, STOC 1985. Association for Computing Machinery, NY (1985). https://doi.org/10.1145/22145.22178
14. Heiss, J., Busse, A., Tai, S.: Trustworthy pre-processing of sensor data in data on-chaining workflows for blockchain-based IoT applications. In: Hacid, H., Kao, O., Mecella, M., Moha, N., Paik, H. (eds.) ICSOC 2021. LNCS, vol. 13121, pp. 133–149. Springer, Cham (2021). https://doi.org/10.1007/978-3-030-91431-8_9

15. Heiss, J., Oegel, T., Shakeri, M., Tai, S.: Verifiable carbon accounting in supply chains. IEEE Trans. Serv. Comput. (2023). https://doi.org/10.1109/TSC.2023.3332831
16. López-Pintado, O., García-Bañuelos, L., Dumas, M., Weber, I.: Caterpillar: A Blockchain-Based Business Process Management System (2017)
17. Marangone, E., Di Ciccio, C., Friolo, D., et al.: MARTSIA: enabling data confidentiality for blockchain-based process execution. In: Proper, H.A., et al. (eds.) Enterprise Design, Operations, and Computing, pp. 58–76. Springer Nature Switzerland, Cham (2024). https://doi.org/10.1007/978-3-031-46587-1_4
18. Marangone, E., Di Ciccio, C., Weber, I.: Fine-grained data access control for collaborative process execution on blockchain. In: Marrella, A., et al. (eds.) Business Process Management: Blockchain, Robotic Process Automation, and Central and Eastern Europe Forum, pp. 51–67. Springer International Publishing, Cham (2022). https://doi.org/10.1007/978-3-031-16168-1_4
19. Mendling, J., Weber, I., Aalst, W.V.D., et al.: Blockchains for Business Process Management - Challenges and Opportunities. ACM Trans. Manag. Inform. Syst. **9**(1) (2018). https://doi.org/10.1145/3183367
20. Müller, M., Ostern, N., Rosemann, M.: Silver bullet for all trust issues? blockchain-based trust patterns for collaborative business processes. In: Asatiani, A., et al. (eds.) BPM 2020. LNBIP, vol. 393, pp. 3–18. Springer, Cham (2020). https://doi.org/10.1007/978-3-030-58779-6_1
21. Narayanan, S., Jayaraman, V., Luo, Y., Swaminathan, J.M.: The antecedents of process integration in business process outsourcing and its effect on firm performance. J. Operat. Manag. **29**(1) (2011). https://doi.org/10.1016/j.jom.2010.05.001
22. Panayides, P.M., Venus Lun, Y.H.: The impact of trust on innovativeness and supply chain performance. Inter. J. Prod. Econ. **122**(1) (2009). https://doi.org/10.1016/j.ijpe.2008.12.025
23. Petto, O., Preindl, T., Kjäer, M.: Interpreted and Confidential Execution of Process Choreographies on a Blockchain. In: Di Ciccio, C., et al. (eds.) Business Process Management: Blockchain, Robotic Process Automation, Central and Eastern European, Educators and Industry Forum. pp. 40–54. Springer Nature Switzerland, Cham (2024). https://doi.org/10.1007/978-3-031-70445-1_3
24. Pisoni, G., Kherbouche, M., Molnár, B.: Blockchain-based business process management (BPM) for Finance: the case of loan-application. In: Prieto, J., et al. (eds.) Blockchain and Applications, 4th International Congress, pp. 249–258. Springer International Publishing, Cham (2023). https://doi.org/10.1007/978-3-031-21229-1_23
25. Quattrocchi, G., Plebani, P.: Trustworthy Collaborative Business Intelligence Using Zero-Knowledge Proofs and Blockchains. In: Islam, S., Sturm, A. (eds.) Intelligent Information Systems. Springer Nature Switzerland, Cham (2024). https://doi.org/10.1007/978-3-031-61000-4_4
26. Sturm, C., Szalanczi, J., Schönig, S., Jablonski, S.: A lean architecture for blockchain based decentralized process execution. In: Daniel, F., Sheng, Q.Z., Motahari, H. (eds.) BPM 2018. LNBIP, vol. 342, pp. 361–373. Springer, Cham (2019). https://doi.org/10.1007/978-3-030-11641-5_29
27. Toldi, B., Kocsis, I.: Blockchain-Based, Confidentiality-Preserving Orchestration of Collaborative Workflows (2023). https://doi.org/10.48550/ARXIV.2303.10500

28. Weber, I., Xu, X., Riveret, R., Governatori, G., Ponomarev, A., Mendling, J.: Untrusted business process monitoring and execution using blockchain. In: La Rosa, M., Loos, P., Pastor, O. (eds.) BPM 2016. LNCS, vol. 9850, pp. 329–347. Springer, Cham (2016). https://doi.org/10.1007/978-3-319-45348-4_19
29. Weske, M.: Business Process Management Architectures. In: Business Process Management, pp. 333–371. Springer, Heidelberg (2012). https://doi.org/10.1007/978-3-642-28616-2_7
30. Weske, M.: Business Process Management: Concepts, Languages, Architectures. Springer, 3rd ed. 2019 edn. (2019). https://doi.org/10.1007/978-3-662-69518-0

Business Processes and Decision-Making

GymPN: A Library for Decision-Making in Process Management Systems

Riccardo Lo Bianco[1,2](✉), Remco Dijkman[1,2], and Willem van Jaarsveld[1,2]

[1] Eindhoven University of Technology, Eindhoven, The Netherlands
{r.lo.bianco,r.m.dijkman,w.l.v.jaarsveld}@tue.nl
[2] Eindhoven Artificial Intelligence Systems Institute, Eindhoven, The Netherlands

Abstract. Process management systems support key decisions about the way work is allocated in organizations. This includes decisions on which task to perform next, when to execute the task, and who to assign the task to. Suitable software tools are required to support these decisions in a way that is optimal for the organization. This paper presents a software library, called GymPN, that supports optimal decision-making in business processes using Deep Reinforcement Learning. GymPN builds on previous work that supports task assignment in business processes, introducing two key novelties: support for partial process observability and the ability to model multiple decisions in a business process. These novel elements address fundamental limitations of previous work and thus enable the representation of more realistic process decisions. We evaluate the library on eight typical business process decision-making problem patterns, showing that GymPN allows for easy modeling of the desired problems, as well as learning optimal decision policies.

Keywords: Process Models · Decision Making · Reinforcement Learning · Process Management Systems · Petri Nets · Graph Neural Networks

1 Introduction

Process management systems play a crucial role in supporting organizational decision-making, particularly in determining which task to perform next, when to perform it, and who should perform it. Traditionally, such decisions have been guided by simple heuristics [3,11]. However, these heuristics often fail to capture the complexity and variability of real-world business processes [18].

In recent years, Deep Reinforcement Learning (DRL) has emerged as an alternative to heuristics and is a promising tool to support organizational decision-making [17]. In particular, the use of DRL to optimally assign resources to activities has been an active area of investigation [20]. Yet, DRL solutions are typically tailored to specific problem formulations, making them difficult to generalize or adapt to new decision-making problems [6]. To address this challenge, the Action-Evolution Petri Net (A-E PN) framework was introduced as an approach to modeling organizational decision-making problems and solving them with DRL [13]. The original A-E PN framework was later extended with Attributed

© The Author(s), under exclusive license to Springer Nature Switzerland AG 2026
A. Gianola et al. (Eds.): EDOC 2025, LNCS 16213, pp. 139–155, 2026.
https://doi.org/10.1007/978-3-032-15140-7_8

A-E PN [14], introducing the use of Graph Neural Networks (GNNs) to learn policies in more complex settings. Despite these advancements, two key assumptions remained. First, the framework assumes that all information about the state of the process can be used to make a decision. This assumption is often unrealistic, as in many cases only a fraction of the process variables are visible to the decision-making algorithm [1]. Second, the framework enables modeling only one type of decision in a business process at a time. However, this limits the expressive power of the framework, because often multiple decisions need to be made in a single business process [9]. To overcome these limitations, this paper presents GymPN, a Python-based software library that implements and extends the A-E PN framework. GymPN introduces two main novelties: (1) support for modeling partial observability of process state, and (2) support for modeling multiple decision types within a single business process. These novel elements allow for a realistic and flexible modeling of business process management problems while retaining the ability to learn optimal decision policies through DRL. Also, since it is released as a Python library, it is easy to install and use. GymPN is built on top of the SimPN library [5], extending its core functionalities to support the new A-E PN elements, including the distinction between action and evolution transitions, a customizable reward structure, and utilities for training and evaluating DRL algorithms as well as heuristics. The library encapsulates the entire DRL pipeline, allowing users to define new problems and train agents with minimal configuration, thereby facilitating the discovery and analysis of optimal decision policies across a wide range of business process scenarios. The library is evaluated by applying it to eight typical organizational decision-making problems, showing that it can learn how to solve these problems in an optimal way.

Against this background, the remainder of this work is structured as follows: Sect. 2 discusses related DRL frameworks and libraries for organizational decision-making; Sect. 3 presents the main theoretical background of the A-E PN framework; Sect. 4 presents the main novelties that are introduced in GymPN based on the A-E PN framework; Sect. 6 provides a set of typical organizational decision-making problems, showing how GymPN is capable of learning optimal assignment policies in every problem instance; Sect. 5 provides a basic overview of GymPN's main features from a software perspective; Sect. 6 presents eight typical business process decision-making problems and shows that GymPN allows the learning of optimal solutions to these problems; Sect. 7 presents the conclusions, reflecting on the current limitations and future research steps.

2 Related Work

The main objective of GymPN is to provide users with an easy way to model and solve business process decision-making problems using DRL. Inspired by the variety of successful DRL-based approaches [15,16,20], GymPN facilitates learning and testing business process decision-making policies, using the Proximal Policy Optimization (PPO) algorithm with minimal technical overhead. In particular, the library draws from the theory of A-E Petri nets proposed in [13] and extended in [14]. By combining a Petri net simulation environment with DRL decision-making capabilities, this work is related to [12], which adopts a similar technique with the specific objective of solving job shop scheduling problems. By contrast, GymPN focuses on business process decision-making problems. To facilitate modeling and solving such problems, GymPN integrates simulation capabilities with the decision-making capabilities of general sequential decision-making libraries. In Table 1, we compare GymPN with several popular academic frameworks designed for sequential decision-making. Each framework is evaluated across several dimensions. The *Framework* column lists the name of the package, while *Algorithms* indicates the types of decision-making methods supported, such as deep reinforcement learning (DRL), heuristics, or exact solvers. *Ease of Use* and *Ease of Modelling* provide qualitative assessments of how user-friendly the framework is and how easily users can define and simulate decision-making environments. The *Agent Type* column specifies whether the framework supports single-agent, multi-agent, or both types of scenarios. *Multi-Action* denotes whether agents can perform multiple actions simultaneously, which is essential for modeling complex business processes. Finally, *Partial Obs.* indicates whether the framework supports partially observable environments, where the agent has limited visibility of the system state.

Table 1. Comparison of Business Process Optimization Frameworks.

Framework	Algorithms	Ease of Use	Ease of Modelling	Agent Type	Multi-Action	Partial Obs.
Gymnasium [22]	DRL	High	Low	Both	Yes	Yes
or-gym [10]	DRL	High	Low	Single	No	Yes
pyknow [8]	Heuristics	Medium	Medium	Single	No	No
POMDPs.jl [7]	Exact, Heuristics, DRL	Medium	Medium	Both	No	Yes
pyomo [4]	Exact, Heuristics	Medium	Medium	Both	No	No
DynaPlex [2]	DRL, Heuristics	High	Low	Single	No	Yes
GymPN	DRL, Heuristics	High	High	Single	Yes	Yes

Compared to the basic Gymnasium (which is used internally in GymPN), our library provides a clear set of primitives that greatly simplify the modeling of business process decision-making problems. These primitives include A-E Petri net modeling capabilities, but also popular higher-level modeling languages, such as the Business Process Model and Notation (BPMN) [19]. Moreover, in GymPN there is no need to specify the state space nor the action space, which greatly reduces the modeling effort. Compared to OR-Gym, which is essentially a collection of Gymnasium environments for operations research, GymPN offers higher flexibility in the modeling phase, while still allowing for easy training and testing of DRL policies. POMDP.jl is suitable for expressing partially observable MDPs but its primitives are only adequate for simple action types. DynaPlex, on the other hand, provides simple training and testing functions for DRL, as well as high flexibility in the types of processes that can be modeled, but modeling new environments is challenging due to the low-level coding primitives. Other packages like pyknow and pyomo allow modeling only fully observable processes, and they do not support DRL policies.

3 Preliminaries

As GymPN supports modeling and simulation of business process decision-making problems based on A-E Petri net theory, this section describes the main elements of the (attributed) A-E PN framework, including the mechanism used to extract observations from the environment for a DRL agent. For brevity, we focus on the elements that are necessary to formalize the novel elements introduced in GymPN. For a complete discussion on A-E PN, the interested reader is referred to the original publications [13,14].

The (attributed) Action-Evolution Petri net is defined as follows.

Definition 1 (Attributed Action-Evolution Petri Net). *Let* $\mathcal{T} = \{'A','E'\}$ *be a finite set of tags representing actions and evolutions, and* $S : \mathcal{T} \rightarrow \mathcal{T}$ *a network tag update function. An Action-Evolution Petri Net (A-E PN) is as a tuple* $AEPN = (A, \mathcal{E}, P, T, F, C, G, E, I, L, l_0, \mathcal{R}, \rho_0, \mathcal{A})$*, where:*

- A *is a finite set of types called attributes.*
- $\mathcal{E}$ *is a finite set of types called color sets.*
- P *is a finite set of places.*
- T *is a finite set of transitions.*
- $F \subseteq P \times T \cup T \times P$ *is a finite set of arcs.*
- $C : P \rightarrow \mathcal{E}$ *is a color function that maps each place* p *into a set of possible token colors.*
- G *is a guard function that expresses, for each transition, the condition necessary to enable that transition.*
- E *is an arc expression function that expresses, for each arc, what type of tokens should be flow in the arc.*
- I *is an initialization function which determines the network's initial marking.*
- $L : T \rightarrow \mathcal{T}$ *is a transition tag function that maps each transition* t *to a single tag. Only transitions with the same tag as the network can fire at any point in time.*
- $l_0 \in \mathcal{T}$ *is a singleton containing the network's initial tag, usually equal to* E*.*
- $\mathcal{R} : T \rightarrow (f : \mathbb{R})$ *associates every transition with a reward function.*
- $\rho_0 \in \mathbb{R}$ *is the initial network reward, usually equal to* 0*.*
- $\mathcal{A}$ *is an attribute function that maps each place* p *into a set of attributes. Each token on* p *must have a color that is composed of the token's time and a value for each of the attributes in* $\mathcal{A}(p)$*.*

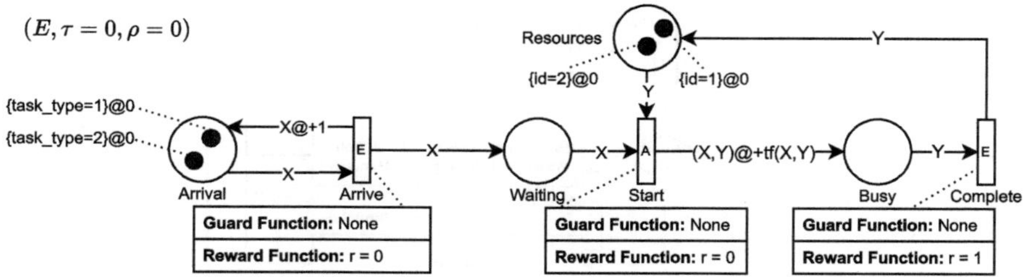

Fig. 1. A task assignment problem expressed in A-E PN notation.

In this work, we refer to the types and placement of tokens in the network (plus the network tag, the clock, and the total reward) with the term *marking*.

As an example, let us consider the A-E PN in Fig. 1, representing a task assignment problem with cases composed of a single activity and two available resources.

In Fig. 1, two tokens are used to represent cases that enter the system (two for each timestep). Two tokens represent resources that need to be assigned to the cases, and different assignments take different times to complete according to the function $tf(x, y)$, defined as:

$$tf(X,Y) = \begin{cases} 1 & \text{if } X.\text{task\_type} = Y.\text{id} \\ 2 & \text{otherwise} \end{cases}$$

A reward of 1 is provided every time a case is completed. Thus, the objective is to minimize the cycle time of cases (to maximize the reward).

The A-E PN relies on the periodic iteration between non-deterministic events, represented by E transitions and triggered when the network tag is E, and sequential decision making, represented by the choice of which tokens' combinations to use to fire A transitions when the network tag is A. The network tag and clock are updated as soon as there are no transitions of the current network tag that are enabled, and the system is in a deadlock (i.e., the simulation terminates) when no transitions are enabled in any of the two tags. In Fig. 1, the network tag (first element of the tuple in the upper left corner), is E, so only the *Arrive* transition is enabled. After the arrival of both cases, the network tag will be updated to A, enabling transition *Start*. In the context of A-E PN, a policy is a function that, given the PN with the relative *marking* (i.e., the tokens contained in every place of the network at a given time), selects an action transition to *fire* (i.e., activate), and the set of tokens to use to fire that transition (in Petri Net terms, a *binding*). Such a function can be rule-based (what we call a heuristic), or it can be learned by a DRL agent. In Fig. 2 we report a visual representation of the interactions between the agent and the A-E PN, enriching the classic RL cycle [21].

In Fig. 2, the A-E PN interacts with the agent every time an action needs to be taken. To this end, the current *marking* of the A-E PN, representing the

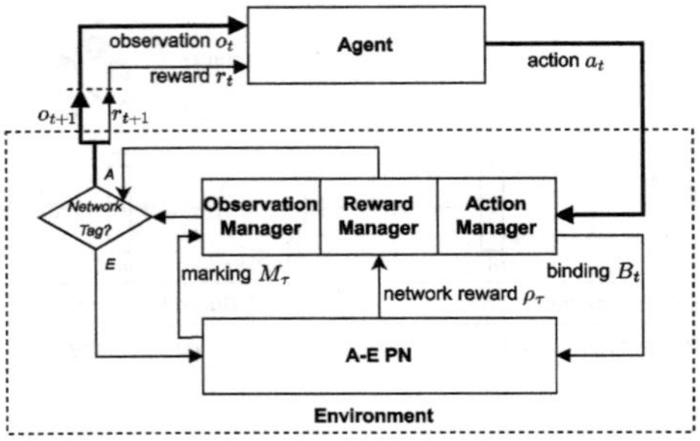

Fig. 2. The classic reinforcement learning cycle integrated with A-E PN.

state of the system, is translated into a suitable *observation* for the agent by encoding only the elements of the simulation that should be exposed to the decision-making algorithm, and the total *reward* cumulated by previous actions is used as a measure of the goodness of the current policy. When provided with a new observation, the agent returns an *action* (integer-valued) that corresponds to a specific binding on an action transition in the A-E PN. The observation is an element of particular relevance to the framework and is defined in [14] as reported in Definition 2.

Definition 2. ***(Assignment Graph)*** *An assignment graph G is a tuple $G = (V, D, Y, A, \phi, \theta)$ where:*

- *V is a finite set of nodes.*
- *$D \subseteq V \times V$ is a set of ordered pairs of vertices, known as (directed) edges.*
- *$Y = \{A\_Transition, E\_Transition, \dots\}$ is a finite set of node types, where A_Transition represents the action type and E_Transition represents the evolution type. Other node types represent the different places in the PN, discriminated on the base of their attributes.*
- *A is a finite set of attributes.*
- *$\phi : V \rightarrow Y$ is a function assigning a type to each node.*
- *$\theta : Y \rightarrow 2^A$ is a function assigning a set of attributes to each type.*

Such a graph representation of the observations translates the action into the selection of a node on the graph (between the nodes corresponding to the bindings enabling the action transitions). The previous versions of the A-E PN framework assumed that all the elements of the state would be included in the assignment graph and that a single action transition would be present in the network. In the next section, we introduce the necessary elements to relax these assumptions.

4 Method

This section is dedicated to the two main novel elements introduced in GymPN. In particular, we dedicate one subsection to introducing the concept of observability and the GymPN approach to model it, and one to the GymPN modeling approach for environments with multiple action types.

4.1 Process Observability

GymPN is a framework that combines elements of simulation with elements of automatic decision-making. When it is possible to expose all the elements of the state of the simulation to the agent, we speak of *fully observable process.* Previous A-E PN implementations only considered this process class. In GymPN, we introduce a modeling mechanism that allows us to represent *partially observable processes* by allowing single token attributes or entire places to be excluded from the observations presented to the agent.

We can formally introduce the concept of observability in a revised version of Definition 1 by adding two more elements to the tuple representing A-E PN.

Definition 3 (Partially Observable Action-Evolution Petri Net). *A Partially Observable Action-Evolution Petri Net (A-E PN) is a tuple* $AEPN = (A, P, T, F, \mathcal{A}, G, E, I, L, l_0, \mathcal{R}, \rho_0, \mathcal{O}_P, \mathcal{O}_\mathcal{A})$, *where* $(A, P, T, F, \mathcal{A}, G, E, I, L, l_0, \mathcal{R}, \rho_0)$ *follow Definition 1, and:*

- $\mathcal{O}_P : P \to \{0, 1\}$ *is a place observability function that maps every place in* P *to a boolean value, where* 0 *indicates that the place is observable and* 1 *indicates that the place is unobservable.*
- $\mathcal{O}_\mathcal{A} : \{(p, a) \mid p \in P, a \in \mathcal{A}(p)\} \to \{0, 1\}$ *is an attribute observability function that maps, for each place* p*, the attributes* $a \in \mathcal{A}(p)$ *to a boolean value, where* 0 *indicates that the attribute is observable and* 1 *indicates that the attribute is unobservable.*

The adjustments introduced in Definition 3 are enough to enable the A-E PN framework to express partially observable processes. The newly defined partially observable A-E PN retains the expressive power to represent the simulated environment and the decision-making problem in a single notation, while allowing for the separation of the elements that pertain to the former from the ones that pertain to the latter. As an example, we can consider the problem presented in Fig. 1. In such a problem, it would be reasonable to exclude the arrival process from the elements that are included in the observation. Given the newly introduced elements in Definition 3, this can be achieved simply by setting $\mathcal{O}_P$ so that $\mathcal{O}_P(\mathit{Arrival}) = 1$. In the next subsection, we provide the details of the algorithm that achieves this effect.

4.2 Multiple Actions

In previous implementations of the A-E PN framework, the focus was on modeling problems with a single action transition. However, in many cases, complex processes require the making of decisions at different stages of the process. In this section, we show how this limitation is lifted in GymPN with minimal modifications to the existing theory of A-E PN.

To introduce the problem of modeling multiple actions, we refer to the two business process decision-making problem patterns in Fig. 3 and Fig. 4. The two images present two archetypal cases of systems with multiple actions. The problem in Fig. 3 includes two action transitions (*Start1* and *Start2*) that do not share any incoming place. We refer to this problem as having *disjoint actions*. On the other hand, Fig. 4 presents two action transitions (*Start1* and *Start2*) that share a common incoming place (*Resources*). We refer to this problem as having *joint actions*.

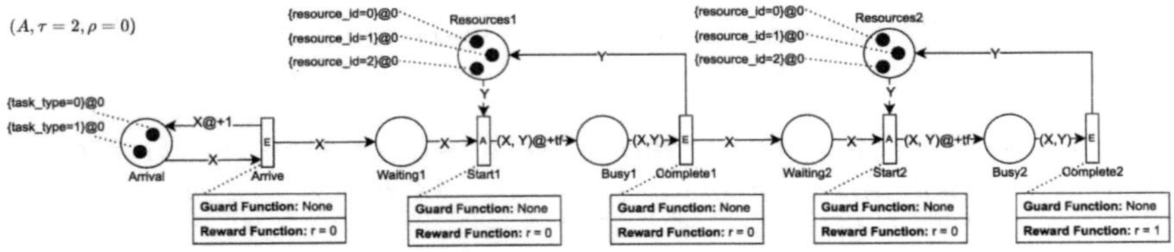

Fig. 3. An example of A-E PN with disjoint actions.

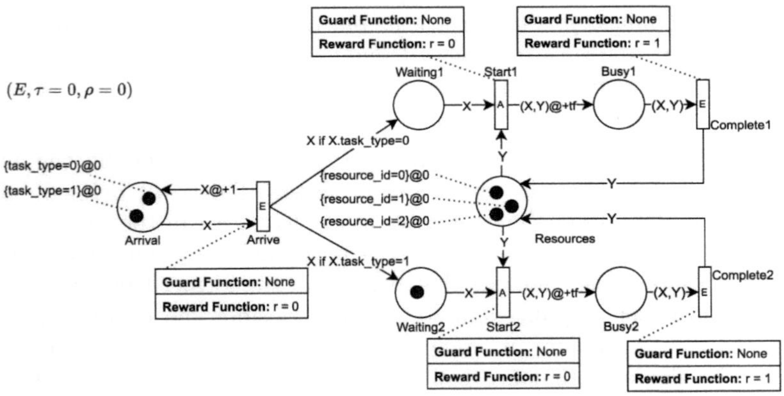

Fig. 4. An example of A-E PN with joint actions.

The translation of a marking of an A-E PN, such as the ones in Fig. 3 and Fig. 4, was originally designed to handle a single action transition in the network. In fact, in its design, no steps were taken to handle situations with joint or disjoint action transitions. In Definition 4, we provide an informal definition of the new mapping algorithm.

Definition 4. *[Mapping from Petri Net to GymPN Assignment Graph] A mapping from (expanded) A-E PN to assignment graph is a function from a marked A-E PN $\mathcal{T}$ to an assignment graph G having one node for each place or transition in $\mathcal{T}$ and one (directed) edge for each arc in $\mathcal{T}$ to the corresponding source and destination nodes in G.*

At a high level, the mapping function operates in three main steps:

1. **Place mapping**: every non-empty place is mapped to a node with the same attributes as the single token in the original place, plus its time.
2. **Transition mapping**: every transition is mapped to a node without attributes.
3. **Arc mapping**: every arc not connected to empty places is mapped to an edge connecting nodes corresponding to the arc's source and destination.

The mapping algorithm from A-E PN $\mathcal{T}$ to assignment graph G is formally described in Algorithm 1. In the algorithm, we use the notation $v(t)$ to refer to the value of attributes of token t, $\tau(t)$ to refer to its time, $v(n')$ to refer to the values associated with attributes of the type of the newly created node n', and $p(t)$ to refer to a place p marked with a single token t. We also assume the existence of the functions *get*_A_transition_type and *get*_E_transition_type, which map the action and evolution transitions in the expanded network to an integer value indicating the original transition in the non-expanded network. A third function *one*_hot is used to map the integer value to its one-hot encoding value. Finally, we introduce two support multi-sets, H_p and H_t, used to store tuples of nodes and transitions in the A-E PN and the corresponding edges in the assignment graph.

The new mapping in Algorithm 1 excludes all unobservable places and attributes from the assignment graph. Moreover, it ensures that the information regarding the original transitions is available in one-hot encoded form, thus enabling the solving algorithm to discriminate between different action transitions.

To better clarify the procedure in Algorithm 1, let us consider the two problems presented in Fig. 3 and Fig. 4. Since handling unobservable features and tokens is relatively straightforward, we focus on use cases with multiple actions. In the case of disjoint actions (Fig. 3), we can consider the marking reported in Fig. 5 (simplified for improved readability). Two activities are ready to be assigned (places *Wait1* and *Wait2*). All resources are available.

The expansion procedure would produce the A-E PN reported in Fig. 6, where every place contains a single token.

The GymPN mapping algorithm applied to the A-E PN in Fig. 6, produces the assignment graph in Fig. 7.

In the same way, we can derive the assignment graph for an A-E PN with joint actions (Fig. 4). To this end, let us consider the marking reported in Fig. 8.

In this case, the expansion procedure would produce the A-E PN reported in Fig. 6.

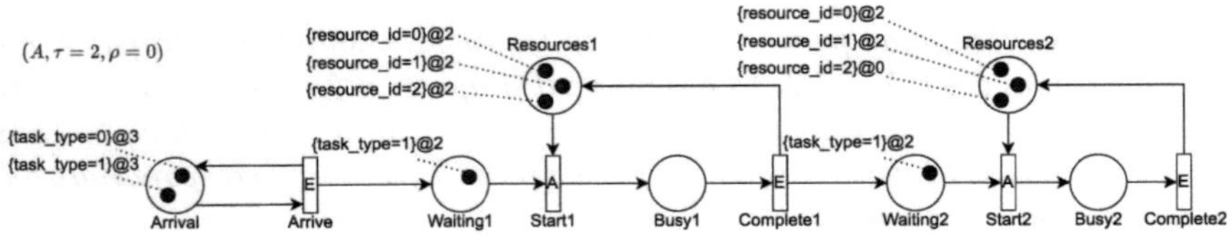

Fig. 5. A-E PN with disjoint actions.

Algorithm 1. Petri Net to GymPN Assignment Graph Mapping

procedure MAP($\mathcal{T}$)
  $V_G \leftarrow \emptyset$, $D_G \leftarrow \emptyset$, $Y_G \leftarrow \emptyset$, $A_G \leftarrow A_{\mathcal{T}}$, $H_p \leftarrow \emptyset$, $H_t \leftarrow \emptyset$
  for $\forall p \in P_{\mathcal{T}}$ **do**
    if $\mathcal{O}_P(p) = 0 \land \exists t$ s.t. $p(t)$ **then**
      $\mathcal{A}_{obs}(p) \leftarrow \{a \in \mathcal{A}(p) \mid \mathcal{O}_{\mathcal{A}}(p, a) = 0\}$
      $v_{obs}(t) \leftarrow \{v(t)[a] \mid a \in \mathcal{A}_{obs}(p)\}$
      $V_G \leftarrow V_G \cup \{n' \text{ s.t. } \phi(n') = \mathcal{A}_{obs}(p) \land v(n') = \{\tau(t)\} \cup v_{obs}(t)\}$
      $H_p \leftarrow H_p \cup (p, n')$
  for $\forall tr \in T_{\mathcal{T}}$ **do**
    if $L_{\mathcal{T}}(tr) =$ 'E' **then**
      $type \leftarrow$ get_E_transition_type(tr)
      $v_{onehot} \leftarrow$ one_hot($type$, num_E_types)
      $V_G \leftarrow V_G \cup \{n' \text{ s.t. } \phi(n') = \text{E\_Transition} \land v(n') = v_{onehot}\}$
    else
      $type \leftarrow$ get_A_transition_type(tr)
      $v_{onehot} \leftarrow$ one_hot($type$, num_A_types)
      $V_G \leftarrow V_G \cup \{n' \text{ s.t. } \phi(n') = \text{A\_Transition} \land v(n') = v_{onehot}\}$
    $H_t \leftarrow H_t \cup (tr, n')$
  for $\forall a \in F_{\mathcal{T}}$ **do**
    if $a[0] \in P_{\mathcal{T}} \land \mathcal{O}_P(a[0]) = 0 \land \mathcal{O}_P(a[1]) = 0$ **then**
      $D_G \leftarrow D_G \cup \{(H_p[a[0]], H_t[a[1]])\}$
    else if $a[1] \in P_{\mathcal{T}} \land \mathcal{O}_P(a[1]) = 0 \land \mathcal{O}_P(a[0]) = 0$ **then**
      $D_G \leftarrow D_G \cup \{(H_t[a[0]], H_p[a[1]])\}$
  return G

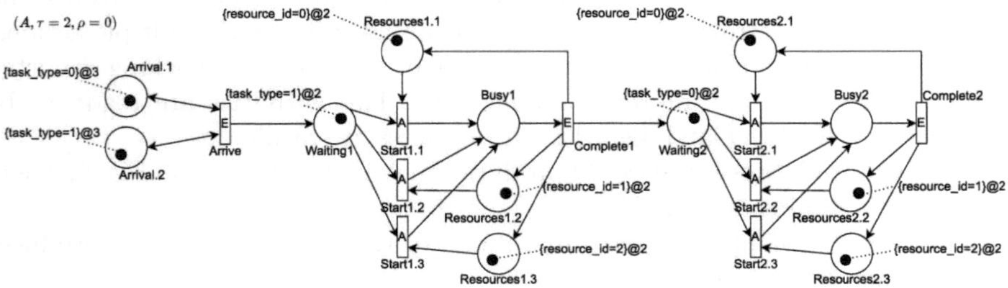

Fig. 6. Expanded A-E PN with disjoint actions.

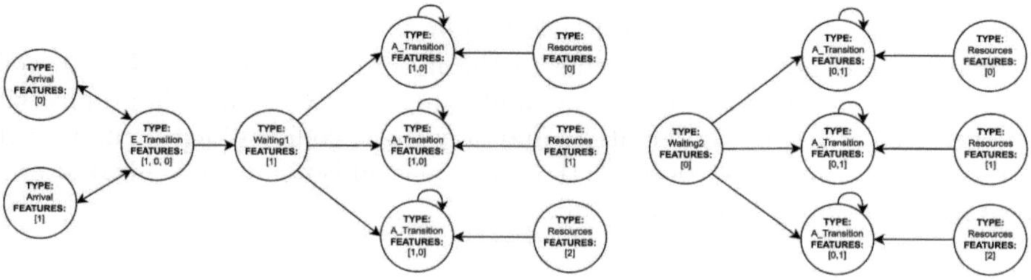

Fig. 7. Assignment graph observation for A-E PN with disjoint actions.

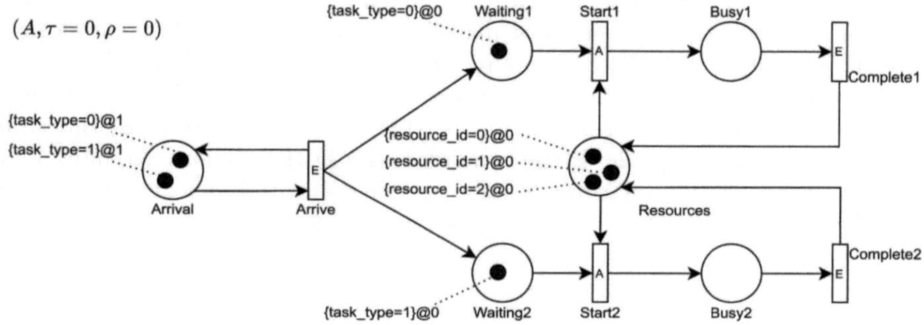

Fig. 8. A-E PN with joint actions.

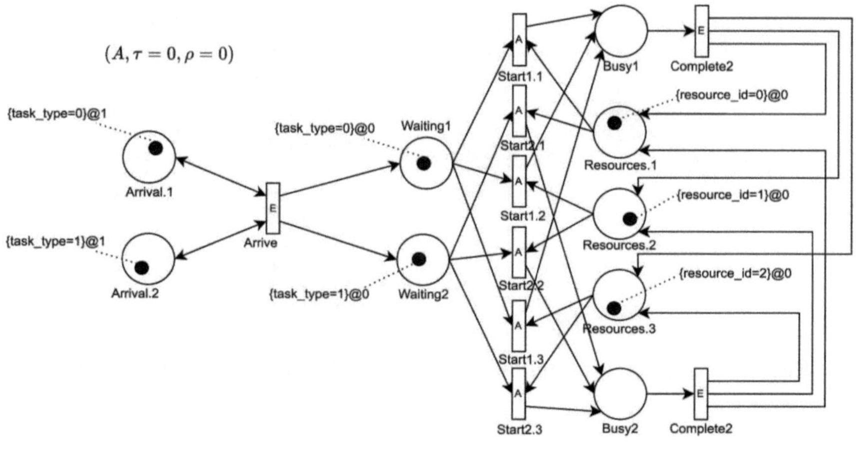

Fig. 9. Expanded A-E PN with joint actions.

The GymPN mapping algorithm applied to the A-E PN in Fig. 6, produces the assignment graph in Fig. 7.

The assignment graphs in the two considered cases clearly discriminate different action types, allowing the policy network to distinguish different action nodes. It can be noticed that, in Fig. 7, two disconnected graphs are produced. However, this is not a problem: due to the nature of the Graph Neural Networks used to approximate the policy and value functions, the two graphs will be considered as a single observation, and only the encoding of action nodes will be used to determine the chosen action. The mechanism allowing this desirable property is described in detail in [14].

5 Implementation

GymPN is a Python library that implements the partially observable A-E PN definition, as well as a collection of utilities to facilitate modeling the desired problem, as well as training and testing DRL and heuristic policies. It consists of three main modules, as illustrated in Fig. 11: the *Simulator* that can be used to model and simulate a business process decision-making problem, the *Gym Environment* that encapsulates the simulator as a DRL problem, enabling it to be solved using the Gymnasium library, and the *Agent* that learns the policy that solves the business process decision-making problem.

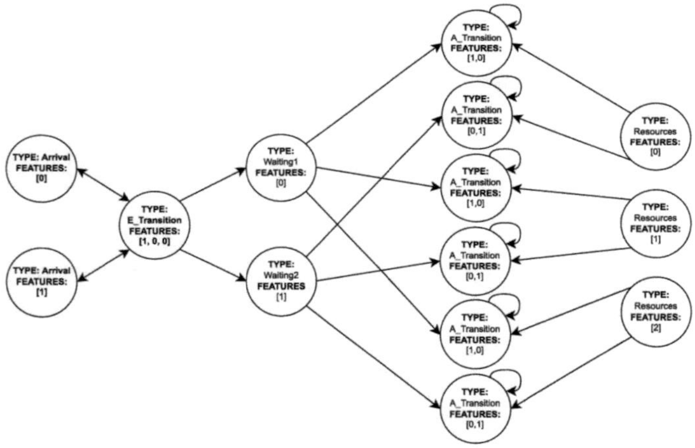

Fig. 10. Assignment graph observation for A-E PN with joint actions.

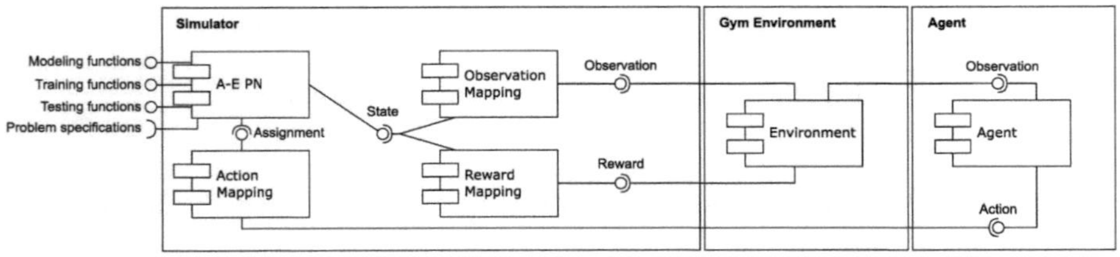

Fig. 11. The GymPN component model.

The Simulator facilitates modeling and simulating a business process decision-making problem. To this end, the simulator contains four specialized modules: A-E PN, Observation Mapping, Reward Mapping, and Action Mapping.

The A-E PN module implements the A-E PN framework described throughout this work, exposing to the user the primitives that are necessary to define the desired business process decision-making problem, and to train and test DRL or heuristic policies. In order to define such a problem, the user is expected to define the corresponding A-E PN in terms of its places, transitions (with relative guard, behavior, and reward functions), and the marking (by adding the desired tokens to the places). Optionally, unobservable places and token attributes can be defined in a similar fashion.

The observation mapping module is responsible for translating the A-E PN state (i.e., its marking) into the assignment graph observation, excluding unobservable elements. The action mapping module is responsible for translating the integer-valued actions returned by the agent into suitable bindings to fire in the A-E PN. The reward mapping module keeps track of the total reward accumulated during a trajectory and returns the correct reward every time an action transition fires.

GymPN implements a Gym environment as a communication layer between the simulator and the agent. The environment module ingests the observations and rewards from the simulator. The former is passed to the agent to perform actions, while the second is used to store information regarding the goodness of the current policy, allowing it to improve during the training.

The agent module represents the decision-making algorithm that encodes the policy. Given an observation, it produces a single integer-valued action. Currently, GymPN implements the well-known Proximal Policy Optimization (PPO) algorithm, while other DRL algorithms will be introduced later.

The GymPN library is available at https://github.com/bpogroup/gympn.

6 Evaluation

The evaluation of the proposed approach relies on business process decision-making problem patterns that demonstrate the possibility of learning optimal policies when multiple actions are present in the problem.

In this section, we consider the problem of task assignment, involving the decision of which resource to allocate to which activity under which circumstances (i.e., in which state of the process). To this end, we consider a set of eight business process decision-making problem patterns. The considered patterns cover the most important workflow patterns reported in [23], namely:

1. **Sequence**: activities in a case appear sequentially.
2. **Parallelism**: two or more activities in a case need to be processed in parallel for the case to continue.
3. **Arbitrary Cycle**: a subset of activities can be repeated multiple times in a case.

4. **Exclusive Choice**: two or more activities in a case appear as mutually exclusive.

To validate the novel mapping algorithm introduced in Algorithm 1, we propose two variations for each of the cited patterns: one with joint actions (i.e., with a single resource pool), and one with disjoint actions (i.e., with separate resource pools). In Fig. 12 we represent the eight example problems using BPMN. In the figure, problems *(a)* and *(b)* represent, respectively, sequences of joint and disjoint actions. Problems *(c)* and *(d)* represent, respectively, parallel joint and disjoint actions. Problems *(e)* and *(f)* represent, respectively, cycles of joint and disjoint actions. Problems *(g)* and *(h)* represent, respectively, exclusive joint and disjoint actions. For example, Fig. 12.a shows a process with two activities that are executed in a sequence, where new cases arrive every time unit (i.e. with a rate $\lambda = 1$). There is one pool with three resources R_1, R_2, R_3 that can perform both activities, but perform differently on each activity. For example, resource R_1 takes 1 time unit to perform activity 1, but 2 time units to perform activity 2. The objective is to maximize the number of cases processed in a trajectory of 10 time units (or, equivalently, to minimize the cycle time of cases).

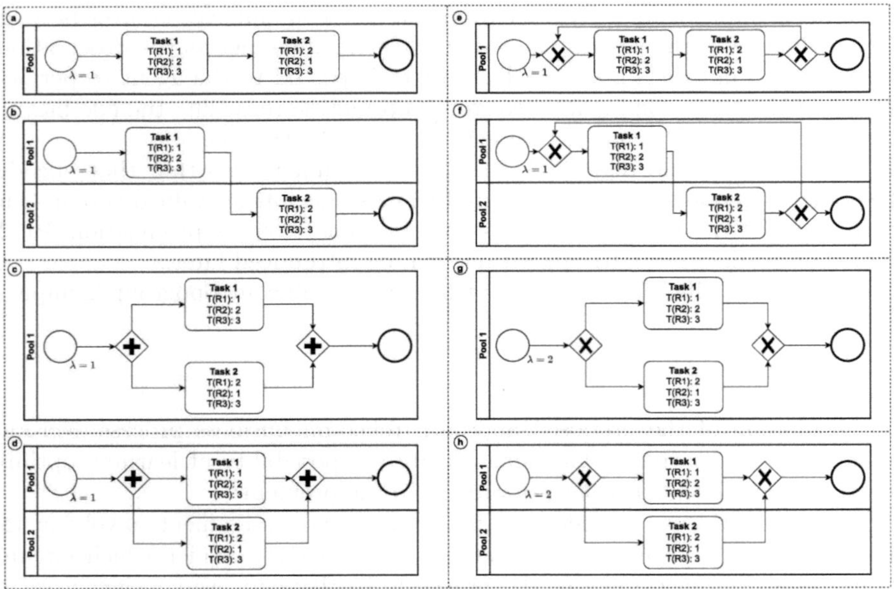

Fig. 12. BPMN diagrams of the eight example problems used for evaluation.

In problems *(a)*, *(b)*, *(c)*, *(d)*, *(e)*, and *(f)* cases are composed of two activities, while in problems *(g)* and *(f)* cases are composed of a single activity. The resource pools contain three resources, each characterized solely by a *resource*_id attribute, similar to Fig. 3 and Fig. 4. An arrival rate of 1 is assumed for every problem, except for problems *(g)* and *(h)*, where the arrival rate is raised to 2 to balance higher resource availability. Each resource has a different completion time for each task type (reported in the activities in Fig. 12). It is easy to see that, in every problem, the algorithm is expected to always assign resource 1 to activities of type 1 and resource 2 to activities of type 2, while resource 3 should remain unused because it takes 3 time units to complete any activity. In Table 2 we report the mean and standard deviation of the cumulative reward over 10 episodes of 10 time units following a random policy and following the (deterministic) trained policy.

Table 2. Performance comparison between Random, PPO, and the Optimum

Problem	Random	PPO	Optimum
(a)	6.1 ± 0.8	9 ± 0	**9**
(b)	7.5 ± 0.5	9 ± 0	**9**
(c)	6.8 ± 0.4	10 ± 0	**10**
(d)	8.8 ± 0.4	10 ± 0	**10**
(e)	2.9 ± 1.4	9 ± 0	**9**
(f)	3.9 ± 0.4	9 ± 0	**9**
(g)	15.1 ± 1.1	20 ± 0	**20**
(h)	17.8 ± 1.2	20 ± 0	**20**

In all instances, the DRL agent learned the optimal policy. Using the deterministic policy (that is, taking action with higher probability instead of sampling from the probability distribution that is the output of the policy network) in problems that do not include stochastic elements results in a variance of 0. All experiments are made available as part of the GymPN library and can be found at https://github.com/bpogroup/gympn/tree/main/examples/paper_examples. In the library documentation, other examples dealing with problem classes different from task assignment are present.

7 Conclusion

This work introduced GymPN, a library for automated decision-making in process management systems. GymPN is built on top of SimPN, a library for simulation with Petri Nets, and the two share the same syntax and basic constructs. Compared to previous versions of the A-E PN framework, GymPN introduces the possibility of expressing partially unobservable processes and handling multiple action transitions. The first novelty required an addition to the attributed A-E PN framework, while the latter required a modification of the expansion algorithm. The novel elements were evaluated by means of a set of problem instances representing the basic workflow patterns in business processes. In all instances, a DRL agent was capable of learning the optimal assignment policy. At the time of writing, the GymPN library still supports only single-agent DRL, and only the PPO algorithm is available as part of the code. In the future, support for multi-agent DRL will be provided, as well as other DRL algorithms. The reason to include different algorithms is motivated by the relatively low data-efficiency of PPO, while alternatives like rollout-based algorithms proved to be more efficient, especially in highly stochastic environments. Although such features will be implemented directly by the authors, we remain confident that the research community will provide further suggestions for improvements.

Acknowledgements. The research leading up to this paper is funded by the European Supply Chain Forum (ESCF) under the Artificial Intelligence Planner of the Future program.

Declaration of Competing Interest. The authors declare that they have no competing interests relevant to the content of this article.

References

1. Ahmadi, Z., De Weerdt, J., Serral Asensio, E.: Context-driven process discovery: enhancing process flow interpretability with contextualized activity hierarchies. Softw. Syst. Model. (2025). https://doi.org/10.1007/s10270-025-01313-1, https://link.springer.com/10.1007/s10270-025-01313-1
2. Akkerman, F.: (2022). https://github.com/WillemvJ/Dynaplex
3. Amaran, S., Sahinidis, N.V., Sharda, B., Bury, S.J.: Simulation optimization: a review of algorithms and applications. Ann. Oper. Res. **240**(1), 351–380 (2016)
4. Bynum, M.L., et al.: Pyomo–optimization modeling in python, vol. 67. Springer Science & Business Media, third edn. (2021)
5. Dijkman, R.M.: SimPN: A Python Library for Modeling and Simulating Timed, Colored Petri Nets
6. Dulac-Arnold, G., et al.: Challenges of real-world reinforcement learning: definitions, benchmarks and analysis. Mach. Learn. **110**(9), 2419–2468 (2021). https://doi.org/10.1007/s10994-021-05961-4, https://link.springer.com/10.1007/s10994-021-05961-4
7. Egorov, M., Sunberg, Z.N., Balaban, E., Wheeler, T.A., Gupta, J.K., Kochenderfer, M.J.: POMDPs.jl: a Framework for Sequential Decision Making under Uncertainty. J. Mach. Lear. Res. **18**(26), 1–5 (2017)
8. Ghlala, R., Kodia, Z., Ben Said, L.: Enhancing decision-making consistency in business process using a rule-based approach: case of business intelligence process. J. Telecommun. Digital Econ. **10**(2), 44–61 (2022)
9. Gul, R., Al-Faryan, M.A.S.: From insights to impact: leveraging data analytics for data-driven decision-making and productivity in banking sector. Humanities Soc. Sci. Commun. **10**(1), 660 (2023). https://doi.org/10.1057/s41599-023-02122-x, https://www.nature.com/articles/s41599-023-02122-x
10. Hubbs, C.D., Perez, H.D., Sarwar, O., Sahinidis, N.V., Grossmann, I.E., Wassick, J.M.: OR-Gym: A Reinforcement Learning Library for Operations Research Problems (Oct 2020), arXiv:2008.06319 [cs]

11. Kumar, A., Aalst, W., Verbeek, H.: Dynamic work distribution in workflow management systems: how to balance quality and performance. J. Manag. Inform. Syst. **18**, 157–194 (2002)
12. Lassoued, S., Schwung, A.: Introducing petrirl: an innovative framework for JSSP resolution integrating Petri nets and event-based reinforcement learning. J. Manuf. Syst. **74**, 690–702 (2024)
13. Lo Bianco, R., Dijkman, R., Nuijten, W., Van Jaarsveld, W.: Action-evolution Petri Nets: A Framework for Modeling and Solving Dynamic Task Assignment Problems, vol. 14159. LNCS, pp. 216–231. Springer Nature Switzerland, Cham (2023). https://doi.org/10.1007/978-3-031-41620-0_13
14. Lo Bianco, R., Dijkman, R., Nuijten, W., Van Jaarsveld, W.: A universal approach to feature representation in dynamic task assignment problems. In: Marrella, A., Resinas, M., Jans, M., Rosemann, M. (eds.) Business process Management Forum, vol. 526, LNCS, pp. 197–213. Springer Nature Switzerland, Cham (2024). https://doi.org/10.1007/978-3-031-70418-5_12
15. Lo Bianco, R., Jaarsveld, W.v., Middelhuis, J., Begnardi, L., Dijkman, R.: Automated decision-making for dynamic task assignment at scale (Apr 2025). https://doi.org/10.48550/arXiv.2504.19933
16. Middelhuis, J., Bukhsh, Z., Adan, I., Dijkman, R.: A rollout-Based Algorithm and Reward Function for Efficient Resource Allocation in Business Processes (Apr 2025). https://doi.org/10.48550/arXiv.2504.11250
17. Middelhuis, J., Bianco, R.L., Sherzer, E., Bukhsh, Z., Adan, I., Dijkman, R.: Learning policies for resource allocation in business processes. Information Systems **128**, 102492 (2025). https://doi.org/10.1016/j.is.2024.102492, https://linkinghub.elsevier.com/retrieve/pii/S0306437924001509
18. Raue, M., Scholl, S.G.: The use of heuristics in decision making under risk and uncertainty. In: Raue, M., Lermer, E., Streicher, B. (eds.) Psychological Perspectives on Risk and Risk Analysis, pp. 153–179. Springer, Cham (2018). https://doi.org/10.1007/978-3-319-92478-6_7
19. Rosing, M.V.: The complete business process handbook: body of knowledge from process modeling to bpm. Elsevier, Waltham, MA, 1st edition edn. (2014)
20. Shyalika, C., Silva, T., Karunananda, A.: Reinforcement learning in Dynamic Task Scheduling: A Review. SN Computer Science **1**(6) (Nov 2020), publisher: Springer Science and Business Media LLC
21. Sutton, R.S., Barto, A.G.: Reinforcement Learning: An Introduction, second edn. The MIT Press(2018). http://incompleteideas.net/book/the-book-2nd.html
22. Towers, M., et al.: Gymnasium: a Standard Interface for Reinforcement Learning Environments (Nov 2024), arXiv:2407.17032 [cs]
23. Van Der Aalst, W., Ter Hofstede, A., Kiepuszewski, B., Barros, A.: Workflow patterns. Distrib. Parallel Databases **14**(1), 5–51 (2003). https://doi.org/10.1023/A:1022883727209

Decision Noise Instrument (DNI): Estimating Decision Noise in Business Processes

Marcus Dees[1](✉), P. H. G. Berkhout[2], Claudio Di Ciccio[3], and Hajo A. Reijers[3]

[1] Radboudumc, Nijmegen, The Netherlands
marcus.dees@radboudumc.nl
[2] UWV, Amsterdam, The Netherlands
peter.berkhout@uwv.nl
[3] Utrecht University, Utrecht, The Netherlands
{c.diciccio,h.a.reijers}@uu.nl

Abstract. Business processes in which decisions are made by human resources suffer from noise. Noise is unwanted variability, which leads to inconsistent and unrepeatable decisions and impacts trust negatively. In this paper, we present the Decision Noise Instrument (DNI) to quantitatively estimate the noise that can be attributed to unknown factors affecting the actors who carry out the business process. For our estimation, we solely use readily available data from business information systems that support the execution of the process. In our method, we limit the influence of factors that cannot be attributed to actors. The DNI makes it possible to compare the noise levels between and within business processes. Based on that comparison, further investigation into the problem and noise reduction efforts can be prioritized. We evaluate the DNI on a claim handling process of UWV, a public service provider in the Netherlands. Our results show that we can estimate differences between the noise levels of several decisions within the selected process of UWV. By drilling down on a decision, the subgroups that have the most impact on the noise level are identified.

Keywords: Business Process Management · Decision analysis · Noise

1 Introduction

Decision making is an integral part of all business processes [19,21]. Examples of processes in which decisions play a key role are diagnostic processes operated by doctors, legal processes executed by judges, and insurance claim processes carried out by insurance experts. These types of processes also have in common that the final decision is typically left to a human decision maker, since they are trusted and expected to make a fair, objective decision. We refer to these types of processes as *decision processes*. Especially for decisions that have a major impact, it is essential that the decision is trusted by all parties who are involved in and subject to the decision process. Variability is in itself not inherently good

© The Author(s), under exclusive license to Springer Nature Switzerland AG 2026
A. Gianola et al. (Eds.): EDOC 2025, LNCS 16213, pp. 156–172, 2026.
https://doi.org/10.1007/978-3-032-15140-7_9

or bad. The variation that occurs within a decision process should, however, be explainable and made accountable. If this cannot be guaranteed then trust in the process itself and the organization executing the process deteriorates.

Noise and bias are the core causes for variability within decision processes, whereby bias is a systematic variation is in a specific direction, and noise is unexpected variation. Kahneman et al. [13] show that human decision makers are unaware of *noise* in their decisions, which means that under the *same observable circumstances* a human actor does not always reach the *same decision.* A part of the variability of decision process can therefore be attributed to decision makers. We use the term *decision noise* when we refer to noise that originates from taking a decision by a human actor, i.e., when the human actor is the source of the noise. In the literature, this is also called *system noise* [13]. The effect of having decision noise in a business process means that not only the behavioral properties or the norms regulating the decision process have an impact on the outcome of the decision, but also *who* takes the decision ultimately matters. The state-of-the-art intervention proposed in [13] is to estimate the overall amount of noise in a decision process by performing a *noise audit.* In a noise audit, a group of resources assesses the same pre-compiled cases. Comparing their decisions allows for estimating the variability in the decision process. The outcome of a noise audit can uncover the amount and the sources of decision noise. However, performing it is no sinecure, as Kahneman et al. suggest in [13, Appendix A].

In light of the above, we present the Decision Noise Instrument (DNI) as a means to estimate decision noise in business processes based on process data. Our method is less labor-intensive than a noise audit, and uses data about decision-making that is already recorded in the information systems supporting the execution of business processes. Our objective is to *automate* the estimation of noise levels between or within decision processes. We use a statistical behavioral model [5] in combination with a simulation model to estimate the decision noise level of a decision process or the *decision checks* that make up a decision process. Our method approximates the *true decision noise* that can be attributed to the human actors by limiting the influence of factors that cannot be attributed to human actors. To gauge the noise level of a decision process, we introduce a measure we call *switching rate.* The estimated noise levels can be compared in order to prioritize further research and efforts to reduce noise within business processes. We perform a case study applying the DNI in the context of the unemployment benefits claim process at the Dutch Employee Insurance Agency UWV (Uitvoeringsinstituut Werknemersverzekeringen). The case study shows that our method is able to estimate the noise levels of different decision checks made within the selected decision process. The results reportedly gave UWV the opportunity to target further investigation in the most noisy decision checks.

The remainder of the paper is structured as follows. In Sect. 2, we discuss related work. In Sect. 3, we explain the method we developed. Section 4 details the design of our statistical technique and how a dataset can be constructed as an input. In Sect. 5, we report on a case study at UWV using our method. Section 6 discusses the generalizability and limitations of our work. Section 7 concludes the paper with directions for future work.

2 Related Work

Our work is directly inspired by the book *Noise: A Flaw in Human Judgement* by Kahneman et al. [13]. Variation exists in human judgment and in business processes executions by human resources. Variability within a process is in itself not a negative property. It can even be a design choice of the process and of the organization [18]. Noise, however, is a source of variability that organizations, in general, should strive to minimize. This is especially true for decision processes. It is the aim of a decision process to create accurate and repeatable decisions *independently* of the human actor taking the decision. That is, from the perspective of the subject in the decision process the outcome of the decision should not depend on the assigned actor.

The influence and impact of decision noise have already been investigated in other domains such as healthcare and sports. In the healthcare domain, noise affecting the decision on the diagnostic test to be performed is investigated by Belle et al. [3] and Dlugos et al. [7]. In the sports domain, noise in the decision-making of football referees is examined by Samuel et al. [17].

Our work aligns with the notion of *fairness* in Artificial Intelligence [2,9], which also seeks to distinguish justified from unjustified variability in decision making. Decision noise analysis is, from this viewpoint, similar: We aim at a model that helps to separate variability into *systematic variability*, which is predictable and explainable, and *idiosyncratic variability*, i.e., noise.

Understanding how noise can be modeled in computational cognitive models is discussed by Li et al. in [14]. The authors state that most models use a static noise level. Better models for decision-making can be obtained by modeling noise in a dynamic way. Li et al. argue that periods of attention to the decision task are alternated with moments of distraction. While our aim is to measure the actual noise level of a decision process, understanding how to model noise can prove to be helpful in designing noise reduction methods.

Recommender Systems (RSs) [1] also have to be able to deal with noise. To train a RS, samples from rating databases are used that can contain *natural noise* and *malicious noise* [15]. Natural noise originates from users not being consistent in giving ratings. A source of malicious noise lies in ratings that are deliberately added to steer a rating in a specific direction, thus creating bias. For RSs, countermeasures have been proposed to deal with noise, including noise-reducing sampling and noise-filtering methods [11]. Some of the techniques discussed could also be viable ways to reduce noise in a business process context.

Bollarino et al. [4] developed a *noise decision scale* aimed at examining organizational factors that have an influence on decision-making and the level of noise. The authors use qualitative surveys to develop and validate their scale. Similarly, in [20], research on reducing noise is presented and different strategies are tested. A survey was used to gather data about the effectiveness of each noise reduction strategy. In our method, we refrain from resorting to labor-intensive approaches like surveys to estimate decision noise levels, and opt for a data-based measurement, as we explain in the next section.

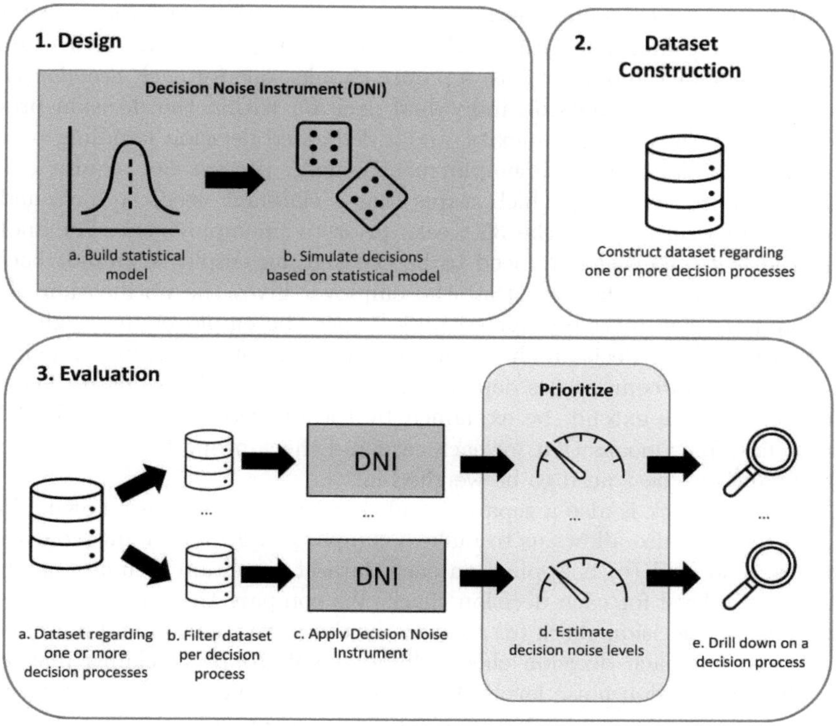

Fig. 1. Overview of the three main phases of our method

3 Method

The most important countermeasure to manage noise, as suggested by Kahneman et al. [13], is to perform a noise audit. The goal of a noise audit is to calibrate a decision process by having several human resources judge the same set of pre-compiled cases. By comparing the judgments of the human resources for each case, the amount of noise in the decision process can be estimated. The noise audit, as proposed in [13], is a manually-intensive exercise. In our work, we propose an automated approach instead. It applies to cases wherein data from the decision process is available, and the assignment of actors to cases is random.

Figure 1 gives an overview of the method we employed to conduct our research. In the first step, we designed the Decision Noise Instrument (DNI). The DNI is an instrument that estimates decision noise based on a dataset taken from the decision process. The DNI combines (a) a multilevel mixed-effects model [5] with (b) a simulation model [10]. Intuitively, the DNI returns the percentage of cases whose decision is expected to change when handled by a different human actor. Secondly, we describe the requirements to construct a dataset that can be used together with the DNI. In the third and final step, we evaluate our method by performing a case study. In particular, we employed the DNI in the real-world setting of the unemployment benefits claim decision process at UWV. We started the evaluation with (a) the extraction and cleansing of the dataset. Next, (b) we split the dataset into separate chunks, one for each *decision check*. A decision check represents an individual decision within the decision process with its own nature and complexity, and a dedicated decision handling process. For example, a claim on the unemployment benefits process can require a check on the *Weeks requirement*, which states that a claimant needs to have had an income in 26 weeks out of the 36 weeks prior to unemployment. For another claim, the *Notice period* may need to be checked: an employee cannot become unemployed between the date that the employer gives the notification of dismissal and the contractually agreed period that the employer must adhere to. Although the above decision checks seem rather automatic, empirical evidence shows that the outcome varies depending on the resource handling it. The variation can, to some extend, be explained by the discretionary space the UWV resource has. This means that for each case and check properties and context of the claimant's request need to be weighed in.

A decision check is also a separate (sub-)decision process on its own. Therefore, our method also allows us to make a comparison *between* multiple decision processes. The DNI (c) is applied on each dataset to obtain estimations of the decision noise level for each decision check. We compare the estimated decision noise levels per decision check (d) to guide further investigation and noise reduction efforts. For each decision check, different subgroups of claims may exist with different decision noise levels. We drill down (e) on each decision check to determine the most crucial subgroups and better steer the forthcoming efforts.

4 Design

The aim of the DNI is to quantify and thereby compare decision noise levels between decision processes, or decision checks within a decision process. In Sect. 4.1, we discuss the design of the DNI. In Sect. 4.2, we explain our approach for the construction of a suitable dataset on which the DNI can be applied.

4.1 The Decision Noise Instrument

The DNI is developed based on the idea that a decision process with a binary outcome can be expressed as a statistical behavioral model. A behavioral model captures the essence of the decision-making process of human resources in a statistical model. This is the first element (1a) of the DNI as displayed in Fig. 1.

Statistical Behavioral Model. We aim to estimate the noise level of a decision process executed by human resources. We assume that each case i for which a decision needs to be made has an objective (and unknown) grant-ability value $G_i \in \mathbb{R}$. Human resources working in the process make their own estimation of the value of G_i. The decision for the case is either 1 (denoting a positive outcome, like *Yes*, *Accepted*, *OK*, etc.), when the estimation by the human resource corresponds to $G_i \geqslant 0$, or 0 (indicating a negative outcome: *No*, *Rejected*, *NOK*, etc.), when $G_i < 0$. If every human resource could estimate the same value of G_i for each case i, the decision process would have no decision noise. However, when two resources make their own estimation and their estimates differ from each other, then the same case i could be associated to $G_i = 1$ for the first resource and $G_i = 0$ for the second resource. The source of variation in this model is the extent to which an individual's estimate deviates from the actual value G. The real value for G is unknown, though, since it is a concept that solely exists within our model. We now assume that G_i of case i is equal to the hypothetical average if all human resources were to make an estimate of it. Let R be the number of resources. The index $r \in [1, R]$ identifies a unique resource. Each resource r has a (structural) deviation T_r. We assume that this deviation is the same for every case processed by r. We postulate that T_r follows a normal distribution with the average equal to 0 and the standard deviation set to σ_T: $T_r \sim \text{Normal}(0, \sigma_T)$. A negative T_r means that r structurally grants cases less often than the average. We assume that the objective grant-ability G_i of case i follows the logistic distribution: $G_i \sim \text{Logistic}(X_i\beta, 1)$. The first argument (the location parameter), can vary depending on application-specific features X_i which are typically collected in a vector and multiplied by a vector of coefficients β, such that the features can each have their own weights. A feature represents a source of variation. An example of a feature is the age of the applicant if, in practice, older people are awarded more often (or less often) than younger people on average. Vector X_i also always includes a constant, which represents the intercept in the regression equation. We set the scale argument to 1 since this assumption does not change the essence of the model.

The decision $D_{i,r}$ of resource r on case i is thus determined as follows:

$$D_{i,r} = \begin{cases} 0, & \text{if } G_i + T_r < 0 \\ 1, & \text{if } G_i + T_r \geqslant 0 \end{cases} \tag{1}$$

To build our statistical model, we need records of the following data: a case i with its properties X_i, a resource r, and the actual decision $D_{i,r} \in \{0, 1\}$ taken by r for case i. We do not observe the variables G and T. The objective is to estimate the model parameters β and σ_T from the available data. Multilevel mixed-effect models are suitable for analyzing this sort of information. More specifically, the described model can be estimated empirically with a logit model with fixed effects for case properties and a random effect for the human resources.

Simulation. The resulting model estimate of σ_T is an estimate of the standard deviation of the individual deviations of the human resources. The value of σ_T expresses the variability in decision making for all human resources that execute the process. That is, σ_T is a benchmark for decision noise within a process that is related to the human resources executing the process. This implies that σ_T could already be used to benchmark decision noise levels.

Domain experts involved in our study expressed a preference towards a more tangible measure than standard deviations. To this end, we introduced the *switching rate* S as a measure of decision noise. We define the switching rate as the percentage of cases that are expected to change outcome in the event that the case were assigned to another randomly assigned resource. The percentage of cases whose outcome depends on the handling resource can be seen as the degree of arbitrariness of the system. A low percentage indicates little arbitrariness, whereas a high percentage indicates a high level of arbitrariness. The *switching rate* $S(\sigma_T, \bar{X}\beta)$ follows from the estimated values for σ_T and $\bar{X}\beta$ and the assumed distributions of the model (i.e. the logistic distribution and the normal distribution). We define S as follows:

$$S(\sigma_T, \bar{X}\beta) = \iint_{-\infty}^{+\infty} |\Lambda(r_1) - \Lambda(r_2)| \cdot \Phi(r_1) \cdot \Phi(r_2)\, dr_1\, dr_2. \qquad (2)$$

In the formula, Λ is the cumulative distribution function of the logistic distribution with expectation $\bar{X}\beta$ and scale 1, and Φ is the probability density function of the normal distribution with expectation 0 and standard deviation σ_T. The integral calculates the difference between two human resources making a decision for the same case. Inspired by Item Response Theory [16], we use it as a means that is also common in psychometric models to measure noise or discrimination.

We approximate $S(\sigma_T, \bar{X}\beta)$ by running a simulation using standard computation methods for the normal distribution and the logistic distribution [10]. Figure 2 shows a contour plot indicating the value $S(\sigma_T, \bar{X}\beta)$ for each combination of the standard deviation σ_T and expected acceptance rate $\Lambda(\bar{X}\beta)$. The maximum switching rate is 50 %. When the expected acceptance rate is close to 0 % (or 100 %) the switching rate is close to 0 %. The statement that the switching rate is bounded by 50 % may seem counterintuitive. One might imagine two decision makers who always make opposite choices, implying 100 % disagreement. However, the switching rate as defined here refers to the probability of disagreement when two decision makers are drawn at random from the population. Technically, let p be the probability of a positive decision. In this setting, the disagreement probability is $2p(1-p)$. This expression is maximized at 0.5, yielding an upper bound of 50 %.

4.2 Dataset Construction

The DNI uses a dataset taken from a decision process as input. Both the decision process and the dataset need to meet specific requirements.

Decision Process Requirements. To avoid variation between human resources that originates from the process itself, we require that the human resources are *randomly assigned* to the decisions that need to be taken. This ascertains that no assignment bias occurs in the dataset. When some bias purposely exists within a process, for example because certain human resources

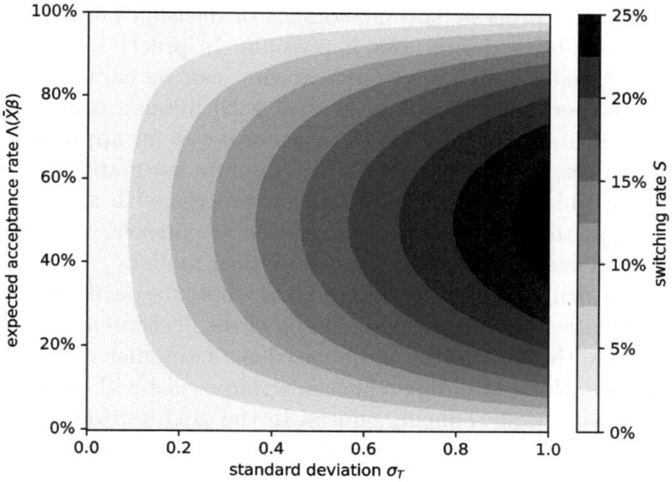

Fig. 2. Contour plot showing the percentage of cases that are expected to change at specific acceptance rates and standard deviation values.

are always assigned a specific type of cases, then the DNI should be applied separately on each set of human resources that deal with the same type of cases.

The mix of cases each human resource is assigned is another source of variation. While the cases have the same type, differences between the cases can still exist. To minimize this type of variation, we advocate, as a starting point, that per human resource at least 20 cases per decision process should be present. In our evaluation, we observed that having at most 15 resources in the dataset is not enough to derive a valid statistical model. We advise having at least 30 different resources in the dataset. This implies that the dataset should consist of at least 600 cases. Our approach is, therefore, only feasible for high-volume decision processes, i.e., when enough human resources have handled a sufficiently large number of cases.

Another requirement for the decision process is that the decisions' outcome should have exactly one of two possible values. For example, a decision process that handles an insurance claim has *accepted* and *rejected* as possible outcomes. In our approach, we calculate the share of cases that is expected to switch outcome, i.e., from accepted to rejected or vice versa.

Dataset Requirements. The dataset should contain at least the following pieces of information: an attribute that identifies a case, an attribute that identifies a human resource, and a decision, having the value 0 or 1 to indicate the binary outcome. In general, the estimation of the decision noise will become more accurate if more sources of variation are excluded from the dataset.

For each decision process, specific sources of decision noise should be identified and removed from the dataset if possible. In practice, this can turn out to be difficult. Also, not all sources of variation can be captured in data. Our approach is, however, robust enough to deal with missing sources of variation. The estimation in itself may become less accurate as an approximation of the true noise. However, it is still possible to compare estimates with each other. Our technique is able to identify the decision process with the biggest amount of noise, as long as the same sources of variation are present within each dataset per decision process and are used in the statistical model.

To be able to drill down on decisions, more context-specific variables should be added to the dataset. After the comparison of the decision noise levels between decision processes, these variables can be used to distinguish differences between subgroups of cases. Understanding which subgroups exist will support in focusing further research and noise reducing efforts. In the next section, we will evaluate both the construction of a dataset and the DNI for a real-life decision process.

5 Case Study

UWV (Uitvoeringsinstituut Werknemersverzekeringen)[1] is a public service provider in the Netherlands. In particular, it is responsible for supporting citizens to get back to work. If this is not immediately or fully possible, UWV provides a temporary income in the form of social security benefits.

Recently, UWV introduced a new guideline to cater for more customization of the decision processes. In particular, the UWV resources would be given more discretionary space to tailor decisions to client-specific situations in a more fitting way. As per the new guideline, the UWV resource should weigh in the situation of the citizen and not solely rely on the rule of law. Thus, the new guideline increases the influence of the UWV resource on each individual decision and thereby decreases the level of determinism of a decision. As an expected consequence, the presence of decision noise might increase.

However, since UWV did not have an instrument to gauge the decision noise that is currently present in their processes, it was not possible for them to determine whether the new guideline would actually raise the noise levels or not. In an attempt to tackle this problem, UWV agreed to run a pilot study with the application of the DNI on one of their claim processes to estimate the magnitude of the decision noise present in it.

5.1 The Unemployment Benefits Claim Process of UWV

Employees in the Netherlands can claim unemployment benefits at UWV. Figure 3 shows a simplified BPMN model of the process for the handling of a claim up until reaching a decision. The client who files a claim is referred to as the *claimant*. The claim is received in the workflow system of UWV (*Register*

[1] https://www.uwv.nl/. Accessed: June 12, 2025.

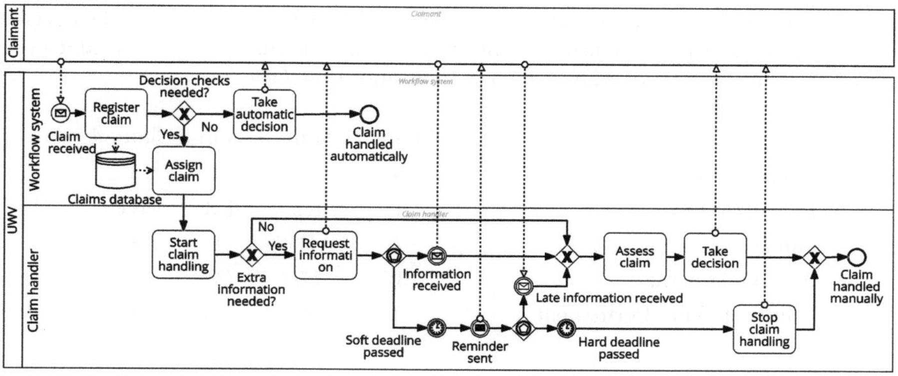

Fig. 3. BPMN model of the unemployment benefits claim process at UWV

claim). Information about former employments and income of the claimant is automatically gathered from other governmental agencies like the taxing service and added to the claim. If all required information is present to make a decision on the claim, then the decision is made automatically (*Take automatic decision*). Otherwise, the workflow system assigns the claim to a randomly selected resource at a UWV office (*Assign claim*). When necessary, extra information is requested that is not part of the claim (e.g., the employment contract of the claimant). When the information is not received within a week, a reminder is sent. If no information is received after two weeks, then the claim handling is stopped (*Stop claim handling*). As soon as the necessary pieces of information are acquired, the UWV resource assesses the claim (*Assess claim*) and takes a decision (*Take decision*) which is delivered to the claimant.

To reach a final decision, one or more decision checks need to be made by a UWV resource. Which decision checks need to be done is automatically derived from the information that is present in the received claim. Examples of decision checks are the *Weeks requirement* and the *Notice period*, which we mentioned in Sect. 3. Other decision checks, with a brief description, are:

- *Interim termination*: the contract is stopped before the contractual end date;
- *Daily wages*: information to calculate benefits amount is missing;
- *No relevant loss*: a claimant must have lost at least 4 working hours per week;
- *Legitimate claim*: did the claimant or the employer cause the unemployment?

The UWV resource who is assigned the handling of the claim is informed about which decision checks need to be done. Each decision check has its own procedure and can be considered a distinct decision process. If one of the decision checks leads to a rejection, the claim itself is rejected. Otherwise, the claim is accepted. As mentioned before, within each case and check, the UWV resource has the discretionary space to weigh in properties and context of the claimant's request. For each of the decision checks, then, we want to estimate the noise level.

Table 1. Sample of four cases and some of the variables from the dataset. The decision checks indicate which check needs to be done for the claim. The decision and other boolean variables are encoded as 1 for *true/yes* and 0 for *false/no*.

Variable	Claim 1	Claim 2	Claim 3	Claim 4
Decision: Accepted	1	1	0	1
Resource	R1	R2	R3	R1
Office	A	B	A	E
Age of claimant	37	55	50	62
Contract type: Permanent	1	0	1	0
...				
Decision check: Weeks requirement	1	1	0	1
Decision check: Notice period	0	0	1	0
...				

5.2 Application of the DNI at UWV

To apply the DNI on the unemployment benefits claim process at UWV, we constructed a dataset based on claims that were received between August 2021 and September 2024. The first step was to remove as many potential sources of variation from the dataset. We did that by filtering out claims for which no decision could be made, i.e., only claims that were accepted or rejected were selected. Next, we retained claims for which exactly one UWV resource was involved in the handling of the claim. Claims that were handed over between colleagues or between offices are not used because multiple resources were involved in taking the decision. Finally, a claimant can file multiple claims during the research period. Only the first claim for each claimant was used. This ensures that any previous knowledge about a claimant is minimized.

Table 1 shows an excerpt of the dataset. The outcome of the decision is assigned with either of two values, which we encoded as 1 for *accepted* and 0 for *rejected.* After the removal of claims that do not meet the described criteria, we obtained a dataset containing 549,772 claims, handled by 1739 unique UWV resources. The average acceptance rate in the research dataset is 85.7 %. Differences exist between the offices where the claims were handled, though, with acceptance rates ranging from 83.0 % to 87.8 %.[2]

As mentioned in Sect. 4.1, independent variables in the regression model are split into fixed factors that are not considered sources of decision noise and random factors which are seen as sources of decision noise. Factors that represent decision noise are factors that are related to how the process is designed and therefore are an integral part of the process. For the selected claim process, these factors are the UWV resource that executes the process and the office where the UWV resource resides. In our dataset, the moment when a claim was received is

[2] The acceptance rates are based on claims with only one decision check.

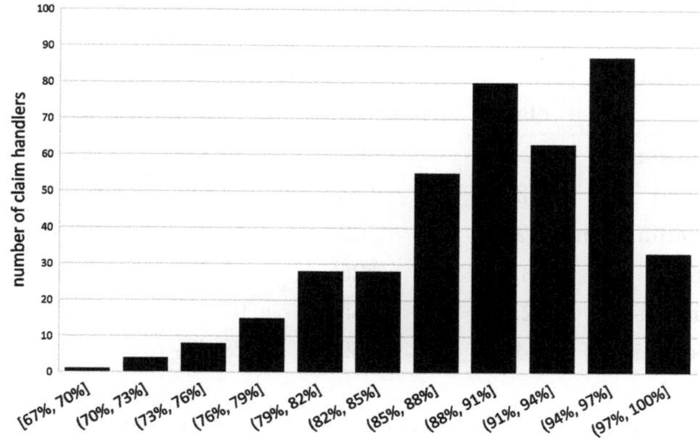

Fig. 4. Distribution of the acceptance rate of UWV resources who handled at least 20 claims subject to the *Weeks requirement* decision check

also a source of decision noise since the research period that we consider spans a period of 3 years. In this time frame, the process itself has changed and the UWV resources who work in the process have changed, too.

We applied the DNI using only the factors that represent decision noise, i.e., the UWV resource, the UWV office and the year and month when the claim was received. These factors were added as random effects to the regression expression. No other variables (i.e., fixed effects) were used. For each decision check a separate dataset was constructed by filtering the complete dataset. We built our statistical model using *Pymer4* [12], a Python implementation of the R package *Lme4*.

Taking the *Weeks requirement* decision check as an example, we filtered out from the dataset the claims that were handled by resources who were not involved in at least 20 claims requiring that check. This ensures that we have enough samples for each resource in the dataset for this decision check. After filtering, the dataset contains 12,892 claims. The average acceptance rate within the filtered dataset is 89.8 %. The dataset holds 407 unique resources from different UWV offices. Figure 4 shows the distribution of the acceptance rate of resources for claims where only the *Weeks requirement* decision check was conducted. The range for the acceptance rate for the 407 UWV resources is between 67 % and 100 %. The oscillation is evidently wide. We investigated to what extent this phenomenon could be attributed to decision noise. Next, we report our findings.

5.3 Results

We applied the DNI on all decision checks. Table 2 summarizes the results we gathered. For each decision check, it shows the number of claims used in the analysis, the number of unique resources involved, the acceptance rate of these claims, the standard deviation σ_T, and the estimated switching rate S. Notice that a comparison among decision noise levels is legit because we estimated them

Table 2. Summary of the UWV dataset

Decision check	# claims	# resources	Acceptance rate	Standard deviation	Switching rate
Weeks requirement	12,892	407	89.8%	0.337	3.4%
Notice period	3393	123	74.6%	0.535	11.0%
Interim termination	2625	102	85.4%	0.339	4.7%
Daily wages	18,297	525	95.3%	0.429	1.7%
No relevant loss	12,071	355	97.1%	0.555	1.7%
Legitimate claim	4505	169	78.4%	0.308	5.8%

Table 3. Subgroups for the *Weeks requirement* based on the variable *Contract type* and the estimated decision noise levels

Subgroup	# claims	# resources	Acceptance rate	Standard deviation	Switching rate
Contract type: Temporary	3254	123	89.7%	0.397	4.1%
Contract type: Permanent	581	22	99.0%	0.919	2.1%

under the same experimental conditions. As we can see in Table 2, the *Notice period* decision check exhibits the highest decision noise level at 11.0 %. The acceptance rate of this decision check is 74.6 % and the standard deviation of the random effect for the UWV resource is 0.535. As can be observed in Fig. 2, these values correspond with a switching rate between 10.0 % and 12.5 %. Next, we drill down on one decision check to uncover relevant subgroups.

5.4 Drilling Down on a Decision Check

Any variable present in the dataset can be used to drill down on, as long as the variable is not part of the integral design of the system and thereby may signify decision noise. Since subgroups are per definition smaller than the complete dataset, it is possible we do not have enough cases for each subgroup to derive the noise level. As mentioned before in Sect. 4.2, we need roughly 600 cases to estimate the decision noise level.

We use the dataset for the *Weeks requirement* decision check again. The variable *Contract type* is part of the dataset. This variable represents the type of contract that the claimant has with an employer. A claimant has either a permanent contract, or a temporary contract. For each value, i.e., subgroup, the average acceptance rate and the noise level is estimated and shown in Table 3.

The subgroup *Contract type: Temporary* has almost a twice as high decision noise level (4.1 %) as the subgroup *Contract type: Permanent* (2.1 %). Keeping Fig. 2 in mind, the expected acceptance rate plays an important role. At 99.0 % the subgroup *Contract type: Permanent* has a 10 % higher acceptance rate than the subgroup *Contract type: Temporary* (89.7 %). The number of claims and resources involved, together with the decision noise level of 4.1 % make it clear that it is best to focus first on further qualitative and quantitative research investigations on the subgroup *Contract type: Temporary.*

The next section will address UWV's response to our analysis, alongside implications for practice and research, and present limitations of our method.

6 Discussion

Having DNI at our disposal, organizations can now benefit from an approach, other than the noise audit, to measure decision noise in their decision processes. However, applying the DNI does come at a cost and carries a responsibility.

Implications for Practice. When the results of the DNI analysis were presented to UWV, the first question raised during the follow-up meeting was which noise level is acceptable from a policy point of view for each decision check. Determining a threshold of this sort is up to the stakeholders, and further case studies are necessary to start building up guidelines in that regard. Organizations should be aware that estimating decision noise will trigger questions like these, and thus should be required to formulate maximum noise level policies.

Another consequence of our approach is when the DNI estimates the switching rate at for example 6 %, then 6 out of 100 cases are expected to have a differing outcome whenever another human resource handles them. This raises the question of whether an organization should actively search for cases that could have had a different outcome. Apart from the practical hurdles of setting up such an investigation, an ethical question arises, too: What should an organization do when these cases are found? Stakeholders should decide what to do before starting the endeavor. In fact, understanding that this ethical aspect of our method exists ahead of time is crucial. Otherwise, it might hinder further consideration.

Implications for Research. Decision noise is present in business processes where human actors take decisions. Other types of processes are suitable for research on decision noise. An illustrative example is the peer-review process in academic publishing. This process is compelling due to the fact that manuscripts are typically evaluated by three or more independent reviewers, allowing for robust analysis of inter-rater variability.

The decision processes we investigate are rooted in laws, policies, and work instructions. The unemployment benefits process from our case study is supported by a workflow system and a rule-based system, which is similar to a decision model expressed via Decision Modeling and Notation (DMN)[3] [6,8]. Although DMN can be used to mitigate decision noise through standardization, transparency, automation, and validation of the decision process, decision noise

[3] https://www.omg.org/spec/DMN. Accessed: September 24, 2025.

affects the decision process as soon as the latter leaves room for arbitrary interpretation.

Other techniques may complement and enrich our approach. Machine Learning, e.g., could be used to estimate decision noise by modeling the systematic component of decisions, analyzing residuals or unexplained variance, comparing human versus model consistency, and using statistical decomposition (variance components, entropy) to quantify randomness. Ideally, alternative decisions could be predicted for every observation in a sample by swapping human resources, thus obtaining a switch rate. Nevertheless, such achievements are attainable only in the presence of rich and high-quality training datasets.

Being able to estimate decision noise more easily also opens up the potential to create decision noise reduction methods. One such effort is supporting the decision-making process of a human resource with a decision support system. The system can make a suggestion, but the human resources must justify when they want to deviate from it. The registered justifications can then be used to improve the decision support system.

Limitations. The DNI, evaluated at UWV, can be generalized to other domains and processes, provided the key conditions discussed in Sect. 4 are met.

However, the DNI has its own limitations. Unlike controlled experimental methods, where multiple assessors evaluate identical cases, DNI relies solely on observational data. This requires the assumption that distinct cases can be treated as sufficiently similar to warrant comparison. The validity of this assumption hinges on the quality and completeness of the available features: if important dimensions of case complexity are missing, the method risks conflating legitimate differences with noise. However, we remark that we assume cases to be randomly assigned to resources. This aspect permits us to hint at the law of large numbers. All unobserved positive and negative factors influencing the outcome should zero out, thereby not interfering with the higher level estimates.

It is worth mentioning that the number of years of experience, i.e., tenure, and the skill set of resources might influence their decisions. If data of sufficient quality is available about these traits, then these factors could be added to the model as a source of variation.

At present, DNI cannot deal with cases that require multiple decisions (or decision checks). The DNI also does not indicate which cases have a higher probability of resulting in a varying outcome. Similarly, the DNI does not indicate which actors exhibit a higher level of decision noise than others.

We built the DNI for decision processes with a discrete outcome and one resource involved. For other configurations, different models are needed, although multi-level mixed-effect models might still be suitable for many of those.

7 Conclusion

Noise is an important aspect of human decision making. Organizations should be aware of decision noise in their processes. Estimating human-induced noise in decision processes is a first step for organizations to enhance fairness and trust in their business processes. Our developed instrument (the DNI) has provided a national governmental agency such as UWV insights into the decision noise levels that exist within a claim process. We plan to gauge the effectiveness of the DNI in other organizations from different domains.

At present, DNI can only deal with binary decisions. However, other types of outcome values, i.e., nominal and continuous decision values, can still be modeled using the multilevel mixed-effects model we applied. For non-binary types of decisions, the instrument should be extended to estimate, instead of a switching rate, the percentage of the value that could change due to the noise level in the decision process. Since we aimed to automate the measurement of noise levels, our method can also be used to monitor the effect of any interventions that are deployed and follow the development of noise levels over time. In future work, we aim to develop a monitoring framework for decision noise levels.

Disclosure of interests. The authors have no competing interests to declare that are relevant to the content of this article.

References

1. Adomavicius, G., Tuzhilin, A.: Toward the next generation of recommender systems: a survey of the state-of-the-art and possible extensions. IEEE Trans. Knowl. Data Eng. **17**(6), 734–749 (2005)
2. Barocas, S., Hardt, M., Narayanan, A.: Fairness and Machine Learning: Limitations and Opportunities. Adaptive Computation and Machine Learning series. MIT Press (2023)
3. Belle, N., Cantarelli, P., Wang, S.Y.: The management of bias and noise in public sector decision-making: experimental evidence from healthcare. Public Manag. Rev. **26**(11), 3246–3269 (2024)
4. Bollarino, S., Ceschi, A., Monti, M., Sartori, R.: Development and validation of a noise in decision inventory for organizational settings. Informing Sci. Inter. J. Emerging Transdiscipline **26**, 173–189 (01 2023)
5. Bryk, A.S., Raudenbush, S.W.: Hierarchical linear models: applications and data analysis methods. Sage Publications, Inc. (1992)
6. De Leoni, M., Felli, P., Montali, M.: Integrating BPMN and DMN: modeling and analysis. J. Data Semant. **10**(1), 165–188 (2021)
7. Dlugos, K.V., Mazwi, M., Lao, R., Honjo, O.: Noise is an underrecognized problem in medical decision making and is known by other names: a scoping review. BMC Med. Inform. Decis. Mak. **25**(1), 86 (2025)
8. Dumas, M., La Rosa, M., Mendling, J., Reijers, H.A., et al.: Fundamentals of business process management, vol. 1. Springer (2013). https://doi.org/10.1007/978-3-662-56509-4
9. Dwork, C., Hardt, M., Pitassi, T., Reingold, O., Zemel, R.S.: Fairness through awareness. In: ITCS, pp. 214–226 (2012)
10. Forbes, C., Evans, M., Hastings, N., Peacock, B.: Statistical Distributions. Wiley (2011)
11. Jain, K., Jindal, R.: Sampling and noise filtering methods for recommender systems: a literature review. Eng. Appli. Artifi. Intell. **122** (2023)

12. Jolly, E.: Pymer4: connecting R and Python for linear mixed modeling. J. Open Source Softw. **3**(31), 862 (2018)
13. Kahneman, D., Oliver, S., Sunstein, C.R.: Noise. A Flaw In Human Judgement. Springer (2021)
14. Li, J.J., Shi, C., Li, L., Collins, A.G.: Dynamic noise estimation: a generalized method for modeling noise fluctuations in decision-making. J. Math. Psychol. **119**, 102842 (2024)
15. O'Mahony, M.P., Hurley, N.J., Silvestre, G.C.: Detecting noise in recommender system databases. In: IUI, pp. 109–115 (2006)
16. Robitzsch, A., Steinfeld, J.: Item response models for human ratings: overview, estimation methods, and implementation in r. Psychol. Test Assess. Model. **60**(2), 223–243 (2018)
17. Samuel, R.D., Galily, Y., Hochman, G.: The "silent" noise: moving forward from bias to noise in football referees' decision-making. Inter. J. Sport Exercise Psychol., 1–26 (2025)
18. Shishkov, B., Mendling, J.: Business process variability and public values. In: Business Modeling and Software Design, pp. 401–411 (2018)
19. Simon, H.A.: Rational decision making in business organizations. Am. Econ. Rev. **69**(4), 493–513 (1979)
20. Srinivasan, S.: Quantifying Effects of Automated Noise Auditing Notices and Decision Structuring on Noise, Accuracy, and Fairness in Human Decision-Making. Master's thesis, Harvard University (2022)
21. Vanthienen, J.: Decisions, advice and explanation: an overview and research agenda. a Research Agenda for Knowledge Management and Analytics, pp. 149–169 (2021)

Learning to Allocate: Dynamic Heuristic Selection for Business Processes

Jeroen Middelhuis(✉), Zaharah Bukhsh, Ivo Adan, and Remco Dijkman

Department of Industrial Engineering and Innovation Sciences, Eindhoven University of Technology, Eindhoven, The Netherlands
{j.middelhuis,z.bukhsh,i.adan,r.m.dijkman}@tue.nl

Abstract. Efficient resource allocation is critical for reducing the mean cycle time in business processes. While traditional heuristics like Shortest Processing Time (SPT) and First-In-First-Out (FIFO) are widely used, their effectiveness depends heavily on process characteristics. This paper introduces a Deep Reinforcement Learning (DRL) approach that dynamically selects heuristics during process execution. Our method learns adaptive heuristic selection, automatically determining when each heuristic should be applied to minimize the overall cycle time based on the current process state. Furthermore, unlike existing methods that encode each resource-to-activity assignment as a separate action, our approach limits the actions to the considered heuristics, reducing the dimensionality and complexity of the learning task. We evaluated our method on six synthetic and five real-world business processes. Our proposed method outperformed the best individual heuristic in six out of eleven scenarios and matched performance in the remaining five. The results demonstrate that adaptive heuristic selection using DRL provides a scalable and effective strategy for resource allocation that adapts to varying business process characteristics.

Keywords: Business process optimization · Resource allocation · Deep reinforcement learning · Heuristic selection · Cycle time minimization

1 Introduction

Efficiently allocating resources to activities within an organization can significantly improve an organization's operations. Consequently, enriching enterprise systems with algorithmic support for resource allocation is an important field of research that has seen an increasing interest in recent years (e.g., [17,19,27]). The most recent papers present algorithms that can effectively optimize the cycle time across various small and large business processes [3,15–17].

Typically, studies benchmark their (learning-based) algorithm against heuristics, such as Shortest Processing Time (SPT) or First-In-First-Out (FIFO). The methods proposed in these papers show good performance. However, often only achieve marginal gains over heuristic policies, which are known to perform well

© The Author(s), under exclusive license to Springer Nature Switzerland AG 2026
A. Gianola et al. (Eds.): EDOC 2025, LNCS 16213, pp. 173–190, 2026.
https://doi.org/10.1007/978-3-032-15140-7_10

for cycle time minimization [7]. For example, in [3], the proposed algorithm outperforms SPT in only four out of ten experiments. Furthermore, the method proposed by [17] outperforms the best heuristic in only two out of six scenarios. These results show that while simple heuristics are strong baselines, their effectiveness is highly context-dependent. For example, in the test scenario with high resource utilization, resources must be assigned as efficiently as possible to avoid queue buildup. In this scenario, the SPT heuristic performs well, while FIFO does not. Conversely, in the test scenario with parallelism, cases should be executed in the order of their arrival. The FIFO policy excels in this scenario, whereas SPT does not. Therefore, the question is not whether to replace heuristics, but rather how to best leverage them in a flexible and adaptive manner.

To facilitate that, this paper proposes a Deep Reinforcement Learning (DRL) approach that dynamically selects heuristics during process execution. Instead of committing to a single heuristic, our method learns when to apply different heuristics based on the state of the process. This hybrid strategy allows the agent to exploit the strengths of individual heuristics in states where they are effective. Previous work on resource allocation often assigns a resource to an activity as a separate decision option [3,9,27]. As we consider larger processes, the number of resources and activities increases. As a result, the number of resource-to-activity assignments explodes, making it difficult and time-consuming for the algorithm to learn which decisions work best. In contrast, our approach constrains the choices (also referred to as the action space) to a small set of proven heuristics. This significantly reduces the complexity of the learning task, thereby accelerating convergence [6]. By reducing the action space, our method improves scalability and learning efficiency.

Our experiments on multiple synthetic and real-world business processes demonstrate that our approach consistently finds the best policy across all eleven evaluated business processes. The DRL agent learns to combine heuristics such that the resulting policy outperforms the best single heuristic in six out of eleven test processes and matches the best heuristic in the other five processes. These results highlight the potential of learning to effectively leverage existing heuristics instead of learning a policy from scratch.

The remainder of this paper is organized as follows. Section 2 reviews related work on resource allocation in business processes and highlights commonly used heuristic benchmarks. Section 3 formalizes the resource allocation problem and introduces key concepts from deep reinforcement learning. Section 4 introduces our DRL approach to dynamically select heuristics during process execution and details the heuristics we include in our model. In Sect. 5, we describe our experimental setup, optimize our hyperparameters, and evaluate our method on both synthetic scenarios and real-world business processes. Finally, Sect. 6 concludes the paper and outlines directions for future research.

2 Related Work

Data-driven business process optimization (BPO) has seen an increasing amount of attention in recent years [20]. Several studies propose to rank assignments by leveraging information contained within event logs [2,10,29] or derived from process models [22,24]. These rankings are then used to make online resource decisions. However, one limitation of these methods is that the assignment rankings are static and not adaptable to the current state of the business process.

To overcome this limitation, dynamic methods make resource assignments based on real-time process states. For instance, [19] predicts processing times to make informed decisions. Recently, reinforcement learning (RL) has emerged as a powerful approach for online resource allocation in business processes. In RL, an agent learns a resource allocation policy by interacting directly with the business process environment. Initial success was achieved with Q-learning, but it struggled with complexity and scalability [9]. DRL, which incorporates neural networks, has addressed these limitations [25,27]. Recent research has demonstrated DRL's applicability across small-scale [13,16,17,27], large-scale [16,17], and real-world business processes [3,15].

Despite these advances, the improvement over standard heuristic benchmarks often remains limited. We identify three heuristic benchmarks for online resource allocation in the literature: SPT [3,9,13,15–17,19,27], FIFO [3,9,15–17,27], and a random heuristic [12,15–17]. The random heuristic is typically used to assess if the proposed approach learns a meaningful policy. We include these heuristics, in addition to other heuristics detailed in Sect. 4.2, as options for a learning agent to choose from. One paper uses the SLACK heuristic [9], which considers due dates for assignments. However, we assume we have no information about due dates, and therefore, we exclude SLACK from consideration.

In this paper, we train a DRL agent to utilize existing effective heuristics by dynamically selecting them to minimize the mean cycle time in business processes. The application of heuristic selection strategies has also been explored in job shop scheduling [28] and dynamic material handling [8]. Our paper specifically studies this approach in the context of business processes, including the formulation of the resource allocation problem and using different heuristics suitable to solve it.

3 Background

This section formalizes the resource allocation problem in Sect. 3.1 and provides background information about DRL in Sect. 3.2. We base our formalization on our previous work [16,17].

3.1 Resource Allocation in Business Processes

A business process is a set of activities $\mathcal{A}$ that must be executed by a set of resources $\mathcal{R}$. The process defines for each activity $act \in \mathcal{A}$ the set of resources $\mathcal{R}_{act} \subseteq \mathcal{R}$ that can execute it. The time it takes for a resource $r \in \mathcal{R}$ to process an activity $act \in \mathcal{A}$ is determined by a probability distribution with mean $\mu_{r,act}$. The business process model defines the sequence of activities that a case $c \in \mathcal{C}$ goes through. A new case arrives according to some stochastic arrival process and is added to the set of ongoing cases $C \subseteq \mathcal{C}$.

An activity instance $k \in \mathcal{K}$ refers to a single execution or occurrence of a particular activity k_{act} within a business process, associated with a specific case k_c. The activity instances belonging to activity $act \in \mathcal{A}$ are part of the subset $\mathcal{K}_{act} \subseteq \mathcal{K}$. We differentiate between the set of all activity instances $\mathcal{K}$ and unassigned activity instances K, where the latter contains all activity instances that must still be executed. Following this, the set of unassigned activity instances waiting at a specific activity is defined as $K_{act} \subseteq \mathcal{K}_{act}$.

To solve the resource allocation problem, we must assign resources $r \in \mathcal{R}$ to unassigned activity instances $k \in K$ to create an assignment (r, k). However, a resource may only be assigned if it is available. The set of available resources is defined as $\mathcal{R}^+ \subseteq \mathcal{R}$. When an assignment is made, the respective resource is added to the set of unavailable resources $\mathcal{R}^- \subseteq \mathcal{R}$, such that $\mathcal{R}^+ \cup \mathcal{R}^- = \mathcal{R}$ and $\mathcal{R}^+ \cap \mathcal{R}^- = \emptyset$. Furthermore, a resource must be eligible to execute a specific activity, as defined by the process model.

Using these definitions, we define the set of all possible resource-to-activity assignment (r, act) as $\mathcal{D} = \{(r, act) \mid act \in \mathcal{A}, r \in \mathcal{R}_{act}\}$. However, we aim to allocate resources to unassigned activity instances in an online manner such that at runtime, the possible assignments are $D = \{(r, k) \mid (r, act) \in \mathcal{D}, r \in \mathcal{R}^+, k \in K_{act}\}$. Making an assignment (r, k) moves r from $\mathcal{R}^+$ to $\mathcal{R}^-$ and puts k in the set of assigned activity instances Z. The assignment (r, k) is then added to the set of ongoing assignments $B \subseteq Z \times \mathcal{R}^-$. Figure 1 shows a specific state of a business process with three resources and two activities and illustrates the defined concepts in this state.

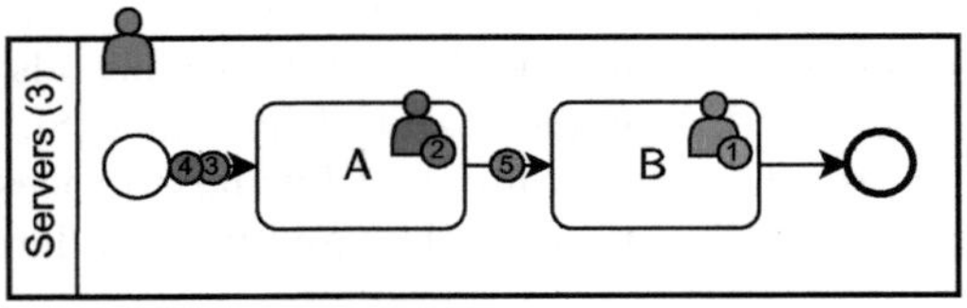

Fig. 1. Example of a process model with three resources ($r_{\texttt{blue}}$, $r_{\texttt{orange}}$ and $r_{\texttt{green}}$) and two activities (A and B). In the current process state, the green resource is available ($\mathcal{R}^+ = \{r_{\texttt{green}}\}$) and the blue and orange resources are unavailable ($\mathcal{R}^- = \{r_{\texttt{blue}}, r_{\texttt{orange}}\}$). Furthermore, there are three unassigned activity instances ($K_{\texttt{A}} = \{3, 4\}$ and $K_{\texttt{B}} = \{5\}$) and two ongoing assignments ($B = \{(r_{\texttt{orange}}, 1), (r_{\texttt{blue}}, 2)\}$). (Color figure online)

The business process execution state $s = (C, K, \mathcal{R}^+, \mathcal{R}^-, B, t)$ describes all information related to the process condition, where $t \in T \subseteq [0, \infty)$ is the current time. The set of all states is defined as S. We transition from one state s to a new state s' by taking an action a, which equals one of the included heuristics. Consequently, the heuristic selects an assignment from the set D allowed in s, after which a stochastic event e from the set of all events E happens according to the process model. This event can either be the completion of an assignment (r, k) from the set of current assignments B, the arrival of a new case c, or a resource $r \in \mathcal{R}^-$ becoming available according to its resource calendar. Upon the completion of an assignment (r, k), the state changes by moving r from $\mathcal{R}^-$ to $\mathcal{R}^+$. Subsequently, as defined by the process model, either a new activity instance k is generated and added to the set of activity instances K, or the case k_c completes. Upon a case arrival, the new case c is added to the set of active cases C, and activity instance k is generated according to the process model and added to the set of activity instances K. When a resource r becomes available according to its probabilistic resource calendar (Sect. 5.4), it is moved from $\mathcal{R}^-$ to $\mathcal{R}^+$. We refer to the time t at which an action a is taken as a_t. Similarly, we refer to the time at which an event $e \in E$ happens as e_t.

The objective of the resource allocation problem is to minimize the mean cycle time of cases in the system, which is the time between the arrival and departure of a case. This objective can be optimized by allocating resources effectively to activity instances.

3.2 Deep Reinforcement Learning

DRL integrates the representation learning capabilities of deep neural networks with the decision-making framework of reinforcement learning (RL) to solve complex, sequential decision-making tasks [25]. In DRL, an agent observes a state s and takes an action a according to a policy $\pi(a|s)$, which maps the states to actions. The state then transitions to the next state, and the agent receives a reward $R(s, a)$. The objective of the agent is to learn a policy that maximizes cumulative rewards. DRL utilizes deep learning to approximate the policy $\pi(a|s)$, the state value function $V(s)$, or the state-action value function $Q(s, a)$.

DRL algorithms generally fall into three categories: value-based, policy-based, and actor-critic methods. Value-based methods, such as Deep Q-Networks (DQN) [18], approximate the value function $Q(s, a)$ using a neural network. Policy-based methods directly optimize a policy $\pi(a|s)$, (e.g., [26]). Actor-critic algorithms, like Proximal Policy Optimization (PPO) [21], combine these approaches by using both an actor (policy) and a critic (value estimator). PPO achieves stable and efficient learning by constraining policy updates within a trust region, making it suitable for the dynamic and uncertain nature of business processes [21].

4 Method

This section details our proposed method. Section 4.1 provides an overview of how our DRL agent interacts with the business process environment, and Sect. 4.2 provides an overview of the heuristics that we include in our model.

4.1 DRL for Heuristic Selection

In this paper, we train a DRL agent for online heuristic selection. The agent learns a policy that selects heuristics in states where they perform well while avoiding using heuristics in states where they do not. We train using the standard RL framework, in which an agent interacts with an environment to create execution trajectories consisting of states, actions, and rewards. Based on what happened in each trajectory, the agent learns which actions lead to good outcomes with respect to the objective function. We use the PPO algorithm to train the agent as it provides a stable and efficient learning mechanism [21]. Figure 2 shows an overview of the interaction between the agent and the environment.

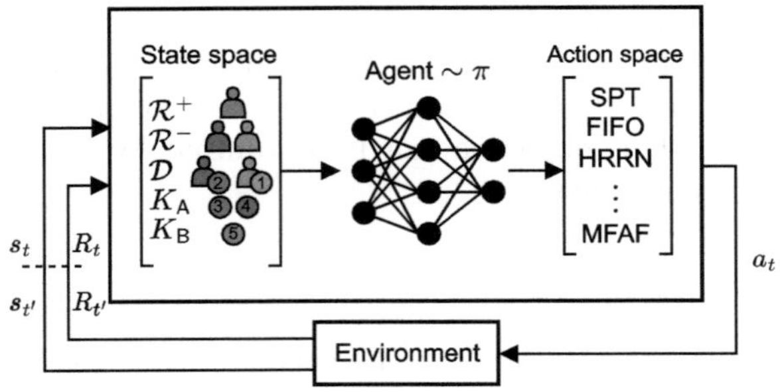

Fig. 2. Agent-environment interaction based on Fig. 1. At time t, the agent observes a state s_t based on which it selects an action a_t, which is a heuristic. The heuristic then chooses an assignment (r, k) which is fed to the environment. Afterward, the environment transitions to the next state $s_{t'}$ and the agent receives a reward R_t.

The agent, which is represented by a neural network, receives a state of the environment on which it bases its decision. This state is fed to the agent, and the agent then predicts the best action in that particular state. This action is then returned to the environment, which then transitions to the next state. Additionally, the agent receives a feedback signal in the form of a reward. We model the agent-environment interaction as a Markov Decision Process (MDP).

State. The first component of the MDP is the state space, which contains all possible states that the agent can observe. While the state contains all information related to the business process execution state, we feed the agent with information relevant to the problem. This representation of the state is called the observation. We model our observation similarly to [16]:

- A binary mapping of the resources $\mathcal{R} \mapsto \{0, 1\}$ indicating resource availability. For resource $r \in \mathcal{R}$, the value is 1 if $r \in \mathcal{R}^+$ and 0 if $r \in \mathcal{R}^-$.
- A binary mapping of the possible assignments $\mathcal{D} \mapsto \{0, 1\}$ indicating if an assignment $(r, act) \in \mathcal{D}$ is currently executing. The feature equals 1 if there is at least one resource $r \in \mathcal{R}^+$ and a case $k \in K_{act}$ for which $(r, k) \in B$; otherwise, it is 0.
- For each activity $act \in \mathcal{A}$, we define a continuous mapping $K_{act} \mapsto [0, 1]$. The mapping is given by $K_{act} \mapsto \min\left(\frac{|K_{act}|}{100}, 1\right)$.

Action. The agent selects an action, which includes the heuristics, in a specific state. The chosen heuristic then selects a specific assignment (r, k) according to its logic, which starts processing in the environment. The action space contains all considered heuristics, which are detailed in Sect. 4.2.

Reward. The reward function guides the agent towards taking desired actions. We return a penalty (i.e., negative reward) to the agent equal to the contribution to the sum of cycle times during the state transition [3,16]. Maximizing this reward function ensures that the objective function is minimized. An overview of the reward function is shown in Fig. 3.

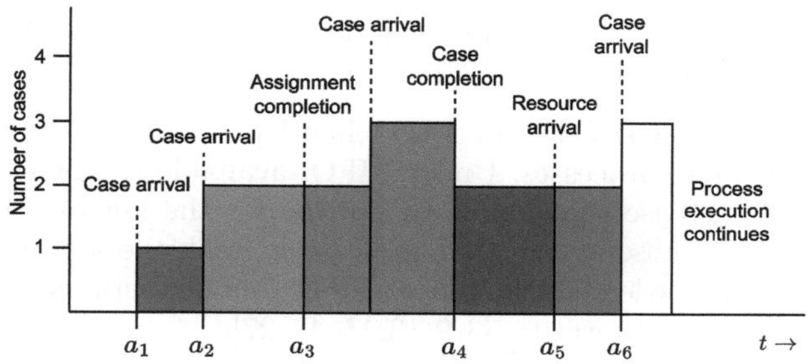

Fig. 3. Overview of the reward function. The agent receives a penalty equal to the accumulated cycle time during the state transition, represented by the colored areas. A state transition occurs only when a new assignment becomes possible. Multiple simulation events may take place between actions, and the penalty corresponds to the surface of the area in this interval.

The figure shows that after each action, the contribution to the cycle time during the state transition is recorded. For example, after the first case arrival, an assignment becomes possible, which triggers the first action a_1. The next case arrival triggers the next action a_2. Before taking action a_2, we compute and return the reward for action a_1, which is a penalty equal to the blue area. Note that not every event triggers an action. For example, after the third case arrival (green area), no assignment is possible, so we continue the simulation.

State Transition. After taking an action, the state transitions to the next state, as defined in Sect. 3.1. From the perspective of the agent, the state only transitions to states in which an action is possible. If there are no actions possible following a simulation event, such as a case arrival or assignment completion, the simulation continues. The agent takes a single action at a time.

4.2 Heuristics

Existing heuristics have been shown to perform well for cycle time minimization. For example, the SPT and FIFO heuristics are often used to minimize cycle time [23] and often result in low mean cycle times in business processes (e.g.,

[9,27]). However, while these heuristics generally work well, the performance depends on the characteristics of the business process [17]. In this paper, we investigate whether a DRL agent can learn to combine existing heuristics such that the resulting policy is better than any individual heuristic. Our DRL agent selects the heuristics at runtime, which then chooses the specific assignment. We include the heuristics below in our model.

Shortest Processing Time (SPT). The SPT heuristic is a well-established heuristic used in resource allocation problems. At each decision step, SPT makes the resource-activity assignment $(r, k) \in D$ with the smallest expected processing time $\mu_{r,k_{act}}$. This approach prioritizes activities that can be completed efficiently, thereby reducing the mean cycle time. SPT has been widely used as a benchmark in resource allocation in business processes, where it has been shown to be an effective strategy [3,9,13,15–17,19,27].

First-In-First-Out (FIFO). The FIFO heuristic is widely used in resource allocation for business processes. Under FIFO, available resources are assigned to an activity of the case that has been waiting for the longest in the process, i.e., an $(r, k) \in D$ is chosen, such that the case k_c with the arrival event e with the earliest time e_t is selected. Similar to SPT, this heuristic is often used as a benchmark in the BPO literature [3,9,13,15–17,27].

Highest Response Ratio Next (HRRN). The HRRN heuristic prioritizes assignments based on their response ratio to reduce the risk of starvation, such that assignments with short expected processing times get priority, but long waiting activity instances are not neglected [11]. This heuristic balances activity waiting time and processing time to calculate a response ratio for each assignment and selects the assignment $(r, k) \in D$ with the highest ratio:

$$\frac{w_k + \mu_{r,k_{act}}}{\mu_{r,k_{act}}}$$

where w_k is the time that an unassigned activity instance k has been waiting.

Longest- and Shortest Queue First (LQF and SQF). Two load-balancing heuristics can be used to distribute cases over the system to avoid resource starvation and reduce bottlenecks. LQF selects the assignment $(r, k) \in D$, for which the assigned activity k_{act} has the longest queue: $\arg\max_{(r,k)\in D} |K_{k_{act}}|$. Similarly, SQF selects the activity with the shortest queue: $\arg\min_{(r,k)\in D} |K_{k_{act}}|$.

Least- and Most Flexible Resource First (LFRF and MFRF). These two heuristics make assignments based on resource eligibility and can be helpful when there is much variability in resource capabilities. Intuitively, the LFRF heuristic is the most effective as it ensures that resources with limited eligibility are utilized. We also include this heuristic's opposite, MFRF, to study if the agent can utilize (or avoid) it. For any $r \in \mathcal{R}$, let $\mathcal{A}_r = \{act \in \mathcal{A} | r \in \mathcal{R}_{act}\}$ denote the set of activities resource r can execute. LFRF selects an assignment

$(r, k) \in D$ for which the resource r has the lowest number of compatible activities: $\arg\min_{(r,k)\in D} |\mathcal{A}_r|$. Similarly, MFRF selects the resource with the highest number of compatible activities: $\arg\max_{(r,k)\in D} |\mathcal{A}_r|$.

Least- and Most Flexible Activity First (LFAF and MFAF). These two heuristics are similar to MFRF and LFRF, but approach the assignment problem from the activity perspective. We expect the LFAF heuristic to be the most effective as it ensures that activities with low resource eligibility are not neglected. We also include the opposite of this heuristic, MFAF. LFAF selects an assignment $(r, k) \in D$ that has an activity k_{act} with the fewest compatible resources: $\arg\min_{(r,k)\in D} |\mathcal{R}_{act}|$. Similarly, MFAF selects the activity with the most compatible resources: $\arg\max_{(r,k)\in D} |\mathcal{R}_{act}|$.

Note that some of the heuristics may enable multiple assignment choices. For example, the FIFO heuristic selects the case that has been in the process the longest. The activity instance related to this case may be executed by multiple resources. On this occasion, we complete the assignment by selecting the enabled assignment with the shortest processing time (i.e., the SPT heuristic). In that way, selecting an action in a specific state always results in the same assignment, thus reducing noise in the learning process. Multiple enabled assignments can have the same (shortest) processing time, in which case we select one randomly.

5 Evaluation

This section presents the evaluation of our proposed method. We begin by detailing the experimental setup and training procedure in Sect. 5.1. Before training our models, we optimized the PPO hyperparameters, as described in Sect. 5.2. We then evaluate our approach on a series of synthetic business processes containing typical workflow patterns in Sect. 5.3. Finally, Sect. 5.4 investigates the scalability and effectiveness of our method when applied to complex real-world business processes. The code, our trained models, and results are available in our repository: https://github.com/jeroenmiddelhuis/BPO_heuristics.

5.1 Evaluation Setup

The training and evaluation of each business process follows the same setup. We train each agent for $1e7$ decision steps, where one decision step corresponds to a single iteration of the reinforcement learning loop shown in Fig. 2. An episode represents one complete simulation run, in which we simulate 2500 cases, following the experimental design of [16,17]. An episode is over when all 2500 cases have been completed (i.e., $C = \emptyset$). After finishing an episode, the environment resets and is initialized as an empty process. The number of decision steps per episode varies depending on both the specific process characteristics and stochastic events during the simulation.

For evaluation, we select the best-performing model found during training and evaluate its performance across 300 independent episodes. We report the mean cycle time and standard deviation based on these evaluation episodes. In our results tables, we highlight the best-performing method in boldface. Additionally, we also bold the results of methods that are not statistically significantly different from the best method, based on a t-test with a 95% confidence level.

5.2 Hyperparameter Tuning

We tuned the PPO hyperparameters to improve the performance of our models using the Optuna framework [1]. We performed this optimization on the real-world process in the BPI2017W event log (described in detail in Sect. 5.4). We conducted 100 trials, training an agent for 1e6 decision steps per trial and evaluating its performance over 100 episodes per trial. Table 1 presents the set of hyperparameters we optimized, their search ranges, and the best-found values.

Table 1. Hyperparameter optimization results for PPO on the BPI2017W process.

Hyperparameter	Range/Set	Best Value
Nr. layers	{1, 2, 3}	2
Nr. neurons per layer	{64, 128, 256}	128
Nr. steps per update	{4096, 8192, 16384}	16384
Batch size	{64, 128, 256, 512}	512
Nr. epochs	{5, 10, 20}	20
Learning rate	$\{3e-5, 3e-4, 3e-3\}$	$3e-4$
Discount factor	{0.99, 0.999, 1}	1
GAE	[0.8, 0.98]	0.873
Entropy coefficient	[0, 0.1]	0.044

The best-performing architecture consists of two layers with 128 neurons each, consistent with [17]. More steps per policy update and a larger batch size result in more stable learning trajectories, which are beneficial for environments with high variability and delayed rewards, such as a business process. Furthermore, in line with the delayed nature of rewards, a discount factor of 1 and a high Generalized Advantage Estimation (GAE) parameter (0.873) are chosen, which indicates that the optimization of long-term rewards is important. The low entropy coefficient (0.044) allows the agent to explore more states during training. The found learning rate ($3e-4$) balances between fast training and stable convergence, while the relatively high learning rate accelerates learning speed. We use the best-found hyperparameters when training our models for both synthetic and real-world business processes.

5.3 Synthetic Scenarios

In this section, we train and evaluate our models on the six synthetic business processes, also referred to as scenarios, proposed by [17] and also used by [16].

Each of these scenarios contains two resources and activities and represents typical process constructs for business processes, such as different utilization levels and employee skill levels. The processing and interarrival times are exponentially distributed. For more detailed information about the scenarios, we refer the reader to [17]. The scenarios are shown in Fig. 4.

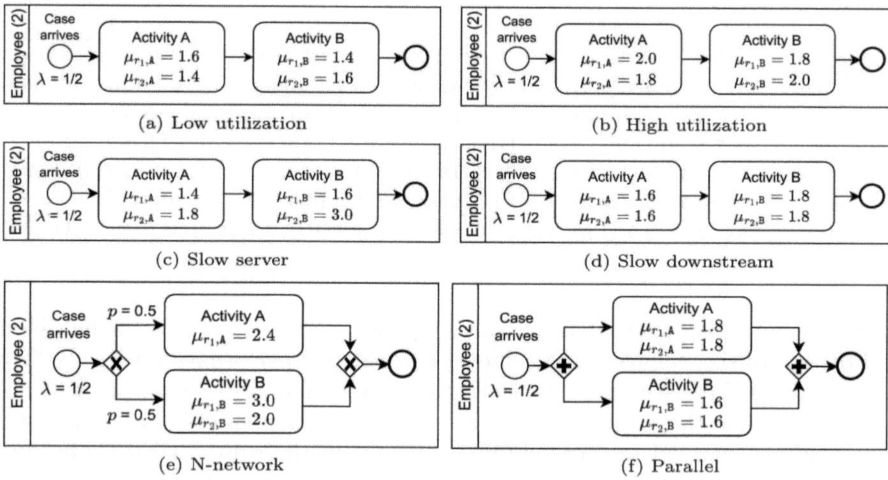

(a) Low utilization (b) High utilization (c) Slow server (d) Slow downstream (e) N-network (f) Parallel

Fig. 4. Six scenarios with two activities and resources adapted from [17]. In each scenario, cases arrive according to a Poisson process with rate $\lambda = 1/2$. Activity *act* is executed by resource r according to an exponentially distributed processing time with mean $\mu_{r,act}$.

The scenarios in Fig. 4 show various process flows that favor different heuristics. In the high utilization scenario, an activity instance is first generated for activity `A` followed by `B`. In this scenario, a policy should assign each resource to the activity at which it performs best to avoid queues building up, which is exactly what SPT does. In contrast, in the parallel scenario, it is more important to select which activity should be executed, as both resources process the activities at the same speed. In this scenario, the most efficient strategy is to complete both activity instances for one case before starting the next case, which is done by FIFO. Given these scenarios, some heuristics will perform well and others will not. We use these scenarios to evaluate whether our agent can learn which heuristics perform well in different contexts and whether the agent can combine their strengths to outperform any single heuristic.

We train two versions of our method on these scenarios, DRL and DRL$_{min}$. In DRL, we train an agent according to our proposed method. In all scenarios, except the N-system, there are always two activities that can be executed by the same two resources. Therefore, each resource and activity has the same level of flexibility. As a result, these heuristics randomly select an activity or resource.

Thus, we train a second version of our method, DRL$_{min}$, with a reduced set of heuristics that excludes these four heuristics. Table 2 shows the results of both models on the scenarios compared to the heuristic benchmarks.

Table 2. Mean cycle time (and standard deviation) for various policies on the scenarios. The best results are highlighted in bold. Multiple bold values indicate no statistically significant difference.

Scenario	DRL	DRL$_{min}$	SPT	FIFO	HRRN	LQF	SQF	Random
Low utilization	**5.7 (0.5)**	**5.7 (0.4)**	5.9 (0.4)	5.8 (0.5)	6.5 (0.6)	6.7 (0.7)	6.4 (0.6)	6.7 (0.7)
High utilization	19.4 (4.8)	**17.9 (4.8)**	19.7 (5.3)	25.7 (10.7)	25.8 (8.1)	35.3 (16.9)	30.5 (13.3)	34.7 (18.2)
Slow server	**11.7 (1.8)**	**11.9 (1.8)**	29.0 (11.5)	18.6 (6.7)	16.1 (3.3)	23.1 (8.3)	21.5 (8.3)	22.4 (7.1)
Slow downstream	**9.9 (1.5)**	**10.0 (1.6)**	14.7 (3.1)	**10.1 (1.8)**	12.2 (2.3)	11.9 (2.3)	11.0 (2.3)	11.8 (2.1)
N-system	**5.9 (0.5)**	**5.9 (0.5)**	7.2 (1.1)	**5.9 (0.5)**	**5.9 (0.5)**	**5.9 (0.6)**	6.9 (1.1)	6.4 (0.8)
Parallel	**9.7 (2.0)**	**9.5 (1.6)**	14.1 (3.3)	**9.5 (1.8)**	9.9 (1.7)	**9.7 (1.8)**	15.5 (4.6)	11.0 (2.1)

The results show that DRL$_{min}$ learns a policy that outperforms the heuristics in three out of six scenarios and achieves competitive performance with FIFO in the remaining three scenarios. In fact, [16] showed that FIFO is on par with the optimal policy in these three scenarios, which both our models can learn. In the N-system and parallel scenario, LQF is effectively the same as FIFO, because the longest queue always contains the longest waiting case. On these scenarios, LQF achieves the same performance as FIFO

Our standard DRL method, which includes all heuristics, performs slightly worse than DRL$_{min}$ in the high utilization scenario. The most likely reason for this is that the added heuristics have similar behavior to SPT because there is no least or most flexible resource or activity in this scenario. These heuristics add noise to the training process, making it more challenging to learn the same policy as DRL$_{min}$. These findings suggest that heuristic selection within the action space plays an important role in improving performance. Figure 5 provides a detailed look at the action distribution of DRL$_{min}$.

Figure 5 shows how many times each action is taken in an episode averaged over 300 episodes. For instance, in the low utilization scenario, the agent selects the SPT heuristic in 41.4% of decision steps. Across all scenarios, the agent learns to combine multiple heuristics into a new policy. Interestingly, while the FIFO heuristic is optimal for the slow downstream, N-system, and parallel scenarios [16], the agent either combines FIFO with other heuristics or uses other heuristics altogether to achieve similar performance.

In most scenarios, the agent uses two or three of the five heuristics available in DRL$_{min}$, except in high utilization, where four heuristics are used. The reason for not using all the heuristics is likely due to the limited number of assignments per scenario (four assignments in all scenarios, except for the N-system, which has three assignments). With fewer assignments, some heuristics choose the same assignments, making certain heuristics redundant. Notably, the SQF heuristic is

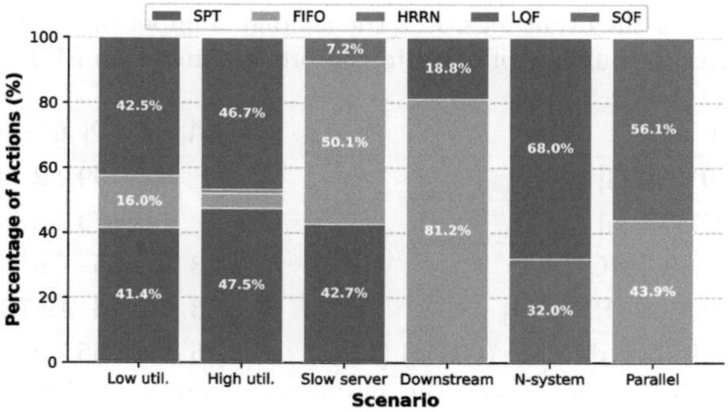

Fig. 5. Scenario action distribution of DRL_{min} averaged over 300 evaluation episodes.

never selected, which can be expected as, intuitively, assigning resources to non-bottleneck activities is inefficient. This intuition is also supported by the results, where it achieves a similar or worse performance than a random heuristic. The agent selects effective heuristics and avoids ineffective ones, demonstrating its ability to minimize cycle time across different business process settings.

5.4 Real-World Business Processes

In this section, we evaluate the scalability of our approach to real-world business processes. We consider five publicly available real-world datasets and mine them to generate a simulation model with probabilistic resource calendars using the approach presented in [3]. The resource calendars cause resources to become unavailable due to, for example, breaks or working schedules. We used this simulation model as its code base was most compatible with our code. We changed the processing time distributions to exponential to increase the variability, and thus complexity, of the resource allocation problem. We found that the resource-case ratio was not balanced, resulting in a process where resources were barely utilized and there were hardly any ongoing cases. As a result, resources spend little time queued and can be served immediately. Therefore, similar to [3], we tuned the arrival rate (which was already tuned in [3] to fit their distributions) such that the process exhibits stable behavior and there are at least several ongoing cases under an SPT policy. The specific arrival rates and distributions used can be found in our repository. The considered event logs and their descriptive statistics are shown in Table 3.

Table 3 shows that the number of assignments $|\mathcal{D}|$ becomes large in the real-world business processes. Previous work typically models each assignment as a separate action (e.g., [9,15,27]). In contrast, in our approach, the heuristics are the actions that then select the assignment. This reduction is especially useful for large processes with many possible assignments $|\mathcal{D}|$, as it significantly reduces the complexity of the learning tasks and accelerates convergence [6]. For example, the BPI2017W log includes 573 assignments, which would require a

Table 3. Overview of the event logs. L is the average number of activity instances per case. $|\overline{C}|$ is the average number of cases in the process under an SPT policy.

Event log	$\|\mathcal{A}\|$	$\|\mathcal{R}\|$	$\|\mathcal{D}\|$	L	$\|\overline{C}\|$
BPI2012W [4]	6	52	199	2.2	37.3
BPI2017W [5]	7	145	573	7.8	38.6
Microsoft (MC)[a]	13	8	55	7.6	43.4
Production (PR) [14]	13	33	76	19.7	19.3
ConsultaDataMining (CDM) [14]	16	179	435	5.2	23.8

[a] https://learn.microsoft.com/en-us/power-automate/process-mining-tutorial

neural network to predict among 573 possible labels (i.e., actions). We reduce the action space to the 9 heuristics included in the model.

For each resulting simulation model, we train an agent and evaluate as described in Sect. 5.1. Each episode contains significantly more decision steps compared to the scenarios because the average case length, L, is longer. Therefore, we reduce the number of cases per episode during training to 1000. This value ensures that the agent sees enough episodes, which is important for learning, while still ensuring sufficient states are visited in each episode. During the evaluation, we simulate 2500 cases per episode. For consistency with the evaluation of the scenarios, we again train two models: DRL and DRL$_{min}$. Table 4 shows the results of our method on the real-world processes.

Table 4. Mean cycle time for trained models, DRL and DRL$_{min}$, compared to heuristics on real-world processes. Best results are highlighted in bold. Multiple bold values indicate no statistically significant difference.

Event log	DRL	DRL$_{min}$	SPT	FIFO	HRRN	LQF	SQF	LFRF	MFRF	LFAF	MFAF
BPI2012W	**8.4**	**8.3**	**8.2**	60.3	9.8	73.8	52.4	9.1	8.5	40.2	52.1
BPI2017W	8.7	**8.3**	8.7	9.6	8.6	11.3	9.9	10.4	9.0	11.4	9.2
MC	143.6	**122.0**	270.2	171.3	157.3	252.8	217.3	358.0	342.6	223.8	406.1
PR	147.6	**144.1**	**145.9**	261.7	164.2	170.4	566.6	172.4	169.9	174.4	468.3
CDM	**64.5**	**65.0**	90.2	336.9	69.0	166.9	348.8	114.9	107.7	369.6	116.6

Table 4 shows that DRL outperforms the best heuristic in two out of five business processes (MC and CDM) and ties the performance of the best heuristic in the other three processes (BPI2012W, BPI2017W, and PR). Training the model with a subset of the heuristics, as seen in DRL$_{min}$, the performance improves. DRL$_{min}$ outperforms the best heuristic in three out of five processes (BPI2017W, MC, and CDM) and achieves the same performance as the best heuristic in the other two processes (BPI2012W and PR).

In line with the scenario results in Sect. 5.3, reducing the number of heuristics in the model improves the performance slightly. One reason for this is that the excluded heuristics do not perform that well individually, as shown in Table 4. While we expected that the agent would learn to avoid these heuristics in certain states, the agent still selects them. The results indicate that the included heuristics in the model affect the performance of the learned policy. Figure 6 shows the action distribution of the best model, DRL_{min}.

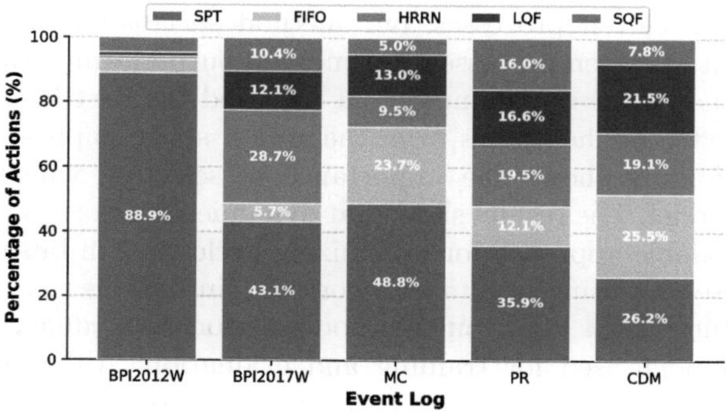

Fig. 6. Real-world business processes action distribution of DRL_{min} averaged over 300 evaluation episodes.

Figure 6 shows that the SPT heuristic is selected most frequently. This pattern aligns with the results in Table 4, where SPT ranks among the top heuristics. Additionally, prior work also showed that SPT is typically among the best-performing heuristics [3,9,17]. Specifically, for BPI2012W, the SPT heuristic is selected 88.9% of the time. This behavior makes sense, as Table 4 also shows that SPT achieves the lowest mean cycle time. In the other event logs, the figure shows that a more balanced strategy is found where the agent learns to combine all the heuristics. Interestingly, for the PR event log, our method learns a policy that is competitive with SPT, as shown in Table 4. The learned policy achieves similar performance to SPT, despite not selecting SPT for the majority of actions (64.1% of actions are not SPT). This demonstrates that, even without directly relying on certain heuristics, the agent can still approximate their performance.

These results show that our method successfully learns the best policy in all tested synthetic and real-world business processes. Therefore, selecting existing heuristics at runtime using DRL is an effective method for minimizing the mean cycle time in business processes.

6 Conclusion

In this paper, we introduced a DRL approach for dynamic heuristic selection for resource allocation problems within business processes. The objective is to minimize the mean cycle time of cases that go through the process. Our method leverages the strengths of existing heuristics by learning to select the most suitable heuristic in each process state. Furthermore, our method learned to avoid heuristics that negatively contribute to the objective function. By constraining the action space to proven heuristics, we significantly reduced the decision complexity compared to prior work that modeled all resources and activities as individual assignments. This reduction is especially important in real-world business processes, where the action space can become increasingly extensive.

We evaluated our method on six synthetic and five real-world business processes. Across all eleven processes, our method successfully learned the best policy. In six out of eleven processes, our method outperformed the best individual heuristic, and in the remaining five, it matched the best heuristic. Notably, excluding less effective heuristics from the action space improved performance slightly. This finding shows the importance of selecting which heuristics to include in the model. The results show that dynamically selecting heuristics is an effective and scalable approach for minimizing cycle time in business processes.

Despite these promising results, our work has limitations that present opportunities for future work. First, our method's performance depends on the simulation environment used for training and evaluation. Although our method performed well within our simulator, its effectiveness remains untested on other simulators, where the models would need to be retrained and evaluated. This limitation highlights the need for a standardized benchmarking environment for resource allocation in business processes. Second, our results showed that the choice of candidate heuristics impacts performance. A systematic analysis of heuristic selection and combination strategies would be valuable in future work.

Acknowledgments. The research leading up to this paper is supported by the Dutch foundation for scientific research (NWO) under the CERTIF-AI project (nr. 17998).

Disclosure of interest. The authors declare that there are no conflicts of interest related to the publication of this article.

References

1. Akiba, T., Sano, S., Yanase, T., Ohta, T., Koyama, M.: Optuna: a next-generation hyperparameter optimization framework. In: KDD (2019). https://doi.org/10.1145/3292500.3330701
2. Arias, M., Rojas, E., Munoz-Gama, J., Sepúlveda, M.: A framework for recommending resource allocation based on process mining. In: BPM Workshops (2016). https://doi.org/10.1007/978-3-319-42887-1_37
3. Bianco, R.L., van Jaarsveld, W., Middelhuis, J., Begnardi, L., Dijkman, R.: Automated decision-making for dynamic task assignment at scale (2025). https://doi.org/10.48550/arXiv.2504.19933
4. van Dongen, B.: BPI challenge 2012 (2012). https://doi.org/10.4121/uuid:3926db30-f712-4394-aebc-75976070e91f
5. van Dongen, B.: BPI challenge 2017 (2017). https://doi.org/10.4121/uuid:5f3067df-f10b-45da-b98b-86ae4c7a310b

6. Dulac-Arnold, G., et al.: Deep reinforcement learning in large discrete action spaces (2015). https://doi.org/10.48550/arXiv.1512.07679
7. Hopp, W.J., Spearman, M.L.: Factory physics (2011)
8. Hu, C., Wang, Z., Liu, J., Wen, J., Mao, B., Yao, X.: Constrained reinforcement learning for dynamic material handling. In: IJCNN. https://doi.org/10.1109/IJCNN54540.2023.10191999
9. Huang, Z., van der Aalst, W.M., Lu, X., Duan, H.: Reinforcement learning based resource allocation in business process management. DKE (2011). https://doi.org/10.1016/j.datak.2010.09.002
10. Kuchař, Š, Vondrák, I.: Automatic allocation of resources in software process simulations using their capability and productivity. J. Simul. (2016). https://doi.org/10.1057/jos.2015.8
11. Latip, R., Idris, Z.: Highest response ratio next (hrrn) vs first come first served (fcfs) scheduling algorithm in grid environment. In: ICSECS (2011). https://doi.org/10.1007/978-3-642-22191-0_60
12. Lo Bianco, R., Dijkman, R., Nuijten, W., van Jaarsveld, W.: Action-evolution petri nets: a framework for modeling and solving dynamic task assignment problems. In: BPM (2023). https://doi.org/10.1007/978-3-031-41620-0_13
13. Lo Bianco, R., Dijkman, R., Nuijten, W., van Jaarsveld, W.: A universal approach to feature representation in dynamic task assignment problems. In: BPM (2024). https://doi.org/10.1007/978-3-031-70418-5_12
14. Meneghello, F., Di Francescomarino, C., Ghidini, C.: Runtime integration of machine learning and simulation for business processes. In: ICPM (2023). https://doi.org/10.1109/ICPM60904.2023.10271993
15. Meneghello, F., et al.: Optimizing resource allocation policies in real-world processes using hybrid process simulation and deep reinforcement learning. In: BPM (2024). https://doi.org/10.1007/978-3-031-70396-6_10
16. Middelhuis, J., Bukhsh, Z., Adan, I., Dijkman, R.: A rollout-based algorithm and reward function for efficient resource allocation in business processes (2025). https://doi.org/10.48550/arXiv.2504.11250
17. Middelhuis, J., Lo Bianco, R., Sherzer, E., Bukhsh, Z., Adan, I., Dijkman, R.: Learning policies for resource allocation in business processes. Inf. Syst. (2025). https://doi.org/10.1016/j.is.2024.102492
18. Mnih, V., et al.: Playing atari with deep reinforcement learning (2013). https://doi.org/10.48550/arXiv.1312.5602
19. Park, G., Song, M.: Prediction-based resource allocation using lstm and minimum cost and maximum flow algorithm. In: ICPM (2019). https://doi.org/10.1109/ICPM.2019.00027
20. Pufahl, L., Stiehle, F., Ihde, S., Weske, M., Weber, I.: Resource allocation in business process executions–a systematic literature study. Inf. Syst. (2025). https://doi.org/10.1016/j.is.2025.102541
21. Schulman, J., Wolski, F., Dhariwal, P., Radford, A., Klimov, O.: Proximal policy optimization algorithms (2017). https://doi.org/10.48550/arXiv.1707.06347
22. Schumann, F., Rinderle-Ma, S.: Optimizing resource-driven process configuration through genetic algorithms. In: BPM (2024). https://doi.org/10.1007/978-3-031-70396-6_1
23. Sels, V., Gheysen, N., Vanhoucke, M.: A comparison of priority rules for the job shop scheduling problem under different flow time-and tardiness-related objective functions. Int. J. Prod. Res. (2012). https://doi.org/10.1080/00207543.2011.611539

24. Si, Y.W., Chan, V.I., Dumas, M., Zhang, D.: A petri nets based generic genetic algorithm framework for resource optimization in business processes. Simul. Model. Pract. Theory (2018). https://doi.org/10.1016/j.simpat.2018.05.004
25. Sutton, R.S., Barto, A.G., et al.: Reinforcement Learning: An Introduction (1998)
26. Williams, R.J.: Simple statistical gradient-following algorithms for connectionist reinforcement learning. Mach. Learn. (1992). https://doi.org/10.1007/BF00992696
27. Żbikowski, K., Ostapowicz, M., Gawrysiak, P.: Deep reinforcement learning for resource allocation in business processes. In: Process Mining Workshops (2023). https://doi.org/10.1007/978-3-031-27815-0_13
28. Zeng, Y., Liao, Z., Dai, Y., Wang, R., Li, X., Yuan, B.: Hybrid intelligence for dynamic job-shop scheduling with deep reinforcement learning and attention mechanism (2022). https://doi.org/10.48550/arXiv.2201.00548
29. Zhao, W., Yang, L., Liu, H., Wu, R.: The optimization of resource allocation based on process mining. In: ICIC (2015). https://doi.org/10.1007/978-3-319-22053-6_38

Modeling and Modeling Methods

Mapping the Pain: How Modelers Experience and Respond to Common Domain Modeling Frustrations

Isadora Valle[1(✉)], Tiago Prince Sales[1], Eduardo Guerra[2], Maya Daneva[1], Luiz Olavo Bonino da Silva Santos[1], Henderik Proper[3], and Giancarlo Guizzardi[1]

[1] University of Twente, Enschede, The Netherlands
{i.vallesousa,t.princesales,m.daneva,l.o.boninodasilvasantos, g.guizzardi}@utwente.nl
[2] Faculty of Engineering, Free University of Bozen-Bolzano, Bolzano, Italy
eduardo.guerra@unibz.it
[3] TU Wien, Vienna, Austria
henderik.proper@tuwien.ac.at

Abstract. Despite the widespread use of domain models, the modeling process remains underexplored, particularly regarding the interactions among agents, products, and activities. Building on prior work that identified 16 recurrent moments of dissatisfaction ("pain points") experienced by modelers during these interactions, this study offers a deeper analysis to clarify the significance of these pain points and support improvements in modeling practice. Through an online survey of 49 modelers, the study provides empirical evidence on the frequency of these moments, the reasons behind the frustrations they cause, and the strategies modelers use to address them. The descriptive analysis offers valuable insights into these aspects, revealing interesting patterns among modelers. These findings have implications for practice and academia, offering a foundation to enhance the modeling experience and improve the value of domain modeling efforts.

Keywords: Pain Points · Domain Modeling · Conceptual Modeling · Modeling Experience

1 Introduction

Although domain models are widely used in organizational and academic settings, the domain modeling process itself is not yet fully understood. While it is well established that this process involves multiple agents (e.g., modelers, domain experts, sponsors), products (e.g., models, languages, tools), and activities (e.g., requirements elicitation, concept negotiation), their interplay and influences on the modeling experience remain under-explored.

Our previous study [26] took an initial step toward addressing this gap by identifying 16 of the most prevalent and impactful pain points of domain modeling. They reflect moments of dissatisfaction that modelers experience throughout

© The Author(s), under exclusive license to Springer Nature Switzerland AG 2026
A. Gianola et al. (Eds.): EDOC 2025, LNCS 16213, pp. 193–209, 2026.
https://doi.org/10.1007/978-3-032-15140-7_11

the modeling process. For instance, such a moment arises when modelers and domain experts struggle to reach a shared understanding of a concept. Dissatisfaction may also occur when modelers feel overwhelmed by the manual effort involved in model verification or layout due to a tool's lack of features.

This study provides a deeper analysis of these pain points to further substantiate their relevance to the field. It investigates their practical occurrence, focusing on their frequency, reasons for frustrations, and the reactions they provoke. By understanding these pain points and their implications for modelers and the modeling process, this research aims to enhance modelers' experiences and improve the modeling practice. Additionally, it provides insights into the interactions among agents, products, and activities, helping practitioners anticipate and address potential challenges. Consequently, it equips the modeling community with knowledge to better plan initiatives, assess costs, identify solutions, refine methods, improve languages and tools, and guide novice modelers.

Our study was guided by the following research questions:

RQ1: *How often do modelers experience the pain points of domain modeling?*
RQ2: *Why do modelers feel frustrated by these pain points?*
RQ3: *How do modelers react when facing these pain points?*

To address these research questions, we conducted an online survey targeting modelers with experience in domain modeling. We got 49 responses from a diverse sample in terms of years of experience, activities performed, and application context. The study focuses on descriptive analysis over statistical inference.

The findings of the study show that all analyzed pain points are prevalent among the participants, with frequencies ranging from sometimes to usually. These frustrations were predominantly associated with *lost time*, *financial losses*, and *difficulties in achieving goals*, rather than concerns about e.g. self-esteem. While some pain points were viewed as unavoidable or even necessary challenges inherent to modeling, modelers continued to value modeling as a problem-solving tool. They also identified training as an effective strategy for addressing most pain points and seemed unwilling to change the modeling language they use.

In [26], we analyzed the pain points related to a specific type of domain modeling, referred to as structural conceptual modeling. These models aim to identify, analyze, and describe key structural regularities–such as types (classes), attributes, relationships, and constraints–within a specific universe of discourse [9]. Examples include models specified using Entity-Relationship diagrams (ER) [4], UML Class Diagrams [14], and OntoUML [9]. This paper also focuses on this type of modeling. Thus, we henceforth use the terms models, modelers, and modeling to refer to structural conceptual models and their associated concepts.

The remainder of the paper unfolds as follows. Section 2 presents the state of the art. Section 3 introduces the pain points of domain modeling. Section 4 details the survey research process employed. Section 5 presents the findings derived from the survey data analysis and provides a discussion of the results. Section 6 addresses potential threats to validity. Finally, Sect. 7 offers concluding remarks and outlines directions for future research.

2 State of the Art

Several studies have focused on identifying pain points, challenges, and pitfalls in modeling-related contexts. In [7], a survey of 304 practitioners identified barriers to conceptual model use, such as the variety of modeling methods, tool cost, investment risk, and tool complexity. While our study also highlights practical challenges, it focuses more on frustrations experienced during the modeling process, rather than on adoption barriers.

A meta-review in [27] analyzed publications on the practical use of modeling languages and the benefits and challenges perceived by practitioners in model-driven engineering (MDE). The main issues identified included limited tool functionalities, organizational resistance, immature methods, and high learning effort. Our study resonates with these findings but provides first-hand accounts of how such challenges are experienced across roles and phases of modeling.

Studies on modeling education [13,16,21,22] have focused on the difficulties novice modelers face when using UML. They identified recurring issues related to understanding domain constraints, mastering language constructs, dealing with abstraction, navigating modeling tools, and accessing support materials. Although these studies primarily address students and early modeling stages, they echo technical frustrations also reported by professionals in our study.

In the context of business process modeling (BPM), a literature review in [1] highlighted difficulties in engaging stakeholders and translating business goals into technical objectives. Similarly, a Delphi study conducted in [12] involving academics, practitioners, and tool vendors revealed concerns around standardization, unclear value, and execution challenges. In [17,18], the authors conducted interviews and focus groups with analysts and managers, identifying issues such as limited stakeholder synergy, insufficient modeling expertise, and the burden of model maintenance. These findings closely align with the pain points reported in our study. In particular, the uncertainty surrounding the purpose and long-term value of process models mirrors the doubts expressed by our participants about the usefulness and longevity of the models they produce.

Beyond identifying pain points, some studies have used them to inform artifact development. For example, the framework for Model-based Software Engineering (MBSE) and the curated set of best practices proposed in [15] were grounded in modeling-related pain points identified by the study. Similarly, the taxonomic theory of modeling difficulties presented in [19] was derived from investigations into modelers' experiences throughout the data modeling process [19,20]. Therefore, while our study does not present a prescriptive solution, it similarly provides an empirical foundation for future artifact design.

Unlike these previous studies that primarily focus on identifying modeling pain points, our research delves into how modelers experience and respond to them in practice. By examining the frequency, reasons for frustrations, and reactions to these pain points, our research provides a better understanding of their effects on the modeling process. This deeper exploration offers insights that can inform future efforts in improving modeling tools, methods, and training.

3 The Pain Points of Domain Modeling

"Pain point" is a term from Marketing describing customers' psychological dissatisfaction when their expectations are unmet during interactions with a product or service [28]. Pain point analysis is used by organizations to identify moments of customer dissatisfaction as experienced during a consumption journey, enabling targeted efforts to improve their experience. Empirical studies have employed pain point analysis across various fields. For example, scientific software development [30], computational notebooks [3], and requirements engineering [6].

In [26], we applied this strategy to modeling, investigating the pain points experienced by modelers. We framed modeling as a dynamic interaction involving various products, activities, and agents to identify instances of dissatisfaction when modelers, acting as service consumers, interact with modeling languages, tools, methods, and related resources. To this end, we conducted a five-phase empirical study employing a multi-method approach [5] to identify 16 of the most prevalent and consequential pain points in the modeling experience. Below, we present these pain points and illustrate situations in which they may arise.

- *Improper Requirements:* I could not properly define the model requirements. E.g., when stakeholders were unsure of their needs or the domain was unfamiliar to me.
- *Resistance to Modeling:* My stakeholders resisted adopting modeling, a modeling language, or a tool. E.g., when they perceived modeling as unnecessary or I failed to demonstrate the value of the model I wanted to create.
- *Expensive Requirements:* It was costly to define the model requirements. E.g., when many requirements had to be defined and agreed among many stakeholders.
- *Effortful Negotiation:* It was costly to negotiate a common definition among experts about a concept of the project's domain of interest. E.g., when I lacked negotiation skills or even my domain experts could not agree among themselves.
- *Effortful Verbalization:* It was costly to verbalize my model in a way that was suitable for the different audiences that should be able to use it. E.g., when the tool I used lacked such a feature or too many different verbalizations were required.
- *Inadequate Explanation:* It was hard to explain my model to my stakeholders. E.g., because they do not know how to model or I am not good at explaining my model.
- *Unclear Conceptualization:* Writing definitions for the elements in my model was hard and boring. E.g., when domain experts were not available or I was unsure how to structure a definition.
- *Complexity Issues:* The model has become too complex and too costly to maintain. E.g., because the tool I chose did not support documentation or the model contained too many elements.
- *Laborious Reuse:* I wanted to reuse an existing model, but I had to redraw it from scratch. E.g., when it was only available as an image or in a different language/tool.
- *Tool Restrictions:* I could not choose the modeling tool I wanted. E.g., due to constraints related to cost, expertise, culture, or bureaucracy.
- *Effortful Diagramming:* It was costly to manually split the model into visually appealing and understandable views (diagrams). E.g., when I was unfamiliar with aesthetic guidelines or the tool did not support diagram creation.
- *Overlooked Documentation:* My colleagues did not consider it important to document the model and did not understand my efforts to do so. E.g., when they lacked modeling knowledge or I failed to show the model's value for maintenance or reuse.

- *Limited Verification:* The tool I chose did not support model verification. My model was large and complex and verifying it by myself was not trivial. E.g., when I had to use a suboptimal tool due to organizational constraints or lacked experience.
- *Unclear Approach:* It was costly to define the model-driven approach. E.g., when my company lacked a modeling culture or I struggled to identify the best method.
- *Disinterest in Use:* I was the only one on the team interested in using and reusing the model. E.g., when I was the sole person who understood it or my colleagues did not know how to leverage its benefits.
- *Unclear Documentation:* I was not sure how to document my model. E.g., when I was uncertain about what to include or how much effort to invest.

4 Research Method

The study employed an online survey, as it offers a cost-effective and efficient means of systematically collecting data, enabling access to a geographically dispersed sample while preserving anonymity. Following the survey research process outlined in [23], we consolidated the 13 steps proposed into the three phases detailed below. Study findings and supplementary materials are available in [24].

Questionnaire Design. The questionnaire was subjected to five iterative revisions by four researchers before approval. The final version was composed of three sections: introduction, user profiling, and pain point report.

The introductory section included a consent form, a brief explanation of structural conceptual models, and a question regarding the respondent's experience with this type of model. Respondents without experience were directed to conclude their participation.

The user profiling section comprised ten mandatory personal questions (PQs) aimed at assessing respondents' background in modeling. These questions were presented in multiple-choice and single-choice formats, structured as follows: PQ1.1 and PQ1.2 addressed respondents' experience and preferences regarding modeling languages; PQ2.1 and PQ2.2 focused on their experience and preferences related to modeling tools; PQ3 inquired about years of modeling experience; PQ4 identified the modeling activities they had engaged in; PQ5 required a self-evaluation of their modeling expertise; PQ6 examined the context in which they applied modeling; PQ7 explored how they learned about modeling; and PQ8 asked about their education level.

The pain point report section was organized into sixteen subsections, each corresponding to a specific pain point. Each subsection featured fifteen standardized questions addressing our research questions. They were organized as follows: a dichotomous question (yes/no) to confirm the respondent's experience with the pain point (RQ1.1), followed by fourteen Likert scale questions (five points) assessing its frequency (RQ1.2), reasons for the frustrations it caused (RQ2.1–2.5), and possible reactions it elicited (RQ3.1–3.8). Respondents answered the Likert scale questions only if they confirmed experience with a pain point. For pain points that required additional context for clarity, we included examples in the description to aid comprehension. Questions RQ2.1–2.4 examine four key potential reasons for frustration: *wasted time*, *financial losses*, *unmet goals*, and *diminished self-esteem*. Questions RQ3.1–3.7 explore seven possible reactions to the pain points: abandoning modeling, taking no action, implementing workarounds, pursuing training, or changing the modeling language, tool, or method. The analyzed reasons and reactions were defined based on insights from interviews and brainstorming sessions conducted in the authors' previous research [25,26].

SurveyMonkey was selected as the platform to host the online survey. Before its launch, five modelers tested it asynchronously. Based on their feedback, rephrasing and spelling adjustments were made, while the structure and design remained unchanged. The final version of the survey is available in [24]. An example of questions for the pain point *Improper Requirements* is shown in Fig. 1.

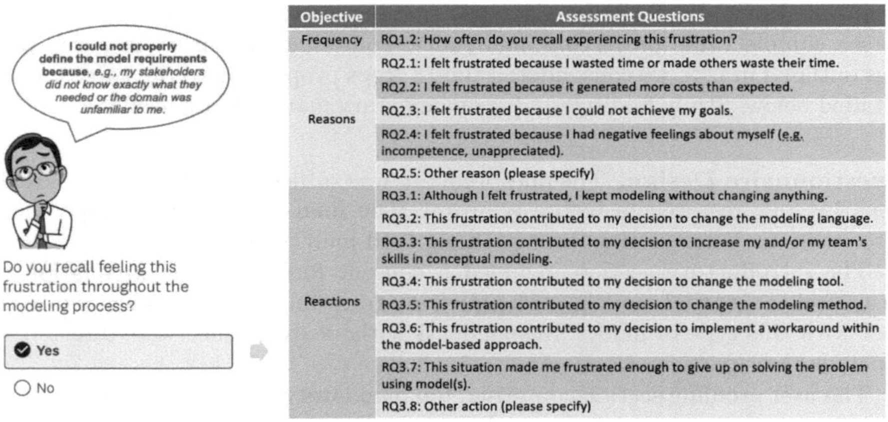

Fig. 1. Subsection related to the pain point *Improper Requirements*

Data Collection. The survey was launched on October 30, 2023, during the EDOC 2023 conference, using a banner and a LinkedIn post on the conference page for promotion. The same strategy was applied at the ER 2023 conference the following week. Afterward, posts were shared in relevant LinkedIn groups and on the authors' pages. Direct invitation emails were also sent to the authors' professional contacts and researchers from the conceptual modeling field identified via Google Scholar. The survey closed on December 13, 2023, after receiving 50 complete responses. However, one participant, who reported no frustrations across all 16 questions, was deemed an outlier and excluded from the analysis.

We acknowledge that our sample size is not statistically representative. However, as an exploratory study, the priority was on recruiting knowledgeable participants over randomly sampling a population [23]. Accordingly, we focused on reaching modelers with diverse experiences rather than maximizing sample size.

Data Analysis. As the survey relied primarily on Likert-scale questions and involved a small sample, descriptive statistics were employed for data analysis [11]. The data were first organized into tables displaying the number of responses for each category within the variables. These tables were then used to visualize data distribution through graphs and charts. When appropriate, measures of central tendency such as mean, median, and mode were included. For open questions (RQ2.5 and RQ3.8), we conducted a thematic analysis using inductive coding [2]. This process uncovered additional reasons for, and reactions to, participants' frustration during the modeling process. The resulting themes and findings are presented in detail in [24].

5 Results and Discussion

The analysis in this section is based on 49 survey responses. Some analyses use these responses as data points, while others treat the 321 pain point reports as individual data points. Throughout the text, the most significant findings are highlighted and labeled with an "F".

5.1 Study Population

All 49 respondents reported having experience in structural conceptual modeling. In a self-assessment of their expertise (PQ5), 2% identified as novice, 6% as beginner, 24% as intermediate, 31% as advanced, and 37% as expert. Regarding years of experience (PQ3), 2% had less than one year, 29% had between one and three years, and 69% had more than three years. Among those with over three years of experience, the reported range spanned from 5 to 40 years, with a mode of 20 years, a mean of 18, and a standard deviation of 8.9.

Throughout their years of experience, respondents have engaged in various modeling tasks (PQ4). The data indicates that 94% have participated in creating conceptual models, while 73% have contributed by reviewing and providing feedback on models created by others. Additionally, 53% have undertaken tasks related to documenting or implementing conceptual models, and 47% have been involved in modifying models initially developed by others. In summary, 82% have participated in multiple modeling activities over their careers, underscoring the diverse skill sets of the survey participants.

The respondents reported engaging in the aforementioned modeling activities across diverse contexts (PQ6), with research (73%), education (65%), and industry (49%) being the most common. Moreover, 78% indicated involvement in modeling across multiple contexts. Among those operating within a single context, the majority (12%) were exclusively involved in industry, while no respondents reported working solely in education.

Regarding respondents' experience with modeling languages (PQ1.1), UML [14] emerged as the most widely used, with 96% reporting familiarity. This was followed by ER/EER [4] (71%), OntoUML [9] (43%), and ORM [10] (22%). Moreover, 84% indicated experience with multiple modeling languages. Among

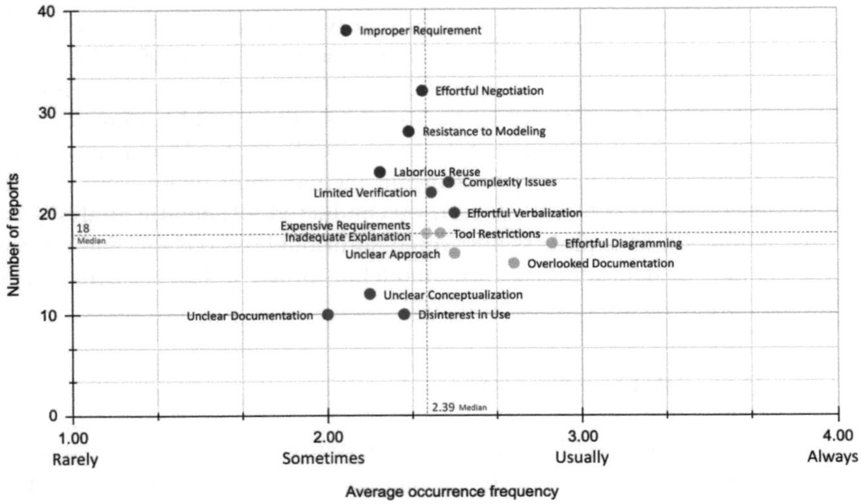

Fig. 2. The frequency with which the pain points are experienced.

those familiar with only one language, UML was the most prevalent, reported by 12%. Regarding their experience with modeling tools (PQ2.1), Draw.io was the most commonly used, with 47% reporting experience, followed by Visual Paradigm (45%), Enterprise Architect (31%), and Lucidchart (27%). Additionally, 63% indicated familiarity with multiple tools, while only two respondents reported no experience with any tool.

Because some pain points are related to language and/or tool issues, respondents were asked to select a specific modeling language and tool as a reference for completing the questionnaire. For modeling languages (PQ1.2), 53% chose UML, 24% chose OntoUML, and 18% chose ER/EER, while the remaining 4% selected other languages. For modeling tools (PQ2.2), 33% chose Visual Paradigm, 24% chose Draw.io, and the rest selected other tools, which did not provide a sufficiently representative sample for analysis.

The study population profile reflects a diverse and experienced sample, aligning with our focus on prioritizing expertise over random sampling [23]. We consider this sample appropriate for supporting our exploratory analysis.

5.2 The Frequency of the Pain Points of Modeling

To assess the frequency of the pain points, we analyzed how many respondents have experienced each pain, and how often. To examine the occurrence of a pain point among modelers, we analyze responses to questions RQ1.1 (Fig. 1) for all 16 pain points. As illustrated in Fig. 2, **each pain point was reported by at least ten participants, providing evidence of its prevalence (F1)**. The most frequently reported ones were *Improper Requirements* (38), *Effortful*

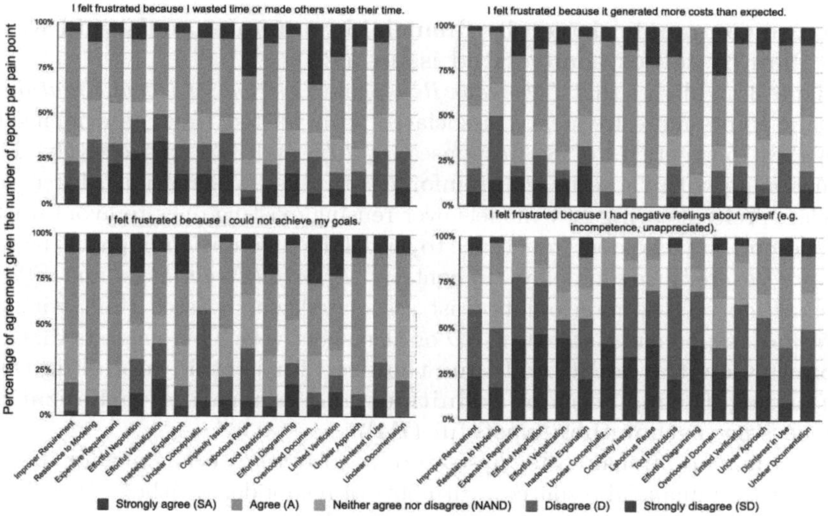

Fig. 3. Reasons for the frustrations behind the analyzed pain points.

Negotiation (32), *Resistance to Modeling* (28), *Laborious Reuse* (24), *Complexity Issues* (23), *Limited Verification* (22) and *Effortful Verbalization* (20).

To examine the recurrence with which modelers experience a pain point, we analyze responses to question RQ1.2 (Fig. 1) for all 16 pain points. As illustrated in Fig. 2, **all pain points were experienced by participants with a frequency ranging from sometimes to usually (F2).** The most frequently experienced ones were *Effortful Verbalization* (2.50), *Complexity Issues* (2.48), and *Limited Verification* (2.41). Conversely, the least frequently experienced pain points are *Disinterest in Use* (2.30), *Unclear Conceptualization* (2.17), and *Unclear Documentation* (2.00). While many respondents reported encountering *Improper Requirements*, *Effortful Negotiation*, *Resistance to Modeling*, and *Laborious Reuse* at some point in their careers, these were not experienced frequently.

5.3 The Frustration Behind the Pain Points of Modeling

To understand why modelers felt frustrated when encountering the pain points and explore the reasons for these frustrations, we analyzed responses to questions RQ2.1–RQ2.5 (Fig. 1) for all 16 pain points. Figure 3 presents the analysis for each source of frustration. As shown, *NAND* (see the legend of Fig. 3 for an explanation of the abbreviations) responses are relatively low across most pain points, suggesting that respondents generally have clear opinions on whether these factors contribute to their frustrations. Among the 321 reported pain points, 55% of respondents *SA* or *A* that they felt frustrated due to wasted time, 61% due to financial losses, 56% due to unmet goals, and 21% due to diminished self-esteem. These findings suggest that **frustrations throughout the modeling process**

are more commonly driven by financial loss, unmet goals, and wasted time than by self-esteem-related issues (F3).

Figure 3 highlights that *Laborious Reuse* and *Overlooked Documentation* are the pain points more frequently associated with wasted time, as evidenced by the highest percentages of *SA* responses, at 29% and 33%, respectively. These findings align with those in [26], reinforcing two key observations. First, most modelers prefer creating new models over reusing existing ones to avoid wasting time. Second, stakeholders' resistance to model documentation impacts the modeling process, resulting in delays. In contrast, *Effortful Negotiation* and *Effortful Verbalization* are the pain points least associated with wasted time, with 47% and 50% of respondents indicating *SD* or *D*, respectively. This suggests that **participants view the additional time required for certain modeling tasks, such as negotiating concept definitions and generating verbalizations, as necessary rather than wasteful (F4).**

Regarding additional costs, *Resistance to Modeling* stands out for its minimal impact on financial resources, with 50% of respondents either *SD* or *D* with its contribution to financial waste. In contrast, *Unclear Conceptualization*, *Complexity Issues*, *Laborious Reuse*, and *Effortful Diagramming* exhibit high levels of agreement, with 75% or more of respondents *SA* or *A* with their association with frustrations related to increased expenses. These four pain points are linked to model documentation in various ways. Textual concept definitions and visually appealing diagrams are key components of documentation, while tasks such as model maintenance and reuse depend on documentation quality. Therefore, **model documentation can help mitigate frustrations arising from wasted financial resources throughout the modeling process (F5).**

Regarding frustration related to goal attainment, *Unclear Conceptualization* stands out, with 58% of respondents *SD* or *D* that difficulties in writing concept definitions affect goal achievement. One possible explanation is that most modelers create models for personal use [25], where they already understand the model's conceptualizations, making written concept definitions unnecessary. However, when modelers' goals depend on others understanding the model, difficulties in formalizing definitions become more relevant.

For most respondents, damaged self-esteem was the least frequent source of frustration when encountering these pain points. However, *Disinterest in Use* emerged as the pain point that affects modelers' self-esteem, with 60% of respondents indicating *SA* and *A*. This pain point reflects modelers' frustration when others involved in a project fail to recognize the benefits of the model. Although modelers typically develop models for their personal use [25], the lack of recognition of the model's utility by others can be discouraging, leading them to perceive their work as undervalued or unappreciated.

An open question (RQ2.5) invited participants to share additional reasons for their frustrations. Their responses highlight challenges related to stakeholders (e.g. "I felt frustrated because my clients consistently showed ignorance about the value of modeling." – *Improper Requirements*), tools (e.g. "It would have been better to do the modeling using a tool more suited to the needs." – *Tool*

Restrictions), autonomy (e.g. "I felt frustrated because I was given responsibility without authority to change things." – *Unclear Approach*), and the nature of the work (e.g. "Because it's a lot of work, sometimes repetitive work." – *Effortful Verbalization*). Additionally, they clarified that, **although frustrating, some pain points are inherent challenges of the modeling process that should be addressed (F6)**, such as *Expensive Requirements*, *Effortful Negotiation*, *Effortful Verbalization*, *Inadequate Explanation*, and *Limited Verification*.

5.4 The Reactions to the Pain Points of Modeling

To understand modelers' reactions to each pain point, we examined the responses to questions RQ3.1–RQ3.8 (Fig. 1) for all 16 of these. Figure 4 and 5 present the analysis for each analyzed reaction. As shown, *NAND* responses are minimal across most pain points, indicating that participants generally have clear opinions on how to address them. Moreover, among the 321 reported pain points, respondents *SA* or *A* that they reacted to the pain points by abandoning modeling (18%), taking no action (43%), implement workarounds (40%), pursue training (49%), or change the modeling language (16%), tool (29%), or method (43%).

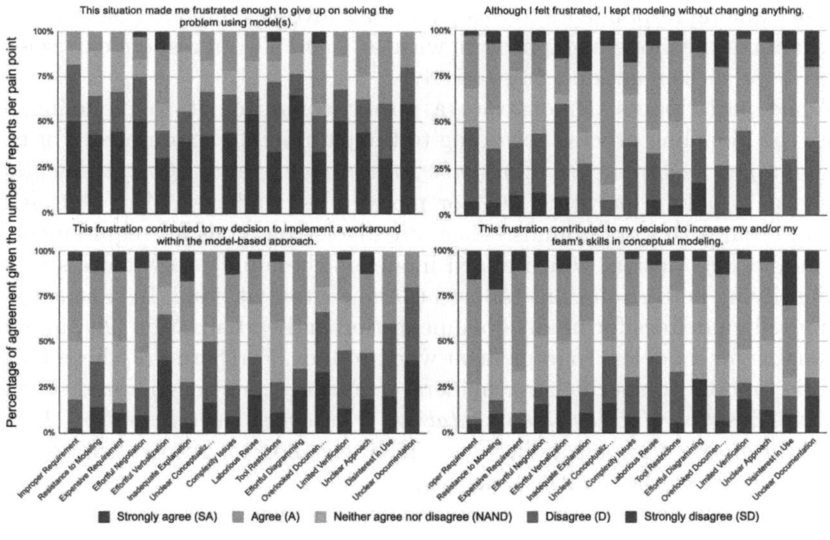

Fig. 4. Reactions to the analyzed pain points (Part 1).

As shown in Fig. 4, the percentage of *SD* responses is notably higher for abandoning modeling as a reaction. This suggests that **study participants are committed to using modeling as a problem-solving tool, even when the process is challenging (F7).** This finding aligns with that in [25] which states that modelers "always choose to solve problems through models, even if they do not rationally know whether modeling is the best option for a given situation". Although participants are unwilling to give up modeling, *Effortful Verbalization*, *Overlooked Documentation*, and *Disinterest in Use* are the pain points that are most likely to prompt this reaction, with 40% of them indicating *SA* or *A*. One possible explanation is that modeling tools still offer limited support for verbalization and documentation, and conveying the value of modeling remains inherently difficult [26]. These challenges create barriers to understanding and using models, making it difficult to persuade others to adopt modeling.

The analysis suggests that respondents may overlook certain pain points, such as *Unclear Conceptualization* and *Disinterest in Use*. Specifically, 83% and 70% of them, respectively, *SA* or *A* to continuing modeling without making any adjustments in reaction to these pain points. This result can also be attributed to the fact that most modelers create models for personal use [25], which reduces the impact of challenges such as difficulties in defining concepts and limited interest among team members in using and reusing the model. In contrast, *Effortful Verbalization* is perceived as the pain point most requiring intervention, with 60% of respondents *SD* or *D* with taking no action. Given that verbalizing the model to enhance its accessibility and comprehensibility for diverse audiences can produce positive outcomes [26], it is reasonable for modelers to address issues related to this task promptly. Further analysis reveals that the most preferred reactions among respondents to this pain point involve increasing modeling skills and changing the modeling approach, with 46% and 50% of respondents selecting *SA* or *A* for these reactions, respectively.

While participants demonstrate a strong commitment to modeling, they adjust the modeling process according to the pain point encountered. For example, *Improper Requirements*, *Expensive Requirements*, and *Effortful Negotiation* are the pain points for which 50% or more of respondents *SA* or *A* that they react to them with workarounds. There are diverse methods for requirement elicitation and negotiation, which afford modelers the ability to explore strategies for identifying better solutions tailored to the context at hand. In contrast, there are limited guidelines for model documentation and verbalization [26], making it challenging for modelers to implement workarounds. Furthermore, these artifacts must be tailored to specific stakeholders, requiring more personalized solutions. This explains why *Unclear Documentation*, *Overlooked Documentation*, *Effortful Verbalization* are the pain points for which over 60% of respondents *SD* or *D* that they react to them with workarounds.

Figure 4 also reveals that respondents broadly view all pain points as opportunities to improve their own or their team's skills in conceptual modeling. This means that **study participants agree that training is a good strategy for addressing most pain points (F8)**. Four of them explicitly mentioned this in their responses to the open question (RQ3.8), citing training as a reaction to *Unclear Approach* (e.g. "Education. Also tried to point out examples of incoherent classification in existing company data structures."), *Improper Requirements* (e.g. "This frustration made me think about investing in the training of non-technical users."), *Resistance to Modeling* (e.g. "Aim to educate stakeholders on what CM is really for.") and *Effortful Verbalization* (e.g. "This situation brought me to invest more in teaching non-technical users."). Although pursuing training had the highest proportion of *NAND* responses, *Improper Requirements* and *Disinterest in Use* emerged as a significant driver of skill development, with 73% and 70% of respondents selecting *SA* or *A*, respectively. Since defining model requirements and encouraging model adoption are complex tasks that rely on modeling expertise, fostering a shared understanding within the team can play a crucial role in addressing these challenges.

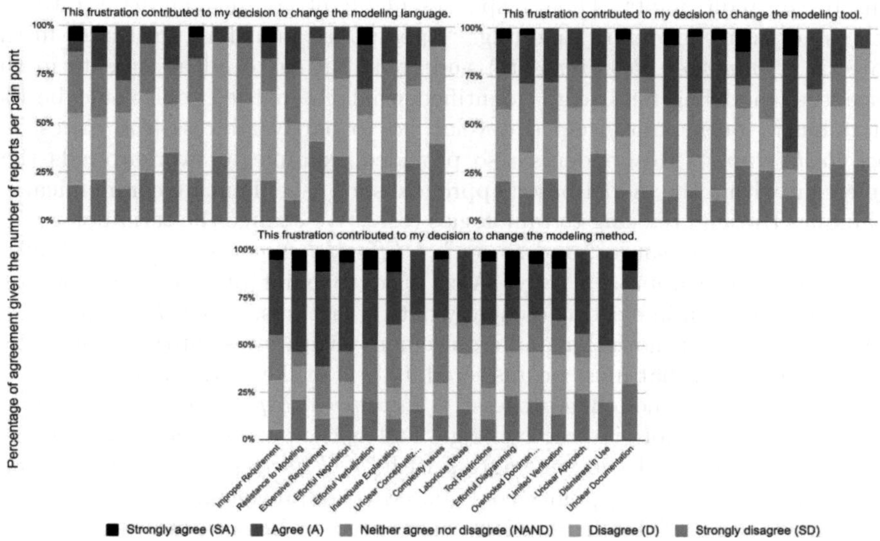

Fig. 5. Reactions to the analyzed pain points (Part 2).

As depicted in Fig. 5, **while participants exhibit some attachment to modeling tools and methods, they are generally more open to modifying these aspects than the modeling language (F9).** In most cases, at least 50% of respondents selected *SD* or *D* when asked about changing the modeling language in reaction to any pain point. The learning curve associated with a modeling language can be long and costly, which may explain modelers' reluctance to switch languages despite existing challenges.

Among the pain points analyzed, *Limited Verification* stands out as a driver of tool-related changes, with 64% of respondents selecting *SA* or *A*. Since this pain point directly stems from tool limitations, modifying the tool appears to be the most effective way to address it. Similarly, *Expensive Requirements* emerges as the pain point that leads to changes in the modeling method, with 61% of respondents in agreement. While the requirements elicitation method plays a role in defining model requirements, the extent to which the modeling method itself influences this process remains unclear.

Conversely, *Unclear Documentation* stands out as the pain point that is unlikely to trigger changes in the modeling language, tool, or method, with over 80% of respondents selecting *SD* or *D*. This suggests that such uncertainties stem more from modelers' experience, domain characteristics, and project scope than from the specific modeling tool, language, or method used. Likewise, writing definitions for model elements is not directly influenced by the modeling language, which explains why respondents show strong resistance to change the language in reaction to *Unclear Conceptualization*, with 92% selecting *SD* or *D*.

An open question (RQ3.8) invited participants to share additional reactions to the pain points. Their responses highlight complementary strategies, such as adjusting modeling time (e.g. "I postponed modeling until later in the project." – *Improper Requirements*) and contributing to advancements in the conceptual modeling field (e.g. "Identified what the needed tool would be like but it hasn't been built. Helped develop [x] to partly address [the issues]." – *Tool Restrictions*). Respondents also provided examples of workarounds they implement within the model-based approach, such as: enhancing communication techniques through revising terminologies (e.g. "We change the terminology, dig up an authoritative source, and so on." – *Effortful Negotiation*) and adopting an example-based approach (e.g. "Also tried to point out examples of incoherent classification in existing company data structures." – *Unclear Approach*), refining agreement negotiation and requirement elicitation strategies (e.g. "After detailing questions that must be answered in term of the model and ones that do not, we continue the modeling process." – *Expensive Requirements*), and making collaborative tasks more interactive (e.g. "Follow the process and iteratively create a verbalization that everyone agrees with." – *Effortful Verbalization*). They highlighted how the pain points contributed to improvements in their modeling strategies (e.g. "This frustration contributed to better study the domain, ask more information to the stakeholders, and postpone the model results." – *Improper Requirements*), persuasive skills (e.g. "This frustration contributed to better explain the benefits of the model." – *Resistance to Modeling*), time management abilities (e.g. "I planned extra time for negotiation meetings in my next projects." – *Effortful Negotiation*), and project selection criteria (e.g. "This situation made me actively search for a new project in a team where there was a modeling culture." – *Unclear Approach*). Finally, three respondents expressed dissatisfaction with how current tools support verbalization, model explanation, and maintenance. For instance, one noted, "Would change to a tool that better conveys meanings if one existed." – *Effortful Verbalization*.

6 Threats to Validity

One concern pertains to the representativeness of the sample in relation to the broader population, affecting the ability to generalize findings [8]. While we acknowledge that our respondents' answers may not universally represent all contexts, there are notable similarities in the settings of our respondents and others engaged in domain modeling. For example, in process modeling, modelers often interact with stakeholders who lack modeling expertise, use models for training and problem-solving, and navigate tool and language constraints. Similarly, researchers in the modeling domain often share overlapping teaching objectives and research interests. Given these parallels, it is reasonable to assume that similar responses could be obtained from other modelers in comparable contexts. Therefore, our sample offers a representative foundation for examining domain modelers' pain points, consistent with the partial generalization criteria proposed in [29]. However, we recognize that the sample size is insufficient to support statistical analysis, and we encourage future research to explore these pain points with a larger sample.

Another concern relates to whether the questions and corresponding answers accurately capture the characteristics under investigation [8]. While we cannot guarantee that all respondents answered the survey questions in a way that fully reflects their true opinions, emotions, or behaviors, we believe the questions effectively capture the intended meaning of the variables under investigation. This is because we followed an established survey development method [23] and conducted five rounds of testing to ensure clarity and minimize misunderstandings. However, due to tool limitations, we could not randomize the research questions, and we observed that the last two pain points were reported as the least experienced. This lack of randomization may have influenced the responses, an issue that should be addressed in future study replications.

7 Conclusion

Despite the widespread use of domain models, the modeling process remains underexplored, particularly regarding the interactions among agents, products, and services. A recent study [26] took an initial step toward addressing this gap by identifying 16 of the most prevalent and impactful pain points that arise as modelers engage with the elements of the modeling process. Building on this work, the present study investigates these pain points in practice by surveying 49 modelers to assess their frequency (RQ1), explore the reasons for the frustrations they evoke (RQ2), and examine how modelers react to them (RQ3).

The findings indicate that the analyzed pain points are prevalent among study participants, with at least ten reporting prior experience with each (F1). Moreover, all pain points were encountered with a frequency ranging from sometimes to usually (F2). Frustrations were more often linked to lost time, financial losses, and difficulties in achieving goals rather than concerns about self-esteem (F3). Although participants found the additional time required for modeling tasks frustrating, they viewed it as necessary rather than wasteful (F4). While some frustrations related to financial losses can be mitigated through model documentation (F5), others are perceived as unavoidable challenges inherent to the modeling process (F6). Despite the difficulties, modelers remained committed to using modeling as a problem-solving tool (F7), recognized training as an effective strategy to mitigate most pain points (F8), and exhibited resistance to changing the modeling language (F9).

This study has practical and academic implications for the domain modeling community. Practically, the insights can help practitioners refine modeling practices and better plan modeling initiatives, while also assisting developers in enhancing tools and languages. Academically, the research advances the field by extending existing studies and providing empirical evidence that can inform improvements in modeling methodologies and training strategies. Additionally, our findings highlight opportunities for future research. For example, future research could further validate and analyze the pain points, examine their relationship with specific modeling goals, explore strategies to mitigate them, and assess their impact on modeling costs. By bridging empirical findings with practical applications, this study equips researchers, developers, and practitioners with a foundation for enhancing the modeling experience and improving the overall value of domain modeling efforts.

Disclosure of Interests. The authors have no competing interests to declare that are relevant to the content of this article.

References

1. Alotaibi, Y.: Business process modelling challenges and solutions: a literature review. J. Intell. Manuf. **27**, 701–723 (2016)
2. Braun, V., Clarke, V.: Using thematic analysis in psychology. Qual. Res. Psychol. **3**(2), 77–101 (2006)
3. Chattopadhyay, S., et al.: What's wrong with computational notebooks? Pain points, needs, and design opportunities. In: Proceedings of the 2020 CHI Conference on Human Factors in Computing Systems, pp. 1–12 (2020)
4. Chen, P.P.S.: The entity-relationship model: toward a unified view of data. ACM Trans. Database Syst. **1**, 9–36 (1976)
5. Easterbrook, S., et al.: Selecting empirical methods for software engineering research. In: Guide to Advanced Empirical Software Engineering, pp. 285–311. Springer, Heidelberg (2008). https://doi.org/10.1007/978-1-84800-044-5_11
6. Fernández, D.M., et al.: Naming the pain in requirements engineering: contemporary problems, causes, and effects in practice. Empir. Softw. Eng. **22**, 2298–2338 (2017)
7. Fettke, P.: How conceptual modeling is used. CAIS **25**, 43 (2009)
8. Fowler Jr, F.J.: Survey Research Methods. Sage publications, Thousands Oaks (2013)
9. Guizzardi, G., et al.: Towards ontological foundations for conceptual modeling: the unified foundational ontology (UFO) story. Appl. Ontol. **10**, 259–271 (2015)
10. Halpin, T.A.: Object-role modeling (ORM/NIAM). In: Handbook on Architectures of Information Systems, pp. 81–103. Springer, Heidelberg (2006). https://doi.org/10.1007/978-3-662-03526-9_4
11. Howell, D.: Fundamental Statistics for the Behavioral Sciences, 9 edn. Cengage Learning, Boston (2016)
12. Indulska, M., et al.: Business process modeling: current issues and future challenges. In: Advanced Information Systems Engineering, pp. 501–514 (2009)
13. Kruus, H., et al.: Teaching modeling in SysML/UML and problems encountered. In: 25th EAEEIE Annual Conference, pp. 33–36. IEEE (2014)

14. OMG: UML 2.0 superstructure specification – Final adopted specification. Technical Report. ptc/03-08-02, Object Management Group (2003)
15. Papke, B., et al.: MBSE model management pain points–Wait, this looks familiar! In: INCOSE International Symposium, vol. 33, pp. 273–289 (2023)
16. Reuter, R., et al.: Insights in students' problems during uml modeling. In: EDUCON, pp. 592–600. IEEE (2020)
17. Rosemann, M.: Potential pitfalls of process modeling: part A. BPMJ **12**(2), 249–254 (2006)
18. Rosemann, M.: Potential pitfalls of process modeling: part B. BPMJ **12**(3), 377–384 (2006)
19. Rosenthal, K., Strecker, S.: Toward a taxonomy of modeling difficulties: a multimodal study on individual modeling processes. EMISA Forum **41**, 31–32 (2021)
20. Rosenthal, K., Strecker, S., Pastor, O.: Modeling difficulties in data modeling. In: Dobbie, G., Frank, U., Kappel, G., Liddle, S.W., Mayr, H.C. (eds.) ER 2020. LNCS, vol. 12400, pp. 501–511. Springer, Cham (2020). https://doi.org/10.1007/978-3-030-62522-1_37
21. Siau, K., Loo, P.P.: Identifying difficulties in learning UML. ISM **23** (2006)
22. Sien, V.Y.: An investigation of difficulties experienced by students developing unified modelling language (UML) class and sequence diagrams. Comput. Sci. Educ. **21**, 317–342 (2011)
23. Sue, V.M., Ritter, L.A.: Conducting Online Surveys. Sage, Thousands Oaks (2012)
24. Valle, I., et al.: Supplementary material (2024). https://github.com/utwente-scs/pain-points-modeling
25. Valle, I., et al.: What do I get from modeling? An empirical study on using structural conceptual models. In: Enterprise Design, Operations, and Computing, pp. 21–38. Springer, Cham (2024)
26. Valle, I., et al.: Unraveling the pain points of domain modeling. Inf. Softw. Technol. **183**, 107736 (2025)
27. Verbruggen, C., Snoeck, M.: Practitioners' experiences with model-driven engineering: a meta-review. Softw. Syst. Model. **22**, 111–129 (2023)
28. Wang, B., et al.: A biclustering-based method for market segmentation using customer pain points. Eng. Appl. Artif. Intell. **47** (2016)
29. Wieringa, R.J.: Design Science Methodology for Information Systems and Software Engineering. Springer, Heidelberg (2014)
30. Wiese, I., et al.: Naming the pain in developing scientific software. IEEE Softw. **37**, 75–82 (2020)

Unlocking Sustainable Value in the Electrical and Electronic Equipment Sector: A Value Network Approach

Frank Stiksma[1(✉)], Luís Ferreira Pires[2], João Luiz Rebelo Moreira[2], Marten van Sinderen[2], and Wilco Engelsman[1]

[1] Saxion University of Applied Sciences, P.O. box 70000, 7500 KB Enschede, The Netherlands
f.k.s.stiksma@saxion.nl

[2] University of Twente, P.O. box 217, 7500 AE Enschede, The Netherlands

Abstract. Extending the lifetime of household appliances, such as washing machines, is often not economically viable. Because environmental costs from the product life cycle are shifted to society, new appliances remain relatively inexpensive and sustainable alternatives are discouraged. In the literature we could not find any work that discusses how value networks in the Electrical and Electronic Equipment (EEE) embed both sustainability and economic value across the product lifecycle. This study aims to develop an approach that supports the design of sustainability-oriented value networks in the EEE sector. Based on interviews and literature, e^3value models are developed that address sustainability. Eco-costs are introduced as a potential means to make environmental impacts more visible and to explore how they might contribute to more responsible value creation and decision-making by network actors. Defined information requirements of value network actors indicate the data that support sustainability-related decision-making, highlighting the enabling role of Digital Product Passports. Further research should address quantitative assessments of eco-costs and their implications across different value network configurations and decision-making scenarios.

Keywords: Electrical and Electronic Equipment · Product Lifetime Extension · Value Networks · Eco-costs · Digital Product Passport

1 Introduction

In the transition towards a circular economy (CE), lifetime extension of Electrical and Electronic Equipment (EEE) products is a strategic priority [1, 2]. Examples of EEE products include household appliances such as washing machines, dishwashers, vacuum cleaners, and coffee machines. However, many EEE products placed on the market end prematurely as electronic waste (e-waste) [3]. Product lifetime extension strategies, such as refurbishment and repair, contribute to the reduction of e-waste, the demand for raw materials, global supply chain risks, and negative environmental impacts [2]. Yet, product lifetime extension in the EEE industry remains a challenge, since customers' decisions

© The Author(s), under exclusive license to Springer Nature Switzerland AG 2026
A. Gianola et al. (Eds.): EDOC 2025, LNCS 16213, pp. 210–227, 2026.
https://doi.org/10.1007/978-3-032-15140-7_12

are often primarily driven by economic considerations and repair costs frequently exceed the price of affordable EEE products [1, 4]. Consequently, in most cases, customers choose to buy new EEE products. Mass production and consumption of EEE products leads to harmful impacts across their entire life cycle, including resource depletion and risks to public health. The business models of value network actors do not adequately reflect these impacts [5]. Instead, they shift the burden of environmental damage and its often invisible costs onto society, which ultimately bears the costs of restoration. As a result, the vicious circle of the current linear economic system of production, consumption, and disposal persists, hampering the adoption of product lifetime extension for EEE [2].

To overcome the current lock-in of the linear economy, a shift towards a circular economy requires network-based value creation [6]. Within value networks, multiple actors work together to create, capture, and deliver value. These networks, embedded in a broader circular ecosystem, aim to balance economic, environmental, financial, and business values [7, 8]. However, in the literature we could not find any work that discusses how value networks in the EEE sector should embed both sustainable and economic values across different product lifecycle phases. Although value network modelling languages such as e^3value exist, their current application focuses predominantly on economic value. Moreover, environmental damage from EEE products across their life cycle is rarely represented as a negative externality in value networks, and it remains unclear how such impacts can be meaningfully incorporated into modelling frameworks.

In this study, we present a possible solution to address this issue. We argue that eco-costs, defined as virtual and monetized prevention costs for ecological damage, could serve as a lever to incentivize sustainable value creation and discourage unsustainable practices in EEE value networks [9]. Accordingly, this study aims to develop an approach that supports the design of sustainability-oriented value networks in the EEE sector. By modelling and analyzing current value network configurations in three different product lifecycle phases, we identify how structural characteristics of the EEE sector may influence or constrain the adoption of more sustainable practices. Drawing on the modelling of current value networks, we propose to make currently overlooked environmental costs explicit to support sustainable and informed decision-making.

In our study, we use the e^3value modelling language as a basis for our conceptual exploration. Although value networks across different EEE product categories exhibit common patterns, we focus on washing machine value networks as a substantial market with significant environmental impacts across the life cycle.

The remainder of this paper is structured as follows. Section 2 outlines the background on sustainability and EEE practices. Section 3 examines how these practices are reflected in current value networks. Section 4 details our approach to sustainable EEE value networks. Section 5 provides information requirements that support value networks in their sustainable decision-making. Section 6 discusses our results. Section 7 presents our conclusion and outlook.

2 Background

2.1 Sustainability in Value Networks

Sustainable business models incorporate proactive multi-stakeholder management, the creation of value for a broad range of stakeholders, and a long-term perspective [10]. In addition to monetary values, ecological and social values are integral to the value proposition, aiming to create value for customers, the environment, and society [11]. Circular business models are a subset of sustainable business models, focusing on resource efficiency, waste reduction, reuse, and closed loops [12]. While concepts such as Green Business Process Management focus on embedding sustainability at the operational level of organizational processes [13], the concept of value networks emphasizes a systemic perspective on how actors' interests and responsibilities align to enable joint value creation [14]. A value network is a goal-oriented network of actors who create, exchange, and receive value to meet a customer's need. Embedding sustainability in value networks requires governance frameworks that balance and integrate economic, ecological, and social concerns [14]. Effective governance requires the use of economic policy instruments such as funding, investments, subsidies, and taxes to stimulate sustainable initiatives [15]. Their success depends on a systemic alignment of incentives and penalties throughout the product life cycle [16]. The guiding principle is that polluting activities, such as production and incineration, are taxed, while product value retention is financially rewarded. Polluting activities across the product life cycle can be subject to taxation by assigning a monetary estimate of the financial compensation required to prevent or remediate future environmental damage [17]. These preventive costs, often called eco-costs, capture a range of environmental impacts, including resource depletion, carbon emissions, ecosystem degradation, and human health risks. Eco-costs are derived from standard reference tables or through Life Cycle Analysis (LCA), capturing the environmental impact of a product across all stages of its life cycle.

2.2 Empirical Analysis of Current EEE Sector Practices

We conducted a literature review to examine how the current systemic characteristics of the EEE sector, including Waste Electrical and Electronic Equipment (WEEE) management, influence the transition to a circular economy. Additionally, we carried out 15 semi-structured interviews. The respondents, based in the Netherlands, Ireland, Germany, and Belgium, represent various stages of the EEE product life cycle, ranging from manufacturing to WEEE management. During one-hour interviews, respondents reflected on the roles of actors, the drivers of their participation in existing value networks, and the underlying EEE system logic. They further proposed interventions and outlined system conditions to support the embedding of sustainability in value networks in the EEE sector.

Respondents argued that value creation in current EEE systems is primarily driven by the maximization of sales and the consumption of large volumes of new EEE products. Business models that focus on competition and transactions, with an emphasis on low prices and margin, are central to how the EEE sector operates. Original Equipment Manufacturers (OEMs) design products that limit product longevity and repairability. Accordingly, the repair infrastructure remains underdeveloped. Low product prices, combined with the labor intensity of circular strategies and the high cost of spare parts, render product lifetime extension economically unattractive. This weak economic rationale is further reinforced by prevailing consumerism and limited consumer willingness to extend the use phase of EEE products. Respondents argued that Extended Producer Responsibility (EPR) schemes shape the EEE system significantly by institutionalizing a waste-oriented end-of-life perspective. Although EPR has contributed to the development of a mature recycling infrastructure, the relatively low cost of EPR fees fails to provide meaningful incentives for producers to invest in durable and repairable product design, resource efficiency, or waste prevention. Moreover, the residual economic and technical value of returned EEE products remains largely underutilized.

In current government policies, ecological values and circular ambitions have been subordinated to short-term economic objectives. According to several respondents, mechanisms to internalize environmental damage in the decision-making processes of actors within the EEE sector are lacking. Consequently, producers have little financial incentives to actively invest in product lifetime extension. The availability of cheap virgin materials and limited market demand for used EEE products further reinforces this inertia.

Respondents emphasized the need for shared responsibility, with all stakeholders in the EEE sector contributing to sustainable outcomes. They advocate for taxing the environmental costs of EEE products through product pricing. As long as resource extraction and disposable production remain cheaper than circular alternatives, equal market conditions for product lifetime extension will be lacking. In addition, respondents call for making lifetime extension economically attractive through fiscal and financial incentives, such as repair vouchers and tax breaks. Respondents further proposed reforming EPR schemes to promote product lifetime extension, alongside broader governance and legislative reforms that support circularity.

3 Current EEE Business Practices

A fundamental principle of a sustainable value network is that it adopts a lifecycle perspective [8]. A product life cycle is typically divided into three main phases. In the Beginning-of-Life (BoL), the customer seeks a new or refurbished washing machine. The Middle-of-Life (MoL) phase centers on product usage, maintenance, and repair services that help extend the product's lifespan. In the End-of-Life (EoL) phase, the customer's priority shifts to accessing appropriate disposal services that enable sustainable processing. Possible circular strategies at this stage include refurbishment and materials recycling. This section presents value networks reflecting typical configurations in the current EEE sector, based on interview data. We developed value models with the e3value modelling language and refer to the user manual for details on its graphical constructs[1]. Each value model corresponds to one of the three life cycle phases. Specifically, we represent value models for the sale of new washing machines (BoL), repair services (MoL), and WEEE compliance and recycling (EoL). These models provide a state-of-the-art understanding of the key actors, their roles, value exchanges, and the customer needs driving the value networks.

[1] https://e3value-user-manual.thevalueengineers.nl/

3.1 Sales Model

As a representation of the BoL phase, Fig. 1 presents the value model capturing customer demand for new washing machines. In the sales-oriented value network, customers' needs for new washing machines trigger a dependency path involving economic value transactions between Customers, Sellers, OEMs, Logistics providers, Component suppliers, and Miners [18]. OEMs play a central role in shaping its structure and value dynamics, notably by controlling the value interfaces with both upstream and downstream actors. They determine how, and under what conditions, value is exchanged across the network. In addition, OEMs have significant influence over product longevity and repairability. The transaction-oriented business models structuring this network are based on product sales in exchange for monetary compensation. Due to the narrow profit margins of most actors, large volumes of EEE products must be sold, which in turn creates incentives for relatively short product life cycles and frequent device replacement.

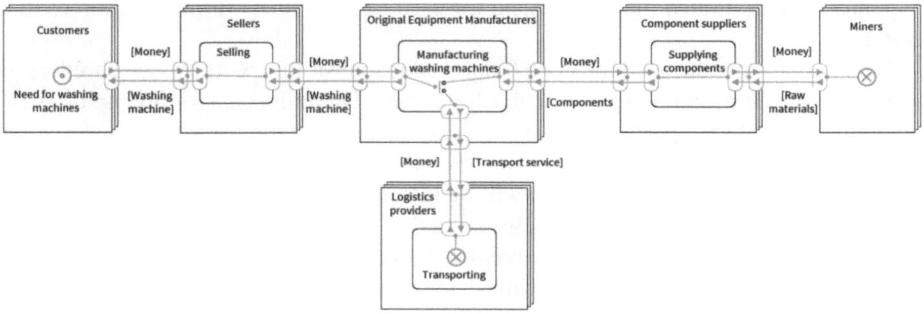

Fig. 1. Sales model

3.2 Repair Service Model

Figure 2 shows a value model that represents the main actors and value exchanges involved in current repair services during the MoL phase. Customer demand for washing machine repair services initiate a dependency path that activates a value network of Repair service providers, OEMs, Spare part providers, and EEE parts manufacturers, along with their associated value exchanges. This model focuses on washing machine repairs by OEM-certified service providers, and assumes OEMs outsource component production to EEE parts manufacturers and provide ongoing service support throughout the product lifecycle. The value network enables professional repairs by providing Repair service providers with access to professional support from OEMs and Spare parts providers. The role of spare part providers in the MoL is to distribute the purchased components from EEE parts manufacturers to Repair service providers. Component suppliers in Fig. 1, by contrast, provide components to OEMs for washing machine production in the BoL phase.

Repair is economically viable mainly for premium-brand washing machines, which typically offer higher repairability and more favorable cost-to-price ratios than lower-end models. OEMs restrict access to repair-related value exchanges for non-certified repairers. Consequently, despite substantial demand for repair services, adoption remains limited due to high repair costs, product designs hampering repair, restricted access to repair resources for non-certified repairers, and legal barriers [1, 4].

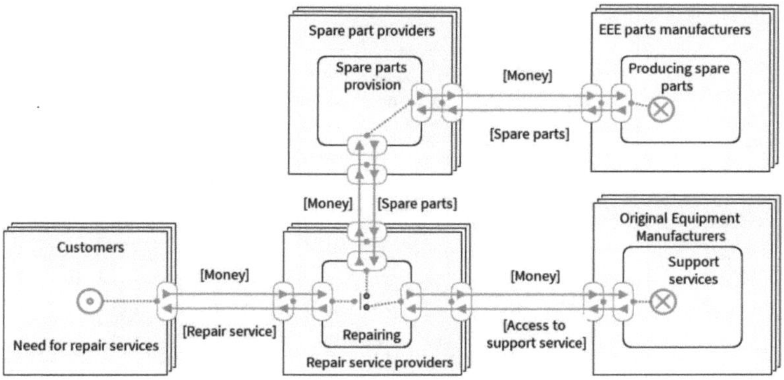

Fig. 2. Repair service model

3.3 WEEE Compliance and Recycling Model

Figure 3 represents the WEEE compliance and recycling model in the EoL phase. In this value model, OEMs operate in accordance with the WEEE Directive 2012/19/EU. Under this directive, OEMs are held responsible for the EoL phase of discarded EEE products, with specific requirements concerning the collection, processing, and environmentally sound disposal of used equipment. Actors in the WEEE compliance value network include OEMs, a Producer Responsibility Organization (PRO), Take-back points, WEEE management centers, Logistics Providers, Disassembly Operators, Recyclers, and Authorized Waste Treatment facilities. OEMs transfer their legal EPR for WEEE management to a central Producer Responsibility Organization (PRO) by paying a waste compliance fee [19]. The PRO distributes WEEE management costs among affiliated producers, typically through a fee based on the quantity and weight of EEE products placed on the market per product category. Acting on behalf of multiple producers, the PRO organizes the collection and processing of end-of-life EEE by contracting take-back operators, recyclers, and waste treatment providers. The value exchanges between PROs and processing actors focus on covering processing costs and ensuring WEEE compliance, but do not incentivize product value retention strategies.

WEEE management centers coordinate the transport, collection, inspection, sorting, and processing of discarded EEE products. During processing, disassembly operators and recyclers recover reusable materials such as steel and copper from washing machines. However, these value activities also produce non-recoverable residues, requiring disposal. This leads to a value transaction with an Authorized Waste Treatment Facility, which provides disposal services in exchange for payment. Furthermore, our model shows that a demand from Secondary Material Providers triggers a value transaction in which recycled materials are purchased from recyclers for financial compensation.

However, e-waste recycling still requires a waste compliance fee imposed by the PRO, regardless of the materials' market value.

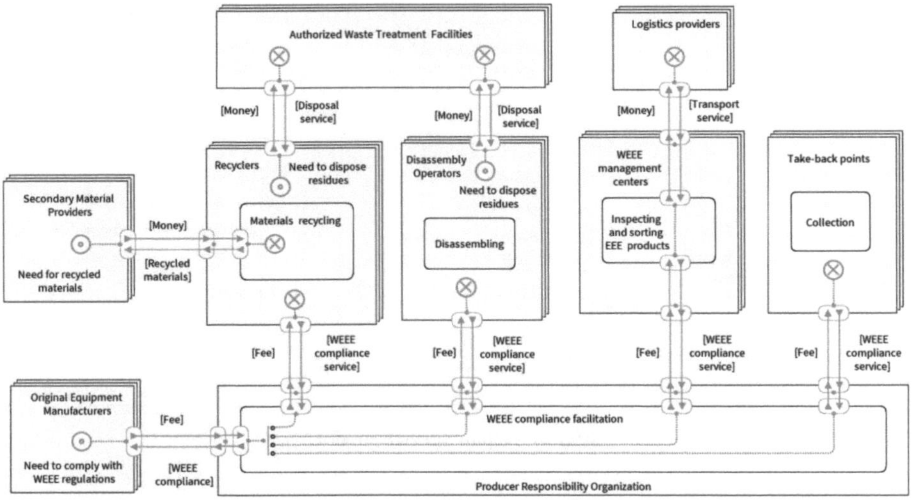

Fig. 3. WEEE compliance and recycling model

4 Sustainable Value Networks

The e3value models presented in Sect. 3 reveal how current value networks in the EEE sector are structured and what drives their behavior across different life cycle phases. We identified several limitations that affect these models. Despite the development of separate life cycle models, an integrated model that represents the product's full life cycle as a coherent system is lacking. Value network configurations across the BoL, MoL, and EoL phases are primarily shaped by sales incentives and compliance requirements. The WEEE compliance model focuses mainly on cost distribution and recycling, offering no meaningful incentives for value retention or reuse. Current value networks and the associated business models of actors in the EEE sector fail to reflect how the negative impacts of value activities affect the environment and society. Environmental degradation and social costs are imposed on actors outside the transactional model. As a result, the models do not represent negative environmental impacts as value exchanges, which hampers the integration of sustainability into the sector. This contributes to keeping repair services economically unattractive and difficult to scale, whereas the sale of new washing machines is more profitable. Moreover, e3value does not clarify which value network actors are responsible for environmental harm or which actors contribute to environmental benefit. Finally, while e3value captures the value objects exchanged between actors, it does not disclose the underlying information that actors rely on for decision-making. This information is essential to support sustainable choices within the value network in the EEE sector.

4.1 Requirements

Based on insights from our literature review (Sect. 2.1), interviews with EEE sector actors (Sect. 2.2), and analysis of current value networks (Sect. 3), we derived requirements, presented in Table 1. These requirements form the basis of our approach to modelling alternative value network configurations that embed sustainability.

Table 1. Design requirements

No	Requirement
R1	Value creation shall be described from a system- or network-centric perspective, where multiple actors co-create value [8, 20–22]
R2	The value network shall support value propositions that address all relevant stages of the product lifecycle [23, 24]
R3	The value network shall offer the complete lifecycle value proposition to the end customer through a single, integrated point of access [25]
R4	The value network shall internalize environmental externalities to align economic operations with sustainability objectives [7, 26, 27]
R5	Economic sustainability shall be a prerequisite for every role within the value network [8, 26, 28, 29]
R6	Product lifecycle scenarios shall be modelled in a way that integrates economic and environmental externalities, enabling value network actors to evaluate sustainability and financial consequences [30]
R7	The value network shall be supported in its information needs across the product lifecycle to enable informed decision-making [8]

4.2 Life Cycle Perspective on Value Networks

To realize future sustainable business models, it is no longer sufficient to focus on a single organization [6]. A broader understanding of the value network is needed, where multiple actors jointly create, exchange and capture value. We apply the e^3value modelling language to represent and evaluate existing value network configurations. Although e^3value in its current form presents limitations in addressing sustainability challenges, we propose conceptual extensions to enable the representation of sustainability in value networks. The life cycle phases reflect the evolving value activities performed by value network actors over time. However, e^3value does not incorporate an explicit temporal dimension since it provides only a fixed configuration of value creation and exchange, which limits its ability to represent circular strategies that unfold over time. We address this limitation by proposing a meta-level solution architecture in which the customer need is central to our modeling approach, in our case, the need for a functioning washing machine. This need serves as a conceptual reference point that links the various life cycle stages as shown in Fig. 4. For each product life cycle phase, distinct value network configurations can be modeled. As such, R1, 2, and 3 are satisfied by modeling value creation from a network-centric perspective and by ensuring that value propositions span the full product lifecycle.

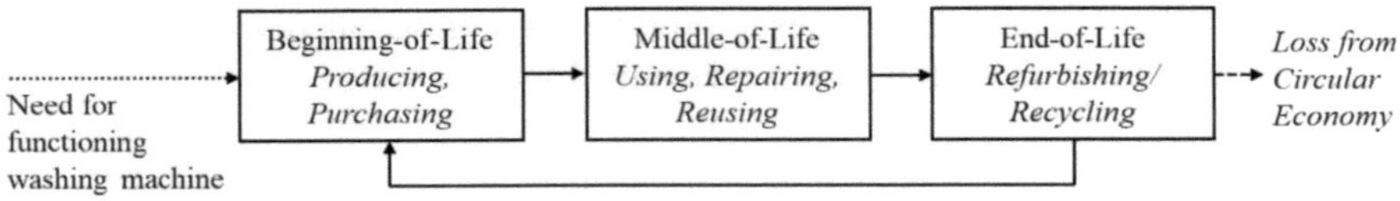

Fig. 4. Customer needs across the product life cycle of washing machines

4.3 Consideration of Eco-Costs in Value Network Design

To satisfy R4, we argue that the concept of eco-costs is well suited for representation into sustainability-oriented value networks in the EEE sector. Eco-costs enable the internalization of negative externalities throughout the lifecycle of EEE products, based on the 'polluter pays' principle [17]. In contrast to other sustainability methods, such as LCA, eco-costs offer a simple and generic way to quantify sustainable value through a single indicator, easily integrated into e^3value models. The core idea behind eco-costs is that society finds it unacceptable for industry to pollute the environment without paying for the damage caused. Eco-costs provide value network actors with incentives to incorporate environmental considerations into their economic decision-making [9]. The eco-costs concept aligns with the objectives and policy frameworks of the circular economy, including the EU Green Deal and Ecodesign regulations. Driven by circular economy policies and regulations, governments are expected to enforce stricter environmental standards and increase pollution taxes [16]. Value networks that internalize environmental impacts are better positioned to support long-term value creation [14]. Eco-costs discourage actors within the value network from producing, consuming, and discarding low-quality EEE products that exert pressure on the environment. We therefore assume that the allocation of eco-costs to actors within the value network enables them to incorporate negative externalities into their economic decision-making. For example, OEMs can avoid high eco-costs by applying circular product design strategies and by using recycled materials. Customers will be able to lower eco-costs by purchasing efficient EEE products and extending their use.

4.4 Sustainable Value Network Designs

Elaborating on requirements 1–4 as a conceptual direction, we designed two possible future sustainable value networks that illustrate how eco-costs could be integrated into existing EEE value networks. We build on the interventions suggested by respondents (Sect. 2.2) and the insights derived from the value network analysis in Sect. 3. As an extension of our sales model in the BoL phase in Sect. 3.1, Fig. 5 presents a potential solution for embedding eco-costs. In Fig. 5, we assume a scenario in which market demand for new washing machines remains high, and value network actors are legally required to internalize eco-costs into their business operations. For this purpose, we introduced a collective entity, namely an Eco-costs Fund Manager. This neutral entity may take the form of a public authority, an EPR organization, a sustainability-oriented financial actor, or a non-governmental organization. The Eco-costs Fund Manager represents the interests of society. Examples of these interests include environmental protection, public health, resource efficiency, and waste reduction.

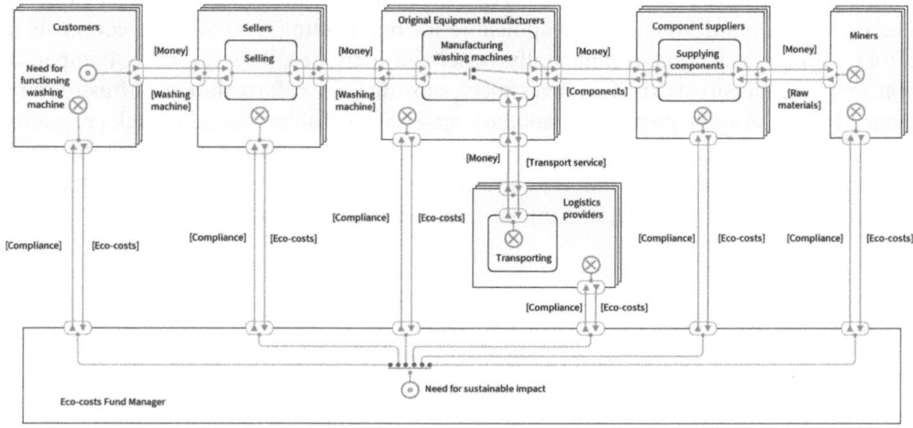

Fig. 5. Internalization of eco-costs in washing machines value network

In our value model, the Eco-costs Fund Manager is responsible for establishing, fairly allocating and receiving eco-costs. These costs are assigned to value network actors based on their environmental performance or their contribution to the prevention of environmental damage. To support this allocation process, the Fund Manager monitors the ecological performance of the value network and incorporates this information into decision-making. Additionally, the Eco-costs Fund Manager collects and manages standardized, accessible lifecycle environmental data essential for alignment, transparency, and informed decision-making among value network actors. Building on the current dominant sales value model, our model in Fig. 5 shows how each actor pays an eco-cost fee to the Fund Manager to comply with environmental regulations. To ensure transparency and effective environmental cost management, we modelled eco-cost fees as separate value exchanges with the Eco-cost Fund Manager, distinct from commercial transactions between other value network actors.

To illustrate how eco-costs and the Eco-costs Fund Manager motivate EEE value networks for sustainable lifetime extension of washing machines, we developed the refurbishment model (see Fig. 6). In this model, we assume a significant increase in demand for refurbished washing machines, driven by CE governance. During our modelling process, we addressed two related challenges. First, we explored how to consistently allocate eco-costs for environmental damage to the appropriate value network actors across the product lifecycle. Second, we aimed to ensure that sustainable activities would be rewarded through financial incentives. We decided to model a value network that consistently charges eco-costs to value network actors whose activities cause environmental damage, including refurbishment.

Additionally, we modeled a separate value transaction where a Refurbisher receives eco-costs compensation from the Eco-costs Fund Manager in exchange for the sustainability impact it delivers. Eco-costs compensation is financed through eco-costs contributions that companies are required to transfer to the Eco-costs Fund Manager to compensate for the environmental harm caused by their business operations (see Fig. 1). The Eco-costs Fund Manager is responsible for reallocating the collected eco-costs to actors who engage in environmentally beneficial activities. The eco-costs compensation includes incentives such as investment subsidies for refurbishment infrastructure, reduced taxes on spare parts and secondary materials, subsidies for take-back programs, reduced rates for lifetime extension services, and market stimulation subsidies [15]. Product value retention strategies that are currently unprofitable for value network actors thus become economically viable, making sustainable choices attractive.

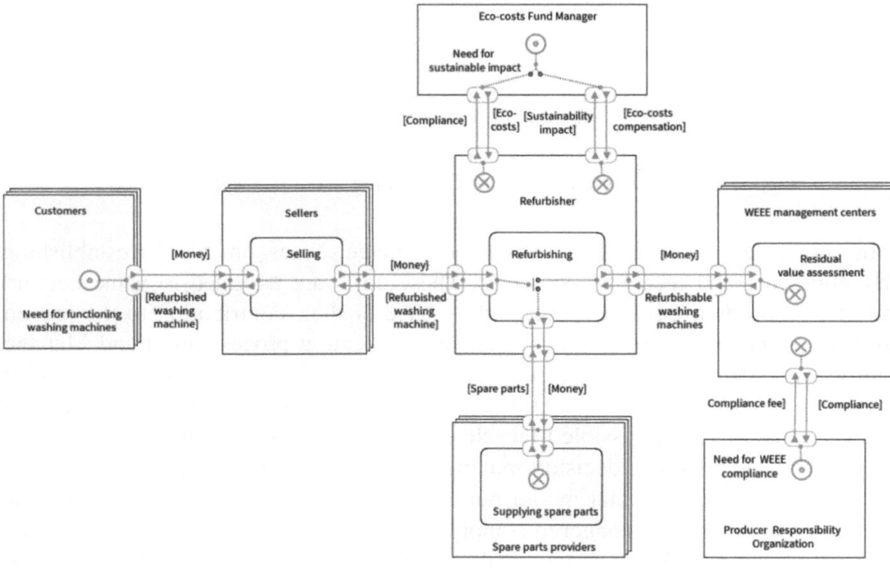

Fig. 6. Refurbishment model

Eco-costs compensation can be modeled as value transactions between the Eco-costs Fund Manager and other value network actors involved in product lifetime extension. Such transactions are only appropriate if the actors demonstrate measurable environmental benefits and contribute to sustainable value creation within the network. Examples include spare parts providers supplying certified reusable components or WEEE management centers identifying the residual value of used washing machines. Due to the specific focus of the refurbishment model, such actors are not linked to the Eco-costs Fund Manager to preserve clarity in the e^3value representation within our value model.

Furthermore, despite the absence of quantitative modelling, interviews with EEE sector actors (Sect. 2.2) suggest that, in practice, the sales model currently provides the most economically sustainable scenario for value network actors. At a smaller scale, washing machine refurbishment also shows potential profitability for both refurbishers and sellers. However, at this research stage it is premature to make definitive claims about the financial feasibility of the sustainability-oriented approach proposed in this study. Proposed economic metrics to assess a value network include such measures as revenues, costs, and net profit per actor, network profitability at the system level, and monetary transfers between actors. Sustainability metrics include incurred eco-costs, avoided eco-costs, and LCA indicators such as global warming potential, material use, waste generation, and ecotoxicity.

5 Information Requirements for Sustainable Value Networks

In our study, the conceptual translation into e3value models was carried out by the authors and reviewed by an e3value expert. Ideally, a joint validation process involving both e3value experts and domain experts would have been preferable. However, empirical validation of our approach is challenging, as the value models explore future-oriented configurations based on assumptions and lack a fixed empirical reference.

We consider the developed value models and the underlying design decisions to be useful for embedding sustainability in value networks within the EEE sector. First, the models implicitly prescribe how actors are expected to behave within the value network. If implemented, each model entails a specific structure of interactions and value exchanges. Second, our models provide a starting basis for reasoning about and quantifying environmental costs. Eco-costs can be linked to elements within the model, potentially using an eco-costs database and LCA data. This offers a promising direction for further exploration, possibly through mechanisms such as Digital Product Passports (DPPs). Third, the models can be used to derive requirements for information systems that support EEE value networks, particularly regarding the information that must be exchanged between actors to realise a joint sustainable value proposition.

In this section, based on our value models in Sect. 4, we further specify the information requirements of value network actors. We argue that, in contrast to conventional practices, sustainability-oriented value networks require actors to have timely and adequate access to relevant information across the entire product life cycle. This information is essential for enabling informed decision-making within their respective value activities.

To meet R7, we suggest that information provided through DPPs enables value network actors to capture and share information within value networks and to make sustainable decisions across different stages of the product life cycle [31, 32]. Based on our interview results (Sect. 2.2), prior work [18], and the modeled value networks in Sect. 4, we derived actor decisions and the corresponding information requirements that should be supported by a DPP. These findings indicate the types of data needed to support sustainability-related decision-making and collaboration within the value network, especially in the MoL phase. To illustrate this, we draw on the refurbishment model in Fig. 6. We specify the information requirements of a customer, a Refurbisher, and an Eco-costs Fund Manager, including the data they contribute and the demands they place on DPPs. Given space constraints, we focus on these three actors in the refurbishment value network. In our reasoning, we assume that modern washing machines are equipped with IoT applications that enable this by providing insights into device usage and condition throughout the lifecycle.

Table 2 explains how a customer aims to make an informed decision when purchasing a refurbished washing machine. This requires access to information on product specifications, refurbishment activities, and the product's environmental impact, which is provided by actors throughout the product life cycle.

Table 2. EEE network actors' decisions and information requirements

EEE network actor	Decisions	Information requirements related to	Delivered by	Added information by actor
Customer	Purchase of refurbished device	Product specifications	OEM	Chain of custody record
		Refurbishment activities, warranty, certification	Refurbisher	
		Environmental impact	OEM, Regulator, Eco-costs Fund Manager	
Refurbisher	Reburbishment feasibility, strategy, warranty, certification	Product, component and materials identification and specifications, regulatory compliance, product service support	OEM	Refurbishment activities, test results, status, certification, warranty, chain of custody record
		Product status and health	OEM, Repairer, Device	
		Product usage history	End-user, Device	
		Service record	OEM, End-user, Repairer	
		Chain of custody record	Life cycle actors	
		Eco-costs metrics	Eco-costs Fund Manager	

(*continued*)

Table 2. *(continued)*

EEE network actor	Decisions	Information requirements related to	Delivered by	Added information by actor
Eco-costs Fund Manager	Eco-costs allocation and compensation	Environmental impact metrics, eco-costs allocation across actors, Eco-cost eligible activities definition	OEM, Regulator	Allocation, compensation, activities, verification, reporting, chain of custody record

To meet the customer's information needs, the refurbisher must have access to DPP information, including service records and a chain of custody. The Refurbisher subsequently adds information to the DPP, such as actor identification, details of refurbishment activities, product status, and quality assurance. Table 2 also clarifies the information required by an Eco-costs Fund Manager to create value for both the refurbisher and the customer.

The elaboration in this section demonstrates how targeted information exchange, as facilitated by DPPs, can influence decision-making within value networks toward more sustainable outcomes.

6 Discussion

Our initial e3value models (Figs. 1, 2 and 3) demonstrate that current value networks are primarily driven by economic and governance considerations. These networks are driven by transactions related to the sale of new washing machines and the fulfilment of WEEE compliance obligations. These current value models generate negative externalities, transferred to society and consequently excluded from the value networks. Modeling sustainable values in e3value requires careful modelling decisions, particularly because e3value cannot explicitly represent non-monetary sustainability aspects, such as value objects related to e-waste reduction and resource scarcity.

We addressed this limitation by introducing eco-costs into our e3value models as possible solution, thereby monetizing sustainable value through the allocation of eco-costs. An Eco-costs Fund manager represents societal interests by allocating eco-costs and compensating for environmentally friendly activities. Eco-costs prompt value network actors to incorporate sustainable values into their business models. In contrast to related studies on eco-costs that focus on specific products such as cork, air cleaners, and street lighting systems [33], we position the eco-costs concept within value networks that represent different life cycle phases of devices, and show how they would work in the context of a washing machine's life cycle.

Furthermore, the absence of a temporal dimension in e3value conflicts with the product lifecycle perspective that underpins sustainable and circular business models. We addressed this limitation by modelling multiple value networks associated with different stages of the product lifecycle, each linked to specific customer needs. Moreover, integrating sustainable values into value networks requires that actors have access to decision-supporting information that spans the entire product lifecycle, enabling them to make sustainable choices from their specific roles. For this purpose, a DPP could contribute to informed decision-making by value network actors. However, a key challenge lies in how DPP-related information provisioning can be represented in e3value models, as these models offer only limited means to represent informational aspects. Our study relates to the work of [34], who use e3value to model a DPP value ecosystem. However, their value objects in the model focus solely on informational transactions, neglecting economic viability and reciprocal value exchanges. An open issue in our design is that the economic feasibility of our sustainable value models across different product life cycle scenarios remains undetermined.

7 Conclusion

This study shows that current dominant value networks in the EEE sector are driven by economic and compliance values. Because the internalization of sustainability values is not economically attractive within the prevailing linear economic business logic, these values are externalized to society and the environment. We showed that by introducing eco-costs as an environmental cost indicator, based on the 'polluter pays' principle, sustainability values can be monetized and integrated into value networks using e3value. We modeled several value networks to explore how the introduction of eco-costs affects the current sales value model for washing machines and the value exchanges between actors, including the introduction of an additional Fund Manager role. In a refurbishment model, we illustrated how eco-costs compensation can stimulate the economic attractiveness of lifetime extension activities. We introduced DPPs as a source of product lifecycle information that enables value network actors to adopt sustainable roles and make informed decisions.

Our study contributes to the literature on modeling sustainability in value networks, particularly in the EEE sector. It offers representatives of the EEE sector and public organizations possible directions for integrating sustainability value into value networks and their underlying decision-making practices. This study builds on existing value network configurations and extends them with sustainability considerations. While our grounded approach offers continuity with current business practices, it may not fully reflect structural changes driven by emerging innovations such as IoT applications in washing machines, Digital Product Passports (DPPs), and product-as-a-service business models. These developments might lead to alternative configurations, with shifts in actor roles, value exchanges, and coordination mechanisms. Furthermore, a remaining limitation of this study is the absence of a quantitative assessment of eco-costs, economic sustainability, and allocation mechanisms across different value network configurations to meet R5. In future research, we will specify the information requirements in a DPP data model, focusing particularly on LCA-related eco-costs and product lifetime data to support actors in making sustainable decisions. This should allow the calculation of the eco-cost impact across different value network configurations and decision-making scenarios, enabling the implications for actors and contributing to R6 to be assessed. This enables analysis of the implications for individual actors and the influence of eco-costs on their decisions, particularly regarding the financial viability of product lifetime extension services. Ultimately, our goal is to develop an e3value-based method for accurately modelling sustainability-oriented value networks for EEE products across their life cycle. This method should serve as an instrument that helps value network actors understand the economic and environmental consequences of their decisions.

Acknowledgements. This research is funded by the Interreg NWE E6 project (grant NWE0200220-E6).

Disclosure of Interest. The authors have no competing interests to declare that are relevant to the content of this article.

References

1. Rudolf, S., et al.: Extending the life cycle of EEE—findings from a repair study in Germany: repair challenges and recommendations for action. Sustainability. **14**, 2993 (2022)
2. Rizos, V., Bryhn, J.: Implementation of circular economy approaches in the electrical and electronic equipment (EEE) sector: barriers, enablers and policy insights. J. Clean. Prod. **338**, 130617 (2022)
3. Baldé, C.P., et al.: Global e-waste monitor 2024 (2024)
4. Svensson-Hoglund, S., Richter, J.L., Maitre-Ekern, E., Russell, J.D., Pihlajarinne, T., Dalhammar, C.: Barriers, enablers and market governance: a review of the policy landscape for repair of consumer electronics in the EU and the US. J. Clean. Prod. **288**, 125488 (2021)
5. Pan, X., Wong, C.W., Li, C.: Circular economy practices in the waste electrical and electronic equipment (WEEE) industry: a systematic review and future research agendas. J. Clean. Prod. **365**, 132671 (2022)
6. Bertassini, A.C., Zanon, L.G., Azarias, J.G., Gerolamo, M.C., Ometto, A.R.: Circular Business Ecosystem innovation: a guide for mapping stakeholders, capturing values, and finding new opportunities. Sustain. Prod. Consum. **27**, 436–448 (2021)
7. Asgari, A., Asgari, R.: How circular economy transforms business models in a transition towards circular ecosystem: the barriers and incentives. Sustain. Prod. Consum. **28**, 566–579 (2021)
8. Trevisan, A.H., Castro, C.G., Gomes, L.A., Mascarenhas, J.: Unlocking the circular ecosystem concept: evolution, current research, and future directions. Sustain. Prod. Consum. **29**, 286–298 (2022)
9. Vogtlander, J.G., Scheepens, A.E., Bocken, N.M., Peck, D.: Combined analyses of costs, market value and eco-costs in circular business models: eco-efficient value creation in remanufacturing. J. Remanufact. **7**, 1–17 (2017)
10. Geissdoerfer, M., Vladimirova, D., Evans, S.: Sustainable business model innovation: a review. J. Clean. Prod. **198**, 401–416 (2018)
11. Abdelkafi, N., Täuscher, K.: Business models for sustainability from a system dynamics perspective. Organ. Environ. **29**, 74–96 (2016)
12. Geissdoerfer, M., Pieroni, M.P., Pigosso, D.C., Soufani, K.: Circular business models: a review. J. Clean. Prod. **277**, 123741 (2020)
13. Sohns, T.M., Aysolmaz, B., Figge, L., Joshi, A.: Green business process management for business sustainability: a case study of manufacturing small and medium-sized enterprises (SMEs) from Germany. J. Clean. Prod. **401**, 136667 (2023). https://doi.org/10.1016/j.jclepro.2023.136667

14. Evans, S., et al.: Business model innovation for sustainability: towards a unified perspective for creation of sustainable business models. Bus. Strategy Environ. **26**, 597–608 (2017)
15. Henriques, J., Ferrão, P., Iten, M.: Policies and strategic incentives for circular economy and industrial symbiosis in Portugal: a future perspective. Sustainability. **14**, 6888 (2022)
16. Milios, L.: Towards a circular economy taxation framework: expectations and challenges of implementation. Circ. Econ. Sustain. **1**, 477–498 (2021)
17. Vogtländer, J.G., Brezet, H.C., Hendriks, C.F.: The virtual eco-costs '99 A single LCA-based indicator for sustainability and the eco-costs-value ratio (EVR) model for economic allocation: a new LCA-based calculation model to determine the sustainability of products and services. Int. J. Life Cycle Assess. **6**, 157–166 (2001)
18. Stiksma, F., van Sinderen, M., Moreira, J.L.R.: Value assessment of consumer electronics with digital product passports: a case study of lifetime extension assessment of disposed washing machines. In: International Conference on Enterprise Design, Operations, and Computing, pp. 81–98. Springer, Heidelberg (2024)
19. Maitre-Ekern, E.: Re-thinking producer responsibility for a sustainable circular economy from extended producer responsibility to pre-market producer responsibility. J. Clean. Prod. **286**, 125454 (2021)
20. Suchek, N., Fernandes, C.I., Kraus, S., Filser, M., Sjögrén, H.: Innovation and the circular economy: a systematic literature review. Bus. Strategy Environ. **30**, 3686–3702 (2021)
21. Fehrer, J.A., Kemper, J.A., Baker, J.J.: Shaping circular service ecosystems. J. Serv. Res. **27**, 49–68 (2024)
22. Derks, M., Berkers, F., Tukker, A.: Toward accelerating sustainability transitions through collaborative sustainable business modeling: a conceptual approach. Sustainability **14**, 3803 (2022)
23. Marconi, M., Favi, C., Pietroni, G., Tamborrini, P.M., Marino, C., Fiore, E.: Toward a collaborative platform for the life cycle design and management of electrical and electronic equipment. In: Presented at the International Conference of the Italian Association of Design Methods and Tools for Industrial Engineering (2024)
24. Haanstra, W., Toxopeus, M., Van Gerrevink, M.: Product life cycle planning for sustainable manufacturing: translating theory into business opportunities. Procedia CIRP **61**, 46–51 (2017)
25. Talmar, M., Walrave, B., Podoynitsyna, K.S., Holmström, J., Romme, A.G.L.: Mapping, analyzing and designing innovation ecosystems: the ecosystem pie model. Long Range Plann. **53**, 101850 (2020)
26. de Pádua Pieroni, M., Pigosso, D.C., McAloone, T.C.: Sustainable qualifying criteria for designing circular business models. Procedia CIRP **69**, 799–804 (2018)
27. Goni, F.A., Gholamzadeh Chofreh, A., Estaki Orakani, Z., Klemeš, J.J., Davoudi, M., Mardani, A.: Sustainable business model: a review and framework development. Clean Technol. Environ. Policy **23**, 889–897 (2021)
28. Tapaninaho, R., Heikkinen, A.: Value creation in circular economy business for sustainability: a stakeholder relationship perspective. Bus. Strat. Environ. **31**, 2728–2740 (2022)
29. Schaltegger, S., Hörisch, J., Freeman, R.E.: Business cases for sustainability: a stakeholder theory perspective. Organ. Environ. **32**, 191–212 (2019)
30. Medina-Salgado, M.S., García-Muiña, F.E., Cucchi, M., Settembre-Blundo, D.: Adaptive life cycle costing (LCC) modeling and applying to Italy ceramic tile manufacturing sector: its implication of open innovation. J. Open Innov. Technol. Mark. Complex. **7**, 101 (2021)
31. King, M.R., Timms, P.D., Mountney, S.: A proposed universal definition of a Digital Product Passport Ecosystem (DPPE): Worldviews, discrete capabilities, stakeholder requirements and concerns. J. Clean. Prod. **384**, 135538 (2023)

32. Berger, K., Baumgartner, R.J., Weinzerl, M., Bachler, J., Preston, K., Schöggl, J.-P.: Data requirements and availabilities for a digital battery passport–a value chain actor perspective. Clean. Prod. Lett. **4**, 100032 (2023)
33. Klaassen, N., Scheepens, A., Flipsen, B., Vogtlander, J.: Eco-efficient value creation of residential street lighting systems by simultaneously analysing the value, the costs and the eco-costs during the design and engineering phase. Energies **13**, 3351 (2020)
34. Gieß, A., Möller, F.: Exploring the value ecosystem of digital product passports. J. Ind. Ecol. **29**, 561–573 (2025)

A Taxonomy and Methodology for Proof-of-Location Systems

Eduardo Brito[1,3](✉), Fernando Castillo[2], Liina Kamm[1], Amnir Hadachi[3], and Ulrich Norbisrath[3]

[1] Cybernetica AS, Estonia Mäealuse 2/1, 12618 Tallinn, Estonia
{eduardo.brito,liina.kamm}@cyber.ee
[2] TU Berlin, Einsteinufer 17, Berlin, Germany
fc@ise.tu-berlin.de
[3] University of Tartu, Narva mnt 18, 51009 Tartu, Estonia
{amnir.hadachi,ulrich.norbisrath}@ut.ee

Abstract. Digital societies increasingly rely on trustworthy proofs of physical presence for services such as supply-chain tracking, e-voting, ride-sharing, and location-based rewards. Yet, traditional localization methods often lack cryptographic guarantees of where and when an entity was present, leaving them vulnerable to spoofing, replay, or collusion attacks. In response, research on Proof-of-Location (PoL) has emerged, with recent approaches combining distance bounding, distributed consensus, and privacy-enhancing techniques to enable verifiable, tamper-resistant location claims.

As the design space for PoL systems grows in complexity, this paper provides a unified framework to help practitioners navigate diverse application needs. We first propose a taxonomy identifying four core domains: (1) cryptographic guarantees, (2) spatio-temporal synchronization, (3) trust and witness models, and (4) interaction and overhead. Building on this, we introduce a methodology to map application-specific requirements onto appropriate PoL architectures. We illustrate this process through three use cases (retail e-coupons, supply chain auditing, and physical e-voting), each showing how different constraints shape protocol choices. Overall, this work offers a structured approach to building secure, scalable, and interoperable PoL systems.

Keywords: Proof-of-Location · Taxonomy · Design Methodology

1 Introduction

Location-based services are increasingly central to digital societies–from supply chain management and civic processes to smart city initiatives [7,20,21]. However, most localization systems (e.g., GPS) and centralized location managers lack cryptographic guarantees of where and when a device was physically present [22,24], leaving them vulnerable to spoofing, replay, and falsification [12,18].

© The Author(s), under exclusive license to Springer Nature Switzerland AG 2026
A. Gianola et al. (Eds.): EDOC 2025, LNCS 16213, pp. 228–244, 2026.
https://doi.org/10.1007/978-3-032-15140-7_13

Proof-of-Location (PoL) protocols address these gaps by enabling tamper-resistant, verifiable spatio-temporal claims [4,11]. Modern approaches combine distance bounding, multi-witness attestation, distributed ledgers, and privacy-preserving techniques (e.g., zero-knowledge proofs) to minimize reliance on centralized trust [5,7,16,25]. Real-world applications span e-voting, supply chain tracking, retail coupons, and digital content authentication [7,22].

Yet, no single PoL protocol satisfies all use-case demands. Some require sub-meter, real-time guarantees (e.g., e-voting), while others tolerate coarser, ex-post proofs (e.g., location-based marketing). Privacy needs also vary, prompting trade-offs between exposure and overhead. Additionally, deployments involving consensus or multiple witnesses eventually increase complexity [7,12,27]. To address these design challenges, this paper makes the following contributions:

1. A **taxonomy** of PoL systems, structured around four core domains: (i) cryptographic guarantees, (ii) spatio-temporal synchronization, (iii) trust and witness models, and (iv) interaction and overhead;
2. A **methodology** for mapping application requirements (e.g., precision, adversary model, privacy) to suitable PoL architectures;
3. **Use-case examples** demonstrating how constraints shape design choices, spanning from retail to civic and logistics contexts.

The rest of the paper is organized as follows. Section 2 reviews the evolution of PoL protocols, from centralized architectures to decentralized and privacy-preserving designs. Section 3 introduces our taxonomy of design domains, followed by Sect. 4, which outlines a methodology for matching application requirements to protocol features. Section 5 applies this framework to concrete use cases, and Sect. 6 closes with conclusion and future directions.

2 Background and Related Work

This section reviews the evolution of the PoL problem, from centralized solutions with trusted anchors, through partially distributed protocols, to fully decentralized and permissionless approaches. It situates this paper's contributions within those developments and identifies the key gaps our work aims to address.

2.1 Trusted and Centralized Architectures

The notion of enabling PoL–that is, providing secure proofs that a device was present at a specific location–dates back to the early 2000s. A foundational contribution is the work by Waters and Felten [24], who proposed a proximity-based system with integrity and privacy guarantees. Their model, shown on the left of Fig. 1, assumed a controlled setup with a verifier, a location manager, and a tamper-resistant device trusted by the verifier. Typical use cases included lending equipment (e.g., university computers) or house arrest monitoring, where the device must remain within physical boundaries. Although dependent on trusted

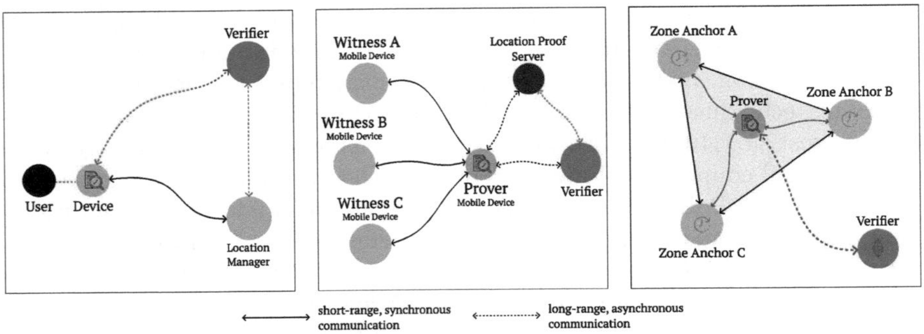

Fig. 1. Evolution of PoL infrastructures from centralised to decentralized models. On the left, centralised systems rely on a trusted location manager to issue location proofs [24]. In the middle, progressively distributed models involve peer-to-peer interactions between provers and witnesses [27]. On the right, decentralized systems eliminate the need for a central authority, enabling direct peer-to-peer attestations and storage in a distributed ledger [11].

wireless LAN infrastructure, this work introduced round-trip time and signal-propagation delays as countermeasures to proxy attacks.

Subsequent efforts, like Saroiu and Wolman [22], further shaped the PoL concept and highlighted applications such as store rewards, location-gated content, and presence verification for voting. Graham and Gray [14] proposed SLVPGP, which shifted trust to tamper-resistant modules. VeriPlace [17] expanded this with a privacy-aware architecture distributing trust across several entities, originally targeting platforms like Yelp. Later works streamlined proof generation via Wi-Fi infrastructure [15] or proposed centralized yet formally secure geo-tamper-resistant designs [1].

Together, these trusted and centralized systems showed that secure location proofs are feasible using short-range wireless signals and trusted anchors. However, their dependence on central authorities limits scalability and exposes them to collusion risks.

2.2 Progression to Distributed Protocols

To reduce reliance on fully trusted entities, more distributed PoL designs began to emerge. VeriPlace [17] already hinted at a multi-entity architecture for privacy without dedicated tamper-resistant hardware, albeit with increased complexity.

APPLAUS [27] was among the first explicitly distributed proposals, combining location privacy with Bluetooth-based local interactions. Provers collected signatures from nearby witnesses and stored the resulting proofs on an untrusted server (middle of Fig. 1). While a Certificate Authority (CA) still issued identities, the location-proof server was distrusted. The work aimed at improving privacy and reducing single points of failure. STAMP [23] and PROPS [13] added group signatures, but faced challenges when provers colluded with witnesses.

SPARSE [19] addressed this by removing the prover's control over witness selection and leveraging crowd density for secure attestations.

Other approaches employed advanced cryptography to secure and anonymize claims. Dupin et al. [12] used secure multi-party computation (MPC) to let multiple semi-honest entities jointly verify location, at the cost of significant computational overhead. These mid-stage protocols showed how trust could be distributed to reduce central dependencies, but often introduced new trade-offs in complexity, resource use, or environmental assumptions.

2.3 Decentralized Systems

With the rise of blockchain technology, decentralized and permissionless PoL architectures gained traction. Amoretti et al. [4] combined short-range wireless protocols with blockchain-backed storage to achieve tamper-evident and censorship-resistant proofs without relying on a trusted server. Nasrulin et al. [18] built on this by formalizing spatio-temporal verification requirements and deploying a permissioned blockchain for supply-chain tracking.

Subsequent work layered privacy onto decentralized ledgers. Wu et al. [25] introduced Zero-Knowledge PoL (ZK-PoL), enabling presence proofs with minimal disclosure [5]. Nosouhi et al. [20] added incentive mechanisms to reward honest witnesses, combining privacy with public blockchains. The FOAM protocol [11], on the right of Fig. 1, advanced zone-based time synchronization, coordinating radio beacons to achieve consensus on clock offsets without centralized control.

Complementary work by Pournaras [21] explored decentralized civic engagement via Proof-of-Witness-Presence, where participants verify each other's presence in smart-city settings. Altogether, decentralized PoL systems now combine local distance bounding, digital signatures, consensus-based ledgers, zero-knowledge proofs, and incentive schemes, as systematized by Brito et al. [7].

In summary, PoL protocols have evolved from early centralized systems with trusted infrastructure, through distributed models mitigating single points of failure, to decentralized frameworks relying on cryptographic primitives and permissionless consensus. While each addresses different real-world scenarios–from retail and crowd-sensing to supply chain–there remains no unified framework for classifying these efforts by core PoL properties. Building on these developments, we propose a consolidated view of PoL across trust models and witness structures, aiming to guide practitioners in navigating design choices, assessing verifiability, and selecting appropriate enabling mechanisms.

3 A Taxonomy of Location-Proof Use Cases

In this section, we propose a structured taxonomy for PoL protocols and their use cases. We begin with core definitions before introducing four major domains of the taxonomy, which are summarized in Table 1.

3.1 Foundations and Basic Definitions

We adopt the standard PoL model with three primary roles [7]:

- **Prover** ($\mathcal{P}$): the party claiming a location statement, e.g. "I was in region R at time t."
- **Verifier** ($\mathcal{V}$): checks whether $\mathcal{P}$'s claim is valid under the given threat model and trust assumptions.
- **Witnesses** ($\{\mathcal{W}_i\}$): optional external participants who measure or attest $\mathcal{P}$'s presence. They may be physical anchors (access points, radio beacons) or other peer devices in the environment.

A *location proof* is a cryptographically bound statement ensuring the correctness of "$\mathcal{P}$ was in R at time t," optionally accompanied by measured distances, timestamps, or other evidence from the witnesses. Following classical interactive proof systems, we define:

- **Soundness.** If the prover is not in R at t, the verifier should reject any maliciously generated proof with overwhelming probability.
- **Completeness.** If the prover is actually in R at t, and all parties, that is the prover and eventual witnesses, behave honestly, the proof should be accepted, with overwhelming probability, by an honest verifier.

For PoL, soundness can subdivide into proximity soundness (preventing distance fraud) and temporal soundness (ensuring correct time references), as elaborated in the following.

Table 1. Taxonomy Summary: Core Domains in PoL Systems

Domain	Key Aspects
(1) Cryptographic Guarantees	Soundness (spatial, temporal), authenticity, integrity, consensus, privacy
(2) Spatio-temporal Synchronization	Source of spatial and time references, required precision, robustness to spoofing or drift
(3) Trust and Witness Model	Prover-managed, verifier-controlled, partially distributed, or fully decentralized
(4) Interaction and Overhead	Interactive vs. non-interactive, proof size, verification cost, real-time vs. offline use

3.2 Domain 1: Cryptographic Guarantees

Under this domain, we collect the specialized security properties that refine completeness and soundness in PoL scenarios:

- **Proximity Soundness (via Distance Bounding).** Constitutes a practical extension to localization techniques to prevent relay ("mafia") attacks, ensuring a remote prover cannot pretend to be close simply by forwarding signals [2,8]. Protocols employ tight round-trip timing or rapid bit exchanges to verify that $\mathcal{P}$ is within a certain distance.

- **Temporal Soundness (via Trusted Time Sources).** Ensures that the timestamp t associated with a location proof reflects the actual moment of the event and cannot be falsified or replayed. This is typically achieved through trusted anchors or time-stamping authorities that bind a verifiable time reference to the proof. Without this guarantee, adversaries could backdate or reuse valid proofs to falsely claim presence at other times [11,18].
- **Authenticity.** Only the legitimate prover and witnesses can generate or attest to location proofs in their own name (no spoofing under another's credentials). This is typically enforced via public-key signatures or secure device identities, like keys backed by Trusted Platform Modules.
- **Consensus and Event Ordering.** In distributed or decentralized systems, additional guarantees are needed to ensure that multiple witnesses or nodes agree on the order and integrity of events across the system [7]. This often requires consensus algorithms such as PBFT [9] or blockchain-based ledgers [18], which collectively maintain an append-only, tamper-evident log of location claims. These mechanisms complement temporal soundness by preventing reordering or deletion of proofs after the fact [4,7].
- **Privacy.** Many use cases require minimal disclosure. For instance, $\mathcal{P}$ might reveal only that it was in a certain region without disclosing exact coordinates or identity. Zero-knowledge proofs [5,16,25] can enforce location membership while hiding extraneous details, albeit at greater computational cost.

In high-assurance scenarios, such as legal forensics, liability tracking, or e-government, additional properties like non-repudiation (ensuring the prover cannot deny a valid proof) and non-transferability (preventing reassignment of proofs to others) may be required. Achieving these guarantees in decentralized, privacy-preserving settings remains an open challenge. Future work may explore new digital signature schemes, identity-bound proofs, or co-signed attestations to address these needs.

3.3 Domain 2: Spatio-Temporal Synchronization

Location proofs revolve around two fundamental aspects: where the prover is and when they are there. Systems thus differ not only in who provides the space and time references but also in how precise those references must be.

Spatial Reference and Precision

- **Reference Mechanism.** This describes how the prover's physical location is determined, which varies across use cases:
  - *Prover-located:* The prover self-reports (e.g., via GPS). Simple to deploy, but prone to spoofing if not combined with secure hardware or distance bounding [24].
  - *Single anchor:* A location server or hardware beacon is controlled by the verifier. It is often used in centralized protocols where trust is placed in a physically secured anchor [22,24].

  - *Multi-witness triangulation:* Multiple independent anchors or peer devices collectively bound the prover's position, characteristic of more fault-tolerant or decentralized systems [7,11,18,27].
- **Spatial Precision.** This captures the granularity of the location claim, how accurately the system must localize the prover. Required precision can range from coarse (e.g., city- or region-level) to fine-grained (sub-meter), depending on the application's sensitivity and risk profile. Systems adopt different approaches based on these needs:
  - *Coarse precision via GPS or single-anchor models:* Suitable for low-risk applications such as retail rewards or general mobility analytics, where city- or district-level location is sufficient [21].
  - *Short-range or specialized radio techniques:* Technologies like UWB or WiFi round-trip timing reduce localization error in room-scale or indoor environments. When combined with distance-bounding protocols, they also support security-critical applications that require proximity enforcement [2,3,8].
  - *Dense witness coverage:* Multi-lateration using multiple vantage points or peer witnesses enables sub-meter multidimensional accuracy with fault-tolerance, often needed in critical infrastructure or industrial settings [7, 10,11].

Temporal Reference & Precision

- **Time Source.** This defines who is trusted to timestamp the prover's location proof. The protocol must determine when the prover was at a location:
  - *Prover's local clock:* Minimal overhead, but untrusted if $\mathcal{P}$ can alter timestamps for replay attacks.
  - *Verifier or Trusted Witness clock:* A central entity timestamps proofs; typical in semi-centralized protocols [24].
  - *Distributed ledger or witness-based clock:* Achieves robust time integrity by ordering events via consensus [7,11]. This suits high-collusion risk scenarios but raises the bandwidth and latency overheads.
- **Temporal Precision.** This captures how exact the timing information must be for the proof to be considered valid. Some applications demand only day-level granularity (e.g., "present sometime on Monday"), while others require second- or even millisecond-level timestamps (e.g., traffic management, real-time access control):
  - *High-precision timing:* sub-second or sub-millisecond typically relies on synchronized protocols like NTP/PTP, or a blockchain with very tight block intervals [26].
  - *Lower-precision needs:* can tolerate simpler clock models or occasional drift (e.g., verifying presence within a 24-hour window) [11].
  - *Replay mitigation:* If the adversary can shift t by even a few seconds to re-use an old proof, the system must maintain strict temporal soundness (e.g., *time bounding* or short validity windows) [18].

Taken together, the location reference mechanism (self-reported vs. anchored vs. multi-lateration) and the time source (local clock vs. anchor timestamp vs. consensus ordering) form the core of spatio-temporal synchronization. The chosen approach must align with each use case's required precision, as well as its threat model (e.g., do we fear adversaries forging sub-meter location or shifting timestamps by seconds?). As higher fidelity in space-time typically demands more infrastructure or more complex protocols, system designers must eventually balance security needs against deployment overhead.

3.4 Domain 3: Trust and Witness Models

This domain captures who is trusted to observe, validate, and attest to the prover's location. It reflects the underlying trust assumptions of the system, whether centralized or distributed, and how witnesses are selected, authenticated, or incentivized. The model also affects the system's resilience to collusion, fault tolerance, and scalability:

- **Prover-Managed.** The prover $\mathcal{P}$ is assumed to be trustworthy or equipped with tamper-resistant hardware, allowing it to self-certify its location. This approach has minimal overhead and works well in controlled environments (e.g., corporate devices), but offers limited resistance to spoofing or collusion [15,17].
- **Verifier-Managed.** A location anchor or server is controlled directly by the verifier $\mathcal{V}$, who certifies the prover's presence. This model dominates early PoL systems [24] and simplifies deployment, but introduces a central point of failure and requires complete trust in the verifier.
- **Partially Distributed.** A limited number of known entities (e.g., location anchors, authorized witnesses) jointly verify location claims. These may be coordinated through a certificate authority or pre-established trust relationships. This model balances decentralization and manageability, and is typical of mid-scale protocols with privacy or availability goals [27].
- **Fully Decentralized or Permissionless.** Witnessing is performed by an open and untrusted set of peers. Verifiability arises from quorum-based or consensus mechanisms (e.g., threshold cryptography, BFT agreement), and often includes incentive layers such as staking, token rewards, or smart contracts to promote honest behavior [7,11,18,20]. This model enables scalability and strong collusion resistance, but also introduces coordination and latency overheads.

3.5 Domain 4: Interaction Model and Overhead

This domain describes how location proofs are constructed and verified–whether they require real-time interaction or can be performed offline, and what computational or bandwidth costs are involved. These choices impact system usability, deployability in constrained settings, and the level of guarantees (e.g., proximity soundness, auditability, scalability):

- **Interactive Proofs (Challenge-Response).** The prover must engage in a time-sensitive exchange with a verifier or witness (e.g., bit-level distance bounding). These are essential in contexts that demand secure proximity guarantees or live validation [2,8].
- **Non-Interactive (Offline) Proofs.** The prover collects signed attestations or zero-knowledge statements from witnesses and later presents them to the verifier without needing further communication. This model is ideal for asynchronous auditing (e.g., supply chains, mobility attestations), but offers weaker proximity guarantees [4,11,18,20].
- **Proof Size and Verification Complexity.** Some zero-knowledge-based PoL protocols [5,16,25] produce large, computation-heavy proofs, especially when encoding distance or privacy constraints. In contrast, lightweight signature-based schemes offer lower overhead but less expressive power and weaker security guarantees [4].

3.6 Summary and Discussion

Table 1 summarizes the domains for classifying PoL systems: cryptographic guarantees, spatio-temporal synchronization, trust and witness models, and interaction or overhead. Each reflects a distinct design concern, from what the proof must guarantee to how location and time are established and verified.

This taxonomy aims to help designers navigate trade-offs between verifiability, privacy, and infrastructure complexity, enabling protocol comparisons across security models and better alignment with application needs.

Nonetheless, the taxonomy abstracts away some real-world complexity. Hybrid architectures that blend interaction models or trust configurations may defy strict categorization. Emerging deployments may feature dynamic witnesses, layered identity systems, or continuous sensing, all of which challenge these static models [7]. New adversarial threats, such as AI-assisted spoofing or environmental emulation, may also shift current assumptions.

Future refinements could extend the taxonomy to address these hybrid and dynamic settings, or incorporate additional dimensions such as usability, legal constraints, or application-specific needs. In the next section, we introduce a methodology for selecting appropriate protocol designs by mapping requirements onto the proposed domains.

4 Methodology for Matching Use Cases to PoL Requirements

Having established our taxonomy in Sect. 3, we now present a five-step methodology for translating application-specific requirements into a concrete PoL protocol design. Each step aligns with one or more domains of the taxonomy and culminates in a set of cryptographic and infrastructural decisions.

4.1 Step 1: Profile the Use Case

The process begins by outlining the application's operational and security requirements across four axes. This step yields a structured requirement profile that will guide further design decisions.

- **Spatial and Temporal Precision.** Define the required granularity of the location proof (e.g., sub-meter, room-level, city-level) and the acceptable time window or resolution (seconds, minutes, or daily presence).
- **Threat Model.** Characterize expected adversaries: are relay attacks, timestamp tampering, or witness collusion realistic threats? What forms of spoofing must the system withstand?
- **Privacy and Disclosure.** Determine the level of information that must be protected. Should the proof reveal exact coordinates, or just region membership? Are there legal or regulatory constraints on disclosure?
- **Deployment Environment.** Identify device and network constraints. Are devices battery-constrained or capable of interactive sessions? Is the network intermittent? Is the system real-time or audit-based?

4.2 Step 2: Classify the Use Case in the Taxonomy

Next, the profile is mapped onto the four taxonomy domains from Table 1:

- **Cryptographic Guarantees.** Identify the required properties: spatio-temporal soundness, authenticity, integrity, consensus, or privacy preservation.
- **Spatio-temporal Synchronization.** Assess how precise and reliable the system's spatial and temporal references must be. Choose between GPS, verifier-managed anchors, or distributed consensus.
- **Trust and Witness Model.** Choose a trust architecture: centralized (verifier-managed), partially distributed (registered anchors), or decentralized (open witnesses with incentives or quorum).
- **Interaction and Overhead.** Establish the acceptable interaction mode and cost model. Is real-time challenge-response feasible? Can the system tolerate large proof sizes or limited connectivity?

This mapping narrows the solution space by identifying which protocol properties are non-negotiable.

4.3 Step 3: Select Cryptographic Building Blocks

With the taxonomy placement in hand, designers can select appropriate cryptographic tools:

- **Distance Bounding** [2,7,8]. Needed for high-precision or proximity-enforcing use cases.

- **Time Anchoring** [7,18]. Achievable through trusted timestamps or consensus-based ordering on a ledger.
- **Standard Authenticity and Integrity Mechanisms** [7]. Public-key signatures, secure enclaves, or hash-chained logs ensure integrity and provenance. Threshold or Group Signatures [6,7] are useful for schemes requiring multiple witnesses to jointly attest a statement.
- **Zero-Knowledge Proofs** [16,25]. Used to prove location assertions without revealing, for instance, fine-grained coordinates.

When resource limitations (e.g., mobile environments) conflict with the above requirements, fallback strategies must be considered–e.g., reducing proof frequency or omitting distance bounding.

4.4 Step 4: Choose Trust and Witness Infrastructure Models

The trust and witness infrastructure models determine how the protocol operates at the system level:

- **Single Anchor (Centralized)** [2,24]. Suitable for low-risk applications with stable infrastructure and strong control over anchor security, but limited in coverage or fault tolerance.
- **Partially Distributed** [17,27]. Combines a small set of trusted anchors to improve coverage and resilience, without full decentralization.
- **Fully Decentralized** [7,11]. Witnessing is open to untrusted participants, relying on threshold consensus or blockchains to enforce integrity. Highly robust against collusion, though more complex to operate and often paired with economic incentives.

The number, coverage, and mobility of anchors must align with the desired spatial precision. Higher granularity generally implies denser and better-placed infrastructure.

4.5 Step 5: Define the Interaction Model and Estimate Overhead

Finally, the designer specifies how location proofs are produced and verified in practice:

- **Interactive Protocols.** Required for real-time checks or distance bounding, but involve latency-sensitive communication and tighter hardware timing constraints.
- **Non-Interactive (Offline) Proofs.** Preferred for post-event validation or intermittent connectivity scenarios, using signed statements or zero-knowledge proofs.
- **Cost and Efficiency.** Analyze whether proof sizes, computation, and bandwidth demands match the device and application context, especially for IoT, edge, or mobile deployments.

This step ensures that the protocol is not only secure, but feasible to run in the intended setting.

4.6 Discussion and Trade-Offs

This methodology shows a structured path from application-level requirements to a tailored PoL design, grounded in the four taxonomy domains introduced in Sect. 3. It enables reasoning about trade-offs between verifiability, privacy, interactivity, and deployment complexity.

For instance, a transit ticketing system needing second-level timestamping and moderate spatial accuracy might rely on a short-range anchor and offline proof submission. In contrast, high-assurance identity verification may call for interactive distance bounding, quorum-based witness validation, and zero-knowledge disclosures.

Nonetheless, this methodology abstracts away several real-world challenges. It assumes that application requirements can be cleanly mapped to static design dimensions, whereas in practice, use cases may evolve over time or operate across multiple modes (e.g., interactive during onboarding, offline during regular use). Hybrid deployments that mix centralized and decentralized witnesses, or dynamically switch between precision levels, are difficult to model with the current framework. Moreover, the methodology does not yet account for economic incentives, user experience constraints, or regulatory compliance workflows, factors that increasingly shape system adoption in practice.

Future work could enrich this methodology with formal decision models or tool-assisted workflows to guide protocol selection. It may also benefit from empirical validation across real deployments, and from integration with broader system concerns such as identity management, data life cycle control, and composability with other attestations (e.g., proof of identity, proof of intent). As the PoL design space expands, a modular, extensible framework for reasoning about trust, precision, and accountability across heterogeneous environments will become increasingly necessary.

5 Illustrative Use Cases

A diverse range of real-world applications benefit from PoL systems, reflecting the growing need for verifiable presence data in modern societies [7]. Among the most prominent PoL use-case domains are:

- **Civic and Governance:** Voter presence verification at polling stations, smart-city crowd-sensing for public resource allocation, or location-based eligibility checks (e.g., verifying residency for local benefits) [21].
- **Supply Chain and Logistics:** Authenticating product handoffs along distribution chains (to thwart counterfeits in pharmaceuticals or high-value goods), and ensuring goods remain in authorized areas [18,20].
- **Delivery and Transport Services:** Proof of package handover (reducing "lost shipment" disputes), ride-sharing liability checks, or verifying IoT sensor deployments [4].
- **Retail and Entertainment:** Issuing location-based promotions, tickets, or exclusive content to users physically visiting a store, stadium, or event [17,22].

- **Content Authentication:** Demonstrating that digital media (photos, videos) were captured at a certain place and time, mitigating deepfake concerns [7].

Collectively, these scenarios span everything from high-stakes (e.g., e-voting with strong adversary models) to low-risk or coarse-grained contexts (e.g., city-level coupons). Some demand sub-meter precision and near-real-time assurance, while others settle for ex-post auditing of day-level location logs. Certain applications must also preserve privacy via selective disclosure or zero-knowledge proofs, whereas others are content with public logs of presence.

To illustrate how our five-step methodology (Sect. 4) applies to different constraints, we now explore three specific examples: *(1) Retail E-Coupon Rewards*, *(2) Supply Chain Auditing with Medium Precision*, and *(3) E-Voting with Strict Proximity*. Each scenario shows a combination of spatial precision, time constraints, threat model, and privacy or resource demands, leading to distinct protocol configurations.

5.1 Use Case 1: Retail E-Coupon Rewards

(1) Requirements. A store issues digital coupons only to customers physically present on-site [17,22]. Spatial precision is coarse (100–200 m), with same-day temporal granularity. Threats are mild (little collusion or relay risk), and privacy demands are low, as the location claim is coarse, voluntary, and not linked to sensitive personal data.
(2) Taxonomy Mapping.

- *Guarantees*: Basic authenticity and integrity; no proximity or time bounding.
- *Synchronization*: Single anchor (e.g., Wi-Fi beacon), day-level timestamp.
- *Trust Model*: Centralized (store-managed).
- *Interaction and Overhead*: Non-interactive; low computation and communication.

(3) Cryptographic Building Blocks. A public-key digital signature scheme suffices. No distance bounding or zero-knowledge is needed.
(4) Trust and Witness Infrastructure. The store acts as a trusted anchor. A BLE or Wi-Fi beacon issues signed proofs upon customer interaction.
(5) Interaction and Overhead. Proofs are collected offline and shown during checkout. System demands are low, with minimal real-time communication.

5.2 Use Case 2: Supply Chain Auditing

(1) Requirements. A logistics provider tracks goods across distribution centers [4,18,20]. Required precision is moderate (± 50 m); timestamps are needed at hour or day-level granularity. Threats include tampering and forgery, but not advanced relays. Privacy is moderate: visibility limited to stakeholders.

(2) Taxonomy Mapping.

- *Cryptographic Guarantees*: Authenticity and tamper-evidence; no sub-meter proximity.
- *Spatio-temporal Synchronization*: Anchors provide signed location and time.
- *Trust Model*: Partially distributed (e.g., partner-operated checkpoints).
- *Interaction and Overhead*: Non-interactive; ex-post verifiability.

(3) Cryptographic Building Blocks. Anchor-issued digital signatures provide basic presence proofs. Ledger-anchored hash chains are used to ensure tamper-evidence and enable aggregation.
(4) Trust and Witness Infrastructure. Each checkpoint hosts one or more trusted anchors, ideally run by different partner firms. These anchors issue signed location-time records, minimizing reliance on a single entity [18].
(5) Interaction and Overhead. Devices collect signed proofs during handovers; verification is deferred to a later auditing phase. Overheads are modest, matching the use case's moderate assurance requirements.

5.3 Use Case 3: E-Voting with Location Binding

(1) Requirements. An election authority wants to ensure that votes are only cast by citizens physically present at designated polling stations during election day [16,21]. Spatial precision is fine-grained (under 10 m) to prevent location spoofing. Temporal precision must support real-time validation to prevent multiple votes. The threat model is strong: relay and collusion attacks are realistic. Privacy is prime to protect voter anonymity and external location leakage.
(2) Taxonomy Mapping.

- *Cryptographic Guarantees*: Proximity soundness (distance bounding), time integrity, and privacy via selective disclosure.
- *Spatio-temporal Synchronization*: Multi-witness triangulation and synchronized clocks; possibly combined with tamper-evident logs or consensus.
- *Trust Model*: Partially distributed (independent anchors) or fully decentralized (to avoid centralized abuse).
- *Interaction and Overhead*: Interactive challenge-response; high computational and coordination complexity.

(3) Cryptographic Building Blocks. Distance bounding protocols [7] are used for real-time proximity soundness. A permissioned ledger or consensus system (e.g., PBFT) enforces temporal ordering and protects against timestamp forgery [7,18]. Zero-knowledge proofs [25] support privacy-preserving presence claims without revealing sensitive metadata.
(4) Trust and Witness Infrastructure. Polling locations are equipped with multiple independent anchors operated by separate trusted entities (e.g., civic oversight bodies or parties). These anchors jointly participate in the proof process and sign ephemeral measurements [7].
(5) Interaction and Overhead. Voters perform real-time distance-bounding with nearby anchors, which may require specialized radio protocols [7]. Collected

measurements are combined and recorded in a ledger for auditability. Proofs are privacy-preserving but computationally heavier. The overhead is justified by the high-stakes and high-threat model of elections.

5.4 Summary and Comparison

Table 2 summarizes the design choices for the three scenarios analyzed. These examples demonstrate how varying combinations of spatial precision, timing constraints, privacy demands, and adversarial strength lead to distinct PoL protocol configurations.

Table 2. Comparison of illustrative PoL scenarios.

Use Case	Precision	Threat Model	Trust Model	Proof Style
Retail Coupons	Coarse (100–200 m)	Low	Centralized	Non-Interactive
Supply Chain	Medium (±50 m)	Medium	Partially Distributed	Non-Interactive
E-Voting	Fine (<10 m)	High	Partially/Full Decentralized	Interactive

6 Conclusion and Future Work

We introduced a structured taxonomy and methodology for designing Proof-of-Location (PoL) systems, spanning four core domains: cryptographic guarantees, spatio-temporal synchronization, trust models, and interaction and overhead. A five-step process maps real-world constraints to concrete protocol features, illustrated through three scenarios–retail coupons, supply chain auditing, and e-voting–each with distinct requirements in precision, trust, and privacy.

Looking forward, challenges remain in scaling PoL systems to real deployments, especially those involving decentralized ledgers, distance bounding, or zero-knowledge proofs. Balancing privacy with efficiency, modeling stronger adversaries, and standardizing verifiable location claims are promising future directions. As trust in location claims becomes as essential as identity, we envision PoL protocols becoming foundational tools across emerging digital societies.

Disclosure of Interests. The authors have no competing interests to declare that are relevant to the content of this article.

References

1. Akand, M.R., Safavi-Naini, R., Kneppers, M., Giraud, M., Lafourcade, P.: Privacy-preserving proof-of-location with security against geo-tampering. IEEE Trans. Dependable Secure Comput. (2021)
2. Akand, M.M.R.: Contribution to Proof-of-Location Systems. Ph.D. thesis, University of Calgary, Alberta, Canada (2023)

3. Alexandru, A.: Secure localization literature review. Not peer-reviewed (2021)
4. Amoretti, M., Brambilla, G., Medioli, F., Zanichelli, F.: Blockchain-based proof of location. In: 2018 IEEE International Conference on Software Quality, Reliability and Security Companion (QRS-C), pp. 146–153. IEEE (2018)
5. Bogdanov, D., Brito, E., Jaakson, A., Laud, P., Rebane, R.M.: Zero-knowledge proof-of-location protocols for vehicle subsidies and taxation compliance. In: International Conference on Availability, Reliability and Security, pp. 343–360. Springer, Heidelberg (2025). https://doi.org/10.1007/978-3-032-00642-4_20
6. Brandao, L.T., Mouha, N.W., Vassilev, A.T.: Threshold schemes for cryptographic primitives. Natl. Inst. Stand. Technol. (2019). https://doi.org/10.6028/NIST.IR.8214
7. Brito, E., Hadachi, A., Kamm, L., Norbisrath, U.: Decentralized proof-of-location systems for trust, scalability, and privacy in digital societies. Sci. Rep. **15**(1), 1–20 (2025)
8. Capkun, S., Hubaux, J.P.: Secure positioning in wireless networks. IEEE J. Sel. Areas Commun. **24**(2), 221–232 (2006)
9. Castro, M., Liskov, B., et al.: Practical byzantine fault tolerance. In: OsDI, pp. 173–186 (1999)
10. Chiang, J.T., Haas, J.J., Hu, Y.C.: Secure and precise location verification using distance bounding and simultaneous multilateration. In: Proceedings of the Second ACM Conference on Wireless Network Security, pp. 181–192 (2009)
11. Corp, F.: Foam whitepaper. https://foam.space/publicAssets/FOAM_Whitepaper.pdf. Accessed 02 Jan 2025
12. Dupin, A., Robert, J.-M., Bidan, C.: Location-proof system based on secure multiparty computations. In: Baek, J., Susilo, W., Kim, J. (eds.) ProvSec 2018. LNCS, vol. 11192, pp. 22–39. Springer, Cham (2018). https://doi.org/10.1007/978-3-030-01446-9_2
13. Gambs, S., Killijian, M.O., Roy, M., Traoré, M.: Props: a privacy-preserving location proof system. In: 2014 IEEE 33rd International Symposium on Reliable Distributed Systems, pp. 1–10. IEEE (2014)
14. Graham, M., Gray, D.: Protecting privacy and securing the gathering of location proofs – the secure location verification proof gathering protocol. In: Schmidt, A.U., Lian, S. (eds.) MobiSec 2009. LNICST, vol. 17, pp. 160–171. Springer, Heidelberg (2009). https://doi.org/10.1007/978-3-642-04434-2_14
15. Javali, C., Revadigar, G., Rasmussen, K.B., Hu, W., Jha, S.: I am alice, i was in wonderland: secure location proof generation and verification protocol. In: 2016 IEEE 41st Conference on Local Computer Networks (LCN), pp. 477–485. IEEE (2016)
16. Li, W., Guo, H., Nejad, M., Shen, C.C.: Privacy-preserving traffic management: a blockchain and zero-knowledge proof inspired approach. IEEE Access **8**, 181733–181743 (2020)
17. Luo, W., Hengartner, U.: Veriplace: a privacy-aware location proof architecture. In: Proceedings of the 18th SIGSPATIAL International Conference on Advances in Geographic Information Systems, pp. 23–32 (2010)
18. Nasrulin, B., Muzammal, M., Qu, Q.: A robust spatio-temporal verification protocol for blockchain. In: Hacid, H., Cellary, W., Wang, H., Paik, H.-Y., Zhou, R. (eds.) WISE 2018. LNCS, vol. 11233, pp. 52–67. Springer, Cham (2018). https://doi.org/10.1007/978-3-030-02922-7_4
19. Nosouhi, M.R., Yu, S., Grobler, M., Xiang, Y., Zhu, Z.: Sparse: privacy-aware and collusion resistant location proof generation and verification. In: 2018 IEEE Global Communications Conference (GLOBECOM), pp. 1–6. IEEE (2018)

20. Nosouhi, M.R., Yu, S., Zhou, W., Grobler, M., Keshtiar, H.: Blockchain for secure location verification. J. Parallel Distrib. Comput. **136**, 40–51 (2020)
21. Pournaras, E.: Proof of witness presence: blockchain consensus for augmented democracy in smart cities. J. Parallel Distrib. Comput. **145**, 160–175 (2020)
22. Saroiu, S., Wolman, A.: Enabling new mobile applications with location proofs. In: Proceedings of the 10th Workshop on Mobile Computing Systems and Applications, pp. 1–6 (2009)
23. Wang, X., Pande, A., Zhu, J., Mohapatra, P.: Stamp: Enabling privacy-preserving location proofs for mobile users. IEEE/ACM Trans. Network. **24**(6), 3276–3289 (2016)
24. Waters, B., Felten, E.: Secure, private proofs of location. Department of Computer Science, Princeton University, Technical Report TR-667-03 (2003)
25. Wu, W., Liu, E., Gong, X., Wang, R.: Blockchain based zero-knowledge proof of location in iot. In: ICC 2020-2020 IEEE International Conference on Communications (ICC), pp. 1–7. IEEE (2020)
26. Xiao, Y., Zhang, N., Lou, W., Hou, Y.T.: A survey of distributed consensus protocols for blockchain networks. IEEE Commun. Surv. Tutor. **22**(2), 1432–1465 (2020). https://doi.org/10.1109/COMST.2020.2969706
27. Zhu, Z., Cao, G.: Applaus: a privacy-preserving location proof updating system for location-based services. In: 2011 Proceedings IEEE INFOCOM, pp. 1889–1897. IEEE (2011)

Ontologies

An Ontology-Driven Domain-Specific Modeling Language for Specification and Evaluation of Resilience Scenarios in Complex Systems

Pedro Paulo F. Barcelos[1,2,3](✉), Rodrigo F. Calhau[4,5], Frederik Gailly[2,3], Geert Poels[2,3], and Giancarlo Guizzardi[5]

[1] Health-RI, Utrecht, The Netherlands
pedro.barcelos@health-ri.nl
[2] Dept. Business Inf. and Operations Management, Ghent University, Ghent, Belgium
[3] CVAMO Core Lab, Flanders Make @UGent, Ghent, Belgium
{frederik.gailly,geert.poels}@ugent.be
[4] LEDS, Federal Institute of Espírito Santo, Serra, Espírito Santo, Brazil
calhau@ifes.edu.br
[5] Semantics, Cybersecurity and Services, University of Twente, Enschede, The Netherlands
g.guizzardi@utwente.nl

Abstract. Resilience is recognized as a critical property of complex social-ecological-technological systems (SETS). Yet, its modeling remains fragmented, often lacking semantic rigor, reusability, and cross-domain applicability. This paper introduces LaDeRR (Language for Describing Risk and Resilience), a novel domain-specific modeling language (DSML) grounded in ResiliOnt—a well-founded core ontology for resilience. LaDeRR enables the formal specification and analysis of resilience scenarios through constructs representing capabilities, vulnerabilities, threats, and emergent resilience configurations. It supports a complete workflow, including textual syntax, RDF-based representation, semantic validation with SHACL, rule-based inference, and automated visualization. LaDeRR explicitly supports both proactive design-time analysis and retrospective modeling, allowing users to formally specify and analyze both ongoing and past resilience scenarios. This dual capability supports improved decision-making and long-term resilience planning. A representative case study in supply chain disruption demonstrates LaDeRR's expressiveness in identifying system vulnerabilities, modeling resilience strategies, and evaluating dynamic scenario outcomes. By integrating ontological precision with robust computational support leveraging logical reasoning, LaDeRR helps bridge the gap between theoretical foundations and applied resilience engineering.

Keywords: Resilience · Ontology-Driven Engineering · Domain-Specific Modeling Language · Resilience Scenario Modeling and Analysis

© The Author(s), under exclusive license to Springer Nature Switzerland AG 2026
A. Gianola et al. (Eds.): EDOC 2025, LNCS 16213, pp. 247–265, 2026.
https://doi.org/10.1007/978-3-032-15140-7_14

1 Introduction

Resilience is a critical requirement for complex systems operating under uncertainty, disruption, and interdependence [2,23,33]. These systems often span interwoven social, technological, and ecological domains—commonly referred to as *social-ecological-technological systems (SETS)*—and include infrastructures, digital platforms, and environmental networks. Despite their importance, resilience in such systems remains loosely defined in both practice and research. The lack of formal modeling frameworks limits efforts to evaluate and improve them in a consistent and meaningful way [4,27].

While enterprise modeling has advanced through the use of ontologies and domain-specific languages (DSLs) to support tasks such as process design [3,13], risk analysis [25,32], capability modeling [7,8], and compliance [1,14], resilience modeling has not similarly benefited. Most existing efforts rely on ad hoc formalisms with limited semantic clarity and interoperability, underscoring the need for an ontologically grounded and reusable modeling language.

Resilience modeling is crucial not only for assessing system behavior under disruption but also for enabling resilience by design—embedding adaptive capacity into system structure. This need spans domains, from supply chains to socio-ecological systems, and calls for a modeling language that supports both evaluation and design across heterogeneous contexts.

We introduce the Language for Describing Risk and Resilience (LaDeRR), a domain-specific modeling language (DSML) focused on resilience. Although tailored for resilience modeling (i.e., domain-specific in scope), LaDeRR is system-independent in application, enabling its use across SETS. Grounded in the ResilIOnt ontology [6], it adopts its ontological categories as modeling primitives and embeds its commitments into the language's semantics and inference behavior.

LaDeRR is supported by a computational tool for validation, inference, and scenario-level evaluation. It integrates ontology reasoning, Shapes Constraint Language (SHACL) validation, and visualization features to support resilience assessments. In addition to evaluating current systems, it enables the registration of past resilience events and the design of future scenarios for strategic planning. This integration of semantic rigor with real-world applicability motivates the following research questions, which address both conceptual and practical challenges in resilience modeling:

- **RQ1.** How can an ontology-grounded domain-specific modeling language be designed to formally represent resilience scenarios across diverse application domains?
- **RQ2.** How can a modeling language leverage formal, rule-based mechanisms to support the correct representation and assessment of resilience in complex systems?
- **RQ3.** How effectively can such a language be applied in a representative case study to model, analyze, and assess the resilience of a complex system?

The remainder of this paper is structured as follows. Section 2 introduces the conceptual foundations of LaDeRR, including its alignment with ontology-driven engineering and the ResiliOnt ontology. Section 3 details the formal design of the LaDeRR DSML, including its core constructs and metamodel. Section 4 presents LaDeRR's computational support, covering inference, validation, and visualization. Section 5 illustrates the application of LaDeRR in a supply chain resilience case study. Section 6 reviews related work on resilience modeling, situating LaDeRR in relation to existing approaches. Finally, Sect. 7 summarizes the main contributions and outlines directions for future research.

2 Foundations of Ontology-Driven Resilience Modeling

According to Guizzardi [16], one of the main attributes of a notation is *domain appropriateness*, which occurs when the notation has constructs to represent the state of affairs in an explicit and clear way. In this context, ontologies play a crucial role, as they are capable of explaining concepts in a domain and avoiding different types of understanding and communication problems, such as false agreements [16]. As a result, notations used in complex domain modeling should be grounded in the principles of ontology-driven engineering, a methodological approach in which formal ontologies guide the development of models, languages, and systems. The adoption of ontologically well-founded theories enables precise semantics, conceptual clarity, and improved interoperability—characteristics that are particularly crucial in domains where ambiguity and inconsistency can hinder system understanding and evaluation [9,16,35].

In the context of LaDeRR, the ontology-driven approach is realized through the design of a DSML for resilience. DSMLs are tailored languages that provide domain experts and system engineers with constructs that reflect the conceptual structure of a domain [12,31]. Unlike general-purpose modeling languages (such as UML), which aim for broad applicability, DSMLs are specialized for particular contexts, offering greater expressiveness and alignment with domain-specific concerns. A typical DSML comprises three main elements: (i) *abstract syntax* (which defines the core concepts and their relationships, often via a metamodel); (ii) *concrete syntax* (the graphical or textual notation used to represent models); and (iii) *semantics* (which specifies how models are interpreted or executed). When developed following ontology-engineering principles, DSMLs benefit from an ontological backbone that ensures semantic rigor and supports advanced reasoning capabilities, particularly for inference and validation.

This ontological foundation is not only beneficial but also methodologically justified in the context of DSMLs. As demonstrated by Carvalho et al. [9], a DSML can achieve precise real-world semantics only when its abstract syntax is explicitly linked to a reference domain ontology that defines the admissible world states and core conceptualizations. This view is further supported by Verdonck and Gailly [35], who propose a structured framework for ontological analysis in DSMLs, emphasizing the need to align abstract syntax elements with formally defined domain conceptualizations. This alignment ensures that the constructs of the language faithfully capture relevant phenomena and reduces ambiguity. Complementarily, Guizzardi's framework for modeling language evaluation [17] shows that *domain appropriateness*—the capacity of a language to truthfully represent a domain—depends on grounding the metamodel in a reference ontology. The author also argues that concrete syntax can benefit from a well-grounded ontological foundation, providing guidelines for improving it based on the ontology. These insights confirm that well-founded ontologies are not merely supportive, but essential to the design of semantically rigorous DSMLs.

While resilience is increasingly emphasized across fields such as ecology, engineering, management, and psychology, it remains semantically ambiguous, with varying definitions across disciplines [6,19,29]. This terminological diversity hinders the development of unified conceptual models, limits empirical comparability, and impedes the design of reusable resilience assessments. To address these issues, the ResiliOnt ontology was created. Developed through a rigorous ontological analysis grounded in the Unified Foundational Ontology (UFO) [18], ResiliOnt establishes a coherent and application-independent definition of resilience, clarifying its essential properties, dependencies, and manifestation conditions [6]. It also formalizes core ontological categories (e.g., capabilities, vulnerabilities, and threats) and the conditions under which resilience occurs.

As the ontological backbone of LaDeRR, ResiliOnt formalizes key concepts relevant to assessing and managing the resilience of systems. It defines resilience as a capability—a positive type of disposition—that emerges from the interplay between different objects' capabilities and vulnerabilities. According to the ontological analysis presented in Barcelos et al. [6], resilience is not an outcome observed only after a disturbance, but rather an intrinsic and risk-dependent capability that exists prior to threat events. It becomes observable only in situations where its protective configuration prevents a loss event. More precisely, resilience is present when a resilient capability preserves another capability that is exposed by a vulnerability, provided that this vulnerability is disabled by an additional capability. This configuration prevents the exploitation of the exposed capability by external threats, thereby safeguarding the object's value. ResiliOnt's formalization makes explicit the necessary and sufficient conditions for the existence and manifestation of resilience, offering a unified, application-independent understanding of the concept.

While LaDeRR does not expose ontological metaproperties directly, its constructs are not mere labels: each one maps to a ResiliOnt concept, thereby making its ontological commitments explicit. In addition, LaDeRR leverages the domain rules defined in ResiliOnt to drive its rule-based inference system and uses its domain constraints to define validation rules.

3 Formal Design of the LaDeRR DSML

LaDeRR is designed to support the formal specification, validation, and evaluation of resilience scenarios in a way that is both ontologically well-founded and applicable across domains. It follows a DSML approach, offering constructs that are semantically grounded in the ResiliOnt ontology and tailored to describe key elements of resilience. The LaDeRR language specification, associated artifacts, and documentation are publicly available at https://w3id.org/laderr/git.

LaDeRR satisfies these conditions: it enables users to define structured abstractions of resilience scenarios—such as entities, capabilities, vulnerabilities, and controls—and to express causal and logical relations between them. Its computational support enables validation and inference over these specifications, allowing modelers to analyze system behavior under disruption and explore alternative resilience strategies. As such, LaDeRR qualifies not only as a domain-specific language, but also as a formal modeling language in the strict sense.

The abstract syntax of LaDeRR is organized around the notion of a `Scenario`, which serves as a container for all modeling elements and represents a temporally and contextually bounded situation in which resilience is to be assessed. Each scenario includes a set of `Constructs` (e.g., individual capabilities or vulnerabilities), which can be typed as one of several predefined classes derived from the ResiliOnt ontology. Constructs may be shared across scenarios or defined locally.

The concrete syntax of LaDeRR is implemented using the TOML format (https://toml.io), chosen for its human-readable structure and compatibility with modern tooling. Each specification is encoded as a structured TOML file that reflects the metamodel hierarchy and relationships, enabling both manual editing and automated parsing by the LaDeRR Engine. This choice facilitates accessibility for domain experts while maintaining alignment with the abstract syntax and ontological semantics.

To express dynamic relationships between constructs, LaDeRR supports typed relations that capture behavioral and causal dependencies. For instance, a `capability` may enable or disable a `vulnerability`, and a `control` may be linked to one or more constructs to represent mitigation structures. Constructs can also be associated with one or more status attributes, indicating their operational state, relevance, or emergence within a scenario. These model elements collectively enable users to represent the dynamic structure of risk and resilience in a structured and semantically precise way.

Figure 1 presents a high-level excerpt of the LaDeRR metamodel in UML, focusing on core domain concepts and their interrelations. At the center of the model is the `Entity` class, which aggregates both `Capabilities` and `Vulnerabilities` as its associated dispositions. These influence and are influenced by additional constructs such as `Threats`, `Controls`, and `Assets`. Threats may `threaten` assets, and controls may `inhibit` threats or `protect` assets, with multiple cardinalities and overlapping constraints allowing expressive combinations.

Capabilities may `sustain` resilience, `disable` vulnerabilities, or be `exploited` by them. Conversely, vulnerabilities may `expose` capabilities, reflecting internal weaknesses that compromise the system's ability to deploy them

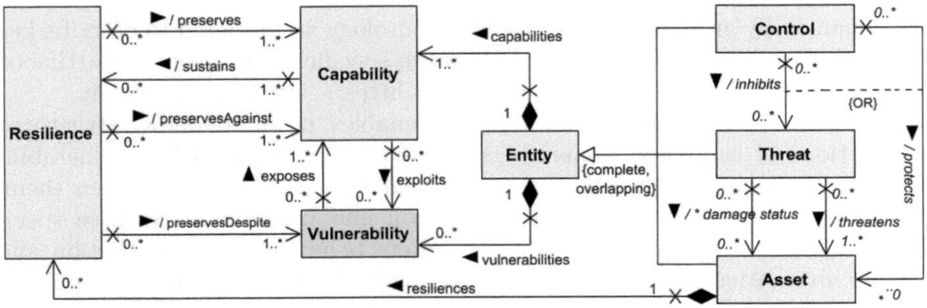

Fig. 1. Excerpt of the UML LaDeRR metamodel illustrating the core constructs and relations used in resilience modeling.

effectively. These bidirectional relations model critical interactions in resilience dynamics and are essential for triggering many of LaDeRR's inference rules.

These interactions are governed by a set of formally defined inference rules that are part of the LaDeRR language design. Expressed in first-order logic, these rules capture the intended semantics of core resilience patterns—such as damage propagation, capability disabling, vulnerability exploitation, and resilience emergence. They act as domain-level constraints that shape valid model interpretations and provide a precise logical basis for semantic reasoning. The complete set of rules is available at the language's git repository alongside the language specification and is directly implemented in the LaDeRR Engine to ensure that derivations during inference reflect the language's ontological commitments.

`Resilience` is linked back to the broader system via preservation relations (`preserves`, `preservesAgainst`, and `preservesDespite`), each capturing a different aspect of resilience logic. The model also reflects how entities collectively participate in resilience modeling by supporting the emergence of resilience instances derived from structured configurations of the other components.

The language design adheres closely to the structure of the ResiliOnt ontology, ensuring that every modeling element in LaDeRR corresponds to a class or property in the ontology, thereby supporting semantic clarity, automated reasoning, and extensibility. In support of these goals, LaDeRR also provides its metamodel as a formal OWL vocabulary, which semantically mirrors the structure defined by the abstract syntax. This vocabulary, available at https://w3id.org/laderr, enables the publication, sharing, and reuse of LaDeRR specifications as machine-processable RDF graphs.

The LaDeRR vocabulary was developed in accordance with the FAIR Principles [36], ensuring that resilience models are Findable, Accessible, Interoperable, and Reusable. Besides serving as the foundation for the LaDeRR Engine's internal reasoning and validation tasks, the vocabulary is intended for broader use in semantic web applications, enabling the standardized exchange and analysis of resilience data across systems and domains.

Moreover, the design accommodates shared model elements across scenarios, enabling the modular reuse of components such as common capabilities or persistent threats. These features make LaDeRR expressive enough for detailed scenario modeling while remaining constrained by ontological rigor to ensure interoperability and correctness. Taken together, the design principles and formal structures presented in this section establish LaDeRR as a robust, ontology-grounded language for resilience modeling. Its alignment with ResiliOnt, support for formal validation and inference, and applicability across multiple domains directly contribute to answering **RQ1**.

4 Inference, Validation, and Visualization in LaDeRR

The LaDeRR implementation consists of a modular architecture that processes specifications and performs inference, validation, and visualization tasks. It takes a LaDeRR specification as input, structured according to the language's abstract syntax and semantically aligned with ResiliOnt, and produces both enriched semantic outputs and human-readable representations of the modeled scenarios.

Modelers can choose between two modes of authoring LaDeRR specifications. In the *manual* approach, all constructs and their attributes are explicitly defined by the user. In contrast, the *minimal* approach allows modelers to define only the essential structure, leaving the engine to automatically complete missing elements based on inference rules and default values. This dual approach supports both expert-driven modeling and lightweight scenario prototyping. In either case, the engine ensures semantic completeness through internal duplication of constructs across scenarios: each construct is treated as scenario-specific, even if declared globally. This duplication enables context-aware reasoning and prevents unintended overlaps between scenarios.

Central to the implementation is the transformation of scenario specifications into an RDF knowledge graph, where each construct and relation is instantiated according to the LaDeRR vocabulary derived from ResiliOnt. This graph-based representation enables automated reasoning and consistency checking through OWL and SHACL technologies.

LaDeRR includes a dedicated rule-based inference engine—the **LaDeRR Engine**, with source code and usage documentation available at https://w3id.org/laderr/engine/git. Implemented in Python, it applies a series of logical inference rules over the RDF model. These rules capture resilience-related patterns, such as enabling and disabling relations, propagation of threats, emergence of resilience, and scenario classification. The full set of inference rules is currently composed of ten formally defined patterns, presented below for reference.

Rules over Dispositions and Entity Interactions

Rule 1. If a *disposition* `disables` another, and the first is `enabled` or the second is `disabled`, then the first must be `enabled` and the second `disabled`.

Rule 2. If an *entity* has both a *vulnerability* and a *capability*, and a second entity has a capability that `exploits` the first entity's vulnerability (which also `exposes` the first capability), then the second entity causes *negative damage* to the first.

Rule 3. If an *entity* has both a *vulnerability* and a *capability*, and a second entity has a capability that `exploits` the vulnerability (which `exposes` the capability), then the scenario becomes `vulnerable` and the second entity causes *positive damage* to the first.

Rule 4. If two entities respectively hold a capability that `disables` a vulnerability, and another capability that `exploits` the same vulnerability, then the first entity `inhibits` the second.

Rule 5. If an *entity* has a *capability* that `disables` a *vulnerability* in another entity, then it `protects` the other entity.

Rule 6. If an *entity* has a *capability* that `exploits` a *vulnerability* in another entity, then it `threatens` that entity.

Rules over Emergence of Resilience

Rule 7. If *capabilities* and *vulnerabilities* form specific configurations—including a capability that `disables` a vulnerability, one that `exploits` it, and one that is `exposed`—then a *resilience* instance emerges and is linked to the affected entity via `preserves`, `preservesAgainst`, `preservesDespite`, and `sustains` relations.

Rule 8. If a *resilience* instance is logically linked to at least one of its components (e.g., preserved capability, exploiting capability, sustained capability, or exposed vulnerability), it must be included in the *scenario* that contains those components.

Rules over Scenario Status and Situation

Rule 9. If the scenario's `situation` is set to `incident`, then all *positive* and *negative* damages must result in actual damage (i.e., `damaged` or `notDamaged`). If it is set to `operational`, they are interpreted as *potential damage* (i.e., `canDamage` or `cannotDamage`).

Rule 10. A *scenario* is marked as `resilient` if no `enabled` *vulnerabilities* are `exploited` by any capability. Otherwise, it is marked as `vulnerable`.

The inference engine implements the formal rules defined as part of the LaDeRR language design, ensuring that derivations are logically grounded in the domain constraints specified in the metamodel. These rules, expressed in first-order logic and included in the official language specification, guide the reasoning process and determine how constructs such as threats, damage, and resilience are derived from base relations. This alignment guarantees that every inferred fact reflects the intended semantics of the language and supports consistent model interpretation across use cases.

The inference process also supports the computation of key scenario-level attributes, such as `status` and `situation`. These attributes are not manually assigned by the modeler but are derived from the logical structure and dynamic configuration of the scenario components. For instance, the `status` of a scenario is set to `vulnerable` if there exist active vulnerabilities that are exploited by active capabilities from other entities; otherwise, it is marked as `resilient`. Similarly, the `situation` attribute distinguishes between `operational` and `incident` contexts based on the type and direction of potential or realized damage relations. These computed attributes play a central role in the evaluation of resilience and are used to categorize and compare scenarios within and across systems.

Validation is performed using SHACL, which ensures that all scenario components comply with structural constraints defined in the LaDeRR vocabulary. This includes type checking, required property enforcement, and cardinality constraints. Validation is executed in two phases: once before inference (pre-inference validation) to detect missing or malformed elements in the user-defined specification, and again after inference (post-inference validation) to verify that the enriched model remains logically consistent and structurally complete. Notably, the validation process serves not only to identify inconsistencies but also to detect incompleteness, helping ensure that mandatory elements are present and aligned with the metamodel. Validation results are reported with severity levels—`Passed`, `Info`, `Warning`, and `Violation`—to guide the modeler in understanding the criticality of each issue. The validation process adopts the Open World Assumption (OWA), allowing specifications to omit certain elements without blocking inference or execution, while still issuing warnings when recommended fields are missing.

To support model transparency and communication, the implementation also includes a visualization component based on Graphviz. Scenario graphs are rendered with styling based on construct type, status, and relationships, enabling users to inspect the model structure and resilience mechanisms at a glance. Visualization is generated automatically from the RDF graph and includes both node-level and scenario-level representations. In addition to visual representations, the LaDeRR Engine optionally generates structured reports that summarize each scenario's constructs, inferred relations, and resilience status. These reports provide tabular views, pie charts, and descriptive summaries to support communication with stakeholders.

Together, these components provide a complete end-to-end workflow: from scenario specification to validation, reasoning, and visualization. The implementation emphasizes traceability, modularity, and extensibility, allowing LaDeRR to be adapted to new domains, extended with additional rule sets, or integrated with enterprise modeling environments in future work.

The elements presented in this section—ranging from the dual authoring modes and RDF-based transformation to the inference engine, validation procedures, and visual reporting—collectively demonstrate how LaDeRR supports the complete modeling lifecycle of resilience scenarios. This end-to-end framework, grounded in ontological principles and enhanced by automation and visualization, directly addresses **RQ2** by showing how formal specification, validation, reasoning, and interpretation are effectively implemented in practice.

5 Case Study: Supply Chain System Resilience Modeling

This work was developed within the context of the *Design for Supply Chain Resilience* (DeSCRe) project, carried out by the Flanders Make core labs at KU Leuven and Ghent University in collaboration with three manufacturing companies. The project aims to investigate and develop methods to enhance supply chain resilience in industrial manufacturing environments.

While the modeling presented in this case study does not correspond to the specific supply chains of the participating companies, it is based on a representative scenario developed within the DeSCRe project. This scenario, described by De Backker et al. [10], proposes a data-driven approach for assessing component-level disruption risks in supply chains using machine learning techniques, including the construction of a *Component Risk Matrix* that combines predicted stockout frequency and severity to support strategic resilience planning.

5.1 Scenario Description and Initial Risk Assessment

The scenario concerns a manufacturing company that assembles complex industrial equipment using components sourced from a diverse set of suppliers. These components vary in criticality, cost, and sourcing strategy. While some are standardized, low-cost parts managed through kanban systems, others are high-cost, custom-made components procured manually from high-risk countries. Historical stockout data indicates that certain critical components frequently delay production due to long replenishment lead times.

The supply chain is increasingly exposed to disruptions caused by geopolitical instability—such as trade embargoes or political tensions—which elevate the likelihood and impact of stockouts. To address these risks, the company performs an internal assessment to evaluate the vulnerability of each component and the operational significance of its role in production. This assessment guides the selection of resilience strategies aimed at reducing exposure to disruptions. Examples include increasing safety stock levels, establishing dual sourcing arrangements, or redesigning products to accommodate interchangeable parts.

The goal is to identify high-risk components and implement protective measures that ensure the continuity of operations even under adverse conditions. Evaluation criteria are based on the organization's ability to deploy capabilities and controls that effectively mitigate the impact of the identified threat across the most vulnerable elements of the supply chain.

This narrative was translated into LaDeRR by identifying relevant entities (e.g., the manufacturing company and geopolitical instability), vulnerabilities (e.g., component stockout risk), and capabilities (e.g., critical component production and disruption capability). Resilience is then defined as the organization's ability to maintain production despite disruptions affecting critical components. This scenario is set as *operational*, meaning it represents a current state of the system rather than a retrospective analysis or a speculative future configuration.

To illustrate LaDeRR's modeling capabilities, we present an excerpt from this scenario using the language's constructs. It is accompanied by visualizations that closely resemble those generated by the LaDeRR Engine. However, while the engine produces automated visualizations using Graphviz, the images shown here were manually created to ensure better visual clarity and a precise fit to the paper's formatting requirements. Additionally, to support reproducibility, all input and output files related to the modeled scenario are publicly available as supplementary material at https://w3id.org/laderr/engine/edoc_examples.

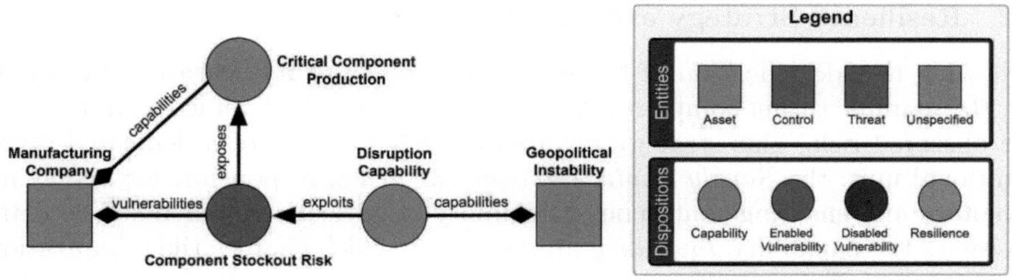

Fig. 2. Excerpt of the supply chain disruption scenario modeled with LaDeRR, with an embedded legend indicating node types.

The excerpt in Fig. 2 models the risk associated with stockouts of a critical component due to geopolitical instability affecting supplier countries. The symbols used in the visualizations throughout this section follow a consistent graphical convention. A legend for the node types is provided in the figure. Entities are represented as squares, with their color indicating their classification: green for assets, red for threats, blue for controls, and gray for entities with an unspecified type. Dispositions are represented as circles: green for capabilities, red for vulnerabilities, and orange for resilience. Light-colored dispositions indicate that they are currently enabled, while dark-colored ones are disabled. Dispositions are visually linked to their owning entities using UML-style composition arrows: a solid line ending in a filled diamond at the entity side. Other relations between elements are shown as directed edges labeled with their respective relation types.

Figure 2 shows how a threat entity, represented by geopolitical instability, disrupts a critical component in the supply chain and how the organization relies on internal capabilities to mitigate this vulnerability. The scenario is deemed *vulnerable* because the asset's capability *Critical Component Production* lacks an associated resilience instance, making it susceptible to disruption.

The model was intentionally created using high-level constructs, such as the generic class `Entity`, without explicitly specifying whether a given entity is an `Asset`, `Threat`, or `Control`. This is because the LaDeRR Engine is capable of inferring these semantic types based on the relationships defined among the elements. When this scenario is processed through the engine, the tool generates a valid and complete semantic specification where all relevant types and derived relations are inferred. Specifically, the engine deduces that the *Manufacturing Company* is an `Asset` and that *Geopolitical Instability* is a `Threat`. It also infers the derived relation `threatens` between the threat and the asset (according to

Rule 6). Furthermore, the engine evaluates the state of the involved capabilities. As a result, it determines that the capability *Critical Component Production* is vulnerable (i.e., it is currently not resilient) and generates the derived relation `canDamage` from the threat entity to the asset. These inferences are not depicted in any of the figures included in this paper but are provided as part of the supplementary material.

5.2 Resilience Strategy and Model Evolution

Following the identification of the potential damage to its operational capability, the manufacturing company adopts a resilience strategy aimed at mitigating the observed risk. This strategy involves the introduction of a dedicated organizational unit: the *Supply Chain Management Team*, responsible for managing inventory and ensuring continuous availability of critical components. The team possesses the capability *Inventory Management*, which enables the organization to maintain sufficient buffer stocks to prevent component shortages. This capability is explicitly modeled as disabling the vulnerability *Component Stockout Risk*, rendering it inactive and unexploitable (Rule 5). All other elements and relations are preserved as in the initial configuration.

Processing this enhanced model through the LaDeRR Engine produces a different set of derived conclusions. Specifically, the engine infers that the vulnerability *Component Stockout Risk* is neutralized by the disabling capability *Inventory Management*. Consequently, the capability *Critical Component Production* is no longer marked as vulnerable (Rule 4). The derived relation `canDamage`, previously generated due to the active vulnerability exploited by the threat, is not produced. Nonetheless, the engine still infers the `threatens` relation between the `Threat` and the `Asset`, since the potential for threat remains conceptually valid even if fully mitigated in this context. This scenario is classified as *resilient* because the asset's operational capabilities are now protected by an automatically inferred resilience instance. The existence of this resilience, connected to the capability *Critical Component Production*, ensures the asset is no longer susceptible to the disruption previously posed by the threat.

This evolution of the model reflects a transition from an exposed to a resilient scenario, demonstrating how LaDeRR can be used not only to assess risk but also to evaluate the effectiveness of resilience strategies in complex systems. When the updated scenario is processed by the LaDeRR Engine, it further shows how the language captures the emergence of resilience constructs and evaluates the presence and effectiveness of system protection through automated inference.

The configuration depicted in Fig. 3 is produced when this enhanced scenario is processed by the LaDeRR Engine. In contrast to the previous scenario, where the asset's capability was vulnerable to the effects of geopolitical disruptions, this model now includes an organizational resilience mechanism.

The enhanced model includes the *Supply Chain Management Team* and its *Inventory Management* capability. Based on its role in disabling the identified vulnerability, the LaDeRR Engine infers this organizational unit to be a `Control`. The processing also leads to the automatic creation of a *Resilience* instance,

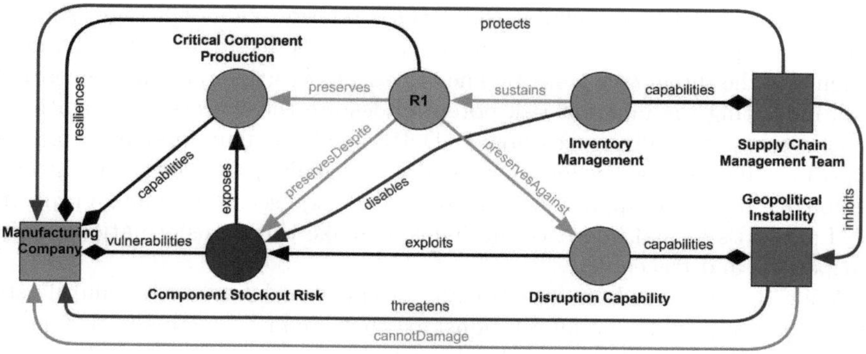

Fig. 3. Resilient version of the supply chain disruption scenario.

represented as R1 in the figure. This resilience instance, depicted as an **orange circle**, is not manually modeled. Instead, it emerges from the structural configuration of the scenario: an asset possesses a capability that is exposed by an active vulnerability and simultaneously protected by another capability that disables that vulnerability, as defined by Rule 7. The relation `resiliencies`, linking the asset to the resilience instance R1, indicates that this resilience belongs to and is structurally associated with the asset it protects. The label R1 is automatically assigned by the LaDeRR Engine as a generic identifier for the inferred resilience instance. Specifically, the capability *Inventory Management* sustains the resilience, allowing it to exist and function effectively. In turn, the resilience R1 preserves the capability *Critical Component Production*, which was previously exposed and unprotected in the earlier scenario.

The relations associated with the resilience, which correspond to the formal pattern defined in Rule 7, include: (i) `preserves`, from the resilience R1 to the capability *Critical Component Production*, representing the protection offered; (ii) `sustains`, from the capability *Inventory Management* to the resilience R1, indicating the capability that maintains the resilience condition; (iii) `preservesDespite`, from R1 to the vulnerability *Component Stockout Risk*, indicating that the capability is preserved despite the risk; and finally (iv) `preservesAgainst`, from R1 to the capability *Disruption Capability*, indicating that the resilience guards against the active disruption imposed by the threat entity.

Given the satisfied inference conditions in this configuration, a set of derived relationships holds, represented as blue arrows in the figure. These include: `inhibits`, from the control `Supply Chain Management Team` to the threat entity *Geopolitical Instability* (Rule 4); and `protects`, from the control `Supply Chain Management Team` to the asset *Manufacturing Company* (Rule 5).

Furthermore, the engine infers that the vulnerability *Component Stockout Risk* is disabled by the *Inventory Management* capability, effectively neutralizing its impact. Consequently, the `canDamage` relation—previously present between *Geopolitical Instability* and *Manufacturing Company*—is no longer generated.

Instead, the model now includes the derived relation `cannotDamage`, signaling that the company's critical capability is no longer susceptible to the disruptive influence of the threat (see Rule 9). The `threatens` relation remains conceptually valid, indicating the inherent risk potential despite the successful mitigation.

This case study illustrates how LaDeRR enables structured modeling and supports resilience analysis for informed decision-making. It shows how the introduction of a targeted capability can transform an exposed system into a protected one. LaDeRR's formal inference mechanisms make this transformation explicit, transparent, and traceable.

While this case study is intentionally designed to be accessible and illustrative, it may appear to model relationships that could be manually deduced by experts. However, LaDeRR's core strength lies in its ability to scale to large and complex scenarios, where human reasoning becomes impractical or error-prone. In such contexts, LaDeRR not only enables the automated inference of resilience (or its absence), but also supports the systematic comparison of alternative strategies to determine which configurations are most effective.

Lastly, while the scenario provides concrete evidence of LaDeRR's applicability, it also raises a threat to validity: being a controlled and representative case, it may not capture the full complexity of enterprise-scale or cross-domain resilience modeling. This limitation was mitigated by basing the scenario on a representative challenge derived from empirical supply chain risk research. Nonetheless, the outcomes confirm that LaDeRR effectively supports the structured specification, validation, and evaluation of resilience scenarios, thereby addressing **RQ3** and laying a foundation for broader application and future validation.

6 Related Work

Resilience modeling has been addressed through ontology development, DSMLs, extensions of general-purpose notations, and model-based engineering frameworks. LaDeRR introduces a DSML grounded in the ResiliOnt ontology, integrating ontological commitments and formal inference rules for specifying and evaluating resilience scenarios. Related contributions are grouped by modeling focus and contrasted with LaDeRR.

Ontology-based approaches aim to establish conceptual foundations. Lestakova et al. [22] define an upper-level ontology for urban resilience, promoting shared understanding and data integration. Payne [26] introduces RPL, a formalism for specifying and verifying reconfiguration policies. These works focus on semantics and verification but lack dedicated modeling support. LaDeRR extends this line by combining ontological rigor with a modeling language and formal reasoning.

Several DSMLs target domain-specific resilience. I®ML [15] models infrastructure resilience via layered abstractions; ReflexLang [11] embeds resilience contracts; coreLang [20] structures threat modeling for ICT; and Sousa's DSML [34] supports adaptive strategies via monitoring. While expressive, they generally lack ontological grounding and rule-based reasoning. LaDeRR differs by defining constructs via an explicit ontology and enabling logic-based inference.

Other approaches extend general-purpose languages. Nordemann et al. [24] propose rBPMN for resilience in workflows; Rodríguez et al. [30] introduce UML profiles with OCL constraints; and Athinaiou et al. [5] revise Secure Tropos for cyber-resilience. These enhance expressiveness but rely on preexisting notations and typically lack formal scenario evaluation. LaDeRR, by contrast, provides a standalone language with ontology-defined semantics and inference support.

Model-based frameworks also address resilience. Pereverzeva [28] combines SysML and MARTE to simulate mitigation strategies; Khan and Risoldi [21] model capabilities and threats over time. They emphasize simulation but omit ontological formalization and logical inference. LaDeRR complements them by enabling structured scenario modeling and evaluation through predefined rules.

While prior work advances resilience modeling via ontologies, abstractions, or simulation, they often separate modeling, semantics, and reasoning. LaDeRR unifies these aspects through an ontology-defined language and inference rules, supporting structured and explainable resilience analysis across domains.

7 Conclusions

This paper introduced LaDeRR, a novel ontology-driven domain-specific modeling language for the specification and evaluation of resilience scenarios in complex systems. Grounded in the ResiliOnt ontology, LaDeRR offers a semantically precise modeling framework that supports structured representation, validation, and reasoning about resilience constructs.

By aligning modeling primitives with well-founded ontological categories and formally specifying the language's abstract syntax, concrete syntax, and inferential semantics, this work addressed **RQ1**, demonstrating how a domain-specific language can be systematically designed to capture resilience scenarios across application domains. Through the implementation of a complete language infrastructure—including authoring support, SHACL-based validation, formal rule-based inference, and graphical visualization—the paper responded to **RQ2**, showing how automated reasoning mechanisms can operationalize the language's semantics and support consistent scenario evaluation. Finally, the application of LaDeRR in a representative supply chain case study answered **RQ3**, illustrating the language's capacity to model both exposed and resilient configurations and to support structured analysis of resilience strategies.

Several directions for further development emerge from this work. On the modeling side, LaDeRR currently supports binary enabling and disabling relations but does not yet accommodate more sophisticated interaction patterns such as conditional triggers, partial mitigation, or the joint action of multiple capabilities. These patterns are essential for capturing distributed or layered resilience strategies, and their formalization would significantly enhance the language's expressiveness. Moreover, while LaDeRR's current focus is on resilience as a form of "capability configuration", its underlying structure suggests potential for generalizing into a broader capability modeling language—one that could address emergence and a wider range of system behaviors and interdependencies.

On the semantic and usability fronts, the absence of a public OWL serialization of ResiliOnt currently limits LaDeRR's formal alignment with foundational ontologies like gUFO. This alignment is planned and will enable broader semantic interoperability with existing tools and vocabularies. In parallel, the addition of visual concrete syntax would extend LaDeRR's accessibility, allowing non-technical users to engage with the language more effectively and supporting its integration into model-driven engineering environments.

These extensions reflect the broader applicability of LaDeRR as both a formalism for resilience modeling and a foundation for capturing, evaluating, and evolving complex system behaviors. As the language matures, it offers a principled foundation for bridging theoretical insights and practical needs in resilience engineering, particularly in domains such as SETS, where complex interdependencies demand transparent, explainable, and scenario-driven forms of analysis.

Disclosure of Interests. The authors have no competing interests to declare that are relevant to the content of this article.

References

1. Abdullah, N.S., Indulska, M., Sadiq, S.: Compliance management ontology – a shared conceptualization for research and practice in compliance management. Inform. Syst. Front. **18**(5), 995–1020 (Oct 2016). https://doi.org/10.1007/s10796-016-9631-4
2. Alkhaleel, B.A.: Machine learning applications in the resilience of interdependent critical infrastructure systems-a systematic literature review. Int. J. Crit. Infrastruct. Prot. **44**, 100646 (2024). https://doi.org/10.1016/j.ijcip.2023.100646
3. Amdah, L., Anwar, A.: A dsl for collaborative business process. In: 2020 International Conference on Intelligent Systems and Computer Vision (ISCV). pp. 1–6 (2020). https://doi.org/10.1109/ISCV49265.2020.9204044
4. Aruväli, T., De Marchi, M., Rauch, E.: Analysis of quantitative metrics for assessing resilience of human-centered CPPS workstations. Sci. Rep. **13**(1), 2914 (2023). https://doi.org/10.1038/s41598-023-29735-1
5. Athinaiou, M., Mouratidis, H., Fotis, T., Pavlidis, M.: A conceptual redesign of a modelling language for cyber resiliency of healthcare systems. In: Katsikas, S., Cuppens, F., Cuppens, N., Lambrinoudakis, C., Kalloniatis, C., Mylopoulos, J., Antón, A., Gritzalis, S., Pallas, F., Pohle, J., Sasse, A., Meng, W., Furnell, S., Garcia-Alfaro, J. (eds.) Computer Security, pp. 140–158. Springer International Publishing, Cham (2020). https://doi.org/10.1007/978-3-030-42048-2_10
6. Barcelos, P.P.F., Calhau, R.F., Oliveira, Í., Prince Sales, T., Gailly, F., Poels, G., Guizzardi, G.: Ontological foundations of resilience. In: Maass, W., Han, H., Yasar, H., Multari, N. (eds.) Conceptual Modeling. pp. 396–416. Springer Nature Switzerland, Cham (2025). https://doi.org/10.1007/978-3-031-75872-0_21
7. Calhau, R.F., Almeida, J.P.A., Kokkula, S., Guizzardi, G.: Modeling competences in enterprise architecture: from knowledge, skills, and attitudes to organizational capabilities. Softw. Syst. Model. **23**(3), 559–598 (2024). https://doi.org/10.1007/s10270-024-01151-7

8. Calhau, R.F., et al.: A system core ontology for capability emergence modeling. In: Proper, H.A., Pufahl, L., Karastoyanova, D., van Sinderen, M., Moreira, J. (eds.) Enterprise Design, Operations, and Computing, pp. 3–20. Springer Nature Switzerland, Cham (2023). https://doi.org/10.1007/978-3-031-46587-1_1
9. de Carvalho, V.A., Almeida, J.P.A., Guizzardi, G.: Using reference domain ontologies to define the real-world semantics of domain-specific languages. In: Jarke, M., Mylopoulos, J., Quix, C., Rolland, C., Manolopoulos, Y., Mouratidis, H., Horkoff, J. (eds.) Advanced Information Systems Engineering, pp. 488–502. Springer International Publishing, Cham (2014). https://doi.org/10.1007/978-3-319-07881-6_33
10. De Backker, T., Vercammen, A., Boute, R.N.: A data-driven component risk matrix to assess supply chain disruption risk. SSRN Working Paper SSRN:5028961, KU Leuven, Faculty of Business and Economics (FEB) (Nov 2024). https://doi.org/10.2139/ssrn.5028961, posted: January 17, 2025
11. Demicoli, J., Steinhorst, S.: Designing resilient autonomous systems with the reflex pattern. In: 2025 Design, Automation & Test in Europe Conference (DATE), pp. 1–7 (2025). https://doi.org/10.23919/DATE64628.2025.10992861
12. Di Sipio, C., Rubei, R., Di Rocco, J., Di Ruscio, D., Iovino, L.: On the use of LLMs to support the development of domain-specific modeling languages. In: Proceedings of the ACM/IEEE 27th International Conference on Model Driven Engineering Languages and Systems, pp. 596–601. MODELS Companion '24, Association for Computing Machinery, New York, NY, USA (2024). https://doi.org/10.1145/3652620.3687808
13. Fan, S., Hua, Z., Storey, V.C., Zhao, J.L.: A process ontology based approach to easing semantic ambiguity in business process modeling. Data Knowl. Eng. **102**, 57–77 (2016). https://doi.org/10.1016/j.datak.2016.01.001
14. Figueiredo, E., Maio, P., Silva, N., Lopes, R.: DSL-based configuration of solid referential management system: a case study. In: 2018 International Conference on Computational Science and Computational Intelligence (CSCI), pp. 890–894 (2018). https://doi.org/10.1109/CSCI46756.2018.00176
15. Filippini, R., Silva, A.: I®ml: an infrastructure resilience-oriented modeling language. IEEE Trans. Syst., Man, Cybern.: Syst. **45**(1), 157–169 (2015). https://doi.org/10.1109/TSMC.2014.2343751
16. Guizzardi, G.: Ontological Foundations for Structural Conceptual Models. No. 05-74 in CTIT PhD Thesis Series, Telematica Instituut / CTIT (2005)
17. Guizzardi, G.: Ontology-Based Evaluation and Design of Visual Conceptual Modeling Languages, pp. 317–347. Springer Berlin Heidelberg, Berlin, Heidelberg (2013). https://doi.org/10.1007/978-3-642-36654-3_13
18. Guizzardi, G., et al.: UFO: unified foundational ontology. Appl. Ontol. **17**(1), 167–210 (2022). https://doi.org/10.3233/AO-210256
19. Hosseini, S., Barker, K., Ramirez-Marquez, J.E.: A review of definitions and measures of system resilience. Reliab. Eng. Syst. Safety **145**, 47–61 (2016). https://doi.org/10.1016/j.ress.2015.08.006
20. Katsikeas, S., Buhaiu, A., Ekstedt, M., Afzal, Z., Hacks, S., Mukherjee, P.: Development and validation of Corelang: a threat modeling language for the ICT domain. Comput. Secur. **146**, 104057 (2024). https://doi.org/10.1016/j.cose.2024.104057
21. Khan, Y.I., Risoldi, M.: Language enrichment for resilient MDE. In: Avgeriou, P. (ed.) Software Engineering for Resilient Systems. pp. 76–90. Springer Berlin Heidelberg, Berlin, Heidelberg (2012). https://doi.org/10.1007/978-3-642-33176-3_6

22. Lestakova, M., Logan, K., Lorenz, I., Pietsch, M., Friesen, J., Steinke, F., Pelz, P.F.: Towards a common ontology for investigating resilience of interdependent urban systems. In: Comes, T., Hölscher, C. (eds.) Proceedings of the Joint International Resilience Conference, JIRC2020, 23.11.2020-27.11.2020, pp. 101–104. University of Twente, Twente (December 2020). https://doi.org/10.3990/1.9789036550956
23. Madni, A.M., Erwin, D., Sievers, M.: Constructing models for systems resilience: challenges, concepts, and formal methods. Systems **8**(1) (2020). https://doi.org/10.3390/systems8010003
24. Nordemann, F., Tönjes, R., Pulvermüller, E.: Resilient bpmn: Robust process modeling in unreliable communication environments. In: Proceedings of the 8th International Conference on Model-Driven Engineering and Software Development - MODELSWARD, pp. 181–192. INSTICC, SciTePress (2020). https://doi.org/10.5220/0008768101810192
25. Oliveira, I., Nicoletti, S.M., Fumagalli, M., Engelberg, G., Guizzardi, G.: Toward an ontology-based modeling for risk management. In: Proceedings of the 18th International Workshop on Value Modeling and Business Ontologies (VMBO 2025). University of Twente, Enschede, The Netherlands (Mar 2025)
26. Payne, R.J.: Verifiable Resilience in Architectural Reconfiguration. Ph.d. thesis, Newcastle University, Newcastle upon Tyne, United Kingdom (2012), supported by EPSRC DIRC project, EU FP7 COMPASS, UK Software Systems Engineering Initiative, and EPSRC TrAmS-2 platform grant
27. Pena, M., Moser, C., Campbell, M.K., O'Connor, A.: Integrating resilience concepts and strategies into transportation planning. Contractor's final project report, National Cooperative Highway Research Program (NCHRP), Washington, D.C. (July 2022), prepared for the Transportation Research Board of the National Academies of Sciences, Engineering, and Medicine under NCHRP Project 08-129
28. Pereverzeva, I.: Formal Development of Resilient Distributed Systems. Ph.d. thesis, Åbo Akademi University, Faculty of Science and Engineering, Computer Science, Turku, Finland (Oct 2015)
29. Reghezza-Zitt, M., Lhomme, S., Provitolo, D.: Defining resilience: when the concept resists. In: Reghezza-Zitt, M., Rufat, S. (eds.) Resilience Imperative, pp. 1–27. Elsevier (2015). https://doi.org/10.1016/B978-1-78548-051-5.50001-2
30. Rodríguez, R.J., Merseguer, J., Bernardi, S.: Modelling and analysing resilience as a security issue within UML. In: Proceedings of the 2nd International Workshop on Software Engineering for Resilient Systems, pp. 42–51. SERENE '10, Association for Computing Machinery, New York, NY, USA (2010). https://doi.org/10.1145/2401736.2401741
31. Roy Chaudhuri, S., Natarajan, S., Banerjee, A., Choppella, V.: Methodology to develop domain specific modeling languages. In: Proceedings of the 17th ACM SIGPLAN International Workshop on Domain-Specific Modeling, pp. 1–10. DSM 2019, Association for Computing Machinery, New York, NY, USA (2019). https://doi.org/10.1145/3358501.3361235
32. Ryan, S.: Domain specific language (DSL) platform for knowledge management. Ph.d. thesis, University of Limerick, Limerick, Ireland (8 2024). https://doi.org/10.34961/researchrepository-ul.26504008.v1, supervised by Prof. Dr.-Ing. Tiziana Margaria and Dr. Nikola Nikolov
33. Salomon, J., Broggi, M., Kruse, S., Weber, S., Beer, M.: Resilience decision-making for complex systems. ASCE-ASME J. Risk Uncert Engrg. Sys. Part B Mech. Engrg. **6**(2), 020901 (03 2020). https://doi.org/10.1115/1.4044907

34. Sousa, T.: Towards modeling and predicting the resilience of ecosystems. In: 2023 ACM/IEEE International Conference on Model Driven Engineering Languages and Systems Companion (MODELS-C), pp. 159–165 (2023). https://doi.org/10.1109/MODELS-C59198.2023.00042
35. Verdonck, M., Gailly, F.: An ontological analysis framework for domain-specific modeling languages. J. Database Manage. **29**(1), 23–42 (2018). https://doi.org/10.4018/JDM.2018010102
36. Wilkinson, M.D., Dumontier, M., Aalbersberg, I.J., et al.: The FAIR Guiding Principles for scientific data management and stewardship. Sci. Data **3**(1), 160018 (2016). https://doi.org/10.1038/sdata.2016.18

Toward an Intent-Based and Ontology-Driven Autonomic Security Response in Security Orchestration Automation and Response

Zequan Huang[1,2(✉)], Jacques Robin[2], Nicolas Herbaut[1], Nourhène Ben Rabah[1], and Bénédicte Le Grand[1]

[1] Center for Research in Informatics (CRI), University of Paris 1 Panthéon-Sorbonne, Paris, France
zequan.huang@esiea.fr, {nicolas.herbaut,nourhene.ben-rabah, benedicte.le-grand}@univ-paris1.fr
[2] Engineering School of Informatics, Electronics and Automation (ESIEA), Paris, France
jacques.robin@esiea.fr

Abstract. Modern Security Orchestration, Automation, and Response (SOAR) platforms must rapidly adapt to continuously evolving cyber attacks. Intent-Based Networking has emerged as a promising paradigm for cyber attack mitigation through high-level declarative intents, which offer greater flexibility and persistency than procedural actions. In this paper, we bridge the gap between two active research directions–Intent-Based Cyber Defense and Autonomic Cyber Defense, by proposing a unified, ontology-driven security intent definition leveraging the MITRE-D3FEND cybersecurity ontology. We also propose a general two-tiered methodology for integrating such security intents into decision-theoretic Autonomic Cyber Defense systems, enabling hierarchical and context-aware automated response capabilities. The practicality of our approach is demonstrated through a concrete use case.

Keywords: Cybersecurity · intent-based networking · ontology · autonomic cyber defense · decision-theoretic artificial intelligence · SOAR

1 Introduction

System and network infrastructures today face increasingly sophisticated threats, posing significant risks. Among the most challenging types of cyber threats are ***Advanced Persistent Threats (APTs),*** orchestrated by well-resourced attackers to gain prolonged unauthorized access to a target network to steal sensitive information or disrupt operations. From a defender's perspective, effective cyber defense encompasses three stages: (a) proactive prevention to deter threats before they occur, (b) real-time detection to identify breaches or anomalies, and (c) post-detection security responses to minimize damage–*i.e.*, attack mitigation. This paper concentrates on stage (c).

In APT scenarios, it is realistic to expect that skilled attackers can always find a way to evade the first line of defense, making post-detection response not just optional

© The Author(s), under exclusive license to Springer Nature Switzerland AG 2026
A. Gianola et al. (Eds.): EDOC 2025, LNCS 16213, pp. 266–283, 2026.
https://doi.org/10.1007/978-3-032-15140-7_15

but essential. Modern ***Security Operations Centers (SOCs)*** still rely heavily on human experts to manually analyze and respond to incident alerts. However, human judgment errors are inevitable during mitigation operations. Despite advancements in ***Security Orchestration, Automation, and Response (SOAR)*** platforms, analysts still face overwhelming alert fatigue, due to the prevalence of false positives generated by insufficiently explained anomaly detection, leading to delayed or missed mitigation [1].

Current mitigation automation tools in SOAR, such as playbooks, operate as procedural checklists of steps and actions [2]. They are primarily concerned with enforcing low-level configurations, without inherently encoding the high-level security intents so far formulated by SOC analysts. Informally, a security intent indicates a desired system or network state in which the identified risk is mitigated. This gap–between operations and objectives–highlights the need for a higher-level security intent layer in security response automation, that aligns closely with human-understandable strategic goals. In other words, next generation SOAR platforms should derive and proceed with security intents "in mind", rather than relying on humans to bear these intents and explicitly instruct them on what mitigation actions to take. This transition represents a major step toward reducing human errors, reaction time, and sub-optimal trade-offs between conflicting security goals, such as availability, confidentiality, and integrity.

Research addressing security response automation has been ongoing since the early 2000s, notably within post-detection ***Autonomic***[1] ***Cyber Defense (ACD)*** [3]. While ACD also encompasses the preventive (a) and detection (b) stages of cyber defense, we refer to post-detection ACD simply as ACD throughout the remainder of this paper. Various decision-theoretic models utilizing ***Artificial Intelligence (AI)*** techniques have been proposed (*cf*. Sect. 3). However, while state-of-the-art approaches acknowledge the dynamic nature of modern IT infrastructures [4], particularly in the era of computer virtualization and service containerization, their impact on security action space has been largely neglected. This oversight mainly stems from limited industry adoption of such decision-theoretic models, caused by factors such as computational complexity [5] and trust [6] constraints. As a result, existing research frequently simplifies security responses into push-button actions executed within controlled test environments. In practice, however, many mitigation actions are more complex, often involving sequences of sub-procedures that rely on specific system or network-level capabilities, which vary depending on the current state of the underlying IT infrastructure.

Therefore, we propose security intent as a promising concept to bridge these gaps. First, intent enables defense systems to maintain a high-level, strategic "understanding" of their objectives before reacting, simulating the reasoning process of human SOC analysts. Second, intent abstracts away intricate implementation details in decision-theoretic mitigation planning, stabilizing its action space and encapsulating the impact of environmental changes (*e.g.*, service update, reallocation, *etc.*) of security functions into the non-stationary model parameters of the underlying IT infrastructure. The goal

[1] We upgrade to the term "autonomic" to denote a level of automation between "automated" and "autonomous". Automated systems require human initiation and follow fixed rules; autonomic systems [7] can adapt and self-manage under limited human oversight; autonomous systems operate entirely independently, without human intervention.

is to facilitate robust handling of increasingly complex and continuously evolving IT infrastructures for autonomic security response.

In this paper, we demonstrate how ***Intent-Based Networking (IBN)*** [8, 9] can be leveraged in ACD to intelligently reconfigure system behavior and security policies in response to active cyber attacks. While IBN was originally developed to simplify network management, we specifically focus on its application for security response. Building upon this perspective, we seek to answer the following Research Questions:

- **RQ1**. What constitutes a suitable and practical operational definition of security intent in the context of Autonomic Cyber Defense?
- **RQ2**. How can such security intents be effectively integrated into Autonomic Cyber Defense, using Intent-Based Networking to enable adaptive and high-level response planning?

To address **RQ1**, we propose a unified definition of security response in the form of structured security intents, grounded in the MITRE-D3FEND™ ontology [10]. D3FEND formalizes cyber defense techniques into actionable concepts that can serve as robust building blocks for our intent definition across diverse attack scenarios (see Sect. 2.2 for an overview of D3FEND). We choose D3FEND over other existing cybersecurity ontologies [11, 12] due to its close alignment with the widely adopted MITRE-ATT&CK™ offensive taxonomy [13], which facilitates understanding of cyber attacks (*e.g.*, APTs) and supports precise intent-driven security responses.

To answer **RQ2**, we introduce a general methodology for integrating our proposed security intent representation into state-of-the-art decision-theoretic ACD models. The integration is two-tiered, comprising (1) an ***Intent Discovery Agent (IDA)***, responsible for autonomically generating security intents based on real-time security observations, and (2) an ***Intent Enforcement Agent (IEA)***, tasked with ensuring these intents remain enforced in dynamic operational environments. We further demonstrate a concrete use case showcasing how such intents can be implemented by the IEA beyond traditional networking contexts (originally envisioned by IBN), using the ***Kubernetes project.***[2]

The remainder of the paper is organized as follows: Sect. 2 presents the background, covering IBN and the D3FEND ontology; Sect. 3 provides a review of related work on both ***Intent-Based Cyber Defense (IBCD)*** and Autonomic Cyber Defense; Sect. 4 details our contribution, including the unified intent definition and the two-tiered integration methodology via the IDA and IEA; finally, Sect. 5 summarizes our conclusions and outlines future research directions.

2 Background

2.1 Intent-Based Networking (IBN)

IBN is a powerful paradigm originally developed to simplify computer network configuration by abstracting low-level, device-specific tasks into high-level, device-agnostic intents. According to the ***Internet Engineering Task Force (IETF)*** [8], intent is defined

[2] Kubernetes is an open-source container orchestration platform that enables dynamic, programmable infrastructure–ideal for evaluating intent enforcement in complex environments.

as "operational goals (to be met) or outcomes (to be delivered) defined in a declarative manner without specifying how to achieve them". In the context of post-detection attack mitigation, intent can be further refined to represent a desired system state in which normal functionality has been restored (outcome to be delivered), and the threat impact has been either eliminated or reduced to a level considered tolerable (goal to be met). In most literature on IBN, we consider that an ***Intent-Based Networking System (IBNS)*** periodically receives intent from human users. The intent lifecycle thus has to be separated into two closed loops (see Fig. 1).

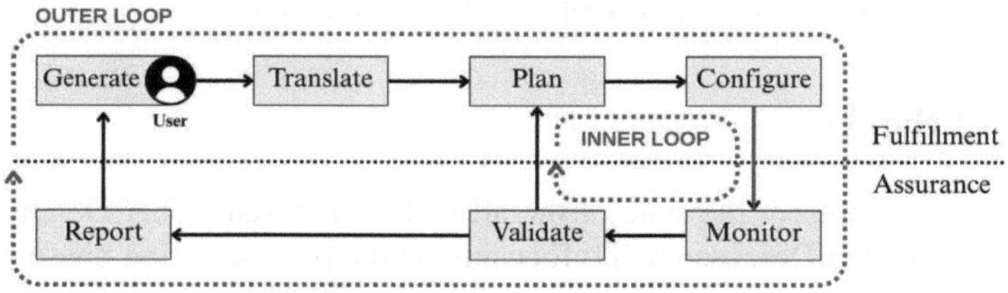

Fig. 1. Intent lifecycle (simplified from [8])

a) **Outer closed loop:** involves user interaction. It interprets the user's intent, implements it, and reports the outcome back to the user.
b) **Inner closed loop:** autonomously detects and counteracts intent drift. It does not involve any user in the loop.

Intents may be transient or persistent. Transient intents conclude once their corresponding operation is executed, *i.e.*, they only traverse the outer loop once. In contrast, persistent intents remain active under continuous lifecycle management until explicitly deactivated or removed.

2.2 MITRE-D3FEND Ontology

Cybersecurity ontologies can serve as robust building blocks for security intent definition. Among them, the MITRE Corporation's D3FEND ontology [10] provides a structured representation of cybersecurity countermeasures and logically relates them to cyber attacks. D3FEND formalizes cyber defense mechanisms into well-defined, actionable concepts–defensive techniques. Identifying which attacks a countermeasure can be employed to counteract is insufficient; it is equally critical to understand, from an engineering standpoint, the concrete mechanisms by which it mitigates those threats [14]. To enhance this understanding, D3FEND is complemented by its offensive counterpart–ATT&CK [13], a conceptual cyber attack taxonomy also developed by the MITRE Corporation, primarily focusing on offensive techniques, which are instantiated by practical attacks.

D3FEND introduces digital artifacts as the basis for conceptualizing and instantiating the relations between offensive techniques (ATT&CK) and defensive techniques (D3FEND) [10]. A digital artifact represents a piece of information or a digital entity that can be acted upon within a cybersecurity context. These attack-defense relationships are covered in D3FEND; let's clarify this with an example: An attacker may establish stealth communication between a compromised server and a remote ***Command and Control (C2)*** server using the ATT&CK technique "Dynamic Resolution", which dynamically resolves malicious domain names to obtain the C2 server's frequently changing IP address. In this scenario, one relevant digital artifact is "Outbound Internet DNS Lookup Traffic", generated by the compromised server as it queries external DNS servers for resolution. From a defensive standpoint, the D3FEND technique "DNS Denylisting" can be applied to block outbound DNS queries to known malicious domains, thereby disrupting the attacker's ability to establish C2 communications.

3 State of the Art

In this section, we present the state of the art in Intent-Based Cyber Defense (IBCD) and Autonomic Cyber Defense (ACD) focusing on the post-detection phase, which are complementary rather than competing. Specifically, IBCD typically lacks *autonomic intent-generation* capabilities, while ACD requires *high-level action abstraction* to adapt to dynamic IT infrastructures. As illustrated in Fig. 2, these two dimensions can be seen as dual aspects of a unified cyber defense.

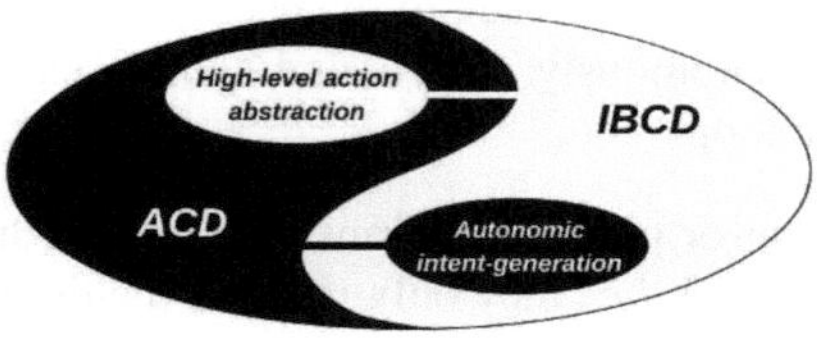

Fig. 2. Yin-Yang Relationship Between ACD and IBCD.

3.1 Intent-Based Cyber Defense (IBCD)

In this sub-section, we analyze existing pioneering efforts that have sought to combine IBN and cybersecurity in various ways. As summarized in Table 1, for our work, we characterize relevant studies according to the following points:

- **Managing Scope:** The operational domain over which the intent is applied.
- **Intent Enforcement Point:** The network components where the security intent is enforced, ranging from low-level devices to high-level orchestrators.
- **Intent Definition:** refers to how the intent is formally defined within the system. This dimension aligns with the concept of intent expression, as introduced in the taxonomy of intent profiling [9, 10]. We go beyond basic intent expression classification (*e.g.*, template-based) by examining the underlying intent representation.
- **User-specified (U) or Machine-inferred (M):** distinguishes *who* or *what* generates the intent:

- **U:** The intent is manually provided by human users (*e.g.*, SOC analysts), based on their expertise and organizational policies.
- **M:** The system can infer intents by interpretating environmental observations (*e.g.*, security alerts), often using AI methods.

From the "Managing scope" column, we observe that most prior works focus predominantly on network-level security. Their defensive schemes affect network traffic possibly involving endpoints,[3] but do not directly impact the internal security posture of the endpoints themselves (*e.g.*, processes, accounts, *etc.*). This emphasis is understandable, since IBN is network centric. However, a resilient SOAR platform cannot rely solely on network-level appliances, it must also support endpoint-level capabilities (*e.g.*, filesystem management), which are currently lacking in existing approaches.

Various representations have been proposed to define and manage security intent, each tailored to different management scopes. Notably, some of them blur the line between declarative expression and rule-based control, thereby undermining the level of abstraction that is central to IBN. For instance, the authors of [16, 17] introduced an

Table 1. State of the art of Intent-Based Cyber Defense

Ref	Managing Scope	Intent Enforcement Point	Intent Definition	U/M
[15]	***Network*** access control in large/distributed network environments	***Network*** routers	Language for ACL (Access Control List) Intents	*U*
[16, 17]	Cloud-native ***network*** security services orchestration across virtualized network infrastructures	***Network*** security functions (*e.g.*, Firewall, Intrusion Prevention System, *etc.*)	Customer-Facing Interface (I2NSF IETF standard)	*U*
[18]	Kubernetes (K8s) ***network*** isolation in multi-domain and multitenant cloud environments for liquid computing	K8s ***network*** policy API	Intra/inter-virtual K8s clusters resource communication authorization intent language	*U*
[19]	Business applications/Security services orchestration in distributed cloud/edge infrastructures	Business applications (*e.g.*, web server) and security services (e.g., VPN, filtering, *etc.*)	Service deployment policy template (*e.g.*, software/hardware capabilities, latency, *etc.*)	*U/M*

(*continued*)

[3] In this paper, a network endpoint refers to any physical or virtual entity that communicates over a network, including servers, containerized applications and so on.

Table 1. (*continued*)

Ref	Managing Scope	Intent Enforcement Point	Intent Definition	U/M
[20]	Multilayer secure ***network*** channel orchestration	Optical ***network*** controllers; ***network*** switches, and routers	Encryption centric requirement submitted through API/CLI interface (*e.g.*, in JSON)	*U*
[21]	Software Defined ***Networking***[4] based Moving Target Defense against reconnaissance attack	Software-Defined ***Networking*** Controller	Template-based, classification-driven network traffic rerouting policy	*U*
[22]	***Network*** security services orchestration based on a service mesh framework in cloud-native K8s environments	***Network*** security functions	Language for security service policy management	*U*

intent-based ***Network Security Functions (NSF)*** orchestration system using the Interface to NSF framework (I2NSF) [23]. An NSF inspects and optionally modifies packets traversing networks, such as a firewall and a network intrusion detection system. In [17], a customer-facing interface based on YANG data model[5] was employed for user intent acquisition. However, this interface supports an event-condition-action scheme, which is typically considered rule-based. Similarly, [15] proposed a language for network ***Access Control List (ACL)***[6] intents to manage router-level packet forwarding policies based on IP prefixes. In this model, users can either directly provide explicit ACL rule updates, or express high-level reachability goals, representing security intents.

Most existing approaches only support user-specified intents. While [19] briefly mentioned the possibility of machine-generated intents, they did not provide further elaboration. As a result, the current state of the art of Intent-based Cyber Defense largely overlooks the possibility of machine-inferred intents. This omission neglects the abstraction power that intent-based models offer, which would significantly simplify the underlying decision-making problem, *i.e.*, selecting the most promising security intent given the current observed context.

[4] Software Defined Networking separates the network control plane from the data plane to enable centralized, programmable network management.

[5] YANG is a hierarchical, schema-based language typically for network management protocols.

[6] A network ACL is a set of rules applied to network interfaces, typically on routers and firewalls, to permit or deny traffic based on criteria such as IP address, protocol, or port number.

3.2 Autonomic Cyber Defense (ACD)

In the context of ACD, decision-making is inherently essential. Recent research has explored various decision-theoretic approaches, leveraging ***Game Theory*** and ***Machine Learning*** [3]. For instance, the authors of [24] investigated the application of model-free Tabular Q-Learning, a type of ***Reinforcement Learning***, applied to a Markov Decision Process to generate a defense strategy (*i.e.*, a mapping from estimated circumstances to actions that guide the defender's decisions) offline[7] within a simulated network environment. At each time step, the defender selects a high-level action such as "restore a host into a known good state", based on uncertain knowledge of the network's current compromise and availability state. Though these actions resemble intent-based abstractions, they emerge not from an explicitly intent-driven model but from the simplification of the simulation environment and its attack surface.

Popular black-box Machine Learning techniques are powerful but lack explainability: they do not explicitly justify why a particular action was taken, relying solely on empirical patterns learned from data. This limitation hinders their integration into human-supervised SOAR platforms. While post hoc explainability methods such as SHAP [25] can attribute feature importance (*i.e.*, the contribution of each input feature to a specific model prediction), they fall short of providing decision-level explanations that are essential for operational trust and oversight by human experts.

In contrast, [26] treats ACD directly as a Partially Observable Markov Decision Process. Their decision-theoretic planner relies on a risk-aware Cyber Security Game simulator [27], which abstracts attacker-defender interactions across coarse-grained infrastructure models, enabling optimal defense action planning based on the inferred risk expectation. More recently, the authors of [4] proposed ***Conjectural Online Learning (COL),*** a model-based Game Theoretic planner that treats the attacker-defender interaction as a non-stationary, partially observed stochastic game. In COL, each player maintains a dynamic conjecture on both the underlying game parameters and the opponent's strategy, both of which may be misspecified. According to the authors, this is the first security application to simultaneously handle learning under misspecified models and bounded computational resources [4]. As a result, COL naturally adapts to changing infrastructures and yields explainable action choices.

Nevertheless, mitigation actions employed by state-of-the-art ACD systems remain simplistic. They typically incorporate straightforward actions, either overlooking practical implementation complexity or relying on a predetermined implementation method, suitable only for simulated environments. However, real-world IT infrastructures typically involve multiple tools for overlapping purposes, each necessitating vendor-specific configurations and possessing distinct advantages and risks. Hence, although [4] assumes non-stationary IT infrastructures, the fact that it still operates over a fixed action alphabet is problematic. Only an intent-based layer, that decouples high-level security goals from concrete, vendor-specific configurations, can make planners like COL practical across diverse and evolving IT infrastructures.

---

[7] Offline learning refers to training the Reinforcement Learning agent entirely during development phase, without further strategy updates during deployment phase.

4 Proposed Contribution

We integrate Autonomic Cyber Defense (ACD) and Intent-Based Cyber Defense (IBCD) into an ***Intent-Based Autonomic Cyber Defense*** framework, which can be viewed either as an ACD enhanced with *high-level action abstraction*, or as an IBCD capable of *autonomic intent-generation* (*cf*. Fig. 2). Adopting the latter Intent-Based Networking (IBN) perspective within an intent lifecycle representation (*cf*. Fig. 1), we designate the outer loop's autonomic intent generator as the ***Intent Discovery Agent (IDA)***, and the underlying Intent-Based Networking System (IBNS)–which consumes each "discovered intent" and implements the remaining components of the lifecycle–as the ***Intent Enforcement Agent (IEA)***. Before detailing these two agents, we first introduce our security intent definition.

4.1 Unified Security Intent

Security observations typically consist of either standalone alerts or incidents, *i.e.*, a chain of correlated alerts. An alert *AL* is defined as structured attack-related data (*e.g.*, in JSON) conforming to a well-defined schema depending on the detection software. We suppose that each alert is mapped to one ATT&CK technique, which is commonly supported in modern intrusion detection solutions.

We propose a unified security intent definition based on the D3FEND ontology. Formally, facing an alert *AL*, a security intent I_{AL} is defined by the following tuple:

$$I_{AL} \triangleq \langle OT, MD, DA_T, DT \rangle$$

where *OT* is the identified offensive technique employed by *AL*. *MD* is the alert technical metadata *s.t.* $MD \subseteq AL$, excluding non-technical fields irrelevant to intent fulfillment (*e.g.*, alert ID). *DT* is a defensive technique. DA_T is the digital artifact targeted both by *OT* and *DT* for offensive and defensive purposes, respectively. Intuitively, the goal of I_{AL} is to prescribe a *DT* that operates on a specific DA_T targeted by *OT*, thereby reaching a desired state where the security risks identified by *AL* are mitigated. The intent I_{AL} embodies a minimal response strategy, aiming to apply the least intrusive yet effective countermeasure. We elaborate this after extending D3FEND for our use case.

A Lightweight Extension of D3FEND for Operational Use

D3FEND exhibits object-oriented features and is based on the Web Ontology Language [28]. Offensive and defensive techniques both rely on digital artifacts to establish their presence on target infrastructure, which comprises both digital and physical artifacts.[8] This dependency is characterized through *properties*, drawn from two partially overlapping[9] property spaces–$Props_O$ and $Props_D$, corresponding to offensive and defensive semantics, respectively. We denote the dependency relation by $OT \overset{Prop}{\rightarrow} DA$, or $OT.Prop = DA$, where $Prop \in Props_O \cup Props_D$.

[8] While attackers might physically infiltrate the target infrastructure, the scope of our defensive techniques is strictly limited to digital artifacts hosted on physical resources.

[9] For instance, *encrypts* exists as both offensive and defensive property with distinct goals.

In D3FEND, the functions of an offensive or defensive technique can be represented as a set of property restrictions over digital artifacts. An offensive technique OT's restriction on property $Prop_O$ over digital artifact DA is denoted as $Restrict_{OT}(Prop_O, DA)$, and is defined as an anonymous superclass of OT that enforces the relation $OT \overset{Prop_O}{\rightarrow} DA$.

We propose a categorization of offensive properties based on their semantic roles, as summarized in Table 2. Each offensive property $Prop_O$ belongs to one category. An offensive property can be prefixed with *may* in a restriction $Restrict_{OT}(may - Prop_O, DA)$. This denotes that an attack instance of OT does not require the engagement $OT \overset{Prop_O}{\rightarrow} DA$ to succeed, *i.e.*, that restriction is *optional* at the OT class level, and can be omitted by its instances. However, if an attack instance of OT does engage DA via $Prop_O$, its corresponding restriction becomes *valid* (or mandatory) and the "*may-*" qualifier of $Prop_O$ is dropped for clarity. Any restriction of a given offensive technique without prefixed offensive property is by default valid for all its attack instances.

Table 2. Categorization of Properties linking Offensive Techniques and Digital Artifacts

Category	Definition	Property Instances
Alter	Modifies existing digital artifacts	*obfuscates, encrypts, may-encrypt, ...*
Generate	Creates new digital artifacts	*forges, produces, may-produce, ...*
Exploit	Leverages existing digital artifacts	*invokes, injects, may-inject, ...*
Remove	Removes existing digital artifacts	*deletes, erases, may-erase, ...*

On the defensive side, each property $Prop_D$ belongs to one of the categories defined as defensive tactics [10]. We focus on intents derived from incident responding tactics (*cf.* Table 3). A defensive technique's restriction $Restrict_{DT}(Prop_D, DA)$ denotes its intended capability to manage DA in accordance with the semantics of $Prop_D$.

Table 3. Categorization of Properties linking Defensive Techniques and Digital Artifacts

Category	Definition	Property Instances
Evict	Removes digital artifacts through which attackers establish their presence on target systems	*terminates, disables, ...*
Isolate	Creates barriers that prevent adversary access to digital artifacts	*blocks, restricts, ...*
Restore	Restores digital artifacts to a known better state	*restores*

Minimal Security Response

Valid restrictions associated with a given attack instance of an offensive technique form a conjunction. Therefore, a minimal security response that disrupts the impact on any engaged digital artifact can invalidate the offensive technique of that attack. We favor minimal security responses because post-detection Autonomic Cyber Defense typically rely on sequential decision-making (see Sect. 4.2). Keeping individual responses minimal not only reduces collateral impact but also preserves strategic flexibility.

Suppose an attack instance has valid restriction $Restrict_{OT}(Prop_O, DA)$; a defensive technique DT **may** invalidate OT (thus the attack) through DA *iff.* There exists a defensive property $Prop_D$ *compatible* with $Prop_O$ *s.t.* $OT \overset{Prop_O}{\rightarrow} DA \overset{Prop_D}{\leftarrow} DT$. The pair $(Prop_O, Prop_D)$ are considered compatible *iff.* Their respective categories are compatible, as defined in Table 4. The compatibility constraint prevents invalid countermeasures (semantic issue of D3FEND [14])–*e.g.*, *restore* a connection *produced* by attacker.

It is important to emphasize the uncertainty inherent in the above formulation. There is no guarantee that even a compatible $Prop_D$ can mitigate the effect of $Prop_O$ on the same digital artifact–its success depends on implementation details and the evolving operational environment. Moreover, from the defender's perspective, identifying valid restrictions associated with a suspected attack is a non-trivial task and not sufficient either: the engaged digital artifacts must be instantiated with concrete attributes (*e.g.*, IP addresses for Network Traffic artifacts) to provide actionable information for the defensive technique to operate on. D3FEND, by design, does not define such attributes, as they depend on the specifics of the underlying IT infrastructure. We argue that the representation of digital artifact attributes must therefore follow use-case requirements.

Table 4. Compatibility of Defensive vs. Offensive Property Categories

Offensive / ***Defensive***	Alter	Generate	Exploit	Remove
Evict	✓	✓	✓	×
Isolate	✓	✓	✓	×
Restore	✓	×	✓	✓

Let $DA.Prop_D^{-1}$ be the set of all defensive techniques DTs *s.t.* $\forall DT \in DTs$: $DT.Prop_D = DA$. Given a defensive technique DT whose set of property-artifact restrictions is exactly $\{Restrict_{DT}(Prop_i, DA_i) | i \in [1, N]\}$, we also define DT's equivalence class $\{DT\} \triangleq \bigcap_{i=1}^{N} DA_i.Prop_i^{-1}$. Defensive techniques belonging to one equivalence class pursue the same defensive objective, but differ in their implementation strategies–just as multiple policies supporting the realization of a single intent.

We illustrate the notion of minimal response through a concrete example (*cf.* Fig. 3). Pluggable Authentication Modules (PAM) handle authentication across various services in Unix-like systems. Attackers can exploit PAM components to intercept credentials or grant unauthorized access. A PAM-based attack invariably modifies *Authentication Service*, in cases where it additionally requires modifying *OS Configuration File*, any of the four defensive techniques (highlighted in blue), if successfully executed, is sufficient on its own to mitigate the attack. Security experts would likely rank their effectiveness[10] as: *System Call Filtering* (most effective) > *Process Termination* > *File Eviction* > *Host Reboot*. While *Host Reboot* and *Process Termination* belong to the same equivalence class, they differ in operational cost and mitigation impact–particularly depending on whether the attacker has established persistence on the host.

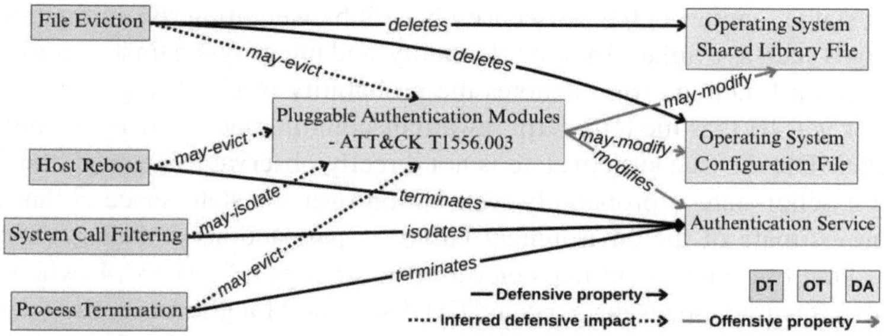

Fig. 3. Truncated representation of ATT&CK Technique T1556.003 in D3FEND.

4.2 Methodology for Intent Discovery Agent (IDA)

The IDA is responsible for autonomic mitigation intent generation. While numerous models fall under the hood of decision theory, the current state-of-the-art models in Autonomic Cyber Defense (*cf.* Sect. 3.2) fundamentally address *sequential strategic decision-making under uncertainty* [3, 29]. This uncertainty arises naturally from the defender's partial knowledge of the operational environment and ongoing attacks. Sequential decision-making is essential, as each attacker-defender interaction yields new insights into the environmental dynamics and adversary behavior, requiring defender to continuously update its strategy. A standalone or static decision-making approach would fail to benefit from such observations, thus risking to become obsolete facing evolving attacks. Furthermore, maintaining a dynamic strategy provides continuous transparency for human supervision across the entire defense lifecycle, supporting oversight under a wide range of possible circumstances.

Preliminary: Standard Action-based ACD Modeling Methodology Before introducing the methodology for our IDA, we present a standard action-based ACD model that aligns with the requirements outlined above. State-of-the-art approaches, as explained in [29], typically rely on ***Partially Observable Markov Decision Process (POMDP)***–modeling only the defender, or ***Partially Observable Stochastic Game (POSG)***–modeling both attacker and defender. Note that a POMDP can be viewed as a single-agent POSG [29], and is defined by the following tuple:

$$\Gamma \triangleq \langle \mathcal{S}, \mathcal{A}, \mathcal{O}, t, r, z, b_1, \gamma \rangle$$

[10] Here, effectiveness reflects a multi-criteria tradeoff, including success probability, operational cost, response time and potentially more context-dependent metrics.

where $\mathcal{S}$ is the state space (*e.g.*, a state could be the number of compromised servers); $\mathcal{A}$ is the action space (*e.g.*, an action might be a playbook for endpoint isolation); and $\mathcal{O}$ is the observation space (*e.g.*, outputs from intrusion detectors). In our case, each observation $o \in \mathcal{O}$ comprises alerts paired with their associated ATT&CK offensive technique. The state transition function $t(s'|s, a)$ denotes the probability of reaching state s' from s by taking action a. The reward function $r(s, a)$ assigns a scalar utility to action a in state s, capturing the net security benefit by weighting risk mitigation–across security goals such as availability, confidentiality, and integrity–against operational cost. The observation function $z(o|s)$ denotes the probability of observing o in state s. The real number $\gamma \in [0,1]$ is the long-term reward discounting factor. b_1 is the initial belief state–In POMDP, the true system state is not directly observable. Instead, the defender maintains a belief state–a probability distribution over the state space $\mathcal{S}$ that captures the current estimate of the environment based on past actions and observations. The defender's goal is to find an optimal deterministic strategy $\pi^* : \mathcal{B} \to \mathcal{A}$ (where $\mathcal{B}$ is the belief space) that maximizes the expected ($\mathbb{E}$) discounted long-term reward (where time t is assumed to be discrete):

$$\pi^* = \arg\max_{\pi} \mathbb{E}_{\pi}\left[\left[\sum\nolimits_{t=1}^{\infty} \gamma^{t-1} \cdot r(s_t, a_t)|b_1\right]\right]$$

Computing π^* typically involves a range of techniques (*e.g.*, Reinforcement Learning). However, algorithmic details are beyond the scope of this paper. We assume the existence of an optimal strategy [30] within the proposed model applied to the cyber defense.

IDA Methodology The concept of intent surpasses that of one-time action due to its potential durability. Suppose an attacker has stealthily controlled a network switch before compromising a connected server. Even if the defender subsequently isolates the server by restricting traffic on adjacent switches (including the compromised one), the attacker may still regain access by reestablishing an unauthorized communication path through the infiltrated switch. To mitigate such risks, persistent intents are monitored by the IEA (see Sect. 4.3), ensuring that they remain consistently enforced. We therefore propose an intent-based extension of Γ inspired and supported by classic IBNSs [9]:

$$\Gamma' \triangleq \langle \mathcal{S}', \mathcal{A}', \mathcal{O}, t, r, z, b_1, \gamma, \boldsymbol{\lambda} \rangle$$

where the state space $\mathcal{S}' = \mathcal{S} \times \mathcal{I}$ with $\mathcal{I}$ denoting the persistent intent store space. An Intent Store $IS = \{(I_1, TTL_1), (I_2, TTL_2), \ldots\} \in \mathcal{I}$ is a collection of active persistent intents $I \in \mathbb{I}$ (the intent space), each associated with a *Time To Live* (*TTL*) value. After each round, the *TTL* of every intent in *IS* is decremented by 1. Intents with $TTL = 0$ are purged from the store at the beginning of each round. The defender maintains an Intent Store to enforce long-term mitigations that remain effective across multiple decision epochs, ensuring resilience against persistent or recurring attacks.

The additional intent observation function $\lambda : \mathcal{O} \to 2^{\mathbb{I}}$ maps an observation o to a candidate intent set $\mathbb{I}_{cand}$. It constrains the action space based on the current observation, thereby reducing planning complexity and minimizing disruption to normal operations. For each alert-technique pair $(AL, OT) \in o$, the function λ:

1. instantiates (via a rule-based or Machine-Learning-based mapper) all digital artifacts instances engaged by OT, using the alert technical metadata $MD \subseteq AL$. Then,
2. identifies, through queries over the D3FEND ontology (*e.g.*, using SPARQL), all defensive techniques that **may** invalidate OT through any operable (sufficiently instantiated) digital artifact DA_T, as defined in Sect. 4.1.

Combining the results of each iteration we get:

$$\mathbb{I}_{cand} = \{\langle OT, MD, DA_T^i, DT_i\rangle | \forall (AL, OT) \in o, MD \subseteq AL, \exists i :$$

$$OT \overset{Prop_O^i}{\rightarrow} DA_T^i \overset{Prop_D^i}{\leftarrow} DT_i, \text{ where}\left(Prop_O^i, Prop_D^i\right)\text{are compatible and } DA_T^i \text{is operable}\}$$

If the security observation lacks sufficient information (depending on the specific use case) to instantiate a digital artifact instance exploited by the offensive technique, then the corresponding artifact will be omitted by λ. This also applies to cases where that property-artifact restriction is optional and not exploited by the suspected attack.

The action space $\mathcal{A}'$ comprises four action types: **(a)** insert a new intent $I \in \mathbb{I}_{cand}$ as persistent[11] to *IS*, **(b)** modify a persistent intent of *IS*, **(c)** execute an intent $I \in \mathbb{I}_{cand}$ as transient (at lower cost), and **(d)** take no action. For each type except (d), the affected intent's *TTL* is (re)set to a default value. For (b), the replacing intent must preserve the offensive context (OT, MD) while updating the defensive measure (DA_T, DT).

Notably, feedback from the underlying IBNS, which identifies cases of misimplemented intents, should be incorporated into the reward function r. This allows the defender to account for the actual implementation status of intents in the Intent Store. For example, *File Eviction* technique can fail due to permission issues, particularly in cases where the attacker has gained control over filesystem privileges without being detected.

We illustrate the proposed methodology in a concrete use case (*cf*. Fig. 4). Suppose an attacker has established persistence on a *Linux* server by creating a scheduled job `maljob` that periodically runs a malicious script `malicious.sh`. This script resolves the DNS name `c2.malicious.com`–whose underlying IP rotates, and connects to the resolved address to maintain its Command-and-Control (C2) channel.

An IDA based on our proposed intent-based model automatically derives intents and can be trained, for instance using Adversarial and/or Reinforcement Learning [3, 29], to learn an optimal mitigation strategy. In our case, when both *Alert-Technique 1* and *Alert-Technique 2* are present in a security observation, the digital artifacts engaged by the ongoing attack are instantiated (highlighted in yellow). The IDA may prioritize blocking the malicious connection between the compromised host and the attacker's C2 server (*Persistent Intent 1*), before evicting the malicious content planted on the host (*Persistent Intent 2*). These two persistent intents are sent to the underlying IEA for intent enforcement, which is detailed in the next section.

4.3 Methodology for Intent Enforcement Agent (IEA)

The IEA receives security intents generated by the IDA and is responsible for their enforcement. It behaves as a typical IBNS, encompassing the full intent lifecycle except

[11] The persistent or transient property of an intent is considered extrinsic.

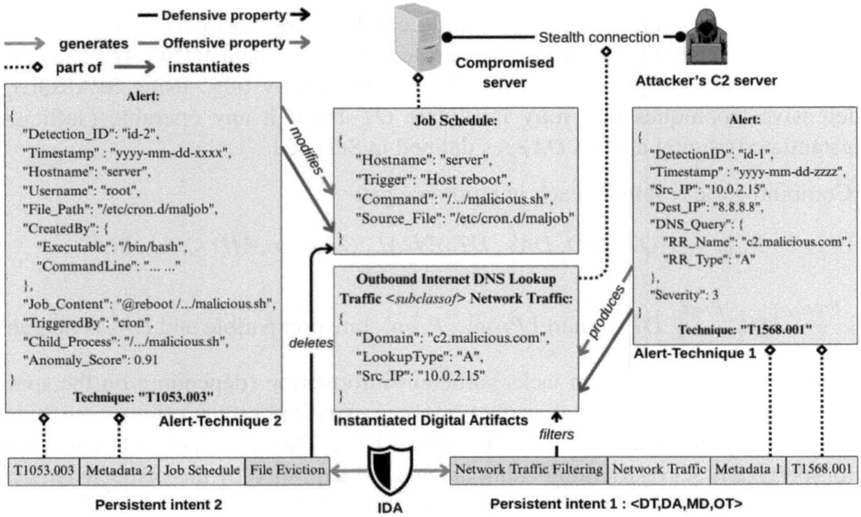

Fig. 4. A concrete use case of intent-based attack mitigation for a persistent attack

intent generation. However, due to the wide range of defensive techniques represented in the D3FEND ontology, the IEA must be highly versatile. To our knowledge, the most versatile existing framework for Intent-Based Cyber Defense–*i.e.*, capable of supporting a broad spectrum of defensive techniques–is the ***Intent-based Closed-loop Security Control (ICSC)*** framework proposed in [17], which builds upon the IETF standard Interface to Network Security Functions (I2NSF) framework (*cf.* Sect. 3.1).

Nevertheless, ICSC is inherently limited to network traffic based security, as it relies exclusively on Network Security Functions (NSFs). The IEA relaxes this constraint by generalizing the framework to include ***Endpoint Security Functions (ESFs)*** as well. An ESF, as opposed to an NSF, enforces control within the internal environment of a network endpoint, regardless of whether the enforcement is executed locally or orchestrated remotely.[12] We thus reinterpret the five core components of the ICSC framework as the combination of an IDA and an IEA, as follows (*cf*. Fig. 5):

- **I2NSF User:** corresponds to our IDA.
- **Our proposed IEA Architecture:**
- ***Security Functions (SFs):*** Enforcement points responsible for executing network-level (NSF) or endpoint-level (ESF) security responses.
- ***Security Controller:*** The central orchestrator that receives intents and invokes appropriate security functions. It translates intents into low-level configurations based on the advertised capabilities of available SFs (see next line).
- ***Developer's Management System:*** provides a platform to register SFs' capabilities. An SF's capability indicates the specific defensive technique(s) that it can realize, along with the operational parameters required for execution.

[12] For instance, user account management may be delegated to external authorities (*e.g.*, Azure Active Directory), which still exert control over internal endpoint behavior.

- ***Analyzer:*** ensures intent assurance (*cf*. Fig. 1). In [17], the Analyzer is also in charge of collecting alerts, but here this role is well assumed by the IDA.

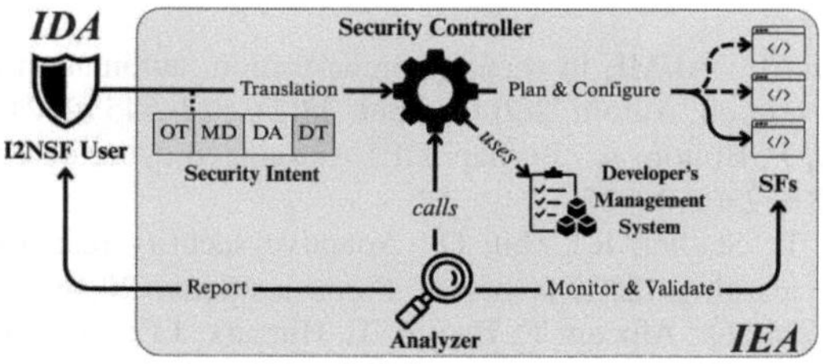

Fig. 5. An adapted overview of the ICSC framework conforming to the intent life cycle

We validate our proposal by implementing the two intents derived in the previous use case (*cf*. Fig. 4). Noting that *Network Traffic Filtering* is network-level and *File Eviction* is endpoint-level, we adopt the Kubernetes platform, which provides both NSF and ESF capabilities. Our testbed consists of a Kubernetes cluster composed of one controller and several Pods. We apply both mitigation techniques to a single infected Pod and demonstrate their effectiveness. Implementation details can be found here.[13]

5 Discussion and Conclusion

In this paper, we envision a next-generation Security Orchestration, Automation, and Response platform in which the role of security analysts gradually shifts from direct decision-making to supervisory oversight. To this end, we bridged two emerging but independently studied paradigms–Intent-Based Cyber Defense and Autonomic Cyber Defense–by introducing a unified, ontology-driven representation of security response intents, along with a two-tiered methodology for their integration into decision-theoretic Autonomic Cyber Defense models. The integration comprises an Intent Discovery Agent and an Intent Enforcement Agent. We illustrated the implementation of the proposed intents through the Intent Enforcement Agent. While this work lays the conceptual and architectural foundation for integrating intent into post-detection Autonomic Cyber Defense systems, we did not evaluate the performance of our proposed methodology. Future work will focus on benchmarking the performance of state-of-the-art Autonomic Cyber Defense systems boosted by Intent-Based Networking, thereby enabling a more comprehensive evaluation across complex infrastructures and dynamic attacks.

Acknowledgements. This work was supported by the French National Research Agency (ANR) under the ANCILE project (Grant No. ANR-23-CE39-0010).

Disclosure of Interests. The authors have no competing interests to declare that are relevant to the content of this article.

[13] https://github.com/Zequan99/EDOC-k8s-DT-implementation/tree/master

References

1. Zidan, K., Alam, A., Allison, J., Al-sherbaz, A.: Assessing the challenges faced by Security Operations Centres (SOC). In: Advances in Information and Communication, pp. 256–271 (2024)
2. Kinyua, J., Awuah, L.: AI/ML in security orchestration, automation and response: future research directions. Intell. Autom. Soft Comput. **28**(2), 527–545 (2021)
3. Vyas, S., Hannay, J., Bolton, A., Burnap, P.P.: Automated cyber defence: a review (2023). arXiv preprint arXiv:2303.04926
4. Hammar, K., Li, T., Stadler, R., Zhu, Q.: Adaptive security response strategies through conjectural online learning. IEEE Trans. Inf. Forensics Secur. **20**, 4055–4070 (2025)
5. Manshaei, M.H., Zhu, Q., Alpcan, T., Bacşar, T., Hubaux, J.P.: Game theory meets network security and privacy. ACM Comput. Surv. (CSUR) **45**(3), 1–39 (2013)
6. Wallace, S., Green, K.Y., Johnson, C., Cooper, J., Gilstrap, C.: An extended TOE framework for cybersecurity-adoption decisions. Commun. Assoc. Inf. Syst. **47**(1), 51 (2020)
7. Lalanda, P., McCann, J.A., Diaconescu, A.: Autonomic computing. In: Principles, Design and Implementation. Springer (2013). https://doi.org/10.1007/978-1-4471-5007-7
8. Clemm, A., Ciavaglia L., Granville L., Tantsura J.: Intent-based networking - concepts and definitions, RFC 9315, IETF (2021)
9. Leivadeas, A., Falkner, M.: A survey on intent-based networking. IEEE Commun. Surv. Tutorials **25**(1), 625–655 (2023)
10. Kaloroumakis, P.E., Smith, M.J.: Toward a knowledge graph of cybersecurity countermeasures. The MITRE Corporation (2021)
11. Sikos, L.F.: Cybersecurity knowledge graphs. Knowl. Inf. Syst. **65**(9), 3511–3531 (2023)
12. Martins, B.F., Serrano, L., Reyes, J.F., Panach, J.I., Pastor, O., Rochwerger, B.: Conceptual characterization of cybersecurity ontologies. In: IFIP Working Conference on The Practice of Enterprise Modeling, pp. 323–338. Springer International Publishing, Cham (2020). https://doi.org/10.1007/978-3-030-63479-7_22
13. Strom, B.E., et al.: Finding cyber threats with ATT&CK-based analytics. The MITRE Corporation, Bedford, MA, Technical Report No. MTR170202 (2017)
14. Oliveira, Í., et al.: Boosting D3FEND: ontological analysis and recommendations. formal ontology in information systems (2023)
15. Tian, B., et al.: Safely and automatically updating in-network ACL configurations with intent language. In: Proceedings of the ACM Special Interest Group on Data Communication, pp. 214–226
16. Kim, J., et al.: IBCS: Intent-Based Cloud Services for security applications. IEEE Commun. Mag. **58**(4), 45–51 (2020)
17. Lingga, P., Jeong, J., Dunbar, L.: ICSC: intent-based closed-loop security control system for cloud-based security services. IEEE Commun. Mag. **63**(4), 169–175 (2025)
18. Pizzato, F., Bringhenti, D., Sisto, R., Valenza, F.: An intent-based solution for network isolation in Kubernetes. In: 2024 IEEE 10th International Conference on Network Softwarization (NetSoft), pp. 381–386 (2024)
19. Robles-Enciso, A., Bernabé Murcia, J.M., Molina Zarca, A., Skarmeta Gomez, A.: Dynamic multi-method allocation for intent-based security orchestration. J. Netw. Syst. Manage. **33**(1)
20. Szyrkowiec, T., et al.: Automatic intent-based secure service creation through a multilayer SDN network orchestration. J. Opt. Commun. Netw. **10**(4), 289 (2018)
21. Hyder, M.F., Ismail, M.A.: INMTD: intent-based moving target defense framework using software defined networks. Eng. Technol. Appl.Sci. Res. **10**(1), 5142–5147 (2020)
22. Settanni, F., Zamponi, A., Basile, C.: Dynamic security provisioning for cloud-native networks: an intent-based approach. In: 2024 IEEE International Conference on Cyber Security and Resilience (CSR), 321–328 (2024)

23. Lopez, D., Lopez, E., Dunbar, L., Strassner, J., Kumar, R.: Framework for interface to network security functions. RFC 8329, IETF (2018)
24. Applebaum, A., et al.: Bridging automated to autonomous cyber defense: foundational analysis of tabular q-learning. In: Proceedings of the 15th ACM Workshop on Artificial Intelligence and Security, pp. 149–159 (2022)
25. Adadi, A., Berrada, M.: Peeking inside the black-box: a survey on explainable artificial intelligence (XAI). IEEE Access **6**, 52138–52160 (2018)
26. Booker, L.B., Musman, S.A.: A model-based, decision-theoretic perspective on automated cyber response (2020). arXiv preprint arXiv:2002.08957
27. Musman, S., Turner, A.: A game theoretic approach to cyber security risk management. J. Defense Model. Simul. Appl. Methodol. Technol. **15**(2), 127–146 (2017)
28. Antoniou, G., Harmelen, F.V.: Web Ontology Language: Owl. In: Handbook on ontologies, pp. 91–110 (2009)
29. Hammar, K.: Optimal security response to network intrusions in IT systems, Ph.D. dissertation, KTH Royal Institute of Technology (2025). arXiv preprint arXiv:2502.02541
30. Krishnamurthy, V.: Partially Observed Markov Decision Processes. Cambridge University Press (2016)

Rethinking Cybersecurity Ontology Classification and Evaluation: Towards a Credibility-Centered Framework

Antoine Leblanc[1,2](✉), Jacques Robin[2], Nourhène Ben Rabah[1], Zequan Huang[1,2], and Bénédicte Le Grand[1]

[1] Center for Research in Informatics (CRI), University Paris 1 Panthéon-Sorbonne, Paris, France
{antoine.leblanc,nourhene.ben-rabah, benedicte.le-grand}@univ-paris1.fr, zequan.huang@esiea.fr

[2] Engineering School of Informatics, Electronics and Automation (ESIEA), Paris, France
jacques.robin@esiea.fr

Abstract. This paper analyzes the proliferation of cybersecurity ontologies, arguing that this surge cannot be explained solely by technical shortcomings related to quality, but also by a **credibility deficit** - a lack of trust, endorsement, and adoption by users. This conclusion is based on our first contribution, which is a state-of-the-art review and categorization of cybersecurity ontologies using the Framework for Ontologies Classification (F4OC) framework. To address this gap, we propose a revised framework for assessing credibility, introducing indicators such as **institutional support**, **academic recognition**, **day-to-day practitioners' validation**, and **industrial adoption**. Based on these new credibility indicators, we construct a classification scheme designed to guide the selection of ontologies that are relevant to specific security needs. We then apply this framework to a concrete use case: the Franco-Luxembourgish research project **ANCILE** (https://www.linkedin.com/company/autonomic-cybersecurity-with-adversarial-learning-and-explanations), which illustrates how a credibility-aware evaluation can reshape ontology selection for operational contexts.

Keywords: Ontology Classification · Credibility · Cybersecurity · Quality Assessment

1 Introduction

In the cybersecurity landscape, ontologies have become the semantic backbone of knowledge bases used by reasoning engines: they structure the representation of vulnerabilities, ground alerts and detections in a shared vocabulary, and allow ***Security Orchestration Automation and Response (SOAR)*** platforms to reason about adversarial tactics and appropriate responses. Without them, interoperability between tools, the traceability of automated decisions, and even the simple comparison of incident reports become fragile and error prone. In short, a well-designed ontology is no longer an academic luxury; it is a critical component of modern cyber hygiene.

© The Author(s), under exclusive license to Springer Nature Switzerland AG 2026
A. Gianola et al. (Eds.): EDOC 2025, LNCS 16213, pp. 284–299, 2026.
https://doi.org/10.1007/978-3-032-15140-7_16

This very importance has triggered an overwhelming proliferation. Since 2014, around a hundred different security ontologies have been published. Figure 1 shows this increasing curve, based on a review of ontologies in cybersecurity domain which is the first contribution of our work.

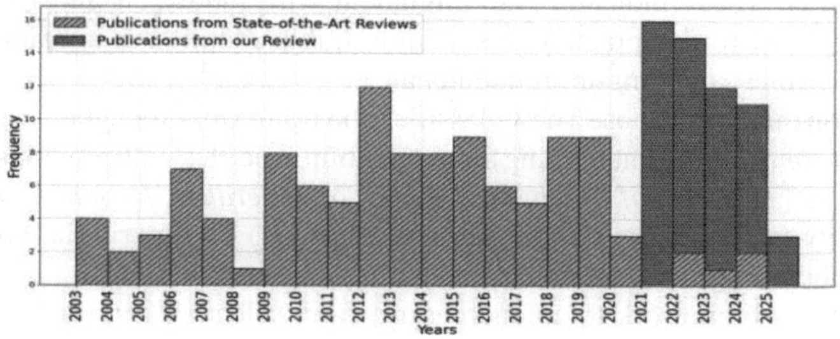

Fig. 1. Number of Published Cybersecurity Ontologies per Year (January 2003–April 2025)

This abundance reveals a lack of reusability, even though this principle is essential for managing data and digital resources according to the ***FAIR principles (Findable, Accessible, Interoperable, and Reusable)*** [1], as argued by Oliveira et al. [2]. This problem of ontologies' abundance has led to our first research question:

- **RQ1.** Why is the reuse of ontologies limited in the cybersecurity domain?

To address this question, we conduct a systematic review of existing cybersecurity ontologies and analyze each one through a structured categorization framework that brings its key properties to light.

Let's now turn to another challenge faced when a cybersecurity team must choose an ontology. They are confronted with a multitude of ontologies in the form of Web Ontology Language (OWL), Neo4j and Prolog implementations, each claiming to cover MITRE ATT&CK™ (a taxonomy of attacker behaviors) [3], MITRE D3FEND™ [4] (a counter-measure ontology mapping how to block or limit ATT&CK tactics)[1], or ISO 27005 [5] – according to Enterprise Strategy Group research, 89% of organizations use MITRE ATT&CK to reduce risk for security operations use-case [6]. However, very few of them are validated by external cybersecurity day-to-day practitioners or widely adopted by operators of ***Security Operations Centers (SOC).*** To guide their choice, teams often rely on intrinsic quality criteria—logical soundness, structural consistency, and syntactic correctness—while overlooking extrinsic properties such as whether the ontology adheres to established standards or how frequently it has been updated. Most of the existing literature has focused on the characterization of ontologies, while few studies have addressed the evaluation of ontology quality in the cybersecurity domain. Moreover, such evaluations remain limited because of the challenges of evaluating their criteria. This led us to formulate a second research question:

[1] While MITRE ATT&CK was initially published as a mere taxonomy, the more recent MITRE D3FEND which is a genuine OWL ontology includes the ATT&CK taxonomy. In what follows, when we refer to MITRE ATT&CK, we mean the sub-ontology of D3FEND that reuses the ATT&CK taxonomy and elaborate it.

- **RQ2.** What additional criteria could be used to characterize cybersecurity ontologies, and how could they be evaluated?

To address this gap, this paper investigates a key complementary criterion: ***Credibility***; and introduce a set of credibility-oriented indicators which constitute our second contribution. Those indicators are alignment with industry standards, validation by independent day-to-day practitioners, demonstrable adoption in operational tools or institutional settings, and long-term maintenance.

Building on this, we propose a new classification framework for cybersecurity ontologies, our *third contribution*, integrating these credibility metrics with previously proposed criteria such as [7]: *Level of application*, Level *of generality*, *Formal expressiveness*, *Logical density* (referred as axiomatization level in [7]) These criteria will be further explained in the background section.

We apply this framework to a concrete use case: selecting an ontology to support ANCILE, a next-generation SOAR framework combining autonomic computing with probabilistic attack detection, attack plan recognition, and automated mitigation, that is being designed in an eponymous Franco-Luxembourgish research project. This application illustrates how the addition of the "credibility" axis reorders the ranking of candidate ontologies and excludes superficially attractive ontologies which lack in fairness and adoption by daily cybersecurity practitioners.

This paper is structured as follows. Section 2 reviews the previous work in classifying ontologies and evaluating their quality; Sect. 3 reviews cybersecurity ontologies and applies a selected framework to those; Sect. 4 explores the concept of credibility, and proposes a refined definition and evaluation metrics tailored to this context; Sect. 5 introduces a new classification framework that incorporates credibility as a core dimension and applies it to a selection of security ontologies; Sect. 6 presents a concrete application of this framework in the context of the ANCILE project, illustrating how credibility-aware selection impacts practical cybersecurity ontology selection; Sect. 7 concludes the paper and outlines directions for future research.

2 Background Knowledge

2.1 Previous Work in Classifying Cybersecurity Ontology

To navigate the growing number of cybersecurity ontologies, it is essential to classify and compare them using a consistent and structured approach. One of the most comprehensive efforts in this direction is **F4OC** proposed by Martins et al. [7]. Their objective is to support the engineering, selection, and integration of ontologies (particularly in domains like cybersecurity) by combining conceptual modeling theory with practical needs from software and knowledge engineering. They propose a five-step, orthogonal pipeline that aligns ontology with practical engineering concerns.

- ***Step 1***. Systematic mapping of the state of the art.
- ***Step 2***. Placement of candidate ontology along Guizzardi's ***level-of-application*** axis [8], defining those as *reference* or *operational* or both. A reference ontology is a well-structured representation of a part of reality, designed for knowledge exchange and reuse, whereas an operational ontology is its concrete implementation in practice.

Throughout the remainder of this paper, the term reference ontology denotes an ontology that either is a reference ontology itself or is explicitly supported by one.
- ***Step 3***. Application of Guarino's [9] and van Heijst's [10] ***level-of-generality*** taxonomy, categorizing ontologies as *Foundational* (its concepts are broad and apply across multiple domains), *Domain* (its concepts are from a particular domain), *Core* (lies between Foundational and Domain), *Task* (its concepts are specific task within a domain), *Application* (lies between Domain and Task). It also checks if the ontology is well-grounded – i.e. its concepts are inherited from a foundational ontology.
- ***Step 4***. Estimation of *formal expressiveness* that combines Uschold-Gruninger's informal / formal ladder [11] and Giunchiglia et al. lightweight / heavyweight distinction [12].
- ***Step 5***. Estimation of *logical density*. – referring to the number of concepts and relations.

Another work, from Oliveira et al. [2], assesses security core ontologies against the four FAIR pillars and checks (a) their implementation language, (b) their artifact availability, (c) whether the ontology reuses concepts from some foundational ontology and (d) their concept vocabulary. Their mapping study shows that only a small fraction of the 57 ontologies they examined satisfy all four indicators, especially struggling with Interoperability and public availability.

Meriah and Rabai [13] introduce a domain-focused scheme that distinguishes six main ontologies built to encode security standards from ISO/IEC 27000 [14]. They also provide recommendations for future ontologies based on this standard.

Martins et al.'s F4OC stands out by proposing a more complete categorization framework of ontologies with features that cover essential properties of ontologies: foundational grounding, complexity, operability, and formality. This is why, in the following sections, we propose to describe existing cybersecurity ontologies by analyzing them according to the criteria of this classification framework.

2.2 A Framework to Evaluate Ontologies

Following the discussion on how to categorize ontologies, Wilson et al. [15] proposed a recent evaluation framework based on a systematic literature review. It assesses ontology quality along four independent axes:

- The *structural intrinsic* axis focuses on the internal consistency of the ontology itself—how well it follows formal language rules, avoids contradictions, and maintains coherence.
- The *domain intrinsic* dimension examines how accurately the ontology represents its subject matter, typically by comparing it to established standards (e.g., ISO, NIST) and testing it with expert reviews.
- The *domain extrinsic* perspective shifts attention to the ontology's real-world usefulness. Here, it's evaluated as a black box—judged by how well it delivers relevant, accurate, and understandable outputs for users like threat analysts.
- Finally, the *application extrinsic* axis treats the ontology as a software component within a larger technical system. The focus is on technical integration and performance, regardless of domain knowledge.

Among the 19 criteria identified among these axes, ***credibility*** stands out as particularly important – it comes from the domain extrinsic axe. It captures how trusted and widely accepted an ontology is within its community—a key factor in distinguishing impactful ontologies from those with limited practical use. A fuller discussion of credibility is provided in Sect. 4.

3 Survey and Characterization of Recent Cybersecurity Ontologies

This section presents our first contribution: a review of cybersecurity ontologies published since 2021, along with their characterization using the F4OC framework.

3.1 Review of Recent Cybersecurity Ontologies

We first searched for review papers in cybersecurity ontologies. Along with proposing F4OC, Martins et al. [7] also cataloged thirty-five cybersecurity ontologies. Other authors examine security ontologies, including Oliveria et al. [2], Adach et al. [16], and Rosa et al. [17]. Jarwar [18] concentrates on a specific context, which is IoT-related ontologies. Finally, a few studies do not directly survey ontologies but address closely related knowledge structures like Rahman et al. [19] who review various taxonomies, or Bratsas et al. [20] and Bolton et al. [21] who focus on knowledge graphs.

Overall, these papers cite a total of 114 papers related to 1 security ontologies. However, the 114 security ontologies related papers cited by these articles were all published before 2021 (except for four ontologies from [18]). To get an up-to-date list of cybersecurity ontologies we conducted a review in the spirit of the work of Martins et al. [7] on cybersecurity ontologies published since January 2021. This resulted in adding ***52 new publications of ontologies*** to our list security and cybersecurity ontologies. We used the search string "TITLE-ABS-KEY("Cybersecurity Ontology" OR "Cybersecurity Ontologies")" on the Scopus database we applied the same inclusion and exclusion criteria as [7]. The inclusion criteria were (IC1) Articles that introduce full-scale cybersecurity ontologies, (IC2) Articles that detail specific modules or subsets of cybersecurity ontologies. The exclusion criteria (EC1) Articles whose low citation count suggests limited relevance, (EC2) Articles that do not actually put forward an ontology.

Among those, two ontologies stand out due to their foundational grounding: the **Common Ontology of Value and Risk (COVER)** [22]and the **Reference Ontology for Security Engineering (ROSE)** [23]. Both are rigorously grounded in the **Unified Foundational Ontology (UFO)** [24]– both implemented in OntoUML – ensuring clear distinctions between the domain-independent concepts of agents, events, dispositions and situations. COVER proposes a formal ontology of risk, highlighting its deep ties to value. ROSE extends it to security, with some modifications, by making explicit how threats, vulnerabilities, and countermeasures interact in ISO 31000-style risk treatment processes [25].

An OWL ontology **CRATELO** [26] (Cyber Risk And Threat Engineering Linked Ontology) combines a DOLCE-SPRAY [27] foundation, Security Core Ontology (SECCO) and an Ontologies of Secure Cyber Operations (OSCO) to capture the full path from threats and vulnerabilities to countermeasures and mission impact, improving the situation awareness of security operations analysts. Because of its foundation on DOLCE, CRATELO is well-grounded. However, it does not rely on any standards.

WAVED [28] (Weakness – ATT&CK – Vulnerability – Engage – D3fend) unifies in a single OWL ontology MITRE ATT&CK tactics, D3FEND counter-measures, ENGAGE [29] engagement activities, the CVE (Common Vulnerabilities and Exposures - a list of disclosed concrete security flaws)[2] and the CWE (Common Weakness Enumeration - recurring software/hardware general weakness classes that are specialized by vulnerabilities)[3] [30]/[31]. Those taxonomies, ontologies and lists are considered de facto standard nowadays because they are openly available, maintained by the trusted MITRE organization, and broadly adopted by tool vendors, government bodies, and practitioners; in the absence of an equivalent rival, they have naturally evolved into the common language of the domain. Thus, WAVED is well rooted into cybersecurity de facto standards, but it lacks foundational grounding.

The Unified Cybersecurity Ontology (UCO) [32] offers a semantic integration of major cybersecurity standards – like Structured Threat Information eXpression (STIX) an open, machine-readable OASIS standard that structures and links cyber-threat intelligence and based on XML [33] – and de facto standards – like CVE – using OWL to support reasoning and interoperability. Unlike STIX, UCO enables advanced queries by linking cyber concepts to general knowledge bases like DBpedia [34] and Yago [35] for instance. However, it lacks foundational grounding.

3.2 Application of Martins et al.'s Framework on Post 2021 Cybersecurity Ontologies for Classification Purposes

We then applied the F4OC framework to those new 52 ontologies, to see the current trends in security ontology engineering. However, it is difficult to evaluate the size or formalization level of ontologies because the available documents describing them do not provide enough details, as explained by [7]. Therefore, we focused only on the first four criteria provided by F4OC: a) Reference Ontology, b) Operational Ontology, c) Well-groundedness and d) level of generality according to [9] and [10].

A summary of key findings is presented in Table 1, highlighting the percentage of ontologies that satisfy each evaluation criterion. For the "level of generality" dimension, we break down the data into four categories core, domain, application, and task specific. The Foundational category is omitted because it does apply to cybersecurity-specific ontologies.

Our review provides some findings regarding the first research question (**RQ1**) by identifying a key barrier to ontology reuse in cybersecurity: the lack of foundational grounding. Although 87% of the most recent ontologies reviewed claim to serve operational purposes, such as supporting reasoning or inference, only 4% demonstrate grounding in a foundational ontology. This gap has significant consequences. Ontologies

[2] Example CVE: *CVE-2017-11882*—A vulnerability in Microsoft Word that allows attackers to execute code just by getting a user to open a malicious document.

[3] Example CWE: *CWE-89*—SQL Injection: a common weakness where attackers can manipulate database queries to access unauthorized data.

developed without a well-established conceptual basis are more prone to inconsistencies, are harder to extend, and are less compatible with broader knowledge ecosystems. A clear example of this is D3FEND, which introduces several useful concepts but lacks ontological rigor, leading to ambiguities and limiting its interoperability [36].

Regarding reuse, we must however nuance our findings because it is not the only aspect to consider. According to [2], Reusability is also assessed by checking if the ontology meets domain-relevant community standard and if it provides rich meta-data.

This lack of foundational grounding motivates the next Subsect. 3.3, where we leverage our characterization framework to propose requirements for selecting a reusable and robust ontology, grounded in both theoretical and operational considerations.

3.3 Selecting a Relevant Ontology for Cybersecurity

While the design of an ontology may be influenced by specific use cases, some properties defined in this framework are broadly desirable and beneficial across various application domains, beyond cybersecurity. First, an ontology which is well-grounded is less prone to error and inconsistencies. Second, a reference ontology has more chance to be reused and respect FAIR principles. Third, an ontology is often built to reason and answer queries, meaning to be operational. Thus, an ontology being well-grounded, being a reference one and being operational is worthwhile to be considered for every project. Filtering the 87 ontologies in our review through those three criteria lenses, *Reference ontology*, *Operational ontology* and *Well-groundedness* singles out CRATELO [26]. Unfortunately, the original artefact appears to be lost; the authors could not retrieve the 2014 code base. We then decided to look for the closest neighbors of CRATELO by relaxing each criterion one by one.

Relaxing the "operational" requirement adds three more candidates, notably COVER [22] and ROSE [23], both grounded in UFO [24] and therefore promising foundations that would, however, still have to be refined with more operational concepts if we wanted an

Table 1. Application of the F4OC to the 52 recent publication of cybersecurity ontologies and the 35 coming from [7].[4]

Number of Ontology	Step 2 (Level of Application)		Step 3 (Level of Generality [7])				
	Reference Ontology	Operational Ontology	Well-grounded Ontology	According to [9] and [10]			
				Core	Domain	Application	Task
35 from [7]	43%	83%	11%	6%	77%	17%	0%
52 from our review	25%	87%	4%	0%	31%	69%	0%

[4] The full results of this analysis are available here https://github.com/AntoineLeblancFr/EdocPAPER.

operational ontology on cybersecurity. Dropping the "well-grounded" criterion widens the net to about twenty ontologies and loosening the "reference" criterion yield no additional ontologies.

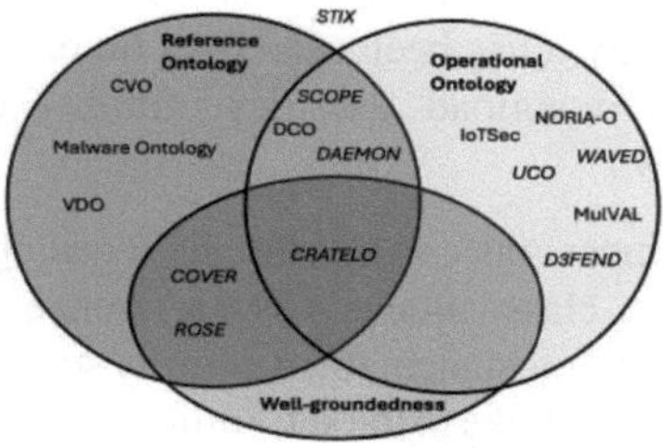

Fig. 2. Classification of cybersecurity ontologies across Reference, Operational, and Well-grounded criteria.

On the one hand, this exercise reveals that there are several ontologies of all ontologies close to what we are looking for except for being well-grounded as expected as only 7% are well-grounded. On the other hand, ontologies found doing this exercise highlight a crucial gap. Pure typological characterization (application versus domain, lightweight versus heavyweight) quickly tells us why an ontology looks right for a project, yet it says nothing about real-world usability. CRATELO, for instance, is structurally ideal but remains silent on standards or de facto industry standards such as MITRE ATT&CK. It is also no longer available in machine-readable form. Conversely, WAVED aligns perfectly with ATT&CK and D3FEND but lacks a foundational grounding and does not rely on a reference ontology, which may lead to logical contradictions and spurious inferences.

To be able to see WAVED as a possible candidate for our use-case, always by following a classification framework, we need to add more criteria to describe the ontology. Here, a criterion that would classify WAVED as valuable would be *credibility*, because WAVED relies on industry-validated de-facto standards. However, credibility is not a categorization criterion but a quality one. This highlights that, in addition to classification, evaluating ontologies is another key factor for selecting the most appropriate one for our use case. We can make the same remarks for STIX – which is an ontological standard –, UCO and D3FEND.

4 Ontologies Evaluation Criteria

4.1 Understanding Ontology Credibility: Concept, Dimensions and Limitations

We define credibility, adopted from the data quality standard: ISO/IEC 25012 [38], as the degree of confidence that users, developers, and experts place in it, particularly when applied to mission-critical domains like cybersecurity.

The definitions of Wilson et al. [39] for credibility rely on the notion of social quality from the work of McDaniel et al. [40]. Their approach decomposes credibility into three sub-dimensions:

- ***Authority*** reflects the degree to which an ontology is integrated within the broader semantic ecosystem, measured by the number of other ontologies that reused it and the extent of shared terminology across these connections.
- ***History*** captures the ontology's longevity and maintenance track record. It includes how long the ontology has been available as an open resource, how often it has been revised, and how frequently it has been used over time.
- ***Recognition*** aggregates download statistics, number of user reviews, and the positivity of those reviews.

Quantitatively, these dimensions can be computed through formulas that normalize each score against the best-in-class value across a reference set of ontologies producing a weighted credibility score. For instance, the Authority score is calculated as the ratio of links to the maximum number of links in the set; similar normalization applies for History and Recognition, each combining relevant variables like years of existence, number of revisions, downloads, and reviews. Together, these definitions reveal that credibility is not a vague or subjective trait but a measurable property, rooted in both social dynamics and technical interdependence. As ontologies become embedded in decision-making systems, credibility may well be the deciding factor between a theoretically perfect yet impractical ontology, and a well-used, battle-tested model that experts are willing to rely on. This calls for a systematic inclusion of credibility metrics in any ontology selection or evaluation process.

The first limitation of these credibility indicators lies in their practical measurability. Recognition demands not only download and review counts but a reliable method for separating positive from negative verdicts—a task easily confounded by balanced, academic prose and thus prone to subjective coding. Authority assumes a well-curated registry where ontologies inter-link according to shared conventions; in practice, such infrastructure is patchy, leaving link statistics sporadic and biased. History likewise hinges on complete version logs: beyond platforms like GitHub or BioPortal, records are often partial, forked, or missing, making cross-ontology comparisons laborious. Collectively, these data gaps undermine the robustness of any credibility score.

Beyond these measurement difficulties, Wilson et al. [39] also raises a more fundamental concern: credibility is context dependent. An ontology that was widely trusted a decade ago may have lost its relevance today, not because it was poorly designed, but because it fails to reflect the evolution of its domain. In cybersecurity, for instance, ontologies developed before 2013 could not incorporate de facto standards like MITRE ATT&CK, which is now a well-known reference. Even if those earlier models were authored by domain leaders, they cannot be considered credible today if they omit critical modern knowledge. Credibility, must therefore be also understood as context-dependent, tied not only to the ontology's internal features but to its temporal and situational relevance.

Yet, this does not mean we should avoid making credibility judgments. On the contrary, we need evaluation methods that acknowledge this temporal dependency and still enabling us to discriminate between outdated and current ontologies.

To address these challenges, we propose measurable indicators to evaluate easily the credibility criterion across periods and contexts.

4.2 Towards a New Definition of Cybersecurity Ontology Credibility

To make the credibility concept as a measurable and context-aware, we propose a decomposition into four dimensions, each reflecting the involvement of a specific stakeholder group in the ecosystem of the ontology's development. This structure acknowledges that credit in an ontology emerges from the validation of several sources: institutions, academia, day-to-day practitioners, and industry. Each dimension contributes a different form of legitimacy, and together they offer a well-rounded view of an ontology's credibility in practice. We define below each dimension, justify its relevance, and propose a practical evaluation indicator.

Institutional Endorsement. Institutions often act as gatekeepers in the development of security ontologies. They provide conceptual scaffolding: defining the key entities, relationships, and taxonomies that the ontology will encode. When an ontology is formally referenced by recognized standards (such as STIX, or NIST), it inherits a high level of legitimacy. The indicator here is deliberately binary: if the ontology is referenced by an established standard or de facto standard, it receives a score of 1; otherwise, it scores 0. While simplistic, this measure captures a powerful signal of trust and relevance at the institutional level.

Academic Recognition. The academic community plays a crucial role in ensuring that ontologies are grounded in rigorous methodology and up-to-date theoretical foundations. This form of credibility is assessed through traditional indicators: the quality of the publication venues (e.g., top conferences or journals in ontology engineering, cybersecurity, or AI). These measures reflect the extent to which the ontology is taken seriously by researchers.

Day to Day Practitioners' Validation. An ontology is considered day-to-day practitioners-validated when it has been reviewed by a panel of domain day-to-day practitioners, each meeting at least two of the following qualification criteria: advanced degree, at least 5 years of professional practice or active membership in a professional standards body.

Industrial Maturity. Nachabe and Jahan [41] suggest re-using the Technology Readiness Level (TRL) scale to gauge ontology maturity; TRL was created to model the technological maturation process of cyber-physical systems like a space shuttle or a satellite. The physical-related steps of this process do not apply to a pure software artefact like an ontology which can become operational in fewer steps. TRL also ignores maintenance steps and requires insider data to verify—a poor fit for an openly published, purely logical artefact. To keep the assessment practical, we introduce a streamlined, evidence-based indicator of industrial maturity that anyone can audit. We propose a three-level ladder:

- **L1 – Visibility:** at least one detailed production deployment is published—for example, a white paper, keynote speech, or deep-dive case study.
- **L2 – Documented deployment:** at least one use-case demonstrating the validity of the ontology has been published.

- **L3 – Independent adoption:** a panel of independent organizations reference the ontology in their technical artefacts (integration guides, architecture documents, RFPs, etc.).

Taken together, these four axes constitute a multi-perspective framework that captures credibility not as an abstract ideal, but as a concrete, measurable, and context-sensitive property. This evaluation method for credibility constitutes our answer to the second research question (**RQ2**).

5 New Ontologies Classification Framework Based on Credibility

Based on this new definition of credibility, we propose a **novel classification** of cybersecurity ontologies, organized into four distinct categories:

- **C1 – Academic Ontology**. The ontology has been published in at least a Q2-ranked journal or a B-tier conference.
- **C2 – Practical Ontology**. The ontology was co-authored by recognized domain day-to-day practitioners or developed with their involvement.
- **C3 – Standardized Ontology**. The ontology explicitly relies on established standards for the definition of all its core concepts.
- **C4 – Industrial Ontology**. The ontology has reached at least the second level of this criterion (L2).

An ontology may belong to multiple categories simultaneously. We applied our classification scheme to the 10 cybersecurity technologies highlighted in Sect. 3.3 (see Fig. 3).

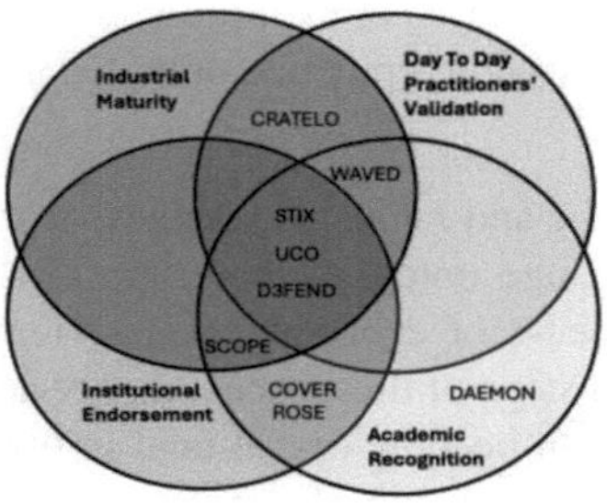

Fig. 3. Classification of cybersecurity ontologies across Industrial Maturity, Expert Validation, Institutional Endorsement, and Academic Recognition.

Thanks to this framework, valuable ontologies that had slipped under the radar—such as WAVED and D3FEND—have now been brought into the spotlight, whereas the original framework largely left them on the sidelines. For instance, WAVED appears to be a very credible candidate due to its reliance on MITRE de facto standards (which are widely adopted in industrial context), on day-to-day practitioners' validation and peer reviewed. Compared to CRATELO which appears at first glance to be the perfect match we see that because of its lack of academic recognition and its lack of reliance on standards, it has become less credible. Nonetheless, some ontologies lack credibility in some dimensions but remain interesting because of their properties highlighted by F4OC, like COVER and ROSE, which are good candidate to be a reference ontology. These new classes allow us to consider more ontologies than F4OC alone, which are credible, and can result in more reutilization of ontologies.

6 A Concrete Use Case: The ANCILE Project

ANCILE (AutoNomic Cyber-security with adversarIal Learning and Explanations) is a Franco-Luxembourgish research project aiming at idealizing, prototyping and empirically evaluating, the next generation of SOAR frameworks. It proposes to architect them as two autonomic computing ***MAPE-K*** pipeline loops [42] in mirror image, one for cyber-defense and one for cyber-attack, allowing their co-improvement through adversarial machine learning in cyberattack-defense simulations.

As shown in the center of Fig. 2, a MAPE-K loop manages a runtime reconfigurable system. **M** stands for a *Monitoring* service that senses data from both the system managed by the loop and the operations environment in which it is deployed, to identify relevant state changes in them. **A** stands for an *Analysis* service that receives relevant state change alerts from **M** and determines whether the current configuration of the system still satisfies its requirements in the new system and/or environment state. If this is not the case, the **M** triggers **P**, a *Planning* service that searches for a reconfiguration of the system that restores the satisfaction of those requirements. **P** then sends a reconfiguration plan to **E,** an *Execution* service that executes it. A MAPE-K loop is thus a continuous loop through a pipeline consisting of *Monitor, Analyze, Plan* and *Execute* steps. The **K** stands for a *Knowledge* base that is shared by the **M, A, P** and **E** pipeline services so that they can interoperate based on a common reference conceptual framework.

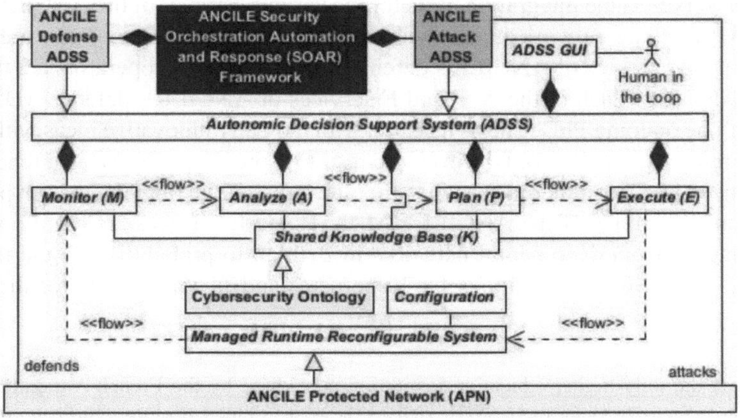

Fig. 4. ANCILE Autonomic SOAR framework architecture

MAPE-K is an abstract autonomic computing architectural pattern that needs to be refined with concrete services specific to a particular application. Hence, in many autonomic systems, **K** takes the form of an application ontology, potentially re-using a domain ontology and/or a task ontology. Such ontology is in turn either queried by or imported inside the knowledge bases or models of the **M, A, P** and **E** inference services of the MAPE-K refinement. This is the case of the ANCILE SOAR framework architecture. in which the cyber-defense MAPE-K loop is an ***Autonomic Decision Support System (ADSS)*** [43], shown at the top-left of Fig. 4, where the humans in the loop are (a) the blue team during adversarial training and (b) the SOC operators during cybersurveillance of a network. The cyber-attack MAPE-K loop is also an ADSS, shown at the top-right of Fig. 4, of where the humans in the loop are the red team during adversarial training. In the ANCILE defense DSS, the alerts from **M** are cyber-attack alerts and the requirements are security quality criteria such as service availability and data confidentiality and integrity. They are collectively analyzed over time by **A** that tries to recognize a known multistep attack plan (*a.k.a.,* kill chain). The reconfiguration planned by **P** concerns the network protected by the ANCILE defense IDSS, one that satisfyingly minimizes the damage of a detected attack on these quality criteria. Such a plan may involve, for example, rerouting traffic from a host suspected to be compromised to another host provisioned to run the same service using an alternative technological stack that cannot be compromised through the same vulnerability. In ANCILE, **E** carries out such mitigation plan by using a ***Software Defined Network Controller (SDNC)*** [44] together with a container orchestrator such as Kubernetes [45].

Cybersecurity experts participating to ANCILE come from four distinct communities: (a) academic researchers as ESIEA[5], (b) cybersecurity tool developers, notably of the open-source OpenSOC SOC platform of ESIEA, and the GCAP-GCenter[6] comprehensive ***Network Detection and Response (NDR)*** solution commercialized by startup Gatewatcher, (c) SOC operators at ***SOC as a Service (SOCaaS)*** centers at both ESIEA and Gatewatcher and (d) cybersecurity standard specification contributors from ***LIST (Luxembourg Institute of Science and Technology)***, *notably.*ISO/IEC JTC 1/SC27. OpenSOC serves as the integration basis for the various services of the ANCILE SOAR. The GCAP-GCenter network attack signature and anomaly alert generators are key elements of the **M** service of ANCILE's defense ADSS. The SOC operators are the target users of ANCILE. Each of the **A, P** and **E** services of ANCILE's defense ADSS is the subject of one ongoing PhD. Thesis research with radically innovative ideas with respect to the current state-of-the-art. However, the resulting prototype SOAR is intended to be industrialized into a commercial product after the project. The implementation platforms and reasoning engines of the ANCILE's **M, A, P** and **E** services are highly heterogeneous, ranging from deep neural networks in Python, to probabilistic logic programs in Prolog, to YAML specifications for Kubernetes and Java programs for the SDNC.

---

[5] ESIEA is the only higher education institution accredited by the French *National InformationSystem Security Agency (ANSSI)* to deliver the post-graduate diploma *"Information System Security Expert"*.

[6] GCAP-GCenter is one of only four NDR solutions that are both certified and qualified by ANSSI as adhering to common criteria and providing sufficient detection capabilities.

Therefore, the ANCILE ontology must satisfy the requirements from four distinct user communities while also remaining agnostic to implementation platforms.

As explained earlier, as a **K** element in two MAPE-K loops, ANCILE's ontology must be an application ontology, reusing a domain ontology and multiple task ontologies since the tasks of the **M**, **A**, **P** and **E** elements in each loop are distinct (*e.g.*, attack detection *vs.* mitigation). Experts from the four communities listed above insist on the FAIR principles, the academic ones further advocate on foundational grounding, the tool developers prioritize credibility and standard contributors value official standard conformity.

As, no existing ontology simultaneously addresses all these concerns according to the new classification framework application in Fig. 5, for ANCILE we have decided to integrate and align those that come close and complement each other to reach cover all of them. This ontology will be well-grounded in UFO and built upon existing efforts like ROSE and COVER. In terms of credibility, we aim to anchor our ontology in widely recognized standards such as ISO 31000 for risk modeling, and integrate established taxonomies like MITRE ATT&CK, CAPEC, CVE, along with ontologies such as D3FEND – all of which are component of the WAVED ontology – and STIX.

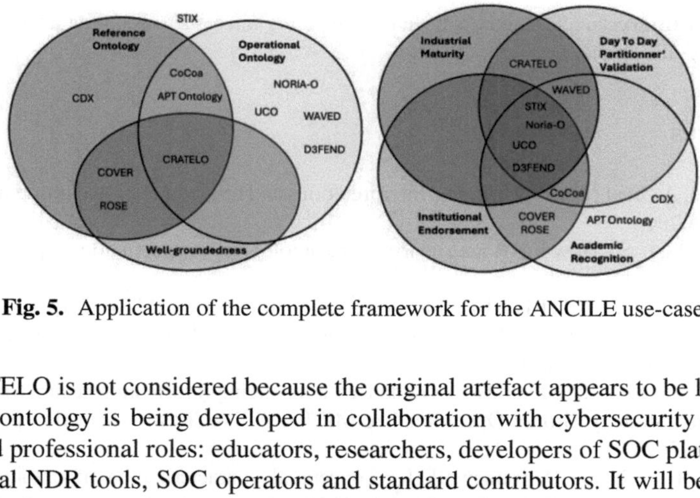

Fig. 5. Application of the complete framework for the ANCILE use-case

CRATELO is not considered because the original artefact appears to be lost. Moreover, our ontology is being developed in collaboration with cybersecurity experts of diversified professional roles: educators, researchers, developers of SOC platforms and commercial NDR tools, SOC operators and standard contributors. It will be deployed in a proof-of-concept, cloning the functionalities of a real-world web application on a different network featuring cutting-edge automation technology, —corresponding to a level 2 of maturity according to our criterion. Through this process, we aim to produce not only a technically sound but also a credible ontology, ready to support high-stakes reasoning in autonomous cybersecurity systems.

7 Conclusion

This study used the F4OC framework to analyze 87 cybersecurity ontologies, revealing most lack foundational grounding and remain tied to narrow, use-case-specific contexts limiting reuse (RQ1). Structure alone being insufficient, we refined Wilson &

McDaniel's notion of "credibility" into four measurable indicators—institutional, academic, expert and industrial—forming a practical evaluation scheme (RQ2). Pairing these indicators with F4OC yielded four credibility-based classes (academic, expert, standardized, industrial), offering a richer lens for ontology selection.

Applying the scheme to the ANCILE SOAR project showed that no single ontology met all requirements, yet several scored highly enough to act as robust starting points for a bespoke model. The work therefore offers a screening tool for practitioners and a roadmap for developers aiming to raise the trust profile of their ontologies.

Key limitations remain: our literature review was not fully systematic, and the history dimension of credibility—stability and evolution—was only partially captured. Future research should address these gaps and extend the evaluation to the full set of ontology quality criteria. Future work needs also to evaluate this credibility criterion with cybersecurity experts and to look for its application to other domains.

Acknowledgements. This work was supported by the French National Research Agency (ANR) under the ANCILE project (grant number ANR-23-CE39-0010).

Disclosure of Interests. The authors have no competing interests to declare that are relevant to the content of this article.

References

1. Jacobsen, A., et al.: FAIR principles: interpretations and implementation considerations. Data Intell. (2020)
2. Oliveira, Í., et al.: How FAIR are security core ontologies? A systematic mapping study. In: RCIS (2021)
3. Strom, B.E., et al., MITRE ATT&CK: design and philosophy. MITRE Corp. (2020)
4. Kaloroumakis, P.E., Smith, M.J.: Toward a knowledge graph of cybersecurity countermeasures. MITRE Corp. (2021)
5. ISO/IEC: ISO/IEC 27005:2022 — Guidance on managing information security risks (2022)
6. Enterprise Strategy Group: Operationalize MITRE ATT&CK with detection posture management (2023)
7. Martins, B.F., et al.: A framework for conceptual characterization of ontologies in the cybersecurity domain. Softw. Syst. Model. (2022)
8. Guizzardi, G.: On ontology, ontologies, conceptualizations, modeling languages, and (meta)-models. Front. Artif. Intell. Appl. (2007)
9. Guarino, N.: The ontological level. Philos. Cogn. Sci. (1994)
10. Van Heijst, G., et al.: Using explicit ontologies in KBS development. Int. J. Hum.-Comput. Stud. (1997)
11. Uschold, M., et al.: Ontologies: Principles, Methods and Applications. Univ, Edinburgh (1996)
12. Giunchiglia, F., Zaihrayeu, I.: Lightweight Ontologies. Univ, Trento (2007)
13. Meriah, I., Rabai, L.B.A.: Comparative study of ontologies based ISO 27000 series security standards. Procedia Comput. Sci. (2019)
14. ISO/IEC: ISO/IEC 27000:2022 — Information security management systems — Overview and vocabulary (2022)

15. Wilson, R.S.I., et al.: A conceptual model for ontology quality assessment: a systematic review. In: Semantic Web (2023)
16. Adach, M., et al.: Security ontologies: a systematic literature review. In: EDOC (2022)
17. Rosa, F., et al.: The security assessment domain: a survey of taxonomies and ontologies (2017)
18. Jarwar, M.A., et al.: Modeling industrial IoT security using ontologies: a systematic review. IEEE Open J. Commun. Soc. (2025)
19. Rahman, M.H., et al.: Manufacturing cybersecurity threat attributes and countermeasures. J. Manuf. Syst. (2023)
20. Bratsas, C., et al.: Knowledge graphs and semantic web tools in cyber threat intelligence. J. Cybersec. Privacy (2024)
21. Bolton, J., et al.: An overview of cybersecurity knowledge graphs mapped to MITRE ATT&CK domains. In: IEEE ISI (2023)
22. Sales, T.P., et al.: The common ontology of value and risk. In: ER (2018)
23. Oliveira, Í., et al.: An ontology of security from a risk-treatment perspective (2022)
24. Guizzardi, G.: Ontological foundations for structural conceptual models, Ph.D. thesis, Univ. Twente (2005)
25. ISO: ISO 31000:2018 — Risk management — Guidelines (2018)
26. Oltramari, A., et al.: Building an ontology of cyber security. In: STIDS (2014)
27. Oltramari, A., et al.: Senso Comune. In: LREC (2010)
28. Akbar, K.A., et al.: The design and application of a unified ontology for cyber security. In: ICISS (2023)
29. MITRE: MITRE engage (n.d)
30. MITRE: Common Weakness Enumeration (CWE) (2025)
31. MITRE: Common Vulnerabilities and Exposures (CVE) (2025)
32. Syed, Z., et al.: UCO: a unified cybersecurity ontology (2016)
33. OASIS: STIX Version 2.1 (2021)
34. Auer, S., et al.: DBpedia: a nucleus for a web of open data (2007)
35. Suchanek, F.M., et al.: YAGO: a large ontology from Wikipedia and WordNet. In: Web Semantics (2008)
36. Oliveira, Í., et al.: Boosting D3FEND: ontological analysis and recommendations (2023)
37. Schulz, S.: The role of foundational ontologies for preventing bad ontology design. In: JOWO (2018)
38. ISO/IEC, ISO/IEC 25012:2008 — Data quality model (2008)
39. Wilson, S.I., et al.: Towards a usable ontology: quality characteristics for an ontology-driven DSS. IEEE Access (2022)
40. McDaniel, M., et al.: Assessing the quality of domain ontologies. Data Knowl. Eng. (2018)
41. Nachabe, L., Jahan, N.: An ontology evaluation tool for the reuse phase. In: KGSWC (2025)
42. Lalanda, P., et al.: Autonomic Computing: Principles, Design and Implementation, Springer (2013). https://doi.org/10.1007/978-1-4471-5007-7
43. Sànchez-Marrè, M.: Intelligent Decision Support Systems, Springer (2022). https://doi.org/10.1007/978-3-030-87790-3_4
44. Xia, W., et al.: A survey on software-defined networking. IEEE Commun. Surv. Tutorials (2014)
45. Kubernetes: Kubernetes documentation (n.d)

Artificial Intelligence and Agents

Automating Access: LLM-Based Permission Request Processing for the Enterprise

Maximilian Niedermeier(✉), Holger Wittges, and Stefanie Rinderle-Ma

Technical University of Munich, TUM School of Computation, Information and Technology, Boltzmannstr. 3, 85748 Garching, Germany
{max.niedermeier,holger.wittges,stefanie.rinderle-ma}@tum.de

Abstract. Every day, across a wide range of industries, companies must adapt employee access profiles to reflect changes in authorization requirements. A key challenge lies in translating the needs of an employee to a technical authorization concept. Due to the rise of generative AI, it makes sense to consider Large Language Models (LLMs) for processing permission requests. This is especially relevant in large-scale access control environments, where the high number of permissions and roles makes oversight difficult for human administrators. Thus, in this contribution, we conduct quantitative research and test whether LLMs are suitable for permission request processing. We find that when embedding an access control document, an LLM performs quite well when translating a permission request into the required permission but struggles with suggesting a suitable role. We show that instead of using an LLM for both permission and role suggestions, it is more efficient to apply a hybrid approach, and first apply an LLM-based permission translation and then algorithmically search for a role that contains the translated permission.

Keywords: Enterprise Security · Role-Based Access Control (RBAC) · Permission Management · Artificial Intelligence (AI) · Large Language Models (LLMs)

1 Introduction

When applying *Role-Based Access Control* (RBAC) [1], security officers regularly receive permission requests from other employees and are responsible for manually assigning the users to appropriate roles that include the required permissions. In existing literature, authorization requests are represented as abstract sets of permissions [2–5] with no intrinsic meaning. Such representations serve well in theoretical approaches, but fail to reflect the way authorization requests are made in practice.

In reality, an employee expresses a permission request in natural language, to be authorized to perform a specific operation in the future. Security officers must

© The Author(s), under exclusive license to Springer Nature Switzerland AG 2026
A. Gianola et al. (Eds.): EDOC 2025, LNCS 16213, pp. 303–320, 2026.
https://doi.org/10.1007/978-3-032-15140-7_17

understand the human request, evaluate it, and, if approved, adjust the access control configuration accordingly. With the growing popularity of *Large Language Models* (LLMs), security officers may increasingly use AI tools to process human permission requests while trying to determine suitable roles.

However, as there is no existing knowledge base on the performance of LLMs when translating authorization requests to RBAC permissions or roles, it is unclear whether solely relying on LLM-based suggestions already shows enterprise-ready results. While existing research on using LLMs for access control, for example, worked on patching access control vulnerabilities [6] and translating natural language access control specifications into formal policies [7–9], we consider the automation of intra-organizational RBAC authorization processes as a gap in research. In particular, we pose the following two research questions:

- *RQ1: To what degree, and in which aspects, does embedding access control documents and increasing model size improve an LLM's ability to process permission requests?*
- *RQ2: To what degree, and in which aspects, does a hybrid approach, that combines an LLM-based permission translation with a role-search algorithm, improve performance in processing permission requests?*

To answer our research questions, we apply quantitative research and conduct the experiment variants as illustrated in Fig. 1. Described by edge *(a)*, we investigate the effects of model size and the impact of an embedded RBAC document on an LLM's ability to translate permission requests into permissions and roles. This variant relies solely on the use of LLMs. Shown in edge *(b)*, we also evaluate the impact of an algorithmic expansion that receives the LLM's permission translation and, using the RBAC document, searches for a role that contains the translated permission. To make our results more reliable, we process each permission request multiple times and use two different data sets.

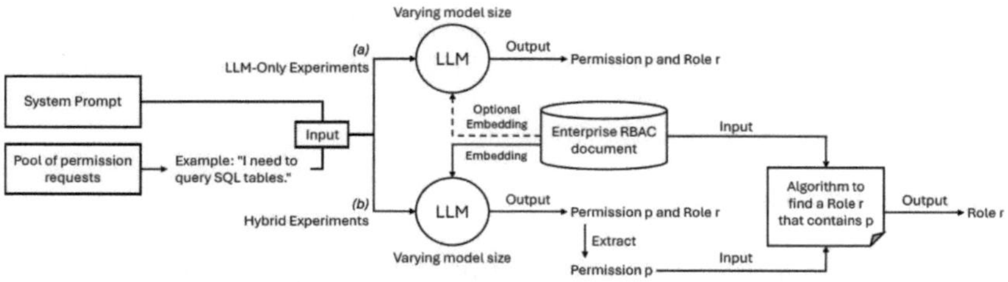

Fig. 1. Experiment variations for researching permission request processing.

The remainder of this paper is structured as follows: First, Sect. 2 shows fundamental concepts of role-based access control, including the application of the principle of least privilege. In Sect. 3, we introduce our evaluation criteria for LLM-based permission request processing. Next, Sect. 4 presents the experiments that rely solely on LLMs for both permission translations and role suggestions. Section 5 then details the experiments that use LLMs for permission translations and an algorithmic expansion for role suggestions. In Sect. 6, we mention the limitations of our research contribution. Finally, in Sect. 7, we conclude our research and show which future research directions we aim to pursue.

2 Background

This section provides background information on access control to help readers without prior knowledge to understand the following paper contents. First, Subsect. 2.1 introduces the basics of role-based access control. Afterwards, Subsect. 2.2 explains how organizations can follow the principle of least privilege.

2.1 Role-Based Access Control

RBAC is a widely adopted access control model, applicable across ERP systems [10–12], healthcare systems [13–15], cloud computing [16–18], and many more. Our explanation is based on the proposed NIST standard by Ferraiolo et al. [19] but only introduces those aspects of the RBAC model which are relevant to understand the following sections of our research article. Figure 2 illustrates the most important components of the RBAC model.

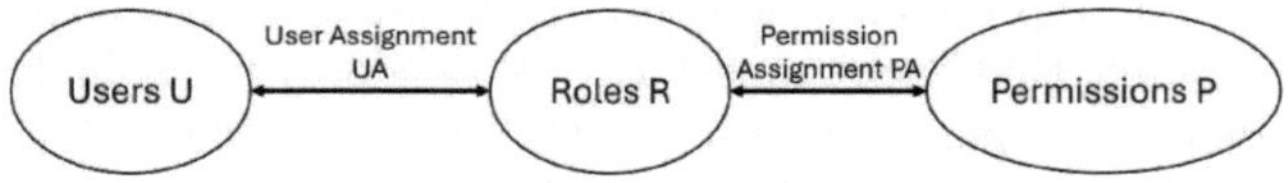

Fig. 2. Important RBAC concepts as well as their interactions.

The three key components of the RBAC model are the users U, the roles R and the permissions P. Instead of directly assigning users to permissions, RBAC relies on a many-to-many relationship $UA \subseteq U \times R$, which assigns the users U to roles R (or vice versa). Similarly, $PA \subseteq P \times R$ is another many-to-many relationship which assigns the permissions P to roles R (or vice versa). This means that roles can be regarded as permission sets that are assigned to users.

2.2 Least Privilege Provisioning in RBAC

The *Principle of Least Privilege* (PoLP) states that users should operate while only being given those privileges that they need to do their job [20]. However, organizations often over-provision roles. For example, as stated in [21], companies may grant project managers administrative permissions, thereby giving them access to projects in which they are not involved.

Fine-grained roles can be created by applying role mining [22]. Solving the basic *Role Mining Problem* (RMP) [23] generates and assigns a minimal number of roles in a manner that fully complies with the PoLP. As shown in [24], the RMP can be regarded as an optimization problem. After creating an initial RBAC configuration through role mining, some employees will eventually change their area of responsibility and, as a result, request new permissions.

Existing literature on inter-domain role mapping [3,5] proposes two courses of action when there is no existing set of roles that exactly covers the requested permissions: One approach, based on *safety* (also called *least privilege*), assigns the user to a set of roles that only includes requested permissions, even if not all of the requested permissions can be assigned this way. Alternatively, the *availability* approach assigns the user a set of roles that includes all requested permissions, along with a minimized number of additional permissions.

3 Evaluation Criteria

In this section, we present evaluation criteria for measuring whether LLMs are suited for processing permission requests. Therefore, we first introduce the underlying assumptions and notations used. First, we let X be the set of unique requests sent to the LLM, and Y be the set of responses generated by the LLM. The black-box behavior of the LLM can then be modeled as a function $f : X \times \mathbb{N}_{\max} \rightarrow Y$, where $\mathbb{N}_{\max}$ is a bounded subset of natural numbers representing the maximum iteration count of sending the same request to an LLM. A permission request $x_i \in X$, where $i \in \{1, \ldots, |X|\}$, is a human request, while a response $y_{i,n} \in Y$ represents a concrete user management suggestion, where $n \in \mathbb{N}_{\max}$. We assume that each request $x_i \in X$ asks only for a single permission.

Next, we define the permissions $P = P_{real} \cup P_{hall}$, where P_{real} represents the permissions existing in an enterprise RBAC document and P_{hall} refers to the permissions hallucinated by an LLM. Similarly, we define the roles $R = R_{real} \cup R_{hall}$, where R_{real} represents the roles available in an enterprise RBAC document and R_{hall} refers to the roles hallucinated by an LLM.

We assume that each response $y_{i,n} \in Y$ includes at most one permission $p \in P$, which is modeled by the function $response\_permission : Y \rightarrow P \cup \{None\}$. Also, we assume that each $y_{i,n} \in Y$ suggests granting at most one role $r \in R$, modeled by the function $response\_role : Y \rightarrow R \cup \{None\}$. We use the function $correct\_permission : X \rightarrow P_{real}$ to model the correct translation from $x_i \in X$ to a permission $p \in P_{real}$. We assume that PA only assigns real permissions to real roles and for each $p \in P_{real}$, there is a role $r \in R_{real}$ such that $(p, r) \in PA$. Lastly, we define $Permissions(r)$ as the set of permissions $P_r \subseteq P_{real}$ assigned to a role through PA if $r \in R_{real}$, else $Permissions(r) = \varnothing$.

Accuracy. We define *Permission Accuracy* (PAcc) as the fraction of permission translations that match the correct permissions across all unique requests and iterations. We define *Role Accuracy* (RAcc) as the fraction of role suggestions in which the suggested role contains the correct permission. Below, we present formal calculations of both metrics:

- $\text{PAcc} = \frac{1}{\mathbb{N}_{\max} \cdot |X|} \sum_{i=1}^{|X|} \sum_{n=1}^{\mathbb{N}_{\max}} 1_{\{response\_permission(y_{i,n}) = correct\_permission(x_i)\}}$

- $\text{RAcc} = \frac{1}{\mathbb{N}_{\max}\cdot|X|}\sum_{i=1}^{|X|}\sum_{n=1}^{\mathbb{N}_{\max}} 1_{\{(correct\_permission(x_i),response\_role(y_{i,n}))\in PA\}}$

Precision. As already investigated by other research projects, e.g. [25,26], LLMs can show non-deterministic behavior. As suggested by Song et al. [27], non-determinism should be taken into account when evaluating LLMs. We thus introduce the two metrics *Permission Precision* (PPrec) and *Role Precision* (RPrec). For each request, these metrics calculate the most frequent permission translation and role suggestion across all iterations and then normalize the number of occurrences. Then, across all unique requests, the averages are calculated. The two metrics can be formalized as shown below:

- $\text{PPrec} = \frac{1}{|X|}\sum_{i=1}^{|X|}\frac{1}{\mathbb{N}_{\max}}\max_{p_a}\left(\sum_{n=1}^{\mathbb{N}_{\max}} 1_{\{response\_permission(y_{i,n})=p_a\}}\right)$
- $\text{RPrec} = \frac{1}{|X|}\sum_{i=1}^{|X|}\frac{1}{\mathbb{N}_{\max}}\max_{r_b}\left(\sum_{n=1}^{\mathbb{N}_{\max}} 1_{\{response\_role(y_{i,n})=r_b\}}\right)$

Hallucination. LLMs can create fictitious contents which is generally referred to as hallucination [28]. We define the *Permission Hallucination* (PHall) and the *Role Hallucination* (RHall) as the fractions of suggested permissions and roles that do not exist. Formally, the two metrics can be described by the formulas:

- $\text{PHall} = \frac{1}{\mathbb{N}_{\max}\cdot|X|}\sum_{i=1}^{|X|}\sum_{n=1}^{\mathbb{N}_{\max}} 1_{\{response\_permission(y_{i,n})\notin P_{Real}\}}$
- $\text{RHall} = \frac{1}{\mathbb{N}_{\max}\cdot|X|}\sum_{i=1}^{|X|}\sum_{n=1}^{\mathbb{N}_{\max}} 1_{\{response\_role(y_{i,n})\notin R_{Real}\}}$

Modesty. It may happen that an LLM admits to not know the correct answer. Because of this, we introduce the *Permission Modesty* (PMod) and the *Role Modesty* (RMod) as the fractions of responses in which the LLM does not provide a concrete permission or role suggestion. We model such a behavior by assigning the permission translation or the role suggestion the value *None*. More formally, we describe the two metrics by the following formulas:

- $\text{PMod} = \frac{1}{\mathbb{N}_{\max}\cdot|X|}\sum_{i=1}^{|X|}\sum_{n=1}^{\mathbb{N}_{\max}} 1_{\{response\_permission(y_{i,n})=None\}}$
- $\text{RMod} = \frac{1}{\mathbb{N}_{\max}\cdot|X|}\sum_{i=1}^{|X|}\sum_{n=1}^{\mathbb{N}_{\max}} 1_{\{response\_role(y_{i,n})=None\}}$

Principle of Least Privilege. Let us first define the *smallest role cardinality* (src): Based on a given request x_i, this function searches for the size of a role that (1) includes the correct permission and (2) has the smallest cardinality of all roles that include this permission. Formally, this can be expressed via:

- $\text{src}(x_i) = \min_{r\in R_{real},\, correct\_permission(x_i)\in \text{Permissions}(r)} |\text{Permissions}(r)|$

We define the *PoLP Violation* (PoLPV) as the fraction of additionally assigned (non-required) permissions, compared to an optimal solution, across all the role-accurate responses of an LLM. We formalize this metric as shown below:

$$-\text{PoLPV} = \frac{\sum_{i=1}^{|X|}\sum_{n=1}^{\mathbb{N}_{\max}}\left((|Permissions(response\_role(y_{i,n}))|-1)\cdot 1_{\{(correct\_permission(x_i),response\_role(y_{i,n}))\in PA\}}\right)}{\epsilon+\sum_{i=1}^{|X|}\sum_{n=1}^{\mathbb{N}_{\max}}\left((\text{src}(x_i)-1)\cdot 1_{\{(correct\_permission(x_i),response\_role(y_{i,n}))\in PA\}}\right)}$$

Adding some small value $\epsilon > 0$ in the denominator prevents a division through zero, which would occur if there were no role-accurate suggestions or if for all role-accurate suggestions, the smallest role contains only one permission. If this is not true, we set $\epsilon = 0$. Referring to Subsect. 2.2, this metric leans towards availability. However, in Sect. 4, we rather hope that the LLM suggests a role with as few non-required permissions as possible. In half of the experiments from Sect. 5, we indeed algorithmically minimize the additional permissions.

4 LLM-Only Experiments

In this section, we conduct quantitative research to assess if LLMs alone are suited for permission request processing. First, Subsect. 4.1 describes the implementation of our experiments, followed by the associated results in Subsect. 4.2. Finally, in Subsect. 4.3, we briefly discuss our findings.

4.1 Implementation

In this subsection, we present the implementation of our pipeline for solely using LLMs in permission request processing (edge *(a)* in Fig. 1). First, we describe the data requirements, and then the data that we use in our experiments. Next, we explain our data preprocessing steps. We break this procedure down into two parts: First, we explain how we generate the used enterprise documents, representing the used RBAC structures, and then we show how to create the permission requests. Afterwards, we explain our approach to prompt engineering. Finally, we detail our technical setup and propose our research design.

Data Requirements. The data used in our (or future) experiments must meet certain conditions: First, it must include the names of the technical roles R, the names of the permissions P and a role-to-permission assignment PA. Also, there must be some amount of requests, each asking for a specific permission $p \in P$. The number of requests should be sufficiently large to allow a quantitative evaluation of LLM-based permission translations and role suggestions.

If no requests from real employees are available, we suggest to use data sets also containing permission descriptions. As shown later in this subsection, permission descriptions can be used to generate permission requests. We prefer this (more neutral) approach over creating purely synthetic requests based on the permission names, as the latter option may introduce biases in wordings.

Data Used. We found two RBAC documentations that fulfill our data requirements, namely the *Microsoft Entra built-in roles* [29] and the *Azure built-in roles* [30]. The Entra built-in roles were found in a © Microsoft GitHub repository licensed under the MIT license[1]. The Azure built-in roles were found in a

[1] https://github.com/MicrosoftDocs/entra-docs/blob/main/LICENSE.

© Microsoft GitHub repository licensed under the Creative Commons Attribution 4.0 International license[2]. We retrieved both documentations on April 17, 2025. Both documentations were modified during our data preprocessing steps.

The Microsoft Entra built-in roles consist of a total of 111 roles. Overall, there are 1552 role-to-permission assignments and on average, each role includes 13.98 permissions. Based on the role-to-permission assignments, we found 563 unique permissions, of which 562 include a description.

The Microsoft Azure built-in roles contain a total of 431 roles, categorized into 19 service domains. The permissions assigned to the Microsoft Azure built-in roles are subdivided into *Actions*, *NotActions*, *DataActions* and *NotDataActions*. In this research paper, we chose to work with the Storage domain. We exclude an outlier role that is assigned *NotActions* to deny specific operations, even if they are covered by a wildcard permission. Then, we use a total of 35 roles that are only assigned *Actions* or *DataActions*. There are 457 role-to-permission assignments, and on average, a role includes 13.06 permissions. Based on the used role-to-permission assignments in the Azure Storage domain, we found 231 unique permissions, of which 202 include a description. The reason behind choosing the Storage domain is that it can be considered a large access control environment, but it contains significantly fewer roles and permissions compared to the Entra data, which allows us to additionally compare different data set sizes.

Data Preprocessing: Creating Enterprise Documents. From each used data source, we created a single JSON structure that captures the role-to-permission assignments from the respective built-in roles. Referring to Subsect. 2.1, these documents represent a permission assignment relation *PA* and capture the names of all roles *R* and permissions *P*, but not the permission descriptions. From now on, we refer to these JSON structures as *Enterprise Documents* (EDs), as they represent real-life enterprise RBAC environments.

We do not differentiate between any types of permissions (such as *Actions* or *DataActions*) but refer to all instances simply as permissions. Figure 3 shows an exemplary snippet of a small role in the ED created from the Azure data set.

```
[
    ...
    {
        "role": "Classic Storage Account Key Operator Service Role",
        "permissions": [
            "Microsoft.ClassicStorage/storageAccounts/listkeys/action",
            "Microsoft.ClassicStorage/storageAccounts/regeneratekey/action"
        ]
    },
    ...
]
```

Fig. 3. An example of a small role with two assigned permissions.

[2] https://github.com/MicrosoftDocs/azure-docs/blob/main/LICENSE.

Data Preprocessing: Creating Permission Requests. Next, from each data source, we created a list of permission requests. These requests were generated by processing the permission descriptions. First, considering all descriptions, we added a punctuation mark (period) at the end of each sentence, if one was not already present. Next, we replaced each quotation mark (") with backticks (“).

We observed that a few descriptions included an annotation, indicating that the associated permission is deprecated, and removed such annotations from the descriptions. We removed descriptions stating that a permission is an internal operation, which, to our understanding, means that it is not used by users. We also removed a few outliers that consisted of more than one sentence, as transforming these descriptions resulted in requests not sounding coherent.

In the Entra documentation, nearly all descriptions start with a verb in the imperative form. There are only few exceptions that begin with “Can”, followed by a verb in imperative form (e.g. “Can perform ...”). From these descriptions, we removed “Can”, so that all descriptions in the Entra documentation then started with a verb in imperative form.

After creating a unique list of descriptions, we noticed that the list length was not equal to the number of unique permissions. The reason therefore was that there are identical descriptions that describe multiple, different permissions. After transforming such descriptions to permission requests, the requests would be identical, but the LLM was supposed to translate them to different technical permission names. This is trivially not possible. Thus, we removed these entries.

Finally, we decapitalized the first letter of each description and added “*I need to* ” at the beginning of a sentence. Then, we put the whole phrase in quotation marks. After applying all rules, for example, the permission description “*Query tables*” was transformed into the permission request *"I need to query tables."*

By applying our data transformation steps, many of the original descriptions from the Azure Storage documentation were converted into requests with grammatical errors. Mostly, such issues resulted from descriptions not starting with a verb in imperative form, but with a verb in the third person singular. For example, one description was transformed into the request *"I need to creates a Backup Instance."* We manually corrected these errors and also fixed other incorrect sentence structures resulting from our data processing steps. Thereby, we created a very small number of duplicated requests, which we removed.

By applying the described data preprocessing steps, we created 546 unique permission requests from the Entra documentation and 173 unique permission requests from the Azure Storage documentation. Finally, from each list, we generated a random sample of 100 requests, which we then used in our experiments.

Prompt Engineering. While the permission requests are user prompts sent to the LLM, the EDs are (in half of the experiments) provided as embedded context. In a real-life business scenario, an RBAC structure can of course change: For example, there could be new roles, modifications to roles or role deletions. In such cases, the ED can simply be adjusted and the embedding can be regenerated.

Next, we designed a system prompt guiding an LLM to translate a request into a permission name and to suggest a role that contains this permission. Each output line should correspond to the following format: `<User Request>;<Permission Name>;<Role Name>`. If the model cannot determine which role has the smallest cardinality, it is instructed to recommend any role that contains the required permission. Also, our system prompt specifies that the LLM should output `NONE` instead of a permission or role name if it does not know the correct answer. Finally, we also provide an exemplary user prompt as well as an exemplary output. We slightly adjust the system prompt depending on the data source the sent permissions are based on (Azure or Entra data set), and depending on whether an ED is supplied to the LLM or not.

Technical Setup and Research Design. Table 1 details our experiment setups, referenced as $E_1 - E_8$. In all of our experiments, we set the frequency penalty, the presence penalty, and the temperature to 0. Also, we set the top p (nucleas sampling) value to 1, and the maximum token limit to 16384 (maximum). We always sent each request individually, reset the chat, and repeated processing this request for $\mathbb{N}_{\max} = 5$ times before moving on to the next request.

We chose to use two different LLMs, namely Mistral Large 2 [31] and Mistral Small 3.1 [32]. We opted for Mistral Large 2 because, according to the referenced documentation, its results are comparable to the performance of GPT-4o. At the time of writing this article, GPT-4o was the default model available to free users of ChatGPT, until reaching usage limits [33]. Thus, evaluating Mistral Large 2 is comparable to an everyday possible business scenario, in which an employee would simply log in to ChatGPT, using it for processing their permission requests. While Mistral Large 2 uses 123 billion parameters, Mistral Small 3.1 "only" uses 24 billion parameters.

In half of our experiments, we used the permission requests based on the Azure Storage documentation as user prompts, while in the other half, we used the requests based on the Entra documentation. In half of our experiments, we provided an LLM with a vectorized, embedded text document that contains the JSON-structured ED corresponding to the sent permission requests. We used the granite-embedding-278 m-multilingual model [34] as an embedding model with a chunk size of 5000 tokens and an overlap of 200 tokens. We chose chunk sizes of 5000 tokens after two test runs of E_1 using 700 and 2000 tokens. The LLM then showed high RMod values of 0.56 and 0.36, often not suggesting any role. We assume that this was due to smaller chunk sizes fragmenting the role structures.

4.2 Results

Before applying the evaluation metrics from Sect. 3 to the outcomes, we slightly changed the output of one experiment: In experiment E_8, one request was always translated to multiple permissions, thereby violating the instructions provided in the system prompt. In this case, we set the translated permission to `NONE`.

We consider the permission translation as permission-accurate if the permission request is translated to the permission belonging to the description from

Table 1. Overview of the LLM-only experiments.

Experiment	LLM	Enterprise Document			Permission Requests		
		Original Source	$\|R\|$	$\|P\|$	Original Source	|Requests|	$\mathbb{N}_{max}$
E_1	Mistral Large 2	Azure Storage Docs	35	231	Azure Storage Docs	100	5
E_2	Mistral Small 3.1	Azure Storage Docs	35	231	Azure Storage Docs	100	5
E_3	Mistral Large 2	-	-	-	Azure Storage Docs	100	5
E_4	Mistral Small 3.1	-	-	-	Azure Storage Docs	100	5
E_5	Mistral Large 2	Entra Docs	111	563	Entra Docs	100	5
E_6	Mistral Small 3.1	Entra Docs	111	563	Entra Docs	100	5
E_7	Mistral Large 2	-	-	-	Entra Docs	100	5
E_8	Mistral Small 3.1	-	-	-	Entra Docs	100	5

which the request originates. In all experiments, we used the ED that corresponds to the sent requests as the ground truth for (1) determining whether a role suggestion is role-accurate, (2) determining whether a proposed permission or role is hallucinated, and (3) calculating the PoLPV values. During evaluation, we did not consider any capitalization in an answer. Table 2 summarizes our results.

Table 2. Overview of LLM-only experiment results. Values that have been rounded down or rounded up are presented as $\lfloor < value > \rfloor$ or $\lceil < value > \rceil$, respectively.

Experiment	Accuracy		Precision		Hallucination		Modesty		PoLP
	PAcc	RAcc	PPrec	RPrec	PHall	RHall	PMod	RMod	PoLPV
E_1	0.63	0.55	1.00	$\lceil 1.00 \rceil$	0.07	0.01	0.06	0.10	$\lfloor 1.06 \rfloor$
E_2	0.54	0.55	1.00	1.00	0.06	0.00	0.00	0.01	$\lfloor 1.07 \rfloor$
E_3	0.30	0.34	1.00	1.00	0.32	0.16	0.05	0.05	$\lfloor 1.07 \rfloor$
E_4	0.16	0.31	1.00	1.00	0.58	0.19	0.06	0.06	$\lfloor 1.10 \rfloor$
E_5	0.52	0.29	1.00	1.00	0.07	0.03	0.16	0.27	$\lceil 1.41 \rceil$
E_6	0.54	0.29	1.00	1.00	0.05	0.00	0.08	0.10	$\lceil 2.23 \rceil$
E_7	0.17	0.39	1.00	1.00	0.64	0.35	0.02	0.02	$\lfloor 2.08 \rfloor$
E_8	0.01	0.35	1.00	$\lceil 1.00 \rceil$	0.95	0.49	0.03	0.02	$\lfloor 1.56 \rfloor$

Accuracy. Providing an ED consistently results in better permission translations ($\text{PAcc}_{E_i} > \text{PAcc}_{E_{i+2}}$ for $i \in \{1, 2, 5, 6\}$). Also, when using an ED, the likelihood of successfully translating a request to the required permission is higher than the likelihood of suggesting a role that contains this permission ($\text{PAcc}_{E_i} > \text{RAcc}_{E_i}$ for $i \in \{1, 5, 6\}$) or similar ($\text{PAcc}_{E_2} \approx \text{RAcc}_{E_2}$).

Precision. Permission translations and role suggestions are highly consistent ($\text{PPrec}_{E_i} = 1$, $\text{RPrec}_{E_i} > 0.99$ for $i \in [1, 8]$) with the temperature set to 0.

Hallucination. In general, there are more permission hallucinations than role hallucinations ($\text{PHall}_{E_i} > \text{RHall}_{E_i}$ for $i \in [1, 8]$). When providing an ED, the probability of hallucinating permissions or roles is low ($\text{PHall}_{E_i} \leq 0.07$, $\text{RHall}_{E_i} \leq 0.03$ for $i \in \{1, 2, 5, 6\}$). When not providing an ED, we find that a larger model hallucinates less ($\text{PHall}_{E_i} < \text{PHall}_{E_{i+1}}$, $\text{RHall}_{E_i} < \text{RHall}_{E_{i+1}}$ for $i \in \{3, 7\}$).

Modesty. We mostly find low modesty scores ($\text{PMod}_{E_i} \leq 0.08$, $\text{RMod}_{E_i} \leq 0.10$ for $i \in [1, 8] \setminus \{5\}$). When providing an ED, larger models admit uncertainty more frequently ($\text{PMod}_{E_i} > \text{PMod}_{E_{i+1}}, \text{RMod}_{E_i} > \text{RMod}_{E_{i+1}}$ for $i \in \{1, 5\}$).

Principle of Least Privilege. When using the Azure data set, the PoLP is respected ($\text{PoLPV}_{E_i} < 1.11$ for $i \in [1, 4]$). However, this property does not hold when using the Entra data set ($1.40 < \text{PoLPV}_{E_i} < 2.23$ for $i \in [5, 8]$).

4.3 Discussion

When provided an ED, an LLM performs quite well when translating permission requests into the correct technical permissions. To put the found PAcc values into a proper context, it is important to note that each permission translation corresponds to a multi-class classification task with $|P|$ possible classes but only one correct class. To further illustrate this, a random guessing algorithm would translate a request correctly with probability $\frac{1}{|231|} \approx 0.0043$ for experiments using the Azure data, and $\frac{1}{|563|} \approx 0.0018$ for experiments using the Entra data.

However, our results also reveal two issues when using the LLM-only approach: First, in our experiments, an LLM struggles to understand the provided ED and is not able to perform a structured search for finding a suitable role. After all, from a human perspective, it does not make sense that the PAcc values are in three cases higher than the RAcc values in case an ED is available. If a permission request was translated to the correct permission, it is a rather trivial task to suggest a role that contains the found permission based on a known RBAC structure. Secondly, it is a problem that whether the PoLP is applied depends on the used data set, as a generalizable solution should not only follow this fundamental security principle in some cases, but in all.

5 Hybrid Experiments with Algorithmic Expansion

Addressing the issue highlighted at the end of the previous section, this section introduces a hybrid approach that uses the ED to algorithmically find the smallest role that contains the permission translated by an LLM. More precisely, Subsect. 5.1 presents our implementation and experiment setup, Subsect. 5.2 shows the corresponding results, and Subsect 5.3 briefly discusses the found results.

5.1 Implementation

In this subsection, we explain the implementation of our hybrid approach (see edge *(b)* in Fig. 1). First, we created a copy of the output files from all experiments using an ED (E_1, E_2, E_5, E_6), as the proposed role-search algorithm only works when an ED is available. Each output file shows a list of permission requests, along with the corresponding permission translations and role suggestions provided by an LLM. We then removed the role suggestions generated by an LLM but kept the LLM-based permission translations.

Algorithm 1. Returning a role containing the translated permission.

function FINDROLE($response\_permission, PA, POLP$)
    // Check if the translated permission is `NONE` or hallucinated.
    if $response\_permission =$ `NONE` $\vee \nexists r \ ((response\_permission, r) \in PA)$ **then**
        return `NONE`
    else
        // Fill a list of roles R with all roles that contain the translated permission.
        $R \leftarrow \{r \mid (response\_permission, r) \in PA\}$
        // Either sort list by ascending or by descending number of permissions.
        if $POLP =$ `True` **then**
            $R \leftarrow \text{sort}(R, \text{ascending by } |Permissions(r)|)$
        else
            $R \leftarrow \text{sort}(R, \text{descending by } |Permissions(r)|)$
        end if
        return $R[0]$
    end if
end function

Next, for each row, we applied Algorithm 1. This function receives the LLM-generated permission, referred to as $response\_permission$, as input and uses the enterprise access control structure defined in the respective ED (referenced as PA) to always return a role that contains the LLM-generated permission. Based on the boolean value $POLP$, the algorithm either returns the smallest role or the largest role containing the translated permission. Including the latter option allows a performance comparison, but for production environments, we strongly advise always generating the smallest possible roles. We did not consider the capitalization of the translated permission when searching for suitable roles.

Table 3. Overview of the hybrid experiments.

Experiment	LLM	Enterprise Document			Requests			POLP
		Source	$\lvert R\rvert$	$\lvert P\rvert$	Source	$\lvert$Requests$\rvert$	$\mathbb{N}_{max}$	
$E_{1H,MIN}$	Mistral Large 2	Azure Storage Docs	35	231	Azure Storage Docs	100	5	True
$E_{1H,MAX}$	Mistral Large 2	Azure Storage Docs	35	231	Azure Storage Docs	100	5	False
$E_{2H,MIN}$	Mistral Small 3.1	Azure Storage Docs	35	231	Azure Storage Docs	100	5	True
$E_{2H,MAX}$	Mistral Small 3.1	Azure Storage Docs	35	231	Azure Storage Docs	100	5	False
$E_{5H,MIN}$	Mistral Large 2	Entra Docs	111	563	Entra Docs	100	5	True
$E_{5H,MAX}$	Mistral Large 2	Entra Docs	111	563	Entra Docs	100	5	False
$E_{6H,MIN}$	Mistral Small 3.1	Entra Docs	111	563	Entra Docs	100	5	True
$E_{6H,MAX}$	Mistral Small 3.1	Entra Docs	111	563	Entra Docs	100	5	False

Table 3 summarizes the experiments based on this hybrid approach. While the last column indicates whether the smallest or largest role was searched for, all other columns were taken over from the original experiments (see Subsect. 4.1).

5.2 Results

We again applied our evaluation metrics as introduced in Sect. 3, now assessing the hybrid experiments. Table 4 shows the corresponding results.

Table 4. Overview of hybrid experiment results. Values that have been rounded down or rounded up are presented as $\lfloor< value >\rfloor$ or $\lceil< value >\rceil$, respectively.

Experiment	Accuracy		Precision		Hallucination		Modesty		PoLP
	PAcc	RAcc	PPrec	RPrec	PHall	RHall	PMod	RMod	PoLPV
$E_{1\text{H,MIN}}$	0.63	0.72	1.00	1.00	0.07	0.00	0.06	0.13	1.00
$E_{1\text{H,MAX}}$	0.63	0.74	1.00	1.00	0.07	0.00	0.06	0.13	$\lceil 1.38 \rceil$
$E_{2\text{H,MIN}}$	0.54	0.67	1.00	1.00	0.06	0.00	0.00	0.06	$\lceil 1.01 \rceil$
$E_{2\text{H,MAX}}$	0.54	0.71	1.00	1.00	0.06	0.00	0.00	0.06	$\lceil 1.40 \rceil$
$E_{5\text{H,MIN}}$	0.52	0.57	1.00	1.00	0.07	0.00	0.16	0.23	1.00
$E_{5\text{H,MAX}}$	0.52	0.59	1.00	1.00	0.07	0.00	0.16	0.23	$\lfloor 2.39 \rfloor$
$E_{6\text{H,MIN}}$	0.54	0.58	1.00	1.00	0.05	0.00	0.08	0.13	1.00
$E_{6\text{H,MAX}}$	0.54	0.65	1.00	1.00	0.05	0.00	0.08	0.13	$\lceil 2.39 \rceil$

Accuracy. Due to using Algorithm 1, the likelihood of suggesting a role containing the required permission is always higher than the likelihood of successfully translating a request to the required permission ($\text{RAcc}_{E_{i\text{H},j}} > \text{PAcc}_{E_{i\text{H},j}}$ for $i \in \{1, 2, 5, 6\}, j \in \{\text{MIN, MAX}\}$). Compared to suggesting the smallest role, suggesting the largest role shows a higher likelihood of suggesting an accurate role ($\text{RAcc}_{E_{i\text{H,MAX}}} > \text{RAcc}_{E_{i\text{H,MIN}}}$ for $i \in \{1, 2, 5, 6\}$). However, the difference in these likelihoods is rather small ($0.02 \leq \text{RAcc}_{E_{i\text{H,MAX}}} - \text{RAcc}_{E_{i\text{H,MIN}}} \leq 0.07$ for $i \in \{1, 2, 5, 6\}$). Compared to using the Entra data, using the Azure data always results in better role suggestions ($\text{RAcc}_{E_{i\text{H},j}} > \text{RAcc}_{E_{(i+4)\text{H},j}}$ for $i \in \{1, 2\}, j \in \{\text{MIN, MAX}\}$).

Precision. Due to using Algorithm 1, the role suggestions are now fully consistent ($\text{RPrec}_{E_{i\text{H},j}} = 1.00 \quad \text{for } i \in \{1, 2, 5, 6\}, j \in \{\text{MIN, MAX}\}$).

Hallucination. Due to using Algorithm 1, there can not be any role hallucinations ($\text{RHall}_{E_{i\text{H},j}} = 0.00 \quad \text{for } i \in \{1, 2, 5, 6\}, j \in \{\text{MIN, MAX}\}$).

Modesty. The acknowledged uncertainty when suggesting roles corresponds to the lines 2–4 of Algorithm 1 ($\text{RMod}_{E_{i\text{H},j}} = \text{PMod}_{E_{i\text{H},j}} + \text{PHall}_{E_{i\text{H},j}}$ for $i \in \{1, 2, 5, 6\}, j \in \{\text{MIN, MAX}\}$). When using a larger model, this admitted uncertainty is higher ($\text{RMod}_{E_{i\text{H},j}} > \text{RMod}_{E_{(i+1)\text{H},j}}$ for $i \in \{1, 5\}, j \in \{\text{MIN, MAX}\}$).

Principle of Least Privilege. When suggesting the smallest roles, the hybrid approach follows the PoLP ($\text{PoLPV}_{E_{i\text{H,MIN}}} < 1.01$ for $i \in \{1, 2, 5, 6\}$). Trivially, this is not the case when always suggesting the largest roles ($1.37 < \text{PoLPV}_{E_{i\text{H,MAX}}} < 2.40$ for $i \in \{1, 2, 5, 6\}$).

5.3 Discussion

Compared to the LLM-only approach, the hybrid approach, while configured to tightly follow the PoLP, increases the likelihood of making role-accurate suggestions ($\text{RAcc}_{E_{i\text{H,MIN}}} > \text{RAcc}_{E_i}$ for $i \in \{1, 2, 5, 6\}$). We therefore consider our hybrid approach superior to an LLM-only approach. As a required permission can be contained in more than one role, making a role suggestion corresponds to a multi-label classification task with $|R|$ possible labels and one or more correct labels. Consequently, it makes sense that using the Azure data set, with fewer roles and thus fewer possible targets, leads to a better performance.

Integrating a larger model into the hybrid approach does not necessarily result in better role suggestions ($\text{RAcc}_{E_{5\text{H},j}} < \text{RAcc}_{E_{6\text{H},j}}$ for $j \in \{\text{MIN}, \text{MAX}\}$), but it reduces the likelihood of making incorrect role suggestions ($\text{RMod}_{E_{i\text{H},j}} + \text{RAcc}_{E_{i\text{H},j}} > \text{RMod}_{E_{(i+1)\text{H},j}} + \text{RAcc}_{E_{(i+1)\text{H},j}}$ for $i \in \{1, 5\}, j \in \{\text{MIN}, \text{MAX}\}$). We consider this combination of metrics an important aspect, as reducing the probability of providing an administrator with wrong suggestions also reduces the probability of accidentally assigning inappropriate roles to users.

6 Limitations

In this work, we did only evaluate LLMs developed by Mistral AI but not any models created by other LLM providers. Also, we did neither evaluate the impact of fine-tuning nor the effects of using reasoning models such as Magistral [35].

Next, we did not investigate if using a different system prompt design would influence our results. For example, previous research [36,37] has already shown that the prompt design affects the performance of LLMs when creating and redesigning process models. In regards to our hybrid experiments, a system prompt that focuses on permission translations instead of also asking for role suggestions may be more suitable. Additionally, in the hybrid experiments, it would be interesting to assess an ED format that does not show the role structures but only a list of all available permissions.

Next, the used data sets include wildcard permissions. For example, the wildcard permission *Microsoft.Resources/deployments/** is actually a set of permissions such as *Microsoft.Resources/deployments/operations/read*. We neither taught an LLM about wildcard permissions nor accounted for hierarchical permission dependencies in our evaluation. Instead, we treated wildcard permissions as explicit permissions, as our work is an initial contribution on the topic of LLM-based permission management, focusing on more fundamental concepts.

Integrating wildcard permissions into our evaluation would affect both the PoLPV scores (as a wildcard permission must be weighted according to the number of contained permissions) and the accuracy metrics. To illustrate the impact on accuracy, assume a permission p covered by a wildcard permission p_w. If p is required but the LLM translates the request to p_w, our current evaluation does not treat this translation as permission-accurate. Similarly, if a role is suggested that includes p_w but not p, the suggestion is not considered role-accurate under our current evaluation. We measured how much a corresponding change in our evaluation metrics would impact the accuracy and, regarding the LLM-only experiments, found an average increase in PAcc of 0.01375. Across all experiments, we observed an average increase in RAcc of 0.038125. However, it remains unclear whether these values would change if the LLMs were explicitly informed about the logic underlying wildcard permissions.

Lastly, our system prompts explicitly instructed the LLMs to only return permissions and roles that are defined within the used set of built-in roles. However, it remains possible that the LLMs returned other roles or permissions that exist in the broader Microsoft cloud platform but are not listed within the used set of built-in roles. These instances were still classified as hallucinations.

7 Conclusion and Plans for Future Work

In this paper, we introduced a novel approach for evaluating the reliability of LLMs in RBAC authorization processes. We find that embedding an RBAC document significantly improves the performance of an LLM when it comes to translating a permission request into the required permission name. However, even if an RBAC document is embedded, an LLM struggles to suggest a suitable role. We created a hybrid approach that algorithmically searches for a role that contains the translated permission. This approach significantly boosts performance when suggesting roles and adheres closely to the PoLP when always returning the smallest role that contains the translated permission. Integrating a larger model into this hybrid approach lowers the risk of giving wrong role suggestions, as the mechanism more frequently admits uncertainty.

In the future, we plan to add an organizational model (UA relation in the RBAC model) to our experiments. This would allow an LLM to identify permissions already assigned to the requesting user. Thereby, after receiving a request, the LLM could already exclude some permissions from further consideration. Also, this would allow us to apply the PoLP more practically by returning the role with the fewest unassigned permissions rather than just the smallest role. Next, as RBAC research also considers multi-domain environments [38], we aim to analyze the influence on performance when querying an LLM about permissions from many different domains. Lastly, we aim to further improve the accuracy of role suggestions by applying a top-k approach. Instead of advising an LLM to translate a request to a single permission, we plan to retrieve the top-k most likely permission candidates. We can then assess whether any existing role sufficiently covers those candidates and evaluate the impact on performance.

Acknowledgments. This research is part of a project funded by the SAP SE University Alliances Program, which aims to investigate Very Large Business Applications

(VLBA). We would like to express our gratitude to the anonymous reviewers, as well as to Nataliia Klievtsova, Florian Eckhard, and Noah Kim, for their valuable feedback on this work. Additionally, we appreciate the support provided by IBM Deutschland Research & Development, which made this research possible by granting us access to the IBM watsonx platform.

Disclosure of Interests. The authors have no competing interests to declare that are relevant to the content of this article.

Data and Code Repository. We created a public GitHub repository (https://github.com/maxniedermeier/LLMs4PRP) that contains the used Python scripts, the preprocessed data sets, and the system prompts.

References

1. Sandhu, R.: Role-based access control. Adv. Comput. **46**, 237–286 (1998). https://doi.org/10.1016/S0065-2458(08)60206-5
2. Du, S., Joshi, J. B.: Supporting authorization query and inter-domain role mapping in presence of hybrid role hierarchy. In: Proceedings of the 11th ACM Symposium on Access Control Models and Technologies, pp. 228–236. ACM, Lake Tahoe (2006). https://doi.org/10.1145/1133058.1133090
3. Chen, L., Crampton, J.: Inter-domain role mapping and least privilege. In: Proceedings of the 12th ACM Symposium on Access Control Models and Technologies, pp. 157–162. ACM, Sophia Antipolis (2007). https://doi.org/10.1145/1266840.1266866
4. Tang, Z., Li, R., Lu, Z.: A request-driven role mapping for secure interoperation in multi-domain environment. In: 2007 IFIP International Conference on Network and Parallel Computing Workshops, pp. 83–90. IEEE, Dalian (2007). https://doi.org/10.1109/NPC.2007.33
5. Zhang, Y., Joshi, J. B.: UAQ: a framework for user authorization query processing in RBAC extended with hybrid hierarchy and constraints. In: Proceedings of the 13th ACM Symposium on Access Control Models and Technologies, pp. 83–92. ACM, Estes Park (2008). https://doi.org/10.1145/1377836.1377850
6. Zhang, L., et al.: ACFix: guiding LLMs with mined common RBAC practices for context-aware repair of access control vulnerabilities in smart contracts. IEEE Trans. Software Eng. **51**(9), 2512–2532 (2025). https://doi.org/10.1109/TSE.2025.3590108
7. Lawal, S., Zhao, X., Rios, A., Krishnan, R., Ferraiolo, D.: Translating natural language specifications into access control policies by leveraging large language models. In: 2024 IEEE 6th International Conference on Trust, Privacy and Security in Intelligent Systems, and Applications, pp. 361–370. IEEE, Washington, D.C. (2024). https://doi.org/10.1109/TPS-ISA62245.2024.00048
8. Yang, M., Atluri, V., Sural, S., Kundu, A.: Extraction of machine enforceable ABAC policies from natural language text using LLM knowledge distillation. In: Proceedings of the 30th ACM Symposium on Access Control Models and Technologies, pp. 157–168. ACM, Stony Brook (2025). https://doi.org/10.1145/3734436.3734447
9. Vatsa, A., Patel, P., Eiers, W.: Synthesizing access control policies using large language models. In: 2025 IEEE/ACM International Workshop on Natural Language-Based Software Engineering (NLBSE), pp. 13–16. IEEE, Ottawa (2025). https://doi.org/10.1109/NLBSE66842.2025.00008

10. Little, A., Best, P.J.: A framework for separation of duties in an SAP R/3 environment. Manag. Audit. J. **18**(5), 419–430 (2003). https://doi.org/10.1108/02686900310476882
11. Anderer, S., Schrader, F., Scheuermann, B., Mostaghim, S.: Evolutionary algorithms for the constrained two-level role mining problem. In: Pérez Cáceres, L., Verel, S. (eds.) Evolutionary Computation in Combinatorial Optimization, LNCS, vol. 13222, pp. 79–94. Springer, Cham (2022). https://doi.org/10.1007/978-3-031-04148-8_6
12. Anderer, S., Scheuermann, B., Mostaghim, S.: Studies on multi-objective role mining in ERP Systems. In: Stützle, T., Wagner, M. (eds.) Evolutionary Computation in Combinatorial Optimization, LNCS, vol. 14632, pp. 81–96. Springer, Cham (2024). https://doi.org/10.1007/978-3-031-57712-3_6
13. Reid, J., Cheong, I., Henricksen, M., Smit, J.: A novel use of RBAC to protect privacy in distributed health care information systems. In: Safavi-Naini, R., Seberry, J. (eds.) Australasian Conference on Information Security and Privacy, LNCS, vol. 2727, pp. 403–415. Springer, Heidelberg (2003). https://doi.org/10.1007/3-540-45067-X_35
14. Santos-Pereira, C., Augusto, A.B., Cruz-Correia, R., Correia, M. E.: A secure RBAC mobile agent access control model for healthcare institutions. In: Proceedings of the 26th IEEE International Symposium on Computer-Based Medical Systems, pp. 349–354. IEEE, Porto (2013). https://doi.org/10.1109/CBMS.2013.6627814
15. Shin, M.S., Jeon, H.S., Ju, Y.W., Lee, B.J., Jeong, S.P.: Constructing RBAC based security model in u-healthcare service platform. Sci. World J. **2015**, 937914 (2015). https://doi.org/10.1155/2015/937914
16. Li, W., Wan, H., Ren, X., Li, S.: A refined RBAC model for cloud computing. In: 2012 IEEE/ACIS 11th International Conference on Computer and Information Science, pp. 43–48. IEEE, Shanghai (2012). https://doi.org/10.1109/ICIS.2012.13
17. Tang, Z., Wei, J., Sallam, A., Li, K., Li, R.: A new RBAC based access control model for cloud computing. In: Li, R., Cao, J., Bourgeois, J. (eds.) Advances in Grid and Pervasive Computing: 7th International Conference, LNCS, vol. 7296, pp. 279–288. Springer, Heidelberg (2012). https://doi.org/10.1007/978-3-642-30767-6_24
18. Tang, B., Li, Q., Sandhu, R.: A multi-tenant RBAC model for collaborative cloud services. In: 2013 Eleventh Annual Conference on Privacy, Security and Trust, pp. 229–238. IEEE, Tarragona (2013). https://doi.org/10.1109/PST.2013.6596058
19. Ferraiolo, D.F., Sandhu, R., Gavrila, S., Kuhn, D.R., Chandramouli, R.: Proposed NIST standard for role-based access control. ACM Trans. Inf. Syst. Secur. **4**(3), 224–274 (2001). https://doi.org/10.1145/501978.501980
20. Saltzer, J.H., Schroeder, M.D.: The protection of information in computer systems. Proc. IEEE **63**(9), 1278–1308 (1975). https://doi.org/10.1109/PROC.1975.9939
21. Vayyavur, R.: Effective application security governance with role provisioning and least privileged access management. J. Artif. Intell. Mach. Learn. Data Sci. **1**(4), 1089–1093 (2023). https://doi.org/10.51219/JAIMLD/raj-vayyavur/258
22. Kuhlmann, M., Shohat, D., Schimpf, G.: Role mining - revealing business roles for security administration using data mining technology. In: Proceedings of the Eighth ACM Symposium on Access control Models and Technologies, pp. 179–186. ACM, Como (2003). https://doi.org/10.1145/775412.775435
23. Vaidya, J., Atluri, V., Guo, Q.: The role mining problem: finding a minimal descriptive set of roles. In: Proceedings of the 12th ACM Symposium on Access control

Models and Technologies, pp. 175–184. ACM, Sophia Antipolis (2007). https://doi.org/10.1145/1266840.1266870
24. Lu, H., Vaidya, J., Atluri, V.: Optimal boolean matrix decomposition: application to role engineering. In: 24th International Conference on Data Engineering, pp. 297–306. IEEE, Cancun (2008). https://doi.org/10.1109/ICDE.2008.4497438
25. Astekin, M., Hort, M., Moonen, L.: An exploratory study on how non-determinism in large language models affects log parsing. In: Proceedings of the ACM/IEEE 2nd International Workshop on Interpretability, Robustness, and Benchmarking in Neural Software Engineering, pp. 13–18. ACM, Lisbon (2024). https://doi.org/10.1145/3643661.3643952
26. Ouyang, S., Zhang, J.M., Harman, M., Wang, M.: An empirical study of the non-determinism of ChatGPT in code generation. ACM Trans. Softw. Eng. Methodol. **34**(2), 1–28 (2025). https://doi.org/10.1145/3697010
27. Song, Y., Wang, G., Li, S., Lin, B. Y.: The good, the bad, and the greedy: evaluation of LLMs should not ignore non-determinism. https://doi.org/10.48550/arXiv.2407.10457
28. Perković, G., Drobnjak, A., Botički, I.: Hallucinations in LLMs: understanding and Addressing Challenges. In: 2024 47th MIPRO ICT and Electronics Convention, pp. 2084–2088. IEEE, Opatija (2024). https://doi.org/10.1109/MIPRO60963.2024.10569238
29. Microsoft Entra built-in roles. https://github.com/MicrosoftDocs/entra-docs/blob/main/docs/identity/role-based-access-control/permissions-reference.md. Accessed 17 Apr 2025
30. Azure built-in roles. https://github.com/MicrosoftDocs/azure-docs/tree/main/articles/role-based-access-control/built-in-roles. Accessed 17 Apr 2025
31. Large enough. https://mistral.ai/news/mistral-large-2407. Accessed 23 May 2025
32. Mistral Small 3.1. https://mistral.ai/news/mistral-small-3-1. Accessed 2 May 2025
33. ChatGPT - Release notes. https://help.openai.com/en/articles/6825453-chatgpt-release-notes. Accessed 23 May 2025
34. Granite Embedding 278m Multilingual model card. https://www.ibm.com/docs/en/watsonx/saas?topic=models-granite-embedding-278m-multilingual-model-card. Accessed 24 Apr 2025
35. Magistral. https://mistral.ai/news/magistral. Accessed 21 Sep 2025
36. Klievtsova, N., Mangler, J., Kampik, T., Benzin, J. V., Rinderle-Ma, S.: How can generative AI empower domain experts in creating process models? In: Wirtschaftsinformatik 2024 Proceedings, 66. AIS, Würzburg (2024)
37. Klievtsova, N., Kampik, T., Mangler, J., Rinderle-Ma, S.: Conversationally actionable process model creation. In: Comuzzi, M., Grigori, D., Sellami, M., Zhou, Z. (eds.) Cooperative Information Systems, LNCS, vol. 15506, pp. 39—55. Springer, Cham (2024). https://doi.org/10.1007/978-3-031-81375-7_3
38. Niedermeier, M., Wittges, H.: Towards role mappings in hybrid cloud environments: a systematic literature review. In: Borbinha, J., Prince Sales, T., Da Silva, M.M., Proper, H.A., Schnellmann, M. (eds.) Enterprise Design, Operations, and Computing, LNCS, vol. 15409, pp. 119–139. Springer, Cham (2025). https://doi.org/10.1007/978-3-031-78338-8_7

Consumer-Centered Selection of Relevant Clinical Trials Using Agent AI

Marcos Burgos[1(✉)] and Zoran Milosevic[2,3]

[1] Independent Researcher, Brisbane, Australia
burgossaavedra.marcos@gmail.com
[2] Deontik, Queensland, Australia
zoran@deontik.com
[3] School of Computer Science and Engineering, UNSW Sydney, Sydney, Australia

Abstract. Current clinical trial matching solutions lack practical, consumer-accessible tools that enable independent trial discovery. This paper presents a solution that makes use of HL7 FHIR standard, and several AI Agents that empower consumers to independently identify relevant clinical trials using their personal health information. The system employs four specialized agents using HL7 FHIR data: (1) extracting medical conditions from consumer records; (2) pre-filtering trials using vector embeddings; (3) structuring unstructured eligibility criteria; and (4) evaluating patient eligibility against trial requirements. The framework generates relevance scores and provides ranked trial recommendations within 5-10 min, which would typically require days of manual effort. Integrated into a web-based platform, this AI-driven approach enables consumers or patients to directly discover pertinent clinical trials without clinical staff intervention, significantly improving access to potentially life-saving research opportunities.

Keywords: FHIR · Clinical Trial · LLM Agent · Healthcare

1 Introduction and Background

Clinical trials are a cornerstone of medical research, providing critical data for clinicians and researchers while offering to consumers and patients access to potentially life-changing treatments. Despite their importance, the recruitment process for clinical trials remains a significant challenge. A primary bottleneck lies in matching eligible patients with suitable trials, largely due to the complex and unstructured nature of eligibility criteria. Currently, trial listings on platforms such as ClinicalTrials.gov rely on manual inspection of inclusion and exclusion criteria, which are typically written in free text and lack standardization. Although filters like age, sex, condition keywords, and location exist, they do not account for nuanced eligibility requirements that must still be interpreted manually.

This limitation is a significant contributor to recruitment inefficiencies. Almost 20% of clinical trials fail before reaching the testing phase due to insufficient enrollment of participants, and only 31% achieve their enrollment goals [1].

© The Author(s), under exclusive license to Springer Nature Switzerland AG 2026
A. Gianola et al. (Eds.): EDOC 2025, LNCS 16213, pp. 321–336, 2026.
https://doi.org/10.1007/978-3-032-15140-7_18

In addition, studies have shown a correlation between the linguistic complexity of eligibility criteria and trial failure rates, as potential participants often struggle to interpret the medical terminology involved [2]. This disproportionately affects niche trials, which are especially vulnerable to failure due to poor recruitment. The time required to screen and eliminate non-eligible participants can consume up to 30% of the overall development timeline, leading to delays of one to six months. Alarmingly, 37% of the clinical research sites do not enroll and 11% do not recruit participants at all [3].

To address this challenge, this paper presents an AI-Agent[1] architecture integrated into an existing web-based platform, developed as part of a digital health project at the University of Queensland [19]. The platform is designed to simplify the clinical trial matching process by transforming unstructured eligibility criteria into a structured format and filtering trials based on patient-provided health data. By doing so, it reduces the cognitive and technical burden on end users, particularly those unfamiliar with medical terminology, by presenting a curated list of trials for which the patient is likely eligible. The application features a user-friendly, jargon-free interface and incorporates intelligent filtering mechanisms aimed at improving recruitment efficiency and accelerating clinical research timelines [4]. As a final result, the web platform then directs patients to the corresponding clinical trial page on ClinicalTrials.gov, where they are required to contact the responsible professionals associated with the trial for further engagement.

The web platform accesses clients' electronic health records through SMART on FHIR, a secure and standardized framework that ensures interoperability across healthcare systems [18]. FHIR (Fast Healthcare Interoperability Resources) is an HL7 standard that uses modern web technologies to structure and exchange clinical, administrative, and financial data [17]. Building on this, SMART on FHIR provides secure authentication and authorization (using OAuth2.0), enabling third-party applications to safely and appropriately access patient records while protecting privacy.

The web platform follows a modular architecture divided into six distinct stages, enabling independent development and future scalability. The process begins with retrieving synthetic patient information from the EPIC sandbox using the HL7 FHIR standard [16], where key details such as name, age, sex, and conditions are extracted and cached in JSON format to enhance performance. Using the patient's demographic information, the platform then queries the ClinicalTrials.gov API to retrieve a list of recruiting or enrolling trials, storing their unique identifier, referred to as NCT ID. Each trial's ID is used to identify the clinical trial, which is then processed through the Computable Publishing API [15] to obtain a FHIR-formatted version, from which inclusion and exclusion criteria are extracted. In the scoring module, the platform compares patient data to trial criteria using Term Frequency—Inverse Document Frequency (TF-IDF)

[1] The architecture makes use of the features which characterize an agent, i.e. autonomy, goal-oriented, environmental perception, learning and adaptation, reasoning and planning, but not all of these features are exploited as part of our agent design.

and cosine similarity, ranking trials by relevance; although BERT was evaluated for its contextual capabilities, TF-IDF was selected due to its efficiency. Additionally, a separate Node.js-based pipeline preprocesses updated clinical trials by structuring eligibility information using the Gemini 1.5 Flash LLM, converting text into a JSON format optimized for accurate matching with patient data [4].

This approach leverages TF-IDF, a statistical measure widely used in Natural Language Processing (NLP) and Information Retrieval to evaluate the importance of a word in a document relative to a collection or corpus of documents. While TF-IDF is effective in identifying significant terms based on their frequency, it lacks the ability to understand context—an essential aspect when dealing with medical terminology, which can vary significantly across sources. For instance, the condition "high blood sugar" might also be described as "hyperglycemia" in clinical trial documents; while both refer to the same medical concept, a term-based approach like TF-IDF may not recognize them as equivalent [5,6]. To address this limitation, this paper presents an alternative approach based on an AI-Agent architecture integrated into the previously described web-based platform. This AI-driven method is capable of interpreting context and systematically evaluating each eligibility criterion against the patient's information to determine whether it is satisfied. By leveraging advanced NLP techniques and domain-specific knowledge, the AI-Agent enhances the accuracy and relevance of clinical trial matching, ensuring that patients are more effectively connected with appropriate studies.

To avoid ambiguity, throughout this paper we use the term AI-Agent to refer to instances of large language models (LLMs) operating within an orchestrated workflow, following the framing suggested by Anthropic [21]. In this paradigm, agents are modular components that perform specific reasoning or transformation tasks, rather than standalone systems. This framing is particularly valuable for clinical trial matching, where modularity allows agents to focus on distinct functions (e.g., extracting clinical conditions, embedding patient information, structuring eligibility criteria, or evaluating trial requirements), robustness is achieved through modular decomposition and sequential processing that progressively reduces complexity and error propagation, and context-awareness is supported by embedding models and LLM reasoning, which help align semantically equivalent concepts such as "high blood sugar" and "hyperglycemia." By embedding this AI-Agent architecture into the web-based platform, the proposed approach bridges the gap between statistical term-based methods and clinically meaningful interpretation, setting the stage for the four specialized agents described in the following section.

2 Related Work

Several recent AI approaches have significantly improved patient-to-clinical trial matching, addressing critical challenges in recruitment and enrollment processes. These include techniques, such as large language models (LLMs) and natural language processing (NLP), to automate and optimize clinical trial eligibility assessments, as listed next.

TrialMatchAI offers an end-to-end solution integrating open-source, fine-tuned LLMs to classify patient eligibility at a criterion-level, achieving remarkable accuracy especially in biomarker-driven clinical trials [7]. Similarly, TrialGPT introduces a zero-shot approach utilizing LLMs for eligibility matching, achieving accuracy comparable to expert manual screening and notably reducing screening times [8].

The MatchMiner-AI system specifically targets cancer clinical trials, leveraging vector embeddings for efficient patient-trial matching and demonstrating rapid and precise matching capabilities [9]. Additionally, Ghosh et al. explored the integration of explainable AI in matching patients to oncology trials, enhancing transparency and trust in AI-driven decision-making processes [10].

Another AI-based framework, DeepEnroll, utilizes deep embedding and entailment prediction to effectively match patients to relevant clinical trials, demonstrating significant improvements over traditional approaches [11]. Chen et al. also emphasized the importance of integrating big data analytics and AI methods to drive precision medicine, drug development, and clinical trial recruitment [12].

Recently, Rajpurkar and Jones reviewed the effectiveness of large language models, highlighting their utility for automating the clinical trial eligibility matching process. Their work underscored the growing adoption and potential of AI in clinical trials, advocating for further exploration and refinement of these methodologies [13].

This related work highlights the considerable potential and increasing effectiveness of AI-driven systems in clinical trial matching. Nonetheless, ongoing challenges such as data standardization, interoperability with existing clinical systems, ethical considerations, and privacy concerns continue to require attention for successful widespread implementation.

3 Solution Approach

The paper proposes an architecture comprising four specialized agents[2] : (1) an agent that extracts medical information from the FHIR Patient Resource to identify relevant clinical conditions; (2) an agent that summarizes the FHIR Patient Resource and utilizes a vector embedding engine to reduce the number of clinical trials assessed by subsequent agents; (3) an agent that transforms unstructured eligibility criteria into a structured format; and (4) an agent that evaluates each eligibility criterion against the patient's information to determine eligibility. This AI-Agent architecture is integrated into an existing web-based platform, which generates a relevance score for each clinical trial, enabling automated ranking from most to least relevant. The large language model (LLM) used is Gemini 2.0 Flash[3], while the vector embedding engine is based on Umls-

[2] This work combines a model-driven approach, based on FHIR standards, with AI-based methods to enhance interoperability and intelligent decision support.

[3] The LLM model can be replaced with other alternatives; however, we selected this one because it is freely accessible and hosted online. Please note that this work has not received external funding.

BERT, specifically, the pretrained model $GanjinZero/UMLSBert_ENG$, which is tailored for capturing semantic similarity in biomedical text. The proposed architecture is illustrated in Fig. 1.

3.1 Condition Extraction Agent (CEA)

This agent extracts relevant medical conditions from the FHIR Patient Resource. The conditions extracted from the Patient Resource in this example are ['Pregnancy', 'Malignant neoplastic disease'] [4] These conditions, along with the patient's birthdate and gender, are used to retrieve a significantly reduced set of clinical trials relevant to the patient from ClinicalTrials.gov. In this scenario, the input is a synthetic FHIR Patient Resource, generated using ChatGPT-4o and provided in Appendix A, which filtered down the trials from 540,505 to just 404. This substantial reduction benefits subsequent AI agents by enabling a more efficient assessment process.

3.2 Patient Embedding Agent (PEA)

This agent first transforms the patient's information from a structured FHIR document into a condensed, human-readable text format, illustrated in Listing 1. This transformation enables the vector embedding engine within the agent to work with the patient's data in a format semantically comparable to clinical trial descriptions, which are typically written in natural language. The vector embedding engine then converts the summarized text into a numerical representation that captures its meaning. This vector is compared against the descriptions of all retrieved clinical trials to assess similarity. In this example, the system selects the 10 most semantically relevant trials for the patient, as shown in Table 1. This step greatly reduces computational effort and improves the accuracy of downstream eligibility evaluation by focusing only on the most promising matches.

3.3 Eligibility Structuring Agent (ESA)

By leveraging the capabilities of the LLM, this agent converts unstructured clinical trial eligibility criteria, illustrated in Listing 2, into a structured format, illustrated in Listing 3. This structured representation is essential for the subsequent agent, which needs to evaluate each eligibility criterion individually. Note that this agent does not make use of FHIR.

[4] This is normally done using FHIR get functionality, but in this case we experimented with LLM solution.

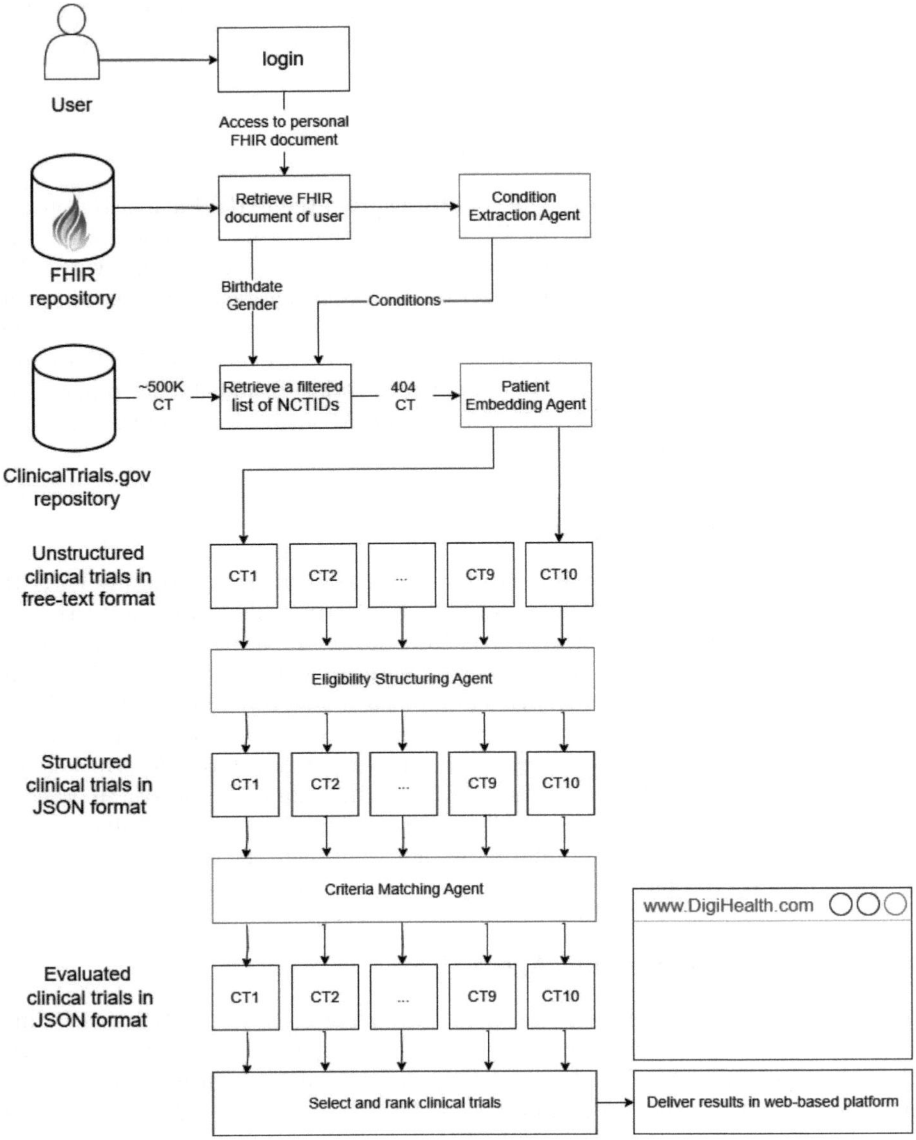

Fig. 1. Proposed architecture using FHIR repository and several agents involved in workflow. (Note: www.DigiHealth.com is a fictive site).

```
This document describes the medical record of a patient named
    Jane Doe, born on May 15, 1990.

Patient Details:
  - Name: Jane Doe
  - Gender: Female
  - Birth Date: May 15, 1990

Conditions:
  - Pregnancy: Diagnosed as active, with onset date March 1, 2025.
  - Cancer (Malignant Neoplastic Disease): Diagnosed as active,
      with onset date November 10, 2024.

Observations:
  - Hemoglobin Level: A Hemoglobin test was performed on April
      10, 2025.
    The hemoglobin level was 11.2 g/dL.

Care Plan:
  - Pregnancy Management Plan: An active care plan exists for the
      patient related to the pregnancy.
    It includes scheduled prenatal check-ups every 4 weeks.

Medication Request:
  - Paclitaxel: An active medication request is in place for
      Paclitaxel, a chemotherapy drug.
    The request was authored on April 1, 2025.
```

Listing 1. Human-readable text format medical summary of patient Jane Doe

3.4 Criteria Matching Agent (CMA)

This agent evaluates each structured eligibility criterion against the patient's FHIR data to determine whether it is satisfied. For each criterion, the agent prompts an assessment using a structured request that includes the patient data and the specific eligibility item. The response follows a predefined JSON format containing an "Answer" field with values yes, not, or unknown, along with a brief explanation in the "Reason" field, illustrated in Listing 4. If any inclusion criterion is marked as not, or any exclusion criterion is marked as yes, the corresponding clinical trial is immediately discarded. The remaining clinical trials are then ranked based on the number of yes and not evaluations in relation to the number of unknowns, giving priority to those with the highest confidence of eligibility—i.e., more definitive answers (yes/not) and fewer unknowns. This scoring approach supports more informed and reliable trial recommendations.

Table 1. Top matching clinical trials ranked by similarity score.

NCT ID	Similarity Score
NCT05973552	0.9174
NCT06302010	0.9134
NCT04551378	0.9125
NCT05916534	0.9112
NCT02895165	0.9101
NCT06510075	0.9076
NCT05676476	0.9060
NCT06001905	0.9057
NCT06135636	0.9057
NCT06685289	0.9047

```
Inclusion Criteria:

- Age > 18 years old;
- Pregnant women whose gestational age >12 weeks and registered
   in our hospital;
- With a certain level of education, can complete the
   questionnaire independently;
- Informed consent to participate in the study.

Exclusion Criteria:

- Patients with mental illness;
- Participated in other clinical studies in the past three months.
```

Listing 2. Unstructured Eligibility Criteria for Study NCT06001905

```
{
  "Inclusion criteria": {
    "1": "Age > 18 years old",
    "2": "Pregnant women whose gestational age >12 weeks and
        registered in our hospital",
    "3": "With a certain level of education, can complete the
        questionnaire independently",
    "4": "Informed consent to participate in the study"
  },
  "Exclusion criteria": {
    "1": "There are patients with mental illness",
    "2": "Participated in other clinical studies in the past
        three months"
```

```
  }
}
```

Listing 3. Structured Eligibility Criteria for Study NCT06001905

```
{'NCT06001905': {
  'pct_yes': 25.0,
  'pct_not': 50.0,
  'final_score': 37.5,
  'result': {
    'inclusion_assessments': [
      {'Answer': 'yes',
       'Reason': "The patient's birth date is 1990-05-15, making
           them older than 18 years old at the time of the other
           events in the data."},
      {'Answer': 'unknown',
       'Reason': 'While the patient is pregnant and registered
           (implicitly by having a care plan), the gestational age
           is not explicitly stated and cannot be determined from
           the provided data.'},
      {'Answer': 'unknown',
       'Reason': "The provided patient data does not contain
           information regarding the patient's level of education,
           which is necessary to determine if they can complete
           the questionnaire independently."},
      {'Answer': 'unknown',
       'Reason': 'The provided data does not contain any
           information about informed consent.'}
    ],
    'final_incl': 'yes',
    'exclusion_assessments': [
      {'Answer': 'not',
       'Reason': 'The patient data indicates pregnancy and
           cancer, but there is no mention of mental illness.'},
      {'Answer': 'unknown',
       'Reason': "The provided data does not contain information
           about the patient's participation in other clinical
           studies within the past three months."}
    ],
    'final_excl': 'yes',
    'final_result': 'yes'
  }
}}
```

Listing 4. Evaluated Eligibility Criteria for Study NCT06001905

3.5 Assessment

Considering that ChatGPT has demonstrated "impressive" accuracy in clinical decision-making tasks [14], this document includes an assessment of the suitability of clinical trial NCT06001905 for a given patient, based on the clinical information provided in a FHIR patient document. The evaluation prompt was: "Assess the suitability of the following clinical trial for the patient using the clinical data contained in the FHIR patient document." The assessment was performed using GPT-4o. The final result indicates that the trial should not be discarded, but additional patient information is required—specifically regarding hospital registration, education level, and informed consent. The complete assessment, including detailed responses for each eligibility criterion, is available in Table 2.

Table 2. Assessment of Each Eligibility Criterion for Study NCT06001905

Criterion Type	Criterion Description	Answer	Reasoning
Inclusion	Age > 18 years old	Yes	Patient's birth date is 1990-05-15, making her 35 years old.
Inclusion	Pregnant, gestational age >12 weeks, registered in our hospital	Unknown	Patient is pregnant with gestational onset on 2025-03-01 (>12 weeks), but hospital unknown.
Inclusion	Certain level of education to complete questionnaire independently	Unknown	Education level or cognitive ability not present in the FHIR document.
Inclusion	Informed consent provided	Unknown	No explicit record of consent found in patient data.
Exclusion	Diagnosis of mental illness	Unknown	No mental illness diagnosis is recorded in the provided FHIR conditions.
Exclusion	Participation in other clinical studies in the past three months	Unknown	No information is available about participation in prior clinical studies.

4 Conclusion and Discussion

The integration of AI agents into clinical trial matching workflows represents a substantial advancement over traditional keyword-based or rule-based systems. By decomposing the complex task of eligibility assessment into modular, specialized agents, the proposed architecture enables interpretable, context-aware evaluations that align closely with the nuanced logic of clinical trial protocols. Each agent contributes to a specific layer of intelligence, from data extraction and semantic filtering to logical criterion verification, creating a pipeline that is not only scalable but also adaptable to the diversity of trial designs and patient scenarios.

A core strength of the proposed system lies in its use of the HL7 Fast Healthcare Interoperability Resources (FHIR) standard. FHIR provides a consistent and extensible structure for representing patient data, allowing agents to operate on interoperable inputs with predictable formats. This interoperability ensures that the system can be integrated with a wide range of electronic health record (EHR) systems and public health datasets, making it more practical for deployment in real-world healthcare settings.

To support interoperability for clinical trial data, the FEvIR (Fast Evidence Interoperability Resources) platform was employed. FEvIR facilitates the transformation of scientific and healthcare knowledge into FHIR-compliant formats.

In this paper, FEvIR was used to convert clinical trials sourced from ClinicalTrials.gov into FHIR format, enabling the extraction of eligibility criteria by using FHIR-related methods [15].

Equally important is the system's delivery through a web-based software application. By embedding the AI-Agent architecture into a web platform, the system ensures accessibility, ease of deployment, and user-friendliness for both patients and clinicians. This design eliminates the need for specialized local installations or advanced technical expertise, enabling users to access trial recommendations from any device with an internet connection. The web-based interface supports interactive features that enhance usability and promote engagement—especially critical for patients who may lack familiarity with medical terminology or healthcare IT systems.

The AI agents' ability to interpret both structured and semi-structured data, and to reason over eligibility criteria at a granular level, introduces a level of precision that manual reviews often lack. For instance, while traditional matching methods might fail to capture contextual equivalences such as "high blood sugar" and "hyperglycemia," the AI agents in this architecture can leverage embeddings and large language models to infer semantic similarity, improving the robustness of matching outcomes.

Moreover, the framework supports transparency and explainability. Each eligibility criterion is assessed individually with a traceable rationale, enabling users and clinicians to understand and verify the decision-making process. This auditability is essential for building trust in AI-powered healthcare tools and ensuring alignment with ethical standards and regulatory expectations.

Another approach, such as that used by Deep 6 AI [20], is clinical trial—centric, it identifies which patients from a predefined patient pool match available clinical trials. In contrast, our user-centric approach focuses on the individual using the web platform, identifying the clinical trials most relevant to that specific patient.

In summary, the combination of modular AI agents, FHIR-based data integration, and a web-based delivery platform demonstrates a powerful paradigm for improving clinical trial recruitment. The architecture enhances accessibility, supports timely and patient-centered decision-making, and holds strong potential to improve recruitment success rates, reduce delays, and accelerate the advancement of medical research. Importantly, this work addresses a concrete problem and demonstrates how it can be solved with appropriate technologies, specifically, the use of the FHIR standard and relevant LLM-based methods, some of which can be encapsulated as AI agents. Furthermore, we anticipate that FHIR-based solutions will enable many more computable approaches that future AI agents can leverage, thereby expanding the range and adaptability of intelligent healthcare applications.

5 Future Work

While the proposed AI-Agent architecture provides a structured and interpretable solution for clinical trial matching based on FHIR patient data, future enhancements can be realized through the integration of emerging communication and context-sharing protocols such as Model Context Protocol (MCP) and Agent-to-Agent (A2A).

MCP aims to equip individual AI agents with secure and standardized access to external data, tools, and systems. In the context of clinical trials, this could allow agents to dynamically retrieve up-to-date patient data from EHR systems, access trial registries like ClinicalTrials.gov, and consult simulation tools for trial planning. For example, a trial design agent might use MCP to extract historical trial success patterns or regulatory guidelines to inform protocol development. Similarly, a patient recruitment agent could query MCP-connected FHIR repositories to identify eligible participants based on real-time clinical data, thereby enhancing both speed and precision.

A2A complements this by enabling secure, interoperable communication between autonomous agents. It allows agents from different vendors or systems to collaborate, discover one another's capabilities, and coordinate their tasks in distributed settings. In a clinical trial workflow, A2A could enable a recruitment agent to inform a monitoring agent about newly enrolled participants, or a compliance agent to review data collected by an analysis agent. This level of collaboration supports complex multi-agent workflows such as distributed trial monitoring, adverse event detection, and coordinated regulatory reporting.

The incorporation of MCP and A2A opens up the possibility of scalable, intelligent, and distributed agent ecosystems, where each agent has specialized responsibilities and operates asynchronously across the clinical trial lifecycle. Moreover, these protocols are designed with modern security standards (e.g., OAuth 2.0, JSON-RPC), multimodal data support, and streaming capabilities, all of which are essential for safe deployment in regulated environments like healthcare.

These advances build directly upon the foundations established by FHIR-based approaches, such as the work by Alper et al. on matching patient data to eligibility criteria using computable FHIR formats. While Alper's work exemplifies rule-based automation rooted in standardized data, MCP and A2A enable more adaptive, collaborative, and context-aware behavior by leveraging that same standardization. For example, FHIR remains the backbone of interoperable data exchange, and MCP serves as a conduit through which AI agents access that FHIR data in real time. A2A then allows those agents to share insights derived from FHIR, enabling team-like collaboration across the clinical trial ecosystem.

In addition to these directions, future work will also focus on analyzing the benefits of advanced prompting strategies (e.g., zero-shot, few-shot, chain-of-thought, or role-based prompts), designing a more robust validation procedure to measure the platform's impact, and evaluating whether an additional agent should be introduced to better support interactions with consumers. Future work could incorporate location as a filtering criterion. In this study, it was considered out of scope, as the location was not restricted because some patients may have the means to travel and participate in clinical trials globally. In future implementations, patients could specify how far from their current location they are willing to travel for clinical trial participation.

Finally, we note that FHIR standard includes a FHIR ResearchStudy Resource, and we will consider it in the future once this Resource is further developed (i.e. gets more mature). ResearchStudy Resource is defined as a scientific study intended to increase health-related knowledge, and clinical trials are research studies that involve people.

Acknowledgments. This paper presents an AI-Agent architecture integrated into an existing web-based platform developed for Team DigiHealth as part of the Digital Health Software Project (COMP3820) at the University of Queensland (UQ). The web-based platform was created by the authors—Marcos Burgos, Shaodong Cui, Jesse Cochrane, Ming Zhun Ku, and Dev Haritwal—as part of the course deliverables. The authors gratefully acknowledge the support of the DigiHealth and teaching team, led by Dr Chelsea Dobbins (UQ), and Prof. Mark Braunstein (CSIRO, Australia), and the guidance provided throughout the development process.

Disclosure of Interests. The authors have no competing interests to declare that are relevant to the content of this article.

Appendix A: Synthetic FHIR Patient Resource Example


```
{
  "resourceType": "Bundle",
  "type": "collection",
  "entry": [
    {
      "resource": {
        "resourceType": "Patient",
        "id": "patient-1",
        "name": [
          {
            "use": "official",
            "family": "Doe",
            "given": ["Jane"]
          }
        ],
        "gender": "female",
        "birthDate": "1990-05-15"
      }
    },
    {
      "resource": {
        "resourceType": "Condition",
        "id": "condition-1",
        "subject": {"reference": "Patient/patient-1"},
        "code": {
          "coding": [
            {
              "system": "http://snomed.info/sct",
              "code": "11687002",
              "display": "Pregnancy"
            }
          ],
          "text": "Pregnancy"
        },
        "clinicalStatus": {
          "coding": [
            {
              "system": "http://terminology.hl7.org/CodeSystem/condition-clinical",
              "code": "active"
            }
```

```
          ]
        },
        "onsetDateTime": "2025-03-01"
      }
    },
    {
      "resource": {
        "resourceType": "Condition",
        "id": "condition-2",
        "subject": {"reference": "Patient/patient-1"},
        "code": {
          "coding": [
            {
              "system": "http://snomed.info/sct",
              "code": "363406005",
              "display": "Malignant neoplastic disease"
            }
          ],
          "text": "Cancer"
        },
        "clinicalStatus": {
          "coding": [
            {
              "system": "http://terminology.hl7.org/CodeSystem/condition-clinical",
              "code": "active"
            }
          ]
        },
        "onsetDateTime": "2024-11-10"
      }
    },
    {
      "resource": {
        "resourceType": "Observation",
        "id": "observation-1",
        "status": "final",
        "category": [
          {
            "coding": [
              {
                "system": "http://terminology.hl7.org/CodeSystem/observation-category",
                "code": "laboratory",
                "display": "Laboratory"
              }
            ]
          }
        ],
        "code": {
          "coding": [
            {
              "system": "http://loinc.org",
              "code": "718-7",
              "display": "Hemoglobin [Mass/volume] in Blood"
            }
          ],
          "text": "Hemoglobin"
        },
        "subject": {"reference": "Patient/patient-1"},
        "effectiveDateTime": "2025-04-10",
        "valueQuantity": {
          "value": 11.2,
          "unit": "g/dL",
          "system": "http://unitsofmeasure.org",
          "code": "g/dL"
        }
      }
    },
    {
      "resource": {
        "resourceType": "CarePlan",
        "id": "careplan-1",
        "status": "active",
        "intent": "plan",
        "title": "Pregnancy Management Plan",
        "subject": {"reference": "Patient/patient-1"},
        "activity": [
          {
            "detail": {
```

```
            "kind": "Appointment",
            "status": "scheduled",
            "description": "Prenatal check-up every 4 weeks"
          }
        }
      ]
    }
  },
  {
    "resource": {
      "resourceType": "MedicationRequest",
      "id": "medrequest-1",
      "status": "active",
      "intent": "order",
      "medicationCodeableConcept": {
        "coding": [
          {
            "system": "http://www.nlm.nih.gov/research/umls/rxnorm",
            "code": "1036970",
            "display": "Paclitaxel"
          }
        ],
        "text": "Chemotherapy drug"
      },
      "subject": {"reference": "Patient/patient-1"},
      "authoredOn": "2025-04-01"
    }
  }
  ]
}
```


Listing 5. Synthetic FHIR Patient Resource of Jane Doe

References

1. Fogel, D.B.: Factors associated with clinical trials that fail and opportunities for improving the likelihood of success: a review. Contemp Clin Trials Commun. **7**(11), 156–164 (2018) https://doi.org/10.1016/j.conctc.2018.08.001.
2. Peterson, J.S., et al.: Growth in eligibility criteria content and failure to accrue among National Cancer Institute (NCI)-affiliated clinical trials. Cancer Med. **12**(4), 4715–4724 (2023). https://doi.org/10.1002/cam4.5276.
3. Chaudhari, N., Ravi, R., Gogtay, N.J., Thatte, U.M.: Recruitment and retention of the participants in clinical trials: challenges and solutions. Perspect Clin Res. **11**(2), 64–69 (2020). https://doi.org/10.4103/picr.PICR.206.19.
4. Burgos, M., Cochrane, J., Ming, Z., Shaodong, C., Haritwal, D.: AI-Driven Application for Optimised Patient-to-Clinical Trial Matching. The Digital Health FHIR project Report, The University of Queensland (2024)
5. Kuang, Q., Xu, X.: Improvement and Application of TF•Method Based on Text Classification. In: Proceeding 2010 International Conference Internet Technology Application (ITAPP), Wuhan, China, pp. 1–4 (2010). https://doi.org/10.1109/ITAPP.2010.5566113.
6. Alodadi, M., Janeja, V.P.: Similarity in Patient Support Forums Using TF-IDF and Cosine Similarity Metrics In: Proceeding 2015 International Conference Healthcare Informatics (ICHI), Dallas, TX, USA, pp. 521–522 (2015). https://doi.org/10.1109/ICHI.2015.99.
7. Abdallah, M., et al.: TrialMatchAI: An End-to-End AI-powered Clinical Trial Recommendation System to Streamline Patient-to-Trial Matching (2025) arXiv preprint, arXiv:2505.08508

8. Jin, Q., Wang, Z., Floudas, C.S., et al.: Matching patients to clinical trials with large language models Nat. Commun., vol. 15, art. no. 9074, (2024). https://doi.org/10.1038/s41467-024-53081-z.
9. Cerami, E., et al.: MatchMiner-AI: An Open-Source Solution for Cancer Clinical Trial Matching (2024) arXiv preprint, arXiv:2412.17228
10. Ghosh, S., Abushukair, H.M., Ganesan, A., Pan, C., Naqash, A.R., Lu, K.: Harnessing explainable artificial intelligence for patient-to-clinical-trial matching: a proof-of-concept pilot study using phase I oncology trials PLoS One, vol. 19, no. 10, art. no. e0311510, (2024). https://doi.org/10.1371/journal.pone.0311510.
11. Zhang, X., Xiao, C., Glass, L.M., Sun, J.: DeepEnroll: Patient-Trial Matching with Deep Embedding and Entailment Prediction (2020) arXiv preprint, arXiv:2001.08179
12. Yu, K.H., Hart, S.N., Goldfeder, R., Zhang, Q.C., Parker, S.C.J., Snyder, M.: Harnessing big data for precision medicine: infrastructures and applications in Proc. Pac. Symp. Biocomput. (PSB), vol. 22, pp. 635–639, (2017). https://doi.org/10.1142/9789813207813.0058.
13. Layne, E., et al.: Large language models for automating clinical trial matching Curr. Opin. Urol., vol. 35, no. 3, pp. 250–258 (2025). https://doi.org/10.1097/MOU.0000000000001281.
14. Rao, A., et al.: Assessing the Utility of ChatGPT Throughout the Entire Clinical Workflow: Development and Usability Study *J. Med. Internet Res.*, vol. 25, p. e48659, (2023). https://www.jmir.org/2023/1/e48659. https://doi.org/10.2196/48659
15. Computable Publishing LLC. Fast Evidence Interoperability Resources (FEvIR) Platform (Version 0.230.0) (2024). https://fevir.net/
16. Epic Systems Corporation: Epic FHIR Test Patients Documentation. https://fhir.epic.com/Documentation?docId=testpatients. Accessed: June 16, 2025
17. HL7 International: FHIR — Fast Healthcare Interoperability Resources. https://fhir.org/. Accessed: June 16, 2025
18. HL7 International: SMART App Launch Framework. https://build.fhir.org/ig/HL7/smart-app-launch/. Accessed: June 16, 2025
19. Braunstein, M., Dobbins, C., Steel, J., Hansen, D.: FHIR Project-based Training for Australia's Digital Health Workforce. Print in preparation
20. Deep 6 AI: About Us — Deep 6 AI: The next generation of AI in clinical trials. https://deep6.ai/about-us/. Accessed: August 17, 2025
21. Anthropic, Building Effective Agents, Anthropic Engineering Blog, Dec. (2024). https://www.anthropic.com/engineering/building-effective-agents

Towards a Toolchain for Formally Capturing and Monitoring Agent Accountability

Thomas Sepanosian[1(✉)] and Zoran Milosevic[2,3]

[1] University of Twente, Enschede, The Netherlands
t.sepanosian@student.utwente.nl
[2] Deontik, Brisbane, Australia
zoran@deontik.com
[3] School of Computer Science and Engineering, UNSW Sydney, Sydney, Australia

Abstract. The increasing deployment of AI agents in enterprise systems presents a critical governance challenge: ensuring clear accountability chains between humans and autonomous systems while supporting their dynamic, adaptive behavior. This paper presents a toolchain that uses the ISO-standard ODP Enterprise Language to formally specify and monitor actor responsibility. Building on our previous DSL work for ODP Enterprise Language formalism expression, we develop a software toolchain that enables domain users to define actor responsibilities and accountability against normative concepts expressed using the basic normative concepts of permissions, obligations, prohibitions, and authorizations. The toolchain supports expressing delegation scenarios between humans and agents, and across multiple agents, accommodating the dynamic nature of AI-driven enterprise systems. Our solution leverages the textX DSL development framework to create a fit-for-purpose toolchain that integrates with contemporary enterprise and AI technologies, providing formal foundations for accountable agent deployment in enterprise distributed systems.

Keywords: ODP · Accountability · DSL · Deontic Reasoning · AI Agent

1 Introduction

The rise of autonomous systems, particularly AI agents powered by Large Language Models (LLMs), is showcasing new avenues for enterprise automation [1], with a range of frameworks aiming to streamline integration [2–4]. However, this shift to greater autonomy exposes a governance gap. The core problem no longer is ensuring a system executes a predefined process correctly, but ensuring it behaves appropriately within a web of permissions, obligations and prohibitions. This requires a shift in perspective, such as assessments of systems beyond verifying merely its correctness, and going from predicate logic to modal

© The Author(s), under exclusive license to Springer Nature Switzerland AG 2026
A. Gianola et al. (Eds.): EDOC 2025, LNCS 16213, pp. 337–353, 2026.
https://doi.org/10.1007/978-3-032-15140-7_19

and deontic logics, capable of reasoning about possibilities and conformance to accepted norms [5]. This need for richer modeling patterns becomes important when considering accountability. As autonomous agents begin to interact and delegate tasks to one another, potentially with humans in the loop, forming complex chains of action, pinpointing responsibility becomes increasingly difficult. When a system of automated trading agents, delegate an order to sub-agents, and it breaches a limit, who is liable? Often, traditional approaches lack the expressive power or semantic constructs to adequately represent these dynamic and normative interactions.

This paper argues that the solution lies in a framework grounded in formal semantics, specifically those of the ISO Open Distributed Processing Enterprise Language (ODP-EL) [6]. We build upon prior work that first established a Domain-Specific Language (DSL) for ODP-EL, proposing it as a means to manage consistency and evolution in long-lived enterprise systems [7]. This DSL is a custom, human-readable textual language to model and specify rules of enterprise systems, following the formally-based ODP-EL constructs. A subsequent paper then targeted this DSL at the problem of accountability in AI agent systems, demonstrating potential for modeling the complex delegation chains that arise between human and AI actors [8].

While prior work discussed the suitability of the DSL to manage enterprise system specifications, the utilization remained descriptive only. The transition from a static, descriptive language to an executable framework for runtime, verification, and enforcement had not yet been made. This paper addresses that gap directly. The primary contribution of this work is therefore twofold. First, we present refinements to the ODP-EL DSL itself, enhancing the grammar, observing its usability, and providing an example that aims to be faithful to the ISO standard. Second, we introduce a software framework built around this DSL. This framework includes a model hydrator, a runtime engine, and visualization tools, which together provide an end-to-end environment for bringing normative specifications to life, serving as an integrated component in the toolchain to manage the life-cycle of enterprise system specifications, moving towards an enforceable runtime contract system.

The remainder of this paper is structured as follows. Section 2 positions our work by providing a critical analysis of established enterprise architecture and process modeling frameworks, highlighting their limitations with respect to formal accountability. Section 3 then details the foundation of our approach: the ODP-EL DSL. It covers the language's evolution through prior work and augmentations. In Sect. 4, we present the main contribution of this paper, the design and implementation of the software framework, detailing the architecture of the model hydrator, the runtime engine, and the visualization tools. Finally, Sect. 5 concludes the paper, summarizing our contributions and outlining directions for future work.

2 Related Work

This section positions our work within the landscape of established enterprise architecture methodologies and modern tools. A comparative summary of their characteristics in relation to normative and accountability modeling is presented in Table 1.

Table 1. Comparative Analysis of Modeling Frameworks and Tools

Framework / Tool	Focus	Normative Concepts	Accountability Concepts	Executability
EA & Process Standards	Method, Structure, Workflow	None native; rely on extensions	Roles, Constraints; no token delegation	Partial
Blockchain / Smart Contracts	Transactional Logic	Low-level code, not a high-level model	Implicit in audit trail; not an explicit model	Yes
Policy Engines (e.g., OPA)	Stateless Authorisation	Limited to stateless queries	External to engine	Yes
ODP-EL	**Purpose, Scope, Policies**	**Native** (*Burden, Permit, Embargo*)	**Native** (*Party, Agent, Delegation*)	**This work**

2.1 Enterprise Architecture and Modeling Frameworks

The challenge of modeling enterprise structure and behavior has been addressed by a wide range of methodologies, each with their strengths and intended use cases.

The Open Group Architecture Framework (TOGAF) [9] is a widely adopted enterprise architecture framework. It provides an approach for designing, planning, implementing, and governing enterprise information architecture. The Architecture Development Method (ADM) is the core methodology within TOGAF, and is used to develop and manage the life-cycle of an enterprise architecture [10]. However, commentators have noted a lack of social-legal notions (e.g. responsibility transfer) [11,12] and an absence of formal semantics for such concerns [13].

ArchiMate complements TOGAF with a graphical metamodel that captures layers (business, application, technology) and, more recently, strategy and outcome concepts [14]. While its Constraint and Requirement elements can flag policy intent, systematic reviews find that security, risk and other normative properties require either extensions or informal annotations [15].

BPMN 2.0 [16], finally, brings executable process semantics to the stack [17]. Its control-flow focus makes it suitable for automation engines, however, commentators have noted that the standard becomes limited when supporting specific domains or non-functional properties [18], leading to extensions that do not always comply with standards, and potentially difficult to adopt [19].

In short, these standards are well established for structural and procedural modelling. We cite TOGAF, ArchiMate and BPMN here purely as baselines for enterprise structure and process modelling. Because none of them contain transferable deontic constructs, they leave a normative gap. When a project requires persistent, transferable permissions, obligations or prohibitions, practitioners tend to rely on auxiliary mechanisms rather than on native language constructs. The token-based approach of ODP-EL offers such constructs natively.

2.2 Contemporary Tools

Blockchain / Smart Contracts. Blockchain and distributed ledger technologies are utilized for creating decentralized, immutable records of transactions, maintaining trust in a distributed system [20]. This technology is often paired with smart contracts, programs that automate agreements when predefined conditions are met [21], used by, Ethereum for instance [22].

The primary benefits of utilizing smart contracts are increased efficiency, reduced cost, and the creation of an immutable audit trail. However, the logic within a smart contract is procedural. The process involves converting a high-level agreement into low-level code. [21]. This highlights a semantic gap; while a smart contract can execute a predefined rule, its procedural nature makes it difficult to model and reason about the abstract, high-level normative concepts. Furthermore, the features of blockchain can introduce challenges. The immutability of a deployed contract, for instance, prevents the adjustments of rules if business circumstances change [23]. Based on this, it could be argued that blockchain and smart contracts are a powerful implementation technology, rather than a comprehensive framework for accountability.

Policy Engines. In the domain of policy enforcement, tools such as Open Policy Agent (OPA) are available for cloud-native environments [24]. As described in its documentation, OPA's core philosophy is to decouple policy decision-making from policy-enforcement. Service query OPA with structured data (e.g., JSON) as input, and OPA evaluated policies written in its DSL, Rego, to return a decision [25]. This pattern is exemplified in modern architectural approaches such as a Data Mesh, where OPA is used as a central engine to enforce global governance rules while allowing for decentralized, domain-specific policy inputs [26].

The practical adoption of OPA is not without challenges however, as its policy language, Rego, has its own complexities. For developers that do not have experience with rule-based programming, there is a learning curve [27]. Furthermore, the focus of OPA is primarily on authorization, as it supports multiple ways of access control, but, as a policy engine, it does not hold any native constructs for more complex, stateful normative concepts. OPA is fundamentally a stateless decision engine; it can answer the question, "Is this action permitted based on the current data?" but it cannot natively model an enduring obligation that is created at one point in time and must be discharged later.

2.3 The Case for ODP and ODP-EL

The critiques of the aforementioned frameworks and tools reveal a gap: a lack of native, formally-defined constructs for modeling social and normative aspects of an enterprise, beyond authorization. While a variety of technologies address fragments of this need, e.g., declarative workflow languages, policy-as-code engines for stateless authorization, and blockchain-based smart contracts for immutability, none provides a unified approach that can express and enforce enduring, transferable obligations. These solutions tend to be narrowly scoped or rely on implicit state rather than explicit token transfer.

The ODP standard (Reference Model for Open Distributed Processing) is explicitly focused on facilitating interconnecting distributed systems in order to gain corresponding benefits. Within ODP, five viewpoints have been specified, with each viewpoint serving as an abstraction for a certain perspective. The enterprise viewpoint concerns itself with "the purpose, scope and policies governing the activities of the specified system within the organization of which it is a part" [28]. Our work focuses on the Enterprise Language (EL), the formal language defined for the Enterprise Viewpoint [6].

Unlike frameworks centered on structural architecture or operational flow, ODP-EL also provides constructs for modeling the social and organizational context, including formally-grounded language for expressing normative rules and relationships. To this end, the Enterprise Language defines a number of *action* types that have different consequences for future behaviour of the system. Distinguishing these different action types provides framework for analyzing the way responsibilities evolve, starting with a *commitment*, defined as an action that results in the object performing it, undertaking some *obligation* [5].

Obligations can then be passed on by their current holder, referred to as the *principal*, performing a *delegation* action, in which the obligation is passed on to an *agent*. The mechanism of passing obligations is supported by a separate object, referred to as a *burden*. In fact, burden is a special kind of *deontic token*, encapsulating obligations, with *permit* and *embargo* being other special types, representing *permissions* and *prohibitions*, respectively. It is also to be noted that delegation is a special kind of *speech act*, which is introduced to capture actions of actors that modify the set of deontic tokens held.

These modelling concepts were developed to support formally describing chains of accountability and responsibility associated with the actions of actors in various interactions. This provides the basis for tracking system actions back to the legally accountable principals, which helps with disambiguating ultimate responsibility of the actors involved in complex distributed systems that increasingly include both humans and automated agents, the examples of latter being AI agents, with either executing simple scripts, or more complex, reinforcing learning agents, exhibiting certain levels of autonomy.

What makes ODP-EL particularly valueable in this context is that, unlike the other tools assessed, it combines capabilities that are not found together. That gap is what the ODP-EL DSL and runtime engine we propose aim to fill:

an integrated toolchain that enables practitioners to design, execute, and evolve normative specifications as living artefacts, rather than static documentation.

The concepts above served as the basis for the key constructs and grammar rules of the DSL for ODP-EL, previously reported [7,8], and are now extended with a runtime engine that operationalizes these constructs.

3 DSL for ODP-EL

The work presented in this paper is built upon a DSL designed to capture the core concepts of ODP-EL. This section details the evolution of this DSL, the rationale for adjustments, and the foundation it provides for our executable framework.

3.1 Prior Work

The initial design of an ODP-EL-based DSL and a roadmap for its toolchain were detailed in prior work, which focused on using DSLs to manage consistency in long-lived enterprise specifications [7]. Consistent with this work, we use DSL to mean a language whose grammar, metamodel, and semantics are restricted to the ODP-EL domain. Compared with a general-purpose language offers advantages as argued in said paper such as keywords mapping to the constructs in the standard, a machine-interpretable grammar which can be turned into an AST which tools can validate, transform and execute, and enhances accessibility for stakeholders by minimizing the need to master a general-purpose programming language.

This work established the DSL's semantic basis in ODP-EL, highlighted the use of ODP-EL constructs such as `policy` and `deontic tokens` for managing system evolution, and demonstrated its implementation using the `textX` meta-language framework. Building on this foundation, subsequent work then proposed the specific application of this DSL to address accountability in LLM-powered AI agent systems [8].

A key design feature of the DSL is its partitioned grammar: `odpel.tx` defines core enterprise concepts (the deontic perspective), while `odppolicy.tx` defines the language for specifying changes to the model (the change perspective). This separation of concerns is a unique strength of the ODP-EL approach. The core `odpel.tx` grammar provides `DeonticTokens` (`Burden`, `Permit`, `Embargo`) as objects that can be created, delegated, and discharged. The `odppolicy.tx` grammar enables controlled system evolution by defining policies that govern how the normative model itself can change. This contrasts with other modeling approaches where change is managed via ad-hoc updates or complete redeployment of a process definition, rather than through a formal, self-describing policy mechanism.

3.2 Validation and Enhancement of the DSL

The original DSL was demonstrated with a `consent.odpl` proof-of-concept, an example based on e-consent within healthcare. While illustrative, this example was not grounded in a formal example. Additionally, while prior research established the DSL, a transition from a static specification to an executable framework required additional steps, including validating the language against a standardized benchmark, and enhancing / refining where necessary. A contribution of this work is to implement a comprehensive example of the library management scenario detailed in Annex B.2 of the ITU-T X.911 standard [6]. This `library.odpl` model was chosen as it provides a credible basis for validating the DSL's fidelity to ODP-EL semantics. Furthermore, its structure utilizes the full deontic logic, from the imposition of a `burden` (the obligation to return an item) to the enforcement of rules, i.e., via an embargo (suspending borrowing rights), making it an useful example to act as a benchmark.

The process of implementing a comprehensive, standard-based example revealed the need for several targeted refinements to the original DSL. These were not sweeping changes, but a series of pragmatic enhancements, each addressing a different aspect of the language's maturity. These changes are available in a forked repository of the original grammar[1]. This included refactoring grammar rules for improved clarity, while not altering the core semantics, and the introduction of the `Agent` construct, which previously was marked as rule to be implemented in the future. The new rule allows the DSL to more fully align with the ODP-EL standard's formal definition of a principal-agent relationship, where an `Agent` is an `ActiveEO` that acts on behalf of a `Party` (the principal).

In the current version of the runtime engine, to be discussed in more detail in Sect. 4, delegation is modeled by transferring a deontic token to a `Party` that fulfills a specific `CommunityRole`, as specified in the first iteration of the DSL. The introduction of the `Agent` type provides the neccesary semantic base for a more explicit model of delegation where responsibility could be assigned directly to a named `Agent` instance. Thus, this lays the groundwork for a more fine-grained and ODP-EL faithful model of delegation.

Distinction Between the ODP-EL Agent, and the LLM Agent. It is important to distinguish the notion of an ODP Agent from that of a contemporary LLM agent.

In the ODP Enterprise Language, a Party represent an entity with legal person hood, such as a natural person, a corporation, or a government body, that can hold rights, be subject to duties, and be held responsible for its actions. An Agent, in contrast, is an ActiveEO that has been delegated authority to perform a task on behalf of a Party, where the principal retains accountability for the actions performed by its agent.

[1] The augmented DSL repository is available at: https://github.com/Thomas-mp4/ODP-EL-textX.

An LLM agent is a system that exhibits (semi)-autonomous, goal-oriented behavior by leveraging a large language model as its core reasoning engine, often in combination with tools, memory, and a defined task environment [29]. It is a technological artifact, not a legal entity. Therefore, within this framework, an LLM-powered system can fulfill the functional role of an ODP agent, but it can not be modeled as a Party.

4 Framework Architecture and Implementation

To operationalize the concepts defined in the ODP-EL DSL, we have designed and implemented a framework that transforms static specifications into executable models. As illustrated in Fig. 1, the framework processes a user-written specification, producing a rich object model that is executed within a runtime environment. Designed with a separation of concerns, the framework consists of several core components. A summary of the components is provided in Table 2. The language and grammar were detailed in Sect. 3. The repository of this framework is published in a GitHub repository[2]

Table 2. Overview of Framework Components.

Component	Description	Key Technologies/Artifacts
Language & Grammar	Formal language for specifying enterprise policies and accountability rules based on ODP-EL.	`textX`, `odpel.tx`, `odppolicy.tx`
ODP Classes	Semantically rich Python classes reflecting DSL constructs, with additional helper functions.	`dataclasses`
Model Hydrator	Transforms DSL source code from an AST into an executable, semantic object model.	Python, Two-Pass Hydrator
Runtime Engine	Executes the hydrated model, managing state and enforcing all specified deontic constraints at runtime.	Python
Runtime Tracer	Captures a structured log of all runtime events to create a history of the simulation.	Python
Visualization Generator	Generates UML sequence diagrams from the trace log to provide a visual and auditable trail of interactions.	Python, Mermaid.js

[2] The toolchain repository is available at: https://github.com/Thomas-mp4/ODP-EL-Toolchain.

4.1 Model Hydrator: From AST to Object Model

A raw Abstract Syntax Tree (AST), as generated by a parser, is a direct representation of the source code's syntax. While `textX` automatically resolves references at the AST level to create a linked tree of parser objects, this tree is not immediately suitable for execution. The nodes of the AST are generic data containers that reflect the source structure; they lack the specific domain logic and behavior required by the simulation engine. For instance, the AST node for the `borrowItem` action is not an instance of the `ODP.behavior.SpeechAct` class that the runtime system is designed to operate on.

To bridge this 'semantic gap', the toolchain introduces a transformation step, hydration. The `Hydrator` component is responsible for traversing the textX-generated AST and building a parallel interconnected graph of Python objects, the executable object model.

To manage these transformations, the Hydrator employs a two-pass pattern. It first traverses the entire AST to instantiate the semantic objects (e.g., `Community`, `CommunityRole`, `SimpleType`). A central `object_registry` is populated, using a fully qualified name (FQN) for each object to ensure unique identification and to prevent name collisions across different scopes. In the second pass, the hydrator re-traverses the model. Using the now-complete `object_registry`, it resolves all relationships between the newly created semantic objects. This pass connects cross-references, such as linking actions to their trigger events and artifacts to their type definitions, creating a fully linked graph of executable objects.

The output of this component is a fully "hydrated" object model where all relationships are explicit object references, creating a complete and executable representation of the model ready for the Runtime Engine.

It is worth noting that `textX` provides a 'Custom Classes' feature, which allows for the direct instantiation of user-defined classes during the parsing process. This effectively merges the parsing and object creation steps into a single stage. The architecture of our toolchain, however, opts for a more granular pipeline by utilizing the `Hydrator`. By treating hydration as a distinct post-processing step, our toolchain gains explicit control over the model's construction, separating the concerns of syntactic parsing from the creation of the final semantic model.

4.2 Runtime Engine: Executable Simulation

The engine provides the runtime environment for the hydrated model, giving executable semantics to the ODP-EL specification. It is responsible for managing the state of the simulation and enforcing the behavioral constraints defined in the model.

The engine manages the runtime state of the "world", maintaining collections of instantiated parties, artifacts, and importantly, deontic token instances. The `perform_action` method is the primary entry point for the simulation. When a Party attempts an action, the engine follows a sequence of validation and

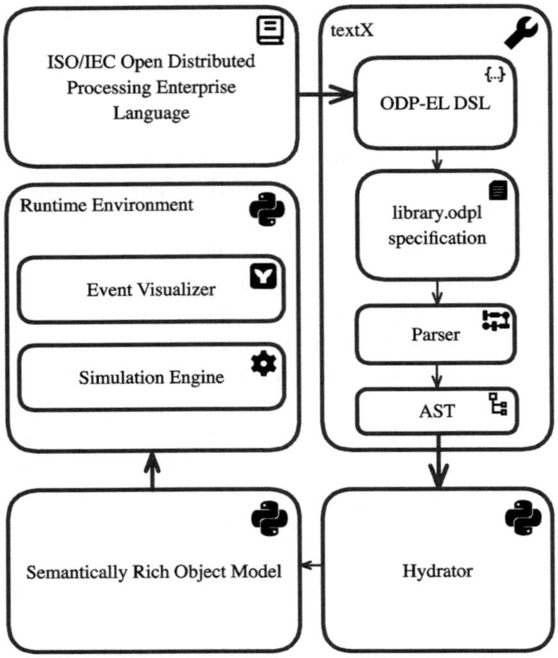

Fig. 1. Architectural overview of the framework.

execution steps. First, it performs precondition checks to enforce constraints; it verifies that the acting Party is not under any relevant Embargo that would prohibit the action, and it evaluates the action's guard condition by passing the current world state into the guard's expression. If all preconditions are met, the action is executed.

To provide clear insight into the dynamic behavior of the system, the framework includes a tracing and visualization component. During execution, the runtime engine is monitored by a tracer that captures a structured history of events. This includes action attempts (both permitted and prohibited), the creation of deontic tokens, and their subsequent state changes. Upon completion, a mermaid generator consumes the event log and transforms it into a UML sequence diagram using Mermaid.js syntax, as shown in Fig 2. This automated visualization provides a clear and auditable trail of the system's execution, making the behavior within the system understandable at a glance.

4.3 Design Considerations for Guard Evaluation and Extensibility

An important design decision in the framework revolves around the evaluation of `guard` conditions. In its current iteration, the DSL grammar is intentionally permissive; a guard's content is captured as a raw string, deferring all parsing and semantic analysis to its runtime environment. This design choice was pragmatic

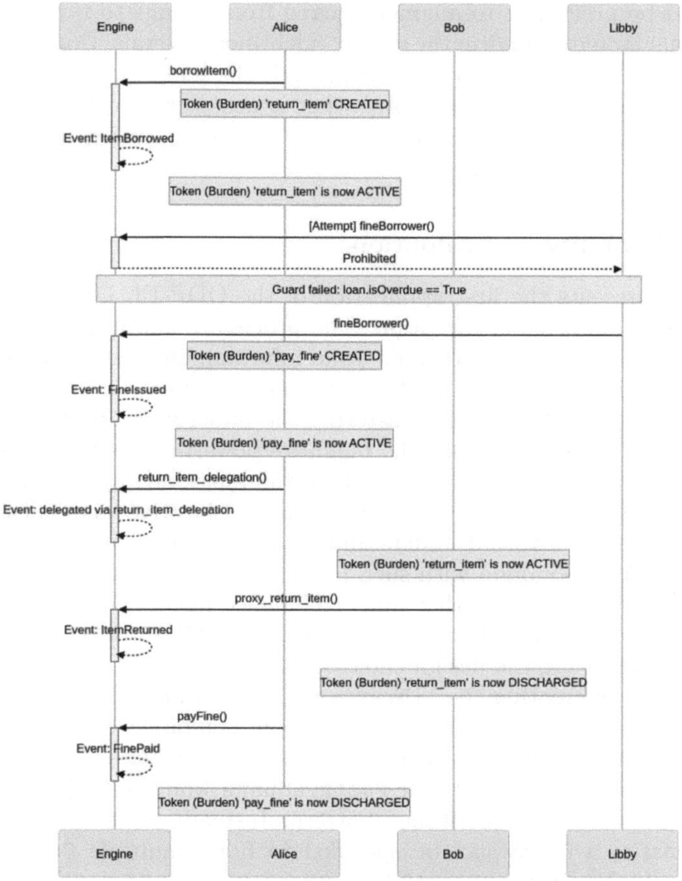

Fig. 2. Sequence diagram from simulation tracer, visualizing system behavior.

for the development of this proof-of-concept, but it also introduces limitations that must be acknowledged.

For this PoC, we implemented a direct evaluation mechanism using Python's built-in `eval()` function. The `Runtime Engine` populates a `context` dictionary with all necessary domain-specific functions, such as `loanCount()`, and executes the guard's string expression against this context. This approach, while functional, results in shortcomings. It introduces tight coupling, due to the guards in this specific example effectively being Python code snippets. Furthermore, because guards are merely strings to the parser, it is not possible to perform static analysis, validation, or type-checking on them at compile time. Errors in guard logic can only be detected at runtime, such as in the aforementioned Hydrator.

It would be preferable to augment `guard` from strings to types expressions. The grammar would formalize the syntax, identifiers, literals, Boolean operators, and the generic shape of a functional call, while the semantic phase would utilize an invariant domain library to resolve what is necessary for instance by linking function identifiers from the expression's AST to their actual implementations in the library.

4.4 DSL Usability and Adoption

This work represents the first application of the ODP-EL DSL by a developer not involved in its original inception. The process of adopting the language to model `library.odpl` scenario served as an informal, qualitative validation of its usability. The experience was that the primary learning curve was not in the DSL syntax itself, but rather in mastering the underlying ODP(-EL) concepts, especially its nuances that make the language powerful. Adopting the language effectively seemed to benefit from a shift in thinking, moving from a procedural or access-control perspective towards a more declarative and normative one. Part of this process involved understanding how the DSL interprets the ODP-EL standard. As is common with such tools, the DSL is not a literal one-to-one mapping, but an adaptation that aims to balance fidelity to the standard with practical usability. A foundational understanding of ODP concepts was therefore helpful in appreciating the design choices made for the DSL.

The process of creating the `library.odpl` model also brought to light some noteworthy design patterns that differ from common object-oriented paradigms. For example, one might typically model a generic `Borrower` as a base class from which roles like `Undergraduate` or `Postgraduate` would inherit. The ODP-EL DSL does not use this inheritance pattern. Instead, as demonstrated in our library scenario, a `Party` can be specified to fulfill multiple `CommunityRoles` simultaneously. For instance, a student is modeled as a `Party` that fulfills both the `Undergraduate` and `Borrower` roles, thereby gaining the capabilities of each. While this pattern addresses intra-community relationships, the DSL also provides the `Import` construct for modularity at a higher level, allowing entire Communities to be reused and composed for inter-community specifications.

Using a comprehensive example from the ITU-T standard provided a useful benchmark that also informed the iterative refinement of the DSL. As the model for the library scenario was developed, some areas for potential improvement in the language became apparent. This led to minor, incremental changes to the grammar to enhance clarity. This iterative feedback loop between using and refining the DSL seemed a pragmatic way to advance the toolchain. At one point, an alternative approach was considered: first building a complete implementation of the library scenario in a general-purpose language to clearly separate static from dynamic concerns, to clearly highlight which parts would be done on the DSL-level, and the engine-level. Ultimately, however, a DSL-first, iterative approach was pursued. This decision was made to keep the focus on developing a proof-of-concept runtime environment that directly served the needs of the DSL.

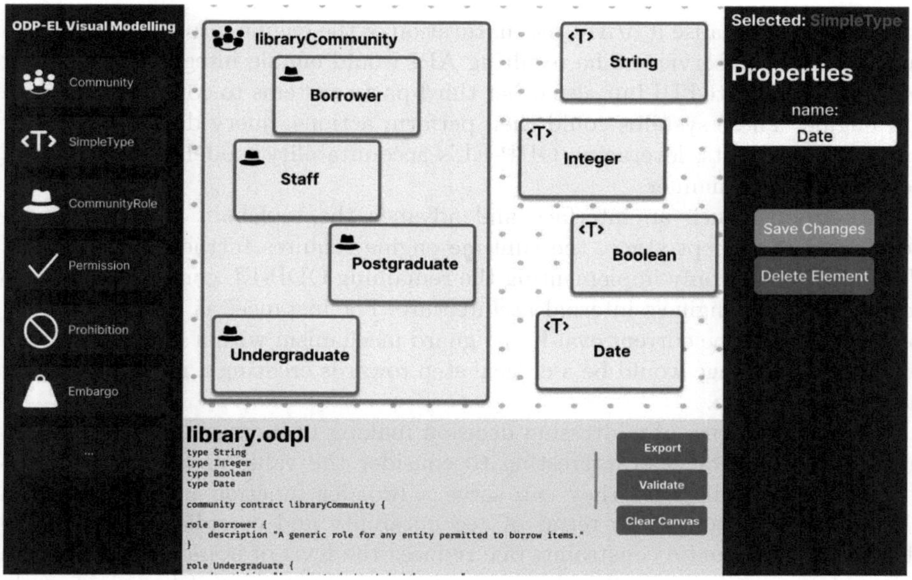

Fig. 3. An illustrative example of a potential ODP-EL DSL GUI.

5 Conclusion and Future Work

This paper presents a toolchain to support the specification of responsibility across the actors in a distributed systems, using a set of accountability concepts, as part of a broader set of ODP-EL concepts [30]. The toolchain makes use of the DSL language constructs initially proposed in [7], and provides additional set of software components needed to support transformation of DSL concepts into Python code. This toolchain enables executable semantics for the DSL by extending functionality beyond the AST representation. We designed and implemented a framework comprising a model hydrator, a runtime engine, and trace visualization tools.

There are several directions we plan to investigate in future.

First, in terms of toolchain enhancement, we are planning to provide a user interface support, in a way to allow creating and manipulating ODP concepts, as illustrated in an example in Fig. 3 using for example a set of icons proposed in the UML profile for ODP standard [31] and also used in [5]. This would significantly lower the barrier to adoption by abstracting away the textual DSL syntax.

A potential architectural approach for such an interface is a decoupled, web-based system. In this model, the ODP-EL engine would be exposed as a backend service with a well-defined API (e.g., REST). A separate front-end application, developed using any modern web framework, would then consume this API to provide the visual modeling environment. This architectural choice is particularly advantageous because it drives the maturation of the engine into a self-contained 'normative microservice'. The resulting API would enable integration, allowing not only a dedicated UI but also other third-party systems to communicate with the engine. These systems could then perform actions, query deontic states, or subscribe to events, leveraging ODP-EL's accountability model in a decoupled, service-oriented manner.

To support such an interface and advance the toolchain beyond its current proof-of-concept stage, the runtime engine requires further consolidation. This involves not only implementing the remaining ODP-EL constructs but also formalizing the engine's internal architecture. For instance, as discussed previously, replacing the current eval-based guard mechanism with a formally-defined expression language would be a critical step towards creating a more robust and analyzable system.

Second, in terms of addressing decision making of increasingly autonomous agents, it would be also interesting to consider the value of the deontic constraints. This is because they can serve a broader function in system design than what we discussed in terms of accountability and compliance. By explicitly specifying deontic constraints one reduces the level of non-determination in the system specification and also supports more dynamic and less rigid workflow. This also implies need for modelling some sort of preference or goal-seeking behaviour as we also discussed in [7]. This may be formalised through the concept of objective, as per ODP Community modelling concept, which is included as part of DSL but was beyond the scope of this work. This in turn can support better integrations with decision processes, human or AI agents, including the way decisions change as a result of environmental constraints or internal intentions of agents. One way of modelling intentions can be through combining possible world semantics mechanism, formalizing decision making over future actions, reflecting obligations and permission behaviour expressions, and augmented with utility functions, to help comparing the desirability of different courses of action, also hinted in [30].

Third, the paper can help us define an implementation path in terms of the use of DSL concepts in specific application domains, such as healthcare. Specifically, we are interested in establishing semantic linkages between the ODP-EL concepts and related concepts within the HL7 FHIR standard. Examples of such links are between FHIR Task Resource, which specifies an activity to be executed, and ODP obligation concept, or FHIR Consent and FHIR Permission Resources, and their relationships with ODP permission and authorizatio concepts. Once developed, these mappings would enable adding the richness of ODP EL deontic concepts to the expression of interactions between various roles involved in healthcare workflows, capturing responsibility of parties and agents in the system, in a way that is grounded in the ODP-EL formalism.

Further, when tailoring of core FHIR concepts for the specific healthcare domains, such as International Patient Summary extensions, there are a set of FHIR own tools, supporting FHIR Shorthand (FSH) DSL. We would like to investigate to what extent it is possible to integrate this and the textX tooling environments to automate expression of responsibility chains as part of clinical workflows, such as those expressed using FHIR worflow constructs. It would be interesting to consider consent use case as previously introduced in [7], in light of the lessons learned in this work.

Acknowledgement. We would like to thank Prof Igor Dejanovic for his inputs regarding the use of textX framework and broader interactions between DSL and GPL approaches.

Disclosure of Interests. The authors have no competing interests to declare that are relevant to the content of this article.

References

1. Sepanosian, T., Milosevic, Z., Blair, A.: Scaling AI Adoption in Finance: Modelling Framework and Implementation Study, in Enterprise Design, Operations, and Computing. EDOC 2024 Workshops, M. Kaczmarek-Heß, K. Rosenthal, M. Suchánek, M. M. Da Silva, H. A. Proper, and M. Schnellmann, Eds. Cham: Springer Nature Switzerland, 2025, vol. 537, pp. 221–236, series Title: Lecture Notes in Business Information Processing. [Online]. Available: https://link.springer.com/10.1007/978-3-031-79059-1_14
2. CrewAI. [Online]. Available: https://www.crewai.com/
3. n8n.io - a powerful workflow automation tool. [Online]. Available: https://n8n.io/
4. LangChain. [Online]. Available: https://www.langchain.com
5. Linington, P.F., Milosevic, Z., Tanaka, A., Vallecillo, A.: Building Enterprise Systems with ODP: An Introduction to Open Distributed Processing, 0th ed. Chapman and Hall/CRC, (2011). [Online]. Available: https://www.taylorfrancis.com/books/9781439866269
6. Gachet, C.: ITU-T Standard - Open distributed processing, (2008)
7. Linington, P., Milosevic, Z., Tanaka, A., Dejanović, I.: Using DSLs to manage consistency in long-lived enterprise language specifications, Software and Systems Modeling, (2024). [Online]. Available: https://link.springer.com/epdf/10.1007/s10270-024-01243-4
8. Milosevic, Z., Dejanović, I.: Enterprise Design, Operations and Computing with AI Agents: Accountability Using DSL, in Enterprise Design, Operations, and Computing, In: Borbinha, J., Prince Sales, T., Da Silva, M.M., Proper, H.A., Schnellmann, M., eds., Cham: Springer Nature Switzerland, 2025, vol. 15409, pp. 21–38, series Title: Lecture Notes in Computer Science. [Online]. Available: https://link.springer.com/10.1007/978-3-031-78338-8_2
9. TOGAF | www.opengroup.org. [Online]. Available: https://www.opengroup.org/togaf
10. Blevins, T.J., Spencer, J., Waskiewicz, F.: TOGAF ADM and MDA, (2004). [Online]. Available: https://pubs.opengroup.org/onlinepubs/ 7699949799/toc.pdf
11. Magoulas, T., Hadzic, A., Saarikko, T., Pessi, K.: Alignment in Enterprise Architecture: A Comparative Analysis of Four Architectural Approaches, Electronic Journal of Information Systems Evaluation, vol. 15, no. 1, pp. pp88-101–pp88-101, (2012). [Online]. Available: https: //academic-publishing.org/index.php/ejise/article/view/244

12. Tambo, T.: Evaluation of TOGAF as a management of technology framework, Conference Proceedings (2016)
13. Dietz, J.L.G., Hoogervorst, J.A.P.: A critical investigation of TOGAF - based on the enterprise engineering theory and practice. In: Albani, A., Dietz, J.L.G., Verelst, J. (eds.) EEWC 2011. LNBIP, vol. 79, pp. 76–90. Springer, Heidelberg (2011). https://doi.org/10.1007/978-3-642-21058-7_6
14. Josey, A., Lankhorst, M., B, I., Jonkers, H., Quartel, D.: An Introduction to the ArchiMate®3.0 Specification (2016)
15. Ellerm, A., Morales-Trujillo, M.E.: Modelling Security Aspects with ArchiMate: A Systematic Mapping Study, in 2020 46th Euromicro Conference on Software Engineering and Advanced Applications (SEAA), pp. 577–584. (2020). [Online]. Available: https://ieeexplore.ieee.org/abstract/document/9226325
16. Business Process Model and Notation (BPMN), Version 2.0 (2013)
17. Völzer, H.: An Overview of BPMN 2.0 and Its Potential Use, in Business Process Modeling Notation, In: Mendling, J., Weidlich, M., Weske, M., eds., Berlin, Heidelberg: Springer, pp. 14–15 (2010)
18. Zarour, K., Benmerzoug, D., Guermouche, N., Drira, K.: A systematic literature review on BPMN extensions, Business Process Management Journal, vol. 26, no. 6, pp. 1473–1503, (2019). [Online]. Available: https://www.emerald.com/insight/content/doi/10.1108/BPMJ-01-2019-0040/full/html
19. Pufahl, L., Zerbato, F., Weber, B., Weber, I.: BPMN in healthcare: Challenges and best practices, Information Systems, vol. 107, p. 102013 (2022). [Online]. Available: https://www.sciencedirect.com/science/article/pii/S0306437922000217
20. Di Pierro, M.: What Is the Blockchain? Comput. Sci. Eng. **19**(5), pp. 92–95 (2017). [Online]. Available: https://ieeexplore.ieee.org/ document/8024092/
21. Mohanta, B.K., Panda, S.S., Jena, D.: An overview of smart contract and use cases in blockchain technology, In: 2018 9th International Conference on Computing, Communication and Networking Technologies (ICCCNT), pp. 1–4 (2018). [Online]. Available: https://ieeexplore.ieee.org/document/8494045/
22. Buterin, V.: Ethereum: A Next-Generation Smart Contract and Decentralized Application Platform, Ethereum Foundation, White paper (2014). [Online]. Available: https://ethereum.org/en/whitepaper/
23. Zheng, Z., et al.:, An overview on smart contracts: Challenges, advances and platforms, Future Generation Computer Systems, vol. 105, pp. 475–491 (2020). [Online]. Available: https://www.sciencedirect.com/science/article/pii/S0167739X19316280
24. Open Policy Agent. [Online]. Available: https://www.openpolicyagent.org/
25. Introduction | Open Policy Agent. [Online]. Available: https://openpolicyagent.org/docs
26. Wider, A., Verma, S., Akhtar, A.: Decentralized Data Governance as Part of a Data Mesh Platform: Concepts and Approaches, in 2023 IEEE International Conference on Web Services (ICWS), pp. 746–754, iSSN: 2836-3868 (2023). [Online]. Available: https://ieeexplore.ieee.org/document/10248262/
27. Everyone Loves Policy as Code, No One Wants to Write Rego, (2024). [Online]. Available: https://www.permit.io/blog/no-one-wants-to-write-rego
28. ITU-T X.901 (08/97) Information technology - Open Distributed Proces (1997)
29. Schluntz, E., Zhang, B.: Building Effective AI Agents. Anthropic. Publ. Anthropic Eng. Blog (2024). [Online]. Available: https://www.anthropic.com/engineering/building-effective-agents

30. ISO/IEC IS 15414, Information Technology - Open Distributed Processing - Enterprise Language 3rd edn (2015). also published as ITU-T Recommendation X.911
31. ISO/IEC IS 19793, Information Technology—Open Distributed Processing—Use of UML for ODP System Specifications, (2014). also published as ITU-T Recommendation X.906

Author Index

© The Editor(s) (if applicable) and The Author(s), under exclusive license
to Springer Nature Switzerland AG 2026

A. Gianola et al. (Eds.): EDOC 2025, LNCS 16213, pp. 355–356, 2026.
https://doi.org/10.1007/978-3-032-15140-7

MIX
Papier aus verantwortungsvollen Quellen
Paper from responsible sources
FSC® C105338

If you have any concerns about our products,
you can contact us on
ProductSafety@springernature.com

In case Publisher is established outside the EU,
the EU authorized representative is:
Springer Nature Customer Service Center GmbH
Europaplatz 3, 69115 Heidelberg, Germany

Printed by Libri Plureos GmbH
in Hamburg, Germany